By SAMUEL ELIOT MORISON

Life and Letters of Harrison Gray Otis (1913)
The Maritime History of Massachusetts (1921, 1961)
The Oxford History of the United States (1927)
An Hour of American History (1929, 1960)
Builders of the Bay Colony (1930, 1963)
The Development of Harvard University 1868-1929 (1930)
The Founding of Harvard College (1935)
Harvard College in the Seventeenth Century (1936)
Three Centuries of Harvard (1936)
The Second Voyage of Columbus (1939)
Portuguese Voyages to America in the XV Century (1940)
Admiral of the Ocean Sea: Life of Christopher Columbus (1942)
History of United States Naval Operations in World War II, 15 vols.
(1947-1962; see Preface for titles of separate volumes)
The Ropemakers of Plymouth (1950)
By Land and By Sea (1953)
Christopher Columbus, Mariner (1955)
The Story of the "Old Colony" of New Plymouth (1956)
The Intellectual Life of Colonial New England (1956, 1960)
Freedom in Contemporary Society (1956)
Strategy and Compromise (1958)
John Paul Jones: A Sailor's Biography (1959)
The Story of Mount Desert Island, Maine (1960)
One Boy's Boston (1962)
*The Two-Ocean War: A Short History of the United States Navy
in the Second World War* (1963)

(With Henry Steele Commager)
The Growth of the American Republic (Fifth Edition 1962)

(Editor)
Sources and Documents on the American Revolution and Constitution (1923, 1950)
Of Plymouth Plantation, by William Bradford (1952)
The Parkman Reader (1955)
Journals and Documents on the Voyages of Columbus (1963)

(In Preparation)
The Oxford History of the American People
The Life of Commodore Matthew Calbraith Perry

The Two-Ocean War

*A Short History of the United States Navy
in the Second World War*

Admiral Ernest J. King USN

The Two-Ocean War

*A Short History of
the United States Navy
in the Second World War*

BY SAMUEL ELIOT MORISON

WITH ILLUSTRATIONS

BACK BAY BOOKS

LITTLE, BROWN AND COMPANY

BOSTON · NEW YORK · TORONTO · LONDON

10 9 8 7 6 5   PB
10 9 8 7 6 5 4 3 2 HC

Library of Congress Cataloging-in-Publication Data

Morison, Samuel Eliot, 1887–1976.
      The two-ocean war / Samuel Eliot Morison.
            p.   cm.
      Includes index.
      ISBN 0-316-58366-9   ISBN 0-316-58352-9 (pbk.)
      1. World War, 1939–1945 — Naval operations, American.   2. United
States.   Navy — History — World War, 1939–1945.   I. Title.
D773.M63   1989
940.54'5973 — dc20   89-12549
                                                                                CIP

MV NY

Published simultaneously in Canada
by Little, Brown & Company (Canada) Limited

PRINTED IN THE UNITED STATES OF AMERICA

To my Wartime Shipmates in

    U.S.S. *Baltimore*

    U.S.S. *Brooklyn*

    U.S.S. *Buck*

    U.S.C.G.C. *Campbell*

    U.S.S. *Honolulu*

    U.S.S. *Montpelier*

    U.S.S. *Tennessee*

    U.S.S. *Washington*

Preface

THIS BOOK has been written in the hope of bringing the exploits of the United States Navy in World War II to the attention of new readers. For I have already written, and Little, Brown and Company have published, a fifteen-volume *History of the United States Naval Operations in World War II*, as follows:

I   *The Battle of the Atlantic*, September 1939–May 1943
II *Operations in North African Waters*, October 1942–June 1943
III *The Rising Sun in the Pacific*, 1931–April 1942
IV *Coral Sea, Midway and Submarine Actions*, May 1942–August 1942
V   *The Struggle for Guadalcanal*, August 1942–February 1943
VI *Breaking the Bismarcks Barrier*, 22 July 1942–1 May 1944
VII *Aleutians, Gilberts and Marshalls*, June 1942–April 1944
VIII *New Guinea and the Marianas*, March 1944–August 1944
IX *Sicily — Salerno — Anzio*, January 1943–June 1944
X   *The Atlantic Battle Won*, May 1943–May 1945
XI *The Invasion of France and Germany*, 1944–1945
XII *Leyte*, June 1944–January 1945
XIII *The Liberation of the Philippines: Luzon, Mindanao, the Visayas*, 1944–1945
XIV *Victory in the Pacific*, 1945
XV *Supplement and General Index*

In this book I have not attempted a uniform condensation of the fifteen volumes, but rather to select the most important battles and campaigns. Consequently, many minor actions, convoy struggles, fights of naval armed guards against U-boats, individual submarine exploits, air clashes in the "central blue," in which sailors fought and died, have had to be omitted. For these, and for illustrations and more charts, the reader is referred to the appropriate volume of my larger History. On the other hand, Chapter I on the Navy between wars is more detailed than the coverage of that period in *The Battle of the Atlantic.*

Whilst research for the larger History has generally served for this, I have consulted all printed works covering the naval war in both oceans which have appeared since my own volumes, and profited by many. Among these, especially valuable were the following:

† E. B. Potter and Chester W. Nimitz *The Great Sea War* (1960)

† M. Fuchida and M. Okumiya *Midway, the Battle that Doomed Japan* (1955)

* Kent R. Greenfield (ed.) *Command Decisions* (1960)

Ernest R. May (ed.) *The Ultimate Decision* (1960)

* Julius A. Furer *Administration of the Navy Department in World War II* (1959)

† Arnold S. Lott *Most Dangerous Sea. A History of Mine Warfare* (1959)

Roberta Wohlstetter *Pearl Harbor Warning and Decision* (Stanford, 1962)

In the * *U. S. Army in World War II* series, Louis Morton *The Fall of the Philippines* (1953); George F. Howe *Northwest Africa* (1957); Maurice Matloff *Strategic Planning for Coalition Warfare 1943-1944* (1959); Philip A. Crowl *Campaign in the Marianas* (1960); Crowl and Edmund G. Love *Seizure of the Gilberts and Marshalls* (1955); Samuel Milner *Victory in Papua* (1957)

* *History of U. S. Marine Corps Operations in World War II,* of which only Volume I by F. O. Hough et al., *Pearl Harbor to Guadalcanal* (1958), has yet appeared

† S. W. Roskill *White Ensign, the British Navy at War 1939-1945* (1960)

† Paul Auphan and Jacques Mordal *The French Navy in World War II* (1959)

† Marc' A. Bragadin *The Italian Navy in World War II* (1957)

† These books are published by the U. S. Naval Institute, Annapolis, Md.

* These books are published by the Superintendent of Documents, U. S. Government Printing Office, Washington, D. C.

S. L. A. Marshall *Night Drop, the American Airborne Invasion of Normandy* (Atlantic-Little, Brown, 1962)

In J. R. M. Butler (ed.) *History of the Second World War. United Kingdom Military Series*, S. W. Roskill *The War at Sea 1939-45* (4 vols., 1954-61); S. Woodburn Kirby *The War Against Japan* (3 vols. 1957-61); John Ehrman et al. *Grand Strategy* (6 vols., not all yet out). These are published by H. M. Stationery Office, London.

In the *Australia in the War of 1939-1945* series, G. H. Gill's Vol. I of *Royal Australian Navy* (Canberra, 1957), and Dudley McCarthy *South-West Pacific Area — First Year* (Canberra, 1959)

K. W. L. Bezemer *Zij Vochten op de Zeven Zeeën* (1960) — the best history of the Royal Netherlands Navy

Jacques Mordal *La Bataille de Casablanca* (Paris, 1952)

Emilio Faldella *Lo Sbarco e la Difesa della Sicilia* (Rome, 1957)

Admiral Karl Doenitz *Memoirs. Ten Years and Twenty Days*. R. H. Stevens trans. (London: Weidenfeld & Nicholson 1959)

Masanori Ito and Roger Pineau *The End of the Japanese Navy* (New York, 1962)

Herbert Feis *Japan Subdued: The Atomic Bomb and the End of the War* (Princeton, 1961)

Tameichi Hara *Japanese Destroyer Captain* trans. by F. Saito and R. Pineau (New York, 1961)

My deepest feeling of gratitude is towards my beloved wife, Priscilla Barton Morison, for her support and encouragement which enabled me to complete this volume, and for many perceptive suggestions when I read it aloud to her in proof.

My obligations to naval officers and historians of the United States and other navies are so many and great that I cannot begin to name them. Special thanks are due to Rear Admiral Ernest M. Eller usn (Ret.), Director of Naval History, for permitting me to use charts and material from my 15-volume History; to two members of his staff, Mr. Jesse D. Thomas and Mr. Donald R. Martin, for doing research on sundry points; and to Captain Ralph C. Parker USN (Ret.) and Vice Admiral Morton L. Deyo USN (Ret.), for helpful advice on the opening and closing chapters.

SAMUEL ELIOT MORISON

44 BRIMMER STREET
BOSTON
February, 1963

Contents

Illustrations

(All photographs not otherwise described are Official United States Navy)

Admiral Ernest J. King USN   *frontispiece*

(Between pages 196 and 197)

Death of *Arizona*, 7 December 1941:
    After her magazine exploded
    Blown in half

Admiral Chester W. Nimitz USN

Admiral Raymond A. Spruance USN

Admiral William F. Halsey USN

U.S.S. *South Dakota* and *Enterprise* during the Battle of the Santa
    Cruz Islands

15 November 1942:
    Japanese transports burning on beach, Guadalcanal
    U.S.S. *Washington*

Vice Admiral Henry Kent Hewitt USN

Rear Admiral Richmond Kelly Turner USN and Staff
        (From a painting by Albert K. Murray)

U.S.S. *Essex* during Operation GALVANIC

Wings over Kwajalein:
    VII Army Air Force Liberator over Kwajalein Island, Octo-
        ber 1944
        (Photo by Army Air Force)

CTF 38 and CTF 58:
    Vice Admiral John S. McCain USN
    Vice Admiral Marc A. Mitscher USN in U.S.S. *Randolph*

List of Charts

Abbreviations

Service designations:

(jg) Junior Grade
RAN — Royal Australian Navy
RN — Royal Navy
RNN — Royal Netherlands Navy
USA — United States Army
USCG — United States Coast Guard; USCGR, Reserve of same
USMC—United States Marine Corps; USMCR, Reserve of same
USN — United States Navy; USNR, Reserve of same
    (All officers and men not otherwise designated may be assumed to be USN)

Terms most frequently used in text:

AGC — Amphibious Force Command Ship
AKA — Attack cargo vessel
A.A.F. — Army Air Force or Forces
ABDA — American, British, Dutch, Australian Command
APA — Attack Transport
APD — High-speed Destroyer Transport
C.A.P. — Combat Air Patrol
C.C.S. — Combined Chiefs of Staff
C. in C. — Commander in Chief
C.N.O. — Chief of Naval Operations
C.O. — Commanding Officer
C.T.F. — Commander Task Force; C.T.G. — Commander Task Group
Cinclant — Commander in Chief, Atlantic Fleet
Cincmed — Commander in Chief, Mediterranean
Cincpac, Cincpoa — Commander in Chief Pacific Fleet, Pacific Ocean Areas
Cominch — Commander in Chief, United States Fleet; Comsopac, Commander in Chief, South Pacific; Comairspac, Commander Air, South Pacific
CVE — Escort Carrier
DD — Destroyer
DE — Destroyer escort

DMS — Fast Minesweeper
dukw — 2 ½ ton amphibian truck
Dumbo — patrol seaplane equipped for rescue

exec. — Executive officer on board a ship

HF/DF (Huff-Duff) — High-frequency Direction-Finder
H.M.A.S. — His Majesty's Australian Ship
H.M.C.S. — His Majesty's Canadian Ship
H.M.N.Z.S. — His Majesty's New Zealand Ship
H.M.S. — His Majesty's Ship (Royal Navy)
H.N.M.S. — Her Netherlands Majesty's Ship

J.C.S. — Joint Chiefs of Staff

Maru (lit. "chubby") is added to the names of Japanese merchant
    ships and many naval auxiliaries
MTB or PT — Motor Torpedo Boat

O.N.I. — Office of Naval Intelligence
op plan — Operation plan
O.T.C. — Officer in Tactical Command

PC — Patrol craft
P.M. — Prime Minister (Churchill)

R.A.F. — Royal Air Force
RCT — Regimental Combat Team
RN — Royal Navy

SC — Submarine chaser
SOPA — Senior Officer Present Afloat

TBS — Talk Between Ships (voice radio)
TF — Task Force; TG — Task Group

UDT — Underwater Demolition Team

YMS — Motor Minesweeper

Landing Craft and Ships [(A), (G), (L), (M), (R) after these mean
    armored, gunboat, large, mortar, rocket]:
LCI — Landing Craft, Infantry
LCP — Landing Craft, Personnel
LCT — Landing Craft, Tank
LCM — Landing Craft, Mechanized
LCVP — Landing Craft, Vehicles and Personnel
LSD — Landing Ship, Dock
LSM — Landing Ship, Medium
LST — Landing Ship, Tank
LVT — Landing Vehicle, Tracked (Amphtrac)

Principal United States Planes (engine number in parentheses):

ARMY

A–20 — Hudson light bomber (2)

B–17 — Flying Fortress heavy bomber (4); B–24 — Liberator heavy bomber (4); B–25 — Mitchell medium bomber (2); B–26 — Marauder medium bomber (2); B–29 — Superfortress heavy bomber (4); P–35, –36, –39, –40 — fighters (1); P–38 — Lightning fighter (2)

NAVY

F4F — Wildcat, fighter (1)

F4U — Corsair, fighter (1)

F6F — Hellcat, fighter (1)

OS2U — Kingfisher float plane (1)

PBM — Mariner, patrol bomber (2)

PBY — Catalina (2) patrol seaplane

PB4Y — Liberator bomber (4)

PV–1 — Ventura medium bomber (2)

SBD–5 — Dauntless dive-bomber (1)

SB2C — Helldiver dive-bomber (1)

TBD — Devastator torpedo-bomber (1)

TBF, TBM — Avenger torpedo-bomber (1)

Japanese Planes

"Betty" — Mitsubishi Zero–1 (2)

"Jill" — Nakajima, Navy (2) medium torpedo-bomber

"Judy" — Aichi, Navy (1) dive-bomber

"Kate" — Nakajima, Navy (2) torpedo-bomber

"Val" — Aichi 99, Navy (1) dive-bomber

"Zeke" — Mitsubishi Zero–3, Navy (1) fighter (also called "Zero")

The Two-Ocean War

*A Short History of the United States Navy
in the Second World War*

CHAPTER I

The Twenty Years' Peace

1919–1939

1. *Naval Limitation, 1922–1937*

ALTHOUGH THE UNITED STATES participated heavily in World War I, the nature of that participation was fundamentally different from what it became in World War II. The earlier conflict was a one-ocean war for the Navy and a one-theater war for the Army; the latter was a two-ocean war for the Navy and one of five major theaters for the Army. In both wars a vital responsibility of the Navy was escort-of-convoy and anti-submarine work, but in the 1917-1918 conflict it never clashed with the enemy on the surface; whilst between 1941 and 1945 it fought some twenty major, and countless minor engagements with the Japanese Navy. American soldiers who engaged in World War I were taken overseas in transports and landed on docks or in protected harbors; in World War II the art of amphibious warfare had to be revived and developed, since assault troops were forced to fight their way ashore. Air power, in the earlier conflict, was still inchoate and almost negligible; in the latter it was a determining factor. In World War I the battleship still reigned queen of the sea, as she had, in changing forms, since the age of Drake, and Battle Line fought with tactics inherited from the age of sail; but in World War II the capital naval force was the aircraft carrier task group, for which completely new tactics had to be devised.

America entered World War I late, almost three years after it began; owing to unpreparedness for battle she had to borrow everybody else's weapons, and in Europe left the reputation of a brave, almost foolhardy, amateur. In World War II, America became not only the "arsenal of democracy" for her Allies (who before had daintily been called "Associates"), but participated with greater man power, weapon power, sea power and air power than any other belligerent except, as respects ground forces, Russia. And American strategists showed themselves at least the equals of those of the Old World in the art of war.

After the earlier conflict ended with defeat of Imperial Germany, America turned her back on Europe, indulged in futile dreams of everlasting peace, and to all intents and purposes disarmed; but World War II was no sooner over than the "cold war" with Communism opened, and we rearmed with new and deadlier instruments of destruction which threaten, whenever and by whomsoever employed, to snuff out civilization itself. Thus, World War I was a hit-and-run war; we struck late but hard, and quickly withdrew into our shell, like a hermit crab; but World War II was a hit-and-stay war; we struck even harder, and stayed in Europe, Asia and Africa. In 1963, American air and ground forces are in Great Britain, Germany, North Africa, Japan, Korea, Formosa, South Vietnam, and a score of Pacific islands formerly in enemy possession; and the United States Navy not only patrols every verge of Asia, and dives under the polar ice, but protects the lifeline between America and all other bastions of freedom.

The important point in "turning our back on Europe" was rejection by the United States Senate in 1920 of the Treaty of Versailles and the League of Nations. Although this action was taken mainly for political and personal reasons — revenge against President Wilson, and Wilson's own stubbornness — the rejection was undoubtedly popular. There was a feeling of national frustration over the unsatisfactory outcome of the Paris Peace Conference, a belief that we had been "sold down the river" by Lloyd

George and Clemenceau, and that adherence to the League would involve us in conflicts contrary to our permanent interests. President Wilson prophesied on 4 September 1919 that the League "is the only conceivable arrangement which will prevent us sending our men abroad again very soon. . . . The only thing that can prevent the recurrence of this dreadful catastrophe." This warning the people heeded not.

Americans nevertheless were devoted to the idea of world peace, and the Harding administration, elected in the fall of 1920, felt obliged to do something spectacular to satisfy that aspiration. This took the form of the Naval Arms Limitation Conference at Washington. In 1916, on the eve of war, Congress had passed an act authorizing the building of a navy which, had it been carried out, would have made it the equal to any other two navies of the world. The British government and people, after the war was over, foolishly regarded this as a challenge to the Royal Navy, which had borne the brunt of blue-water fighting. The war had thrown such financial burdens on the British that they could not match us ship for ship; and, so far as anyone could see, America would always be on their side. Yet British pride and sense of history were too powerful to brook a superior rival; for history seemed to prove that Britain's allies in one war would be her enemies in the next.

The suggestion from London of a naval limitation agreement between the five leading naval powers (Great Britain, the United States, Japan, France and Italy) was eagerly taken up at Washington. There the conference opened spectacularly on 12 November 1921 with an American offer to scrap a large part of the naval tonnage then building, if other powers would forgo building warships themselves; and as the United States had the capability to build the world's most powerful navy, the delegates of those nations hailed Secretary Hughes's offer with almost indecent joy. The results of this conference, after weeks of deliberation, were the famous treaties signed 6 February 1922 setting up the 5:5:3 ratio in battleship and aircraft carrier tonnage between England, America and Japan; France and Italy each receiving a 1¾ ratio; a ten-year "holiday" on building capital ships, and a restriction on the burthen of all battleships to 35,000 tons.[1] Although this ratio allowed Japan to become the strongest naval power in the Western Pacific (since America had two, and Britain three, oceans to defend), Japanese consent had to be purchased by a supplementary agreement on military bases. The United States renounced strengthening, in a military sense, any of her bases, such as Guam and Manila, that lay west of Pearl Harbor; and England renounced strengthening any of hers east of Singapore or north of Australia. This provision actually reversed the ratio to 5:3:2 in favor of Japan, as the United States and Great Britain learned to their sorrow twenty years later.

The American government and people confidently expected that this agreement would prove the entering wedge for limitation of other types of combatant ships, and to general disarmament on land and sea; but three later conferences, called to effect these objects, ended in nothing of importance except an agreement to limit cruisers to 10,000 tons, which we respected and Japan flouted.

Having, as they fondly thought, started the ball rolling toward universal peace, the British and American people allowed their armed forces to drift into obsolescence. For about ten years this hardly mattered, but in the 1930's the German, Italian and Japanese governments began planning war as a short cut to wealth and power, and building up their armed forces. If "England slept," America not only slept but snored. The Army was neglected as much or more than the Navy, which Congress did not allow to be built up even to what the treaties permitted. Congress would probably have done even less but for the Navy League, a civilian organization founded in 1902, dedicated to keeping the Navy in

[1] See NOTE at end of this chapter for details.

proper shape. Ironically, the League celebrated its first Navy Day on 27 October 1922, immediately after the administration had consigned some of our best ships to the wreckers' yards.

Several factors, besides a general revulsion against war and aversion from Europe, conspired to bring about this lamentable state of affairs. The recession of 1921-1922 and the depression of 1929-1933 made Congress unwilling to vote money for armaments that might never be used. Pacifist propaganda in this era was very powerful; one remembers with shame the sneers and jeers at Congressional hearings, directed toward conscientious officers who were trying to obtain a few million dollars for Army buildup, fleet maintenance and new construction.

President Coolidge, although he hated the sea and even disliked reviewing a naval regatta from the presidential yacht, did more for the Navy than any President between Wilson and Roosevelt. Disappointed and irritated that the second Naval Limitation Conference at Geneva in 1927 could not agree to cut down the world's navies further, he urged the then chairman of the House of Representatives' committee on naval affairs to introduce legislation which would bring the United States Navy to full parity with the British. Chairman Butler did so, submitting a program that called for the building of 71 new ships (including 5 aircraft carriers and 25 cruisers) in nine years. The peace societies then got into action, congressmen were overwhelmed with protests, and the program was pared to 15 heavy cruisers and one carrier. Even this bill was rejected in the Senate. President Coolidge returned to the subject in his Armistice Day address of 1928, the "cruiser bill" was re-introduced, and this time became law. That was the origin of the *Astoria*, *Indianapolis* and *Brooklyn* classes; but no keels were laid before 1930 (no *Brooklyn* keels until 1935), and only two of these ships were in commission before 1934.

President Hoover, a Quaker and a congenital pacifist, trusted to a sort of incantation — the Kellogg-Briand treaty "outlawing war"

— to keep the peace. He found the British premier, Ramsay Mac-
Donald, very congenial. After MacDonald on 24 July 1929 had
announced that the Royal Navy would stop work on two heavy
cruisers, four destroyers and two submarines, Hoover, when pro-
claiming the Kellogg-Briand treaty in force, announced that the
keels of three cruisers authorized as far back as 1924 would not
be laid, pending another effort to limit navies. The Hoover administration has the sad distinction of being the only one since the
eighteenth century in which not a single naval combatant ship was
laid down.

Another influence that kept the Navy weak was the propaganda
by Brigadier General William Mitchell USA to the effect that armies
and navies — even aircraft carriers — were obsolete; that land-
based air bombers could overcome all the ships and armies in the
world. When a prophet habitually prophesies around the clock,
he is sure to score some bull's-eyes as well as numerous misses; but
"Billy" Mitchell, although now canonized by airmen for his few
hits, made a very high percentage of bloopers — such as:

> The surface ship as an element of war is disappearing.
> Airplane carriers are useless instruments of war against first-
> class powers.
> Effectiveness [of antiaircraft guns] is constantly diminishing
> [and] never can improve much.
> A superior air power will dominate all sea areas when they
> act from land bases, and no seacraft, whether carrying aircraft
> or not, is able to contest their aërial supremacy.
> An attempt to transport large bodies of troops, munitions
> and supplies across a great stretch of ocean, by seacraft, as was
> done during the World War from the United States to Eu-
> rope, would be an impossibility.

This line of argument appealed to the people and to Congress,
since aircraft were not only the newest weapons but relatively
cheap. And some practice sinkings of moored, unarmed and defenseless naval hulks by air bombing in 1921 were cited as proof

that no ship could ever threaten our shores if we had a powerful air force. Yet, when the Army's planners first asked for appropriations for B-17s, the Flying Fortresses that played so great a rôle in World War II, the Deputy Chief of Staff (General Stanley D. Embick) told them to forget it, since Congress deemed long-range bombers "aggressive."

As a result of this public attitude, which Congress represented, and of presidential indifference, the Navy from 1920 to 1933 remained static, with an average complement of 7900 officers and 100,000 enlisted men, manning about a million tons of warships. The Royal Navy was almost identical in strength. "Except for cruisers," wrote Fleet Admiral King, "hardly any combatant ships (no battleships or destroyers) were added to our own fleet during that period and few were under construction. . . . Moreover, advances in the science of naval construction were hampered by the lack of opportunity to prove new design." Although the naval limitation treaty helped the American taxpayer by suspending battleship construction for ten years, almost all other naval construction stopped too. Battleships were not only the most expensive warships (until the super-carrier came on the scene), but took the longest to build. Before Pearl Harbor, construction of a battleship required an average of 39 months; after that, 32; fleet carriers before Pearl Harbor required 32 months; after it, 15. Submarines and destroyers before Pearl Harbor required 13 to 14 months; after it, five to seven months.

Many senior officers of the Navy envisaged the battles of the next war as long-range gunfire duels between battle lines, as at Jutland, an action so intensively studied at the Naval War College in Newport that one witty officer called Jutland "a major defeat of the United States Navy."

Actually, only one major battle in which our Navy engaged during the war, the night action off Guadalcanal on 14-15 November 1942, was decided by gunfire. All the others were won by ships' torpedoes, and by bombs and torpedoes delivered to the target by aircraft. Accurate gunfire, nevertheless, proved to be indispensable in World War II, both to repel air attack and for shore bombardment to cover an amphibious assault.

Although air bombing of an objective supplemented rather than superseded naval bombardment, it was largely the development of air power that doomed the "battlewagon" to a secondary rôle. In the face of unwelcome attention from bomber planes, she could no longer hold a battle line. Very few ranking officers of any navy appreciated this. Germany put mighty efforts into producing *Bismarck* and *Tirpitz;* and although Admiral Ozawa reached the same conclusion as the progressive American naval leaders, Japan built 18.1-inch-gunned *Musashi* and *Yamato*, and concentrated on battleships in its attack on Pearl Harbor, assuming that their elimination would leave the Japanese Navy supreme.

Battleships were very useful in World War II. All those present at Pearl Harbor on 7 December 1941 were "old enough to vote," but five of the seven sunk or badly damaged, after being raised, repaired and modernized, proved indispensable in covering amphibious operations and for shore bombardment; even *Arkansas, New York* and *Texas* were still "dishing it out" in the European theater at the age of thirty or more in 1944. That is not what they were designed to do; but no matter, many classes of naval vessels have proved useful in unintended directions. The submarine was originally conceived by us as a coast defense vessel, to torpedo enemy ships approaching our shores; it proved incapable of doing that at Luzon in December 1941, but in the Pacific war the submarine proved to be especially potent in sinking the enemy merchant fleet. Destroyers — originally "torpedo boat destroyers" — superseded the torpedo boats to become, first, the "cavalry of the sea" for scouting, and finally, a protective screen for convoys and carriers. Motor torpedo boats were supposed to sneak up on capital ships after dark and torpedo them, a feat seldom performed in

World War II; but they became very effective as small, fast gunboats.

Nevertheless, a much too big slice of the thin appropriation pie was spent on battleships between wars. This was due, fundamentally, to Captain Alfred Thayer Mahan's teachings to the effect that all other classes of warships would be so outranged and outgunned by them in fleet actions as to be useless. And it was fed by a belief that lighter men of war — cruisers, destroyers, auxiliaries and patrol craft — could be constructed quickly in an emergency.

Not only in harping on battleships, but in other matters too, the Navy itself must share the blame with Congress and the public for unpreparedness. One cause was overemphasis on ship-to-ship competition. Gunnery competition, instituted by President Roosevelt in 1902 as a result of the Navy's bad shooting in the Spanish-American War, was extended to torpedo firing, propulsive engineering and communications, the whole comprising the "battle-efficiency competition." For several years this helped the Navy, and probably the net result was beneficial — certainly it was better than no competition at all. But the rivalry thus engendered became almost an end in itself. In order to ensure fairness, rules were standardized and contests held under optimum conditions of fair weather and smooth seas, off the New England coast in summer and in the Caribbean in winter, such as are seldom encountered in battle. A somewhat complacent attitude, to the effect that the United States Navy could outshoot every other Navy, developed. But competition and battle practice were useful in discovering defects in ordnance and matériel, and in improving the design of warships.

To quote a recent letter from Vice Admiral Deyo to the writer:

The surface Navy, despite lack of funds from Congress or interest by its civilian heads, produced a reasonable semblance of a balanced fleet and operated effectively as one in its training. The spur of officer selection and ship competition was most noticeable. But gradually the means became the end. Thus, while everyone worked hard, we began going in circles. The Fleet became more and more tied to bases, operating out of Long Beach–San Diego on a tight fuel budget, chained to the increasingly artificial, detailed mandates of the Office of Fleet Training whose word was law. The pencil became sharper than the sword, everyone tried to beat the target practice rules and too many forgot there was a war getting closer. There was a waiting line for top commands, and tenure of office was so short — often only a year or less — that high commanders came and went, leaving little impression. Paper work wrapped its deadly tentacles around cabin and wardroom. Smart ship handling, smart crews, eager initiative received little attention, as did the reverse. Glaring defects in guns, ammunition, torpedoes, battle tactics, went unnoticed so long as the competition rules made due allowances and gave everyone similar conditions.

Fortunately the "battle-efficiency competition" was abolished in 1935 by the then C.N.O., Admiral Standley, and our ships began to train under conditions that more nearly approximated what they were to face in war. Even so, there was little if any practice in night fighting, on which the Japanese Navy specialized. That they were so doing in the East China Sea was apparent in 1937-1939 to the United States Asiatic Fleet, whose C. in C., Admiral Yarnell, repeatedly called it to the attention of the C.N.O. in Washington; but nothing was done. And, although our development in central-directed gunfire subsequent to 1934 was outstanding, no improvements were made in our torpedoes.

Poor design and performance of our torpedoes was due partly to obsolescence (leftover stock from World War I), partly to economy (it was a major offense to lose a live torpedo), partly to between-wars inefficiency of the Bureau of Ordnance, and partly to politics in the torpedo factory at Newport. Rhode Island politicians regarded civilian labor there as part of their patronage, and supported the local union in resisting efficiency. As one United States naval officer remarked ruefully, "If I fired an incompetent or insubordinate workman, the Secretary of the Navy was visited next day by both Rhode Island senators and a congressman insisting that he be reinstated." After war broke with Japan we discovered the hard way that not only our torpedo exploders and depth-regulation mechanisms were fatally defective, but that the enemy had an oxygen-propelled torpedo which carried half a ton of TNT (compared with our 780-pound charge), and could travel eleven miles at 49 knots, compared with our range of 7.5 miles at 26.5 knots. And, while the United States Navy, expecting to fight daylight Jutlands at long range with high-caliber guns, took the torpedo tubes off its cruisers, the Japanese kept theirs, and prepared for the close-range nocturnal "hugger-mugger" clinch, making abundant use of torpedoes. With these tactics they reaped rich rewards during the battles around Guadalcanal in 1942-1943. The United States Navy, in contrast, was like a city police force equipped only with high-powered rifles, but with no weapons to meet thugs jumping patrolmen at night with automatic pistols and blackjacks.

2. *Naval Aviation and Amphibious Training*

Nevertheless, the Navy strove to attain excellence within the required framework. After 1930, under the lead of wise and aggressive Chiefs of Naval Operations such as Admirals William V. Pratt and William H. Standley, the Fleet made substantial progress in several directions, especially naval aviation. The Navy's first aircraft, a bamboo-and-canvas single-engined biplane, the Curtiss A–1, dates from 1910. Pilot Eugene Ely landed it successfully on an inprovised flight deck of cruiser *Pennsylvania* on 18 January 1911. The Navy's small air arm did so well in World War I that in May 1919 the General Board declared for an immediate development of fleet aviation: "a naval air service must be established capable of accompanying and operating with the Fleet in all waters of the globe." That year the catapult was invented to enable spotting planes to take off from the decks of battleships and cruisers. The use of planes on board ship incorporated the new weapon and the newly trained aviators with the existing naval organization, instead of keeping it at arm's length, as the Army did with the A.A.F. These young aviators, unhampered by obsolete equipment or doctrine, injected new life into ships' wardrooms, and there was enough time before war again broke for many to become senior officers and some to reach flag rank. This early integration of air power with the United States Navy, and our Navy's successful resistance to every effort to deprive it of the air arm, was the basis for the remarkable performances of American aircraft carriers and their planes in World War II.

It was also in May 1919 that Lieutenant Commander Albert C. Read USN, pilot of *NC–4*, with a crew of four, flew the first airplane to cross the Atlantic.[2] The first seaplane tender, *Wright*, and the first aircraft carrier, appropriately named *Langley* after another American poineer in aviation, were commissioned in 1921. The Bureau of Aeronautics (Buaer) was added to the Navy bureaus that same year. The creation of an Assistant Secretary of the Navy for Aviation followed. Aircraft and carriers participated, from 1923 on, in the annual fleet "problems," which were maneuvers aimed at some definite objective, such as attacking the Panama Canal. *Langley's* performance in the 1925 problem so impressed the C. in C. that he pressed the speedy completion of *Lexington* and *Saratoga*. Both carriers participated in fleet maneuvers and problems from 1929 on; and in 1938 *Saratoga* launched a successful "surprise attack" on Pearl Harbor, a hint probably not lost on Admiral Yamamoto of the Imperial Japanese Navy. Commen-

[2] Commander Read called at the Azores; the first nonstop flight was made from Newfoundland to Ireland by two Royal Air Force officers, J. W. Alcock and A. W. Brown, 14-15 June 1919. Charles Lindbergh's, the first nonstop solo flight, was in 1927.

surate improvement went on in carrier aircraft types (fighters, torpedo-bombers, dive-bombers), but the Japanese Navy improved the first two types faster than we did. U.S.S. *Ranger*, first of our aircraft carriers to be built as such from the keel up, was completed in 1934.

The performance of these vessels and their planes brought about a new conception of the aircraft carrier's place in naval warfare. Formerly their functions were to scout for and provide an "air umbrella" over the Battle Line. Now rôles were reversed; the carrier became the nucleus of a striking force capable of projecting fire power deep into enemy-held waters, and the proud battlewagon, when not employed in shore bombardment, joined the protective screen to the carrier.

Other important developments came in connection with amphibious training. A military expedition the object of which is to land troops on enemy-held territory and establish a beachhead there, is called an amphibious operation. This, the most ancient form of naval warfare, in which the Greeks, Phoenicians and Norsemen distinguished themselves, became discredited in World War I and for years thereafter was neglected by all naval powers except Japan. This neglect arose from the misleading claims made by air-power fanatics, and from the costly failure of the Dardanelles operation in 1915. Both combined to create the impression that land-based aircraft and modern coast defense guns would slaughter any landing force before it reached the beach.

Credit for the revival of amphibious training, and for adapting amphibious tactics to an age of air power and increased gunfire potential, is due to the United States Marine Corps; primarily to Major Earl H. Ellis usmc, who disappeared mysteriously when reconnoitering the Palau Islands in 1923. He was probably murdered by the Japanese because he knew too much; but he had already planted the seed. He pointed out that Japan's insular spiderweb would have to be swept up in case of war, and that the

Marines would have to wield the broom — provided the Navy could get them there and cover their landings with gunfire. He even anticipated that we would have to take Okinawa before defeating Japan. Major Ellis's plans were approved by General Lejeune, Commandant of the Marine Corps, in 1921, a Marine expeditionary force was organized, and in 1923 it performed the first amphibious attack "problem" on Culebra Island east of Puerto Rico. Next year a bigger problem, with 1700 troops engaged, resulted in a complete foul-up. This convinced the Navy that far more study and training were required before an amphibious assault could dislodge a determined enemy. New landing craft types, even the precursor of the LVT amphibian tractor, were tried out, and in 1933 the Fleet Marine Force was established. Next year it issued a *Tentative Manual for Landing Operations* which Marine Corps historians regard as "the Pentateuch and the Four Gospels" of amphibious warfare. As Bob Sherrod writes, the establishment of Fleet Marine Force marks the evolution of the Marine Corps "from a simple, rough-and-ready gang, which could fight banana wars . . . to a specialized organization with a primary mission" — the seizure of beachheads as bases for military operations.[3] General John H. Russell, acting Commandant of the Corps, was largely responsible.

Gradually the Marines drew more of the Navy and Coast Guard into their maneuvers. After France fell, and the Army realized that no future American Expeditionary Force could land at Brest on stone jetties and proceed to the battle area in *40 hommes, 8 chevaux* boxcars, it too consented to learn from the Marines, and began to take part in their amphibious exercises.

[3] *History of Marine Corps Aviation in World War II* (1952) p. 30.

3. *Pacific Ocean Strategy*

Until September 1939, when World War II broke in Europe, the Navy hardly knew what it would be called upon to do in the Atlantic; but for over forty years it had known what would be expected of it in the Pacific. Responsibility for the Philippines, which (together with a formidable insurrection) we bought from Spain in 1898, involved us in Far Eastern power politics and made war with Japan difficult to escape, if not inevitable. And, as an example of the haphazard, nonstrategic nature of the decision to buy the Philippines, we failed to acquire island approaches to the archipelago on which Spain had put a "For Sale" sign — excepting Guam, which was of slight value without nearby Saipan and Tinian.

Out of the welter of events in the Pacific between 1900 and 1941 there emerged two major factors — the growing disorganization of China and the increasing power of Japan. We tried to arrest the one by the "Open Door" policy of John Hay, which meant dissuading European powers and Japan from annexing parts of China or acquiring special privileges in her ports. Then came the Russo-Japanese War of 1904-1905 in which Japan acquired Korea and a new area of influence in Manchuria. It was generally expected that this would not long satisfy Japan, and that the Philippines would be her next objective.

As early as 1903 our great authority on naval strategy, Captain Mahan, urged that the United States Navy concentrate in the Pacific. The joint Army-Navy Board, precursor of the Joint Chiefs of Staff, so recommended in 1905; it proposed that the Battle Fleet be based on Subic Bay, Luzon. President Theodore Roosevelt declined to support this. Had he done so, and if Congress had built up shore installations there as a "deterrent," it is possible that Japan would never have attacked us. But one can never tell when something intended as a deterrent may instead become a mere irritant. Basing the Battle Fleet in the Philippines might have provoked Japan to a sneak attack on Subic Bay, before the opening of the Panama Canal in June 1914 permitted warships to be shifted rapidly from one ocean to another.

Japan again increased her power by joining World War I as the ally of Britain, and, with very little exertion and minimum loss, acquiring Germany's insular empire — the Marshall and Caroline Islands, and all the Marianas except Guam. President Wilson, more farseeing about Japan than Theodore Roosevelt had been, protested against these acquisitions at the Paris Peace Conference, and the 1916 naval program, which he strongly supported, had the deterrence of Japan principally in view. Wilson was overruled on the first point, and the planned big navy, as we have seen, was scrapped after the war. Japan kept her insular spiderwebs, on which dozens of airfields and numerous naval bases could be built and were built after 1936. In the event of war with Japan, the United States Navy's "Orange" plan looked to the Army to defend Manila and hold out for an estimated three to four months until the Battle Fleet could cross the Pacific and raise the siege. Japanese possession of the mandated islands made this task impossible unless key positions in the Marshalls and Carolines were first secured, and the spiders cleaned out; that increased the estimated time for the Army to hold out in Luzon to nine months. And, as we have seen, a part of the 1922 Washington agreement was our renouncing the right to strengthen our bases in Guam and the Philippines.

An impossible situation in grand strategy had been created for us, largely by our own folly. We were promising to defend the integrity of China and of the Philippines, without anything near the military means to implement such a policy.

In the meantime the liberal, Western-oriented groups in Japanese politics, which had been participating in the collective security measures of the League of Nations, were being harassed and terrified by a movement roughly parallel to Hitler's Nazis. *Kodo-Ha*, as it was called, aimed to place Japan under Army control, "liberate" China, India, the Philippines and all East Asia from "foreign imperialists," and place all Asiatic countries under Japanese hegemony. Liberal politicians were assassinated, and in 1931 the Japanese Kwantung Army moved into Manchuria. Secretary Stimson was unable to persuade President Hoover to do more than protest against the Japanese invasion of Manchuria, and of Shanghai later in the same year. A commission of the League of Nations condemned the Japanese action and demanded that she retire from Manchuria; Japan's reply was to withdraw from the League of Nations and to announce that on her part the naval limitation treaties would end in 1936.

Harbinger of fairer weather for the Navy was the appointment of the Honorable Carl Vinson of Georgia, in 1931, to be Chairman of the Naval Affairs Committee of the House of Representatives; a position that he still held, as chairman of an enlarged House Armed Services Committee, in 1962. Mr. Vinson was not only well disposed toward the Navy; he made himself an expert on its technique and supported its aspirations to help defend the country. "No Member of Congress," writes Rear Admiral Furer, "has ever shown a greater understanding of naval needs . . . nor a greater mastery of the practical politics necessary to get the legislative branch of the government to recognize these needs, than Carl Vinson." Among the promoters of a powerful Navy Carl Vinson deserves a high place. But the No. 1 architect of victory was the former Assistant Secretary of the Navy in World War I, who became President of the United States on 4 March 1933. Franklin D. Roosevelt brought a New Deal for the armed forces as well as for the nation. Yet he was not yet ready to end appeasement of Japan.

4. Naval Buildup under Roosevelt, 1933–1939

Even though Japan had bowed out of naval limitation, both Britain and America regarded themselves bound by the treaties. But the United States Navy had been allowed to fall so low that there was a vast gap to be filled before even treaty strength could be attained. Congress finally began responding to frequent prods from President Roosevelt, Mr. Vinson and the leading admirals. The first new construction authorized in years — of the *Brooklyn* class light cruisers, *Craven* class destroyers, carriers *Enterprise* and *Yorktown* and four submarines — came as a corollary to the National Industrial Recovery Act of 16 June 1933, the avowed purpose being to relieve unemployment.

This buildup taxed the ingenuity of the Navy bureaus (especially Ships and Yards and Docks) because during the lean decade many shipbuilding and other firms that depended on naval orders had been liquidated, and their designers, draftsmen and skilled workers had obtained other jobs or gone on relief. Thus the rearmament program started almost from scratch and could not be greatly accelerated until wartime. For example, the Vinson-Trammel Act of 1934 provided an eight-year replacement program which would require ten years to attain "treaty strength."

The first five "treaty 10,000-ton" heavy cruisers of the *New Orleans* class, which had been authorized five years earlier, joined the Fleet in 1934. Despite nation-wide unemployment, Congress for several years refused to increase the authorized personnel of the Navy, which in 1935, with only 8063 officers and 82,500 men, had to operate ships with about 80 per cent of their proper complement. Two years later a new ceiling of 100,000 bluejackets was established. Between 1935 and 1940 the *Atlanta* class of antiaircraft cruisers was designed and several types of fleet auxiliaries, including minesweepers, were transferred from the drafting boards to the building ways. All battleships of the *North Carolina, South Dakota* and *Iowa* classes were designed in these years; but only *North Carolina* and *Washington* were completed before we entered the war — our first battleships in eighteen years. These ships were characterized by 16-inch main batteries, thick armored decks for protection from air bombing, heavy fragment protection around important control stations, modern 5-inch antiaircraft guns in twin mounts, and the forerunners (found by battle experience to be inadequate) of the present types and numbers of close-range antiaircraft weapons.

In August 1939, when Admiral William D. Leahy was relieved as C.N.O. by Admiral Harold R. Stark, he could look back with some satisfaction at the increase of naval strength during the two and a half years of his incumbency. But, as he wrote in his last report, "The Navy must be sufficiently strong in every essential element, and it must be adequately trained," in order to take the offensive in the event of war and "defeat the enemy fleet wherever it can be brought to action." In several respects the Navy was not well rounded. Very few fast, modern auxiliaries had been finished. On 1 July 1939 the Navy had only two transports, three cargo ships, three oilers and one ammunition ship in commission; and on 1 December 1941 Cincpac had only one transport and one oiler ready to accompany the fleet's trans-Pacific trek, if and when war broke out. But the chief worry that Leahy bequeathed to his successor was the subject of bases.

It was probably a good thing in the long run that the United States Navy was ill-provided with bases in the Pacific, in comparison with the Imperial Japanese Navy and the Royal British. Want of them made American officers more self-reliant, and their ships more self-sufficient. Nevertheless, failure to develop adequately what bases we had meant a rapid withdrawal of American sea power from the western Pacific when the Japanese struck. After Japan denounced the naval limitation treaty in

1936, the United States was free to strengthen all bases, anywhere. But all that could be got out of Congress was a few million dollars for seaplane bases at Wake and Midway islands, and at Kodiak (Alaska) and Dutch Harbor in the Aleutians. These were indeed useful; only the first-named was lost to the enemy. In 1938 a special board headed by Admiral Hepburn recommended the building of a fully equipped fleet and air base at Guam, to help defend the Philippines. Congress, after a heated debate, turned this down, largely for fear of provoking Japan. And the little that was done to strengthen the defenses of Manila Bay proved to be wholly inadequate.

Immediately upon the outbreak of war in Europe, in September 1939, the appropriate bureaus of the Navy drew up comprehensive estimates of warship requirements. The problem was no longer one of designing the best ship of a limited size, but of selecting the most desirable combination of basic characteristics. With the aid of previous experience, designs were completed for new types of destroyers, cruisers, and aircraft carriers. By 7 December 1941, plans had been completed for the *Fletcher* class destroyers, the 6-inch *Cleveland* class cruisers, the 8-inch *Baltimore* class heavy cruisers, the *Essex* class aircraft carriers, the first destroyer escorts, and a dozen different classes of auxiliaries. In order to meet the demands of modern warfare, more ammunition was required for an increased number of guns, more crews to man the gunmounts, more fuel capacity for a wider cruising radius, more powerful machinery to deliver greater shaft horse power and develop more speed. Increased tonnage was inescapably necessary to carry the added weight, with sufficient reserve buoyancy and stability for the ship to survive serious damage. New main propulsion plants, using high-pressure, high-temperature steam, were introduced during the prewar period. These reached such a state of development that United States ships were able to travel enormous distances without shipyard upkeep and overhaul — in many cases over 100,000 miles within a single year. Vast improvements in the diesel engine industry provided another source of propulsive power which would be utilized to the staggering total of 35 million out of a total of some 90 million shaft horse power during the war.

A number of experimental laboratories and testing stations, maintained by various bureaus of the Navy, were staffed with technicians and scientists. Among such establishments were the Taylor ship-model basin, wind tunnels, powder, gun, torpedo, mine and aircraft factories, ordnance proving grounds, as well as testing and experimental stations. A Naval Research Laboratory was established in 1928 for high-level work. Owing to meager appropriations, it lost primacy in radar to the Royal Air Force laboratory in England; but that eventually benefited us too, and our research laboratory helped the Royal Navy in other fields. The National Research Council collaborated with the Naval Research Laboratory and also with the research activities of private industry. This laid foundations for the phenomenal success of the Navy in mobilizing American scientists and scientific resources for wartime purposes.

During Franklin D. Roosevelt's first administration and the first two years of his second (1937-1939), progress in national defense was substantial but slow. A five-day week law, designed to spread employment, made construction lag. Nor did our foreign policy substantially change. What the Japanese called the "China Incident" of 7 July 1937 inaugurated their invasion of China proper, in the course of which they sank United States River Gunboat *Panay* without producing a noticeable dent on the American people's determination to avoid war.

The widely publicized report of a committee headed by Senator Gerald Nye, in 1934, "proved" by innuendo that bankers and munitions makers ("merchants of death") had got America into World War I, and Congress responded to the public opinion

thereby created by passing a series of neutrality acts. These renounced most of the neutral rights for which we had fought
England in 1812 and Germany in 1917. Sale or transport of munitions to a belligerent was forbidden (1935), loans to belligerents
were prohibited (1936); these were applied to the civil war in
Spain, but sale of munitions was permitted on a "cash and carry"
basis (1937). And the President was authorized to prohibit American ships from entering "danger zones" so as to prevent "incidents"
(1939). Thus, to peace by naval limitation and peace by incantation
(the Kellogg-Briand pact) we added peace by an ostrich-like
isolation.

When war broke in Europe in September 1939, the vast majority of the American people wished to stay out of it. American
sympathies were strongly pro-Ally, but it was assumed that Hitler's
Third Reich was a big bluff, and that the French Army and Royal
Navy could defeat him in short order.

NOTE ON "SCRAPPING" UNDER THE 1922 TREATIES

There were a few exceptions allowed to the 5:5:3 ratio: the most
fortunate for us being permission to convert two 43,500-ton battle
cruiser hulls, still on the ways, into carriers *Lexington* and *Saratoga*,
of 33,000 tons each — despite a treaty limitation of 25,000 tons on
aircraft carrier construction. Japan by way of compensation converted battle cruiser *Akagi* and battleship *Kaga* (substituted for
Amagi, destroyed in the great earthquake) to carriers. In accordance with the 1922 treaties, the United States Navy scrapped the
76 per cent completed battleship *Washington*, six 43,200-tonners of
South Dakota class 11 to 38 per cent complete, and four battle
cruisers building, sisters to *Lexington* and *Saratoga*. On these ships
three hundred million dollars had already been spent. In addition,
"Dreadnoughts" *Delaware*, *North Dakota*, *Michigan* and *South
Carolina* (twelve years old), were scrapped and 15 pre-Dread-

noughts, some as old as the Spanish-American War, were broken up, used as targets, or made museum pieces. Originally the United States Navy was also to have scrapped *Colorado* and *West Virginia*, retaining only *Maryland* as a postwar 16-inch-gunned battleship; England to have kept *Hood*, and Japan *Nagato*, to balance *Maryland*. Japan, however, presented a plea to keep new battleship *Mutsu*, since Japanese schoolchildren had contributed their pennies to pay for her; so there was another compromise, whereby the United States Navy kept *Colorado* and *West Virginia* and England built two new equalizers, *Nelson* and *Rodney*. The Royal Navy in accordance with the treaty scrapped 14 "Dreadnought" battleships and 6 "Dreadnought" battle cruisers, 7 to 15 years old, totaling 415,000 tons, and renounced building four "super-*Hood*" class battle cruisers. Japan used as a target and sank the completed 40,000-ton battleship *Tosa*, gave up constructing two more battle cruisers, and scrapped 8 pre-Dreadnought battleships, 11 to 16 years old. A re-examination after World War II makes the balance fairer than it seemed at the time; 8 of the 18 battleships retained by the United States Navy were completed in 1917 or later, but only 3 of the 16 battleships retained by the Royal Navy, and 5 of the 6 battleships retained by Japan, were that new. Both Britain and Japan had in the blueprint stage eight 18-inch-gunned battleships, which they gave up building. I am indebted to Mr. Samuel A. Smiley of Falls Church, Virginia, for information on this subject.

CHAPTER II

Short of War

1939–1941

1. *Impact of the European War*

THE SIXTH YEAR of the appeasement of Hitler by England and France ended on "1 September 1939" when he invaded Poland. For another year American policy toward the European war was dictated by the public's overwhelming desire to keep out of it, at almost any price. At the same time that President Roosevelt announced American neutrality, he declared a "limited emergency" (8 September). The immediate effects of this on Congress, as respects the Navy, were to increase authorized enlisted strength to 191,000, and to allow the President to recall reserve officers and men to active duty as needed.

Our first positive action toward the war, typically if paradoxically negative, was to organize the Neutrality Patrol. This was decided at the Congress of American Republics at Panama, on 2 October. Hitler had been nourishing "fifth columns" of Nazis in many Latin American republics, and the gravest danger to the Americas at that time appeared to be German subversion. The idea behind the Neutrality Patrol was to create and protect a neutral zone extending an average of 300 miles off the American coastline, except off Canada; for Canada loyally declared war when her mother country did. West of this line, belligerents were forbidden by the Congress of American Republics to conduct military operations. Eight groups of the United States Navy, mostly destroyers and cruisers, covered the North American sector from Newfoundland to Trinidad. This, writes Captain Roskill RN, "was unquestionably an unfavorable move from the Allies' point of view." On the other hand, Admiral Doenitz, commander of the German U-boat fleet, regarded the Neutrality Patrol as an outrageous limitation on the operations of his submarines.

Although naval and military men are often accused of trying to fight a new war with the tactics of the last one, the reverse was true here; neither Germany nor England realized that World War II in the Atlantic would closely resemble World War I. In both wars, Germany tried to disrupt England's communications and sink Allied tonnage with U-boats, whilst England counterattacked the submarines and imposed a surface blockade of Germany. But neither side thought it would be like this in 1939. Germany had fewer than fifty submarines ready for offensive operations when war broke, and a very low production schedule. The Royal Navy was not provided with mines to protect British harbors or with nearly enough ships for escort-of-convoy and antisubmarine work. The reasons given for this lack, by Admiral Sir William James, are equally applicable to the United States Navy when it entered the war more than two years later: it was thought better to spend limited budgets on battleships, carriers, and other big ships that took a long time to build, rather than on a multitude of escorts and other small craft which, it was believed, could be improvised when war broke out.

Another lesson of the last war was the necessity of convoying merchant shipping, and the folly of trying to cope with submarines by hunting them all over the place — "looking for a needle in a haystack," as Captain Mahan described such tactics. The Royal Navy did organize merchant convoys to the extent of its supply of escorts; but, spurred by Winston Churchill and other civilians, it also wasted time and effort on hunter groups. After a big fleet carrier, H.M.S. *Courageous*, had fallen victim to a U-boat while engaged in one of these hunts, the British stopped them; and after the United States entered the war, Admiral King set his face sternly against anything of the sort.

To anticipate: The entire experience of the war demonstrated that the heavily escorted merchant convoy, supplemented by an escort carrier group on its flank, was by far the best way to get U-boats, because the merchantmen acted as bait. The convoy was not a defensive weapon, as so often charged by ignorant or prejudiced people, but the best sort of offensive, besides being the only way to insure safe transportation of men and matériel.

With the aid of the land-based Coastal Command of the R.A.F., now under Admiralty control, the Royal Navy did well against U-boats in 1939-1940, the winter of the "phony war" on the European Continent. German moored magnetic mines and surface raiders proved more destructive than submarines at this period. The Royal Navy quickly learned to cope with these, and passed on its findings to us, which enabled the United States Navy to repair its former neglect of mine warfare.

2. *The Fall of France and "Short of War" Strategy*

Up to mid-1940 it was the general opinion in the United States that the French Army and British Navy between them could defeat Hitler. The blitzes that Hitler exploded in the spring of 1940, culminating in the fall of France in June, administered a rude jolt to this attitude. It took time for the implications to sink into the public mind; but we now know that the fall of France was the greatest upset to world balance of power between 1871 and 1949, when China went Red.

With Germany in control of such French outposts as Brest, Lorient, Saint-Nazaire and La Pallice, her U-boats' cruising radius was doubled; and the air blitz laid on England at the same time carried the grave threat of Hitler's acquiring bases in the British Isles. If North Africa too were brought under German control, there was a fair prospect that Nazi governments would be set up in South America and the French and Dutch West Indies be taken over.

Naturally there were repercussions in the Far East. The Tokyo press reacted violently to the United States holding its annual fleet exercise in the Pacific. At the conclusion of this 1940 Fleet Problem, and at the request of the State Department, the Fleet was ordered to remain based on Pearl Harbor, in the hope of its exercising a "deterrent effect" on Japanese aggression. The Imperial government had already proclaimed the "Greater East Asia Co-Prosperity Sphere," aiming at Japanese political, economic and military hegemony over Indochina, Thailand, Netherlands East Indies and the Philippines. On 27 September 1940, Japan formally joined the European Axis in the Tripartite Pact, which stipulated that if one of the three got into war with the United States the other two would pitch in. For the United States Navy this posed the problem of fighting a two-ocean war with a much less than one-ocean Fleet.

President Franklin D. Roosevelt had a political calculating machine in his head, an intricate instrument in which Gallup polls, the strength of armed forces and the probability of England's survival; the personalities of governors, senators and congressmen, and of Mussolini, Hitler, Churchill, Chiang, and Tojo; the Irish, German, Italian, and Jewish votes in the approaching presidential election; the "Help the Allies" people and the "American Firsters," were combined with fine points of political maneuvering. The fall of France, fed into the F.D.R. calculating machine, caused wheels to whir and gears to click with dynamic intensity. Out came a solution: the "short of war" policy (1) to help keep England fighting in Europe, (2) to gain time for American rearmament, and (3) to restrain Japan by diplomacy and the Fleet's "deterrence." Whether Roosevelt really believed that this policy would "keep us out of war" is debatable. But he had to assume that it would, until after the presidential election of 1940, in which he flouted tradition by running for a third term, and until events abroad convinced the American people that war was their only alternative to a shameful and ultimately disastrous appeasement.

In any case, an essential and most beneficial part of the "short of war" policy was to build up the Navy. On 14 June 1940, the day that Hitler took Paris, President Roosevelt signed a naval expansion bill that had been under discussion for months. Three days later, Admiral Stark asked Congress for four billion dollars more to begin building a "two-ocean navy," and got it. The Navy then had about 1,250,000 tons of combatant shipping; this bill authorized a more than double increase. But, as Admiral Stark said, "Dollars cannot buy yesterday." For two years at least, the Americas would be vulnerable in the event of a German victory in Europe.

To meet this emergency, President Roosevelt adopted the political strategy of helping England and (after June 1941) Russia in their war with Germany. This meant violating all the old international laws of neutrality. Hitler had completely flouted neutral rights by his invasion of Denmark, Norway, Belgium and Holland; hence Germany forfeited the right to demand neutrality of others. Most Americans were loath to discard a concept so deeply rooted in the national tradition — they had just been trying to embalm neutrality in acts of Congress! But they were willing to build a two-ocean Navy, hoping that a wall of ships in the blueprint stage or on the building ways would deter Hitler from setting up satellite states in America.

On 15 June 1940, the day after approving the first of these new navy bills, President Roosevelt appointed a group of eminent civilian scientists members of a new National Defense Research Committee. These included Vannevar Bush, President of the Carnegie Institution of Washington; James Bryant Conant, President of Harvard University; Karl T. Compton, President of the Massachusetts Institute of Technology; Frank B. Jewett, President of the National Academy of Sciences; and Rear Admiral J. A. Furer. Since late 1939 Dr. Bush had been working on the mobilization of American scientists for war, but it took the fall of France to bring matters to a head. From this N.D.R.C. stemmed most of the essential civilian research done for the armed forces during the "short of war" period, and during the war itself.

At the same time, in order to emphasize the nation's danger and obtain nation-wide support, President Roosevelt appointed two leading Republicans Secretary of the Navy and Secretary of War. Frank Knox, who had been Republican candidate for Vice President in the last election, quickly acquired a grasp of naval business and became one of the best secretaries the Navy ever had. The office of Under Secretary of the Navy was created and first filled by Knox's future successor, James V. Forrestal, on 22 August 1940. Henry L. Stimson, who had been Secretary of War under President Taft and Secretary of State under President Hoover, became Secretary of War again in July 1940. Upon his urgent recommendation, Congress passed the Selective Training and Service Act on 16 September. This was the first time that the United States had adopted compulsory military training in time of peace.

During the summer and fall of that year, President Roosevelt initiated several important steps in high-level strategy in the Atlantic. He held a conference with Mackenzie King, Prime Minister of Canada, in August. A United States–Canada Mutual Defense Pact included complete reciprocity in the use of the naval shipyards of both countries. Now that the British Commonwealth was the one power fighting Germany, it became urgent to keep her strong and pugnacious while the American "two-ocean navy" was being built. President Roosevelt and Winston Churchill concluded on 2 September the naval bases–destroyers deal. Britain ceded to the United States sovereign rights for ninety-nine years over sites for naval, military and air bases in the West Indies in exchange for fifty four-stack destroyers built during or shortly after the last war. The Argentia (Newfoundland) and Bermuda bases were also granted to the United States as free gifts.

Information from United States naval attachés in the Axis countries furthered the "short of war" policy. For instance, Commander A. E. Schrader reported from Berlin on 18 December 1940 that Hitler already had seven to nine million men available to be called to the colors, that there was no possibility of an internal revolt against him, that all six of the occupied countries were being systematically plundered for Germany's benefit, and that the British "heart of oak" was admirably taking the German air blitz on a "chin of armorplate." He even predicted that Germany would next attack Russia to annex the Ukraine and the Caucasus, and warned that the whole world would be "an empty shell" if Germany won. One of our military attachés in Berlin obtained a copy of Hitler's plan for an attack on Russia six months in advance; the important news went to Stalin via Roosevelt and Churchill, but Stalin refused to believe it.

Postwar revelations of discussion in the German high command prove that President Roosevelt's estimate that Hitler would overlook direct American aid to England, rather than declare war, was absolutely right. The arrogant Nazi government chose to accept the destroyer deal and plenty more, because it knew very well that the United States at war would be far more formidable than the United States "short of war." And the time gained by us for preparation was of inestimable value.

The next unneutral measure was Lend-Lease. By existing neutrality legislation it was still illegal for American merchant ships to trade with, or for private investors to lend their money to, belligerent countries. Whatever war supplies Britain or Canada procured in the United States had to be paid for with cash, and carried in their own ships; and they were "scraping the bottom of the barrel." The Lend-Lease plan was briefly this: The United States would embark on an all-out military and naval defense program, both by giving orders to private firms and by building new government plants; but would lend or lease as much production as could be spared to Great Britain. Congress passed the first Lend-Lease Act on 11 March 1941. "This decision," said the President on 15 March, "is the end of any attempt at appeasement in our land; the end of urging us to get along with the dictators; the end of compromise with tyranny and the forces of oppression."

It was not quite that; certainly not, respecting Japan; but the Nazis had to "take it." Hitler, who attacked Russia in June 1941, informed his navy chief in July that it was "vitally important to put off America's entering into the war for another one or two months." He wanted no "incidents" calculated to provoke America. But he got plenty, as we shall see.

Even more important in early 1941 was the ABC–1 Staff Agreement which constituted the basic agreement for Anglo-American coöperation if and when we entered the war, and the basic strategic decision of the war: to "beat Hitler first." In July 1940, Admiral Harold R. Stark, Chief of Naval Operations, sent Rear Admiral R. L. Ghormley to London for "exploratory conversations" with the Admiralty. These were so fruitful in acquiring information about antisubmarine and other aspects of the war that, on the advice of C.N.O., a secret staff conversation with the British was convened at Washington at the end of January 1941. Rear Admirals Ghormley and Richmond Kelly Turner and Captains Alan G. Kirk and DeWitt C. Ramsey represented the United States Navy; Major General Embick, Brigadier General Sherman Miles and Colonel L. T. Gerow, the Army; Air Vice Marshal John C. Slessor was there for the Royal Air Force; Rear Admirals Roger Bellairs and Victor Danckwerts for the Royal Navy. After long deliberations, this conference concluded the "ABC–1 Staff Agreement" of 27 March 1941. This provided that, if and when the United States entered the war, it would exert "the principal U.S. military effort" in the European theater. America would try to avoid war with Japan, but, even if that proved impossible, operations in the Pacific would be conducted in such a manner as "to facilitate" the effort against the European Axis. Naturally this decision pleased the British, but the Americans initiated it. The reasons behind so sound a decision — which, as Slessor wrote, continued to govern our combined action throughout the war, although "at times a bit frayed at the edges" — were (1) Germany had a far greater military potentiality than Japan; (2) Germany already controlled almost the entire Atlantic coast of Europe and threatened the Americas; (3) England was already fighting Germany and could be assisted immediately, whilst Japan at that time was fighting only China, which foreign aid could not reach — Japan having already seized the Chinese coast, part of Indochina, and the Burma Road.

The two staffs also agreed that, if and when the United States entered the war, the American Joint Chiefs of Staff and the British Chiefs of Staff would meet as the Combined Chiefs of Staff to make strategic plans and decisions for the Allied nations. And other decisions about command structures, areas of responsibility, and exchange of information were loyally carried out on both sides. Thus, even before America entered the war, the basic strategic decision had been made, and machinery had been set up for close coöperation. This forehandedness prevented an infinite amount of friction, misunderstanding and fruitless effort, such as had taken place in World War I.

One Washington agreement went into effect immediately — that the United States Navy share responsibility for escorting transatlantic convoys as soon as the Atlantic Fleet could do so.

The Atlantic Fleet was reactivated 1 February 1941 under Admiral Ernest J. King as Commander in Chief — "Cinclant" for short. "Ernie" King, born in Ohio in 1878, a graduate of the Naval Academy in 1901, was not only a great naval officer but a military strategist. He had shown outstanding ability in almost every branch of the Navy — ordnance, engineering, assistant chief of staff to the C. in C. in World War I, logistics, submarines, naval aviation, General Board, C.O. of a reefer, of destroyers, of a naval air station, and of *Lexington*. A hard man with little sense of humor, he was more respected than liked in the Navy; his eagerness to get things done quickly with no unnecessary palaver, coupled with an abrupt and often rude manner, infuriated many Americans and dismayed his British opposite numbers. No officer on either side or in any armed service had so complete a strategic view of the war as King's. Neither General Marshall nor any of the British had time or energy to concentrate on the war in the Pacific; but King not only grasped that and the Atlantic war; he had a better strategic savvy of the land phases of the European war than most of the generals. Secretary Stimson hated him, Winston Churchill and Sir Alan Brooke hated him, Admiral Sir Andrew B. Cunningham hated him, many even in the United States Army and Navy hated him. But Tojo, Hitler, and Doenitz had even greater reason to hate King, because, with Churchill, Roosevelt and Eisenhower, he was a principal architect of Allied victory.

By the time the "short of war" measures were being organized, German U-boats were coming in increasing numbers off the assembly line, enabling Admiral Doenitz to set up new "wolf-pack" tactics. His submarines, in groups of eight to twenty, were sent out fanwise into the North and South Atlantic, and, daily controlled by radio from the command post in Lorient, would shadow a convoy by day and attack by night. On the night of 3-4 April 1941 one of these wolf-packs sank 10 out of 22 ships in a slow transatlantic convoy. Admiral Stark at once saw that the United States Navy would have to pitch in to help escort-of-convoy, or the lend-lease aid would never reach its destination.

On 4 April he transferred the new carrier *Yorktown,* three battle-ships, four light cruisers and two destroyer squadrons from the Pacific to the Atlantic Fleet. On 9 April the minister of Denmark (now occupied by the Germans) at Washington invited the United States to become the protector of Greenland, which she promptly did; and Greenland became a base for weather stations and for air-fields, both important in the antisubmarine campaign. On 18 April Admiral King issued his Operation Plan 3-41 in which he ordered that any belligerent warship or aircraft — other than those of powers which had West Indian colonies — which approached within 25 miles of the Western Hemisphere (Greenland included) to be "viewed as actuated by an intention immediately to attack such territory." The Fleet was ordered to be in constant readi-ness for combat, but to make no attack without orders from C.N.O. In May came the break-out of German battleship *Bismarck,* sunk after a long chase by torpedo bombers and gunfire of the Royal Navy on the 27th. That day President Roosevelt declared an "Un-limited National Emergency." The decimation of transatlantic convoys by U-boats continued. Hitler invaded Russia on 22 June. After a tardy invitation from a sulky Icelandic government, United States Marines occupied Iceland on 8 July. The United States Navy formally began escort duties by protecting merchant ships, of what-ever flag, in convoys from East Coast ports to Iceland. On 16 Sep-tember the Navy began helping the Canadians to escort transatlantic convoys to a mid-ocean meeting point ("Momp") south of Iceland, where the Royal Navy took over.

First blood for Germany was narrowly averted on 20 June 1941 when *U-203* sighted battleship *Texas* between Newfoundland and Greenland and, assuming that she had been lend-leased to England, tried to attack but could not catch her. On 4 Septem-ber United States destroyer *Greer* and *U-652* played a cat-and-mouse game with depth charges and torpedoes. Both missed, but the President took this occasion to have orders issued to shoot on sight any ship interfering with American shipping. It worked both ways; on the black night of 17 October U.S.S. *Kearny,* one of Captain Hewlett Thébaud's destroyer division escorting a slow convoy, was torpedoed. She lost eleven men, but reached port. On 30 October a naval oiler, *Salinas,* was torpedoed in mid-ocean, but survived. The first sinking of a combatant ship came next day when U. S. S. *Reuben James* (Lieutenant Commander H. L. Edwards) was sunk by *U–562* while helping to escort a fast convoy from Halifax, with a loss of 115 officers and men.

Thus, "short of war" was not so very short for the Atlantic Fleet. Autumn and winter escort work in the North Atlantic was arduous and exhausting for men and ships. That section of it covered by United States destroyers, between Newfoundland, Greenland and Iceland, is the roughest part of the western ocean in winter. Winds of gale force, mountainous seas, biting cold, body-piercing fog and blinding snow squalls were the rule rather than the exception. The continual rolling and pitching, coupled with the necessity for constant vigilance night and day — not only for enemy attack, but to guard against collisions with other escort vessels and the convoy — wore men down. The so-called "rest periods" at Hvalfjordur and Argentia were rests merely from enemy attack, not from the weather; for in both ports the holding ground was bad and the weather terrible. Destroyers dragged all over these harbors in winter gales, and vigorous effort was required to avoid fouling other vessels and running aground.

The strain was not only physical but psychological. These officers and men were enduring all the danger and hardship of war; yet it was not called war. They were forbidden to talk of their experiences ashore, or even to tell where they had been and what they were doing, and so had none of the satisfaction derived from public recognition. After going through cold hell at sea, they would reach port to find other young men making money in safe industries, and college football stars featured as heroes of the day.

Barroom isolationists and (it is suspected) enemy agents worked on the men in Boston, taunting them with "fighting England's battles" and tempting them to desert. But our bluejackets had seen for themselves the new terror that the Nazi had added to the perils and dangers of the deep. Few realized better than they the threat to America in this German strike for sea supremacy. And the fact that morale in the destroyers remained high, throughout this period of bitter warfare that yet was not war, attests the intelligence, the discipline, and the fortitude of the United States Navy.

3. *Japan Moves Toward War*

As we have seen, the United States Fleet, commanded by Admiral James O. Richardson, had been based at Pearl Harbor, as a "deterrent" to Japanese aggression, since April 1940. Admiral Richardson, after expressing to the President in no uncertain terms his dislike of Pearl Harbor as a fleet base, was relieved by Admiral Husband E. Kimmel on 1 February 1941; and on the same day the United States Fleet was renamed the Pacific Fleet.[1] It was still an unbalanced fleet, incapable of promptly performing its assigned mission in the revised Orange (now called Rainbow 5) plan of capturing key points in the Marshall and Caroline Islands with the help of the Marine Corps, and then relieving the Philippines. There, it was assumed, the Army under General Douglas Mac-Arthur, who was also Field Marshal of the armed forces of the Philippine Commonwealth, would be holding out against the Japanese. Kimmel, an energetic, devoted naval officer, applied himself to fleet training, both of ships and planes, so as to provide a core of

[1] The Pacific Fleet, as then constituted, included all ships in the Navy except (1) the Atlantic Fleet which was set up on 1 Feb. 1941; and (2) the Asiatic Fleet under Admiral Thomas C. Hart, a very small fleet with no ship larger than a cruiser, based at Manila Bay.

experienced officers and petty officers for the flood of new construction that the two-ocean navy and other recent acts provided. He frequently sent out task groups to exercise the men and the guns but he made a practice of mooring most of the Fleet in Pearl Harbor over weekends, to keep officers and men happy. It must be remembered that the average young American of that era, conditioned by twenty-one years of antimilitarist indoctrination by movies, books, preachers and teachers, could be induced to enlist in the armed forces, or reënlist if his term had expired, only by making things pleasant for him — not too much work and plenty of recreation. That situation, besides the two-thousand-mile haul for supplies, was why Admiral Richardson objected to the fleet's being based away from California.

The situation in Oahu of the United States Army, responsible for the defense of the Territory, was similar. Lieutenant General Walter Short had two divisions under his command. He too was deeply concerned with training and replacement. Flying Fortresses (B–17s) as fast as built were flown to Oahu for their final arming and equipment, after which most of them flew on to Manila via Wake Island and Guam. There seems to have been no expectation that they might be needed in Hawaii.

In contrast to the United States Pacific Fleet, the Japanese Combined Fleet was well balanced, thoroughly trained and spoiling for a fight. Owing to the operation of the 5:5:3 ratio, and to Japan's kicking over even that in 1936 and embarking on an intensive building program, the Japanese Navy was more powerful in combatant ships than the United States Navy in the Pacific; more powerful even if one added the British and Dutch warships in that ocean.[2] It had plenty of freighters convertible to transports, fleet oilers, or other auxiliaries; it was rugged from annual ma-

[2] On 1 Dec. 1941: Pacific Fleet, 9 battleships, Japan, 10; Pacific Fleet, 3 carriers, Japan, 10; United States Pacific and Asiatic Fleets, 13 heavy and 11 light cruisers, Japan, 18 and 17; Pacific and Asiatic Fleets, 80 destroyers, Japan, 111; Pacific and Asiatic Fleets, 55 submarines, Japan, 64.

neuvers in rough northern waters. Japanese gunnery and navigation were excellent; their torpedoes were far more speedy, accurate and destructive than those of any other navy, and their carrier planes were superior in the fighter and torpedo-bomber categories.

Admiral Yamamoto, Commander in Chief Combined Fleet, had been attached to the Japanese embassy in Washington, where he was respected for his naval knowledge, and also for his excellent game of poker. Knowing America's military potential very well, he begged Prince Konoye, the prime minister who preceded General Tojo, to endeavor to avoid war; but when war was decided upon, Yamamoto set his ingenious brain to work on the best method of neutralizing the United States Navy at the start. He had, in fact, been working on that problem since January 1941, when he decided that a surprise air attack on the Pacific Fleet at Pearl Harbor was the answer.

The decision, for a man of Yamamoto's intelligence, was strange; for as strategy it was not only wrong but disastrous. The Pacific Fleet, as we have seen, had been sent to Pearl Harbor as a "deterrent," and as such it was fatally effective. The Japanese war lords had made up their minds in 1940 to take advantage of the European situation and conquer all European or American colonies or dependencies in eastern Asia. The only deterrents that they feared were the B–17s at Manila and the Pacific Fleet at Pearl Harbor. In view of the weakness of that Fleet (of which they were well apprised), and the length of time that it would take to reach Philippine waters, it is unaccountable that Yamamoto thought its destruction necessary before war fairly began. Apparently he felt that Japan could not suffer a "fleet in being" (one of Mahan's concepts) on her flank, even though thousands of miles distant. Actually the Fleet would have been as much of a deterrent in California harbors as at Pearl, but harder to get at. And if we had based it at Singapore, as the British urged us to do, it would have been even more vulnerable, besides being in an impossible position logistically.

The Japanese war plan, brought together at a Supreme War Council on 6 September 1941, was as follows: First, prior to a declaration of war, destruction of the United States Pacific Fleet and the British and American air forces on the Malay Peninsula and Luzon. Second, while the British and American Navies were decimated and disorganized, a quick conquest of the Philippines, Guam, Wake, Hong Kong, Borneo, British Malaya (including Singapore), and Sumatra. Third, when these were secure, the converging of Japanese amphibious forces on the richest prize, Java, and a mop-up of the rest of the Dutch islands. Fourth, an intensive development of Malayan and Indonesian resources in oil, rubber, etc.; and, to secure these, establishment of a defensive perimeter running from the Kurile Islands through Wake, the Marshalls, and around the southern and western edges of the Malay Barrier to the Burmese-Indian border. With these bases the Japanese Navy and air forces could cut all lines of communication between Australia, New Zealand and the Anglo-American powers, which would then be forced to sue for peace. Fifth and finally, Japan would proceed completely to subjugate China. Over half the world's population would then be under the economic, political and military control of the Emperor.

This scheme of conquest was the most enticing, ambitious and far-reaching in modern history, not excepting Hitler's. It almost worked, and might well have succeeded but for the United States Navy.

This being Japan's plan, it is astonishing to find her American apologists claiming that she was goaded, provoked and coerced into making war on us by the Roosevelt administration. What F.D.R. did (with the support of Congress and popular approval, as judged by acts of Congress, Gallup polls and the newspapers) was to impose embargoes on iron, steel, oil, and other strategic materials going to Japan, and to "freeze" Japanese financial assets in America. This process, applied gradually, began in mid-1940 and finally reached effectiveness at the end of July 1941, after Japan had announced her determination to occupy southern Indochina.

Now, in the second half of 1941, the British and the Dutch co-operated in both freeze and embargoes; and as Japanese oil stocks dwindled, the government found itself in a dilemma. It must either renounce an imposing plan of conquest, on which the army insisted, to get oil from the United States and the Netherlands East Indies; or it must fight the United States, the Dutch and the British, to conquer oil for more conquests. It chose the second alternative deliberately, as the more honorable and potentially profitable. Better to defeat America in a quick blitz, as Hitler had France, and then, impregnable, get on with the conquest of China.

It is now perfectly clear that nothing short of force could have stopped Japan from embarking on her Southeast Asia plan, or have persuaded her to withdraw from China. But war might have been at least postponed, allowing the United States to catch up somewhat in the arms race, if Prince Konoye's proposal in August 1941 of a summit conference between himself and President Roosevelt had been accepted. Joseph Grew, our sapient and sensitive ambassador at Tokyo, was for it; F.D.R. was for it; but Secretary of State Cordell Hull opposed it on the grounds that Konoye was a slippery character, and that a summit conference should take place only to cap a prior agreement on principles, such as Japan's abandoning the Tripartite Pact. Hull did not understand that for Japan that treaty with Germany and Italy was part "face," part minatory gesture, and that she did not intend to honor it if it did not suit her. Prince Konoye sincerely wished to start liquidating Japan's dreams of conquest; but he was on a spot, with a ministry of jingo militarists, and Hull gave him no help to get off. As prince of the royal house he had the Emperor's ear, and Hirohito himself was anxious for peace. So there was a chance that if Konoye brought a promise from Roosevelt to lift the oil embargo and unfreeze the assets, in return for Japan's promising to start a military evacuation of Indochina and eventually of China itself, the prince might have persuaded the Emperor to expel the militarists from the cabinet. Of course it is even more likely that Konoye would have been assassinated; but he was willing to take the chance, and he should have been given the opportunity. In any event, a summit conference would have gained time; it could not have met until late October, and Japan could hardly have dispatched the Pearl Harbor striking force while it was sitting.

After toying with the summit idea for almost two months, Hull persuaded F.D.R. to reject it definitely on 2 October. Konoye then resigned, and General Tojo became prime minister. And as the Japanese Supreme War Council had in the meantime set up the grandiose war plan already described, any complete change of Japanese policy would have been difficult to carry out, even by the Emperor.

The negotiations at Washington dragged along fruitlessly. On 10 November Winston Churchill declared in a speech that he did not know whether "the effort of the United States to preserve peace in the Pacific will be successful"; and he promised that "if the United States should become involved in war with Japan, a British declaration would follow within the hour." That threat did not deter the Japanese government for a moment.

You can always keep the peace if you are willing to pay the asking price; and it is a matter of high strategic decision whether the price demanded is worse than refusal with its risk of war. Tojo's price for peace, his ultimatum as he called it, was presented by his ambassador at Washington on 20 November 1941. America must concede Japan a free hand in Indochina and China, and render Chiang no more assistance. She must restore trading relations with Japan and send no more military forces to the South Pacific or the Far East, even to the Philippines. In return for these extraordinary concessions, which could only have been accepted by a nation defeated in war, all Japan offered was to send no more armed forces into Southeast Asia, and to evacuate French Indochina after peace had been imposed on China.

Tojo had already twice postponed the deadline at which war would begin if the United States did not knuckle under. Time was running out, and time was what the leaders of the American armed forces, especially General Marshall, Admiral Stark, and General MacArthur in the Philippines, most wanted. Largely to please them, the Department of State drafted a three months' *modus vivendi*, according to which Japan would start a token withdrawal from Indochina and America would partially resume trade with Japan, as a preliminary to a fresh approach to the China problem. Of the friendly governments to which this was submitted on 25 November, Chiang Kai-shek "violently opposed" it, and the British, Dutch and Australian governments were lukewarm or unfavorable; many people high in the United States government, too, thought that this proposal smelt of Munich. The President decided, on Hull's advice, that the slight prospect of Japan's agreeing to this *modus vivendi* did not warrant the risks to Chinese and American morale that backtracking at this time would involve. Actually, Tojo had already rejected the essential idea of the *modus vivendi* — halting conquest in return for oil — in a dispatch of 20 November, so the whole thing was bad diplomacy.

Hull's next move was even less fortunate. On 26 November he presented to the Japanese ambassadors at Washington an outline of a "proposed basis for agreement" which went absolutely counter to Tojo's plans; for it required an eventual Japanese evacuation of China and recognition of Chiang in return for restoration of trading relations with the United States. While such stipulations made no sense at that crisis, it must be emphasized that this note was not an ultimatum, an alternative to war. There was no threat, express or implied, that the President would ask for a declaration of war on Japan if Tojo rejected it. The cold war could have gone on indefinitely, so far as Washington was concerned (and we now know how long a cold war can go on), provided Japan made no fresh aggressive move. And it is doubtful whether Congress would have considered as *casus belli* a Japanese move into Thailand, British Malaya or the Netherlands East Indies.

On 26 November, the very day that Hull's outline was presented, the Japanese striking force for Pearl Harbor sortied from Tankan Bay in the Kuriles. The "day of infamy" was already set for 7 December, and several other Japanese task forces were set in motion to strike or invade Hong Kong, Malaya, Thailand and the Philippines. If Washington had knuckled under completely before 5 December, the Pearl Harbor force would have been recalled; but the conquest of the Philippines, Malaya and the Netherlands East Indies would have gone on according to schedule. Those were Japanese objectives from which they could not have been dissuaded, no matter how abject the appeasement.

History is studded with ironies, but never were there greater ironies that these: The fundamental reason for America's going to war with Japan was our insistence on the integrity of China; yet all our efforts and sacrifices, instead of strengthening friendly relations with China, have resulted in making her our greatest potential enemy. America in 1939-1941 wanted neither world power nor world responsibility, only to be let alone; but world power and responsibility were forced upon her by the two nations, Germany and Japan, that badly wanted both. And those nations are now numbered among America's firmest allies. In terms of the ancient Greek drama, the gods of Olympus must be roaring with laughter over the state of the world twenty years and more after the Pearl Harbor attack, which one might think had been especially arranged by them to destroy American complacency.

CHAPTER III

Disaster at Pearl Harbor

7 December 1941

1. Last Days of "Peace" in the Pacific

THE PEARL HARBOR STRIKING FORCE, under Vice Admiral Chuichi Nagumo, was strong, well organized, and intensively trained for the double purpose of wiping out the major part of the Pacific Fleet at Pearl Harbor, and destroying all military aircraft on Oahu. It included the six newest and largest carriers of the Imperial Navy[1]; a screen of nine destroyers and a light cruiser; a support force of two battleships and two heavy cruisers; three fleet submarines to patrol the flanks, and a supply train of seven or eight tankers. These ships departed the Inland Sea in deuces and treys so as not to arouse suspicion, rendezvoused at desolate Tankan Bay in the Kuriles, and sailed for Pearl Harbor 26 November. Course was shaped over a part of the North Pacific generally avoided by merchant shipping, and the advance screen of destroyers was ordered to sink at sight any American, British or Dutch vessel encountered. The weather was foul, many men were washed overboard, fueling at sea was accomplished with difficulty; but Striking Force pounded along according to schedule.

Admiral Nagumo did not relish his assignment and rather hoped that his force would be detected by 5 December, in which case Yamamoto had instructed him to abandon mission and return. But

---

[1] *Akagi, Kaga, Shokaku, Zuikaku, Horyu, Soryu,* carrying 423 combat planes.

only one ship, a Japanese freighter, was encountered; and not one aircraft. By listening to the Honolulu commercial broadcasts, the Admiral was assured that nobody ashore anticipated the lethal strike that he was about to deliver. His sailors had been hopped up by anti-American propaganda to a black, bitter hatred of Americans; and it apparently never occurred to anyone that to attack an unsuspecting people, when your government was still negotiating, and in defiance of the Hague Convention of 1907 which Japan had ratified, was dirty ball. Treaties, for the Japanese government of that time, were to be honored or broken according to the Emperor's presumed interest. Early on 6 December the latest report from the Japanese consulate in Honolulu on American ships present in Pearl Harbor was received via Tokyo. The Battle Fleet was there all right, but no carriers — a great disappointment.

At 2100 that evening Striking Force reached the meridian of Oahu at a point about 490 miles north of the island. All hands on the carriers who could be spared from duties below were summoned to the flight decks, officers made speeches, and the actual flag which had been displayed from Admiral Togo's flagship before the Battle of Tsushima in 1905 was raised to the masthead of *Akagi*. It was a high moment of frenzied patriotic emotion. Course now was shaped due south, the oilers and supply ships were left behind, and during a night of thick overcast through which the moon (three days after full) showed a faint light, Striking Force charged forward at 26 knots. Heavy cruisers *Tone* and *Chikuma* thrust ahead to catapult two float planes for reconnaissance. They reported everything calm in Pearl Harbor; not one ship under way. Nagumo reached his launching point, lat. 26° N, long. 158° W, about 275 miles north of Pearl Harbor, at 0600. It was still dark, and the carriers pitched badly in the swell, but the launching of the first attack was effected without mishap, and the 183 planes orbited waiting for their strike commander, Captain Fuchida, to give the word to go. Again emotion welled high in Japa-

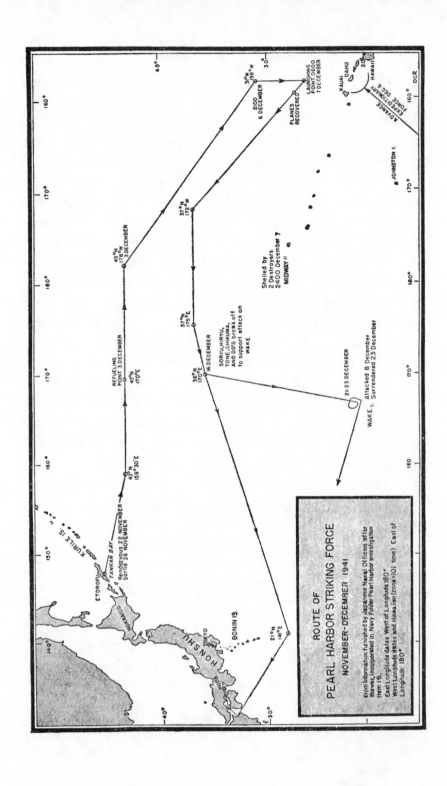

ROUTE OF
PEARL HARBOR STRIKING FORCE
NOVEMBER–DECEMBER 1941

From information furnished by Japanese Naval Officers after
the war, incorporated in Navy Folder Pearl Harbor investigation
Item 16.

East Longitude dates West of Longitude 180°
West Longitude dates and Hawaiian (zone +10½ time) East of
Longitude 180°

nese breasts; all who could came topside and shrilled "Banzai!" into the gray dawn.

2. *The Unsuspecting Victim*

First blow of Japan against the United States was scheduled not for the Emperor's "eagles" but for his Advance Expeditionary Force of submarines. These, 27 in number, left Kure and Yokosuka around 19 November and fueled at Kwajalein in the Marshalls. Five of the I-boats carried midget two-man submarines. These had the mission of penetrating Pearl Harbor, while the big ones took stations on 6 December about Oahu, to torpedo any American ship that escaped the air strike. The midgets were cast off at midnight 6-7 December, a few miles outside the harbor's mouth.[2]

Before taking up the story of what happened on that "day of infamy," let us see what the high commands at Hawaii and Washington were doing to prevent surprise. The answer is, Almost nothing.

Admiral Stark in Washington sent Admiral Kimmel in Pearl Harbor a "war warning" on 27 November, to expect "an aggressive move by Japan within the next few days . . . against either the Philippines, Thai, Kra Peninsula or possibly Borneo." He ordered Kimmel to prepare to execute "defensive deployment preparatory to carrying out" the existing war plan.[3] The Chief of Naval Operations did not mention Hawaii as a possible target, and neither Ad-

---

[2] One of these was sighted by Lieutenant James O. Cobb about 3 miles off Diamond Head, by daylight on the 6th. Since it was near one of our "submarine sanctuaries," he felt obliged to radio ashore for permission to attack, but by the time permission arrived the I-boat had submerged. After the war he met the submarine's skipper, who remembered the occasion.

[3] In addition, Kimmel received a dispatch from C.N.O. on 28 Nov.: "Hostile action is possible at any moment," but ordered him to "undertake no offensive action until Japan has committed an overt act."

miral Kimmel nor Lieutenant General Walter Short, commanding the Army in Hawaii, believed it to be menaced. They did not even notify the commanders of their respective air arms, Rear Admiral Bellinger and Brigadier General Martin, of the "war warning" dispatch. There had been no Army-Navy air raid drill since 12 November. On 2, 3, 4 and 5 December air patrols were sent out as much as 400 miles to the northwestward, not with any idea of discovering an enemy but to train pilots and break in new PBY Catalinas; but on the 6th the air reconnaissance was again reduced to little more than harbor-mouth patrol. General Short took the war warning as indicating danger only from local sabotage, and ordered all Army planes to be parked wing-to-wing; he so informed Washington, but, owing to a recent renumbering of the three degrees of alert, Washington assumed that his alert was complete instead of local. In general, routine patrol and training schedules were maintained after 27 November, and the usual leaves and liberties were granted for that weekend and the next. Pearl Harbor and Oahu were unprepared, mentally and physically, for what happened on the 7th. As one officer expressed it, "there was a state of mind of being fed up with the unproductive vigilance of the several months preceding."

One very important new measure Admiral Kimmel did take in good time. On 28 November he sent carrier *Enterprise* from Pearl Harbor, under Rear Admiral Halsey, to deliver Marine Corps fighter planes to Wake Island; and Halsey, to his credit, ordered his men to shoot down any suspicious ships or planes encountered. On 4 December Halsey delivered the planes, and on the 7th was on his way back to Oahu. Also, on 5 December, Admiral Kimmel sent a task force built around carrier *Lexington*, under Rear Admiral Newton, to deliver 25 scout bombers to Midway Island. *Saratoga*, the third Pacific Fleet carrier, had left Pearl Harbor for upkeep and repairs on the West Coast. Thus the three carriers, whose destruction would have been far more disastrous than that of the entire Battle Fleet, were absent on 7 December — a slight concession that the god of battles made to us on that fateful day.

Now let us turn to Washington. There, Army and Navy Intelligence had been "reading the Japanese mail" — intercepting, decrypting and translating dispatches between Tokyo and its representatives in Washington and elsewhere. These told them that war was likely to break out in the Far East on the weekend of 29 November; but whereabouts, or on what date, the Japanese government was too cagey to admit even in the top-secret diplomatic code. Every bit of intelligence received from this and many other sources was ambiguous; neither date nor target was mentioned. And when Sunday, 30 November, passed and nothing happened, a sort of numbness seemed to creep over official Washington. Commander Arthur H. McCollum of the Office of Naval Intelligence felt that the situation was serious enough to send another war warning to Hawaii on 4 December, but Admiral Stark declined to do so; felt there had been too much crying "Wolf!"

The two Japanese dispatches decrypted and translated before 7 December which might have suggested an attack on Pearl Harbor, were orders from Tokyo to an agent in Honolulu, to report not only all ship movements in and out of Pearl Harbor, but where each ship was berthed within the harbor. Admiral Kimmel might have perceived the significance of these now famous "berthing orders," but he never had the chance. Naval Intelligence discounted them because similar orders were being sent to Japanese agents in all principal world ports, and in that context these particular demands on Honolulu no more indicated an attack on Pearl Harbor than an attack on San Diego, the Panama Canal, New York, London, Rio or Sydney. Nevertheless, the failure to transmit this material to Pearl Harbor is a black mark against Washington. One may argue, as Admiral Turner did at the hearings, that the 27 November war warning should have been enough to put Kimmel on his toes. But as Roberta Wohlstetter well says, "There seems little doubt that if the sender had been more alarmed, the warning itself would have been more alarming." [4]

On Saturday, 6 December, Tokyo began transmitting to its Washington embassy in diplomatic code a long note for the State Department, breaking diplomatic relations. Army Intelligence had the first thirteen parts decrypted, translated, and in the hands of Brigadier General Sherman Miles, head of Army Intelligence, and Captain Theodore S. Wilkinson, head of Naval Intelligence, by 2230. These thirteen parts were a long rehash of Japanese-American relations, accusing us of warmongering in East Asia. President Roosevelt received and read them that evening and exclaimed, "This means war!" But the note gave no hint of a projected attack on Hawaii, or anywhere in particular. General George C. Marshall, Army Chief of Staff, and Admiral Stark, Chief of Naval Operations, were not informed that evening by the officers whose duty it was to do so.

Admiral Stark and Rear Admiral Turner, the Navy War Plans chief, were in Stark's office at 0915 Sunday, 7 December, when Captain Wilkinson, chief of Naval Intelligence, and Commander McCollum, head of his Far East Section, brought in the translation of Tokyo's Part 14, the "snapper" which broke off diplomatic relations. But even Part 14 did not declare war or threaten immediate attack. About an hour later, Commander McCollum brought in the "time of delivery" message, an order from Tokyo to its ambassadors to destroy all coding machines after presenting the fourteen-part note to Secretary Hull at 1300. Sunday was an

---

[4] *Pearl Harbor: Warning and Decision* (1962), p. 336. And, as Mrs. Wohlstetter says on p. 383, "If our intelligence system . . . failed to produce an accurate image of Japanese intentions . . . it was not for want of the relevant materials. Never before have we had so complete an intelligence picture of the enemy." And on p. 392: "What these examples illustrate is . . . the very human tendency to pay attention to the signals that support current expectations about enemy behavior."

odd day, and one P.M. a strange hour, for presenting a diplomatic note. What could it mean?

McCollum and his assistant, Lieutenant Commander A. D. Kramer, and Colonel Rufus S. Bratton of Army Intelligence, guessed the answer by consulting a time chart on the wall. One P.M. in Washington was 0730 at Pearl Harbor. That might be only a coincidence, but it might also mean an attack there, and there only — for one P.M. in Washington is nighttime at Manila and Guam. Wilkinson suggested that Admiral Stark at once call Admiral Kimmel on the telephone. Stark demurred, feeling that since the Army was responsible for the defense of Hawaii, General Marshall should do it. Marshall, contacted on returning from his Sunday morning horseback ride, came into Stark's office at about 1115. In tense silence he read all fourteen parts, agreed that they meant immediate war, and that Pearl Harbor and Manila should be alerted at once. Marshall's communicator said he could get the word to Pearl in twenty minutes. Rear Admiral Leigh Noyes, Director of Naval Communications, offered to send it through Navy channels. Stark declined (again Navy-Army punctilio), and the message — JUST WHAT SIGNIFICANCE THE HOUR SET MAY HAVE WE DO NOT KNOW, BUT BE ON THE ALERT ACCORDINGLY — was filed at noon, 0630 in Hawaii. General Marshall called the Army communication center thrice to make sure that the message had been filed and sent, and was assured that it had been sent, which it had — but by Western Union! There was a foul-up that morning in Army radio, and the officer in charge entrusted the message to commercial channels. A boy on a bicycle delivered it to General Short some hours after the attack was over.

The night of 6-7 December was not uneventful in and around Oahu. While officers and men on leave enjoyed themselves in Honolulu, as sailors do on a Saturday night, a routine patrol was maintained off Pearl Harbor entrance. At 0355 U.S.S. *Condor* sighted a periscope less than two miles off shore and passed the word by blinker to destroyer *Ward*, also on patrol. The two captains discussed the contact by radio. Their talk was overheard at Bishop's Point radio station ashore, but nobody there thought it worth while to relay this to naval headquarters; nor did the captains.

Almost three hours passed, and Pearl Harbor slept. At 0633 a patrolling Catalina sighted the same or another midget submarine, dropped smoke pots on the spot, and informed *Ward*. The destroyer closed, shot at, depth-charged and sank the midget at 0645. *Ward's* commanding officer, Captain Outerbridge, sent the word at 0651 to naval district headquarters where, owing to an unexplained delay, Lieutenant Commander Harold Kaminsky, the duty officer, never got it until 0712. Kaminsky, one of the few communicators really on the ball that morning, made frantic efforts to pass this word to fleet headquarters, but he had only one telephone operator, a Hawaiian who spoke little English, and found it difficult to raise anyone at that hour of a Sunday morning.

In the meantime, at 0700, another PBY had sunk a second midget a mile off Pearl Harbor entrance; but, contrary to instructions, reported the incident in code. So this message was not ready for circulation until 0730, when the Pacific Fleet staff duty officer telephoned it to Rear Admiral Bellinger's operations officer at Ford Island. They discussed these reports over the telephone with Admiral Bloch, the naval district commandant. All three, who suspected these contacts to be false, were still talking about them when the bombs began to drop.

Thus, the Navy, largely through faulty or lax communications, lost an opportunity to alert the Fleet that midget submarines were lurking about Pearl Harbor in the early morning. Admiral Kimmel himself, on 14 October, had warned the Fleet that "a single submarine attack may indicate the presence of a considerable surface force probably composed of fast ships accompanied by a carrier." But this was imbedded in a very prolix and involved fleet letter, which nobody except Kaminsky appears to have digested.[5]

And the Army lost an even better chance to give advance warning of the main air attack. It was responsible for five or six mobile search radar stations, spotted around the coast of Oahu. Search radar had saved England from destruction during the German air blitz of 1940, and it might have done so here; but these Army radars were being operated on Sunday only from 0400 to 0700, and at all times on a training basis, to train radar operators, not with any serious idea of watching for enemy aircraft.

The radar set at Opana on the northern point of Oahu was manned on the morning of 7 December by Privates Lockard and Elliott. Between 0645 and 0700 they tracked what we now know to have been a Japanese cruiser plane reconnoitering ahead of the bombers to make sure that the Battle Fleet was really in harbor. One of the lads reported this to radio information center at Fort Shafter near Honolulu, where the duty officer was an inexperienced second lieutenant, also under training. He ordered them to secure for the day. Instead of so doing, the two privates, eager to improve their technique, continued to work the radar. Elliott, at the controls at 0702, saw on the screen "something completely out of the ordinary" — blips indicating an enormous flight of planes, bigger than anything he had ever observed. The flight was then 132 miles north of Oahu, approaching at 182 m.p.h. He telephoned the switchboard operator at the information center, who insisted on calling the duty officer to hear what the privates had to say. The green lieutenant listened in a bored manner and told them to "forget it." For he had heard that a flight of our B–17s was ex-

---

[5] One midget actually penetrated Pearl Harbor, the gate to which had carelessly been left open, and was sunk therein by a destroyer. One ran aground and was captured, and the rest disappeared without leaving a trace. Nor did the big I-boats accomplish anything, owing to our aggressive patrolling after the air attack. I–70 was sunk by planes from *Enterprise* 10 December. Two proceeded to the West Coast and sank a few merchant ships, giving the West Coast a big scare.

pected to arrive from the mainland that morning. But these could only have been a dozen planes at most, and the Opana radar screen showed a flight numbering over a hundred.

Note that if even one of the people responsible, either in Washington or on Oahu, had been really brisk, the Fleet and Army could have had at least an hour's warning, and hundreds of lives would have been saved. It seems that the Fates were determined to humble American pride.

3. *The Assault*

Shortly after 0700 the sun, rising over the Tantalus Mountains, cast its first rays on Pearl Harbor, heightening the green of the canefields that stretch up the slopes above Aiea and deepening the blue of the lochs, as the arms of this harbor are called. Even for Oahu, favored by nature, this was an uncommonly bright and peaceful Sabbath morning. On board ships the forenoon watch was piped to breakfast while the men it would relieve at 0800 concluded their various duties, such as cleaning brass and wiping dew off the machine guns and the 5-inch dual purpose guns. Of these, only about one in four was fully manned. The main batteries were not manned, nor were the plotting rooms, directors, and ammunition supply; ready ammunition was in locked boxes whose keys were in the hands of the Officer of the Deck. All ships had at least one boiler lighted, but few had enough steam up to get under way in a hurry. Among the 70 combatant ships and 24 auxiliaries in the harbor, only one, a destroyer, was under way.

At about 0740 the first Japanese attack wave, 40 torpedo-bombers, 49 high-level bombers, 51 dive-bombers and 51 fighters, sighted the Oahu coastline. They then deployed — the fighters to destroy parked planes at Wheeler Field and Kaneohe, the high-

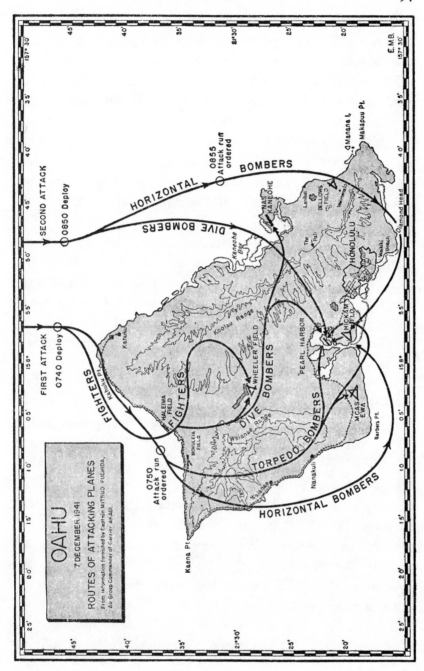

OAHU
7 DECEMBER, 1941
ROUTES OF ATTACKING PLANES
From information furnished by Captain MITSUO FUCHIDA,
Air Group Commander of Carrier AKAGI

level bombers for Hickam Field, the torpedo planes and dive-bombers for "Battleship Row." By 0750 they were ready to strike and Captain Fuchida, the strike commander, gave the word.

The sound of church bells at Honolulu, ringing for eight o'clock mass, came over the harbor, whose calm surface was only lightly rippled by the breeze. Many officers were at breakfast, others were just rising; seamen were lounging on deck talking, reading, or writing letters home. As the hour for morning colors approached, sailors in white uniforms removed the jack and ensign from their lockers, a bluejacket on the signal bridge hoisted the Blue Peter, and boatswains were set to pipe the preparatory signal at 0755.

A few seconds before or after that hour — nobody could remember which — the air suddenly seemed filled with strange planes, hovering, darting, diving. A brisk dive-bomber got in the first lick, on Ford Island naval air headquarters, where Commander Ramsey, the operations officer, who had been discussing the midget submarine sinkings over the telephone, thought it was accidental, from an overzealous Army plane. Hardly anyone, for seconds or even minutes, even after seeing the red "meat ball" on the fuselages, recognized the planes as Japanese. Some thought they were United States Army planes camouflaged as Japanese to give the Navy a scare. Others assumed that this was an air drill and thought it too realistic. Across the harbor, Rear Admiral William R. Furlong, in minelayer *Oglala*, who had studied Japanese plane types, recognized the torpedo-bombers when they zoomed up the main channel between him and Ford Island; and as he happened to be senior officer present afloat, he ordered the signal hoisted, "All Ships in Harbor Sortie." Almost simultaneously, someone in the signal tower ashore made the same observation and telephoned to Cincpac headquarters, "Enemy air raid — not drill." The Navy air arm on Ford Island took a little longer to realize the truth, so it was not until 0758 that Admiral Bellinger broadcast a message which shook the United States as nothing had since the firing on Fort Sumter: —

AIR RAID PEARL HARBOR — THIS IS NO DRILL.

Now, to quote John Milton, "All hell broke loose." The Sabbath calm was shattered by bomb explosions, internal explosions, and machine-gun fire, with the hoarse signal of General Quarters as obbligato. At least two battleships were already doomed and hundreds of American seamen dead by 0758.

Let us now concentrate on the first phase of the attack, from 0755 to 0825, during which about 90 per cent of the damage was done.

Battleship Row was located along the southeast shore of Ford Island, a few hundred yards across the main channel from the Navy Yard. The battlewagons were moored, some singly and others in pairs, to massive quays a short distance off the island shore. *Nevada* occupied the northeasterly berth, with an ammunition lighter outboard. Next came *Arizona*, with tender *Vestal* outboard. Southwest of them were *Tennessee* and *West Virginia* side by side, and the next pair was *Maryland* and *Oklahoma*. *California* alone had the southernmost berth. *Pennsylvania* was in drydock across the harbor, where five cruisers were also berthed. Twenty-six destroyers and minecraft were moored in groups in various parts of the harbor.

The Japanese aviators knew exactly where to find the battleships, completely unprotected from torpedo attack, and made first for *Arizona* and the two pairs. The major attack was made by twelve "Kate" torpedo-bombers launching torpedoes from low altitudes — 40 to 100 feet above the water. Four more Kates followed. Almost simultaneously, "Val" dive-bombers began combing battleship row fore and aft, dropping not only conventional bombs but converted 16-inch armor-piercing shells which penetrated the decks and exploded below. Then five more planes attacked cruiser *Raleigh* and three other ships moored on the northwest side of Ford Island. Most of these planes, after they had dropped bombs or topedoes, flew back over their targets, strafing viciously in order to kill as many sailors as possible.

Imagine the consternation that this sudden onslaught created among the officers and men on board! A surprise attack in war is bad enough to cope with, but this was a surprise attack in time of peace when, so far as anyone in Hawaii knew, diplomatic negotiations at Washington were continuing. What made defense even more difficult was the absence on weekend leave of many senior officers and chief petty officers to whom juniors were accustomed to look for orders and guidance. Yet the junior officers and bluejackets' reaction, against fearful odds, was superb. Between explosions one could hear sailors knocking off the padlocks from ready ammunition chests with axes and mauls. Dive-bombers swooped so near that sailors could see the Japanese pilots' toothy grins, and in exasperation hurled monkey wrenches at them. At what moment return gunfire was opened is still uncertain. Some said within a minute, others within five; but photos taken by the Japanese as late as 0805, when *California* was torpedoed, show not a single black burst of ack-ack in the sky, and all but one or two of the first wave of torpedo-bombers got away unscathed. The Navy's machine guns at that time were not very effective — the 3-inch was not rapid-fire enough, and the 1.1-inch was liable to heat and jam after a few rounds; it was not until next year that the 20-mm Oerlikon and 40-mm Bofors were installed.

Oklahoma, outboard of the southernmost pair of battlewagons, one of our 1916 "Dreadnoughts," never had a chance to fight back. While the crew were running to battle stations, a few moments after the first bomb exploded on Ford Island, three torpedoes blasted huge holes in her and she promptly listed 30 degrees. There was no time to set Condition Zed (complete watertight integrity), or to counterflood, or to bring machine guns to bear. Before 0800 the senior officer on board ordered Abandon Ship. Men crawled over the starboard side as she rolled over, and two more torpedo hits completed her doom. Fifteen minutes later, parts of her bottom were facing the sky. Many survivors climbed on board *Maryland* alongside, to help her fight. She, protected by *Oklahoma* from the torpedoes, got off with only two bomb hits, and became the first of the stricken Battle Fleet to return to active service. *Oklahoma* lost 415 officers and men killed out of 1354 on board.

Tennessee and *West Virginia* made the next couple on Battleship Row. The latter, outboard, took six or seven torpedoes, the first before 0756, and two bombs. An exceptionally well-trained crew, who loved their "Wee Vee," as they called the ship, saved her from the fate of *Oklahoma*. Ensign Brooks, officer of the deck, saw the first bomb hit Ford Island and immediately ordered "Away Fire and Rescue Party!" This brought everyone topside on the double, and saved hundreds of lives. She listed so rapidly that the guns on the starboard side, which opened fire promptly, could be served only by organizing a double row of ammunition handlers — one to pass and the other to hold the passer upright. Lieutenant Ricketts ordered counterflooding on his own initiative, and, ably assisted by Boatswain's Mate Billingsley, corrected a 28-degree list to 15 degrees; this allowed her to settle on the bottom almost upright. Captain Bennion, disemboweled by fragments from a bomb that exploded on *Tennessee* alongside, was *in extremis;* his only thoughts were for his ship and crew until his life flickered out a few minutes later; but his fighting spirit lived on. All hands fought fires, although frequently dive-bombed and strafed. "Their spirit was marvelous," reported the surviving executive officer. "Words fail in attempting to describe the magnificent display of courage, discipline and devotion to duty of all." *West Virginia* lost 105 killed out of about 1500 on board.

Tennessee, moored inboard, naturally suffered less. She received two bombs early in the action, but most of her damage came from fires started by flaming debris from *Arizona,* exploding 75 feet astern. Fire-fighting continued all the rest of that day and the following night, and she did not sink. Her losses were only 5 killed; and within three weeks she, in company with *Maryland* and *Pennsylvania,* sailed to the West Coast for a complete overhaul.

Arizona was moored inboard of a short repair ship which afforded her slight protection. Within one minute of the opening attack the battleship was literally torn apart by torpedo and bomb explosions. A bomb exploded in the forward magazine before it could be flooded, wrecking half the ship, killing Captain Van Valkenburgh and Rear Admiral Kidd who were on the bridge, and causing the ship to settle so fast that hundreds of sailors were trapped below. Even so, the machine guns topside opened fire on the enemy planes, and she was not abandoned until 1032. Owing to lack of warning and to the magazine explosion, *Arizona's* casualties were over half those suffered by the entire Fleet at Pearl Harbor — 1103 officers and men killed out of some 1400 on board. Her remains, and most of theirs, are still there today; she has never been formally decommissioned, and every day a color guard faithfully raises and lowers the ensign on a mast built on a platform over the wreck.

Battleship Row tapered off to a lone battlewagon at each end. Southernmost was *California,* flagship of Admiral Pye and, at the age of twenty, youngest of the Battle Fleet. At 0805 she was the last to be hit, but in the worst condition to take it — completely "unbuttoned" in preparation for an admiral's inspection — so that the two torpedoes that hit her, together with one bomb that exploded below and set off a magazine, were enough to cause her to settle into the mud. Prompt counterflooding, directed by Reserve Ensign Fair, prevented her from capsizing, which would have meant a far greater loss of life than the 98 officers and men actually killed. *California* was also restored to the Fleet and performed excellent service in the latter half of the war.

Nevada, at the northern end, oldest battleship present — well past her 25th birthday — had a little more grace than her immediate neighbors; Color guard began making morning colors and the band struck up "The Star-spangled Banner" before anything lethal came her way. A Kate that had torpedoed *Arizona* skimmed across her stern during the ceremony and the rear gunner tried to strafe the sailors at attention, but managed only to rip the ensign. A second strafer came in, but the band finished the national anthem without a pause; nobody broke ranks. Ensign Taussig, officer of the deck, then ordered Battle Stations, set Condition Zed, and *Nevada* went into action with her machine guns and port 5-inch battery. One and possibly two torpedo-bombers were hit, and the rest gave *Nevada* a wide berth; but one torpedo tore a hole in her side, 45 by 30 feet. Prompt counterflooding corrected the list, and as her power plant was intact, Lieutenant Commander Francis J. Thomas, senior officer present, eighth in the chain of command — made the wise decision to get under way. In the meantime she had taken two bomb hits amidships, causing many casualties and great damage. Ordinarily, four tugs were required to get a battleship under way from the mooring quays, but *Nevada* did it unaided; Chief Boatswain E. J. Hill jumped onto the quay, cast off the lines under strafing fire, and swam back to the ship. Down the ship channel she stood, fighting off dive-bombers of the second Japanese attack wave who concentrated on her, and at one time surrounded by a curtain of smoke and spray so dense that spectators thought her gone; but most of the bombs were near-misses. A proud and gallant sight she made, with her tattered ensign streaming from the fantail. She could easily have gone to sea, but in the confusion Admiral Bloch or Kimmel, fearing lest she sink and block the channel, sent her an urgent signal not to leave the harbor. Commander Thomas then decided to anchor off Hospital

Point. Just as she was about to drop the hook, dive-bombers attacked and made three hits, one of which "opened the forecastle like a sardine can" and killed the entire anchoring detail, including Boatswain Hill. *Nevada* then slid gently aground. The Captain now came on board and ordered her towed across the harbor to Waipio Point where, despite strenuous effort at damage control, she flooded and settled. Fifty officers and men had been killed, and the old battlewagon was thoroughly wrecked topside. Floated in February, she steamed to Puget Sound under her own power and, after modernization, rejoined the Fleet in 1943.

Pennsylvania, flagship of the Pacific Fleet, was happily in dry dock at the Navy Yard and so could not be reached by torpedo-bombers. She threw up powerful antiaircraft fire, took but one severe bomb hit, and lost only 18 men. But several bombs meant for her hit destroyers *Cassin* and *Downes* in the same dry dock, and pretty well demolished them.

Thus, in half an hour the Japanese bombers accomplished their most important objective, wrecking the Battle Line of the Pacific Fleet beyond any possibility of offensive action within a year.

Too much praise cannot be given to the officers and bluejackets in these and other ships. Once they had recovered from the initial surprise they served their vessels nobly, and the damage control parties were especially effective. There was no flinching, no attempt to escape. On the contrary, from the moment of the first alarm, officers and men on leave in Honolulu and elsewhere began hastening to their stations. Dozens of barges, gigs, launches and small yard craft took men out to their own ships, evacuated the wounded from the stricken vessels, and helped fight fires, with complete disregard for their own safety. Chief Jansen, commanding *YG–17*, one of the yard's garbage lighters, received high praise for closing *West Virginia* to fight her fires until they were quenched, when he moved over to another post of danger, alongside *Arizona*. Ensign Sears of *West Virginia* was taken to the wrong ship but jumped overboard and swam to his own to bear a hand. Chief Boatswain Hill of *Nevada,* and every one of his detail, and the exposed gunners of the 5-inchers, fought like one man, and that man a hero; and almost every one of them lost his life. So, while we deplore the surprise, let us never forget the heroic reaction. "That strife was not inglorious, though the event was dire."

During the initial phase of the attack, between 0755 and 0825, the enemy inflicted severe punishment on military aircraft in Oahu. A flight of dive-bombers worked over Ford Island and in a few minutes Patrol Wing Two lost 33 planes, almost half its number. At Ewa, the Marine Corps air base, halfway between West Loch and the ocean, some 50 planes were based. Captain Ashwell, officer of the day, was having breakfast when he heard aircraft, stepped out, sighted the first flight of torpedo-bombers making for Battleship Row, immediately recognized them; and, as he ran to the guardhouse to sound an alarm, saw 21 "Zeke" fighter planes roaring in over the Waianae mountains. They struck Ewa before sprinting Ashwell reached his goal. Swooping low, they attacked with short bursts of gunfire the planes parked wing to wing, and destroyed over thirty in a couple of minutes. By the time a second attack came in the Marines had organized defense, dragging one undamaged plane to a good position to use as a machine-gun mount, breaking out spare machine guns from ordnance rooms and wrenching them off damaged planes to set up elsewhere. These were able to keep the would-be strafers at a healthy distance, and threw back a third attack by 15 Zekes. Only four men were killed in these attacks, but the Marine air arm on Oahu was almost completely destroyed.

Yamamoto had also placed the Indian sign on Kaneohe, a Navy patrol wing station on the windward side of Oahu. A squadron of Vals made for the Catalinas parked there at 0755. Almost everyone was asleep; the duty officer thought they were Army planes gone berserk, and telephoned to Pearl Harbor for help. Another strike came in at 0820, blasted a hangar and destroyed three Catalinas inside; an hour later, a third strike mopped up. As a result, 27 of the 36 PBYs at Kaneohe were destroyed, and six more damaged; the three saved were out on patrol when the attack came in.

Three principal Army airfields on Oahu caught it badly. At Hickam, adjoining Pearl Harbor Navy Yard, a dozen A–20s, 33 B–18s and 6 B–17s were lined up in the open, wing to wing. A few seconds after 0755, bombers earmarked to destroy them barreled in. One bomb crashed through the roof of the mess hall and exploded in the midst of the breakfast tables, killing 35 men. Others destroyed the parked planes. It was even more difficult to fight back ashore than on board ship, since many antiaircraft guns spotted around Hickam and in the Navy Yard, all operated by the Army, were not manned, and none had ready ammunition. Soldiers had to run to the depots and break down doors to get bullets; others wrenched machine guns off planes and blazed away. At Wheeler Field, in the central valley of Oahu, 62 P–40s and other planes too were parked as close as possible, in lines only 20 feet apart. Most of these were destroyed by 25 dive-bombers which attacked at 0802. Two small squadrons of P–40s at Bellows Field near Lanikai were also pretty much wiped out. Army Air Force had 231 aircraft on Oahu when the attack came in, but at close of day had only 166 units left, half of them damaged. Navy and Marine Corps had only 54 left out of about 250.

From 0825 to 0840 there was a lull, broken only by a few laggards from the first wave. Then the second wave struck. It consisted of 50 Kates equipped for high-level bombing, 80 Val dive-bombers, and 40 fighter planes. These came in around Diamond Head, concentrating largely on Hickam, on *Nevada*, and on other ships already hit. But this second wave of Japanese attackers was met by a lethal barrage of antiaircraft fire and did comparatively little damage. The destroyers which were moored in groups of three to five in East Loch, the cruisers tied up at docks in Southeast Loch, and the minecraft moored off the Naval Hospital in Middle Loch were under way by this time, and escaped serious damage.

At 0945 all Japanese planes over Oahu returned to their carriers. All but 29 got back, though some 70 were shot full of holes. One plane crash-landed on the island of Niihau, where the pilot, with the aid of a local Japanese, managed to terrorize the unarmed native populace for a week. At the end of that time a burly Hawaiian grappled with the pilot and, although shot by him in divers places, managed to kill him with bare hands and a stone.

By the end of two morning hours on 7 December, the Navy had lost over 2000 officers and men killed and 710 wounded, about thrice as many as in the two wars of 1898 and 1917-1918. The Army and Marine Corps together lost 327 killed and 433 wounded. In addition, some 70 civilians were killed — mostly men who happened to be on one of the airfields, but some in Honolulu where a few naval antiaircraft shells, whose fuses in the confusion had not been cut, exploded on city streets.

The rest of this terrible day was passed in expectation of worse to come. Japanese ships were reported to be on every side of Oahu, preparing to land troops. In the Hawaiian Islands were 160,000 people of Japanese blood; surely from among them Black Dragon bands had been recruited, to assassinate Americans? Japanese maids and butlers, it was said, told their employers to "scram," as their house had been assigned to a Japanese general. Every one of these rumors was later found to be false, and not one disloyal act was committed by the local Nipponese. General Short, for whom that day marked the end of a distinguished Army career, promptly executed his plans for deployment in the event of enemy attack. At about 1000, Army contingents in trucks or afoot began to move toward the supposed danger spots, now that the danger had passed.

Sunset over the Pacific inaugurated a hideous night for all hands. Fire-fighting continued on many of the stricken ships. Surgeons and nurses in the overcrowded hospitals were up all night attending the wounded and dying; hundreds of women and children whose husbands' quarters had been bombed huddled miserably in the university auditorium, or in a storage tunnel at Red Hill. Trigger-happy sentries and machine-gunners fired at everything that moved, supposing it to be a Japanese invader. Saddest of all accidents was the shooting down at night of four dive-bombers from carrier *Enterprise*. These had landed at Ford Island during the morning lull and were then sent out to search for the enemy. When they returned after nightfall with running lights on, an anti-aircraft gunner, who failed to get the word because the airbase communications had been ruptured, opened fire and started a panic of shooting all around the harbor.

Daybreak 8 December revealed a "dismal situation waste and wild" — half the aircraft on the island destroyed, seven battleships sunk or badly damaged, three destroyers reduced to junk. And the atmosphere was one of tormenting uncertainty. Nobody knew where the Japanese task force was; the one radar fix on it was interpreted 180 degrees wrong, so many a ship and most of the flyable planes were sent scurrying southward.

But, as the days elapsed, one saw that the situation might well have been worse. Our three aircraft carriers were safe; the repair shops, which did an amazingly quick job on damaged ships, were almost untouched, as was the fuel-oil tank farm, filled to capacity, whose loss would have tied up the Fleet for months.

Nevertheless, the armed forces and the nation had been struck a treacherous, devastating and humiliating blow. When someone in Washington proposed that a medal be issued to Pearl Harbor combatants, one of the survivors replied, "Better make the ribbon of black crepe."

4. *Who Was Responsible?*

The Pearl Harbor disaster made a tremendous emotional impact on the American people. The Japanese high command, by their idiotic act, had made a strategic present of the first order to the United States; they had united the country in grim determination to win victory in the Pacific. Isolationism and pacifism now ceased to be valid forces in American politics; but some of their exponents, and many well-meaning people too, became violent propagandists for the bizarre theory that the Roosevelt administration, with the connivance of leading generals and admirals in Washington, knew perfectly well that the attack was coming and deliberately withheld knowledge of it from Kimmel and Short in order, for their own foul purposes, to get us into the war.

Even if one can believe that the late President of the United States was capable of so horrible a gambit, a little reflection would indicate that he could not possibly have carried it off. He would have needed the connivance of Secretaries Hull, Stimson and Knox, Generals Marshall, Gerow and Miles, Admirals Stark, Turner and Wilkinson, and many of their subordinates, too — all loyal and honorable men who would never have lent themselves to such monstrous deception. More reflection might suggest that if Roosevelt and his cabinet ministers and armed service chiefs had schemed to get us into the war, their purpose would have been better served by warning the Hawaiian commanders in time to get the Fleet to sea and the planes airborne. Even a frustrated attempt to strike Pearl Harbor would have been sufficient *casus belli* to satisfy the most isolationist congressman. Actually, the administration and the heads of the armed forces, as we have seen, were doing their best to prevent or postpone a war with Japan. Roosevelt even sent a personal appeal to Hirohito on the evening of 6 December.

After any overwhelming disaster there is a search for the culprit; and this search is still being pursued, for partisan purposes, after two Navy and two Army investigations and a lengthy congressional one have combed every phase of omission and commission. No military event in our or any other country's history, not even the Battles of Gettysburg and Jutland, has been the subject of such exhaustive research as the air assault on Pearl Harbor.

A principal reason why Washington and Pearl Harbor were caught unawares was their inability to imagine that Japan would do anything so stupid and suicidal. But Joseph Grew in Tokyo — one of the most alert and perceptive ambassadors in United States history — warned Washington on 3 November 1941 against any possible misconception "of the capacity of Japan to rush headlong into a suicidal conflict with the United States. National sanity would dictate against such an event, but Japanese sanity cannot be measured by our own standards of logic. . . . Japan's resort to [war] measures . . . may come with dramatic and dangerous suddenness." Grew's warning fell on deaf ears.

Three weeks later, almost everyone in a responsible position in Washington expected Japan to make an aggressive move on the weekend of 29 November; but not on Pearl Harbor. And the curious lethargy into which official Washington seemed to fall after the "war warning" is partly explained by the decrypting of a whole series of dispatches from Tokyo to its ambassadors, to the effect that the deadline was approaching, time was running out, etc. There were no fewer than 19 such messages between 2 and 26 November, yet nothing had happened.

The Army and Navy cryptographers in Washington were experts, but grossly overworked. The stuff was coming in faster than they could deal with it, and one could not tell which dispatch was important and which was not until all were decrypted.[6] A message from the Japanese consulate at Honolulu dated 6 December, which ended, "There is a considerable opportunity . . . to take advantage for a surprise attack against these places" (Pearl Harbor and vicinity), was not decrypted until after the attack. The "berthing plan" message and Honolulu's replies were not assigned their proper significance at Washington, because they were mixed in with hundreds of messages, which had to be decrypted and translated, from all parts of the world. Observers in China, for instance, were sending as many as fifty messages a week, warning of forthcoming Japanese attacks on Siberia, Peru, and other unlikely places.

Army and Navy Intelligence officers in Washington were somewhat in the position of a woman with a sick child trying to take instructions from a doctor over the telephone while the neighbors are shouting contrary advice in her ear, dogs are barking, children screaming, and trucks roaring by the house. The noise overwhelmed the message. Personalities also entered into it. Rear Admiral Turner, Navy War Plans officer, was highly opinionated and difficult to work with. He actually forbade the Japanese language officers who did the decrypting and translating, or even the Chief of Naval Intelligence, to make estimates from the dispatches, insisting on doing that himself. And Turner, until late November, was obsessed by the idea that Japan was going to attack Russia, not American or British possessions.

Intelligence data received in Washington was handled in a manner that dissipated its impact. Copies of all decrypted messages that the translators thought significant, sometimes running to 130 a day,

---

[6] In the subsequent "conspiracy" theory of the surprise, much is made of one of the decoding machines being given to the British instead of to Kimmel. It was actually exchanged for machines that the British invented, and Washington wanted, for decrypting certain German ciphers; and since Britain had interests in the Far East at least equal to ours, the exchange was natural and proper. Another machine destined for Pearl Harbor was being constructed when war began. Admiral Hart already had one at Cavite.

were placed in locked briefcases and carried by special messengers to the President, the Secretaries of State, War, and Navy, and about six top-ranking members of the armed forces. The recipient, without taking notes, had to read these signals in the presence of the messenger, who returned them to Army or Navy Intelligence office, where all copies but one were burned. This system, devised for security, denied to all these important people the opportunity to digest data and draw conclusions. It was nobody's particular and exclusive business to study all intelligence material and come up with an estimate. Nobody got anything but excerpts and driblets.

It must also be remembered that in the late months of 1941 all high Army, Navy and State Department officials in Washington were deeply concerned with the "short of war" conflict in the Atlantic, and with Europe, where it then seemed probable that Hitler would gobble up Russia as he had France, order American merchantmen to be sunk, and step up his subversive activities in Central and South America.

Every one of the Japanese messages decrypted and translated before 7 December was ambiguous. None mentioned Pearl Harbor. None even pointed clearly at Japanese intent to attack the United States anywhere. Thus, no clear warnings were sent to Hawaii because Washington saw no reason to anticipate an attack on Hawaii. Washington, moreover, was determined not to begin a war with Japan. That was the meaning of the passage in the diary of War Secretary Stimson, recording the cabinet meeting of 25 November, after one of Tojo's deadline messages had been decrypted and translated. "The President predicted that we were likely to be attacked perhaps next Monday. . . . The question was how we should maneuver them into the position of firing the first shot." This quotation has been made much of by those trying to prove conspiracy between F.D.R. and his cabinet to get us into war. Mr. Stimson's use of the verb "maneuver" was unfortunate, but his intent is clear — we were not going to provoke the Japanese by an overt act; peace would continue until and unless they chose to strike. This was exactly the same attitude as President Lincoln's about Fort Sumter; or, to go further back, Colonel Parker's classic speech to the Minutemen at Lexington on 19 April 1775: "Don't fire unless fired upon, but if they mean to have a war, let it begin here."

Pearl Harbor, besides lacking the complete Intelligence picture, had the additional handicap of divided responsibility. General Short was charged with the defense of Oahu, including Pearl Harbor and antiaircraft batteries ashore; Admiral Bloch, commandant Fourteenth Naval District, was responsible for the defense of the Navy Yard, and Admiral Kimmel for that of the Fleet. Relations between them were friendly but inadequate; each one, as we have seen, assumed that the others were doing something that they didn't do.

A series of false assumptions, both at Washington and Oahu, added up to something as serious as the sins of omission. In Hawaii, the Navy assumed that the Army had gone on full alert, and that the radar warning net was completely operational. The Army assumed that the Navy was conducting an effective air reconnaissance around the island. Admiral Kimmel assumed that aërial torpedoes could not operate in the shoal waters of Pearl Harbor. Both Army and Navy Intelligence officers assumed that Japan was sending all her naval forces south, and that in any event Japan would not be so stupid as to attack Pearl Harbor. In Washington, Colonel Bratton of Army Intelligence assumed that the Pacific Fleet would go to sea after the 27 November "war warning," so to him the intercepted reports of ships' positions by the Japanese consulate registered waste effort; and Captain Wilkinson of Naval Intelligence assumed that these reports were simply evidence of the Japanese inordinate love for detail. Rear Admiral Turner of War Plans assumed that this and all other relevant intelligence was going to Admiral Kimmel, and General Gerow of Army War Plans assumed that Kimmel and Short were exchanging every scrap of what they did get, which was considerable. Washington was as vague and uncertain about what was going to happen on the first or second weekend after 27 November as Pearl Harbor itself. It was a case of the blind *not* leading the blind; false assumptions at both ends of the line.

The gravest charge against Admiral Kimmel and General Short is that they virtually ignored the "war warning" dispatch of 27 November from Washington. Admiral Kimmel, as we have seen, did send air reinforcement promptly to Wake and Midway Islands. He had already (with Admiral Bloch's coöperation) set up the surface and air patrol off the mouth of Pearl Harbor which encountered the midget submarines. He had, on 14 October, warned the Fleet against a submarine attack as a herald of something worse. Thus, the charge whittles down to this: that he did not repeat this warning and beef-up air patrol after 27 November. He thought that he had done everything that could reasonably be expected, in view of the intelligence received. Nevertheless, an "unwarranted feeling of immunity from attack" prevailed in Oahu at the crucial moment, as Admiral King observed; and it is not unfair to hold Kimmel and Short responsible.

Finally, we have to consider the "East Wind, Rain" dispatch which, by people bent on proving dastardly deception by Washington, has been blown up to a definite word from Tokyo that Pearl Harbor was about to be attacked. Actually, it was nothing of the sort. On 19 November, Tokyo notified the principal Japanese representatives abroad, in a dispatch that Washington decrypted, that if all other means of communication failed, they would be ordered to destroy codes in a plain-language weather broadcast. In this broadcast, "East Wind, Rain" would mean, "Japanese-United States relations in danger"; "North Wind, Cloudy" would mean the same as to Russia; "West Wind, Clear" would mean the same as to England. There was no mention of Pearl Harbor, or any other target; not even a clear forecast of war. This "Winds" message, however, was taken seriously in Washington where a number of officers were alerted to watch Japanese broadcasts for the false weather forecast. Whether or not that was ever sent is disputed; but in no case would it have told Washington or Hawaii anything more than what they already knew, viz., that Japanese embassies had been ordered to destroy their codes.

Fundamentally, however, it was the system, the setup both at Washington and at Pearl, rather than individual stupidity or apathy, which muffled and confused what was going on. No one person knew the whole picture that the intelligence data disclosed; no one person was responsible for the defense of Pearl Harbor; too many people assumed that others were taking precautions that they did not take.

There is an old saying, "Give every dog two bites"; but Kimmel and Short were not even allowed one; they were relieved from active duty forthwith. Admiral Turner, however, was conceded two bites — Pearl Harbor and the Battle of Savo Island, after which he became a highly successful practitioner of amphibious warfare. General Marshall functioned brilliantly as Chief of Staff; and Admiral Stark, as Commander United States Naval Forces Europe in London, acquitted himself very well. Admiral Kimmel and General Short were so shaken by the attack that they had to be relieved anyway; but they might, with justice, have been given honorable commands elsewhere.

Since World War II the methods and systems of obtaining military intelligence and, what is more important, evaluating it and seeing that the proper people get it, have been vastly improved. But let us not forget that we were surprised by the North Koreans in June 1950; surprised when China entered the war later that year; surprised in 1961 by discovery of the attempt to overthrow Castro in Cuba; surprised by the building of the East Berlin wall.

In a tense international situation, such as we have been in ever since the end of World War II, it is important not only to gather intelligence but to see that the right people get it, and to have it evaluated intelligently. It is vital to ascertain not only the capabilities of a potential enemy but his intentions.

So, I conclude this sad story of disaster with the warning which Sophocles, over twenty-three centuries ago in his tragedy of the Siege of Troy, placed in the mouth of Ajax: —

> Far-stretching, endless Time
> Brings forth all hidden things,
> And buries that which once did shine.
> The firm resolve falters, the sacred oath is shattered;
> And let none say, "It cannot happen here."

CHAPTER IV

Disaster in the Far East

July 1941–May 1942

1. *Loss of the Philippines, December 1941–May 1942*

ONE OF THE STRANGE THINGS in popular psychology is the different reaction of the American people to disaster at Pearl Harbor, and to disaster at Manila. The one completely overshadowed the other; it seemed so overwhelming that people could take in no bad news elsewhere. Yet the attack on Pearl Harbor was the lesser of the two evils. It was a hit-and-run raid, and the hit was not decisive. By 1000 December 7 the Japanese planes had retired, and they never returned; nor was there any attempt by the enemy to land troops on Oahu and take over. All we had to do was to count the losses, begin salvage and bury the dead. In the Philippines, the events of 7 December here (8 December there) were not so devastating as at Oahu, but they proved to be but the first of a series of body blows — and what blows! General MacArthur's Army forced to evacuate Manila and Admiral Hart's Fleet to evacuate Cavite; after a rear-guard campaign the entire Philippine archipelago surrendered to Japan; General MacArthur retired to Australia. Nor were these all. Defeat at Pearl Harbor brought no immediate consequences except the capture of Wake Island; but the Japanese blitz in the Philippines was followed by the seizure of Guam, Hong Kong, Thailand, North Borneo, Singapore; and, after a last-ditch campaign in the Java Sea, the entire Netherlands East Indies. Our inability to defend the Philippines in 1941-1942 cost us tens of thousands of lives, and uncounted billions of dollars, before the archipelago could be liberated in 1944-1945.

If surprise at Pearl Harbor is hard to understand, surprise at Manila is completely incomprehensible. Some eight or nine hours after General MacArthur was informed of the attack on Pearl Harbor, his planes were caught grounded, and his air force was as badly destroyed as that of the Army at Pearl Harbor. Yet General MacArthur was given a "second bite"; his mistakes on 8 December were overlooked — fortunately.

Again and again, since the turn of the century, American military commanders in the Philippines had warned that, with the meager forces assigned, they could not possibly defend the archipelago against Japan. Their plan, in case of war, was to abandon Manila, retire the army to Bataan, but to defend Manila Bay from Corregidor and other small island fortresses until the Pacific Fleet managed to arrive on the scene.

This plan and attitude changed after General MacArthur became Commander United States Army Forces Far East in July 1941. The General convinced Army authorities in Washington that, if properly reinforced before war broke out, and if the clash could be postponed until the spring of 1942, his army and the United States Asiatic Fleet could keep the Japanese out of Luzon until the Pacific Fleet arrived. His opinion was based on the hope, and expectation, that his command would receive at least one hundred B–17s. The performance of these Flying Fortresses was so outstanding that in October 1941 General MacArthur advised the War Department that the "citadel type of defense" of the Philippines, as envisaged by the "Rainbow 5" war plan, be changed to a dynamic and offensive plan. MacArthur's enthusiasm was infectious; General Marshall told him to go ahead with new plans, which provided for an offensive strike by B-17s on the Formosa airfields when and if war came with Japan. The Chief of Staff at a press conference in Washington on 15 November 1941 told selected correspondents that we were on the brink of war with Japan, that our position was "highly favorable" in the Philippines, where we had 35 B-17s — "greatest concentration of heavy bomber strength anywhere in the world" — which could counterattack, set the "paper cities" of Japan afire, and make the Philippines garrison independent of sea power.

General MacArthur's opposite number on the naval side was Admiral Thomas C. Hart, Commander in Chief of the Asiatic Fleet. Small, taut, wiry and irascible, Admiral Hart was a year older than Admiral King and had served 44 years in the Navy. In the autumn of 1940 he transferred most of his small fleet from China to Manila Bay. The Asiatic Fleet in the existing war plan was responsible for the naval defense of the Philippines. It must support the Army there "so long as that defense continues." Its total strength, when war broke, was a heavy cruiser *Houston*, two light cruisers, 13 World War I destroyers, 28 submarines, and a number of auxiliaries. Obviously, all that this fleet could do in the event of a Japanese invasion of the Philippines was to retire, or fight a delaying action. "Tommy" Hart, a real fighter, preferred the second alternative, but on 20 November the Navy Department ordered him to fall back. The Admiral then began deployment southward of all except his submarines, which were wanted to repel invasion, and Seaplane Wing 10 of PBYs, which were wanted for reconnaissance. On 8 December, four destroyers, six river gunboats, five "bird" class minesweepers, two fleet oilers, floating dry dock *Dewey* and a couple of tugs were still in Manila Bay. The 4th Marine Regiment was also in barracks at Cavite. Admiral Hart tried his best to remove Marines of the China embassy guard in time, and did get most of them out in river gunboat *Wake;* but merchant ship *President Harrison,* sent for the rest, was captured by the Japanese on 8 December.

Both commanders in the Philippines took the 27 November war warning very seriously and expected the blow to come soon. Ocean search by the PBYs was stepped up, and General MacArthur ordered all Flying Fortresses around Manila to be flown to Davao Field, Mindanao, for safety from a surprise air attack. But by 7 December only about half of them had gone, because room had to be left at the small Mindanao base for more B–17s expected presently from Hawaii. Nevertheless, the new war plan called for a counter-attack on the Formosan airfields as soon as Japan made war, or declared war.

News of the Pearl Harbor attack reached Admiral Hart's head-quarters in Manila at 0230 December 8 (East Longitude date), which was 0800 December 7, Hawaiian time. There was nothing he could do but alert the Asiatic Fleet to prepare for air attack. General MacArthur got the word about an hour later, and official confirmation arrived from Washington at 0530. At dawn a flight of 22 planes from Japanese carrier *Ryujo* attacked U.S. seaplane tender *William B. Preston* in Davao Gulf, Mindanao. That overt act inaugurated war in the Philippines. At 0930 two flights of bombers from Formosa struck Baguio and the Tugugarao airfield in northern Luzon. So there was no possible doubt that we were at war with Japan, or that the Philippines were on her list for con-quest. Yet, in the face of this, there was hesitation at Manila about unleashing the B–17s against Formosa, or the fighter planes to intercept a bomber strike from Formosa that might reasonably be expected at any moment. General Sutherland, General Mac-Arthur's chief of staff, and General Brereton, commanding Mac-Arthur's army air forces, have given each other the lie as to why the planned attack on Formosa was not promptly executed. Each claims that he wanted to do it but that the other dragged his feet, or his wings, insisting that first there be a photographic reconnaissance of the Formosa airfields. And why had that not been done earlier? The surprise at Manila has never been thoroughly investigated, and Dr. Louis Morton, the official Army historian, failed to get to the bottom of it. This naval historian can only venture a guess — that the real trouble was bad blood between Sutherland and Brereton, of which, unfortunately, General MacArthur seems to have been ignorant.

Whatever the cause, by 1130 almost all B–17s and fighter planes were grounded on Clark, Nichols, Iba and other fields of the airdrome complex around Manila. The ground crews then began arming the bombers for a raid on Formosa, which had finally been ordered to take place that afternoon, and the pilots went to lunch. A force of 108 twin-engined Japanese bombers, escorted by 34 fighters, was then well on its way from Formosa to Manila.

At about 1130, warnings of this approaching strike, from observers in northern Luzon, began to reach the Air Force plotting board at Nielson Field. Thence, about a quarter of an hour later, a warning message was ordered sent to Clark and other fields by teletype. Some claim that it never did go out; that the radio operator was at lunch. Nevertheless, one pursuit squadron of American fighter planes took off promptly from Iba Field, and another was just about to take off from Clark, at 1215, when the first group of 27 Japanese bombers appeared. Their delighted pilots found the B–17s all lined up like "sitting ducks," dropped their bombs from about 22,000 feet altitude, and were off and away. Then came a similar formation which bombed for fifteen minutes, completely unmolested by American antiaircraft, whose ancient ammunition (vintage 1932) and corroded bomb fuses could not reach so high. Finally came a full hour's strafing attack by 34 fighter planes. The scene was one of horror and destruction, relieved by many acts of individual heroism similar to those of the victims at

Pearl Harbor. Iba Field was struck by 54 Japanese planes, just as the pursuit squadron, which had gone forth a little before noon, was about to land. That squadron gave a good account of itself but lost all but two of its planes. Total losses to our side were 18 of the 35 B–17s present destroyed, 56 fighter planes, 25 miscellaneous aircraft, and many installations destroyed, 80 men killed and 150 wounded at a cost to the enemy of only seven fighters. After one day of war, and despite ample warning, the Far Eastern Air Force as an effective combat unit had been eliminated.

After this debacle there was no possibility of a counterattack, and Japan retained the initiative she had so easily won. December 9 was comparatively quiet, but the 10th was Navy Day for the enemy, who sent part of an 80-bomber and 52-fighter group to rub out the Cavite Navy Yard. While a substantial segment of this attack group neutralized airfields, some 54 bombers flew back and forth over Cavite at 20,000 feet elevation, beyond the range of our 3-inch antiaircraft guns, bombing at will. The Navy Yard and a large part of the city of Cavite were completely destroyed, as were a dockside submarine, a minesweeper, and the entire reserve stock of submarines' torpedoes.

On 12 December, all the PBYs of Patwing 10, returning from a fruitless search for an enemy carrier force that wasn't there, were destroyed by Japanese Zero fighters at their Olongapo moorings. The surviving aviators were sent south. The United States Navy had completely lost control of the waters and air surrounding Luzon; no supplies or reinforcements could reach MacArthur's army, ever. Let us humbly remember this humiliating fact and not bury it under the memory of MacArthur's gallantry, or the Navy's part in spearheading his return to the Philippines.

Across the South China Sea the Royal Netherlands Navy and the Royal British were faring no better.

Japan actually began hostilities in that quarter two days before her strike on Pearl Harbor. Minelayer *Tatsumiya Maru*, beginning on the evening of 6 December (East Longitude date), laid 456 mines in British territorial waters between Tiuman Island and the Malay Peninsula, not far from Singapore. This was done to protect the forthcoming Japanese landings on that peninsula from interference by British ships in Singapore. Netherlands submarine *O–16*, and probably *K–XVII* too, were sunk in this minefield in mid-December.

Worse things had already happened. Japanese bombers based on Indochina sank H.M. battleship *Prince of Wales* and battle cruiser *Repulse* on 10 December. By that time Japanese forces had already landed on the Malay Peninsula, taken Hong Kong from the British, and Guam from us. Nor is this all that happened on the 10th, which should be regarded as an even greater "day of infamy" than the 7th at Pearl Harbor. On that day the Japanese executed the first of their five amphibious landings on Luzon, at Aparri. The others coming up were at Vigan and Legaspi (11th and 12th), Lingayen (21st) and Lamon Bay (24th). The pitifully few ships and aircraft of Admiral Hart's fleet were unable to prevent the enemy from landing whenever and wherever he chose, or even to delay his timetable of conquest. Not that Asiatic Fleet failed to try. Its submarines were deployed to intercept the landings, and sank a couple of transports or freighters; but that did not stop the Japanese. Our efforts only served to prove that a properly equipped amphibious force cannot be stopped by submarines alone. And a Japanese amphibious group led by Rear Admiral Tanaka in light cruiser *Jintsu*, of whom (and of which) we shall hear much more, landed at Davao, Mindanao, on 20 December and then proceeded to take Jolo.

Japanese air forces so completely controlled the air over Manila Bay that reinforcements could not be brought in by sea, and the B–17s fleeted up from Mindanao were soon expended. On 21 De-

JAPANESE INVASIONS
OF THE
PHILIPPINE ISLANDS
DECEMBER 1941

■ US Airfields

Nautical Miles
0   50   100   150

cember Rear Admiral Francis W. Rockwell, Commandant Sixteenth Naval District, established new headquarters in a tunnel on "The Rock," Corregidor. On Christmas Eve General MacArthur decided to evacuate Manila (daily being bombed) and to deploy his army in the ultimate defense area, the Bataan Peninsula. Admiral Hart at the same time ordered the only two destroyers left in Manila Bay to Java, where Rear Admiral William A. Glassford, in cruiser *Marblehead*, was rallying the Asiatic Fleet. Hart himself departed for Java in submarine *Shark* the day after Christmas, leaving tender *Canopus* and a handful of minecraft, gunboats and motor torpedo boats, under Admiral Rockwell, to be expended. That they were, covering the flanks of the Army in its stubborn defense of Bataan.

There was no lack of individual bravery. A colorful character, Commander Francis J. Bridget of an already expended PBY squadron, organized a weird Naval Battalion of about 200 men from grounded aviators, Marines, Filipinos or anyone who would join. Wearing white Navy uniforms dyed bright yellow, these tough hombres not only protected General MacArthur's headquarters at Mariveles from capture by one Japanese landing force several times their strength, but forced a second Japanese group to hole up in caves on the coastal cliff, whence they were "disinfected" by Lieutenant John D. Bulkeley's PT boats. It was no use. On 21 February 1942 submarine *Swordfish* took President Quezon of the Philippine Commonwealth out of danger, and on 11 March, on orders from Washington, Lieutenant Bulkeley's PT carried General MacArthur and Admiral Rockwell to Mindanao, whence B–17s flew them to Australia.

General Jonathan M. Wainwright, left in command of the Army, evacuated Bataan on 8 April, to Corregidor. "The Rock," gallantly defended by Colonel S. L. Howard's 4th Marines and the remnants of the Army, held out for another month. Finally on 6 May came the bitterest event of all, when General Wainwright, hoping to prevent further effusion of blood, surrendered Corregidor and all armed forces in the Philippines to the enemy.

This was the greatest surrender in American history, not excepting Appomattox. But unlike that one, in which the Southern dream of empire faded, Corregidor inspired a grim determination on the part of General MacArthur to return, and of the country to see that he did return, in sufficient force to reverse the verdict. A new bond of brotherhood between Americans and Filipinos was forged, and it has never since been sundered.

2. *The ABDA Command*

By the new year Japan could afford to neglect the Philippines, since both United States and Commonwealth forces there were completely neutralized, and to the southward Japan was fast realizing her bold scheme of conquest.

England, the Netherlands and America had to fight for the Malay Barrier, a name then applied to the string of big islands from the Malay Peninsula to New Guinea, most of them belonging to the Netherlands East Indies. If Japan got possession of these rich territories, teeming with oil, rubber and other strategic materials, she would be well-nigh self-sufficient; and, once in control of the Molucca, Sunda, Lombok and other straits between the islands, the warriors of Nippon might pour into the Indian Ocean and threaten British India and Australia.

In April 1941 an attempt was made to arrive at an international staff agreement about the conduct of war in the Far East, similar to the Anglo-American one at Washington. Representatives of the United States, Great Britain, the Netherlands, Australia and New Zealand met at Singapore. This conference came to no useful result, largely because of divergent views about Singapore itself. The British had spent vast sums on creating the military and naval

base there, and regarded it as a symbol of empire, a pledge to the
Antipodes that England in her time of greatest peril had not forgotten them. Rear Admiral Turner and other Americans took a dim
view of Singapore as a strategic base. Owing to its lack of defenses
on the land side, they predicted that Singapore could not long hold
out in the event of war with Japan, nor did it. Even after H.M.S.
Prince of Wales and *Repulse* had been sunk, the British continued
to insist that Singapore must and could be defended. Divergent aims
bedeviled the new ABDA (American-British-Dutch-Australia)
combined command, set up on 15 January 1942, throughout the six
stormy weeks of its existence. The British wanted more troops to be
poured into Singapore, and to use the combined naval forces to
escort them; the Dutch wished to protect their East Indies; the
Australians to prevent an invasion of their country; and the Americans to prepare a comeback.

Thus ABDA as a combined command was very creaky at the
joints. Communication and language difficulties were never solved.
No combined system of signaling was worked out. The native
Indonesians, unlike the Filipinos, were apathetic or hostile. The supreme ABDA commander, Field Marshal Sir Archibald Wavell,
had proved himself in Africa to be one of England's most distinguished soldiers, but here he failed, as anyone under like conditions would have failed. Under Wavell, Admiral Hart commanded
the combined naval forces, a Dutch lieutenant general the ground
forces, and a British air chief marshal the air forces. The Asiatic
Fleet was now based at Surabaya on the north coast of Java, and its
principal units were organized into the ABDA striking force under
Vice Admiral Helfrich of the Royal Netherlands Navy. Port Darwin, Australia, 1200 miles distant, was the nearest service and supply base for the United States Asiatic Fleet.

Two powerful Japanese attack groups, the Eastern under Vice
Admiral Takahashi, and the Western under Vice Admiral Ozawa,
composed of heavy cruisers and destroyers escorting army trans-

ports, and with Admiral Nagumo's still intact carriers of the Pearl Harbor Striking Force in wide-ranging support, slithered into the Netherlands East Indies like the arms of two giant octopi. The Western octopus worked down the South China Sea to North Borneo and Sumatra; the Eastern to East Borneo, the Celebes, Ambon, Timor and Bali. Aircraft would pound down a beachhead, amphibious forces would then move in and activate another airfield and soften up the next objective for invasion. Nothing possessed by the three Allied powers could stop this grim process. Dutch and United States submarines inflicted considerable damage, but the enemy forces were overwhelming. The Allies, owing to their diverse interests, dissipated their forces in various directions and on gallant but futile missions.

Commander Paul Talbot in *John D. Ford,* with three other World War I destroyers, broke into the Japanese force landing at Balikpapan, Borneo, on the night of 23-24 January 1942, and sank four *Marus* and a patrol craft; but this did not delay the Japanese timetable by even a day. By 3 February Japanese airplanes, now established at Kondari in the Celebes, began raiding Surabaya, forcing Admiral Hart to send his tenders south to Tjilatjap; none too soon, for light cruiser *Marblehead* was so badly mauled off Banka next day that she had to be sent home. Another air-surface battle between planes from carrier *Ryujo,* and an ABDA striking force under Admiral Doorman RNN on 15 February, forced the ships to retire through Gaspar Strait to the Java Sea. And on that very day, Singapore surrendered — as bitter a draught for Britain as Pearl Harbor had been for America.

3. *The Battle of the Java Sea, 27 February 1942*

Now, in quick succession, the Japanese occupied Timor and Nagumo's carrier planes bombed Port Darwin, heavily damaging the

Allied supply ships, and forcing the abandonment of that port as a supply base. The octopi would soon put the final squeeze on Java.

By the time they were ready for that, ABDA command had been "reorganized upon the floor," like the person described in T. S. Eliot's "Sweeney among the Nightingales." Admiral Hart had been a good skipper in a bad storm, using the little that he had to fight to best advantage, but on 12 February, owing to the Netherlands government's desire that in their East Indies a Dutch admiral should be in command, "Tommy" Hart was relieved by Admiral Helfrich RNN. This change did not help the desperately bad situation. All fighting ships and sailors had been worked beyond their capacity. Facilities for repairs were inadequate at Surabaya, and almost nonexistent at Tjilatjap on the south coast of Java, which most of the Asiatic Fleet now had to use as base, owing to frequent air attacks on the north-coast ports.

Field Marshal Wavell was ordered home, and on 25 February departed. General Brereton of the United States Army Air Force had already gone, together with most of the planes that he had managed to evacuate from the Philippines. Units of the British, of United States and of the Netherlands Navy remained. ABDA no longer existed in fact, only in theory. Dutch officers were now in full control of all armed forces left in the area.

Rear Admiral Karel Doorman RNN now commanded the Striking Force of the three Allied navies, based at Surabaya. It was far from negligible as a fighting array: heavy crusiers *Houston* and H.M.S. *Exeter*, light cruisers H.M.A.S. *Perth*, H.M.N.S. *De Ruyter* and *Java;* four American, three British and three Dutch destroyers. Collectively, these ships were not strong enough to stop the major Japanese thrust, and they had never worked together as a team. Two massive amphibious forces were approaching — 56 transport types under Rear Admiral Ozawa to the westward, and 41 under Rear Admiral Nishimura to the eastward. And the eastern one, which Doorman hoped to intercept since it seemed headed for Surabaya, was covered by a formidable support force under Rear Admiral Takeo Takagi, which included heavy cruisers *Nachi* and *Haguro*, and two destroyer squadrons with light cruiser flagships (*Naka* and *Jintsu*) under Rear Admirals Nishimura and Tanaka. Vice Admiral Nagumo's Pearl Harbor Striking Force was hovering in the Indian Ocean to prevent reinforcement from that quarter and took no part in the battle. The air component was supplied by the Japanese cruisers' float planes. Their spotting and (after dark) illuminating may well have tipped the scales, for Doorman had no aircraft whatsoever. He had left his float planes ashore on the 26th, expecting a night battle, and when he called for air support from Java, the air commander there stupidly sent his few light bombers and fighters to make a fruitless attack on the Japanese transports.

Admiral Doorman, a fine type of fighting sailor, was about to enter Surabaya for rest and replenishment when he received reports of two Japanese convoys, the nearer but 80 miles distant. At 1525 February 27 Striking Force reversed course to give battle in waters between the north coast of Java and Bawean Island, which the Japanese had already taken. Doorman had no time to issue a battle plan, much less to distribute it; and there was confusion and delay from the necessity of translating every signal. About the only command that Doorman could get across during the battle was "Follow me!" and every ship that could, did. His object was simple enough, to beat off or get around Takagi's fighting ships and raise havoc among the transports waiting just over the northern horizon. Takagi's object, naturally, was to prevent this and clear the way for the invasion of Java.

The battle was such a series of thrusts and parries, bursts of gunfire and shoals of torpedoes, over a period of five or six hours, that it is difficult to follow. If you care to go with me, keep one eye on our chart. If you do not, skip to read only the result.

At the lower right of the chart, note the Allied order of battle:

three British destroyers (*Encounter, Electra, Jupiter*) in the van; H.N.M.S. *De Ruyter* (Doorman's ship) followed by H.M.S. *Exeter*, U.S.S. *Houston*, H.M.A.S. *Perth*, H.N.M.S. *Java* in column; two Dutch destroyers (*Witte de With* and *Kortenaer*) on the left flank, and four Americans (*John D. Edwards, Alden, John D. Ford, Paul Jones*) in the rear.

It was a calm, clear day with high visibility and a slight swell. At 1612 the enemy was sighted, in three columns — Tanaka's *Jintsu* and seven destroyers on the right flank; Takagi's two heavy cruisers *Nachi* and *Haguro* in the center, Nishimura's *Naka* and six destroyers on the left flank. At 1616 firing commenced between the two heavy groups at the extreme range of 28,000 yards, almost 14 miles. Tanaka's destroyer squadron closed *Electra* and *Jupiter* to 18,000 yards and straddled them, but they could not reach him with their 4.7-inch guns. As Doorman's course, if continued, would enable the Japanese to emulate Admiral Togo's famous Tsushima "crossing of the T," the Netherlands admiral changed course from northwest to west to parallel the enemy, and endeavored to close range so that his three light cruisers could use their 6-inch guns. In the gunfire duel that ensued, the Japanese, with planes spotting for them, had the advantage, and at 1631 made the first hit, fortunately a dud, on *De Ruyter*. Takagi now ordered the first torpedo attack; and he had 17 ships to launch from, as all Japanese cruisers carried torpedoes. Over a period of 19 minutes, 1633-1652, the Japanese launched 43 of their fast, powerful "long lances," but made not one hit; the range was too great. Both forces sped westward at about 25 knots or more, firing furiously but not hitting. This battle showed something that became increasingly evident during World War II: the ineffectiveness of naval gunfire at high speed and great range.

Again the Japanese took the initiative. At 1700, bold Tanaka peeled off to cross Doorman's bows and make a second torpedo attack. He would have had little chance to score against the thin

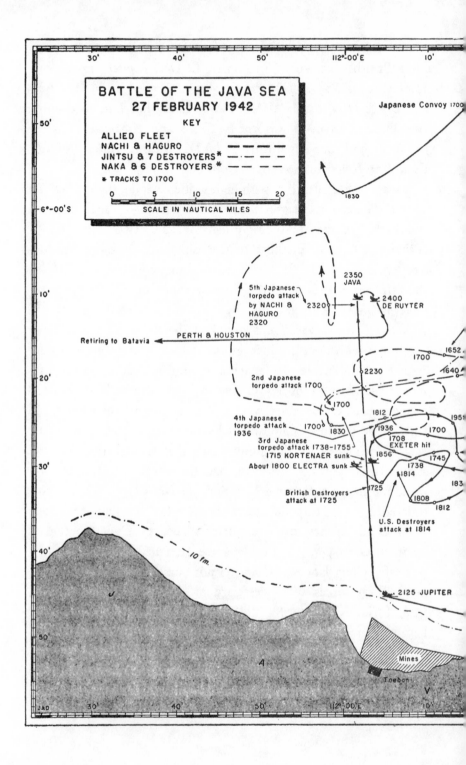

BATTLE OF THE JAVA SEA
27 FEBRUARY 1942

KEY

ALLIED FLEET
NACHI & HAGURO
JINTSU & 7 DESTROYERS *
NAKA & 6 DESTROYERS *

* TRACKS TO 1700

0   5   10   15   20
SCALE IN NAUTICAL MILES

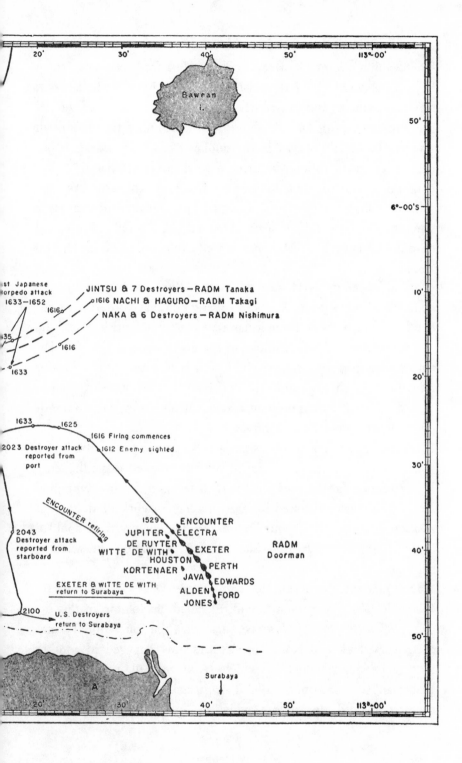

20' 30' 40' 50' 113°·00'

Bawran i.

50'

6°·00'S

10'

st Japanese
orpedo attack
1633–1652
    °1616
JINTSU & 7 Destroyers — RADM Tanaka
°1616 NACHI & HAGURO — RADM Takagi
NAKA & 6 Destroyers — RADM Nishimura

435
°
    °1616

°1633

20'

1633   1625
2023 Destroyer attack
reported from
port
1616 Firing commences
1612 Enemy sighted

30'

ENCOUNTER retiring
1529 ENCOUNTER
2043
Destroyer attack
reported from
starboard
JUPITER ELECTRA
DE RUYTER
WITTE DE WITH EXETER
HOUSTON
KORTENAER PERTH
JAVA EDWARDS
ALDEN FORD
JONES
RADM
Doorman

40'

EXETER & WITTE DE WITH
return to Surabaya

2100 U.S. Destroyers
return to Surabaya

50'

A Surabaya

20' 30' 40' 50' 113°·00'

frontal silhouette of Doorman's column, but for a cruiser's 8-inch hit, at 1708, on H.M.S. *Exeter*, which put six of her eight boilers out, slowed her down and caused her to sheer out of line, about 90 degrees to port. *Houston*, *Perth* and *Java*, assuming that Doorman (whom they could not see in the smoke) must have ordered a 90-degree left turn, followed suit; and so flagship *De Ruyter*, after continuing west for a minute or two, had to do the same. As a result, the Allied force became scattered in a confused pattern right slap into Tanaka's torpedo water. He could hardly fail to score, and he did. At 1715 H.N.M.S. *Kortenaer* exploded, jackknifed, and sank.

Takagi, seeing his chance with the Allied force in confusion and slowed down to 15 knots by *Exeter*'s mishap, ordered his entire force in for the kill. Doorman sent the three British destroyers to counterattack through smoke to the northwestward, where Tanaka's squadron was milling about and trying pot shots. By this time, in the gathering dusk, the entire battle area was shrouded in smoke, through which only an occasional blinker signal from Admiral Doorman reached his ships.

Electra, which received this latest order at 1725, scored a hit on *Jintsu*, but in return was stopped dead by a shell exploding in a boiler room. Tanaka now drove in to try and finish off limping *Exeter*, but was frustrated by the nimble footwork of destroyers *Jupiter*, *Witte de With* and *Encounter*. The enemy then doubled back to gang up on *Electra*. She fulfilled the tragic implication of her name at 1800.

Doorman in the meantime had ordered *Exeter*, escorted by *Witte de With*, to Surabaya, and reformed his column in this order: *De Ruyter, Perth, Houston, Java*, with the four United States destroyers flank and rear. The cruisers now engaged in another long-range gunfire duel, in which *Houston* took two duds. As Doorman was steering south, Takagi assumed that he was retreating, advised the convoy (which had turned north) to resume course for the landing beaches, and sent Nishimura's squadron to finish off the Allies. Nishimura scored not one hit with the 24 torpedoes his squadron launched.

Doorman now ordered the United States destroyers to cover his retirement. Their squadron commander, T. H. Binford, regarding attack as the best means to cover, turned north to torpedo *Nachi* and *Haguro*. Unfortunately the American torpedoes had been set so that they could only be fired broadside, and under these circumstances to close to a proper range would mean almost certain destruction by the cruisers' gunfire before launching. Binford therefore took a chance shot at 10,000 yards, and all torpedoes missed. After a short gunfire duel with destroyer *Asagumo*, possibly holing her, the "four-pipers" hastened to catch up with Admiral Doorman.

That great sea-dog never acknowledged defeat. At 1830 he had radioed to Admiral Helfrich ashore: "Enemy retreating west, where's the convoy?" At that very moment Takagi ordered the convoy to reverse course and stand northward — it was then only 30 miles away. The Japanese did not underestimate the ability of Doorman, now steering northwesterly, to get at the convoy; and if the Allies had had any air reconnaissance they might have evaded Takagi's ships and struck a fatal blow. But the dice were loaded against them.

At about 1927 the converging cruisers sighted each other again in the gathering darkness. *Nachi* led *Haguro*, *Jintsu* and several destroyers; 13,000 yards to the southeastward was *De Ruyter* followed by *Perth*, *Houston*, *Java* and four American destroyers; H.M.S. *Jupiter* was stationed about a mile on *De Ruyter's* port bow. *Perth* and *Houston* opened fire at 1933, but their shells fell short. The enemy fired star shells to illuminate, and at 1936, when Captain Waller RAN of *Perth* saw a row of flashes in the enemy column, he rightly suspected that they meant torpedo launchings and swung hard right to course 60°. The other ships followed suit and this, the fourth, Japanese torpedo attack was successfully evaded.

Doorman now planned to escape these troublesome ships and get at the convoy by following the coast of Java west. So, at 1955, he swung his column south and at flank speed steamed toward the Java coast, which soon loomed up in the moonlight. There could be no escape, since he was continually illuminated by Japanese float planes dropping flares. When his column reached shoal water, at 2100, Admiral Doorman turned right to parallel the coast. The United States destroyers at this point left the formation and turned east for Surabaya; Doorman had instructed them to do that when their torpedoes were expended, as now they were. As Doorman's force continued westward along the coast, it skirted a newly laid Dutch minefield whose exact position had been broadcast at frequent intervals. At high speed the cruisers, followed by two destroyers, cleared the mined area safely; but at 2125 an explosion racked H.M.S. *Jupiter*, and she dropped out, victim either of a floating mine that had broken loose, or of an internal explosion. She sank four hours later.

Shortly after *Jupiter* exploded, Admiral Doorman turned his four cruisers north again. Although he now had but one destroyer with him and no air support, this brave officer determined to make one last desperate thrust to thwart the invasion of Java. It was a suicidal move. Zigzagging slightly, the column steamed northward, hoping to avoid further attention from the enemy. Over an hour passed and nothing happened, except that destroyer *Encounter* dropped out to pick up survivors from *Kortenaer* on life rafts. Then *Nachi*, *Haguro* and several destroyers were sighted in bright moonlight on the port beam, steering south. Takagi reversed course to parallel Doorman, and the two columns exchanged long-range gunfire for twenty minutes, hoping for a lucky hit. Salvos came slowly now, since both sides were low on ammunition and their crews were near exhaustion. At 2320, when the two columns were almost parallel, 8000 yards apart, the Japanese cruisers launched 12 torpedoes. *De Ruyter* and *Java*, caught in the wide spread, burst into flames, exploded and stopped dead. *Java* lived for only fifteen minutes; *De Ruyter* defiantly floated for about three hours. Their captains and Admiral Doorman followed the hard ritual of the sea and went down with them.

Before he lost contact with *Perth* and *Houston*, Doorman had ordered them not to stand by him but to retire to Batavia. They headed for Tanjong Priok, where they signaled to Admiral Helfrich the tragic results of the Battle of the Java Sea.

In one afternoon and evening, half the ships of Admiral Doorman's Striking Force had been destroyed; the Japanese had not lost a single ship, and only one destroyer was damaged. The convoy was never touched.

The main factors in this battle, any one of which would have doomed the Allies to defeat, were complete lack of air power, bad communications, and the enemy's superiority in torpedoes. The most surprising thing about the battle was its duration. Before World War II, most strategists thought that gun and torpedo fire had been developed to such a degree that naval battles would be decided in a few minutes, at the end of which one side would either be annihilated or so crippled that it could fight no more. Several battles in this war — notably, Savo Island — were of that description. But in the Battle of the Java Sea the two opponents slugged each other intermittently over a period of some seven hours before one had to break off and admit defeat. That it lasted so long was due to Admiral Doorman's stubborn determination and the admirable manner in which men of the three navies under his command fought and fought until they could fight no more.

Java Sea was indeed a decisive battle. There was nothing now to stop the Japanese invasion. And when brave Doorman went down, his country's colonial empire was doomed; even the eventual Allied victory could not eradicate the effects of this Japanese triumph. Never again would the Netherlanders rule over these beautiful islands and their volatile people.

4. *Bloody Sequel, March–April 1942*

One Allied disaster after another followed the Java Sea battle. Seaplane tender *Langley*, pioneer carrier of the United States Navy, was sunk by air bombing south of Tjilatjap on 27 February while trying to bring in plane reinforcements. On the last night of February, U.S.S. *Houston* and H.M.A.S. *Perth*, survivors of the Java Sea, gallantly charged into Banten Bay, adjoining Sunda Strait, to break up one of the major Japanese amphibious forces that was being landed. If only Doorman and his other ships had been with them, they could have realized the ABDA dream of breaking up a Japanese invasion force at its most vulnerable moment. But, alas, it was so late, they were so few, and Admiral Kurita's Western Covering Group, built around four heavy cruisers, was too strong.

Destroyer *Fubuki* almost caught *Houston* and *Perth* as they entered Banten Bay. She fired torpedoes at them at a range of about 2700 yards, missed them but hit and sank a couple of Japanese transports on their port hand. The cruisers swung around the bay, shooting up transports as they passed; one was sunk outright and three others had to be beached.[1]

As they roared through the narrow channel between Panjang Island and Saint Nicholas Point, the two cruisers ran into a fatal trap. On the port hand a Japanese destroyer squadron blocked

[1] John Toland *But Not in Shame* (1961) states that from Japanese sources all four transports were sunk by Japanese torpedoes from the heavy cruisers. This cannot be correct; the cruisers were too far away to score with torpedoes, and Panjang Island lay between them and the transports.

Sunda Strait, their escape hatch; on the starboard hand, freshly replenished, oversize heavy cruisers *Mogami* and *Mikuma* opened up on the two depleted, exhausted "treaty" cruisers. The Japanese shooting, from almost point-blank range, was inaccurate but so overwhelming that only a miracle could have changed the result. H.M.A.S. *Perth* came under fire at 2326. At 0005 March 1 she took a torpedo in her forward engine room that almost lifted her out of the water, then another, and in a few moments she went down, taking Captain Waller and hundreds more.

Now every Japanese ship concentrated on putting *Houston* away. She was already listing dangerously to starboard. Around 0010 she took a salvo in her after engine room which burst all the steam lines and scalded to death the entire engine room force. A torpedo hit forward smashed up main battery plot, whose crew was wiped out by a shellburst as they ran topside. Turrets went to local control, and for a few moments the gunners profited by a mistake that the enemy made, illuminating his own ships; they hit three different destroyers and sank a minesweeper. A shell hit No. 2 turret just as powder bags were being loaded, starting a fire which forced Captain Rooks to have both magazines flooded. Now the two 8-inch turrets had no ammunition except what was already in the hoists. Three torpedoes hit the ship on her starboard side and shrapnel from small-caliber fire ricocheted about her superstructure. Around 0025, standing near a machine-gun mount, Rooks and the gun crew were killed by a bursting shell. Men stood by the other guns and fired every bit of ammunition until all was expended. Then, as the ship lost headway, Japanese destroyers swarmed about her, machine-gunning the quarterdeck and the port hangar where many of the survivors from below had congregated. Commander David Roberts, the exec., ordered Abandon Ship, and Seaman Stafford, standing on the careening fantail, sounded the call on his bugle, at 0033. Within ten or twelve minutes *Houston* rolled over and sank. Swimming survivors could see her ensign defiantly flying until it dipped below the waters of Sunda Strait.

On this same bloody first of March, H.M.S. *Exeter* tried to lead U.S. destroyer *Pope* and H.M.S. *Encounter* through the Surabaya minefields to safety. All three were sunk by enemy naval gunfire and carrier bombing planes.

Japanese troops swarmed over Java, and on the 9th the Dutch commanding general surrendered the Netherlands East Indies.

Admiral Nagumo's carrier force was now free to raid the Indian Ocean, where Admiral Sir James Somerville RN, one of England's senior and most versatile flag officers, awaited him with the British Far Eastern Force — five old battleships, three small carriers, eight cruisers and 15 destroyers. The Japanese had it pretty much their own way from 25 March to 8 April, striking Colombo and Trincomalee, sinking carrier *Hermes* and two heavy cruisers, and about 136,000 tons of merchant shipping. In four months' time Nagumo had operated one third of the way around the world. He had conducted strikes against ships and shore installations at Pearl Harbor, Rabaul, Ambon, Darwin, Java, and Ceylon. He had sunk five battleships, an aircraft carrier, two cruisers and seven destroyers; had damaged several more capital ships, disposed of some 200,000 tons of fleet auxiliaries and merchant men, and hundreds of Allied aircraft. Yet not one ship of his Striking Force had been even damaged by enemy action. There was no longer any doubt as to what type would be the capital ship of the future.

The Malay Barrier was now shattered. Except for isolated pockets of resistance, such as Corregidor, the colonial empires of the United States, the Netherlands, and Great Britain, as far west as India and as far south as Australia, had joined that of the French, already liquidated. Within four months of the Pearl Harbor strike, Japan had achieved her Greater East Asia Co-Prosperity Sphere. She was poised to lash backward into China; or, if America and

Britain did not throw in the sponge, forward by the right flank into India and by the left flank into the Aleutians and Hawaii.

Were our efforts, then, to defend the Malay Barrier a waste of men and matériel? Admiral King is reported to have characterized the whole Southwest Pacific campaign as "a magnificent display of very bad strategy." He never said what he thought good strategy would have been; probably he meant abandoning Singapore and concentrating on defending Java, which might possibly have worked. Be that as it may, the Allies did well to fight for the Malay Barrier, although fighting alone could not save it. Recent experience of the French showed the moral cost of too easy and complacent a capitulation. Another such in Southeast Asia might have been too much for the Allies to bear.

So, while we mourn *Houston* and the other gallant ships of three navies that went down with most of their officers and men after fighting so bravely and well, we should not regard their efforts as vain; their desperate exploits should forever be held in proud and affectionate remembrance by the ABDA nations — America, Britain, the Netherlands and Australia.

CHAPTER V

Destruction in the Atlantic

1942

1. *Transatlantic Convoys, January–April 1942*

THE JAPANESE ATTACK on Pearl Harbor was as much of a surprise to Hitler as to the United States; he had been trying to persuade Japan to attack Russia. The *Chicago Tribune* on 4 December printed a purloined document in which the ABC Conference decision of March to beat Germany first was embodied, and the German chargé at Washington promptly transmitted this to Berlin. But the revelation, instead of encouraging Hitler to continue his policy of avoiding war with the United States as long as possible, caused him to declare war on the United States (11 December 1941). Mussolini obediently followed, and that afternoon Congress declared war on Germany and Italy.

Admiral King, appointed Commander in Chief United States Fleet (Cominch) on 20 December 1941 at the age of sixty-three, was relieved ten days later as Commander in Chief Atlantic Fleet (Cinclant) by Admiral Royal E. Ingersoll. As the functions of the Chief of Naval Operations overlapped those of a shore-based Cominch, President Roosevelt gave King the C.N.O. job too, on 12 March 1942.

King was a "man of adamant," as Mahan described Sir John Jervis. Tall, spare and taut, with piercing brown eyes, a powerful Roman nose and deeply cleft chin, he looked the part and filled the part of Commander in Chief of the Fleet. King was a sailor's sailor. He believed that what was good for the Navy was good for the United States, and indeed the world. In that sense and that alone he was narrow. But he had a firm grasp of naval strategy and tactics, an encyclopedic knowledge of naval detail, an immense capacity for work, and complete integrity. Endowed with a superior intellect himself, he had no toleration for fools or weaklings. He hated publicity, did not lend himself to popular buildup, and was the despair of interviewers. Unlike Admiral Stark's decisions, King's were made quickly and without much consultation; when anyone tried to argue with him beyond a certain point, a characteristic bleak look came over his countenance as a signal that his mind was made up and further discussion was useless. Although he had nothing of the courtier in his make-up, King acquired and retained the confidence and esteem of President Roosevelt. The two men were in a sense complementary. Each had what the other lacked, and in concert with General Marshall, who shared the qualities of both, they formed a perfect winning team. The Republic has never had more efficient, intelligent and upright servants than these three men.

Admiral King made Rear Admiral Russell Willson his chief of staff, and brought with him to Washington from the Atlantic Fleet Rear Admiral Richard S. Edwards as deputy chief of staff, Captain Francis S. Low as operations officer, and Commander George L. Russell as flag secretary. As assistant chiefs of staff he appointed Rear Admirals Richmond K. Turner and Willis Augustus Lee. When Turner went to Guadalcanal he was relieved as assistant chief of staff for plans by Rear Admiral Charles M. ("Savvy") Cooke. Apart from Edwards, Willson, Russell and Cooke, and Vice Admiral Frederick J. Horne, who became Vice Chief of Naval Operations in March 1942, Admiral King kept a continual turnover on his staff. Senior officers were constantly being brought in from different theaters of war, retained on duty with Cominch-

CNO for a few months, then sent back to sea. Thus the fighting Navy point of view was maintained at Washington.

Since escort-of-convoy was every day becoming more important, and required heavy communications facilities, Admiral King took the direction of it with him from Newport to Washington. Shortly after becoming Cominch, he exchanged views on the subject with the Admiralty. This resulted in transatlantic convoy routes being shifted southward, and the Canadian Navy being given a greater share in escorting slow convoys to a "momp" [1] at long. 22° W (about five hundred miles from Northern Ireland), where Royal Navy escorts could take over, and the Canadians proceed to Londonderry to fuel. The fast Halifax–U.K. convoys were escorted by United States destroyers to Momp, where they, too, were relieved by the Royal Navy, refueled at Londonderry, and escorted a fast convoy home. This change of the turnaround point from Iceland to Ireland was most welcome to bluejackets; Londonderry, a dour Presbyterian city, seemed like Coney Island after Reykjavik, and the green Irish countryside looked like heaven after the barren wastes of Iceland. Repair facilities also were superior, since Londonderry was already an important base of the Royal Navy, and the main British center for antisubmarine training. The British "dome teacher," in which sailors were trained to the use of antiaircraft guns in a sort of planetarium, was of immense value to American gunners, as were the British "tame submarines" on which escort vessels practised both day and night attacks.

Admiral Ingersoll as Cinclant exercised complete responsibility for troop convoys, the first of which sailed from Halifax 10 January 1942 and arrived Londonderry about two weeks later. It was desirable to build up United States Army forces in the United Kingdom immediately, so that there would be no shortage of troop-lift, as in 1918, when the Army was ready to strike. In

1 Abbreviation for Mid-ocean Meeting Point.

February the Navy organized a series of troop convoys, partly with British transports, and a heavy American escort, including battleships and cruisers as well as destroyers. These convoys also enjoyed all the blimp and airplane escort that was available at each end of the route. Heavy weather was often encountered, and an occasional sound contact on a submarine was made, but a speed of 12.5 to 14.5 knots was maintained and not a ship or a soldier was lost.

Fueling at sea was another problem. The old "short-legged" 1200-ton destroyers had been designed in the light of World War I experience, when all that was expected of an escort was a 48-hour run outbound or inbound. But the necessities of escort duty in 1941-1942 were such that every United States destroyer had to cover the route Argentia–Momp–Iceland, or the reverse, which required at least ten days' steaming. It was impossible for such ships, in winter weather, to conduct the active, aggressive patrolling enjoined on all by the fate of U.S.S. *Kearny* and *Reuben James*. Before the war, fueling at sea had been practised largely in calm weather, and only from battleships; now it had to be done from merchant tankers. On one transatlantic convoy four tankers, rigged for ocean fueling abreast or astern, made twenty fuelings of escorts, four or five times on some of them.

The scarcity of suitable escorts was the greatest handicap during this period. Coast Guard Cutter *Campbell*, employed as escort in November 1941, proved so effective that most of her sister ships of the "Treasury" class were diverted to this duty. These big seagoing cutters had everything that a destroyer had except speed and torpedoes; and seldom does an opportunity arise to use torpedoes in escort-of-convoy. U.S.C.G.C. *Alexander Hamilton* was torpedoed and sunk ten miles off Iceland 29 January 1942, when towing a disabled storeship.

Air cover at this period could only be provided at each end of the transatlantic route, and from Iceland. In antisubmarine warfare, air search proved so valuable for locating and destroying U-boats that every effort was made to extend and enlarge the coverage. By the end of 1942, a squadron of four-engined Liberators operating out of Greenland proved a great help in mid-ocean, but even they left a big "dark pocket" around the Azores, where U-boats operated with impunity and even refueled from special submarine "milch cows" sent out for that purpose. The Navy was eager to light up this pocket by occupying the Azores and installing airfields there, but Dr. Salazar, premier of Portugal, would not allow this until late 1943, when he had decided that the Allies were going to win; and the Allies could not violate their own principles by seizing part of a neutral country.

A convoy is beautiful, whether seen from a deck or from the sky. The inner core of stolid ships in several columns is never equally spaced, for each has her individuality; one is always straggling or ranging ahead until the commodore becomes vexed and signals angrily, "Number So-and-so, take station and keep station!" Around the merchant ships is thrown the screen like a loose-jointed necklace, the beads lunging to port or starboard and then snapping back as though pulled by a mighty submarine elastic; each destroyer nervous and questing, all eyes topside looking for the enemy, sound gear below listening for him, radar antennae like cats' whiskers feeling for him. On dark nights only a few shapes of ships a little darker that the black water can be discerned; one consults the radar screen to ascertain that the flock is all there. To one coming topside for the dawn watch, it is a recurring wonder to see the same ships day after day, each in her appointed station, each with her characteristic top-hamper, bow-wave, lift and dip; the inevitable straggler, the inveterate smoker, the vessel with an old shellback master who "knew more about shipping forty years ago than any goddam gold-braid in a tin can," and whose sullen fury at being convoyed translates itself into belated turns, unanswered signals and insolent comebacks. When air cover is furnished there are darting, swooping planes about the convoy; upon approaching port, the stately silver bubble of a blimp comes out, swaying in the breeze and blinking a cheery welcome.

There is nothing beautiful, however, about a night attack on a convoy, unless you see it from a submarine's periscope. A torpedo hit is signaled by a flash and a great orange flare, followed by a muffled roar. Guns crack at imaginary targets, star shell breaks out, a rescue ship hurries to the scene of the sinking, and sailors in other ships experience a helpless fury and dread. If the convoy has a weak escort it can only execute an emergency turn and trust that the rest of the wolf-pack will be thrown off or driven down; if the escort is sufficient a "killer group" peels off, searching relentlessly with radar and sonar, while everyone stands by hoping to feel underfoot the push of distant depth charges that tells of a fight with a submerged enemy.

The only American-escorted convoy that lost heavily during the first four months of 1942 was ON–67 of 35 ships in eight columns which crossed westward during the full moon of February. The ocean escort, consisting of the United States destroyers *Edison, Nicholson, Lea* and *Bernadou,* under Commander A. C. Murdaugh USN, steamed south to join from Iceland. Shortly after they took over, at 1305 February 22 two ships were torpedoed and sunk. In the early hours of 24 February, four more were torpedoed and two sank. All day the screen made wide sweeps and aggressive patrols, which continued throughout the night. Two U-boats were sighted in the moonlight and depth-charged, but both escaped. Commander Murdaugh's officers were alert and zealous, but deficient in attack technique.

Escort units, composed usually of two United States destroyers and four Canadian corvettes, directed by such seasoned commanders as W. K. ("Sol") Phillips in *Mayo,* P. R. Heineman in *Benson*, H. C. Fitz in *Niblack*, John B. Heffernan in *Gleaves* and R. W. Hungerford in *Bristol*, were getting the ships across safely — but they were not sinking any U-boats. When March came in like a lion, weather became more deadly than the submarine. A convoy cannot heave-to like a single steamship, because vessels act so differently hove-to that collisions and wide scattering would result. It has to keep going somewhere, somehow. Except for two ships sunk out of Convoy ON–68, the casualties in March were caused by the weather.

2. *The Assault on Coastal and Caribbean Shipping,* *January–July 1942*

A prompt attack by U-boats on American coastal shipping should have been anticipated, since they had done just that during World War I. No U-boats happened to be in position to raid American coasts when Germany declared war on the United States in December 1941, but Admiral Doenitz chose five of his best "aces" (and followed them by six more) to devastate the American East Coast shipping lanes. These originate in the Saint Lawrence River, cross the Gulf of Maine, pass New York (where at least fifty ships arrived and departed daily), and extend past the Capes of Delaware, the Chesapeake, and Hatteras, into the Caribbean, the Gulf of Mexico, and down past the bulge of Brazil.

Operation PAUKENSCHLAG ("Roll of the Drums"), as the Germans called it, opened on 12 January 1942, when a British steamer was torpedoed and sunk about 300 miles east of Cape Cod by *U–123*. Two days later, enemy submarines moved into the shipping bottleneck off Cape Hatteras. Three tankers in succession were sunk on 14 and 15 January. Next day the U-boats sank a Canadian "Lady boat" and two freighters, then three tankers in succession and three more before the end of the month. Thirteen vessels in all, measuring 95,000 gross tons (and 70 per cent of this tanker tonnage), were lost in a little over two weeks.

No more perfect setup for rapid and ruthless destruction could have been offered the Nazi sea lords. The massacre enjoyed by the U-boats along our Atlantic Coast in 1942 was as much a national disaster as if saboteurs had destroyed half a dozen of our biggest war plants. The damage in the Eastern Sea Frontier was wrought by no more than 12 U-boats operating at any one time, and every month the Germans were building 20 or more new 740- and 500-tonners. Each U-boat carried fourteen torpedoes, including some of the new electrically propelled type that showed no air bubbles in the wake, so could not be sighted or dodged. In addition they carried guns of sufficient caliber to sink most merchant vessels by shellfire alone. The 500-tonners carried enough fuel for a cruise of at least 42 days. Allowing two weeks for the outward passage and the same for homeward to a French port, they could spend two weeks in the Atlantic coastal lanes. Their usual tactics, in the early months of 1942, were to approach a trade route at periscope depth, lie in wait on the surface at night, and launch torpedoes from seaward against a vessel whose silhouette might be seen against shore lights.

One of the most reprehensible failures on our part was the neglect of local communities to dim their waterfront lights, or of military authorities to require them to do so, until three months after the submarine offensive started. When this obvious defense measure was first proposed, squawks went all the way from Atlantic City to southern Florida that the "tourist season would be ruined." Miami and its luxurious suburbs threw up six miles of neon-light glow, against which was silhouetted southbound shipping that hugged the shore to avoid the Gulf Stream. Ships were sunk and seamen drowned in order that the citizenry might enjoy pleasure as usual. Finally, on 18 April 1942, the Eastern Sea Frontier ordered waterfront lights and sky signs doused, and the

Eastern Defense Command of the Army ordered a stringent dim-out on 18 May.

If one or two torpedoes did not fatally hole the attacked ship, the submarine finished her off by shellfire. In the spring, when the nights became shorter and the ineffectiveness of our anti-submarine warfare had been demonstrated, the U-boats became bolder and attacked in broad daylight, even surfaced. Although they invariably attacked without warning, they commonly gave the crew a chance to get away before opening gunfire, and re-frained from machine-gunning survivors in lifeboats, as had been done freely in the early part of the war. Survivors were often questioned as to the identity of the ship and the nature of her cargo, were sometimes offered water, provisions or cigarettes and dismissed with a standardized joke about sending the bill to Roosevelt or Churchill. The healthy and sunburned German sub-mariners appeared to be having a glorious field day. They later referred to this period as "the happy time."

This assault temporarily stunned the defense forces of the United States and Canada. Such protection as the Navy furnished to shipping was pitifully inadequate. Destroyers could not be spared from the transatlantic route. The entire antisubmarine fleet when the U-boats struck along the East Coast consisted of three 110-foot wooden subchasers (SC) and two 173-foot patrol craft (PC), together with a score of Eagle boats left over from World War I and a few converted yachts. Orders for sixty PCs and SCs had already been placed, but they were not due for completion until the summer and fall of 1942. Consequently there were no escorts to organize coastal convoys; and Admiral King judged, rightly, that a convoy without escort was worse than no convoy at all. The question has often been asked why the Navy was so unprovided with these indispensable small craft for antisubmarine warfare. The reason was its desperate concentration on building destroyers and larger ships to fight an impending two-ocean war.

Small craft were neglected in the belief that they could be improvised and rapidly reproduced in quantities at small shipbuilding yards. It was the same with antisubmarine aircraft. Vice Admiral Adolphus Andrews, Commander Eastern Sea Frontier — which extended from the Canadian border to Jacksonville, Florida — had no naval planes at his disposal in December capable of searching far out to sea. Offshore air patrol was therefore undertaken by the nine available planes of the Army Air Force. But by 1 April 1942 the antisubmarine patrol had been built up to 84 Army and 86 Navy planes at 19 bases between Bangor, Maine, and Jacksonville.

The total number of Allied, American and neutral merchant vessels sunk in the North Atlantic in January 1942, between our coast and the Western Approaches to the British Isles, was 58; only three of these were in transatlantic convoys. The tonnage lost was 307,059 gross, of which 132,348 tons consisted of tankers of 5,000 to 12,000 tons each; the rest were mostly freighters up to 10,000 tons each. In February, the score was almost identical for the same area; but the sinkings in the Eastern Sea Frontier alone passed the 100,000-ton mark, and new zones were raided: east coast of Florida, and, in the latter half of the month, the Caribbean. Admiral Andrews's attempt to hunt U-boats with two or three destroyers taken out of transatlantic duty was a costly failure. *U–578* sank destroyer *Jacob Jones* off the Delaware Capes on the last day of February.

The aggregate loss increased in March 1942: 28 vessels of 159,-340 tons sunk by U-boats in the Eastern Sea Frontier alone; 15 more of 92,321 tons (over half of it tanker tonnage) in the Gulf and Caribbean; 86 vessels and almost half a million gross tons for the entire Atlantic. The coastline from Norfolk to Wilmington was the scene of numerous sinkings. Submarines lay off Diamond Shoals buoy "pickin' 'em off"; at least three U-boats maintained patrol off Cape Hatteras, lying on the bottom by day and hunting at night. Some of the details of these sinkings,

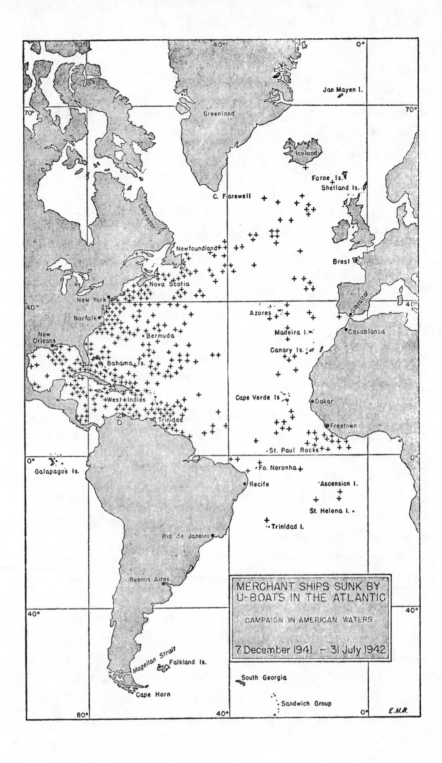

MERCHANT SHIPS SUNK BY
U-BOATS IN THE ATLANTIC

CAMPAIGN IN AMERICAN WATERS

7 December 1941 — 31 July 1942

especially of the tankers, are pitiful to relate: oil scum ignited by signal flares on life preservers, men attempting to swim in a heavy viscous layer of fuel oil, men trying to swim underwater to avoid flames. A Chilean freighter was torpedoed and sunk 30 miles off Ambrose Channel, New York, and only one man survived. A tugboat and three barges, shelled by *U–574*, sank on the last night of March off Cape Charles and there were only two survivors. The same night, a tanker was sunk off Cape Henry when maneuvering to pick up a pilot; on the following night, between Cape Charles and Cape Henlopen, an unarmed collier was sunk by a submarine's gunfire at a range of about 600 yards. Her crew of 27, denied any opportunity to abandon ship, were slaughtered by machine-gun fire and only three men survived.

A poor substitute for coastal convoys, nicknamed the "bucket brigade," was set up on 1 April 1942. Net-protected anchorages were established at places where there were no harbors, such as Cape Hatteras and Cape Fear, so that ships could be escorted by daylight from one harbor to another by such small craft as were available in the naval districts. By mid-May enough proper escorts were available to organize convoys between New York and Halifax, N.S., and between Hampton Roads and Key West. By August a completely interlocking convoy system had been organized: two main lines (New York–Guantanamo and New York–Key West) with local branch lines from all important points on the East Coast, Gulf, Caribbean, Brazil and West Africa feeding in.

As soon as Admiral Doenitz learned that coastal convoys were being organized along the Eastern Sea Frontier, he diverted U-boats southward, into the Gulf Sea Frontier. Organized 6 February 1942, with headquarters at Key West,[2] this naval frontier covered the Straits of Florida, most of the Bahamas, the entire Gulf of Mexico, the Yucatan Channel and most of Cuba. Available defense

[2] Removed to Miami 17 June 1942.

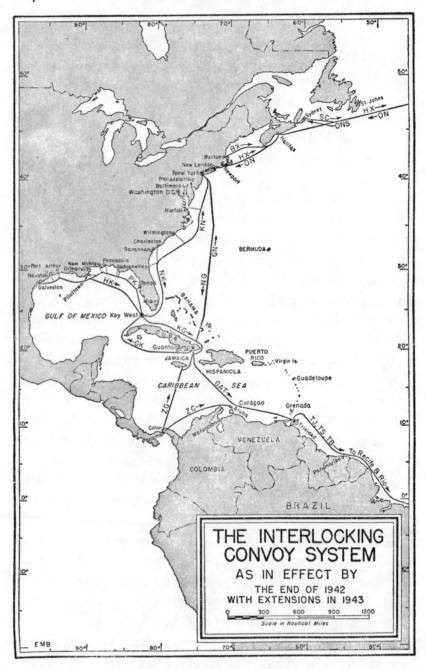

THE INTERLOCKING
CONVOY SYSTEM

AS IN EFFECT BY

THE END OF 1942
WITH EXTENSIONS IN 1943

0   300   600   900   1200

Scale in Nautical Miles

forces were a small converted yacht, three Coast Guard cutters, and, in emergency, the craft used for instruction at the Key West Sound School. Air protection was almost nil. The first U-boat known to enter this frontier, *U–128*, signaled her presence on 19 February 1942 by sinking tanker *Pan Massachusetts* about forty miles SE of Cape Canaveral. Two more ships were sunk on the 21st by *U–504*, and one on the 22nd. This was merely a foretaste of woe. By traveling at night surfaced and submerging during daylight hours, the U-boats bucked the Stream through the Straits of Florida into the Gulf or else chose the Windward Passage— Yucatan Channel route. One of their most fruitful hunting grounds in May and June 1942 lay off the Passes of the Mississippi. This U-boat blitz gave the Gulf Sea Frontier the melancholy distinction of having the most sinkings in May (41 ships, 219,867 gross tons) of any one area in any month during the war, and 55 per cent of this was tanker tonnage, which made it all the worse. And it was wrought by not more than six submarines operating at one time.

The Navy was not idle while these things went on. Every submarine spotted was hunted; but the hunters, few in number, had not yet acquired the necessary technique to kill. Between 8 and 10 May, the following measures were taken: night patrol by a radar-equipped Catalina between Cape Canaveral and Fowey Rocks, a squadron of Hudson bombers based on Jacksonville, and six B–25s staged in to Miami; merchantmen routed from the Canal to New Orleans through the Old Bahama Channel and past Key West. Several of those sunk in the Yucatan Channel, or in the Gulf between there and the Passes, had disregarded routing orders. A detachment of B–25s was sent to Havana, to patrol the Yucatan Channel, and preparations were made to take over the San Julian airfield near Cape San Antonio and to build an airfield on Grand Cayman. A Yucatan Channel patrol began on 21 May.

Rear Admiral James L. Kauffman, appointed Commander Gulf Sea Frontier on 3 June 1942, did much to make this a less profitable hunting ground for U-boats. "Reggie" Kauffman, who had had plenty of experience with submarines in his Iceland command, believed that the best way to sink them was by organized killer groups of properly equipped ships and planes that would go out on any favorable contact and stick to it until they scored. He lost no time in organizing such a group from the frontier craft at his disposal, and between 10 and 13 June they enjoyed a memorable and successful hunt, which in the end sank *U-157*. Everybody enjoyed the hunt and it paid dividends in training and morale; but the experiment was not repeated. For the diversion of large numbers of aircraft and armed vessels for several days left shipping unprotected, and it was proved that better results could be obtained by using the same number of craft to beef-up escort units.

U-boats showed the utmost insolence in the Caribbean, their happiest hunting ground, which they began working over in February. With devilish economy, Admiral Doenitz concentrated on two particularly soft spots — the Dutch islands of Curaçao and Aruba, where over half a million barrels of gasoline and oil derivatives were produced daily; and Trinidad, through or by which most of our shipping to and from South America, and all the bauxite trade, had to pass. Rear Admiral John H. Hoover, Commander Caribbean Sea Frontier at San Juan, had to do the best he could with even less than most sea frontier commanders.

At Aruba, where one Dutch motor whaleboat, three 7.5-inch coast defense guns and a few Army Air Force medium bombers defended this valuable oil industry, a submarine shelled a shore refinery on 16 February 1942. On the same day a successful attack was made on the light-draft tankers that carried oil from Lake Maracaibo to the islands, and on seagoing tankers just departing; six were sunk. *U-161* sneaked into the Gulf of Paria on 18 February, and torpedoed two big ships anchored at Port of Spain. Kapitänleutnant Albrecht Achilles ("Ajax," as this bold bantumweight skipper was called) steamed boldly out through the Bocas, surfaced and showing running lights. He then entered Castries Harbor, Saint Lucia, where *U–161* torpedoed a Canadian passenger steamer and a freighter lying alongside the dock.

A glance at the map will show the peculiar strategic importance of Trinidad. It blocks off the Gulf of Paria, an inland sea which, if properly protected, is an ideal center for handling traffic between the Atlantic and Gulf ports of the United States and the Guianas, Brazil, the River Plate and Africa. Tanker traffic between the Dutch West Indies and Europe or Africa passes the same way. Trinidad itself has an oil industry, and nearby there are oilfields in Venezuela. Port of Spain was the clearinghouse for bauxite, an ore essential for the manufacture of aluminum. The bauxite mines in British and Dutch Guiana were situated up the Demerara, Berbica, Cottica and Surinam Rivers, at the mouths of which were bars that admitted a maximum draft of 17 feet. In order to economize shipping, a small fleet of British and Dutch bauxite ships maintained a shuttle service between the Guianas and Trinidad, where they transferred their cargoes to big ore carriers, diverted from the Great Lakes. Already important at the opening of the war in Europe, Trinidad gradually built up until in 1943 it was one of the world's greatest centers of sea traffic.

The right to establish ground facilities for naval, army and air bases in Trinidad had been ceded to the United States as part of the original destroyer-naval base deal of 2 September 1940. N.O.B. Trinidad was commissioned 1 August 1941, with Captain A. W. Radford USN, our future C.N.O., as commanding officer. During the first few months of the war the chief concern of his command was to push construction, which was delayed by enemy activities, such as the sinking of a freighter that was bringing two million dollars' worth of equipment to Port of Spain. The arrival of *SC–453*, a 110-foot subchaser, first vessel of the "Hummingbird Navy" to be equipped with sound gear, was an event comparable to the addition of an *Essex* class carrier to the Pacific Fleet. But the deadly count went up and up — 31 ships of 154,779 gross tons sunk in the Caribbean Sea Frontier (west) in February and March 1942; 41 ships of 198,034 tons in April and May; 42 ships of 218,623 tons in June and July. During June, German submarines disposed of more shipping in the Gulf, the Caribbean and approaches thereto than they had sunk the world over during any month of 1940-41.

ADMIRAL LOW'S GRAPH OF THE ANTISUBMARINE WAR

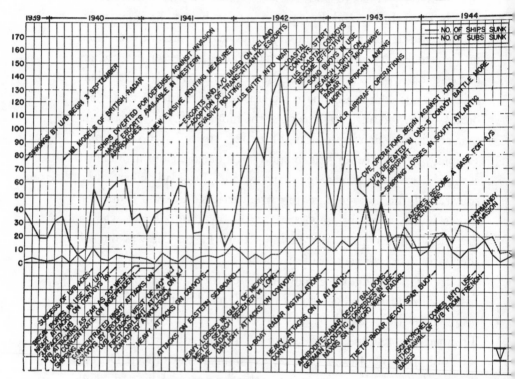

Panama, the only sea frontier with a foot in each ocean, had a baffling task. Relative to its responsibilities and extent, it was the most poorly provided with means of defense. On the Atlantic side alone, this frontier included the entire coast from the Yucatan Peninsula to Punta de Gallinas, Colombia. But its prime, overriding charge was defense of sea approaches to the Panama

Canal and of shipping in transit — the Army protected the Canal from sabotage, land attack or air attack. They also had to cope with a difficult political situation. Only the ten-mile wide Canal Zone was under United States' control; the rest of the frontier was divided among several independent republics, officially at war with Japan and Germany but somewhat dubious as to who would win. In any case, these republics had no naval vessels capable even of inshore patrol; thus, the entire burden of their defense fell on the United States Navy. The same was true of the two republics in Hispaniola. Authorities in the British and Dutch West Indies were most coöperative. Venezuela, Colombia and Mexico were rather "sticky" and the French islands remained stiffly neutral until a commissioner from De Gaulle took over in 1943. Mexico finally declared war on the Axis after one of her fully lighted tankers had been sunk by a U-boat off Miami; Colombia, too, became a loyal ally after some of her small freighters had been sunk. Cuba was our most useful ally in North America, excepting Canada; her fleet of small gunboats took care of her coastal traffic and helped to escort the Florida-Havana seatrains. *CS–13*, an 83-foot Cuban Navy subchaser which sank *U–176* in the Old Bahama Channel in May 1943, was the only small craft of any navy to kill a submarine in American waters.

Enemy submarines entered Panama Sea Frontier in June, 1942, a very favorable moment for attack. Reinforcements for the Pacific Fleet were constantly passing through the Canal. Rear Admiral Clifford E. Van Hook had at his disposal only four old destroyers, *Borie*, *Barry*, *Tattnall* and *Goff*; gunboat *Erie*, two PCs, two small converted motor yachts, and 24 Catalinas. In view of the Japanese attacks on the Aleutians and Midway during the first week of June, the Frontier had to prepare for a possible carrier or submarine raid on the Pacific side, and its most watchful care was extended in that direction. It was a rude shock when *U–159* sank eight ships in four days, two of them right off the Canal entrance. On 17 June, a British tanker bringing diesel oil to Cristobal was shelled by two U-boats and sunk within 75 miles of her destination. Shortly after, two ships were sunk off Santa Marta, and on 2 July the redoubtable "Ajax" Achilles in *U-161* put into Puerto Limon, Costa Rica, and torpedoed a steamer loading at a dock. That concluded this blitz on the Panama Canal approaches. No more than five submarines had disposed of an average of a ship a day for two weeks, and retired without damage — without even being attacked, except from the air.

Many new precautionary and defense measures were now adopted. Puerto Limon was closed by a net. The first Canal Zone-Guantanamo convoy sailed 10 July. Air patrol out of Coco Solo was reinforced with radar-equipped PBYs and so extended that any submarine contact could be followed night and day for 36 hours. Four Catalinas were stationed at Grand Cayman, two at Port Royal Bay, Jamaica, and a few short-range patrol planes operated from Almirante, Panama. VI Army Air Force covered the Colombian Coast and Venezuela up to Curaçao. A seaplane base with tender was set up at Puerto Castillo, Honduras.

Before these measures were completed, a well-coördinated attack resulted in Panama Sea Frontier's first kill. On 11 July net tender *Mimosa*, about 60 miles off Almirante, was attacked by *U-153* with five torpedoes, some of which passed right under her keel. All available ships and planes were then ordered to that position. Destroyer *Lansdowne* (Lieutenant Commander William R. Smedberg III) on the 13th sank *U-153* with four depth charges, fifteen minutes after relieving one of the patrol craft; an exploit that started "Smeddy" on his career to flag rank.

This was only the eighth kill of a German submarine by United States naval forces since we entered the war. The first, of *U-656*, had been made on 1 March 1942 off Cape Race, Newfoundland, by Ensign William Tepuni USNR, when piloting a Lockheed-Hudson of Squadron VP-82 based on Argentia. Donald Francis Mason, Chief Aviation Machinist's Mate of the same squadron, has the credit of the second, *U–503*, on 15 March, near the southeast corner of the Grand Bank of Newfoundland. One month later destroyer *Roper* (Lieutenant Commander H. W. Howe) became the first United States naval vessel to make a kill, of *U–85*, off Wimble Shoal near Hatteras. *U–352* on her first war patrol was caught in shoal water off Cape Lookout by Coast Guard Cutter *Icarus* (Lieutenant Commander Maurice Jester uscg) on 9 May 1942. The other two kills in the first half of 1942 were that of *U–157*, victim of Kauffman's killer hunt, and *U–158*, sunk off Bermuda 30 June. The first two weeks of July brought a couple more, Smedberg's *U–153*, and *U–701*. The latter was caught flatfooted off Diamond Shoal Lightship by an A.A.F. bomber and killed with three depth charges. Eight kills in six and a half months — about as many U-boats as were being produced every ten days!

Admiral Doenitz was naturally delighted with the performance of his boys. On 15 June he reported to Hitler the gratifying number of sinkings compared with the small number of submarines employed, and predicted "vast possibilities through the rapid increase in number of U-boats and the use of supply submarines." He dwelt on the poor quality of American defenses, the heavy destruction of tankers and the failure of new construction to replace shipping losses. In a press interview that summer Doenitz declared: "Our submarines are operating close inshore along the coast of the United States of America, so that bathers and sometimes entire coastal cities are witnesses to that drama of war, whose visual climaxes are constituted by the red glorioles of blazing tankers."

No frantic boast, this; burning tankers were not infrequently sighted from fashionable Florida resorts, and on 15 June two large American freighters were torpedoed by a U-boat within full view of thousands of pleasure-seekers at Virginia Beach.

3. *The Organization of Antisubmarine Warfare*

Having described the havoc wrought by the U-boats during the first six months of the war, we may now relate some of the principle countermeasures adopted, which bore fruit in the latter half of the year and in 1943. Of these, by far the most important were the building of more escort vessels (although the best of these, the DE or destroyer escort, did not come out until 1943), and the interlocking coastal convoys which we have already mentioned.

The amount of study, energy and expense necessary to combat a few hundred U-boats is appalling. The major naval effort of the Allied navies in the Atlantic was so employed for two years. In money terms alone, counting the sunken ships and cargoes, time lost at sea, and expense of operating naval vessels and planes to protect the seaways, the efforts of the American republics and the British Empire amounted to some hundreds of billions of dollars; whilst the lives lost by submarine action reached tens of thousands. Beaten Nazis may take comfort in reflecting that no army, fleet or other unit in World War II, with the exception of their own people who murdered defenseless civilians, wrought such destruction and misery as the U-boats.

There was no administrative center of the Navy's efforts against the U-boats until March 1942, when Admiral King designated Captain Wilder D. Baker to set up an antisubmarine section of his staff in Washington. This section was responsible for matériel, supply, development and training.

An important step toward unified control of merchant shipping was taken on 15 May 1942, when the Convoy and Routing Section of C.N.O., headed by Rear Admiral M. K. Metcalf, became a section of Cominch headquarters. About 1 July "C. and R." assumed full responsibility for the routing and reporting of all merchant shipping in the United States strategic area, and for troop convoys. Cinclant, Admiral Ingersoll, provided the escorts and many of the transports; C. and R. organized the convoy, and, in conjunction with the British Admiralty, laid down its route.

Until Tenth Fleet was organized in May 1943, Admiral Ingersoll directed antisubmarine warfare. Living on board his flagship U.S.S. *Vixen*, steaming from one Atlantic port to another as occasion required, he kept his finger on the U-boat pulse. The public knew nothing of him; even to most of the Atlantic Fleet he remained a shadowy, almost a legendary figure. But to Admiral Ingersoll's sagacity and seasoned "sea-cunning," to use an Elizabethan phrase, the Allied nations owed in large measure their progress against the submarine in 1942-1943.

Besides improved depth charges, which were tossed off a vessel's stern, two ahead-thrown weapons were adopted by the United States Navy in 1942: "hedgehog" and "mousetrap." Hedgehog, adapted from a British design which Captain Paul Hammond USNR called to the attention of the Royal Navy, consisted of a steel cradle from which projected six rows of spigots firing 24 projectiles. As the ship fired these ahead before breaking her sound contact with a submarine, it gave her a better chance of inflicting damage. Depth charges went off at the determined depth, whether they hit anything or not, but hedgehog shells exploded only on contact. The smaller mousetrap, which fired a pattern of four to eight small rocket projectiles, was developed for PCs and SCs. Antisubmarine ships also mounted the usual types of naval ordnance suitable for their burthen. Machine guns proved to be useful in clearing a surfaced submarine's deck, but there is no record of any U-boat being sunk with a gun smaller than 3-inch.

Both the British and ourselves, between the two wars, invented supersonic echo-ranging sound which they called "asdic" and we named "sonar." Housed in a streamlined retractable dome which projected beneath the ship's bottom but was operative only at moderate speeds owing to water noises, sonar could be employed in two ways: listening for the U-boat's propeller noises, and echo-ranging with a sharp "ping" which the U-boat's hull returned, the time giving the range and the direction indicating the bearing. The echo reached the operator with varying degrees of pitch, depending on the nature and movements of the target. This variation in the pitch, known as the "doppler effect," told a trained operator with a sensitive ear whether the target was a ship or a whale, whether it was stationary or moving, and its direction and speed.

In order to thwart sonar, German submarines were equipped with *Pillenwerfer*. This device shot out from a special tube a multitude of small, stationary gas bubbles, which returned an echo similar to that of a submarine. Trained sound operators, however, could detect a submarine's echo from that returned by *Pillenwerfer*. There were many other pitfalls for inexperienced operators. Schools of blackfish, whales, wrecks, coral reefs, and even a layer of water of different temperature echoed in a way which only an expert could distinguish from echoes on a steel hull. Snapping shrimps on the ocean bottom made a curious crackling noise that disturbed sound-listeners. The Navy's monthly *Anti-Submarine Warfare Bulletin* had to print special articles about the habits of cetaceans and crustaceans in order to diminish false alarms.

Intensive training was necessary for a bluejacket to operate sonar, or an officer use it intelligently. Atlantic Fleet Sound School, originally established in 1939, at the submarine base in New London, was shifted to Key West. During the first three months of 1943, 250 officers passed through the eight-weeks course, 1033 enlisted men began basic sound training, and 969 were graduated. In addition, the Key West Sound School trained 1016 officers and men of seven different foreign Navies during the war. And the West Coast Sound School at San Diego kept up a steady enrollment of about 1200 students.

In order to study details of fights with submarines and ascertain the causes of success or failure, an Atlantic Fleet Anti-Submarine Warfare Unit was commissioned 2 March 1942 at Boston. Collection and correlation of data, analysis and deduction, were its primary functions; but it also trained instructors for the Key West Sound School, the Subchaser School at Miami, and for the various "attack teachers," British mechanical devices set up at naval bases from Iceland to Brazil. Thus the Boston Unit became a sort of teachers' college for antisubmarine warfare.

In every aspect of this planetary struggle, men of science worked in laboratories, inventing, developing and testing new weapons, devices and military equipment for the armed forces. One group of civilian scientists worked side by side with naval officers, even on board ships and in planes. This was the Anti-Submarine Warfare Operations Research Group (Asworg), an offshoot of the National Defense Research Committee. James B. Conant, then President of Harvard University, and other scientists, visited England during the Battle for Britain and returned convinced that one of the main factors which saved England from destruction under the long sustained assaults of the Luftwaffe was a group of "operational" scientists, working closely with R.A.F. fighter command to coördinate coast warning radar with fighter plane defense. As Professor P. M. S. Blackett pointed out, "Relatively too much scientific effort has been expended hitherto in the *production* of new devices and too little in the *proper use* of what we have got." When assigned to antisubmarine warfare, scientists were called upon to answer such questions as "What pattern of depth charges at what settings has the best mathematical chance of killing a submarine? What sort of track should a ship steer to have best chance of regaining a lost underwater contact? How large an expanse of ocean, under varying atmospheric conditions, can a ship or a plane profitably patrol in one hour? What disposition of escorts around a convoy gives optimum protection?" Answers to these and a thousand other questions on antisubmarine warfare could not be left to mere trial and error, or the Battle of the Atlantic might be lost before the right answer was found. And it was not sufficient for scientists to invent a new device; they must observe its use in action, in order to make improvements.

At Captain Baker's suggestion, Asworg was organized 1 April 1942, with Professor Philip M. Morse, sound physicist of M.I.T., as director. Asworg was centered at Washington, but individual members were sent to Norfolk, Argentia, sea frontier headquarters, Trinidad and Brazil. And very important work was done at these outlying bases. It sounds odd today, when all armed services are scientifically indoctrinated; but in 1942 "practical seamen" had a deep suspicion of "long-haired scientists" that had to be overcome. Dr. Morse, however, "sold" Asworg by laying down the principle that no scientist was to claim credit for anything, since he took no responsibility for the ultimate decision; that his duty was simply to help the fighting Navy improve its antisubmarine technique.

The Asworg mathematicians and analysts worked out a whole complex of search problems, including patterns of "box search" by ships, on Greek key patterns, for regaining underwater contact with a submarine; they worked up data on effective search speed, altitude, and airborne time for patrol planes; they proved that three destroyers searching abreast were more than three times as effective as a single destroyer, that an "air umbrella" over a convoy gave far less protection than a wide-ranging air search on front and flanks; they drafted blueprints for the Atlantic Narrows air patrol that caught several German blockade runners, and for the Straits of Gibraltar patrol; they worked up countermeasures which stymied the German acoustic torpedo as soon as it appeared.

Radar was invented by Sir Robert Watson-Watt, but some of its developments and refinements were produced in the United States from sheer necessity. By the summer of 1942 almost every combatant ship in the Atlantic Fleet had been equipped with some form of radar, and an improved model, the SG — in which the scope gives a picture of what lay ahead — had passed the test of experiment and was ready to be installed in October. For aircraft, the value of radar was even greater than for ships, because it enabled planes to pick up a surfaced submarine far beyond visible distance, to deliver a surprise attack, and to home in other planes and ships. The first sets installed in planes were on meter-wave. The Germans invented a search receiver for it which ended its usefulness as a detecting device, and inventing a microwave plane radar to take its place became urgent. That was done, and a variety of 10-cm sets did the trick; the Germans never could figure out a way to detect or jam these. Microwave radar made possible the large number of kills by aircraft in the spring and early summer of 1943. Hitler referred to it peevishly, in his New Year's 1944 address, as "one invention of our enemy" which had thwarted his submarine fleet.

A convoy is no stronger than its ears and eyes. Radar furnished our convoys with cat's eyes, sonar with ears, while the high-frequency direction-finders (HF/DF, pronounced "Huff-Duff"), by picking up and plotting radio transmissions of U-boats at sea, acted as highly sensitive, elongated cat's whiskers. The Royal Navy was the first to adopt this method of locating submarines. Estimated positions of U-boats, plotted at Washington and London, were sent out to sea on "Fox" schedule, which was a secret radio bulletin transmitted several times a day on a fixed schedule. While HF/DF fixes were seldom accurate within 50 or 100 miles, they enabled an escort commander to order an evasive change of course which, by Admiral Doenitz's admission, frequently frustrated his wolf-packs.

There is no better example of the effectiveness of the land-based HF/DF than that of the following submarine kill. About noon 30 June 1942, HF/DF ranges were obtained by the stations at Bermuda, Hartlant Point, Kingston and Georgetown. Operations officers at N.O.B. Bermuda plotted the bearings, which made a perfect fix. Lieutenant Richard E. Schreder usnr in a Mariner of Squadron VP–74, patrolling out of Bermuda, was then about fifty miles away. Immediately notified, he laid his course accordingly and found *U–158* idling on the surface with the crew sunning themselves on deck. He dropped a depth charge which stuck to the superstructure and detonated as the submarine went down, for keeps.

The next step was the shipborne HF/DF, which began to be installed in key escort vessels in October 1942. The Germans long ignored the danger of this to them; their U-boats continued to chatter among themselves and to Doenitz when closing a convoy, thus revealing their position.

As the number of escort craft increased it was necessary to provide special training for the young reservists who were to man them. A Submarine Chaser Training Center was commissioned at Miami in March 1942, with Lieutenant Commander E. F. McDaniel as commandant. His school opened with about 50 pupils, but by 1 January 1944 10,396 officers and 37,574 enlisted men had been trained there for the United States Navy alone. These included the crews of 285 DEs, 256 PCs, 397 SCs, and 150 other craft. McDaniel was a lean, thin-lipped officer whose eyes burned with hatred of the enemy and all his works, and whose heart glowed with devotion to the Navy, especially the antisubmarine part of it. He had a sense of organization and a natural teaching ability. His "faculty," like his "student body," was constantly changing; for McDaniel would have for instructors none but officers who had actually hunted submarines, and back to sea they went after a few months.

Before this Miami institution was many months old, the United States began to deliver subchasers under lend-lease to Allied European and American nations, and the task of training their crews too was thrown on McDaniel. In 1942-1943, 360 officers and 1374 men were trained there for fourteen different foreign navies.

4. *Air Power, Auxiliaries and Amateurs*

The Army Air Force, which controlled almost the entire supply of United States military land-based planes in 1941, did not expect to include antisubmarine warfare among its duties. Army pilots were not trained to fly over water or protect shipping or bomb small moving targets like submarines. And the Navy did not have the planes to fill the rôle so successfully assumed by the British Coastal Command. This was due not to lack of foresight, but to a principle decided on in 1920, that the Army should control land-based and the Navy sea-based aviation. Consequently the Army received the entire American production of military land planes; while the Navy received the entire production of seaplanes and carrier types, and the numbers were inadequate for both kinds. When British experience showed the value of large land-based bombers in antisubmarine warfare, the Army modified this agreement. On 7 July 1942, General Marshall consented to a reallocation of production that promised the Navy a fair share of Liberators and other long-range bomber types. But by that time the submarines had done their worst off the Atlantic Coast.

The Navy badly wanted four-engined land-based bombers for antisubmarine work, and the Army responded to the best of its ability. By the end of July 1942, the Army had 141 planes available for antisubmarine work in Eastern Sea Frontier, and the naval air arm had grown to 178 planes and 7 blimps. These were spread among 26 fields along the coast from Argentia to Jacksonville.

This coverage was far from effective, partly because the Army and Navy had different communications system, partly because of a deficient command organization. At General Marshall's suggestion, Antisubmarine Army Air Command was formed in October 1942, with Brigadier General Westside T. Larson as commander. Admiral King, however, had no intention of permanently sharing with the Army what he considered to be a naval responsibility, the protection of shipping. He conceived of Army participation in antisubmarine air warfare as a temporary expedient. So, as fast as the Navy obtained land-based planes and trained pilots, they were moved into sea frontiers and Iceland and Greenland, to relieve the Army Air Force of this special duty. But it should be remembered that the Army Air Force came to the Navy's assistance at a critical moment, stood by as long as it was needed, contributed to the technique of antisubmarine warfare, and killed several submarines.

The naval air squadrons based at Argentia, under the successive command of Rear Admirals Bristol and Brainard, were particularly useful in covering convoys during the critical moment of changing escort groups, and also in killing submarines. Amphibious Catalinas found a new sphere of usefulness in air-sea rescue work, and by the time the war ended many were trained and equipped for that purpose alone. Throughout the war, the PBY was the Navy's workhorse of the air. It did everything — search, reconnaissance, transport, bombing, rescue. It was slow, ungainly, a big target for the enemy — but what a plane!

Air search and attack, because of the delicate instruments and the mathematical factors involved, were peculiarly subject to improvement through the efforts of the operational scientists. The Navy set up early in 1943 the Anti-Submarine Development Detachment (Asdevlant) at Quonset Point, Rhode Island, to which many scientists were attached. This opened a new and brilliant chapter for naval air in antisubmarine warfare.

In addition to the efforts, methods and procedures to master the U-boats that we have already described, there were several auxiliary operations which accomplished little good, yet must be mentioned for their brave efforts. Probably the most useful was the Northern Ship Lane Patrol, consisting of big converted yachts such as *Migrant* and *Guinevere*, which patrolled the main convoy routes to a considerable distance off shore, and reported some useful information on submarines that enabled convoys to elude them. Second was the Coastal Picket Patrol, nicknamed the "Hooligan Navy." Organized by the Coast Guard in May 1942, this consisted of auxiliary yachts and motor boats under 100 feet in length. These were taken over by the Coast Guard, often with their civilian owners as skippers, manned mostly by yachtsmen who could not pass qualifications for the Navy, armed with small guns and depth charges, and sent forth to hunt U-boats. This was too late to help repel Doenitz's first blitz along the East Coast, but they patrolled faithfully during the hard winter of 1942-1943. The "Hooligans" were too small, slow and feebly armed to make any kills. At top strength, in February 1943, there were no fewer than 550 of these boats patrolling between Eastport, Maine, and Galveston, Texas. From that time the numbers were progressively reduced, and their duties assumed by 83-foot Coast Guard cutters.

The Civil Air Patrol, organized in March 1942, was much the same thing in the air. Civilian pilots ineligible for the armed forces — some even veterans of World War I with wooden legs — contributed their planes and their services, and many of the ground crews were women. All served without pay. At the height of its strength the C.A.P. had several hundred planes operating from bases between Bar Harbor, Maine and Corpus Christi, Texas. They never killed a submarine, but they spotted survivors from sinkings in rafts and lifeboats, and performed many auxiliary services for the armed forces. Down to September 1943, when it was disbanded, C.A.P. had reported the positions of 173 enemy submarines, 91 vessels in distress, and rafts or lifeboats containing 363 survivors.

In addition to their direct services, the C.A.P. and the "Hooligans" trained hundreds of young boys to be pilots, sailors and coastguardsmen. Both organizations are outstanding examples of fusing civilian with military effort. At least 90 per cent of their personnel consisted of men and women who had to earn their livings, and who could have made big money in war industries or the merchant marine. But they were people who wanted to serve, not to gain; they proved that the call to work and sacrifice is stronger, and produces better service, than the lure of money.

There was also a "Mystery" or "Q" ship project which consumed an inordinate amount of effort and lost the lives of about one quarter of the sailors who volunteered, without accomplishing anything. These were heavily armed vessels disguised as peaceful merchantmen which, on the approach of a U-boat, were supposed to unmask powerful batteries and sink the submarine. The Q ships had done some good in World War I, but not nearly so much as the thriller books written about them claimed; and the U-boats of World War II were too fast and smart to be taken in by such a ruse. Nevertheless, in early 1942, the situation was so serious that Admiral King very reluctantly, in response to pressure from President Roosevelt, organized a Mystery Ship program. The first three sailed from New England ports in March. U.S.S. *Atik* was sunk with all hands by a U-boat off the Capes of the Chesapeake when only four days out. *Foam* met a similar fate in May off Nova Scotia. Two others which never made a contact and a third which made three unsuccessful attacks were finally converted to weather-reporting ships; and a fourth, a three-masted schooner, almost sank in a hurricane and was decommissioned.

The building of new merchant ships to replace and surpass those lost by enemy action, under the Maritime Commission and the War Shipping Administration Board headed by Rear Admiral Emory S. Land, was highly successful, and got under way before formal war began. The first Liberty ship of 10,800 deadweight tonnage, *Patrick Henry*, was launched in September 1941; the first Victory ship, of about the same size but 50 per cent faster, two years later. In 1942, 727 ships of 55.5 million tons were constructed. By April 1943 the Maritime Commission was building 140 ships of a million tons per month; and by the end of the year these figures were doubled and the time of construction had been lowered from 244 days to an average of 42 days for a Liberty. These ships were manned by merchant mariners, for whom training schools had to be organized.

Although the best protection of merchant ships from the enemy was to travel in convoy, many had to ply routes for which no escort could be spared, and sailed alone. For their protection, the Navy began in early 1942 to provide merchantmen with one or more guns and a naval armed guard of bluejackets. This led to a great deal of friction between the merchant mariners and the naval ratings who were not under union control or interested in pay, bonuses or overtime.[3] Of course the merchant marine might have been absorbed by the Navy or made an auxiliary service like the famous Seabees. This was not done, mainly for two reasons. It would have antagonized the National Maritime Union, headed by the truculent Joe Curran; and it would have required far more man power; naval regulations would have about doubled the number of each crew. And many "ancient mariners" with decayed teeth or ruptures, who made good seamen for a merchant ship, could never have passed the Navy's physical requirements.

As the war continued, naval armed guards and ships' crews, facing a common danger, learned to coöperate; and there were several instances of armed merchant vessels driving off and even sinking submarines.

By June of 1942 the United States Navy and the Army Air Force were coming to grips with the U-boat problem, but were far

[3] The Navy bluejackets' pay started at $50 per month; the merchant seaman's at $100 for a 44-hour week (85 cents for every hour over that), plus $100 war bonus in the Atlantic, plus various sums around $100 for each different combat area entered. On 15 Mar. 1943 this last bonus, greatly to the indignation of the National Maritime Union, was commuted to a flat rate of $125 per man for every air raid occurring when the ship was in port, whether or not the ship was hit. Although the merchant seaman was not paid when on the beach, continuous employment was guaranteed during the war. He did not, however, receive the family allowances and retirement pay of the naval seaman.

from attaining mastery. The shortage of escorts was still critical; no DE had yet joined the Fleet. No killer groups of escort carriers had yet been organized. On the other side, Admiral Doenitz had not exhausted his repertoire, and tough days were to come for the convoys. The Admiral, who relieved Raeder as commander in chief of the German Navy in January 1943, later regarded the next two months as the peak of U-boat achievement.

A fair example of a transatlantic convoy crossing in June 1942 and of the comparatively slight improvement in antisubmarine warfare to that time, is furnished by the story of Convoy ONS–102, from Londonderry to Halifax. There were 63 ships in eleven columns, protected by nine escorts — U.S.S. *Leary,* three big Coast Guard cutters, one Canadian destroyer, and four Canadian corvettes. Commander P. R. Heineman was escort commander in U.S.C.G.C. *Campbell.* Speed of advance was 8 knots. At 0725 June 16, two contacts were made through HF/DF, and two escorts were detached to run them down. Both made unsuccessful depth-charge attacks, but the convoy was left at peace that night. The following night two U-boats managed to worm in between the convoy columns, and at 0125 torpedoed a ship. A few minutes later *Campbell,* patrolling two and a half miles ahead, sighted a submarine headed for the convoy, distant 500 yards. This U-boat submerged and was depth-charged, unsuccessfully. Admiral Brainard, at Argentia, Newfoundland, now sent four Canadian corvettes to help Heineman. One of them, H.M.C.S. *Agassiz,* sighted a U-boat a mile ahead at 2242 June 20. It dove, and *Agassiz* attacked with depth charges, one of which made such a terrific explosion that several merchantmen thought themselves torpedoed and fired star shell. The resulting illumination revealed a second submarine in the middle of the convoy. The nearest merchant ship, which had a naval armed guard, attacked with gunfire and forced it to submerge. Escorts dashed about the now brightly illuminated convoy throwing depth charges to no purpose. Radar broke down, and the U-boat escaped. Convoy ONS–102 was lucky to get through with the loss of but one ship.

Commander Heineman, one of the best of our escort commanders, was red-faced about the whole thing, and reported seven different classes of errors that prevented him from getting a U-boat. The most important was the lack of uniform antisubmarine doctrine. Escort vessels needed a definite set of principles concerning how to hunt a submerged U-boat in order to make best use of available detection gear and weapons. A good beginning was made by the issuance on 9 July 1942 of a Cominch information bulletin on antisubmarine warfare, the result of intensive study by officers of the Boston Anti-Submarine Warfare Unit and its attached scientists. In clear, precise language it described the German submarine and its capabilities, and laid down rules and methods for escort-of-convoy and patrol operations, for sound, sight and radar searching, and for surface, air and joint attacks.

Looking backward, the increasing number of escorts, uniform doctrine, the training and analysis systems set up, and plain hard experience seem to be the most important contributions toward controlling the U-boat menace during the first half of that woeful year 1942. Convoys were increasingly successful in protecting trade routes, but escorts were not killing enough U-boats. Only 21 of these, together with seven Italian submarines, were sunk by both Allied navies during the first six months of 1942; and only five of these kills were by United States forces. During the same period Germany built 123 new U-boats, and in June 1942 there were 60 of them, on an average, patrolling the Atlantic.

This period of antisubmarine warfare closed with a stern warning, delivered by General Marshall to Admiral King on 19 June 1942:

The losses by submarines off our Atlantic seaboard and in the Caribbean now threaten our entire war effort. The following statistics bearing on the subject have been brought to my attention.

Of the 74 ships allocated to the Army for July by the War Shipping Administration, 17 have already been sunk. Twenty-two per cent of the Bauxite fleet has already been destroyed. Twenty per cent of the Puerto Rican fleet has been lost. Tanker sinkings have been 3.5 per cent per month of tonnage in use.

We are all aware of the limited number of escort craft available, but has every conceivable improvised means been brought to bear on this situation? I am fearful that another month or two of this will so cripple our means of transport that we will be unable to bring sufficient men and planes to bear against the enemy in critical theatres, to exercise a determining influence on the war.

Admiral King's and the Navy's response to this challenge will be related in a later chapter. For we must now turn to the Pacific, where the tide of war had already turned in the great Battle of Midway.

CHAPTER VI

Carrier Strikes, Coral Sea and Midway

December 1941–June 1942

1. *Wake Island and the Tokyo Raid,*
December 1941–April 1942

"THE PACIFIC SITUATION is very grave," signaled President Roosevelt to Winston Churchill on 9 March 1942. The first four months of 1942 were the grimmest period of the war for the Allies, everywhere. It looked as if America's entry would mean only one more victim for the Axis and Japan to strike down and tear apart. In Eastern Europe, after a winter's stalemate, the German armies had resumed their victorious advance toward the Caucasus. Crippling attacks by U-boats and Italian midget subs in Alexandria Harbor had reduced the British Mediterranean Fleet to a squadron of cruisers and destroyers. In the broad Atlantic and the Caribbean, merchant shipping was being sunk by submarines much faster than it could be replaced. In the Middle East, Hitler had turned Rommel loose on the British, with devastating effects. In the Far East, the Japanese were about to throw the Americans, British and Dutch out of their last strongholds. Then came a ray of light for the Allies out of the Coral Sea, dawn broke over Midway, Russia successfully defended Moscow and Stalingrad, Auchinleck won the First Battle of El Alamein in the Libyan desert, and hope returned to the forces of freedom.

In the Central Pacific, the first few months after Pearl Harbor were dark indeed. Wake Island, the most important outpost be-

tween Oahu and Guam, was garrisoned by a little over 500 officers and men, mostly Marines, under Commander W. Scott Cunningham USN and Major James Devereux USMC. With the help
of a squadron of fighter planes and a few coast defense guns,
none larger than 5-inch, they beat off a Japanese invasion on 11
December — the only occasion in the entire war when an amphibious assault was thrown back with loss. But the Japanese came
back with greater force on 23 December, and captured Wake,
after a strong Naval relief force under Rear Admiral Frank Jack
Fletcher, built around carrier *Saratoga*, had been recalled by
Cincpac.[1] The American combatant prisoners were sent to Shanghai, the Japanese commander beheading a couple of them en route
to amuse his men. About one hundred civilian workers were de-
tained on Wake, to work for the enemy. These were later executed.

On the last day of 1941, when Admiral King became Cominch
at Washington, Admiral Chester W. Nimitz became Cincpac. At
his first meeting with Admiral Kimmel's former staff at Pearl
Harbor, he assured them of his confidence and announced that they
would serve him too. That act alone raised morale at Pearl Harbor
from an all-time low. Nimitz, calm in demeanor and courteous in
speech, with blue eyes, a pink complexion, and tow-colored hair
turning white, was a fortunate appointment. He restored confidence to the decimated Pacific Fleet. He had the prudence to wait
through a lean period; to do nothing rash for the sake of doing
something. He had the capacity to organize both a fleet and a
vast war theater, the tact to deal with sister services and Allied
commands, the leadership to weld his own subordinates into a
great fighting team, the courage to take necessary risks, and the

---

[1] Admiral William S. Pye, who had relieved Admiral Kimmel. This fiasco, however, was more the fault of Admiral Fletcher, who wasted time on unnecessary
fueling, when he should have pressed on to relieve Wake.

wisdom to select, from a variety of intelligence and opinions, the correct strategy to defeat Japan.

For the time being nothing was practicable but hit-and-run raids, such as the British were making in Europe. In the Pacific, aircraft carriers served this strategy of weakness. Admiral Halsey's *Enterprise* group raided Kwajalein in the Marshall Islands on 1 February 1942, sank a transport, badly damaged nine other ships and killed the Japanese atoll commander. Next, Admiral Wilson Brown's *Lexington* group raided Rabaul. The Japanese air force based there hit back, and on 20 February an air battle between Japanese and American planes was joined. Our airmen won this round, John S. Thach and "Butch" O'Hare particularly distinguishing themselves. On 10 March Wilson Brown, his force augmented by *Yorktown*, launched planes from a point off Port Moresby, and flew them over the Owen Stanley Range to pound the Japanese at Lae and Salamaua on the north coast of Papua.

That raid, however, paled in comparison with the Halsey-Doolittle one on Tokyo, in April. As the Fleet then had no carrier bombers with enough range to operate from outside the limit of the Japanese offshore air patrol, the Army Air Force lent sixteen B–25 Mitchells, which made a deckload for carrier *Hornet* (Captain Marc A. Mitscher). *Enterprise* (Captain George D. Murray) went along to provide combat air patrol; Rear Admiral Raymond A. Spruance commanded the cruisers and Captain Richard Conolly the destroyers of the screen. Although B–25 pilots could be trained to take off from a carrier, the deck was too short for recovery; so the planes had to fly 668 miles from *Hornet*'s launching point to Tokyo, bomb the city, and thence fly another 1100 miles to friendly Chinese airfields. The strike group, led by Lieutenant Colonel James H. Doolittle USA, were airborne by 0824 April 18, and over the city by noon. They completely surprised the Japanese, as we had been surprised by them at Pearl Harbor, and not one B-25 was lost over Japan; but some made crash landings in China or splashed off the coast, and two pilots picked up by the Japanese were executed — an unpleasant practice which persisted through the Pacific war, and led to some of the officers responsible being hanged when it was over.

This "answer to Pearl Harbor" did not inflict one thousandth part of the damage it was supposed to revenge; but it gave the American public, which had had nothing but bad news for nineteen weeks, a great lift. The Japanese authorities, who never guessed where the bombers came from (President Roosevelt's announcement that they flew from "Shangri-la" didn't help much) pinned down hundreds of planes to defend Tokyo. And, what is more important, the event expedited plans for an overextension that led to the Japanese defeat at Midway.

2. *The Battle of the Coral Sea, 3–8 May 1942*

"Strategic Over-stretch" Captain Liddell Hart calls it; "Victory Disease" a Japanese admiral named it after the war. Imperial General Headquarters, not content with the most rapid, stupendous conquest made in modern times, now embarked on a plan for still further aggression. First, Tulagi in the Solomons and Port Moresby in Papua would be seized to secure air mastery of the Coral Sea. The Combined Fleet would cross the Pacific to "annihilate" the United States Pacific Fleet, and at the same time capture Midway Island and the Western Aleutians; then set up a "ribbon defense" anchored at Attu, Midway, Wake, and the Marshalls and Gilberts. This effort, had it not been thwarted by the Battle of Midway, would have been followed by invasion of New Caledonia, the Fijis and Samoa, to isolate Australia.

The one really sound part of this grandiose plan, even though it failed, was Admiral Yamamoto's challenge to the Pacific Fleet. He knew that the destruction of the Fleet must be completed before 1943, when American war production would make it too late. With Pacific Fleet wiped out, Japan could make her ribbon defense impregnable and organize her conquests; Americans would tire of a futile war and negotiate a peace which would leave Japan master of the Pacific. Such was the plan and the confident expectation of the war lords in Tokyo.

The Coral Sea is one of the world's most beautiful bodies of water. Typhoons pass it by; the southeast trades blow fresh across its surface almost the entire year, raising whitecaps which build up to long surges that crash on Australia's Great Barrier Reef in a 1500-mile line of white foam. Lying between the Equator and the Tropic of Capricorn, it knows no winter, and the summer is never uncomfortably hot. The islands on the eastern and northern verges — New Caledonia, the New Hebrides, the Louisiades — are lofty, jungle-clad and ringed with coral beaches and reefs. Here the interplay of bright sunlight, pure air and transparent water may be seen at its best; peacock-hued shoals over the coral gardens break off abruptly from an emerald-hued fringe into deeps of brilliant amethyst. Under occasional overcasts the Coral Sea becomes a warm dove-gray instead of assuming the bleak dress of the ocean in high latitudes. Only in its northern bight — the Solomon Sea — does the Coral Sea wash somber shores of lava and volcanic ash. That bight had been dominated by Japan since January 1942, from her easily won base at Rabaul. It was now time, in the view of her war planners, that she swing around the New Guinea bird's tail, and move into the dancing waters of the broad Coral Sea.

Cincpac Intelligence smoked out the gist of this plan by 17 April, and Admiral Nimitz saw to it that Task Force 17, a two-carrier group (*Lexington* and *Yorktown*) under Rear Admiral Fletcher, was there to spoil it. That is why the Coral Sea, where no more serious fights had taken place in days gone by than those between trading schooners and Melanesian war canoes, became the scene of the first great naval action between aircraft carriers — the first naval battle in which no ship on either side sighted the other.

The Japanese operation plan was not simple; her naval strategists believed in dividing forces. There were three main divisions: (1) a left prong (Rear Admiral Shima) to occupy Tulagi in the lower Solomons and establish a seaplane base whence Nouméa could be neutralized; (2) a right prong (Rear Admiral Kajioka's Port Moresby invasion group, floating a sizeable army in a dozen transports, covered by heavy cruisers and light carrier *Shoho*) to start from Rabaul, whip through Jomard Passage in the Louisiades, and capture Port Moresby; (3) Vice Admiral Takagi's big carrier striking force, including *Shokaku* and *Zuikaku*, veterans of Pearl Harbor, to enter the Coral Sea from the East, and destroy anything the Allies might offer to interfere with this plan. The whole was to be directed from Rabaul by Commander in Chief Fourth Fleet, Vice Admiral Inouye.

Admiral Nimitz did not have even half this force at his disposal; but he put together under Admiral Fletcher's command all he had and gave him no more specific orders than to stop the enemy. Fletcher in *Lexington*, familiar with the Coral Sea, came steaming west from Pearl Harbor. *Yorktown*, already known as the "Waltzing Matilda of the Pacific Fleet," was ordered to cut short a period of upkeep at Tongatabu, waltz over to the Coral Sea, and rendezvous with "Lady Lex." Most of the ships of "MacArthur's Navy," not yet named Seventh Fleet, also joined. These were three cruisers — H.M.A.S. *Australia* and *Hobart*, U.S.S. *Chicago* — and a few destroyers, under the command of Rear Admiral J. G. Crace RN.

The ensuing action was full of mistakes, both humorous and tragic, wrong estimates and assumptions, bombing the wrong ships, missing great opportunities and cashing in accidentally on minor ones.

The Japanese won the first trick. Admiral Shima's group occupied Tulagi unopposed, on 3 May. They took the second, too,
on 4 May, when *Yorktown*'s planes bombed Tulagi and did only
minor damage. At the same time, however, Japan missed her best
chance to win this game, through false economy. To save an ex-
tra ferrying mission, *Shokaku* and *Zuikaku* were ordered to
deliver nine fighter planes to Rabaul; this delayed the two big
carriers two days, so that on the 4th they were too far away to
counterattack Fletcher.

Nothing much happened on the 5th and 6th, when each big
carrier force was searching for its enemy without success. At one
time they were only 70 miles apart. That 6th day of May, when
General Wainwright surrendered Corregidor in the Philippines,
marked the low point of the entire war for American arms. But the
next day opened with a bright dawn. This transition from Corregidor to the Coral Sea is startling and dramatic.

At dawn on the 7th *Shokaku* and *Zuikaku* sent out a search mission for an enemy force they suspected to be in the Coral Sea. The
search planes sighted Fletcher's retiring fueling group, fleet oiler
Neosho and destroyer *Sims*, and made the second big mistake of
this error-crowded battle by reporting them to be a carrier and a
cruiser. Admiral Takagi promptly ordered an all-out bombing attack on this hapless couple and sank them both. This caused Rear
Admiral Hara, the carrier division commander under Takagi,
"much chagrin," cost him six planes, and saved the American carriers from attack.

The American planes, however, were off on a similar wild-
goose chase. That particular "boo-boo" had resulted from the report of a *Yorktown* search plane, at 0815 May 7, of "two carriers
and four heavy cruisers" about 175 miles northwest of the American force. Fletcher, naturally assuming that this meant Takagi's
Striking Force, launched full deckloads to go after it. When these
aircraft were already airborne it was discovered that the "two car-

riers and four heavy cruisers," owing to a disarrangement of the pilot's code contact pad, should have been reported as "two heavy cruisers and two destroyers." [2] Nevertheless, by good luck the *Lexington* and *Yorktown* fliers encountered light carrier *Shoho*, piled in on her, and put her under in a matter of ten minutes — a record for the entire war. "Scratch one flattop!" signaled *Lexington*'s dive-bomber commander.

It was not the right flattop, but the loss of *Shoho* so discouraged Admiral Inouye that he ordered the Port Moresby invasion group, instead of pressing on through Jomard Passage, to jill around at a safe distance north of the Louisiades. Thus, our attack on the wrong carrier thwarted the enemy's main object.

More grim humor on the 7th was furnished by "Crace's Chase." Fletcher gallantly weakened his carriers' screen by detaching Rear Admiral Crace RN with his two Australian cruisers, U.S.S. *Chicago* and a few destroyers, to find and attack the Port Moresby invasion force. Crace handled this mixed group so efficiently as to beat off 31 land-based bombers from Rabaul without receiving a scratch; and he also fought off three United States Army Air Force B–17s from the Townsville (Queensland) base, which thought his ships were Japanese. To cap this comedy, the thwarted Japanese planes claimed to have sunk two battleships and a heavy cruiser.

Toward evening of the same day, 7 May, Takagi sent a search-attack mission to find and bomb Fletcher's carriers. They missed the flattops, but had a rough experience. First they were intercepted by Fletcher's fighter planes and lost nine of their number; then, after dark, six tried to land on *Yorktown*, mistaking her for Japanese; and eleven more were lost trying to make night landings on their own carriers.

---

2 Post-battle information downgraded this contact still more, to two old light cruisers and three converted gunboats, which were escorting a seaplane tender to one of the Louisiades.

On 8 May came the payoff. The two major carrier groups under Fletcher and Takagi (or, to use the actual O.T.C.'s of the carriers, Fitch and Hara),[3] which had been fumbling for one another for the better part of three days and nights, finally came to grips. Each located the other and attacked. Never were forces more even. The Japanese admiral with the Irish name had 121 planes; "Jakey" Fitch had 122. Hara had a screen of four heavy cruisers and six destroyers; Fitch, now Crace was away, had but one more of each type. Nature, however, gave the Japanese carriers one great advantage. They were in a belt of heavy overcast which had moved into the Coral Sea from the Solomons, whilst the Americans were out in the clear under brilliant sunshine. Thus, the *Yorktown* attack group, 41 planes strong, missed *Zuikaku* under a rain squall, concentrated on *Shokaku* and obtained only two bomb hits; but one of these bent the flight deck so that she could no longer launch planes. Half *Lexington*'s attack group failed to find the fog-enshrouded enemy; the other half gave *Shokaku* another bomb hit. Takagi, who by this time (noon 8 May) believed that both American carriers were sinking, decided he could dispense with the damaged carrier and sent her back to Truk.

His assumption was about half correct. The Japanese attack group, amounting to about 70 planes, gave both American carriers a severe working-over. *Yorktown* took one bomb hit which killed 66 men; *Lexington* took two torpedoes and two bomb hits. The end of the battle found "Lady Lex" listing, with three fires burning but her power plant intact. There was every prospect of damage control quenching the fires, when suddenly she was racked by two internal explosions which forced Captain Frederick Sherman to abandon ship. This was done skillfully, some 150 wounded being lowered in basket stretchers into motor whale-

---

[3] Before the battle opened on the 8th Fletcher wisely made Rear Admiral Fitch, in *Lexington*, the O.T.C.; for Fitch had the more carrier experience. Similarly, Takagi made Hara in *Zuikaku* his O.T.C. Takagi wore his flag in *Myoko*; Fletcher's flagship was *Minneapolis*.

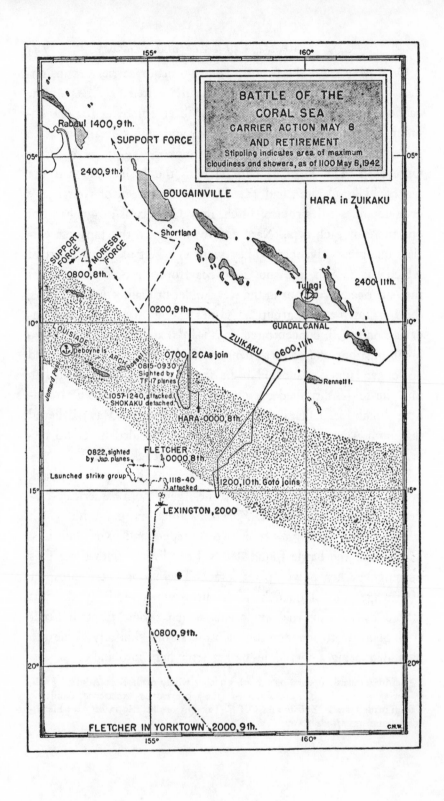

BATTLE OF THE
CORAL SEA
CARRIER ACTION MAY 8
AND RETIREMENT
Stippling indicates area of maximum
cloudiness and showers, as of 1100 May 8, 1942

Rabaul 1400, 9th.

SUPPORT FORCE

2400, 9th.

BOUGAINVILLE

HARA in ZUIKAKU

Shortland

SUPPORT
FORCE

MORESBY
FORCE

0800, 8th.

0200, 9th.

Tulagi

2400, 11th.

LOUISIADE

Deboyne Is.

Rossell

ARCH

ZUIKAKU

GUADALCANAL

0700, 2 CAs join

0600, 11th.

Jomard Pass.

0815-0930,
Sighted by
TF-17 planes

Rennett I.

1057-1240, attacked,
SHOKAKU detached.

HARA-0000, 8th.

0822, sighted
by Jap. planes

FLETCHER
0000 8th.

Launched strike group

1118-40
attacked

1200, 10th. Goto joins

LEXINGTON, 2000

0800, 9th.

FLETCHER IN YORKTOWN, 2000, 9th.

C.R.W.

boats, while the able-bodied slid down lines into the water, where they were picked up by destroyers. Rear Admiral Tom Kinkaid, who handled these rescue operations, showed the qualities that helped him to emerge as one of our great flag officers.

Lady Lex, beloved as few warships have been by her crew, some of whom had been on board since she was commissioned in 1927, finally had to be sunk by a friendly destroyer's torpedoes. Her loss gave the Japanese the winning score in tonnage sunk; but that does not register the effect of the battle. Admiral Inouye, fearful of risking the Port Moresby Invasion Force south of Papua without air cover, ordered it to retire to Rabaul; and never again in this war did the keel of a Japanese warship vex the Coral Sea south of the Louisiades. Thus the battle was really won by the Americans owing to their biggest mistake, the sighting and bombing of *Shoho;* her loss led Inouye to throw in the sponge. Even the big carriers' battle turned out ill for the Japanese, because *Shokaku* took two months to repair, and *Zuikaku* took over one month to replace her plane losses. Thus, neither big flattop could take part in the great battle coming up. But *Yorktown* could and did.

3. *The Battle of Midway — First Blood, 3 June*

Even before the sea warriors of Japan began roaring into the Coral Sea, word had reached Admiral Nimitz at Pearl Harbor of a second offensive that threatened to be much the more powerful and dangerous. Imperial General Headquarters issued the order that put the wheels in motion on 5 May 1942: "Commander in Chief Combined Fleet will, in coöperation with the Army, invade and occupy strategic points in the Western Aleutians and Midway Island." The objectives were three-fold. The named islands were wanted as anchors in the new "ribbon defense," and Midway too as a base for air raids on Pearl Harbor. But most of all, Admiral Yamamoto intended this operation to draw out and "annihilate" the United States Pacific Fleet, in its hour of greatest weakness, before new construction could replace the losses of Pearl Harbor. The success of this battle was central to the entire Japanese strategic concept of the war. Had Japan won, Port Moresby, Fijis, anything else she wanted, would have fallen into her lap. But the yet small Pacific Fleet declined to accept the sacrificial role.

Midway, situated 1136 miles WNW of Pearl Harbor, is the outermost link of the Hawaiian chain. The entire atoll, smaller even than Wake, is but six miles in diameter. Only two islets, Sand and Eastern, the first less than two miles long and the other a little more than one, are dry land. It had been a Pan American Airways base since 1935, and a Naval Air Station since August 1941.

A comparison of the Combined Fleet thrown into this operation with what Admiral Nimitz could collect to withstand it indicates that Yamamoto's expectations of "annihilation" were justified. He commanded (1) an Advance Force of 16 submarines, (2) Nagumo's Pearl Harbor Striking Force, with four big carriers, (3) a Midway Occupation Force, some 5000 men in 12 transports, protected by two battleships, six heavy cruisers, and numerous destroyers, (4) a Main Body under Yamamoto's immediate command, comprising Japan's three most modern battleships and four older ones, with a light carrier; and (5) the Northern Area Force, with two light carriers, two heavy cruisers and four big transports, for the bombing of Dutch Harbor and occupation of Adak, Attu and Kiska. This added up to 162 warships and auxiliaries, not counting small patrol craft and the like — practically the entire fighting Japanese Navy. The total number that Admiral Nimitz could scrape together was 76, of which one-third belonged to the North Pacific Force and never got into the battle.

Nevertheless, Nimitz had certain assets which helped tip the scale. The senior commander of the Carrier Striking Force which did most of the fighting was Rear Admiral Fletcher in *Yorktown* (repaired at Pearl Harbor in two days, when by peacetime methods it would have taken ninety), and Fletcher had learned a thing or two at the Coral Sea. Junior to him, and in temporary command of Halsey's Task Force 16,[4] which had pulled off the Tokyo strike, was Rear Admiral Raymond A. Spruance. He, though not an aviator, showed in the forthcoming battle the very highest quality of tactical wisdom, the power to seize opportunities. *Enterprise* and *Hornet*, the carriers under him, had two superlative commanding officers, Captains George D. Murray and Marc A. Mitscher. In Midway itself, where 32 Navy Catalinas and six of the new torpedo-bombing Avengers, 54 Marine Corps planes, and 23 Army Air Force planes (19 of them B–17s) were based, we had an "unsinkable aircraft carrier." Finally, Nimitz had the inestimable advantage of knowing when and where the enemy intended to attack. But for early and abundant decrypted intelligence, and, what was more important, the prompt piecing together of these bits and scraps to make a pattern, "David" United States Navy could never have coped with the Japanese "Goliath."

Admiral Nimitz's orders to Fletcher and Spruance were to "inflict maximum damage on enemy by employing strong attrition tactics," which meant air strikes on enemy ships. He cannily ordered them to take initial positions to the northeastward of Midway, beyond search range of the approaching enemy, anticipating that the 700-mile searches by Midway-based planes would locate the Japanese carriers first. To this he added a special Letter of Instruction: "In carrying out the task assigned . . . you will be governed by the principle of calculated risk . . . the avoidance of exposure of your force to attack by superior enemy forces

4 Admiral Halsey had been hospitalized after the Tokyo strike.

without good prospect of inflicting . . . greater damage on the enemy." No commander in chief's instructions were ever more faithfully and intelligently carried out.

Yamamoto really threw away his chance of a smashing victory by dividing his mammoth forces several ways, and by fitting his operation plan to what he assumed the Americans would do. Dividing forces was a fixed strategic idea with the Japanese. They loved diversionary tactics — fleets popping up at odd places to confuse the enemy and pull him off base. Their pattern for decisive battle was the same at sea as on land — lure the enemy into an unfavorable tactical situation, cut off his retreat, drive in his flanks and then concentrate for the kill. Their manual for carrier force commanders even invoked the examples of Hannibal at Cannae and Ludendorff at Tannenberg (probably studied in Schlieffen's works) to justify such naval strategy as Yamamoto tried at Midway. Thus, the preliminary air strike on Dutch Harbor, set for 3 June, was a gambit to pull the Pacific Fleet up north where it could not interfere with the occupation of Midway Island, due to take place at dawn 6 June. When the Pacific Fleet hastened south after a fruitless run up north, which could not be earlier than 7 June, Japanese carrier planes and Midway-based aircraft would intensively bomb the American ships. These, if they did not promptly sink, would be dispatched by gunfire from Yamamoto's battleships and heavy cruisers.

So very, very neat! But Nimitz, insteaded of falling for this trap, had three carriers already covering Midway as Nagumo approached. It was the "Nips" who were nipped.

The Japanese Aleutian prong struck first, on 3 June, with the triple object of deceiving Admiral Nimitz into the belief that this was the main show, destroying American installations at Dutch Harbor, and covering an occupation of the Western Aleutians. Besides separate occupation forces, Vice Admiral Hosogaya had light carriers *Ryujo* and *Junyo,* three heavy cruisers and a suitable number of destroyers and oilers. On our side, we had the North Pacific Force commanded by Rear Admiral Robert A. Theobald in light cruiser *Nashville*, with sister ships *St. Louis* and *Honolulu*, two heavy cruisers, a destroyer division, a nine-destroyer striking group, six S-class submarines and a flock of Coast Guard cutters and other small craft. Cincpac Intelligence smoked out Japanese intentions in this quarter, and informed the Admiral of them on 28 May, but "Fuzzy" Theobald, as usual, thought he knew better — that the enemy was going to seize Dutch Harbor. Consequently he deployed the main body of his force about 400 miles south of Kodiak, instead of trying to break up the Western Aleutians invasion force. This bad guess lost him all opportunity to fight; for Hosogaya's two light carriers, under the tactical command of Rear Admiral Kakuji Kakuta, slipped in between Theobald's force and the land, began bombing Dutch Harbor at 0800 June 3, and returned through a fog-mull for another whack at this Eastern Aleutians base next day, completely unmolested from the sea. The Japanese could have landed at Dutch Harbor, for all the protection it had from Theobald. Considerable damage was inflicted on this base, but it was far from being knocked out.

On 7 June undefended Attu and Kiska in the Western Aleutians were occupied by the Japanese according to plan, but Adak was not taken, because it seemed to be too near Unmak. Army P–40s based on the new A.A.F. field at Unmak had given Kakuta's carrier planes quite a run for their money.

Turning now to the main show, Old Man Weather seemed determined to help the Japanese here, as in the Coral Sea. Admiral Nagumo's Striking Force, built around carriers *Akagi, Kaga, Hiryu* and *Soryu,* veterans of Pearl Harbor, advanced toward Midway under heavy cloud cover; they could even hear the island-based search planes buzzing overhead, but themselves were not seen. The force allotted to occupy Midway was, however, sighted by a Catalina on 3 June. Captain Simard's island-based air force reacted quickly, though ineffectively. It made but one hit, on an oiler, at 0143 June 4. That was the first blow in this battle south of the Aleutians.

4. *The Battle of Midway — the Fourth of June*

All night 3-4 June the two opposing carrier forces were approaching each other on courses which, if maintained, would have crossed a few miles north of Midway Island. Day began to break around 0400. It was still overcast over the Japanese, clear over the Americans. A light wind blew from the southeast; another break for the Japanese, since wind is almost as important for aircraft carriers as for the old frigates. Contrary to what was desirable in the sailing navy — to get the weather gauge of your enemy — the lee gauge was now wanted, because a carrier has to steam into the wind to launch or recover planes. Thus, Fletcher and Spruance, having the weather gauge, had to lose mileage during flight operations. *Yorktown*, having to recover a search mission, had to lag behind when the big news arrived, shortly after 0600 June 4.

This news was a Midway-based PBY's contact report of two Japanese carriers, headed southeast. For four hours this was all the information that Fletcher and Spruance had of Nagumo's location and course; but it was enough. Fletcher promptly ordered Spruance, with *Enterprise* and *Hornet*, to "proceed southwesterly and attack enemy carriers when definitely located," promising to follow as soon as his search planes were recovered. Both admirals knew very well that Nagumo's Striking Force was Yamamoto's jugular vein, and that their only hope was to cut it.

Ten minutes after Fletcher issued that pregnant order, the next phase of the Battle of Midway opened, over the island itself. One hundred and eight Japanese planes, divided evenly between fighters, dive-bombers and torpedo-bombers, took off from the four carriers before sunrise. Midway search radar picked them up 93 miles away, and every fighter on the island was scrambled to intercept; but they were too few, and the Marine Corps "Buffaloes" too weak and slow, to stop the Japanese. The bombing of Midway began at 0630 and continued for twenty minutes. It did considerable ground damage, without breaking up the runways; and Midway antiaircraft fire was very good. Between that and the Marine fighters, 15 of which were lost, about one third of the Japanese attack group was shot down or badly damaged. In the meantime, four waves of American Midway-based bombers had flown off to counterattack Nagumo's carriers. They, too, lost heavily; but, as we shall see, their sacrifice was not in vain.

Now came the most decisive moment in a battle filled with drama. Admiral Nagumo, when sending off that 108-plane strike on Midway, reserved 93 aircraft armed with bombs and torpedoes to deal with enemy ships, if he could find any. Usually the Japanese were smarter than we in air search, but this time they failed, largely because, according to the Japanese plan, no American carriers should have been around for a couple of days. So Nagumo sent only a few cruiser float planes on routine search, and by 0700 they had found nothing. At that moment Lieutenant Tomonoga, commander of what was left of the 108-plane strike then returning to their carriers, signaled to Nagumo that Midway needed another pounding. Immediately after, there came in on the Japanese carriers the first Midway-based bombing attack, which seemed to second Tomonoga's motion — obviously Midway had plenty of bite left. So the Admiral "broke the spot," and ordered the 93 planes struck below to be rearmed with incendiary and fragmentation bombs for use against the island. Fifteen minutes elapsed, and the Admiral was dumfounded to receive a search plane's report of "ten enemy ships" to the northeast, where no American ships were supposed to be. What to do? Nagumo mulled it over for another quarter-hour, canceled the former change-bomb plan, and ordered the 93 planes again rearmed and readied to attack ships. That took time, and it was already too late to fly those planes off to attack enemy ships, because flight decks had to be kept clear to receive the rest of the Japanese aircraft which had been bombing Midway.

At 0835, when the returning bombers began landing on the Japanese carriers, American birds carrying death and destruction were already winging their way from *Enterprise* and *Hornet*. Spruance had taken over from Halsey, as chief of staff, Captain Miles Browning, one of the most irascible and unstable officers ever to earn a fourth stripe, but a man with a slide-rule brain. Browning figured out that Nagumo would order a second strike on Midway, that he would continue steaming toward the island, and that the golden opportunity to hit his carriers would arrive when they were refueling planes for this second strike. Spruance accepted these estimates and made the tough decision to launch at 0700, when about 175 miles from the enemy's calculated position, instead of continuing for another two hours in order to diminish the distance. Spruance also decided to make this an all-out attack — a full deckload of 20 Wildcat fighters, 67 Dauntless dive-bombers and 29 Devastator torpedo-bombers — and it took an hour to get all these airborne. Fletcher properly decided to delay launching from *Yorktown*, in case more targets were discovered; but by 0906 his six fighters, 17 SBDs and 12 TBDs were also in the air.

Imagine, if you will, the tense, crisp briefing in the ready-room, the warming-up of planes which the devoted ground crews have been checking, arming, fueling and servicing; the ritual of the take-off, as precise and ordered as a ballet; planes swooping in graceful curves over the ships while the group assembles. This Fourth of June was a cool, beautiful day; pilots at 19,000 feet could see all around a circle of 50 miles' radius. Only a few fluffy cumulus clouds were between them and an ocean that looked like a dish of wrinkled blue Persian porcelain. It was a long flight (and, alas, for so many brave young men, a last flight) over the superb ocean. Try to imagine how they felt at first sight of enemy flattops and their wriggling screen, with wakes like the tails of white horses; the sudden catch at their hearts when the black puffs of anti-aircraft bursts came nearer and nearer, then the dreaded Zekes of Japanese combat air patrol swooping down out of the central blue; and finally, the tight, incredibly swift attack, when a pilot forgets everything but the target so rapidly enlarging, and the desperate necessity of choosing the exact tenth of a second to release and pull out.

While these bright ministers of death were on their way, Nagumo's Striking Force continued for over an hour, as Miles Browning had calculated, to steam toward Midway. The four carriers were grouped in a boxlike formation in the center of a screen of two battleships, three cruisers and eleven destroyers. Every few minutes messages arrived from reconnaissance planes that the enemy was approaching. At 0905, just before the last of the planes returning from Midway were recovered, Nagumo ordered Striking Force to turn 90 degrees left, to course ENE, "to contact and destroy the enemy Task Force." His carriers were in exactly the condition that Spruance and Browning hoped to find them — planes being refueled and rearmed in feverish haste.

Now came a break for Nagumo. His change of course caused the dive-bombers and fighters from *Hornet* to miss him altogether. *Hornet*'s torpedo-bombers, under Lieutenant Commander John C. Waldron, sighted his smoke and attacked without fighter cover. The result was a massacre of all fifteen TBDs. Every single one was shot down by Zekes or antiaircraft fire; only one pilot survived. The torpedo squadron from *Enterprise* came in next and lost ten out of fourteen; then *Yorktown*'s which lost all but four; and not a single hit for all this sacrifice. No wonder that these torpedo-bombers, misnamed Devastators, were struck off the Navy's list of combat planes.

The third torpedo attack was over by 1024, and for about one hundred seconds the Japanese were certain they had won the Battle of Midway, and the war. This was their high tide of victory. Then, a few seconds before 1026, with dramatic suddenness, there came a complete reversal of fortune, wrought by the Dauntless dive-bombers, the SBDs, the most successful and beloved by aviators of all our carrier types during the war. Lieutenant Commander Clarence W. McClusky, air group commander of *Enterprise*, had two squadrons of SBDs under him: 37 units. He ordered one to follow him in attacking carrier *Kaga*, while the other, under Lieutenant W. E. Gallaher, pounced on *Akagi*, Nagumo's flagship. Their coming in so soon after the last torpedo-bombing attack meant that the Zekes were still close to the water after shooting down TBDs, and had no time to climb. At 14,000 feet the American dive-bombers tipped over and swooped screaming down for the kill. *Akagi* took a bomb which exploded in the hangar, detonating torpedo storage, then another which exploded amid planes changing their armament on the flight deck — just as Browning had calculated. Fires swept the flagship, Admiral Nagumo and staff transferred to cruiser *Nagara*, and the carrier was abandoned and sunk by a destroyer's torpedo. Four bomb hits on *Kaga* killed everyone on the bridge and set her burning from stem to stern. Abandoned by all but a small damage-control crew, she was racked by an internal explosion that evening, and sank hissing into a 2600-fathom deep.

The third carrier was the victim of *Yorktown*'s dive-bombers, under Lieutenant Commander Maxwell F. Leslie, who by cutting corners managed to make up for a late start. His 17 SBDs jumped

Soryu just as she was turning into the wind to launch planes, and planted three half-ton bombs in the midst of the spot. Within twenty minutes she had to be abandoned. U.S. submarine *Nautilus*, prowling about looking for targets, pumped three torpedoes into her, the gasoline storage exploded, whipsawing the carrier, and down she went in two sections.

At 1024 Japan had been on top; six minutes later, on that bright June morning, three of her big carriers were on their flaming way to death. But Nagumo did not give up. He ordered *Hiryu*, the one undamaged carrier, to strike *Yorktown*. Her two attack groups comprised 18 dive-bombers, 10 torpedo-bombers and 12 fighters. Most of them were shot down by C.A.P. and antiaircraft fire, but three Vals of the first strike made as many bomb hits, and four Kates, breaking low through a heavy curtain of fire, got two torpedoes into *Yorktown* at 1445. These severed all power connections and caused her to list 26 degrees. Fifteen minutes later Captain Buckmaster ordered Abandon Ship. *Yorktown*'s watertight integrity had been impaired in the Coral Sea battle, and her repairs were so hasty that he feared she would turn turtle.

Admiral Fletcher, who shifted his flag to cruiser *Astoria* after the first attack, had already sent out a search mission to find the fourth Japanese carrier. Almost at the same moment that *Yorktown* was torpedoed, these planes found *Hiryu*. As a result of their contact, "Waltzing Matilda" was revenged just as her dancing career ended. *Enterprise*, at Spruance's command, turned into the wind at 1530 and launched an attack group of 24 SBDs, including ten refugees from *Yorktown*, and veterans of the morning's battle. Led by the redoubtable Gallaher, they jumped *Hiryu* and her screen at 1700. The carrier received four hits which did her in, and she took down with her Rear Admiral Yamaguchi, an outstanding flag officer who, it is said, would have been Yamamoto's successor had he lived.

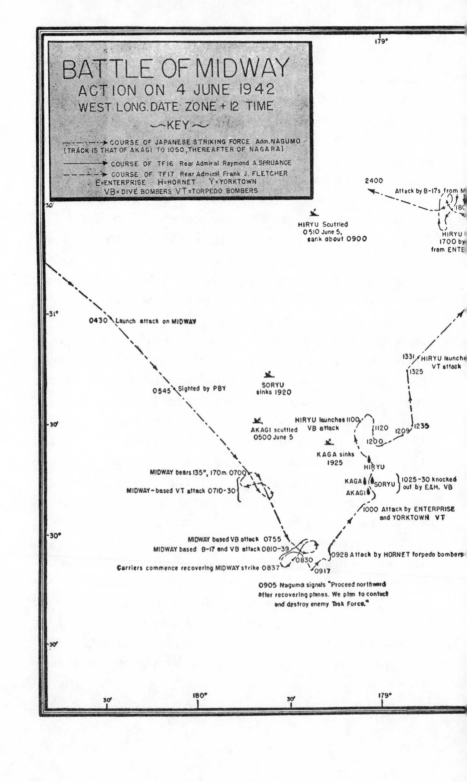

BATTLE OF MIDWAY
ACTION ON 4 JUNE 1942
WEST LONG. DATE ZONE +12 TIME
~KEY~

—·—·—·—➤ COURSE OF JAPANESE STRIKING FORCE Adm. NAGUMO
(TRACK IS THAT OF AKAGI TO 1050, THEREAFTER OF NAGARA)
————➤ COURSE OF TF16 Rear Admiral Raymond A. SPRUANCE
——▲——➤ COURSE OF TF17 Rear Admiral Frank J. FLETCHER
E=ENTERPRISE H=HORNET Y=YORKTOWN
VB= DIVE BOMBERS VT =TORPEDO BOMBERS

179°

2400

Attack by B-17s from M

HIRYU Scuttled
0510 June 5,
sank about 0900

HIRYU
1700 by
from ENTE

0430 Launch attack on MIDWAY

1331 HIRYU launche
VT attack
1325

0545 Sighted by PBY

SORYU
sinks 1920

HIRYU launches 1100
VB attack
1120
1200
1209 1235

AKAGI scuttled
0500 June 5

KAGA sinks
1925

HIRYU

MIDWAY bears 135°, 170m. 0700

KAGA SORYU
AKAGI

1025-30 knocked
out by E&H. VB

MIDWAY-based VT attack 0710-30

1000 Attack by ENTERPRISE
and YORKTOWN VT

MIDWAY based VB attack 0755
MIDWAY based B-17 and VB attack 0810-39

0830

0928 Attack by HORNET torpedo bombers

Carriers commence recovering MIDWAY strike 0837

0917

0905 Nagumo signals "Proceed northward
after recovering planes. We plan to contact
and destroy enemy Task Force."

30°

180° 30° 179°

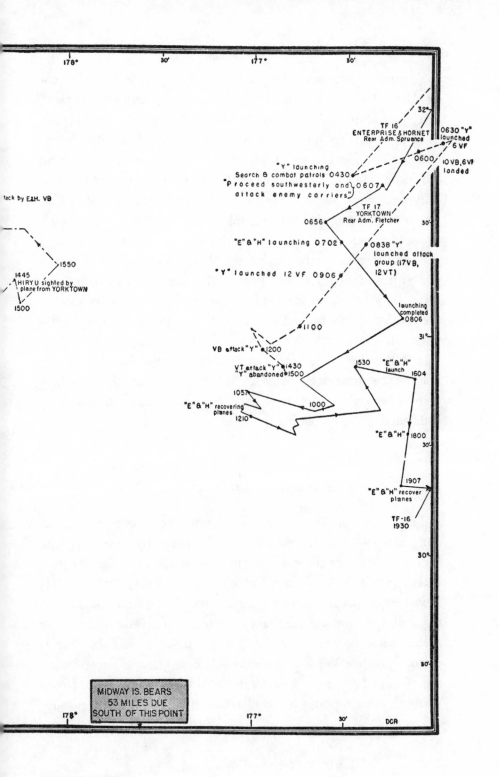

178°   30'   177°   30'

32°

TF 16
ENTERPRISE & HORNET
Rear Adm. Spruance

0630 "Y"
launched
6 VF

0600

10 VB,6 VF
landed

"Y" launching
Search & combat patrols 0430
"Proceed southwesterly and 0607
attack enemy carriers"

tack by E&H. VB

TF 17
YORKTOWN
Rear Adm. Fletcher

0656

30'

"E" & "H" launching 0702

0838 "Y"
launched attack
group (17VB,
12 VT)

"Y" launched 12 VF 0906

launching
completed
0806

1550

31°

1445
HIRYU sighted by
plane from YORKTOWN

1100

1500

VB attack "Y" 1200

VT attack "Y" 1430
"Y" abandoned 1500

1530   "E" & "H"
launch

1604

1057

1000

"E" & "H" recovering
planes
1210

"E" & "H" 1800

30'

1907

"E" & "H" recover
planes

TF-16
1930

30°

30'

30°

30°

MIDWAY IS. BEARS
53 MILES DUE
SOUTH OF THIS POINT

178°   177°   30'   DCR

Yamamoto, who according to plan was keeping well to the rear his Main Body, built around the mastodonic battleship *Yamato*, first reacted to these events aggressively. He ordered Kakuta's three light carriers down from the Aleutians, and Kondo's heavy cruiser Covering Group to join Main Body next day, to renew the battle. He still had overwhelming gunfire and torpedo superiority over anything that Spruance and Fletcher could offer. But, after news arrived that his four splendid carriers were either sunk or burning derelicts, he bowed to the logic of events and at 0255 June 5 ordered a general retirement. He had lost his entire fast carrier group, with their complement of some 250 planes, most of their pilots, and about 2200 officers and men. In all its long history, the Japanese Navy had never known defeat; no wonder that Yamamoto fell ill and kept close to his cabin during the homeward passage. Never has there been a sharper turn in the fortunes of war than on that June day when McClusky's and Leslie's dive-bombers snatched the palm of victory from Nagumo's masthead, where he had nailed it on 7 December.

5. *The Battle of Midway — Epilogue*

The Fourth of June — day that should live forever glorious in our history — decided the Battle of Midway. By destroying the four Japanese carriers and their air groups, the American aviators had extracted the sting from Combined Fleet. Everything that followed now appears to be anticlimax; but the situation during the night of 4-5 June was far from clear to the people at Midway, to Fletcher and Spruance, or, for that matter, to Nimitz and Yamamoto. Spruance knew that the Japanese supporting naval forces, which nobody had yet located, included carriers. With *Yorktown* disabled, the air groups of his own carriers decimated, and no support in sight, he had to balance the possible damage he could inflict by pressing westward that night against the risks involved. Consequently he retired *Enterprise* and *Hornet* to the eastward, and did not reverse course until midnight. It was fortunate that he refused to tempt fate further; for, had he steered westward that evening, he would have run smack into a heavy concentration of Yamamoto's battleships and cruisers around midnight, and have been forced to fight a night gunfire battle — just what the Japanese wanted.

Prior to ordering a general retirement at 0255 June 5, Yamamoto canceled a scheduled bombardment of Midway by Admiral Kurita's four heavy cruisers. Two of these, *Mikuma* and *Mogami*, which had sunk *Houston* and *Perth* in the Java Sea, were attacked by the bombers Captain Simard had left on Midway — six SBDs and six old Marine Corps Vindicators. Both cruisers were damaged, and *Mikuma* next day was sunk by dive-bombers from *Hornet*.

By 1000 June 5 Spruance's carriers were about 50 miles north of Midway. Five hours later they launched 58 SBDs to search for targets, but found only one destroyer. After continuing to a point some 400 miles west of Midway, and increasing his score only by the sinking of *Mikuma*, Spruance turned east on the evening of the 6th to keep a fueling rendezvous.

After the battle was over Yamamoto blamed his defeat on the failure of his advance screen of 16 submarines to accomplish anything. The fault, however, was the Admiral's. He had deployed them to catch the Pacific Fleet where he counted on its being, instead of where it was. Nevertheless, a Parthian shot by one of these boats scored for Japan in the last play of this big game. Her victim was *Yorktown*, abandoned after her hits on 4 June — unnecessarily, as proved by the fact that she floated for 24 hours with no human hand to help. She was taken in tow on the 5th by minesweeper *Vireo*, too small to cope with the carrier's 19,800-ton bulk. As *Yorktown* inched along toward home on 6 June, submarine *I–168* penetrated her destroyer screen and got two torpedoes home. A third torpedo sank destroyer *Hammann*, which was then alongside the carrier to furnish power and pumps for her salvage crew; she went down in four minutes, taking 81 officers and men with her. The two other torpedo hits finished old "Waltzing Matilda." During the night her list suddenly increased, and at dawn it was evident she was doomed. The escorting destroyers half-masted their colors, all hands came to attention, and at 0600, with her loose gear making a horrible death rattle, *Yorktown* rolled over and sank in a two-thousand-fathom deep.

Midway was a victory not only of courage, determination and excellent bombing technique, but of intelligence, bravely and wisely applied. "Had we lacked early information of the Japanese movements, and had we been caught with carrier forces dispersed . . . the Battle of Midway would have ended differently," commented Admiral Nimitz. So, too, it might have ended differently but for the chance which gave Spruance command over two of the three flattops. Fletcher did well, but Spruance's performance was superb. Calm, collected, decisive, yet receptive to advice; keeping in his mind the picture of widely disparate forces, yet boldly seizing every opening, Raymond A. Spruance emerged from this battle one of the greatest admirals in American naval history.

The Japanese knew very well that they were beaten. Midway thrust the war lords back on their heels, caused their ambitious plans for the conquest of Port Moresby, Fiji, New Caledonia and Samoa to be canceled, and forced on them an unexpected and unwelcome defensive role. The word went out from Imperial Headquarters that the name Midway was not to be mentioned.

Admirals Nimitz, Fletcher and Spruance are, as I write, very much alive; Captain Mitscher of *Hornet*, Captain Murray of *Enterprise* and Captain Miles Browning of the slide-rule mind have joined the threescore young aviators who met flaming death that day in reversing the verdict of battle.[5] Think of them, reader, every Fourth of June. They and their comrades who survived changed the whole course of the Pacific War.

[5] The squadron commanders killed were Lieutenant Commanders Lance E. Massey of *Yorktown*, Eugene E. Lindsey of *Enterprise*, John C. Waldron of *Hornet*, and Marine Corps Majors Floyd B. Parks, Loften R. Henderson and Benjamin W. Norris of the Midway-based Marine Aircraft Group.

CHAPTER VII

Guadalcanal

August 1942–February 1943

1. *The Landings, 7–8 August 1942*

THE GUADALCANAL CAMPAIGN, the most bitterly contested in American history since the Campaign of Northern Virginia in the Civil War, comprised seven major naval engagements, at least ten pitched land battles, and innumerable forays, bombardments and skirmishes. It began as a gleam in Admiral King's eye, in early February 1942. He saw clearly that the Japanese must not be permitted to consolidate the formidable prizes that they were then in the course of gathering. To the basic prewar strategic decision to beat Germany first, King always remained faithful; but he insisted that it would be fatal to adopt a purely defensive attitude in the Pacific, as General Sir Alan Brooke (Chief of the Imperial General Staff) and other British strategists demanded. Limited offensives against the Japanese must be begun, and bases secured by us for future advances. Otherwise, the Japanese would certainly advance from Rabaul in the Bismarck Archipelago into Papua and New Guinea, then into Australia, Samoa, and even New Caledonia.

The Joint Chiefs of Staff did not take kindly to the Admiral's "defensive-offensive" strategy, as he called it; they regarded it as a diversion. They were trying to block Churchill's diversion of our buildup for the main attack on Germany into North Africa; wasn't this the same sort of thing in the Pacific? King vigorously denied it. The Bismarck Archipelago, he pointed out, blocks a main road (General MacArthur would say the only road) to Tokyo, and Guadalcanal is the tollgate. If we don't pay the toll, the Japanese will — and sail through in the contrary direction to Nouméa, Fiji and Queensland.

On 3 May, as we have seen, the Japanese seized Tulagi, opposite Guadalcanal. Washington countered by allowing Vice Admiral Robert L. Ghormley, recently appointed Commander South Pacific Force, to move into Espiritu Santo and start a base there (28 May). The Free French had already allowed us to use Nouméa.

Japan's defeat at Midway caused General Tojo to shift his attention once more to the Southwest Pacific. A new Eighth Fleet under Vice Admiral Mikawa was created to spearhead a fresh advance from Rabaul, new airfields were built at Rabaul to accommodate an air flotilla, and troops were alerted to march on Port Moresby, Papua, across the Owen Stanley Mountains. In order to enable land-based bombers to cover this advance, more airfields would have to be constructed in the Solomons. Tulagi was fit only for a seaplane base.

Admiral King, with this intelligence in hand, overcame General Marshall's objections, and obtained a Joint Chiefs of Staff directive on 2 July 1942 for Operation WATCHTOWER. The South Pacific Force would first seize Tulagi and Guadalcanal. General MacArthur (in command of Southwest Pacific Forces and Area at Brisbane) would then assume responsibility for taking the rest of the Solomons and finally Rabaul. That would remove one major barrier, the Bismarck Archipelago, to the recovery of the Philippines and the defeat of Japan.

On 5 July South Pacific reconnaissance planes gathered a bit of news that sparked off Operation WATCHTOWER: the Japanese were beginning work on an airfield — the future Henderson Field — on Guadalcanal. Admiral King put his foot down, ordered WATCHTOWER to start within a month; and how right he was! The

Japanese expected to have the new Guadalcanal field ready for 60 bombers by 1 August, and by the end of the month to base a whole air flotilla there. That would menace our entire position in the South Pacific. Had we not attacked when we did, a new sea-borne invasion of Port Moresby would have started in mid-August.

Preparations were so hasty and the forces available so lean that the officers concerned nicknamed this Operation SHOESTRING. And won on a shoestring it was, since the main Allied effort at the time was directed to Operation TORCH in North Africa.

Vice Admiral Ghormley, who remained in Nouméa, had over-all command. Under him, Rear Admiral Frank Jack Fletcher commanded the Expeditionary Force, as well as a carrier supporting force built around *Enterprise, Saratoga* and *Wasp*. Rear Admiral Richmond Kelly Turner, the rough, tough but highly intelligent flag officer who helped make the prewar strategic decision of March 1941, now became Commander South Pacific Amphibious Force. This comprised, on the naval side, two Australian heavy cruisers and one light cruiser, four United States heavy cruisers and 19 destroyers; and for ground forces, about 19,000 Marines under Major General Alexander A. Vandegrift USMC, embarked in 19 transports. Almost the entire Pacific Fleet at that time was involved. The operation was quickly mounted at Wellington, Sydney, San Diego and Nouméa; the Marines rehearsed in the Fijis at the end of July. This meant too short a period for training.

WATCHTOWER was the first amphibious operation undertaken by United States forces since 1898; and the feeling among the participants was anything but confident. The Japanese in Malaya, the Philippines and Java had acquired a reputation of invincibility, especially in jungle fighting. Despite their defeat at Midway, they still had plenty of ships and planes to throw into the Solomons. Furthermore, there is something sinister and depressing about that Sound, soon to be renamed Ironbottom, between Guadalcanal and Florida Islands. Men who rounded Cape Esperance in the darkness before dawn of 7 August remember that "it gave you the creeps." Even the land smell failed to cheer sailors who had been long at sea; Guadalcanal gave out a rank, heavy stench of mud, slime and jungle. And the serrated cone of Savo Island looked sinister as the crest of a giant dinosaur emerging from the ocean depths.

Everything went well, for a time. Surprise, one of the most essential conditions of a successful landing in enemy territory, was complete. The landings on Guadalcanal were effected in full daylight against slight and scattered opposition, and the incomplete airstrip was occupied at 1600. Tulagi, where the bulk of the defense force was located, took more time and effort, but was practically secured by the morning of 8 August.

On D-day, 7 August, there developed the first serious counterattack, a raid of some 43 Japanese bombers, with fighter cover, from Rabaul — in three groups. Intercepted successfully by Wildcats from Fletcher's three carriers, then operating southwest of Guadalcanal, they did no damage this time. But on the 8th, nine Japanese torpedo-bombers bored into the transport area, and one burning plane crashed transport *George F. Elliott*, which had to be abandoned.

By midnight 8-9 August, the beachheads and airstrip on Guadalcanal, and the three wanted islands on the Tulagi side of the Sound, were secured. Prospects looked bright indeed. Then, shortly after midnight, there opened the Battle of Savo Island, probably the worst defeat ever inflicted on the United States Navy in a fair fight.

2. *The Battle of Savo Island, 9 August 1942*

Early in the morning of 7 August news of the American landings reached Vice Admiral Mikawa at Rabaul. His decision was prompt and intelligent — to send reinforcements to the Tulagi-

Guadalcanal garrison, and to assemble a task group to attack the American ships unloading there. A few hundred troops were hastily assembled at Rabaul and embarked in transport *Meiyo Maru*, which was sent off to the endangered island with a light escort. When this transport was steaming about 14 miles off Cape St. George shortly before midnight 8 August, she encountered United States submarine *S–38* (Lieutenant Commander H. G. Munson), a veteran of the Java campaign, and was torpedoed and sunk. So much for that.

Mikawa's naval reaction is a very different story. One hour after receiving the bad news from Tulagi, he began collecting from Kavieng and Rabaul a task group to attack the American Expeditionary Force. It was a "scratch team," the ships had never trained together before, but it proved to be good enough for the task in hand. Heavy cruisers *Chokai* (flagship), *Aoba*, *Kako*, *Kinugasa* and *Furutaka*, light cruisers *Tenryu* and *Yubari*, and one destroyer, *Yunagi*, made rendezvous in St. George Channel around 1900 August 7 and started hell-bent for Guadalcanal. Mikawa's battle plan, sent by blinker to each ship, was to enter Ironbottom Sound in the small hours of the 9th, strike the warships guarding the expeditionary force, shoot up the unloading transports, and retire. An excellent plan; but the chances of detection were great, as the striking force had to steam in full daylight down the "Slot" between the central Solomon Islands before entering the cover of darkness.

Owing to a series of blunders on our side, the Slot was not properly covered by air search on 8 August, and the one sighting of Mikawa's force that day, by an Australian Hudson pilot at 1026, was so mishandled by him, as well as by the authorities who passed it along, that Admiral Turner did not receive it until over eight hours had passed. This contact report, moreover, was misleading, in that the pilot mistook two Japanese cruisers for seaplane tenders.[1] On that basis Turner made the bad guess that the Japanese were not coming through that night, but intended to set up a seaplane base at Santa Isabel Island, some 150 miles from Savo, and attack later.

Dogmatically deciding what the enemy would do, instead of considering what he could or might do, was not Turner's only mistake on that fatal night. He allowed his fighting ships to be divided into three separate forces to guard three possible sea approaches by the enemy. Rear Admiral Norman Scott with two light cruisers and two destroyers patrolled the transport area between Tulagi and Guadalcanal, and never got into the battle. The two western approaches, on each side of Savo Island, were guarded by six heavy cruisers and four destroyers (besides two more destroyers thrust out as pickets) under Rear Admiral Victor Crutchley RN. This British flag officer in the Australian Navy was a gallant and jovial figure, sporting a full red beard to hide a wound scar. He had taken part in the Battle of Jutland and won the Victoria Cross. For reasons unknown, Crutchley neither conferred with his cruiser captains before the battle, nor issued a battle plan; and his disposition was faulty. The cruisers were divided into two groups: the southern, under himself in H.M.A.S. *Australia*, with her sister ship *Canberra*, U.S.S. *Chicago* and two destroyers, guarded the southern entrance to the Sound; U.S.S. *Vincennes*, *Astoria*, and *Quincy*, with two destroyers, under the tactical command of Captain Riefkohl in *Vincennes*, guarded the northern entrance.

Turner was so certain that the enemy would not attack that night that he made the further mistake of summoning Crutchley, in *Australia*, to a conference on board his flagship *McCawley*, some 20 miles away, in Lunga Roads, Guadalcanal. This action of Turner's stemmed from the worst of all blunders that night: Admiral

---

[1] Seaplane tender *Akitsushinia* was coming down the Slot on 8 August to establish a seaplane base at Gizo Island; possibly the Hudson sighted her.

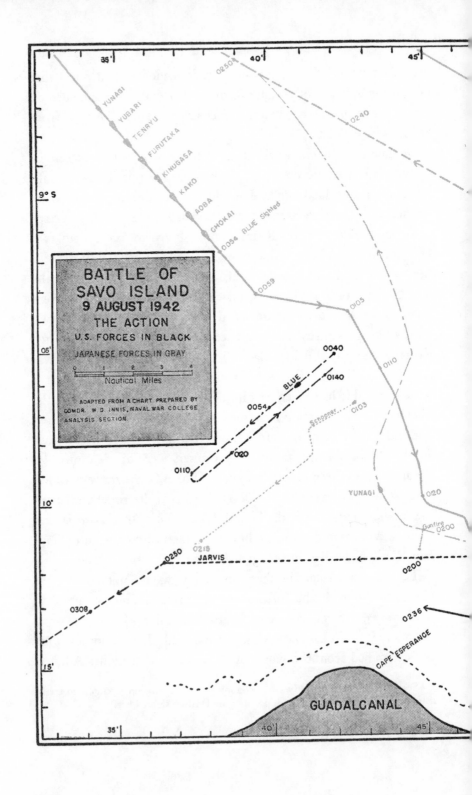

BATTLE OF
SAVO ISLAND
9 AUGUST 1942
THE ACTION
U.S. FORCES IN BLACK
JAPANESE FORCES IN GRAY

0   1   2   3   4
Nautical Miles

ADAPTED FROM A CHART PREPARED BY
COMDR. W. D. INNIS, NAVAL WAR COLLEGE
ANALYSIS SECTION.

YUNAGI
YUBARI
TENRYU
FURUTAKA
KINUGASA
KAKO
AOBA
CHOKAI

0250

0240

0054 BLUE Sighted

0059

0105

0110

0040

0140

0054

BLUE

020

0110

Schooner   0103

YUNAGI

0120

Gunfire 0200

0218

JARVIS

0250

0200

0308

0236

CAPE ESPERANCE

GUADALCANAL

9° S

05'

10'

15'

35'   40'   45'

35'   40'   45'

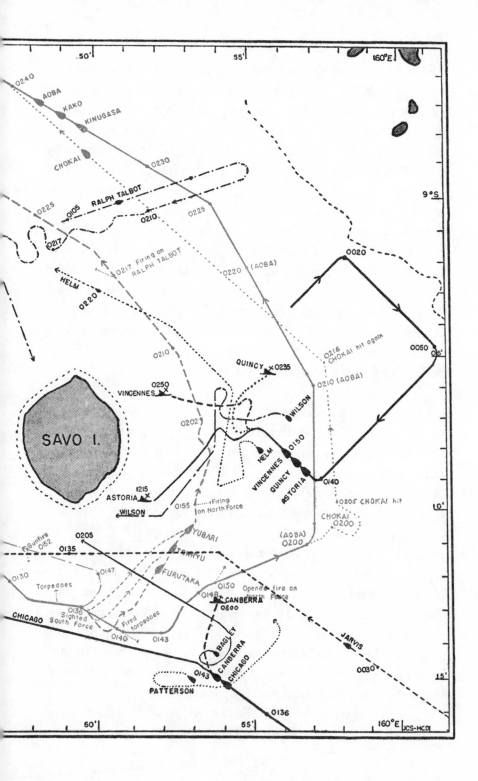

SAVO I.

AOBA
0240
KAKO
KINUGASA

CHOKAI
0230

0225
0105
RALPH TALBOT
0210
0225
0217
0217 Firing on
RALPH TALBOT
0220 (AOBA)

9°S

HELM
0220

0210

QUINCY × 0235
VINCENNES ×
0250

0202

0020

0216
CHOKAI hit again
0210 (AOBA)

0050
0°5'

WILSON
0150
HELM
VINCENNES
QUINCY
ASTORIA
0140

0205 CHOKAI hit

0202

1215
ASTORIA ×
WILSON
0155
Firing
on North Force

CHOKAI
0200

LO'

0205
0135

0130

Gunfire
0152

0147

YUBARI

TENRYU

FURUTAKA

0150
0148

Opened fire on
North Force

(AOBA)
0200

Torpedoes

0136
Sighted
South Force
Fired
torpedoes
0140
0143

CANBERRA
0800

BAGLEY

JARVIS

CHICAGO

CANBERRA
CHICAGO
0143

0030

15'

PATTERSON

0136

160°E JCS-HCDI

Fletcher's decision to retire his three-carrier task force from its covering position, depriving the landing force of air cover next day. He did so on the flimsy ground that his fighter-plane strength had been reduced 21 per cent in two days' operations, and that his ships needed fuel — of which they were far from dangerously short. Probably the real reason was that "Frank Jack" had already lost *Lexington* and *Yorktown*, and did not intend to lose another carrier. He commenced this withdrawal at about 1810 August 8 without consulting Turner, who was below him in the chain of command. That was why Turner felt he had to confer with Crutchley and Vandegrift, to decide whether the partly unloaded transports should depart that night, or risk more Japanese air attack without air protection. Consequently, cruiser *Australia* and the O.T.C. were not on hand when badly needed, and the depleted cruiser group south of Savo Island was commanded by Captain Bode of *Chicago*, who acted as if dazed.

This was a hot, overcast and oppressive night, "heavy with impending doom," as a novelist would say. At 2315, when Turner's flag conference opened, the two cruiser groups off Savo Island were steaming at low speed on their monotonous patrol courses. Officers and men were dog-tired after two full days of incessant action. They had been at General Quarters for forty-eight hours.

At 2345 came the first disturbance: three unidentified planes reported by picket destroyer *Ralph Talbot*. Turner did not get this report; but the cruiser captains who did, and who even saw the planes overhead, assumed with incredible optimism that they were friendly. These planes had been catapulted by Mikawa's cruisers at 2310 to tell him what to expect, and to illuminate targets for his gunners. They droned unmolested over the sleepy American ships for an hour and a half, sending exact information of their movements that was very helpful to the Japanese admiral.

At 0040 August 9, Admiral Mikawa, having sighted Savo Island in the darkness, summoned his men to battle stations. He was using hooded blinkers, invisible outside his column, to signal his ships. Three minutes later, lookouts in flagship *Chokai* sighted a ship, obviously enemy, on their starboard bow. This was picket destroyer *Blue*. Mikawa wisely decided that this was no moment to alert the enemy by shooting. He ordered a slow-down to 22 knots, and the Japanese column padded silently by, every gun trained on *Blue*, just in case she opened up. Nobody in the destroyer suspected a thing. Her SC radar did not register, and her lookouts were looking the wrong way.

After another tense half-hour, the Japanese sighted ahead two American cruisers and two destroyers. At 0136 Mikawa ordered Commence Firing. Two minutes later a flock of torpedoes leaped out of their tubes, aimed at *Chicago, Canberra* and *Bagley*. For five minutes more the Japanese force approached undetected. Not until 0143 did Commander Frank Walker of destroyer *Patterson*, the only American ship properly awake that night, sight them. Immediately she broadcast the tocsin: —

WARNING, WARNING, STRANGE SHIPS ENTERING HARBOR!

Too late, too late! Three Japanese float planes, alerted by Mikawa, now dropped brilliant flares which silhouetted the American southern group; and at that moment the Japanese heavy cruisers opened gunfire. A few seconds later H.M.A.S. *Canberra*, with General Alarm sounding and her guns still trained in, was hit by two of the torpedoes launched at 0138. Next (range less than one mile) she was literally taken apart by 24 shell hits in less than one minute. Her captain and gunnery officer were killed, unquenchable fires spread, and this fine Australian cruiser had to be abandoned and eventually scuttled. *Chicago* was similarly surprised. Captain Bode, who in Crutchley's absence was O.T.C. of this group, was awakened out of sound sleep by gunfire, and, with a column of five heavy cruisers to shoot at, steamed off in pursuit of

Mikawa's lone destroyer,[2] little the worse for one shell hit and one torpedo explosion well forward. *Chicago* was out of the battle.

Having dealt with these two cruisers and their destroyers, Mikawa divided his yet untouched column to put the pincers on the northern group of American cruisers. They had heard *Patterson's* warning at 0143, but no other word; shut off from the southern group by a heavy rain squall, they could not see what was going on and Captain Bode in the confusion forgot to signal their O.T.C. *Vincennes* was followed in column by *Quincy* and *Astoria*, with destroyers *Helm* and *Wilson* on their flanks. All were on the northwesterly leg of their box patrol when, at 0148, *Chokai* launched torpedoes at *Astoria*, the nearest. Captain Greenman was catching a little sleep after some 40 hours spent on the bridge. His gunnery officer, Lieutenant Commander Truesdell, commenced firing the main battery on his own initiative, at 0152½. *Chokai's* torpedoes missed; but she poured salvo after salvo of 8-inch shell into hapless *Astoria*, which became a blazing shambles. She went dead in the water and, defying all efforts of her damage control crews, sank next day.

Quincy, next astern of *Astoria*, was the least prepared for action and took the worst beating; but, in the opinion of the Japanese, she put up the best fight of any Allied ship that night. A searchlight from *Aoba* which brilliantly illuminated her at about 0150 found her guns still trained in, fore and aft. Promptly she trained them on the target and got off two 9-gun salvos, from which two shells hit *Chokai*, one of them demolishing the Japanese admiral's staff chartroom. In avoiding collision with *Vincennes* ahead, she appeared to the enemy to be bearing down on them to ram. Although enveloped in flames from midships aft, a shellburst having

---

[2] This was *Yunagi*, which Mikawa had detached to deal with the picket destroyers. U. S. destroyer *Jarvis*, badly hit in the air attack of 8 August and ordered to Sydney, was limping through the battle area at the time. She received additional damage from *Yunagi* and was sunk with all hands at noon 9 August by torpedo planes from Rabaul.

lighted a plane on her fantail, her forward guns continued to fire. Now the doomed cruiser was caught by crossfire between the two Japanese columns. Turret No. 2 exploded after a shell hit, No. 4 fire room took a torpedo, engine rooms became sealed deathtraps, the sick bay was wiped out, a shell ignited the ammunition for a 5-inch gun, fires raged throughout. The only question now was whether she would burn to death or sink. Captain Moore, mortally wounded by a shell hit that killed almost everyone on the bridge, ordered the helmsman to try to beach her on Savo Island; then he gave up the ghost. The senior surviving officer — seventh in the chain of command — ordered Abandon Ship. At 0235 *Quincy* rolled over and sank, first piece of the steel carpet that now underlies Ironbottom Sound.

Leading the northern cruiser column and last to be engaged was *Vincennes*. At 0150 Captain Riefkohl and his executive officer were still speculating about *Patterson's* warning, and what the sound of distant gunfire and airplane flares meant, when Japanese searchlights fastened on their ship. Riefkohl assumed that they were from the southern group, having strayed off its patrol course, and even signaled *Chicago* by radio to shut off the searchlights! An 8-inch salvo from *Kako* ended that line of thought. *Vincennes* replied in kind at 0153, and her second salvo made a hit on *Kinugasa*; enemy gunfire simultaneously exploded the planes on the American cruiser's fantail and their flames provided a brilliant illumination which helped the enemy, as he swept by, to destroy *Vincennes* methodically by gunfire and torpedoes. She took three of these in two fire rooms, floundered to a halt, and, pounded by repeated gunfire, with direct hits on every gun turret, went down into the depths a few minutes after *Quincy* took the plunge.

By this time the Japanese force was in disorder, owing to each ship's maneuvering to fire at best advantage, and Admiral Mikawa was not certain where they all were. So at 0220 he ordered all ships to re-form northwest of Savo Island, intending apparently to execute the second part of his battle plan and fall on the almost undefended transports. But Mikawa was uneasy in his mind, as he confessed after the war. At 0240 he thought better of returning to the fray, and ordered all ships to make for Rabaul at top speed. His reason, strangely enough, was a fear of being bombed in the approaching daylight by planes from Admiral Fletcher's carriers, which by that time were hightailing to safety.[3]

Even though Mikawa lacked the strategic savvy to gather more fruits of victory, a resounding victory it was. In a battle lasting exactly 32 minutes he had sunk or put in a sinking condition four heavy cruisers and chased away a fifth, with negligible damage to his own force, and at a cost of only 35 men killed and 57 wounded.

An investigation by the United States Navy so evenly distributed the blame that nobody was punished. Military commanders, wrote Churchill, "should not be judged by results, but by the quality of their effort"; and it was well that Admiral Turner was retained, since he became the leading practitioner of amphibious warfare in the Pacific. Admiral Crutchley, exonerated because not present, retained his position in the Australian Navy, and was even knighted. Captain Riefkohl of *Vincennes*, who had made about as many mistakes as a commanding officer could make, was broken in spirit by the loss of his ship. He used to go about, like Kipling's "Matun the Old Blind Beggar," telling "over and over the story" to anyone who would listen, of how his ship had prevented Mikawa from attacking the transports by wrecking the flag chartroom (*Quincy* did that) and that the battle should be called an American victory. Captain Bode of *Chicago*, whose stupidity was largely responsible for that cruiser's inglorious part in the battle, committed suicide.

[3] Captain Forrest Sherman of *Wasp*, on hearing a flash report of the action, begged permission to turn back and launch planes at daylight to pursue the Japanese ships, but was denied. However, the 17-year-old submarine *S-44* (Captain John R. Moore) encountered cruiser *Kako* off Kavieng on 10 August and sank her with four torpedoes — first retribution for Savo Island.

Many lessons were learned from this disastrous battle. *Canberra* and *Astoria* might have been saved but for their heavily upholstered wardroom furniture, and the layers of paint and linoleum on their bulkheads and decks. All inflammable furniture and bedding was now ordered ashore, and every ship in the Navy was ordered to scrape down her interior to bare steel; day and night for the rest of 1942, sounds of chipping hammers were never still. Improved fire-fighting technique and the "fog nozzle," far superior to a solid stream of water, were developed; communications were improved; and officers adopted a more reasonable battle-readiness condition which relieved them and their men from continual tension.

Thus, Savo Island was neither a decisive battle nor an unprofitable defeat, although the cost was heavy — four heavy cruisers and one destroyer sunk, 1270 officers and men killed and 709 wounded. It opened a bloody and desperate campaign for control of an island that neither side really wanted, but which neither could afford to abandon to the enemy.

3. *The Battle of the Eastern Solomons, 24 August 1942*

Guadalcanal is mountainous, covered with dark-green rain-forest jungle, interspersed with patches of light-green kunai grass, whose tall, saw-toothed blades can inflict a nasty wound on walkers. Along the north coast, where the Japanese had built their landing strip, there is a narrow plain where the Australians had planted coconut groves. The fuzzy-haired Melanesians, whose labor converted the ripe nuts into copra, were uniformly hostile to the Japanese, who had pushed them around too violently, and friendly to the Allies. They, as well as the Australian "coast watchers" who concealed themselves in the Japanese-held central and upper Solomons, were an important factor in the eventual Allied victory.

The main factor, however, was the Marines. When the transports and surviving naval vessels departed on 9 August, they had landed over 16,000 Marines, but less than half their supplies and weapons had been unloaded. The Leathernecks pulled in their belts and lived on two meals a day, using the large stores of rice which the Japanese had obligingly left; but they could not continue to fight without naval support — witness what had happened at Wake. For the present, they concentrated on setting up a five-mile long defense perimeter from the Tenaru (Ilu) River to the native village of Kukum, and, by using abandoned Japanese equipment, turning the airstrip, then no more than a piece of level ground, into Henderson Field. It was ready for the first flight of Marine Corps planes on 15 August. On the same day the Marines received their first reinforcements — aviation gas, ammunition, and a "Cub" unit to service planes — in three fast destroyer-transports; and these returned on the 20th with rations.

During the twelve days following the Battle of Savo Island, the Japanese lost their best opportunity to reinforce their small garrison and run us off the island. They had full sea-and-air command; there was nothing to stop them but submarines — and Marines. But the high command was more interested in its Papuan operation; and General Hyakutake at Rabaul, estimating that only 3000 Marines were on the island, thought that a thousand more Japanese could do the trick. Accordingly, the Ichiki Detachment, originally slated to occupy Midway, was loaded in the six destroyers of Rear Admiral Raizo Tanaka's squadron and landed east of the Marines' perimeter, in the night of 18-19 August. Two days later Colonel Ichiki and his 815 men were completely wiped out by a part of the 1st Marines under Lieutenant Colonel E. A. Pollock, who lost only 34 men killed. This Battle of the Tenaru River, a model of perfectly coördinated effort, freed the Marines' eastern flank and had far-reaching effects. The Corps' first stand-up fight with the much-touted jungle-fighting Jap, it proved that the American was the better fighting man, even on his enemy's chosen terrain. From that time on, United States Marines were invincible.

It also proved what a mistake it is to commit forces piecemeal, but the Japanese war lords did not heed this lesson; not even Yamamoto did. An old Chinese proverb says, "A lion uses all its might in attacking a rabbit." Yamamoto had acted on that principle at Midway, but the rabbit won; and he reverted to the piecemeal doctrine, saving his best capital ships for a future all-out offensive. His biggest commitment came now, in the third week of August: 3 carriers, 3 battleships, 9 cruisers, 13 destroyers, 36 submarines and several auxiliaries to cover a reinforcement of only 1500 men to the garrison in western Guadalcanal. The reinforcement unit, under Rear Admiral Tanaka, was to run down the Slot and land the troops at night. In the meantime, a fleet carrier force under Vice Admiral Kondo, spearheaded by *Shokaku* and *Zuikaku*, with two battleships and three heavy cruisers, advanced into waters northeast of the Solomons to engage whatever ships Admiral Ghormley ventured to deploy. Admiral Hara's light carrier *Ryujo*, thrusting ahead, would play the dual role of flying off bombers to pound Henderson Field, and baiting the American carrier planes into attacking her, while formidable air groups from the two big carriers punished Frank Jack Fletcher's flattops. Six submarines steamed ahead to scout, six others were deployed southwest of the Santa Cruz Islands, and four groups of three each thrust down to the south and west. It looked like a sure thing.

Warned by Australian coastwatchers and American reconnaissance planes, Admiral Ghormley now ordered Fletcher's strong carrier force (*Enterprise, Saratoga, Wasp*) north to cover sea lanes into the Solomons. By daybreak 23 August they were east of Malaita, and about 150 miles from Henderson Field. Admiral Kondo did not yet know their exact position, and Fletcher, misinformed by Pacific Fleet Intelligence that the Japanese force still lay north of Truk, decided at the close of the 23rd that there would be no battle for several days. So he sent the *Wasp* group to a fueling rendezvous. This was a bad move; for Yamamoto had already ordered Kondo to press ahead and engage him.

At 0905 August 24 an American PBY spotted carrier *Ryujo* about 280 miles northwest of Fletcher's now two-carrier force. At 1345 Fletcher took the offensive, launching 38 bombers and torpedo planes to snap at the bait. Within one hour, his search planes discovered *Shokaku* and *Zuikaku* some 60 miles farther north than *Ryujo*. Fletcher attempted to divert his strike to the big carriers; but communications that afternoon were abominable and he could not reach the pilots. Commander N. D. Felt's air group attacked *Ryujo* successfully, and at 2000 she was swallowed up by the sea.

Admiral Nagumo decided that the hour had come to avenge Midway. At 1507 and 1600, two attack groups rolled off the decks of *Zuikaku* and *Shokaku*.

Poseidon and Aeolus had arranged a striking setting for this battle. Towering cumulus clouds, constantly rearranged by the 16-knot southeast tradewind in a series of snowy castles and ramparts, blocked off nearly half the depthless dome. The ocean, two miles deep at this point, was topped with merry whitecaps dancing to a clear horizon, such as navigators love. The scene — dark shadows turning some ships purple and sun illuminating others in sharp detail, a graceful curl of foam at the bow of each flattop, the long bow of *North Carolina* (a recent arrival from the Atlantic), *Atlanta* bristling like a porcupine with antiaircraft guns, heavy cruisers stolid and businesslike and the destroyers thrusting, lunging and throwing spray — was one for a great marine artist to depict. To practical carrier seamen, however, the setup was far from perfect. Those handsome clouds could hide a hundred vengeful aircraft; that high equatorial sun could provide a concealed path for pouncing dive-bombers; that reflected glare of blue, white and gold bothered and even blinded the lookouts, and made aircraft identification doubtful. Altogether it was the kind of weather a flattop sailor wants the gods to spread over the enemy's task force, not his own.

As at Midway and Coral Sea, each carrier group, in a tight circle about two miles in diameter, was independent of the other. *Enterprise* operated ten miles northwest of *Saratoga*. Later they combined.

Fletcher was ready for Japanese bombers with 51 Wildcats, mostly from *Enterprise*, stacked in three layers as Combat Air Patrol. At 1629 August 24 the attack group was only ten miles away. Dive-bombers and torpedo planes helped C.A.P. to intercept it. About 24 dive-bombers got through, one diving about every seven seconds. *Enterprise* took three bombs — which killed 74 men, ruptured her decks and wrecked the 5-inch guns; but good damage control saved the ship. *North Carolina* also attracted enemy attention, but she drove off or shot down 14 bombers that got through C.A.P. By 1647 this main attack was finished, and *Enterprise* at 1749 headed into the wind to recover planes. But "Big E's" troubles were not over; delayed effects of two bombs stifled the steering engine and jammed her rudder. By amazingly quick and courageous work this was brought under control at 1859, just when the second Japanese attack wave should have come in; but it missed the carriers altogether.

None of the attackers got through to *Saratoga*, but she hit back at the enemy. Five TBF and two SBD under Lieutenant Harold H. Larsen were scrambled to counterattack. At 1745 they attacked Kondo's Advance Force, badly damaging seaplane carrier *Chitose*, and were back on board "Sara" by 1930. They had no fighter cover, and they were only seven, on a mission for which tenfold the number of planes would have been assigned later in the war. Gallant lads these; none braver.

Admiral Fletcher now decided to call it a day, and turned southward toward a fueling rendezvous. His two carriers, amazingly, had lost only 17 planes. Kondo sent his van of battleships and cruisers in pursuit, but gave it up and retired before midnight.

Neither commander regarded the battle as finished, but to all intents and purposes it was, except for Admiral Tanaka's reinforcement unit. His destroyers pranced up and down off Lunga Point that night, bombarding the Marines' perimeter. Next morning, 25 August, the Marines' own air group, from Henderson Field, badly damaged Tanaka's flagship *Jintsu* and a transport; while a B–17 actually sank a destroyer, which caused amazement on both sides. The Battle of the Eastern Solomons was over.

It is generally accounted an American victory, though far from clean-cut, since two big Japanese carriers remained afloat and undamaged. But the study of this engagement by American airmen and technicians led to great improvements in aircraft tactics and carrier construction in the immense pilot-training and shipbuilding programs under way. An unfortunate epilogue was the torpedoing of *Saratoga*, about 260 miles southeast of Guadalcanal, by submarine *I–26* on 31 August. She was saved, but her repairs took three months to complete. Admiral Fletcher, flying his flag in her at the time, was now relieved, and during the rest of the war received commands more commensurate with his abilities.

4. *The Battle of Cape Esperance, 11–12 October 1942*

This Guadalcanal campaign ran from one crisis to another. After the Battle of the Eastern Solomons each side concentrated on reinforcing its island garrison. Admiral Ghormley initiated an almost continuous reinforcement by freighters, covered by combatant ships and by planes. The Japanese kept thrusting reinforcements into the island after dark in fast destroyers, covered by naval bombardments which made night life hideous for the Marines. Ashore there was fighting every day in the week, and two big offensives. The one laid on by the island commander, General Kawaguchi, 12-14 September, was known as the Battle of the Bloody Ridge, in which the Japanese lost a cool thousand men, against 40 dead Marines. This was followed by a westward thrust by the Marines themselves, along and around the Matanikau river on their west flank, which lasted for two weeks from 23 September.

Apart from these battles, a curious tactical situation developed: a virtual exchange of sea mastery every twelve hours. The Americans ruled the waves from sunup to sundown. Big ships discharged cargoes, little ships dashed through the Sound, landing craft ran errands between Lunga Point and Tulagi. But as the tropical twilight performed a quick fadeout and the pall of night fell on Ironbottom Sound, big ships cleared out like frightened children running home from a graveyard and small craft holed up in Tulagi Harbor. Then the Japanese took over. The "Tokyo Express" of troop-laden destroyers and light cruisers dashed in to discharge soldiers or freight where their troops controlled the beach, and, departing, tossed shells in the Marines' direction. But the Rising Sun flag never stayed to greet its namesake; by dawn the Japanese were well away and the Stars and Stripes reappeared. Such was the pattern cut to fit the requirements of this strange campaign; any attempt to reshape it meant a bloody battle. The Japanese rarely, and then only disastrously, attempted daytime raids with ships; the Americans more frequently interfered with the Tokyo Express, but any such attempt was apt to be fatal — as was that of destroyer-transports *Little* and *Gregory* on 5 September. Both were sunk.

It was not easy to get American reinforcements to Guadalcanal. To protect a convoy of six transports carrying the 7th Marine Regiment, which departed Espiritu Santo on 14 September, Admiral Ghormley committed two carriers, *Wasp* and *Hornet*. Japanese submarines *I-19* and *I-15*, which had missed their opportunities in the Battle of the Eastern Solomons, now hit the jackpot.

The one penetrated *Wasp*'s destroyer screen on 15 September, got three torpedoes into her, and sank that big carrier. The other took a crack at *Hornet*, missed her, but got one torpedo each into destroyer *O'Brien* and the *North Carolina*. Both survived, though *O'Brien* sank on her way to the West Coast. Admiral Turner, in command of the transport echelon, decided to push on; and never was the old naval adage "Stout hearts make safe ships" better tested. The Marines, 4000 in number, were safely landed at Guadalcanal on 18 September.

Some effort had to be made to break this deadlock. Could not more help be obtained from the Southwest Pacific? A conference to discuss this subject was held at Nouméa on 28 September. Admirals Nimitz, Ghormley and Turner, General MacArthur's chief of staff General Sutherland, and General "Hap" Arnold, head of the Army Air Force, attended.

MacArthur had 55,000 troops, American and Australian, in Port Moresby. The Japanese attempt to take Port Moresby by marching troops across the Owen Stanley Range had been halted on 17 August, and Nimitz thought that MacArthur might now spare troops for Guadalcanal. Sutherland rejected this idea flat; he expected the Japanese to start another Coral Sea operation. Nobody on our side knew that on 31 August the Japanese high command had decided to throw everything it had into Guadalcanal, and until that island was secured, to leave their Papuan army out on a limb. The two Admirals at the Nouméa conference, even without that knowledge, warned that unless Guadalcanal were reinforced the enemy could push us off the island whenever he really tried.

Try he did, and thrice; but not quite hard enough, as we were trying a little harder. The next naval battle, that of Cape Esperance, was sparked off by the dispatch of a reinforced regiment of the Americal Division to Guadalcanal, in two big transports and eight destroyer types, on 9 October. Admiral Turner commanded this echelon, and Ghormley sent up a cruiser group to run interference. The cruisers were commanded, in *San Francisco*, by Rear Admiral Norman Scott, a young and brilliant flag officer. He had had three weeks to give his task force intensive training in night action, and it paid off well.

For a week or more, the Japanese had been running nightly Tokyo Expresses to northwestern Guadalcanal, and a particularly strong one was due on the night of 11-12 October: two seaplane carriers and six destroyers carrying troops and a vast amount of ammunition and matériel, commanded by Rear Admiral Joshima. In addition, Rear Admiral Goto brought down the Slot a bombardment group of three heavy cruisers and two destroyers. These were reported by a B–17 to Admiral Scott in the early afternoon of the 11th. He built up speed to intercept them west of Savo Island, launched his cruisers' float planes to track them, and Goto was completely surprised when Scott's cruisers opened gunfire at 2346. The American task force (five destroyers, heavy cruisers *San Francisco* and *Salt Lake City*, and light cruisers *Boise* and *Helena*) was just executing a countermarch, southwest of Savo Island and north of Cape Esperance, Guadalcanal, from which this battle is named. The range of *Aoba* at the head of the Japanese column, to *Helena*, was only 4800 yards.

So far, so good; but this might have been called the Battle of Mutual Errors. Scott, fearing that his cruisers were firing on van destroyer *Duncan*, ordered Cease Fire only one minute after firing began. Fortunately the American cruiser commanders, emulating Nelson at Copenhagen, turned deaf ears to this order and their gunners continued to pump shells into the enemy ships. Admiral Goto, thinking that Scott's column was Joshima's Reinforcement Group (then safely within the Sound), did the same, and ordered his column to turn right. A few seconds later the Admiral was mortally wounded by a shell explosion near his flag bridge. By

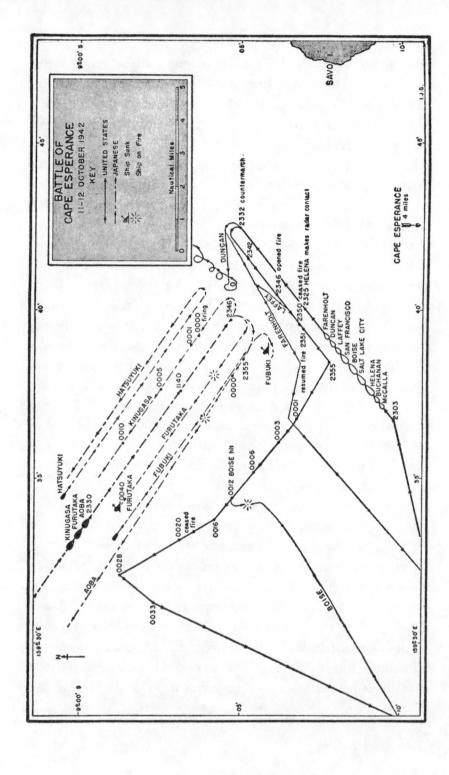

BATTLE OF
CAPE ESPERANCE
11–12 OCTOBER 1942

KEY

⟶ UNITED STATES
⟶ JAPANESE
⊘ Ship Sunk
✳ Ship on Fire

Nautical Miles
0 1 2 3 4 5

that time, both *Aoba* and *Furutaka* were burning brightly. At 2351 Scott discovered his error and ordered Resume Firing. Four minutes later he swung his column northwest to parallel the Japanese. Partly as a result of Goto's bad guess and sudden death, the enemy never returned an effective fire, and lost cruiser *Furutaka* and destroyer *Fubuki* to gunfire and torpedo hits. On our side, *Duncan* was mortally wounded and *Farenholt* badly so; *Boise* was badly pounded by two enemy cruisers, her No. 1 turret breached and a magazine exploded. But the luck of the Irish and good damage control saved the "Galloping Ghost," as the men called Captain "Mike" Moran's cruiser, to fight another day. The main action was over at 0020 October 12.

In the meantime Admiral Joshima was setting ashore the contents of his Reinforcement Group. At 0250 a float plane from *Boise* sighted his formation steaming out of the Sound. Bomber planes summoned from Henderson Field sank two of his destroyers, which were combing the scene of the action for survivors.

Norman Scott fought the Battle of Cape Esperance with cool, determined courage, and, despite an intricate countermarch, never let the situation deteriorate into a mêlée. He became the hero of the South Pacific during the short month that remained of his valiant life. Unfortunately, because it is human to conclude that the result justifies the means, some fallacious conclusions were drawn from the Battle of Cape Esperance: that the single-column formation was all right, and that American gunfire could master any night battle situation. Actually, Scott's disposition was dangerously unwieldly and prevented the destroyers from exploiting their proper weapon, the torpedo. And because the surprised enemy did not get off his usual torpedo attack, that was assumed to be no longer a serious threat. One learns more from defeat than from victory.

The Japanese did accomplish their main mission, landing not only troops but heavy artillery while Goto and Scott were fighting. On the other hand, the 164th Infantry Regiment, Americal Division, whose journey to Guadalcanal was the reason for Scott's being where he was, landed safely on 13 October, bringing relief to the weary Marines in the perimeter.

Tokyo Express for the night of 13-14 October was a bombardment mission built around battleships *Kongo* and *Haruna*, under command of Admiral Kurita. They delivered a 90-minute shoot, which killed many Marines, blooded the newly arrived GIs, holed the airfield with yawning chasms, destroyed almost the entire supply of aviation gasoline and 48 aircraft.

The bombardment might have lasted even longer but for the PTs, the first motor torpedo boats to arrive at Tulagi. These piled in against the battleships, shooting and firing torpedoes briskly; and although no hits are recorded, they made Admiral Kurita so nervous (a quality he later showed in greater degree at the Battle off Samar), that he retired at 0230 October 14.

The following night, of 14-15 October, was another bad one for Americans ashore. Admiral Mikawa personally entered "Sleepless Lagoon" (as the Marines were beginning to call it) in cruiser *Chokai*, followed by lucky *Kinugasa*, to churn up the Henderson Field community with 752 eight-inch shell and cover the landing of another echelon of troops.

Dawn of the 15th revealed a humiliating spectacle. In full view were enemy transports lying-to off Tassafaronga, unloading troops and supplies with as much ease as if they had been in Tokyo Bay; and, hovering around and over them, destroyers and planes.

General Geiger, Marine air commander, was told there was no gas at Henderson Field. "Then, by God, find some!" he roared. Men scoured the dispersal areas, collected some 400 drums of aviation gas from swamps and thickets where they had been cached, and trundled them to the field. Even two disabled B-17s had their tanks siphoned dry. By these pint-pot methods enough fuel was procured to enable planes to make the ten-mile hop to the targets off Tassafaronga and back. Army, Navy and Marine pilots bombed and strafed the transports all day long 15 October, fighting off Zekes and dodging the darting tongues of antiaircraft tracers. Flying Fortresses flew up from Espiritu Santo and lent a hand. High over the revitalized airfield, Wildcat bullets and antiaircraft shells brought down twelve bombers and five fighters. Everybody who flew claimed damage that day, and for once they were right. Three large Japanese transports not yet completely unloaded had to be beached and became a total loss. By 1550 things had become so hot that the Japanese task force commander decided to retire. Not one transport escaped damage; not one troop unit landed without casualties and loss of equipment. This field day cost the Americans only three dive-bombers and four fighter planes.

That night, all hands ashore breathed easier. Even a downpour of 800 eight-inch shells from cruisers *Myoko* and *Maya* and 300 five-inch from Tanaka's destroyers failed to quench the spark of hope kindled by the feeling that the enemy had done his worst. But, alas, he had not.

On 15 October Admiral Nimitz expressed his estimate of the situation in three sober sentences: "It now appears that we are unable to control the sea in the Guadalcanal area. Thus our supply of the positions will only be done at great expense to us. The situation is not hopeless, but it is certainly critical."

The extremity of the American situation in mid-October is illustrated by gallant if pitiful efforts to keep the lifeline intact. Twin-engined Douglas Skytroopers became flying workhorses; each brought up from Espiritu Santo about enough gas to keep twelve Wildcats aloft for an hour. Submarine *Amberjack*, fitted to carry 9000 gallons of gasoline and ten tons of bombs, did her part. A barge-towing Allied expedition was made up of two cargo ships, motor torpedo boat tender *Jamestown*, fleet tug *Vireo* and two destroyers, each towing a barge carrying 2000 barrels of gasoline and 500 quarter-ton bombs. On 15 October, 75 miles from Guadalcanal, these lucrative targets were sighted and reported by a Japanese search plane. The bigger ships hastily returned to Espiritu Santo, but around noon *Meredith* was sunk by a 27-plane raid from carrier *Zuikaku*.

Mid-October marked the nadir of misery for the American at Guadalcanal.

5. *The Battle of the Santa Cruz Islands,* 26–27 *October 1942*

Admiral Nimitz was also confronted with the pressing problem of leadership in the South Pacific. Admiral Ghormley, a meticulous, conscientious officer with a long record of achievement, lacked the personal qualities needed to inspire American fighting men in a tough spot. Admiral Nimitz on 15 October decided that "the critical situation requires a more aggressive commander," and named Vice Admiral William F. Halsey.

Since May, "Bill"[4] Halsey had been on the binnacle list with dermatitis, but mid-October found him back to battery. On 18 October, with feelings of "astonishment, apprehension and regret," he relieved his old friend Ghormley. He brought his own staff, headed by Captain Miles Browning who had fought under Spruance at Midway. Halsey had already won a reputation for leadership, confidence and agressiveness. The announcement that he was now Comsopac was received on board ships of that force with cheers and rejoicing.

Other positive measures were taken. Admiral King released from Atlantic Fleet a task group powered by new battleship *Indiana*, which came through the Panama Canal to the South Pacific. A flock of 50 Army fighter planes migrated from the Central to the

---

[4] "Bill" was corrupted by news reports to "Bull"; but nobody who knew Halsey personally ever called him that.

South Pacific. Twenty-four submarines were ordered thither. Two squadrons of Army B–17s droned across the Equator to join the brood under Rear Admiral Aubrey W. Fitch, now Comairsopac at Espiritu Santo.

In Washington, Admiral King had his hands full. Our predicament in the Solomons was more than matched by that of the Atlantic Fleet. German submarines during October sank 88 merchant ships of 585,510 tons in the Atlantic, and the North African invasion was already at sea. British forces in Egypt and India were still being supplied by ships sailing around the Cape of Good Hope. Guadalcanal had to be fitted by the Joint Chiefs of Staff into a worldwide strategic pattern. The island could not be secured without drawing on forces committed to the buildup in the United Kingdom for a cross-channel operation in 1943, a date the British wished to postpone. Admiral King and General MacArthur argued against risking disaster in the Solomons and New Guinea in order to provide for a vague future operation in Europe. President Roosevelt broke this deadlock on 24 October by sending a strong message to each member of the Joint Chiefs of Staff, insisting that Guadalcanal must be reinforced, and quickly.

It could not be done too quickly, for the Japanese high command had now given the capture of Henderson Field top billing. Their plan was to devote the third week of October to softening up the Marines in preparation for "Y-day," the 22nd, when the Rising Sun was to be planted on Henderson Field by General Maruyama. The Combined Fleet, impatiently circling north of the Solomons, would then "apprehend and annihilate any powerful forces in the Solomons area, as well as any reinforcements." This reversed the classic strategy of first securing sea control which the Japanese had tried, unsuccessfully, in the Eastern Solomons battle. Admiral Yamamoto would better have stuck to Mahan. For the Marines and the GIs refused to be softened, and the stout fight they put up for a week (19-26 October) to defend Henderson Field, and the consequent postponement of Y-day, gave Admiral Kinkaid time to bring up carrier *Enterprise* and take a decisive part in the sea action.

The Japanese Guadalcanal garrison, now augmented by the 4500 troops landed by recent Tokyo Expresses, opened attack 20 October against the Marines' western flank on the Matanikau river. This was followed by an enveloping movement against the central and eastern flanks of the American perimeter. Each was beaten off with heavy loss, over a period of six days. And in this Battle for Henderson Field the GIs proved that they too could defeat jungle-fighting Japanese, if properly trained and led, as indeed they were. Lieutenant Colonel Timboe of the 164th belongs to the Hall of Fame with Lieutenant Colonels McKelvy, "Chesty" Puller, Sam Griffith and General Vandegrift of the Marine Corps.

During these ground actions there were several minor actions in Ironbottom Sound, and at least one Tokyo Express failed to deliver the goods; but these were overshadowed by the carrier-fought Battle of the Santa Cruz Islands, now making up.

Northeast and east of the lower Solomons are two small groups of islands, the Stewarts and the Santa Cruz. The center of the United States Navy's position in this forthcoming battle was about 280 miles east of the one and 125 miles north of the other; roughly 160 miles east of the spot where *Enterprise* was hit in the Battle of the Eastern Solomons two months earlier. The Santa Cruz Islands, glorified as the site of "Bali-hai" in the musical comedy *South Pacific*, were so infested with malignant malaria, and so rugged in terrain, that the Army Engineers sent there early in August to build an airfield had to give up and leave.

Admiral Yamamoto, who directed the show from Truk, really expected to clean up this time. He had four carriers, five battleships, 14 cruisers and 44 destroyers to throw in; he knew that *Wasp* had been sunk and that *Saratoga* was under repair, but did not know that "Big E" was back, under fighting Tom Kinkaid, with *South Dakota* in her screen. This new battleship, freshly provided with dozens of the new 40-mm antiaircraft guns, was commanded by one of the Navy's most remarkable characters, Captain Thomas L. Gatch. No ship more eager to fight ever entered the Pacific; for the skipper, by constant target practice on towed planes, ignoring lapses in spit-and-polish, and exercising a natural gift for leadership, had welded his green crew into a splendid fighting team. They "looked like a lot of wild men," said one of his officers, and they all adored Tom Gatch.

Combined Fleet was losing its edge, and the ships were running out of fuel, waiting for the Japanese ground forces to take Henderson Field. A premature paean of victory — later retracted — from the liaison officer on Guadalcanal, at 0126 October 25, sparked off the naval battle. Yamamoto did not know where the American carriers were; but a far-ranging Catalina from Espiritu Santo sighted Nagumo's spoiled children of victory, carriers *Shokaku* and *Zuikaku*, at noon. Kinkaid acted on this contact by launching a combined search-strike from *Enterprise* that afternoon. But they located nothing, as the Japanese had cagily reversed course, again waiting for certain news of victory ashore.

In the small hours of 26 October Admiral Kinkaid, who had been steering northwesterly at 20 knots, began to receive plane contacts on enemy carriers 200 miles away. In the gray hours before dawn Admiral Halsey on Nouméa riffled through the dispatches, glanced at his operations chart, and sent out these words:

ATTACK — REPEAT — ATTACK!

The sun rose at 0523 on a fair day — low broken cumulus clouds scattered over half the sky, the ocean rising and falling in a gentle swell, a languid 8-knot breeze from the southeast scarcely raising ripples on the sea's smooth surface. It was weather to the taste of dive-bomber pilots who could lurk in the clouds, but to the distaste of antiaircraft gunners — no cloud has a silver lining for them. Already *Enterprise* had launched a search mission, each SBD armed with a 500-pound bomb "just in case." At 0740, two bomber pilots sighted light carrier *Zuiho*, used their bombs, and knocked her out so far as this battle was concerned.

One hour earlier a Japanese search plane had sighted *Hornet*. Admiral Kondo, again Japanese O.T.C., ordered strikes to be launched at her immediately from his three viable carriers. Twenty minutes later *Hornet* followed suit. The two hostile groups passed one another in the air, each eying the enemy and wondering which would find a flight deck on its return. Half *Enterprise*'s group was shot down 100 miles short of its target by a dozen Zekes which had peeled off especially to get them.

Now came the most tense moment for the opposing commanders, Kinkaid and Kondo. Each had found the other, each was lashing out at the other.

Flagship *Enterprise* was the hub of a tight little circle rimmed by battleship *South Dakota*, heavy cruiser *Portland*, antiaircraft cruiser *San Juan* and eight destroyers. Ten miles to the southeast cruised Rear Admiral George D. Murray's flagship *Hornet*, similarly surrounded by floating gun platforms. Stacked in layers overhead were 38 fighters of Combat Air Patrol, all under *Enterprise* fighter-direction.

The Japanese strike, first to depart, was also the first to arrive at its target. At 0859 the American C.A.P. sighted Val dive-bombers at 17,000 feet. At about the same moment *Enterprise* entered a local rain squall which concealed her from the approaching enemy; but *Hornet* was in the clear and the enemy concentrated on her, commencing at 0910. Vals dove down, loosing a series of explosive bombs. *Hornet* and her protectors blackened the sky with shell-bursts. One bomb hit the starboard side of the flight deck aft. The Japanese squadron commander, crippled by a shellburst, made a spectacular suicide crash. His plane hit the stack, glanced off and burst through the flight deck, where two of its bomb detonated. Even more deadly were the torpedo-carrying Kates, which bored in low from astern, slugging nastily at *Hornet*'s tender groin. Two torpedoes exploded in the engineering spaces. The carrier, in a thick cloud of smoke and steam, lurched to starboard, slowed to a stop, lost all power and communications. She was now immobile — deaf, dumb and impotent. Three more quarter-ton bombs hit the flight deck. She was still writhing from this onslaught when a flaming Kate with a doomed pilot made a suicide run from dead ahead, piled into the port forward gun gallery, and blew up near the forward elevator shaft. In all, some 27 Japanese planes jumped this carrier, and only two got home; but that was a cheap price to pay for depriving the Pacific Fleet of one third of its carrier strength.

At 0925, when *Hornet* looked like a bad risk, 52 planes of her air group led by Lieutenant Commander "Gus" Widhelm were approaching the Japanese force. Eleven bombers under Lieutenant James E. Vose fought their way through to the pushover point, drew a bead on *Shokaku,* and roared down through flak with Zekes still on their tails. It was worth the risk. Three to six 100-pound bombs ripped the Japanese carrier's flight deck to shreds, destroyed the hangar and ignited severe fires. *Shokaku* was out of the war for nine months. *Hornet*'s second wave missed the Japanese carriers, but exploded two bombs on cruiser *Chikuma* and knocked her out — for a time.

Thus, by 1030 October 26, one large and one small Japanese flattop had been scratched, and *Hornet* almost finished; but *Zuikaku* and *Junyo* were still intact, and Admiral Kondo had already ordered their planes to go get Big E. His earlier strike would have done so, but for superb ship handling by Captain Hardison, and magnificent shooting by the "wild men" of *South Dakota.* She in this action secured for battlewagons the place of honor that they occupied during the rest of the war — defending carriers from attack. *Enterprise* took three bombs which killed 44 men but inflicted no lethal damage on the ship.

Forty minutes later, at 1101, *Junyo*'s dive-bombers tumbled out of the low overcast. One of them planted a bomb on *South Dakota*'s No. 1 turret; an armor-piercing bomb went right through the thin skin of antiaircraft cruiser *San Juan*, exploding below her keel and jamming her rudder.

Enemy planes kept dogging *Hornet*, when under tow by cruiser *Northampton;* she took three more hits, and had to be abandoned. Two Japanese destroyers then sank her. Had the later expedient of attaching powerful fleet tugs to each carrier group been in effect, she would have been towed out of enemy range and salvaged.

Kondo now shaped a retiring course northward, hoping to renew battle on the 28th; but Kinkaid by that time was too far away for him to make contact. The Battle of the Santa Cruz Islands was over. Measured in terms of sinking, the Japanese could claim victory. The loss of the new, powerful *Hornet* was serious, and left the United States Navy with only two carriers in the Pacific, "Sara" and "Big E," both under repair. But Japanese air strength had been reduced by about 100 planes, and some of the best pilots. The land battle, which the naval battle was supposed to cover, had failed. Moreover, this Santa Cruz set-to gained precious time for the Americans to prepare for the next expected onslaught.

6. *The Naval Battle of Guadalcanal,*
12–15 November 1942

As usual, that was not long a-coming. Admiral Yamamoto, contemptuous of earlier air and ground efforts to capture Henderson Field, now issued a new op plan to secure sea supremacy in the

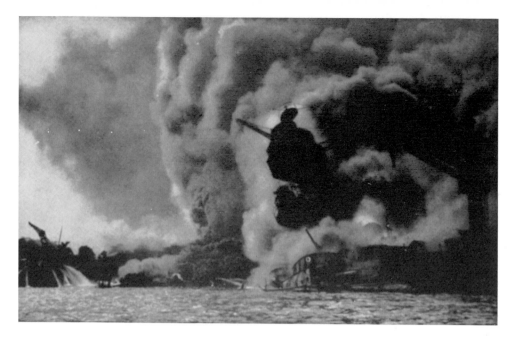

After her magazine exploded

(Stern of *Tennessee* at left)

Blown in half

Death of Arizona, *7 December 1941*

Admiral Chester W. Nimitz USN

Admiral Raymond A. Spruance USN

Admiral William F. Halsey USN

U.S.S. South Dakota *and* Enterprise *during the*
Battle of the Santa Cruz Islands

Japanese transports burning on beach, Guadalcanal

U.S.S. *Washington*

15 November 1942

Vice Admiral Henry Kent Hewitt USN
Commander Task Force 34, 1942; Commander Eighth Fleet, 1943

From a painting by *Albert K. Murray*

Rear Admiral Richmond Kelly Turner USN *and Staff*
In the background: Colonel N. D. Harris USMC, Commander J. S. Lowis, Captain J. H. Doyle

U.S.S. Essex *during Operation* GALVANIC

Photo by Army Air Force

Wings over Kwajalein

VII Army Air Force Liberator over Kwajalein Island, October 1944

Vice Admiral John S. McCain USN

Vice Admiral Marc A. Mitscher USN in U.S.S. *Randolph*

CTF 38 and CTF 58

U.S. motor torpedo boat laying smoke

U.S.S. *Savannah* hit by radio-guided bomb

Salerno

Solomons. Admiral Halsey, exasperated over the loss of *Hornet*, drafted a plan to thwart him. Between 2 and 10 November the enemy brought in 65 destroyer loads and two cruiser loads of troops to western Guadalcanal. One of these detachments, landed at Koli Point east of the American perimeter, was exterminated by the Marines; Henderson Field flyers inflicted major damage on three destroyers, helped by the Tulagi PT squadron; minesweeper *Southard* sank one submarine. But by 12 November the Japanese garrison on Guadalcanal outnumbered the Americans for the first time.

The big American reinforcements, due to arrive on 11-12 November, were (1) three combat-loaded freighters escorted by Rear Admiral Scott in antiaircraft cruiser *Atlanta*, with four destroyers; and (2) four more transport types (including Admiral Turner's flagship *McCawley*), escorted by Rear Admiral Daniel J. Callaghan in *San Francisco*, with three more cruisers and five destroyers. Since intelligence reports indicated that the Japanese were about to dispatch an exceptionally strong and noxious Tokyo Express, Admiral Halsey deployed 24 submarines in and around Solomons waters and sent Tom Kinkaid's carrier task force (*Enterprise*, battleships *Washington* and *South Dakota*, two cruisers and eight destroyers) to cover Turner and counter Yamamoto. If Big E, still under repair at Nouméa, could not get there in time, the battleships and four destroyers would be detached for independent action, under the command of Rear Admiral Willis A. Lee in *Washington*. That is exactly what happened — and mighty fortunate that it did. Halsey inadvertently afforded "Ching" Lee his one big moment in the war, even though he later deprived him of an even greater opportunity in the Battle for Leyte Gulf.

Scott's reinforcement contingent unloaded successfully on 11 November, and Turner's was about half empty at 1317 on the 12th when word came from a coastwatcher at Buin that a formidable flock of fighter-escorted bombers was flying down the Slot. Their attack on the transports in Lunga Roads an hour later opened the Naval Battle of Guadalcanal. This first round resulted very ill for enemy aircraft. Admiral Turner, a past master at handling ships in such manner as to thwart air attack and bring all his own antiaircraft fire to bear, suffered only slight damage, and, helped by Wildcats from Henderson Field, allowed very few of the two-engined Bettys to return.

Tense calm followed the afternoon's elimination shoot. As Turner steamed back to the unloading area through floating remains of downed planes, he realized that the enemy had just begun to show his hand. Abundant intelligence from search planes and coastwatchers indicated that the Tokyo Express that night would include two battleships and at least four cruisers and ten destroyers — too much for Callaghan's two heavy and three light cruisers and eight destroyers to take on with much prospect of success. Yet, with Kinkaid's carrier-battleship force too far away to help, there was nothing else to do but for Callaghan to block, and block hard.

At dusk 12 November Turner pulled out his transports, Callaghan escorting them for a few hours only before he had to return to face the Japanese onslaught. "Uncle Dan" Callaghan, austere, deeply religious, a hard-working and conscientious officer who possessed the high personal regard of his fellows and the love of his men, had reached the acme of his career. There was something a little detached about this man, since his thoughts were often not of this world; something, too, that recalled the chivalrous warriors of other days. One could see him as Ossian's dark-haired Duth-maruno, with beetling-browed Turner in the role of Fingal, exhorting him, when they parted that night: "Near us are the foes, Duth-maruno. They come forward like waves in mist, when their foamy tops are seen above the low-sailing vapor. . . . Sons of heroes, call forth the steel!"

Callaghan passed through Lunga Channel into Ironbottom Sound, his ships in single column. Four destroyers were in the van, then cruisers *Atlanta* (with Rear Admiral Scott embarked), *San Francisco, Portland, Helena* and *Juneau.* Four destroyers brought up the rear. This disposition was supposed to be best for navigating restricted waters and for ship-to-ship communication. But it prevented the rear destroyers from making an initial torpedo attack; and, for reasons unknown, Callaghan did not place in the van two destroyers which had the latest SG radar — the kind that showed a picture on the screen.

Fast approaching was a beefed-up Tokyo Express — two battleships, screened by a light cruiser and 14 destroyers, under Vice Admiral Hiroaki Abe. Their mission was to knock out Henderson Field and slaughter the Marines with high explosive shells. Abe was not looking for a naval battle. He assumed that the Americans as usual would be gone with the sun, allowing him to prowl the Sound and bombard at will.

It was now Friday the thirteenth, last day of life for eight ships and many hundred sailors, including two rear admirals. The Americans' first radar contact, at 0124, showed Abe's battlewagons almost surrounded by his destroyer screen, approaching from the direction of Savo Island. Callaghan did not alter course to cross the enemy's "T"; that was his big mistake. At 0141 destroyer *Cushing,* leading the American column, sighted two Japanese destroyers about to cross her bows. She turned hard-a-port to unmask her torpedo batteries and avoid a collision. This maneuver threw the American column into partial disorder, which in a few minutes' time became almost complete. Now surprise was lost. Callaghan delayed eight minutes before opening gunfire, owing to the confusion engendered by *Cushing's* turn and his fear of hitting friends. This gave Abe precious time to change his high-caliber bombardment shells for armor-piercing. If one American shell had exploded on his battleships while their decks were heaped with shells, they would have been destroyed.

At 0150, just as a Japanese destroyer's searchlight picked up the bridge of *Atlanta*, she began shooting. Other Japanese destroyers and the two battlewagons then deluged the helpless cruiser with shellfire. One snuffed out the lives of Admiral Scott and his staff on the bridge. *Atlanta* was out of the battle, which now became an unplanned, wild and desperate mêlée in black darkness, fitfully lighted by gunfire flashes, torpedo explosions and star shell.

So far as there was any order in this action, it was Callaghan's cruiser column, minus *Atlanta*, thrusting between two battleships, *Hiei* to port and *Kirishima* to starboard, while destroyers of both sides milled about, shooting at targets of opportunity. Although neither Japanese battleship was hit early in the action, Admiral Abe didn't like it and countermarched. *Hiei* sank *Cushing*, which had launched six torpedoes fruitlessly at her, and then had a brush with destroyer *Laffey*, so close that her 14-inch guns could not depress sufficiently to hit the destroyer, whose torpedoes were too close to arm; but *Laffey*'s machine-gun fire riddled the battleship's bridge and killed her C.O. A Japanese destroyer got a torpedo into *Laffey*, and sank her. *Sterett*, next destroyer astern, torpedoed Japanese destroyer *Yudichi* and then herself received three hits that put her out of the battle. *Hiei* at one time was burning from stem to stern, and she went dead in the water, but *Kirishima* took only one hit.

Admiral Callaghan, informed that his flagship *San Francisco* was shooting at disabled *Atlanta*, ordered "Cease Firing Own Ships!" When that order took effect, his ship was the first to suffer. *Kirishima* and two other Japanese ships hurled an avalanche of gunfire at her. Admiral Callaghan and almost every member of his staff, and Captain Cassin Young, were killed. Cruiser *Portland* (Captain Laurance DuBose), next astern, took a torpedo hit which bent her stern plates so that they acted as a giant fixed rudder; she could only steam in circles. As she sheered out of the column she let fly at *Hiei*, range 4000 yards, with both forward turrets. Still churning loopwise, she found crippled destroyer *Yudichi* at first light, and finished her off. That concluded the night's performance for "Sweet Pea," as her sailors called this great fighting ship. *Helena*, next astern, did some useful shooting that helped speed the enemy on his way; but *Juneau*, the rear cruiser, was put out of action by a torpedo that exploded in her forward fire room.

Of the four rear destroyers, brand-new *Barton* had exactly seven minutes of life in combat. Two torpedo hits broke her in two, and down she went with most of her crew. *Monssen* was reduced to a burning hulk by some 37 shell hits. *Fletcher*, the tail-end Charlie with SG radar, useless in that position, threaded her way through the maelstrom, shooting, and emerged without even her paint being scratched.

Four bells of this sinister midwatch struck at the height of the battle. An infernal spectacle presented itself to the survivors. Greenish light from flares and star shell dimmed that of the silent stars. Red and white trails of tracer shell arched and crisscrossed overhead, magazines exploded in blinding bouquets of white flame, oil-fed fires sent up twisted columns of yellow flame and black smoke. Around the horizon smoldering hulks of abandoned ships now glowed dull red, now blazed up when fires reached fresh combustibles. Geysers from shells that missed their targets rose from the surface of the sea, now fouled with oil and flotsam.

At 0226 November 13, Captain Hoover of *Helena*, the senior undamaged cruiser, ordered all ships that could move to retire via Sealark Channel. Only *San Francisco*, *Juneau* and three destroyers were able to comply, and at 1100 submarine *I-26* sank *Juneau*, taking down almost 700 men, including the five Sullivan brothers.

A bloody postscript, this, to the most desperate sea fight since Flamborough Head; recalling Anglo-Dutch battles of the seventeenth century, when each side slugged the other until all but one went down. Ship losses were fairly well balanced; two American light cruisers and four destroyers as against two Japanese destroyers and a battleship so badly damaged that airmen could sink her next day. But the Japanese bombardment mission was completely frustrated; Yamamoto admitted as much by relieving Admiral Abe and depriving him of any further sea command. Callaghan, on the other hand, completed his mission; he had saved Henderson Field from a bombardment which would have been more serious than those of mid-October, and would certainly have stopped the American air operations, which next day disposed of eleven troop-laden transports.

Thus, in the end, mistakes were canceled out by valor. Let none deny praise to those who fell that bloody night, with two great seamen and gallant gentlemen, Daniel J. Callaghan and Norman Scott.

Dawn rose on a glassy, metallic sea, stippled by the floating litter of death and destruction. The mountains of Guadalcanal turned to purple and then to lush green. Sailors on crippled warships of both nations stood or slept by their remaining guns, grimly aware that between ship and ship no quarter would be given. Eight damaged ships, five of them American, were visible between Savo Island and Guadalcanal; *Atlanta* had edged painfully over to Kukum and landed her survivors, but she was past saving and had to be scuttled.

Each side now prepared for another night action. Admiral Kondo, who had been cruising off Ontong Java, pushed south with his yet uncommitted heavy cruisers and destroyers to gather up battleship *Kirishima* and cover a super-Tokyo Express commanded by Rear Admiral Tanaka, composed of eleven destroyers escorting eleven troop-laden transports. Admiral Kinkaid's carrier *Enterprise* and two new battleships were boiling up from the south, Big E ringing day and night with hammer blows and the sputter of welders' arcs to repair the forward elevator. Kinkaid decided that the best thing he could do for the cause was to fly off nine Avengers and six Wildcats to beef up General Geiger's air forces on Guadalcanal, and to do what good they could en route. They found *Hiei* limping along north of Savo Island, and got two torpedoes into her, proceeded to Henderson Field, refueled, picked up some Marine SBDs, and this time made the battleship go dead in the water. B–17s from Espiritu Santo added an "egg" or two to the collection, and at about 1800 she plunged, stern-first. *Hiei* was the first enemy battleship to be sunk by American forces.

That night the Americans on Guadalcanal were subjected to heavy bombardment by two heavy cruisers which Admiral Mikawa had sent down from Rabaul.

As 14 November dawned, airmen, ground crews and stranded sailors rolled out of their foxholes, and Henderson Field warmed up to one of the busiest days in its hectic history. The first strike holed a retiring light cruiser and heavy cruiser *Kinugasa*, which bombers from the deck of *Enterprise* then sank.

American airmen, both land- and carrier-based, now concentrated on Tanaka's transports that were barreling down the Slot. In a series of bold attacks they succeeded in sinking six transports with all their supplies. But Tanaka the Tenacious refused to retire. He pressed on to Guadalcanal with four destroyers and four big transports. These landed their troops before dawn by running onto the beach, whence the ships never got off; but Tanaka and his destroyer escort scampered safely back to Shortlands. Seven more destroyers, which he had detailed to rescue survivors from the sunk transports, picked up almost 5000 men and carried them to safety.

As the third day of this almost continuous naval battle came to an end, orders were given which led to another night action. Kinkaid, as Halsey had planned, detached battleships *Washington* and *South Dakota* and four destroyers from *Enterprise*'s screen to thrust into Ironbottom Sound and clean up. Rear Admiral Willis Augustus Lee, O.T.C. of this group, knew exactly how to handle battleships, and had studied how to make the best use of radar. Coming south to meet him was Admiral Kondo in *Atago*, with the yet undamaged *Kirishima*, another heavy and two light cruisers, and more destroyers under Tanaka, bent on delivering the heavy bombardment on Henderson Field that Abe had been ordered to perform but Callaghan had prevented. Kondo, whom Commander Hara describes as "the British gentleman sort of man," had missed chances in the previous battle, but had been kept in as a favorite of Yamamoto. After this battle he was out.

At 2215 November 14 Admiral Lee entered Ironbottom Sound by the northern passage. A first-quarter moon was shining. Lookouts could pick up looming heights on every side and shore outlines appeared on radar screens, but neither eyes nor radar discerned any trace of enemy. A rich odor like honeysuckle floated out from the land over the calm waters, a pleasant change from the fecal smells usually exuded by the Guadalcanal jungle. This seemed a good omen to the sailors.

Lee badly wanted exact intelligence of the enemy. Light cruiser *Sendai* of Rear Admiral Hashimoto's advance screen had sighted him at 2210 — the Japanese, with their excellent night binoculars, usually picked us up first. Kondo now adopted a typically Japanese battle plan, splitting his 14-ship task force four ways, moving up big units at flank speed while *Sendai* shadowed Lee. The battle opened at 2317 when Lee, steering westerly from Ironbottom Sound toward its southern entrance, opened fire on *Sendai*. The Americans missed, and *Sendai* doubled back to the northward. Next, the destroyers in Lee's van encountered two Japanese destroyers, steaming so close to Savo Island that American radar was useless. The ensuing destroyer duel was disastrous to the Americans. Both *Preston* and *Walke* were sunk, and the other two went out of action.

Lee pressed on with two battleships only — his men tossing out life rafts to the destroyer sailors as they passed over their ships' graves. Captain Gatch was back on the bridge of *South Dakota*, but his luck and hers had run out. At the worst possible moment she suffered an electrical power failure, so that she was little help to Lee, except that she absorbed numerous hits which might have crippled his other battleship. *Washington*, superbly handled by Captain Glenn Davis, picked up *Kirishima* on her radar, and at midnight opened up on her at 8400 yards' range. Nine of her 75 sixteen-inch shells and 40 five-inch shells scored; and within seven minutes the Japanese battleship, steering gear wrecked and topsides aflame, was out of the battle. Admiral Lee now directed lone *Washington* to the northwestward to draw off the enemy cruisers and destroyers that were punishing *South Dakota*, and succeeded in so doing. At 0025 Kondo decided he had had enough, and retired. *Washington* and *South Dakota* rejoined south of Guadalcanal at 0900; helpless *Kirishima* had already been scuttled. The Naval Battle of Guadalcanal, which opened on the afternoon of November 12, was over by 0100 on the 15th.

This night battleship action was vastly better fought by the United States Navy than the unorganized brawl of two nights earlier. Admiral Lee had a positive doctrine that he maintained, despite the loss of his entire destroyer screen. He made quick, accurate analyses from the information on his radar screen. *Washington*, conned by Captain Glenn Davis and directed by Admiral Lee with a skill and imperturbability worthy of her eponym, saved the day for the United States.

The conclusion of this great battle marked a definite shift for America from defensive to offensive, and for Japan one in the opposite direction. Fortune now for the first time smiled on the Allies everywhere: not only here but in North Africa, at Stalingrad, and in Papua. President Roosevelt, while mourning the loss

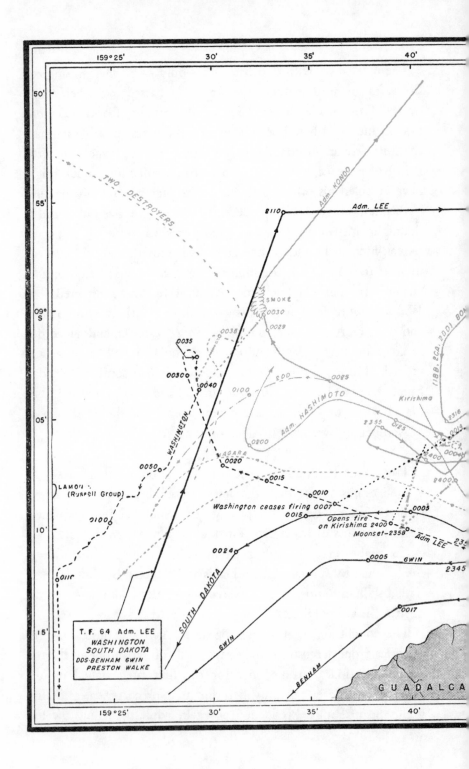

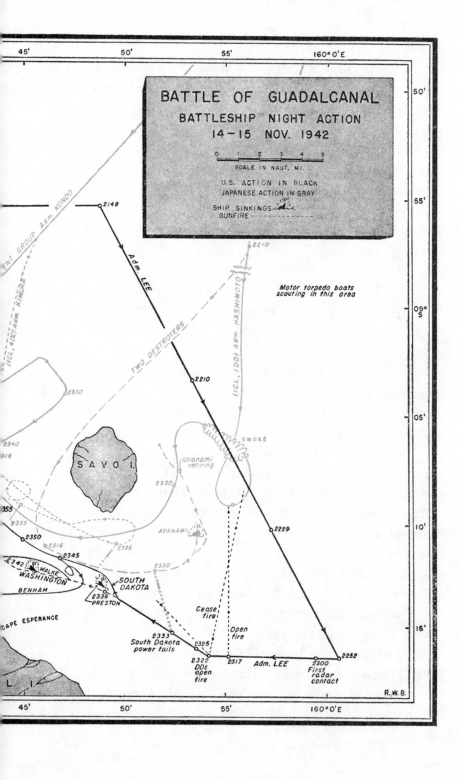

BATTLE OF GUADALCANAL
BATTLESHIP NIGHT ACTION
14–15 NOV. 1942

SCALE IN NAUT. MI.

U.S. ACTION IN BLACK
JAPANESE ACTION IN GRAY

SHIP SINKINGS
GUNFIRE

of his friend Dan Callaghan, announced, "It would seem that the turning-point in this war has at last been reached." Churchill chose this moment to proclaim "the end of the beginning." And a captured Japanese document admitted: "It must be said that the success or failure in recapturing Guadalcanal Island, and the vital naval battle related to it, is the fork in the road which leads to victory for them or for us."

From 15 November 1942 until 15 August 1945 the war followed the right fork. It was rough, tough and uncharted, but it led to Tokyo.

7. The Battles of Tassafaronga and Rennell Island, 30 November 1942–30 January 1943

After losing the Naval Battle of Guadalcanal in November, the Japanese Navy proposed to abandon the island. Tojo, having switched his major South Pacific objective from New Guinea to the Solomons, refused to change back. So the struggle continued.

Captain Morton L. Deyo of Cincpac staff wrote a trenchant memorandum to Admiral Nimitz on 10 October. Commenting on the defeat at Savo Island and the far from satisfactory events that followed, he declared that unrealistic training of our destroyers and cruisers and the almost exclusive employment of them in escort of convoy had prevented the development of a tough, offensive spirit. He suggested the formation of a cruiser-destroyer group in the South Pacific, to be given a solid month of training, especially night fighting, and then thrown up the Slot to break up the Tokyo Expresses.

Belatedly, Admiral Halsey did just that, about a week after the Naval Battle of Guadalcanal. He appointed Rear Admiral Kinkaid commander of a new striking force, composed of heavy cruisers *Minneapolis, Pensacola, New Orleans* and *Northampton*, light cruiser *Honolulu* and four to six destroyers, based at Segond Channel, Espiritu Santo. Kinkaid took command 24 November, before the task force had all been collected, worked up an operation plan, conferred with the officers — and then was detached by Admiral Nimitz! Cincpac wanted Kinkaid to command the North Pacific Force based on Dutch Harbor, where "Fuzzy" Theobald was making a mess of things. As commander of the striking force, Kinkaid was relieved by Rear Admiral Carleton H. Wright, to whose unhappy lot it fell, on the second day of his command, to lead his yet untrained task force against a Tokyo Express led by the redoubtable Tanaka.

This Japanese reinforcement plan was comparatively modest. Tanaka's force, consisting of destroyers only, would dash into Ironbottom Sound and off Tassafaronga would jettison rubber-wrapped drums of provisions, shove troops overboard to be recovered by small craft operating from the shore, and quickly retire. On this particular night Tanaka had six destroyers crammed with troops and supplies, and two more not so encumbered. At 2225 November 30, before arriving off Tassafaronga, he encountered Admiral Wright's much stronger task force. The ensuing battle reflected slight credit on the United States Navy, but great luster on the Imperial Navy of Japan.

The surface of Ironbottom Sound that calm night was like a black mirror, and the American float planes detailed to illuminate Tokyo Express were unable to rise from the water. But Wright had the advantage of radar, and destroyer *Fletcher* in his van had the latest kind. At 2316 she picked up Tanaka's force, broad on the port bow, steaming slowly along the Guadalcanal shore toward the dumping-off place. The squadron commander in *Fletcher* asked permission for his four van destroyers to fire torpedoes; Wright hesitated for four minutes before granting it, and so lost the battle. For, by the time the torpedoes were launched, about 2321, the Japanese column had passed the Americans on a contrary course and the range was too great for American torpedoes to overtake them. Immediately after his last torpedo smacked the water, Wright ordered cruisers to open gunfire, and the flashes of his guns sparked off Tanaka's reaction. Despite initial handicaps of surprise, cluttered decks and enemy gunfire, Tanaka's disciplined crews in the first moments of battle managed to launch more than twenty fast-running torpedoes. And a large share of the American gunfire concentrated on one Japanese destroyer, *Takanami*, the only enemy ship sunk in this battle.

Not one American torpedo found its target, but at 2327 the Japanese "long lances" began to rip the bowels of Wright's cruisers. *Minneapolis* took two violent explosions and was out of the fight. *New Orleans*, maneuvering to avoid her, ran smack into another torpedo that sliced off her bow and everything up to No. 2 turret. *Pensacola*, turning to port to avoid her two burning sisters, became silhouetted by them for the enemy's benefit and took a torpedo hit directly below her mainmast, which became a torch blazing with oil from a ruptured fuel tank. *Honolulu* escaped by smart seamanship on the part of the officer of the deck, Lieutenant Commander George F. Davis.[5] *Northampton*, after firing 18 salvos from her 8-inch battery, took two torpedo hits, and sank, after more than three hours' frantic efforts by Damage Control to save her. By 0130 December 1, all Japanese ships except sinking *Takanami* were hightailing out of Ironbottom Sound, undamaged.

The three stricken heavy cruisers, saved by remarkable energy and ingenuity of their crews, were sent to major bases for repairs, and joined the Fleet again by next fall. But it is painfully true that the Battle of Tassafaronga was a sharp defeat, inflicted on an alerted and superior cruiser force by a surprised and inferior destroyer force whose decks were cluttered with freight. Tanaka

[5] Her C.O., Captain Robert W. Hayler, had a lot to do with this, but generously gave Commander Davis all the credit.

was prevented from delivering the goods, and that was held against him by the higher command.

By 3 December this remarkable flag officer was ready for another reinforcement dash into the Sound. General Imamura, who had succeeded to the top army command at Rabaul, now had some 60,000 troops, and planned to get two divisions of them into Guadalcanal. Successful runs were made on the nights of 3-4, 7-8, and 11-12 December, hampered but not defeated by PT boats based at Tulagi. *PT-59*, Lieutenant (jg) John M. Searles, sank a 2000-ton blockade-running submarine, *I-3*, on the 9th; and three PTs, commanded by Lieutenant (jg) Lester H. Gamble USNR, sank Tanaka's newest flagship, destroyer *Teruzuki*, on the 12th.

Japan had good reason to be proud of her destroyers; and their success was well earned. For forty years the Imperial Navy had put much thought and great effort into improved torpedoes, night fighting, and torpedo tactics. The 2300 ton *Fubuki* class destroyer, such as those of Tanaka's squadron, were equipped with nine torpedo tubes fitted for the deadly "long lances," the crews were trained to reload them in a matter of minutes, and the C.O.'s were all torpedo experts. American and British destroyers enjoyed no comparable matériel, technique, or training. Nevertheless, faulty tactics and stupid strategy doomed to failure Japan's effort to hold Guadalcanal.[6]

During the last weeks of November and the first of December, Allied forces on the island were both relieved and increased. The 1st Marine Division, which had fought almost incessantly for 17 seven-day weeks, was relieved by two regiments of the Second

[6] Rear Adm. Tanaka "Japan's Losing Struggle for Guadalcanal" U.S. Naval Inst. *Proceedings* LXXXII (1956) 698. On pp. 830-831 he discusses Japan's defeat at Guadalcanal, which may be summarized as lack of an over-all operation plan, committing forces piecemeal, "terrible" communications, "unendurable" relations with the Army, belittling the enemy, and inferiority in the air. "We stumbled along from one error to another," he concludes, "while the enemy grew wise."

Marine division. The balance of the Americal Division came up, and its commander, Major General Alexander M. Patch, relieved General Vandegrift on 9 December.

During the rest of December the Japanese refrained from sending anything but submarines to relieve their now starving Guadalcanal garrison. But they were building a new launching platform at Munda in the central Solomons for more and shorter air thrusts against Guadalcanal. It was constructed, very cannily, in a large coconut plantation, the trees being kept standing until the last minute. By 5 December a 2000-foot runway was ready. Since air bombing did not seem to stop the Japanese beavers, Halsey ordered bombardment missions on Munda by light cruisers and destroyers, beginning on the night of 4 January, 1943.

On that very day Tojo decided to evacuate Guadalcanal, but this decision was imparted only to the top Japanese commanders, and remained unknown to Allied forces until the operation was completed. A Tokyo Express run on the night of 10-11 January, 1943, cost us two PT boats and the Japanese a destroyer. On the night of 14-15 January, Rear Admiral Koyanagi, Tanaka's relief, led down the Slot nine destroyers, with a rear guard to cover the Japanese evacuation, and delivered it.

By 23 January, aërial reconnaissance had reported a large number of transports, freighters and destroyers at Rabaul and Buin, and carriers and battleships milling around Ontong Java, north of Guadalcanal. These were preparations for the final evacuation; but Admiral Halsey, assuming that they meant another major attempt at reinforcement, sent up four loaded transports powerfully covered and escorted, in the hope to tempting Yamamoto to another naval battle. C. in C. Combined Fleet declined the gambit; but, with the new Munda airfield as base, he laid on two successful bombing attacks which cost us the only heavy cruiser which had survived the Battle of Savo Island.

Rear Admiral Robert C. Giffen's covering group for the reinforcement echelon comprised heavy cruisers *Wichita*, *Chicago* and *Louisville*, three light cruisers, eight destroyers and two of the *Sangamon* class escort carriers, which had demonstrated their worth off Casablanca. "Ike" Giffen, a tough, colorful officer, had had slight experience in dealing with enemy aircraft. Thus, when Japanese torpedo-bombers jumped his task force in the twilight of 29 January, he was in a bad formation to meet air attack, his ships had no orders what to do, and (worst of all) he had left his escort carriers behind in order to meet an unimportant rendezvous, so had no air cover. He plugged doggedly ahead, trusting to antiaircraft fire alone, while the Japanese aviators pressed their attacks repeatedly. At 1945 *Chicago* was hit and went dead in the water. Giffen then countermarched, *Louisville* (Captain C. Turner Joy), took the stricken cruiser in tow, and, escorted by six destroyers, headed south at slow speed. At 1600 January 30, the Japanese caught up with them. Crippled *Chicago* now had air cover from *Enterprise*, which Admiral Halsey had ordered up; but the Combat Air Patrol provided by Big E was not strong enough to protect an almost stationary target. At a point a few miles east of Rennell Island, nine torpedo-toting Bettys ganged up on *Chicago* and put four "fish" into her already damaged starboard side. She sank in twenty minutes. This Battle of Rennell Island was the last of seven naval battles of the Guadalcanal campaign.

The American transports unloaded troops and matériel at Lunga Point without molestation, as did a second convoy of five transports which arrived 4 February 1943.

By that time, the Japanese were almost out of Guadalcanal. They had chosen the night of 1-2 February to begin the final evacuation, which had been going on in driblets for two or three weeks. American aircraft and destroyers and PTs were dispatched and a minefield was laid to stop these ships, which Admiral Halsey and General Patch still believed to be bringing troops in, not taking them out. Two more echelons, on the nights of 4-5 and 5-6 February, completed the job of removing over 11,000 men. American ground forces never realized what had happened until 9 February, when they covered the entire western end of the island without finding one living Japanese. That afternoon, General Patch radioed to Admiral Halsey:

TOTAL AND COMPLETE DEFEAT OF JAPANESE FORCES ON GUADALCANAL EFFECTED TODAY . . . TOKYO EXPRESS NO LONGER HAS TERMINUS ON GUADALCANAL.

So now 2500 square miles of miasmic plain and savage jungle-covered mountains were in American hands, after six months of toil and suffering. The American ground force losses were not great; the Japanese lost far more heavily. The number of sailors lost on each side in the sea battles, the aviators lost over the Slot, the Sound and Henderson Field, have never been computed. Exactly 24 combatant ships, exclusive of PTs, patrol craft, auxiliaries and transports, were lost by each side. Tactically, Guadalcanal was a profitable lesson book for the United States Navy, Army and Marine Corps. Strategically, it stopped the enemy in his many-taloned reach for the Antipodes, and concluded task No. 1 of Operation WATCHTOWER — an arduous climb to Rabaul.

Guadalcanal should ever remain a proud name in American military history, recalling desperate fights in the air, furious night naval battles, frantic work at supply or construction, savage fighting in a sodden jungle, nights broken by screaming bombs and the explosion of naval shells. Hail to all who fell! The jagged cone of Savo Island, forever brooding over the once blood-thickened waters of Ironbottom Sound, stands as a perpetual monument to the men and ships who here rolled back the enemy tide.

CHAPTER VIII

North Africa and Sicily

(Operations TORCH and HUSKY)

January 1942–August 1943

1. Strategic Discussions, January–June 1942

IN THE PACIFIC the British too were at war with Japan, but they could contribute only to land operations in Burma and India, leaving the naval warfare to the United States. In the European theater, however, England was the senior partner. She had been fighting Germany and Italy since 1939-1940, most of the time alone; she had taken a terrific beating without flinching, and knew the weight of German might. This naturally gave her a great advantage in strategic discussions.

Whilst China remained the great enigma in the Pacific, in the European theater it was Soviet Russia. She had been fighting Germany from the summer of 1941, when Hitler decided to strike her down before resuming his blitz on England. When America entered the war, only the British in North Africa and the Russians were actually engaging the German Army. It was therefore a prime necessity for the Western Allies to keep Russia fighting until they were ready to establish a second front in the west. To get help to Russia, Britain and the United States at great sacrifice maintained convoys to Murmansk and Archangel. These were a Royal Navy responsibility, but about half the merchant ships and an even greater proportion of the cargoes were American. Convoy PQ-17, the worst damaged, lost 22 out of 33 ships to U-boats and

Norway-based German dive-bombers in July 1942. Freighters charged with lend-lease goods for Russia were also being sent around the Cape of Good Hope to ports on the Persian Gulf; and other cargoes in Soviet-flag ships (cautiously let alone by the Japanese) were crossing the Pacific to Vladivostok. But Russia, demanding more, had mobilized left-wing opinions in England and the United States behind the cry, "A Second Front — Now!"

The British Chiefs of Staff and Winston Churchill set their faces firmly against any premature invasion of the Continent, and with good reason. Thrice in this war — from Norway, Greece and Dunkirk — they had been thrown out of the Continent; next time they went in, they wished to be certain to stay. England by early 1942 had mobilized almost her entire man power, which added up to a small army but a first-rate Navy; so why not use the Navy to carry commandos on distant, peripheral operations until such time as the Allies had the requisite men and weapons for a massive invasion of the Continent? Churchill called this strategy "tightening the ring"; England's tradition was behind it. She had got at Napoleon by the back door of Spain, and Churchill always believed that his Gallipoli strategy, if implemented by proper amphibious tactics, could have defeated Germany in World War I. That was the only major war since Marlborough's time when England had gone into the Continent in a big way, and it had led to useless losses which all responsible Englishmen were determined not to repeat. Finally, the Royal Air Force was a convert to the Douhet-Billy Mitchell theory that the quick way to win a modern war was to bomb the hell out of your enemy's civilian population — destroy their homes and their morale. While Churchill and the British Chiefs of Staff were not entirely convinced that this could be done against Germany, they were determined to give it a good try.

The British, accordingly, concluded that it would make no sense to invade the Continent in 1942, perhaps to revive the agony of trench warfare, as long as there was any chance of persuading the Germans by other means into rising against Hitler and demanding peace.

With the policy of bombing Germany into submission, General H. H. ("Hap") Arnold, head of the Army Air Force, was thoroughly in accord. But the other American service heads favored a direct approach by ground forces, and began pressing for a massive cross-Channel operation to establish an army in France, thence to strike into the heart of Germany. The British admitted that this would have to be done eventually, but hoped to make it as painless as possible after a long stretch of "bleeding Germany to death" by air-bombing and jabs around the periphery. This basic difference in British and American strategic thinking was never really resolved until victory crowned the necessary compromise. The J.C.S., especially Marshall and King, continued to work for long-range commitments and a war of massed power aimed at the enemy's heart. The British Chiefs of Staff, always hoping that "something would turn up" to render a major continental campaign unnecessary, argued for a strategy of opportunism, attrition and peripheral attacks.

It had been agreed, in March 1941, that Germany was to be Number One enemy, even if Japan came in; but nothing had been decided as to how Enemy Number One was to be beaten That was debated at the three-weeks "Arcadia" Conference of the Combined Chiefs of Staff with President Roosevelt and Winston Churchill in Washington, in December 1941 and January 1942. Churchill came over with a plan in his pocket, of which the essence was: —

1. Continue all possible material aid to Russia.
2. Clear Axis forces out of Libya.
3. Invade Morocco and Algeria, to clear Axis forces out of the rest of North Africa.

This last, he argued, was essential. And Mr. Churchill finally had his wish — though not without a great deal of argument by the Joint Chiefs of Staff for the direct approach.

His three-weeks stay at the White House — interrupted only by short trips to Canada and Florida — was beneficial for Anglo-American coöperation. The two leaders had met but once before, briefly, at Argentia. They now had an opportunity to thrash things out and take each other's measure. In many ways Roosevelt and Churchill were extraordinarily alike; it has been well said that each had more in common with the other than with his military advisers. But there was one essential difference. F.D.R. did not pretend to be an authority on military strategy; the P.M. did. Just as Jefferson Davis felt he knew more about strategy than Johnston or Lee because he had been an officer in the Mexican War; so Churchill felt that his service in Queen Victoria's army, and subsequently as First Lord of His Majesty's Admiralty, made him an authority on strategy. It was often difficult for the British Chiefs of Staff to dissuade him from carrying out some of his peripheral plans for landing in Norway, Dakar, Rhodes, and so on. Roosevelt, too, would have enjoyed romantic military adventures, but he had a natural common sense on strategy and his military advisers kept him on the "straight and narrow." Both men were political maestros, adept at creating and using public opinion, and both had to deal with the opposition inevitable under democratic governments. Both — but Roosevelt to the greater extent — were regarded as "traitors to their class" and hated by the sort of people with whom they had grown up; but both had the enthusiastic support of the masses. Never has there been such a team in coalition warfare as "Winnie" and "F.D.R." Compared with the relations between these two, the principal protagonists in World War I — Lloyd George, Wilson and Clemenceau — were mutually suspicious strangers, and Hitler and Mussolini were a pair of gangsters, each fearing the other would win the most loot.

Before the Arcadia Conference met at Washington, the United States Army planners, led by General Embick, a member of the Supreme War Council during the First World War, had been doing some intensive thinking on ways and means of defeating Germany. After considering every possible method of getting at the heart of the Reich, they reached the conviction that the only way was to mount a large-scale Anglo-American assault in the British Isles and throw it across the Channel, the sooner the better. They were willing to contemplate small peripheral operations to "blood" American troops and "do something"[1] while preparing for the great push; but they opposed, as long as they could, a large-scale invasion of North Africa, as a diversion which would draw off forces needed for the invasion of Hitler's heartland.

The Arcadia Conference disbanded 14 January 1942 without deciding on any campaign for that year; but the British and American joint staffs continued planning as if the North African invasion would come off in May or June. The series of disasters in the Far East, the U-boat blitz, and the victories of Rommel over Auchinleck in Libya, made this timetable impossible to keep, and on 3 March the Combined Chiefs of Staff agreed to scrap it. In view of the beatings the Allies had already taken in Europe and in Asia, any invasion of North Africa must be done in sufficient force to ensure success. But where was the force to come from? The British agreed that we must place garrisons in Nouméa, Fiji, Johnston and Palmyra Islands to guard the lifeline to Australia, and shipping was in short supply — shortly to become shorter, thanks to the U-boats.

On the C.C.S. agenda, North Africa was now replaced by what was known as the "Marshall Memorandum." This was a plan for (1) a cross-Channel beachhead to be established in Normandy in

---

[1] General Marshall told the writer after the war that the one great lesson he learned in 1942 was that the political leaders must "do something"; they could not afford the imputation of fighting another "phony war" that year.

1942 (Operation SLEDGEHAMMER), to be followed by (2) an all-out cross-Channel offensive in 1943 (Operation ROUNDUP), and a push across the Rhine. This plan was accepted in principle by the British Chiefs of Staff on 14 April, after General Marshall and Harry Hopkins had gone to England especially to "sell" it. But, as Marshall realized, this was not, from the British point of view, a firm commitment. The more they looked at it, the less they liked it, especially the 1942 curtain-raiser. In any cross-Channel movement that early, the major part of the troops would have to be British; so the United States could not insist. Large numbers of landing craft would be required; and although, in the United States, Amphibious Force Atlantic Fleet was established with a training center at Little Creek, Virginia, and a construction program for 2500 craft for SLEDGEHAMMER and 8200 for ROUNDUP was set up on 4 April, these had to compete with so many other urgent shipbuilding demands that the target date could not possibly be met.

In May and June events came thick and fast. Molotov visited both Churchill and Roosevelt to plead for a "second front"; Rommel captured Tobruk, which rendered action in North Africa urgent, and the War and Navy Departments made frantic efforts to get more tanks and planes to the British in Egypt, and to the Russians by the dangerous Murmansk route. Churchill visited Washington again, in June, to tell Roosevelt flatly that England could not and would not undertake a cross-Channel operation in 1942.

2. The "Torch" Is Lighted, July

That opened a crisis in Anglo-American relations. The Joint Chiefs of Staff, especially Admiral King and General Marshall, felt that if the British would not set a firm date for a major invasion of

Europe, we were entitled to renege on the "Beat Germany First" decision of 1941, to stop preparing for an invasion that might never take place, and concentrate on the Pacific war. This proposed right-about-face in strategy would greatly have pleased General MacArthur, who in a long message to General Marshall of 8 May 1942 argued seriously that the "second front" should be established under his own command in the Pacific, where it would take the heat off Russia by seriously engaging the armies of Japan. But Japan was not then at war with Russia, nor would be until August 1945. Not only MacArthur, but King, Marshall, and Secretary Stimson strongly opposed the launching of a North African invasion in 1942, as certain to divert and absorb men, ships, aircraft and matériel that would postpone the direct cross-Channel assault indefinitely.

The President himself decided that to turn our backs on Europe was too drastic. Before Churchill left Washington they had convinced each other that something formidable must be laid on in the Atlantic theater for 1942. Since the British would not accept SLEDGEHAMMER, an invasion of North Africa was the only practical alternative. On 24 July 1942 the Combined Chiefs of Staff in London voted timidly and tentatively for Operation TORCH, a simultaneous occupation of Morocco and Algeria, but to postpone a definite decision until mid-September. President Roosevelt, sick of this wrangling and procrastination, used his authority as C. in C. Army and Navy to make it definite next day. Churchill, naturally, accepted what he had wanted all along. On the 26th, General Marshall informed General Eisenhower that he was to be Commander in Chief Allied Expeditionary Force in North Africa. The torch was lit.

This TORCH decision was one of the most momentous in the war. It set up what was supposed to be only a secondary front; but the force of logic, the natural desire to build on foundations that have already cost one dear, pulled more and more Allied forces into the Mediterranean theater — over a million Americans alone. In consequence, the cross-Channel operation was impossible before 1944; and we came measurably close to having it postponed another year.

At this time the Vichy government of France was in control of French Morocco, Algeria and Tunisia; no De Gaullist movement had developed there and no German armed forces were in occupation. Spanish Morocco opposite Gibraltar was under Franco's control, and so neutral. Libya or Tripolitania, the Italian colony between .Tunisia and Egypt, was the battleground between Rommel and Auchinleck, who checked the Germans at the First Battle of El Alamein on 2 July, and was then relieved by the colorful Montgomery, because Churchill felt that Auchinleck had not done well enough. Egypt, nominally independent, was still under strong British occupation and control. On the north side of the Mediterranean, Gibraltar was British, Spain neutral, Southern France neutral under Vichy; Italy, the Balkans and Greece were under Axis control. Malta, after a heroic defense, held firm, and continued an indispensable strategic base for the Allies, and a thorn in the Axis.

The declared objectives of Operation TORCH were to gain control over French Morocco (where the one modern port Casablanca offered an excellent base for antisubmarine warfare), and of Algeria and Tunisia, as bases for further operations against the Axis. Planning began immediately at Combined Headquarters in Norfolk House, London. General Eisenhower arrived there in early August; Admiral Sir Andrew B. ("A.B.C.") Cunningham RN was appointed Allied Naval Commander. D-day was set for 8 November, the very latest date in the fall when amphibious landings on the ironbound outer coast of Morocco were considered possible. The entire operation was broken down as follows:

1. *Western Naval Task Force* — Rear Admiral H. Kent Hewitt USN; lifting and covering Western Task Force U. S. Army,

Major General George F. Patton USA: consisting initially of about 35,000 troops. This all-American section of TORCH was mounted at Norfolk, Virginia. Owing to its geographical separation from the rest of the operation, Western Naval Task Force was given a free hand by Eisenhower and Cunningham. It was divided in three groups for as many separate landings: (*a*) NORTHERN, Rear Admiral Monroe Kelly, to land at Mehedia and thrust up the Wadi Sebou to Port Lyautey; (*b*) CENTER, Captain Robert R. M. Emmet, to land at Fedhala near Casablanca; and (*c*) SOUTHERN, Rear Admiral Lyal A. Davidson, to land at Safi.

2. *Center Naval Task Force* — escorted and covered by the Royal Navy: about 39,000 American ground forces, mounted in the United Kingdom; to capture Oran in Algeria.

3. *Eastern Naval Task Force* — about 23,000 British and 10,000 American troops, mounted in the United Kingdom, escorted and covered by the Royal Navy; to capture Algiers.

We shall have most to say about the Western Naval Task Force, as it was all American, and many of its doings were original, almost fantastic. Except for the landings at Guadalcanal in August, this was the first amphibious operation conducted by the United States in forty-five years; and it is no exaggeration to say that it was one of the boldest ever undertaken.

Amphibious operations are divided into two main categories, of which the most common is the shore-to-shore. In this the troops are lifted a short distance in landing or beaching craft, which take them directly to the beaches; as, for instance, in Operation NEPTUNE-OVERLORD, the great cross-Channel movement of June 1944. In the other kind, ship-to-shore, of which TORCH is a good example, the troops are lifted over long distances in transports, and put ashore in small landing craft that the big ships carry on deck. This was the first time in history that a ship-to-shore operation had been projected across an ocean. It was extremely risky. There was danger of attack by the yet unmastered U-boats during the ocean passage, and while unloading. There was danger from high surf at the target — all landing places faced the Atlantic surges. The beaches selected were commanded by coast defense guns; the French had plenty of ground, air and naval forces to defend their positions in Morocco, and nobody knew what their attitude would be. Secret diplomacy had been at work for months to persuade the French there to welcome us as liberators; but they were all under command of Marshal Pétain at Vichy, and nobody knew whether he would respond to German pressure or to Allied persuasion.

One of the most amazing things about this bold operation was the secrecy with which so great an expeditionary force — 107 sail in the Western Task Force alone, and even more in the two others — was assembled and transported. The Germans knew that something was in the wind, but never guessed what. Hewitt's Western Naval Task Force they knew nothing of; and by careful work with HF/DF, the Navy was able to spot all U-boats then in the Atlantic and route this great force so that it avoided them all. Nevertheless, after it arrived, some U-boats slipped silently in to make easy kills.

All troops of the Western Task Force embarked at Norfolk, and with a strong naval escort sortied 23 October. The Air Group (carrier *Ranger* and converted escort carriers *Suwannee, Sangamon, Santee* and *Chenango,* commanded by Rear Admiral Ernest D. McWhorter) sortied from Bermuda and joined at long. 50° W on the 28th. There were two fuelings at sea, and every ship was a floating school of amphibious warfare. Nobody on board had ever participated in such an operation, and very few had even been in combat.

3. *The Assault on Fedhala and Casablanca, 7–11 November*

On 7 November the sun set at 1745, and enough stars appeared for a fix. At 2300 Commander James M. ("Shady") Lane, navigator of *Brooklyn* (in which your historian sailed) announced that we were closing "High Barbaree." Africa was never so dark and mysterious to ancient sea-rovers as she seemed that night, veiled in clouds and hushed in slumber. Not a light gleamed, not a dog barked, but the wind came off shore, blowing out to the ships the smell of charcoal smoke and of parched dry grass. What countless strategems of this sort have been practised on this very coast, since remotest antiquity! We might have been Portuguese caravels, with sails furled and yards on deck, waiting for the Pole Star clock to register two hours before dawn to move in and slaughter infidels. It has always been thus. You want a couple of hours' darkness to land and surprise the enemy, and then daybreak, so you can tell friend from foe, gold from brass, and wench from wife.

At a quarter-hour before midnight, flagship *Augusta* signaled "Stop," and the transports coasted into their planned unloading positions off Cape Fedhala, eight minutes in advance of schedule. Before eight bells ushered in 8 November, one could hear the clank and clash which told one that the transports were already lowering landing craft. . . . An hour passed. Assault troops were now leaping ashore, rifles in hand, running up the beach and striking for their first objectives. . . . A searchlight shot up from ashore, and then another — the French had heard the humming of landing craft engines and thought they were planes. At morning twilight *Brooklyn* moved toward her fire support position, to knock out a powerful coast defense battery known to Americans as "the Sherki." It and other shore batteries opened fire on us.

A few moments later, there came over the air from the flagship

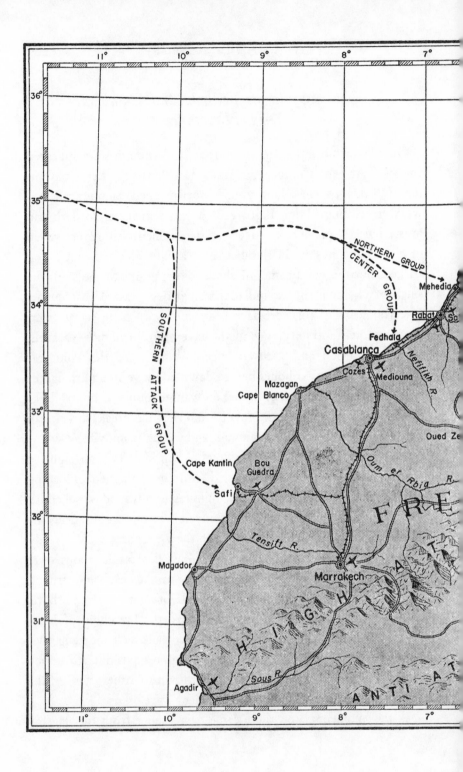

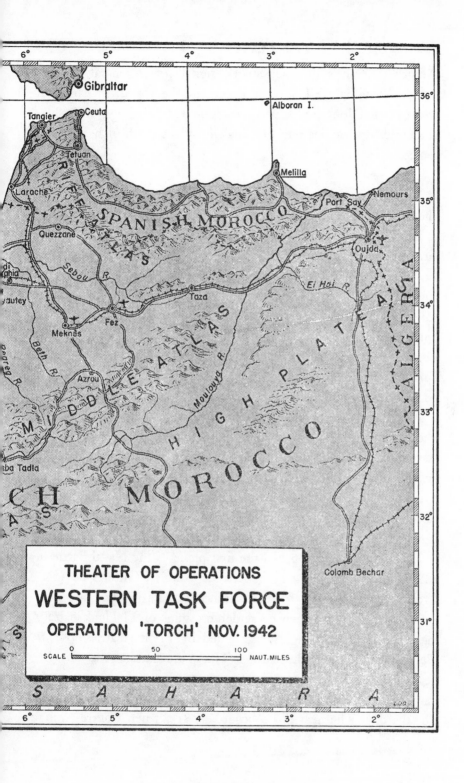

THEATER OF OPERATIONS
WESTERN TASK FORCE
OPERATION 'TORCH' NOV. 1942

SCALE 0   50   100   NAUT. MILES

Admiral Hewitt's long-anticipated signal for a general engagement: "Play Ball!" This little corner of the world, so dark and
silent for five long hours, was now split with blinding gun flashes,
shattered by machine-gun fire, shaken by the crash of heavy ordnance.

It was essential to silence batteries at each end of Fedhala, as
they enfiladed the beaches and their approaches. *Brooklyn* scored
a direct hit on one of the four guns at Sherki, and another on the
fire control station. Ground troops then moved in. The batteries
on Cape Fedhala were harder to find and still more difficult to
knock out; they opened up intermittently on the landing craft and
killed several men. But the landings went on, wave after wave of
small craft, until by 1700 on D-day, 8 November, 7750 officers
and men were ashore. French resistance here was almost nil, but
surf, a falling tide and inexperienced crews brought heavy damage
to landing craft; some 150 out of a total of 350 were expended.

From 0615, when it was barely light enough to launch planes,
the Navy's carrier-based aircraft began to fight. *Ranger*'s Wildcats
destroyed grounded planes at the three principal French airdromes
in Morocco, while her dive-bombers hit the submarine basin in
Casablanca Harbor, and both took part in the naval actions we are
about to relate. *Suwannee*, commanded by Captain "Jocko" Clark,
handled combat air and antisubmarine patrol for the Center Group.

Shortly after 0700 opened the first phase of the Naval Battle of
Casablanca. This was a fight between Admiral Giffen's covering
group (battleship *Massachusetts*, heavy cruisers *Wichita* and *Tuscaloosa*) and four 8-inch coast defense guns of El Hank battery
near the Casablanca lighthouse, aided by French battleship *Jean
Bart* immobilized in the harbor. The shore battery was only silenced temporarily; but *Jean Bart*, whose four 15-inch guns might
have raised havoc in the transport area off Fedhala, was silenced
for the day. The next phase began at 0815, when Contre-Amiral

Michelier, commanding French naval forces at Casablanca, took advantage of a moment when Giffen's big ships were 16 miles off shore to hurl his seven destroyers at the American transports.

Even at this late hour the French did not know whether the ships landing troops on their soil were German, British or American; and they didn't much care; the French Navy's honor was at stake, it was determined to fight. The sortieing destroyers made a few hits on landing craft and destroyer *Ludlow*, but before they could reach the vulnerable transports they were engaged by *Augusta*, *Brooklyn* and two destroyers. The French ships, led by Contre-Amiral Gervais de Lafond in destroyer-leader *Milan*, put up a stout and clever fight, laying a thick smoke screen in and out of which they dodged to shoot; but they were too few and feebly armed, even when assisted by light cruiser *Primauguet* and by eight submarines which had escaped the earlier bombardment of their mooring basin. American gunfire was faster, heavier and more accurate, and carrier-based aircraft had command of the air. Destroyers *Fougueux* and *Boulonnais* blew up and sank; *Primauguet* took a bad beating from the cruisers' gunfire, and was later finished off by air bombing; *Brestois* and *Frondeur* met the same fate. A hit by El Hank battery on *Wichita*, which wounded 14 men, was the only lethal one received by the American ships before action broke off at 1145.

The final score for this day of battle was very onesided. But by the day's end the French Navy had plenty of fight left. El Hank was still intact, and the 15-inch guns of *Jean Bart* were again ready for action.

4. *Mehedia and Safi Assaulted, and Cease-Fire, 7–15 November*

The objective of the Northern Attack Group, commanded by Rear Admiral Kelly in battleship *Texas* and carrying about 9000 men, mostly of the 9th Infantry Division under General Truscott, was to capture the important airdrome of Port Lyautey, several miles up the shoal and winding Wadi Sebou. Escort carrier *Sangamon* carried the fighter and bomber components, and her sister ship *Chenango* stood by waiting for a chance to fly army planes to the airdromes.

It was assumed that the town of Mehedia, with an ancient but well-fortified Kasba citadel at the mouth of the Sebou, must be taken before the river could be used. The Kasba took the initiative at 0700, shelling boat waves and transports, forcing transports to pull out to a point some 15 miles off shore. The result, as General Truscott reported, was that the landings were turned "into a hit-or-miss affair" which "would have spelled disaster" against a determined enemy. The French here were too strong (some 3500 Moroccan *tirailleurs* and Foreign Legionnaires and 14 tanks) and were alerted too early, and our troops got ashore too late, to have a walk-over as at Fedhala. The Kasba, despite efforts of cruiser *Savannah*, did not fall until 10 November — and then to the Army.

The leading naval exploit of this attack was the gallant passage of destroyer *Dallas* (Lieutenant Commander Robert Brodie), a twenty-two-year-old four-piper, up the Sebou. After her net-cutting party had severed the stout wire of the boom at the river-mouth, *Dallas*, carrying a raider detachment of 75 men and guided by a local French pilot, crashed through the rest of the boom at first light 10 November, under fire from the Kasba, threaded her way between sunken hulks, dragged her keel through the soft mud of the river bottom, silenced French guns that fired at her, and landed her raiders without a casualty. Coöperating with a battalion of the 2nd Armored Division United States Army, which marched overland, the raiders captured the airdrome in short order, and by 1030 it was being used by P–40s from *Chenango*.

Everything clicked in the southern attack, on Safi, a little town at a gap in the cliffs 150 miles south of Casablanca, where the French had constructed a small artificial harbor. It was selected as objective partly to box off French forces in Southern Morocco, but mainly as the one place to land tanks. One quay in the harbor was long enough and the water alongside deep enough to berth tank carrier *Lakehurst*, a converted seatrain. She had to be used, as no LST had been completed in time to take part in this operation. There was no other harbor in Morocco that she could enter, except Casablanca — and it was for the capture of Casablanca that these tanks were wanted.

The harbor and all possible beaches were well covered by French artillery. To permit *Lakehurst* to enter and discharge her tanks two 1919-vintage destroyers, *Bernadou* (Lieutenant Commander R. E. Braddy) and *Cole* (Lieutenant Commander G. G. Palmer) were shorn of most of their superstructures and loaded with 350 assault troops to rush into the harbor and take it over before daylight. It worked. *Bernadou*, guided by Ensign J. J. Bell in a rubber scout boat, was just entering the harbor at 0428 November 8 when the French shore artillery started giving her "the works." Cruiser *Philadelphia* and battleship *New York* then started throwing 6-inch and 14-inch shells at the Batterie Railleuse, four 130-mm coast defense guns north of the town, which was making most of the trouble. *Bernadou* miraculously came through unhurt, sweeping the jetties and piers with machine-gun fire, and grounded near the harbor head. Her assault troops clambered down landing nets onto the rocks, and a few minutes later were chasing

Foreign Legionnaires away from the water's edge. *Cole* followed with landing craft trailing, and tied up at a quay. The town of Safi was captured by the raiders, Marrakech airdrome was neutralized by flyers from escort carrier *Santee,* and in the afternoon seatrain *Lakehurst* made a dignified entry and began discharging tanks. They started rumbling along the road to Casablanca on 10 November; but before they had got very far word came through from Admiral Darlan that this little Franco-American war was over.

General Patton's staff on 10 November had drawn plans for an all-out assault on Casablanca next day, and Contre-Amiral Michelier had prepared for desperate resistance. But at 0700 November 11, fifteen minutes before this attack was to start, the French army commander sent Patton a flag of truce. He had received a cease-fire order from Admiral Darlan at Algiers. This was the result of protracted negotiations between that French admiral (Marshal Pétain's second in command in the Vichy government), Robert Murphy of the American Foreign Service, and General Mark Clark USA. Darlan's order, issued at 1120 November 10, brought peace between French and Allied forces in North Africa, but plenty of trouble for metropolitan France.

There was no surrender, no transfer of sovereignty; merely a cease-fire which developed into full coöperation between Allied and French authorities, military and civil. The French naval administration at Casablanca immediately placed port facilities, installations, tugs, pilots and divers at our disposal. Thus, after three days' sharp fighting, the traditional friendship was renewed under the happiest circumstance of making common cause against the Axis powers.

But we had not yet heard from the Axis.

On the evening of 11 November 15 transports and cargo ships of Admiral Hewitt's Western Naval Task Force were still at anchor in Fedhala roadstead. *U–173* worked in between them and the shore, evading their screen and a protective mine field; it torpedoed and sank transport *Joseph Hewes,* then torpedoed but failed to sink oiler *Winooski* and destroyer *Hambleton.* The following evening *U–130,* by using the same tactics, made three victims — transports *Edward Rutledge, Tasker H. Bliss* and *Hugh L. Scott.* Their cargoes were mostly lost, and over a hundred men were killed or died of wounds. On the 15th U.S.S. *Electra* was torpedoed about 17 miles off Fedhala by *U–173,* but, more fortunate than her British namesake in the Java Sea, she did not sink. That U-boat hung around Casablanca too long for its health. Through good teamwork between destroyers *Woolsey, Swanson* and *Quick,* it was sunk off the harbor entrance on 16 November. By that time almost every ship of Admiral Hewitt's group which had not departed was safely inside Casablanca Harbor.

As a definite seal to Darlan's cease-fire order of 10 November, the French admiral, secretly assured by Marshal Pétain of his approval, drew up a formal accord with General Eisenhower and Admiral Cunningham, which was ratified by Churchill and Roosevelt on the 15th. By virtue of this pact, Admiral Darlan became head of the civil government in North Africa and General Giraud, who had escaped from a German prison and been brought to Gibraltar in a submarine commanded by Captain Jerauld Wright, became head of the French armed forces in North Africa. This "Darlan deal" — denounced as a base truckling to Vichy by General de Gaulle and by British and American left-wingers — ensured French coöperation with the Allies, saved very many lives, and prevented an inestimable amount of sabotage and obstruction to Allied military operations.

5. *The Capture of Oran and Algiers,*
8–11 November

Simultaneously with Admiral Hewitt's landings in Morocco, and equally powerful and important, were those of American and British troops, escorted by the Royal Navy, near Oran and Algiers. Both forces were mounted in the United Kingdom, drawing on the United States Army contingents which General Marshall had hoped to use in a cross-Channel operation.

In the small hours of the morning of D-day, 8 November, H.M.S. *Hartland* and *Walney* (former United States Coast Guard cutters transferred to the Royal Navy in 1941) dashed into Oran Harbor carrying a small United States Naval and Marine guard and 400 picked American troops. Unlike *Bernadou*'s assault on Safi, this enterprise was a dismal failure. The local French, alerted, raked both vessels with point-blank fire, sank them, and killed about half their crews and passengers.

The main landings of troops lifted by Center Task Force (Commodore Thomas Troubridge RN), the 1st Infantry Division and part of the 1st Armored Division, United States Army, took place on two sets of beaches, each side of Oran. Those in the Gulf of Arzeu were noteworthy for the use of two British "Maracaibos" — shoal-draft oilers from Venezuela, fitted with a big bow ramp for landing tanks; these were prototypes of the famous LST. The two columns of troops converged on Oran, where all resistance ceased 9 November.

Algiers was taken by the Eastern Naval Task Force, Rear Admiral Sir Harold M. Burrough RN, lifting the Eastern Assault Force, comprising regimental combat teams of the 9th and 34th Infantry Divisions United States Army, and two brigade groups of the British Army, which here outnumbered the American contingent two to one. This force, too, was mounted in the United Kingdom and escorted by the Royal Navy. Five of the transports were American, one of which, *Thomas Stone*, was crippled by a U-boat's torpedo on 7 November, off the Spanish coast. The ships, boat crews and troops of this Force had had only a few days' amphibious training, with the result that the landing, though unopposed, was a complete foul-up. The same state of affairs characterized the unopposed landings from British transports west of Algiers. No fewer than 98 of the 104 landing craft used in all sectors of the Eastern Naval Task Force were expended; a loss so scandalous that the Army put in a bid for taking charge of all future landing operations.

French resistance ceased in and around Algiers on D-day, 8 November, but the Axis picked up the ball, and over a period of a week the big transports unloading were subjected to severe bombing and torpedo attacks by land-based Junkers and Heinkels. U.S.S. *Leedstown* was the principal casualty; she had to be abandoned, and sank.

As a result of this massive three-pronged amphibious operation, North Africa west of Tunisia was denied to the Axis, valuable airdromes, military, naval and antisubmarine bases were secured, and foundations laid for driving the Germans out of North Africa. The Royal and United States Navies had learned far more about amphibious operations than they ever could have done from the most prolonged training and rehearsal; later assaults in the European theater would have failed but for the lessons learned in TORCH. Those lessons were: —

(1) The need of better seamanship and design in small landing craft: the original plywood and rampless "Higgins Boat" proved inadequate, and the Navy henceforth concentrated on building

steel, diesel-powered and ramped types, such as the LCP(R), LCVP and LCM.

(2) The pressing need of big beaching craft — the Landing Ship Tank (LST), Landing Craft Tank (LCT) and Landing Craft Infantry (LCI), to bring in tanks, vehicles and large units of troops quickly.

(3) From the Navy's point of view, the advisability of renouncing tactical surprise in order to deliver gunfire support and land by daylight — a point of view the Army was not yet ready to accept. Owing to the half-hearted, sporadic resistance offered by the French, we had yet to experience a stoutly contested amphibious operation. The Germans would provide that at Salerno, and the Japanese at Tarawa, before the end of 1943.

Bold as Operation TORCH was, and successful within its sphere, it could well have been a little bolder and secured Tunisia too, as Admiral Cunningham wanted. There the Germans beat us at the draw. Admiral Esteva, head of the French government in Tunisia, was well disposed to the Allies but overpowered by German troops arriving by ferry plane. Frenzied efforts were made by the Germans to convert this country into an African bastion, since the British army led by General Montgomery, after winning the Second Battle of El Alamein on 3 November, was slowly and deliberately pursuing Rommel westward. This year 1942 closed on a static situation in Tunisia. The Anglo-American First Army was bogged down in Algerian mud; Montgomery's forces were dusted down by sandstorms; the Germans had occupied the ports of Bizerta, Sousse, Sfax and Gabes.

The Royal Navy, respecting the powerful air forces that the enemy had deployed, was not yet ready to challenge Axis control of the Straits of Sicily. Malta stood firm. But the Axis had won the race for Tunisia.

6. *The Casablanca Conference*

The military campaign for Tunisia, which lies outside the scope of this volume, did not end until 13 May 1943. Axis forces 275,000 strong, which had been pushed into Cape Bon, then completed their surrender to American II Corps (Major General Omar N. Bradley) and British Eighth Army (General Sir Harold Alexander). On 17 May the first Allied trans-Mediterranean convoy since 1941 left Gibraltar, and on the 26th it reached Alexandria without loss. The Suez lifeline now reopened; no longer did ships bound for the Indian Ocean and Australia have to round the Cape of Good Hope.

If TORCH put the Navy on its toes, the Tunisian experience was equally valuable for the Army. There it learned how to fight seasoned German troops, and developed the competence of corps and divisional commanders for a much bigger show. There Generals Bradley and Patton first had a chance to prove their exceptional, though diverse, military qualities. In all three elements — ground, sea and air — British and Americans had learned how to win battles together. Thus, whilst one can argue that TORCH was a mistake, and that the Marshall plan of cross-Channel operations in 1942-1943 should never have been allowed to lapse, almost everyone who studies the Tunisian campaign must conclude that the postponement was correct. We were simply not ready to launch, and still less to follow up, a massive assault on *Festung Europa* in 1942-1943.

Since that had to be postponed, a question arose as before: What could the Allies do in 1943 to engage the Axis and take pressure off Russia? A plenary Combined Chiefs of Staff conference, with President Roosevelt and Premier Churchill, met at Casablanca between 14 and 23 January 1943 to consider that and other questions. This conference ended in a strategic compromise. The

British removed their objection to America's exploiting the initiative she had won in the Pacific; America consented to take part in another Mediterranean operation, and to postpone the cross-Channel invasion until 1944. Both agreed that "the defeat of the U-boat must remain a first charge on the resources of the United Nations," since if that failed, everything would fail. In consequence of that decision, the United States gave "Triple-A" priority to the construction of destroyer escorts, escort carriers and antisubmarine aircraft, placing landing and beaching craft in a lower category. That is why a worldwide shortage of such craft occurred in 1944.

Admirals King and Pound now persuaded the Conference to make Sicily the next objective in order to secure the Mediterranean line of communications, increase pressure on Italy, and divert German forces from the Russian front. The Conference also adopted a rough plan for Operation HUSKY, an Anglo-American invasion of Sicily for July 1943, with General Eisenhower as supreme commander, Admiral Cunningham naval commander and Air Chief Marshal Tedder air commander. American strategists hoped that Sicily would put a stopper on Mediterranean campaigns, so that we could get on with the big cross-Channel invasion. The British, on the contrary, looked on Sicily as another rung of the ladder to what Churchill called the "soft underbelly" of the Axis. Thus, as Admiral King predicted, once we started in the Mediterranean, we would have to go on and on. And the "underbelly" turned out to be boned with the Apennines, plated with the hard scales of Kesselring's armor, and shadowed by the wings of the Luftwaffe.

The other important decision at Casablanca, and the only one made public, was a resolution to accept nothing less than "unconditional surrender" of Germany, Italy and, by implication, Japan. The P.M. and F.D.R. were jointly responsible for the principle, and Roosevelt for the publicity and the phrase, which he remembered vaguely from the history of the Civil War.[2] It was received with joy and acclamation in the Allied countries, where it dispelled the fear of a "Darlan deal" with Hitler, Mussolini and Hirohito, or the adoption of something like a Wilsonian "Fourteen Points," the meaning of which could be argued indefinitely. The decision to utter this rallying slogan was not lightly made. The American, Russian and British people, especially the last two, had suffered so severely that they had to be promised complete victory; no Peace of Amiens, no mere truce which would leave Germany strong enough to start up again. And the Americans felt the same about Japan. But did not "unconditional surrender" help the Axis leaders to persuade their people to fight *à l'outrance*, as the only alternative to virtual "slavery"? Possibly so; probably not. Italy's surrender in 1943 was highly conditional, and both the Nazis and the Japanese war lords, right up to the moment of their complete defeat, imagined that they could make a "deal." In my opinion "unconditional surrender" did not prolong the war a day, and can in no way be considered responsible for our postwar troubles.

7. *The Shipping and Submarine Situation, August 1942–May 1943*

The Casablanca conferees, meeting in an atmosphere of euphoria following the success of TORCH, had eyes bigger than their stomachs, and laid out a strategic menu that they could not digest. Although HUSKY did come off at the target date, it was at the expense of other things — a quick follow-up in the Pacific after the

---

[2] F.D.R. apparently thought that General Grant's initials were expanded to "Unconditional Surrender" owing to the Appomattox affair; he was, however, given the nickname owing to his successful demand for the unconditional surrender of Fort Donelson in February 1862.

securing oi Guadalcanal and Papua, a drive from India toward Akyab in Burma; and the build-up of American forces in Britain for the now postponed cross-Channel operation. Shipping was the bottleneck for everything, and Admiral Doenitz was doing very well in his efforts to squeeze that neck.

In Chapter V, above, we left the antisubmarine situation in June 1942 considerably improved, but it did not long stay improved. Doenitz started a new U-boat blitz in August, which reached its acme in March 1943. He now had echelons of wolf-packs strung across all transatlantic convoy routes between Iceland and the Azores, especially in what we called the "Black Pit" outside the range of land-based aircraft. These tactics were exceedingly difficult to beat; and beaten they were not for eight months. In August 1942, the Allies lost 102 merchant ships of over half a million gross tons to submarine attack, in Atlantic and Arctic waters. Not one transatlantic merchant convoy escaped attack. During the next four months an average of almost a ship a day was lost on the North Atlantic convoy routes, and sinkings in the Caribbean and among unconvoyed merchants ships trying to round the Cape of Good Hope (access to Suez still being closed) were also heavy.

Although the convoy system had been extended, much transatlantic traffic was still carried in unescorted merchant ships with naval armed guards. Their fine fighting spirit is illustrated by the battle of Liberty ship *Stephen Hopkins* (Paul Buck, master) with two armed German ships, Raider "J" armed with six 5.9-inch guns, and blockade-runner *Tannenfels*. These two attacked *Hopkins* at lat. 28° S, long. 20° W, on 27 September 1942. Ensign K. M. Willett USNR and his naval armed guard, operating the freighter's one 4-inch gun, scored 35 hits on Raider "J" and forced her abandonment. After a German shell had exploded the magazine for Willett's gun, the ship's second mate and crew operated two 37-mm guns forward, firing at *Tannenfels*, which was raking their decks with machine-gun fire — Captain Buck maneuvering his ship so as to bring all possible gunfire to bear. This unequal battle continued for almost three hours, when *Stephen Hopkins*, aflame from stem to stern and holed below her waterline, plunged with colors flying; but Raider "J" had preceded her to the bottom. The one undamaged American lifeboat, without charts or navigation instruments, made the coast of Brazil after a voyage of 31 days, with only 15 men of the Liberty ship's crew still alive.

In January, while the C.C.S. and their guests were basking in the sunshine at Casablanca and planning great doings for 1943, one of the worst winters on record was lashing the Western Ocean. Hardly a day passed without snow squalls or bone-chilling rain. Heavy seas broke continuously over vessels' bows, icing their superstructures in the high latitudes. These conditions were even worse for merchant ships than for U-boats, which could get under. During most of the winter the weather was so foul that long-range land-based planes could not fly, and several of those that did never returned. Merchant ship losses by marine casualty alone, for the five months November 1942-March 1943, reached the unprecedented figure of 92 vessels in the Atlantic; 166 for all parts of the world. Sinkings from U-boat attack reached an all-time high in November 1942: 106 ships of 637,907 gross tons. In January 1943, a convoy escorted by four British corvettes from Trinidad to Gibraltar lost seven out of nine tankers.

As a sample, here is what happened to a couple of transatlantic convoys early in 1943. Westbound Convoy ON-166, 63 ships, escorted by Captain P. R. Heineman's unit, comprising U.S.C.G.C. *Spencer* and *Campbell*, five British and Canadian corvettes, and Polish destroyer *Burza*, between 12 and 25 February lost seven merchant ships, but sank two U-boats, one by *Spencer* with depth-charges, one by *Campbell* through ramming and gunfire, after *Burza* had depth-charged it. The escort unit had barely entered the uneasy shelter of Argentia, Newfoundland, when it was ordered out, augmented by U.S.S. *Greer*, to take charge of eastbound

Convoy SC–121, of 56 ships. Thrice in four days (6-9 March) this unfortunate convoy was set upon by wolf-packs. At least seven ships were torpedoed and all but one sunk, with unusually heavy loss of life, including that of the British convoy commodore. The sea was so rough that even *Greer's* veteran sailors on one occasion could not pick up survivors from lifeboats and rafts, and had to let them go. Both in this and the next slow convoy (122), which lost nine ships, and in HX–229 which lost 11 ships on 8-10 March, there were numerous acts of heroism and self-sacrifice on the part of merchant seamen as well as coastguardsmen and bluejackets.

Few outside the two Navies and merchant marines realized how serious the situation had become in March 1943. The U-boats, in this and other areas, sank 108 ships that month, totaling 627,000 tons, and lost only 15 of their number. So many Allied escort vessels were under repair that the group organization was disintegrating. So many U-boats were at sea (an average of 116 operating daily in the North Atlantic) that evasive routing was futile; a convoy avoided one concentration of wolf-packs only to fall into the fangs of another. No enemy ever came so near to disrupting Atlantic communications as Doentiz did that month.

All this had a very damaging effect on Britain's imports. These, the Joint Chiefs of Staff had agreed, early in 1942, must be kept above a certain norm in order to keep her people fighting, producing, and even eating. British imports, owing largely to the work of the U-boats, had declined from a prewar average of over 50 million tons[3] to 23 million in 1942; and by the end of that year Britain was "eating her own tail." In November F.D.R. promised the P.M. to allot England enough newly built merchant ships to raise her imports to a marginal 27 million tons next year. But it was some months before this relief came forth. And as most of the

---

[3] Deadweight tonnage, in tons of 2,240 lbs. each. Apply factor of 1.5 for equivalent in gross tonnage.

follow-up TORCH convoys from the United Kingdom to North Africa had to be under the Red Ensign, food stocks in Britain fell off to a three-months supply in January 1943. In order that England might not "live from hand to mouth," Churchill reduced by half sailings to the Indian Ocean around the Cape, a drastic measure which brought Bengal to the verge of famine.

It was, unfortunately, typical of the hit-or-miss methods of wartime administration that the J.C.S. first heard of the President's promise from Sir John Dill, the C.C.S. representative in Washington. Thus Lieutenant General Brehon Somervell of the U. S. Army Service of Supply, attended the Casablanca Conference both uninstructed and confused. He neither knew what the President had promised, or what his country was able to do about it; and he made a fuzzy sort of agreement with his British opposite number which might be interpreted that we were to give the British 300,000 tons of shipping, or 7 million tons. In March 1943, with the situation clouded by protracted German resistance in Tunisia and U-boat achievements in the North Atlantic, this misunderstanding blew up in everybody's face. To implement the President's promise would require, in April-June, not only 9 million tons of cargo ships to Britain for the rest of 1943, but 14 sailings per month to the Mediterranean to support HUSKY, and 25 sailings per month to the Indian Ocean for the planned drive on Akyab. Churchill wrote severely to Roosevelt "We cannot live from hand to mouth on promises limited by provisos." Admiral King and the other members of the J.C.S. felt, on the contrary, that the important thing was to get on with the war; Britain must tighten her belt. A nasty situation was developing between the military heads of both countries when President Roosevelt took it out of their hands and gave it to a special board of civilians, presided over by Harry Hopkins. On 29 March, Hopkins, Lewis Douglas (then deputy chief of War Shipping Administration), and Sir Anthony Eden, the British Foreign Minister, met with the President at the White House. Douglas presented the case for maintaining the level of British imports if we wished to avoid weakening the entire war effort; he further declared that American armed services' estimates of necessary shipping were generally inflated, and that they wasted tonnage scandalously.[4] Roosevelt decided in Britain's favor, and gave strict orders that his November promise be implemented, as it was. The British import program rapidly revived, and in May the President directed the War Shipping Administration to transfer 15 to 20 new freighters a month to the Red Ensign.

But this presidential promise could never have been kept, and the British people would have approached famine in 1943 but for a dramatic reverse of fortune in the antisubmarine war in April and May.

First came success in antisubmarine operations. The glorious battle of a British escort group under Commander P. W. Gretton RN, to westbound Convoy ONS-5, is regarded both by the Allies and the Germans as a turning-point in the North Atlantic struggle. Doenitz deployed no fewer than 51 U-boats to destroy this 42-ship convoy. The battle raged almost continuously in foul weather from 28 April to 6 May. Thirteen merchantmen (including three Americans) were sunk; but an escort that never numbered more than nine ships sank five U-boats; and two Catalinas — one Canadian and one American — disposed of two more.

This victory was followed by another in the Bay of Biscay offensive which Air Vice Marshal Sir John Slessor of Coastal Command had been conducting since March. His plan was to train bomber planes based on southern England, operating in con-

---

[4] For instance, freighters at places like Nouméa swung around the hook for weeks and even months for lack of unloading facilities. Not until the Okinawa operation in 1945 did the Navy set up a proper administration for controlling shipping, seeing that the turnaround was expedited, and that cargo space was not wasted.

nection with Royal Navy corvettes, to catch U-boats going and coming near their French outports on the Bay. Aircraft-mounted microwave radar, which the Germans could not detect, picked up surfaced U-boats at night, then the new Leigh searchlight illuminated them; and if they were not sunk, a surface unit was homed in to do the job. In May 1943, the results of this Bay offensive, added to others, meant 38 U-boats sunk — 12 more than were built; and three less than the number of merchant ships lost in the Atlantic and Arctic Oceans. The Bay offensive, continuing to the end of the year with American Liberators pitching in to help, broke the back of Doenitz's submarine campaign.

There was also a vast improvement in organization and method. On 1 May 1943, Admiral King organized Tenth Fleet, with himself as commander and Rear Admiral Francis S. Low as chief of staff, to combine "all existing antisubmarine activities." Low — tough, intelligent and hard-working — was a perfect *alter ego* to King, who did not have the time to give this branch of warfare the detailed attention it required. He ruled with an iron hand, but had the respect of his subordinates, who were never allowed to doubt what he wanted, and were never let down.

The destroyer escort (DE) program finally bore fruit. Some 250 of these new escort vessels had been authorized in January 1942, but the shifting of priority work in American shipyards to beaching and landing craft for the cross-Channel operation that never came off so delayed the program that by 2 June only 42 had been launched. They were now produced in such abundance that by December 260 DEs were in commission.

There was a similar delay in building escort carriers. These CVEs, capable of carrying about 24 operating planes, were badly wanted as additional protection to convoys. The first, U.S.S. *Bogue*, got into action in March 1943.[5] At the same time the production of land-based aircraft types suitable for antisubmarine

[5] See Chap. XII for some of their exploits.

work so increased that in the second half of 1943 the Navy was able to relieve the Army Air Force of antisubmarine duties which it had assumed at a time of desperate need. Liberators (PB4Ys, same as the Army B–24s) had a radius of 900 miles from Newfoundland or the British Isles, and smaller bombers had a radius of 500 miles from Greenland or Iceland; but there was still a mid-ocean "black pit" where no air protection could reach a convoy unless brought to it by a CVE. This was not lighted up until late 1943 when Portugal gave the Allies permission to base antisubmarine planes on the Azores.

8. *Operation* HUSKY, *July 1943*

Not even Mr. Churchill expected Operation HUSKY to be soft. As an historian he knew that Greeks, Carthaginians, Romans, Byzantines, Saracens, Normans, Angevins and Spaniards in succession had had their will of this great and fair island, but each conquest had taken years to complete. Sicily had never been so defensible, at least in theory, as in 1943. It contained about a dozen airfields, and its garrison was formidable, at least on paper. The greater part of the island is mountainous, difficult to traverse except by main roads. The Strait of Messina is so narrow that reinforcements can easily be poured in from Italy.

The command setup for Operation HUSKY may best be presented in a diagram: —

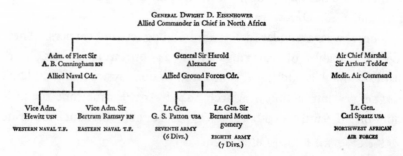

	GENERAL DWIGHT D. EISENHOWER Allied Commander in Chief in North Africa	
Adm. of Fleet Sir A. B. Cunningham RN Allied Naval Cdr.	General Sir Harold Alexander Allied Ground Forces Cdr.	Air Chief Marshal Sir Arthur Tedder Medit. Air Command
Vice Adm. Vice Adm. Sir Hewitt USN Bertram Ramsay RN WESTERN NAVAL T.F. EASTERN NAVAL T.F.	Lt. Gen. Lt. Gen. Sir G. S. Patton USA Bernard Mont- gomery SEVENTH ARMY EIGHTH ARMY (6 Divs.) (7 Divs.)	Lt. Gen. Carl Spaatz USA NORTHWEST AFRICAN AIR FORCES

General Eisenhower, preoccupied with the Tunisian campaign and bedeviled by the rivalries of De Gaulle, Giraud and other French leaders in Africa, was unable to give much attention to planning HUSKY. Most of the essential work was done at Hewitt's and Cunningham's headquarters in Algiers, and General Patton's at Mostaganem, 165 miles distant — much too distant for proper planning. For D-day, the night of 9-10 July was chosen because the moon set around 0230; the Air Forces wanted moonlight for their paratroop drop, and the Army wanted darkness to commence landing at 0245. Nine Allied divisions (four American, four British and one Canadian) were available for the initial assault, and about the same number of German and Italian divisions were expected to be on hand to oppose. The plan finally selected in mid-May, after much wrangling, provided for Hewitt's Western Naval Task Force to land on three sets of beaches near Licata, Gela and Scoglitti on the southwest coast of Sicily, and the Brit⋅h ⋅o land on beaches around the southeastern cape of the island. Patton would drive across the island to secure Palermo, and then swing east to Messina, while Montgomery drove north to Syracuse, Augusta, Catania and Messina.

This was a poor strategic plan, better calculated to push the Axis forces out of Sicily than to trap them in Sicily. But its chief weakness lay in the refusal of the United States Army Air Forces to coöperate, largely because General "Tooey" Spaatz was wedded to the concept of "strategic" air operations — which meant the A.A.F. fighting its own war. He planned to devote practically his entire strength to fighting the Luftwaffe and the Royal Italian Air Force; and not until two weeks before D-day did Spaatz even let Hewitt and Patton know that this was his intention. The A.A.F. and R.A.F. opened this Sicilian campaign on 2 July with an implacable, day-and-night hammering of enemy headquarters and of ten or twelve Sicilian airfields, which were rendered temporarily unusable. But the amphibious expedition sailed and landed with no promise of tactical support from the air, and almost none did it obtain.

An important air unit, which came under Seventh Army, not the A.A.F., and which greatly helped, was the 82nd Airborne Division (Major General Matthew B. Ridgway usa). This, the first paratroop division in the United States Army, made its combat debut in husky. Its mission was to seize high ground and the Ponte Olivo airfield behind the landing beaches, confuse the defense and prevent a prompt counterattack on the beachhead. This division no more than the Navy could obtain night fighter protection from the Army Air Force. The A.A.F. did have night-flying fighter planes and pilots, but had other uses for them.

"The capture of Sicily was an undertaking of the first magnitude," as Churchill wrote. Measured by the strength of the initial assault, it breaks all records for amphibious operations; even the Normandy landings next year exceeded it only if follow-up echelons are counted. Admiral Hewitt had 580 ships, and Admiral Ramsay had 795 ships under their respective commands. In addition Vice Admiral Sir Algernon Willis rn commanded a Royal Navy covering force of six battleships, six cruisers and 24 destroyers. The nature of the operation was part ship-to-shore, part shore-to-shore, this last being made possible by the arrival in North Africa of the first big beaching craft,[6] the 1500-ton, 328-foot Landing Ship Tank (LST), the 550-ton, 112-foot Landing Craft Tank (LCT), and the 200-ton, 158-foot Landing Craft Infantry Large — LCI(L). The biggest of these, the LST, modified from a British design, were built at Newport News, trained in Chesapeake Bay, and early in 1943 began crossing the Atlantic on their own bottoms, as the LCI did too. LCTs came over on the decks of LSTs or on freighters. Admirals Conolly and Hall,

---

[6] These three types, and the Landing Ship Medium (LSM), are designated "beaching craft" to distinguish them from the landing craft proper that are small enough to be carried on the decks or davits of transports. Dimensions here given are those of the three types used in husky; later ones varied somewhat.

who had specially interested themselves in these types, experimented with them to ascertain their capabilities, and used them extensively in HUSKY.

According to Thucydides, the Greeks who invaded Syracuse in 413 B.C. had most to fear from the Sicilian cavalry, against which, for want of a Landing Ship Horse, their only defense was archery. Enemy tanks, the modern cavalry, are now the bane of amphibious landings. In order to prevent their working havoc on the GIs it was necessary to land our own tanks and antitank guns with or immediately after the assault troops. That was the main function of the LST and LCT. These craft were supposed to be able to ground on a beach and lower their ramps, over which tanks, guns and vehicles could roll ashore. The LCI beached and then lowered bow gangways, not unlike the "brows" of a Greek bireme, for infantry to land without boating or swimming. Unfortunately, most of the Sicilian beaches were protected by sand bars with enough water to float landing craft but not an LST. The dukw, an amphibious truck which could carry 25 troops or 2½ tons of cargo, swim in the water and roll over the land, and required only one driver, also made its European debut in HUSKY. The great advantage of the dukw was its ability to carry supplies from a ship to an inland dump without handling at the water's edge.

The Axis was partly, but not completely, surprised by the Sicilian assault. Hitler, swallowing a clever British "plant" to the effect that the real objectives were Sardinia and Greece, dispatched reinforcements to both places; but Marshal Kesselring, the German commander in Italy, was not fooled and sent a panzer division to Sicily as reinforcement. That added up to two German and four Italian combat divisions, in addition to six Italian coastal divisions which were composed mostly of over-age Sicilian reservists.

There were over 300,000 men under arms in Sicily when the Anglo-American expeditionary force landed on 10 July 1943,

TYRRHENIAN

932

799 782 767

422 C. Gallo

93 501 C.S.Vito 359 Carini PALERMO 22 C. Zafferano
Gulf of Gulf of Termini
470 Castellammare Monreale 70 23 36
75 Termini
TRÁPANI M.Erice Lascari
I. Lévanzo 23 Castellammare 2379 5886
38° AEGADES IS. Milo Segesta 24 MADO
I. Favignana Calatafimi Camporeale 5292 Caltavuturo
I. Grande Chinisia 1148 1440 L
C. Lilibeo 1450 1312 1949 Corleone e 21
Marsala Salemi Gibellina 1211 o Lercara
86 Castelvetrano 22 MONTI Prizzi 21 3303 Castronovo 20
98 23 SICANI 3120
54 Mazara Bivona 1650 Cammarata 2805
81 38 Campobello S. Stefano Casteltermini 19
Selinunte 2120 Quisquina 20 3 1466 S. Cataldo 2050
31 Sciacca 20 2211 1510 2380 Serradifalco 18
37 38 Ribera Platani R. Aragona SEVENTH 1542 nicatti 12
68 XX 2 Raffadali 18 Summatina
40 79 COMMITTED 91 31 17 AGRIGENTO Favaro 12
134 ON 20 JULY Porto Naro Campobello
42 80 62 212 XX 82 Empedocle 16 Palma Ravanusa
COMMITTED 27 Marina
75 ON 18 JULY di Palma
Torre di Goffe
29 M. SOLE XX 3 Licata
145 Gulf

SICILY
1943

U.S. & British Lines of Advance in Black
Numbers (10)–(24) Indicate Day of July When Occupied
Heights in Feet, Soundings in Fathoms
Nautical Miles

0   10   20   30   40
0   10   20   30   40   50
Statute Miles

KEY

══════════ Principal roads
++++++++++ Railroads
– – – – – – 100-meter contour, marking edge of plain
············ 50-fathom line

309

205

420

F.J.W.

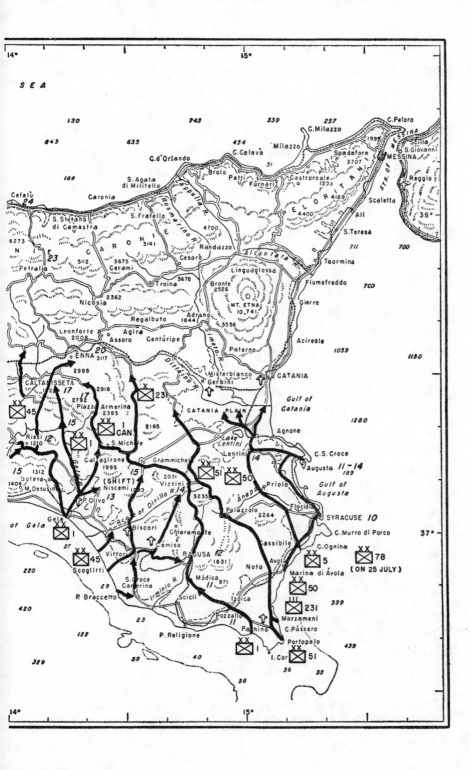

and the Luftwaffe, the German Air Force, had about 1000 serviceable planes within flying distance of the landings. On the other hand, Mussolini prudently kept his Navy in protected harbors such as Spezia, the German Navy was represented by only a few U-boats and motor torpedo boats, and the Italian air force consisted largely of obsolete planes. Another asset to the invaders was the friendly attitude of the Sicilians, and of the Mafia or "Black Hand." Gangsters and peasants alike hated Germans, were fed up with the Duce, and looked on their invaders as liberators.

Admiral Hewitt's Western Naval Task Force, mounted at or staged through six different harbors along the Algerian and Tunisian littoral, ran into a sharp and sudden *mistral* north of Malta that blew up a high breaking sea. This tested the endurance of the new beaching craft and the seamanship of their crews; both met it magnificently.

Carrying to a lower level the diagram at the head of the last section, Hewitt's Western Naval Task Force was divided three ways from west to east: Rear Admiral Conolly's Joss Force, to land Major General Truscott's 3rd Infantry Division[7] on beaches near Licata; Rear Admiral John L. Hall's Dime Force, to land Major General Terry Allen's 1st Infantry Division on beaches near Gela; and Rear Admiral Alan G. Kirk's Cent Force, to land Lieutenant General Omar N. Bradley and II Corps staff, and Major General Troy Middleton's 45th Infantry Division, on beaches near Scoglitti. Conolly, Hall and Kirk, as well as Admiral Hewitt, were experienced practitioners of amphibious warfare. Kirk had relieved Hewitt as Comphiblant, and as such trained his Cent Force in Chesapeake Bay. Hall, who came to Africa as Hewitt's chief of staff, had been Comphibforce Northwest African Waters since early in the year.

[7] All these divisions were "reinforced" and had so many "attached" units that the average number of officers and men in each of these three landings was 24,000.

Up to a certain point the story of these three landings is similar. Although their targets were miles apart, the military objective was the same: to establish a beachhead as a base from which to begin the march on Palermo and Messina. It had to be deep enough so that boats, ships and beaches would be outside enemy artillery range.

On the evening of 9 July the Western Naval Task Force, still undetected, was fast approaching the Sicilian shore. Beacon submarines, to help the vessels find their targets with infra-red blinkers, were stationed about five miles off each set of beaches. In addition, Joss Force had destroyer *Bristol* five miles south of the submarines, and a PC south of her; three lampposts to help the new beaching craft find their way.

There is nothing in warfare to be compared with the hushed tension of the final approach in a night landing. Everything ahead is uncertain. There is no sound but the rush of waters, the throbbing of your ship's engines and of your own heart. You can see nothing but the ship ahead and the ship astern. The shore, if dimly visible, is shrouded in darkness. A few mistakes on our part, or clever thrusts by the enemy, may utterly wreck a vast, long-planned effort. There can be no drawn battle, no half-success, in an amphibious landing; it is win all splendidly or lose all miserably.

The enemy was not entirely surprised, but unready. Many officers of Italian coastal divisions, in view of the foul weather, turned in; and German search-radar crews could not believe the enormous "blips" they saw on their screens. Small groups of beach defenders commonly deserted their pillboxes in panic when they saw the imposing and terrifying spectacle revealed by the first light of dawn. There had been nothing like it in Sicilian history since the Athenian expedition against Syracuse, "no less famous for its wonderful audacity, and for the splendor of its appearance, than for its overwhelming strength," as Thucydides wrote. As

Sicilians later described the scene to me, "There were thousands of vessels in the roadstead; one couldn't see the horizon for the ships." The Allies had ringed a good third of Sicily with a wall of ships, no power on earth could prevent them from establishing beachheads, and it would take more power than the Axis had to keep them from taking the island.

Conolly's Joss landings around Licata were noteworthy for the skill with which the LCIs and LCTs beached in rough surf to land troops and tanks, and for naval gunfire support. Every large troop unit carried a shore fire control party which communicated by "walkie-talkie" radio with a destroyer or cruiser of Rear Admiral Laurance DuBose's Support Group (cruisers *Brooklyn* and *Birmingham*, destroyers *Buck* and *Ludlow*) and frequently asked them to put a few shells on a spot where the enemy showed resistance. By noon General Truscott was setting up his command post in the city of Licata. Already 3000 Italian troops had been taken prisoner. The Joss Force landings were smooth and successful, securing the left flank of the Allied assault, and a port for follow-up.

Rear Admiral Hall's Dime Force, which landed around Gela, encountered the toughest opposition, and had the satisfaction of repelling two enemy tank assaults with naval gunfire. Here most of the troops came in big transports and were taken ashore in landing craft. The first boats hit the beach exactly at H-hour, 0245. Everything went smoothly until dawn brought enemy air attacks. At 0458, just as daylight began to spread over the sea, destroyer *Maddox*, on antisubmarine patrol several miles off shore, was attacked by a Stuka. A bomb exploded under her propeller guard, demolishing the stern and exploding the after magazine. Within two minutes *Maddox* rolled over and sank, taking down her C.O., Lieutenant Commander Sarsfield, and most of her crew.

Cruisers of the Dime Force Support Group, without waiting for fire-support parties to issue invitations, catapulted their float planes to look for targets. One of these cruisers was *Boise*, repaired better than new after her battering in the Battle of Cape Esperance, and with Captain L. Hewlett Thébaud as C.O.; the other was *Savannah*, Captain R. W. Cary. Since their float planes had no fighter protection, most of them were shot down by Messerschmitts; but one at 0830 reported two columns of about 25 Italian tanks each approaching the beachhead. *Boise's* 6-inch fire stopped one column and destroyer *Shubrick* deprived the other of several units. *Boise* also silenced a shore battery that was enfilading the beach, and Admiral Ramsay kindly lent Admiral Hall H.M. monitor *Abercrombie*, to plant a few 15-inch shells on Niscemi, eight miles inland. Thus naval gunfire played the role of the Athenian archers against Sicilian cavalry in the famous invasion of 413 B.C.

One of the bottlenecks in amphibious operations has always been the congestion of supplies on the beaches. Army shore parties are supposed to carry the bales, boxes and other stuff to supply dumps; but they hate the job, and never do it fast enough. By nightfall D-day the Gela beaches were so congested that some landing craft had to return to their ships fully loaded; others, which had managed to find a spot to beach, swamped through their open ramps because nobody would help their exhausted crews to unload. The enemy had almost complete control of the air over the beachhead, while A.A.F. and R.A.F. flew "strategic." A renewal of tank counterattacks at daylight was certain, but how could they be met? *LST–313*, carrying all antitank guns of Dime Force, had been destroyed at sunset on D-day by a Messerschmitt. Other LSTs carrying tanks could not get into the beach over the bars. Thus the main burden of supporting the 1st Infantry Division in a really tough assault by a German tank column on 11 July fell on the Navy. Intermittently, over a period of ten hours, two cruisers and eight different destroyers fired on enemy tanks and infantry, advancing or retreating, destroyed half the tanks and demoralized

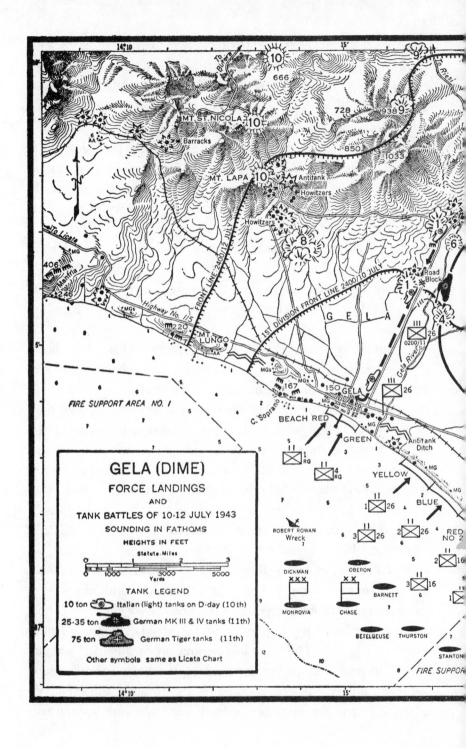

GELA (DIME)

FORCE LANDINGS

AND

TANK BATTLES OF 10-12 JULY 1943

SOUNDING IN FATHOMS

HEIGHTS IN FEET

TANK LEGEND

10 ton — Italian (light) tanks on D-day (10th)

25-35 ton — German MK III & IV tanks (11th)

75 ton — German Tiger tanks (11th)

Other symbols same as Licata Chart

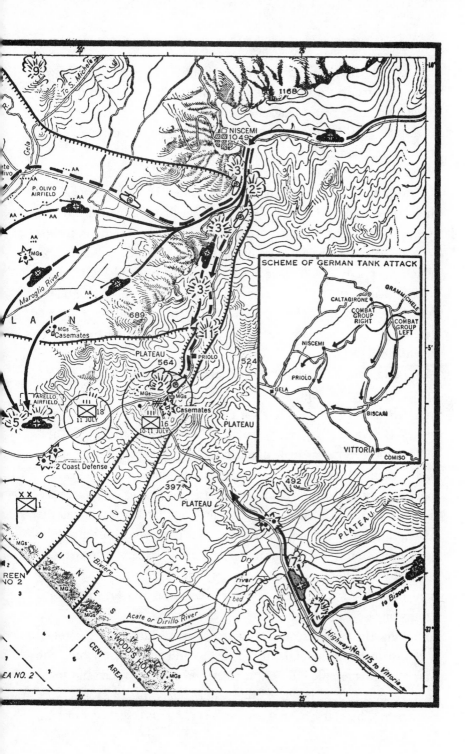

NISCEMI
1049

P. OLIVO
AIRFIELD

689

PLATEAU
564

PRIOLO

524

PLATEAU

FARELLO
AIRFIELD

MGs
Casemates

Casemates

11 JULY

10-11 JULY

PLATEAU

2 Coast Defense

397

492

PLATEAU

PLATEAU

DUNES

Acate or Dirillo River

Dry

river

bed

Highway No. 115 to Vittoria

to Biscari

REEN
NO 2

WOOD'S HOLE

CENT AREA

EA NO. 2

Maroglio River

To S. Michele

Gela

MGs

L A I N

1168

SCHEME OF GERMAN TANK ATTACK

CALTAGIRONE

GRAMMICHELE

COMBAT
GROUP
RIGHT

COMBAT
GROUP
LEFT

NISCEMI

PRIOLO

GELA

BISCARI

VITTORIA

COMISO

the foot soldiers. Next day naval gunfire supported our own advancing troops, up to eight miles inland. "So devastating in its effectiveness," wrote General Eisenhower, was this shooting, "as to dispose finally of any doubts that naval guns are suitable for shore bombardment."

On the other hand, the paratroops won naval converts owing to the magnificent job done by Colonel James M. Gavin's RCT of the 82nd Airborne Division. This was the first troop airdrop ever attempted at night, so it is not surprising that the 3400 paratroops were dispersed along 60 miles of coast. But a part of one battalion which dropped behind Gela held up a German tank column on D-day, harassed the retreating tanks on the 11th, and greatly contributed to the confusion between the Italian and the German defenders. We shall later see Airborne playing a vital role in the Normandy operation.

In Admiral Kirk's Cent Force area, centered on the fishing village of Scoglitti, high surf and outlying rocks were very troublesome to landing craft. Here is a sample incident. A boat from transport *Thomas Jefferson*, commanded by Ensign G. P. Limberis USNR, seeking a small beach in pitchy darkness, hit instead a rocky point. The troops, understandably, flinched from debarking in heavy surf on a rockbound coast; but "after much persuasion," reported the ensign, "every man in my boat was on the beach, and crew and myself salvaged the two .30-caliber machine guns and a few rounds of ammunition." Four Italians who manned a nearby machine gun were so astounded at this exploit that they promptly surrendered. Presently Limberis and his men heard shouts and screams in the water. Two boats in the second wave, following the same erroneous course, had collided and swamped when their coxswains sighted the rocks and tried to sheer off. The first-comers scrambled down the steep and slippery rocks and managed to pull four GIs out of the water, but some 38 others were drowned. The third boat wave, at 0415, barely escaped crashing and put its troops ashore safely on the rocky point, but lost five boats out of seven. The combination of heavy surf, want of definite landmarks, and inexperienced boat crews made landing craft casualties in Cent area almost as great as in the Moroccan landings of Operation TORCH.

The saddest event in the American sector was the shooting down of transport aircraft towing gliders carrying American paratroops. General Ridgway decided on the morning of 11 July to lay a big airdrop on Farello, which, as he did not know, was already occupied by American troops. His opposite number ordered a similar one in the British sector. There was not enough time to inform ships and army units ashore what was coming. The route for the transport planes and gliders lay right along the battle front, and over the ships, whose antiaircraft gunners were trigger-happy after two days of frequent air attack. Between 2150 and 2300 the Germans sent in a heavy air raid — 24th of that busy day — wherein the Axis committed 381 planes against ships off the assault beaches. Right on top of that came our own transport planes. Recognition signals were of no avail in the tracer-filled night sky; antiaircraft gunners ashore and on shipboard fired at friend and foe alike. Twenty-three of the 144 planes which took off from Tunisia failed to return and 37 were badly damaged; almost one hundred officers and men were killed or missing. A special board was convened by General Eisenhower to study this airdrop, and a similarly shot-up one over the British sector. It concluded that these tragic fiascos were caused by not allowing sufficient time to notify friendly ground and naval forces, flying over them during an enemy bombing attack, and at such low altitudes as to make I.F.F. inoperative.[8] These errors were not repeated.

In justice to the Air Forces, we must remember that their

[8] I.F.F. ("Identification Friend or Foe") was a radio device by which friendly planes flashed a coded signal so that they would not be mistaken for enemy.

main efforts against enemy airfields and lines of communication were so successful that air attacks on the amphibious forces were kept to a minimum, and none were delivered in the American sector after 13 July. The British sector, lying nearer mainland airdromes, continued to catch it nightly under the waxing moon, and as soon as the United States naval forces came around to Palermo, the Luftwaffe found them again.

9. *Sicily Secured, July–August 1943*

For reasons of space, I shall have to pass rapidly over the British landings of Vice Admiral Sir Bertram Ramsay's Eastern Task Force, between Formiche, on the west side of Cape Passero, and Cassibile, not far south of Syracuse. The Royal Navy's part was conducted with the same verve and efficiency as that of the United States Navy. The British had the easier meteorological conditions for landing, as their beaches were sheltered from the wind on D-day, but they suffered more from enemy air attack. The American troops met stouter initial opposition, but after 15 July it was the other way round. Although the British and Americans landed on different sections of the coast, a close coördination was maintained between upper levels of command, and the two navies got along so well that a more intimate intermingling could be attempted in the next operation.

Before that could start, Sicily had to be conquered.

On the night of 12-13 July, after the beachheads were secure and enemy dispositions had been felt out, General Alexander's staff drew up a plan and issued directives. Montgomery was to thrust one army corps due north to Catania, while a second corps took the road to Enna and continued to the north coast at San Stéfano, "to split the island in half." Patton's Seventh Army would pivot on its left and overrun the central and western parts of the island. In other words, "Monty" was to wield the sword and "George" hold the shield. This unfortunate reversal of the rôles proper and congenial to their respective characters was the result of Alexander's belief that American troops were not much good.

Marshal Kesselring flew to General Guzzoni's headquarters at Enna on 12 July to find out what was going on. What he saw and heard deflated his optimism. The Allied landings everywhere had been successful. In two days' time, 80,000 men and 8200 vehicles, tanks and guns had been landed. The German tank attack had failed ignominiously. Syracuse and Augusta had fallen to the British. Several airfields were already in Allied possession. Kesselring realized that there was nothing left but to fight a delaying action. He flew back to Rome and informed Mussolini that, owing to the failure of his troops to stop the landings, it would be impossible to defend Sicily. Il Duce beat his breast and bellowed, "It must not be!" but it was; and two weeks later the King of Italy straightened his short back and fired Mussolini. His successor, Marshal Badoglio, issued a brash statement about prosecuting the war "with renewed vigor," but nobody believed that; and he told the little king that the war was absolutely and completely lost.

Seventh Army overran the western half of the island in record time. General Patton made a triumphal entry to Palermo on 22 July, riding between cheering throngs, and appropriately set up Seventh Army headquarters in the palace of *Il Re Ruggiero*, the twelfth-century Norman king. Only a few hours later, the United States Navy arrived at Palermo, in the shape of Motor Torpedo Boat Squadron 15, Lieutenant Commander Stanley M. Barnes. Next came Captain Charles Wellborn's Destroyer Squadron 8 (*Wainwright*, flag), and several minesweepers. On 27 July, when Palermo Harbor was first opened to Allied shipping, Admiral Hewitt organized these and the few other United States warships left in Sicilian waters into "General Patton's Navy" to support Seventh Army. As such, it had plenty to do: defending Palermo from an Italian Navy raid, giving gunfire support to Patton as he advanced along the coast, providing amphibious craft for "leap-frog" landings, and ferry duty for heavy artillery, supplies and vehicles to relieve congestion on the coastal road.

Rear Admiral Davidson commanded the support force. This tall, lanky flag officer, firm in decision and quiet of speech, never lost his temper. He inspired confidence. His flagship *Philadelphia*, with cruiser *Savannah* and six destroyers, steamed into Palermo during the forenoon watch 30 July. There was no chance of their collecting barnacles on their bottoms. General Patton asked for gunfire support next day and was obliged with a vigorous bombardment of shore batteries near San Stéfano. From Palermo, Patton pushed east along the coastal road to Messina, using the Navy to make short hops from place to place along the shore; but the Germans always kept one jump ahead of him.

In the British sector, Montgomery was held up for a week by stout German defense of the plain south of Catania. In contrast to Patton, "Monty" (as Admiral Cunningham has written) made no use of amphibious opportunities, and very little of naval gunfire support. Consequently General Patton, approaching Messina by two legs of the triangle, reached it first, on 17 August. But that was slight satisfaction, as Montgomery's slow and cautious advance along the coast gave the Axis sufficient time to evacuate three good German divisions with all their weapons and most of their armor across the Strait of Messina. The Italian Army, too, got out.

In the land campaign by Seventh Army it has been well said that the ordinary, run-of-the-mine GI now proved himself to be a first-class fighting man. The dash to Palermo, the battle of Troina, and other actions in Sicily deserve to be among the proudest in American military annals. One only regrets that, owing to General Alexander's bad judgment, General Patton was not allowed to wield the sword instead of the slow-moving, methodical Montgomery.

Leadership in the Western Naval Task Force was superb. Admirals Hewitt, Kirk, Hall and Conolly, to mention only the force commanders, showed intelligence in planning and skill in execution that marked them for honors and promotion. Yet the heroes of the western landings were the crews of the landing and beaching craft, mostly very young reservists, many of whom had never even smelled salt water before 1943. These were the last link in a chain that started in American shipyards and factories, which included military bases painstakingly developed in North Africa, warships and transports and three reinforced Army divisions, with their supplies, vehicles, armor and equipment. All these troops and the bulk of their matériel depended, to get ashore safely, on beaching or small landing craft. Boats under reserve ensigns or enlisted coxswains had to negotiate five miles or more of strange waters, often with nothing but a wobbly compass to guide them through the night, to locate targets in the dark, beach their craft, and provide their own support against enemy gunfire while discharging troops and equipment. Surprisingly few mistakes were made. The beaching craft, with slightly more experienced leadership, had even more complicated and difficult tasks. If these crews had failed, the entire American part of Operation HUSKY would have failed, and the British would have been left to carry the war into Sicily unsupported. All honor, then, to these lads of the last link, since they proved themselves to be brave, strong and resourceful. Although their names are not recorded on bronze tablets, let their deeds be kept in fresh memory by the nation and the cause that they served.

CHAPTER IX

Forward in the Pacific

March 1943–April 1944

1. *Alternate Plans for Defeating Japan*

WE LEFT the Pacific on 9 February 1943, with Guadalcanal secured. Three weeks earlier the Papuan campaign had been concluded. General Eichelberger, whom MacArthur had ordered "to take Buna or not come back alive," led his Australian and American troops through a stinking malarial jungle, and captured Gona (9 December), Buna (2 January), and Sanananda (18 January 1943). The naval aspect of this campaign was limited to bringing supplies from Australia via Milne Bay to an Allied base on the north coast of Papua, mostly by small armed Australian and Dutch merchant vessels, covered by American PTs. Rear Admiral Barbey's VII Amphibious Force was training in Australia, but as yet it had no LSTs or other beaching craft.

All this was part of Operation WATCHTOWER which started with Guadalcanal, and whose object was to breach the Bismarck barrier, the route to Japan favored by General MacArthur. He wished the entire weight of the Pacific Fleet to be placed under his command, to cover troop movements along this "New Guinea-Mindanao Axis" to the Philippines. Admirals King and Nimitz did not deny the value of that route, but wished to use an alternate one as well; to project a series of amphibious operations across the Central Pacific, via the Gilbert, Marshall, Caroline and Mariana Islands. Their chief argument against the MacArthur plan was very cogent.

As long as the Micronesian "spider webs" which Japan had spread over the Central Pacific were in her possession, enemy air forces could attack everything that moved along the New Guinea–Mindanao Axis. These webs must be swept up with the Pacific Fleet broom, and a second and shorter route opened to Tokyo.

A third plan which might have been incorporated with Mac-Arthur's never came off. This was for a British comeback through the Indian Ocean and the Straits of Malacca to recover Burma and Singapore and control the South China Sea. Admiral King was eager to have this done by Admiral Lord Mountbatten, the British commander in Southeast Asia whom both he and General Marshall admired. Unfortunately it was postponed again and again, because whenever Lord Louis managed to build up landing craft and naval forces, they were taken away from him to feed the hungry maw of the Mediterranean.

The main thing, in early 1943, was to get on with Operation WATCHTOWER. But nothing substantial was done for five months. The Joint Chiefs of Staff could promise no reinforcement to the Pacific Fleet while U-boats remained a major threat, Tunisia was still being fought over, and the invasion of Sicily was coming up. But the principal reason for this delay was the same shipping shortage that bedeviled the Allies in Europe, and lack of aircraft carriers. When the *Essex*-class carriers began to come out, in answer to the prayers of Pacific sailors, we were ready to go.

2. *In Aleutian Waters, March–August 1943*

During this pause there were fleet and troop movements as far north as the Bering Sea. No operations in this region of almost perpetual mist and snow accomplished anything of importance or had any appreciable effect on the outcome of the war. It was a theater of military frustration. Both sides would have done well to leave the Aleutians to the few Aleuts unfortunate enough to live there. But the Japanese, as part of the Midway offensive, had occupied Attu and Kiska, the two westernmost islands, as northern anchors to their "ribbon defense"; and as such, American strategists felt obliged to set them adrift.

For over nine months after Midway, events in this sector were a sequence of naval bombardment by us which did no damage, reinforcement missions by the enemy which accomplished nothing, and operations by United States submarines which usefully diminished the Japanese merchant marine. Finally, on 26 March 1943, a really interesting event broke: the Battle of the Komandorski Islands. A small task group under Rear Admiral Charles H. McMorris fought a retiring action against a Japanese force of twice its size and fire power; the battle lasted without a break for three and a half hours of daylight; the contestants slugged it out with gunfire at ranges of eight to over twelve miles, without intrusion by air power or submarines. It was a miniature version of the sort of fleet action that the Navy, after World War I, expected to fight in the next war, with the important difference that neither side did the other any great damage.

Admiral McMorris's task group had been cruising on a north-south line west of Attu for several days in order to intercept Japanese reinforcement of that island. He flew his flag in twenty-year-old light cruiser *Richmond* (Captain T. W. Waldschmidt); with him were heavy cruiser *Salt Lake City* (Captain Bertram J. Rodgers), repaired and freshly overhauled since the Cape Esperance battle, and four destroyers under Captain Ralph S. Riggs.[1]

At 0800 March 26, a clear calm day with temperature just above freezing, this task group ran slap into Vice Admiral Hosogaya's Northern Area Force of two heavy cruisers (*Nachi*, flag), two light cruisers and four destroyers, about halfway between Attu

---

[1] *Bailey*, Lt. Cdr. J. C. Atkeson; *Coghlan*, Cdr. R. E. Tompkins; *Dale*, Cdr. A. L. Rorschach; *Monaghan*, Lt. Cdr. P. H. Horn.

and Kamchatka. The ensuing action, fought south of the Komandorski Islands, resembled the Battle of the Java Sea a year earlier. Hosogaya here, like Takagi there, was escorting and covering a reinforcement group of transports and freighters; and McMorris here, like Doorman there, first tried to get at the transports, but soon had to fight for his life. The outcome was very different.

At 0840, before the American ships had had time to change from scouting line to battle order, the enemy opened fire on *Richmond* at 20,000 yards, made a close straddle on the second salvo, then shifted gunfire to *Salt Lake City*. Throughout the action this heavy cruiser received almost all the enemy's attention. She commenced return fire with her forward turrets at 0842, and at a range of over ten miles made hits on *Nachi* with her third and fourth salvos, starting fires that were quickly brought under control.

Nachi now launched a salvo of eight torpedoes which failed to score because of the extreme range; and the same thing happened to all other Japanese torpedoes launched in this fight. *Salt Lake* was now doing some fancy shooting at long range, and all that time nimbly darting and pirouetting like a ballet dancer to throw off the enemy aim. Captain Rodgers "chased salvos" [2] with notable success. Flagship *Richmond* and the destroyers conformed their movements to hers; old "Swayback Maru," as the sailors called *Salt Lake City*, was Queen of the North Pacific that day.

The second Japanese heavy cruiser, *Maya*, at 0910 made her first hit on *Salt Lake*. It failed to stop or even slow her down. Ten minutes later, she and *Nachi* were swapping punches at a range of almost twelve miles. McMorris now turned his force north, hoping to make an end run around the Japanese warships and get at the transports; but Hosogaya was too fast for him. At 1002 *Salt Lake* briefly had steering trouble, and a few minutes later she took another hit. There was a big laugh on *Richmond*'s

[2] This means, changing your course quickly to cover the spot where the enemy's last salvo exploded in the water, so that when he corrects his aim he will miss again.

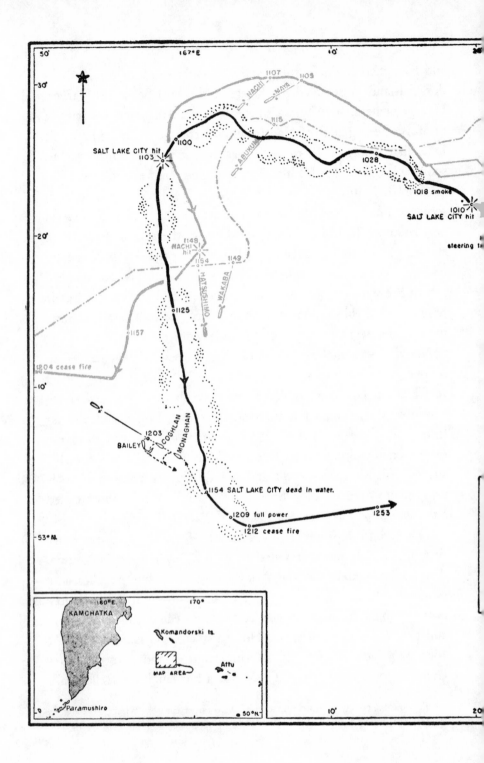

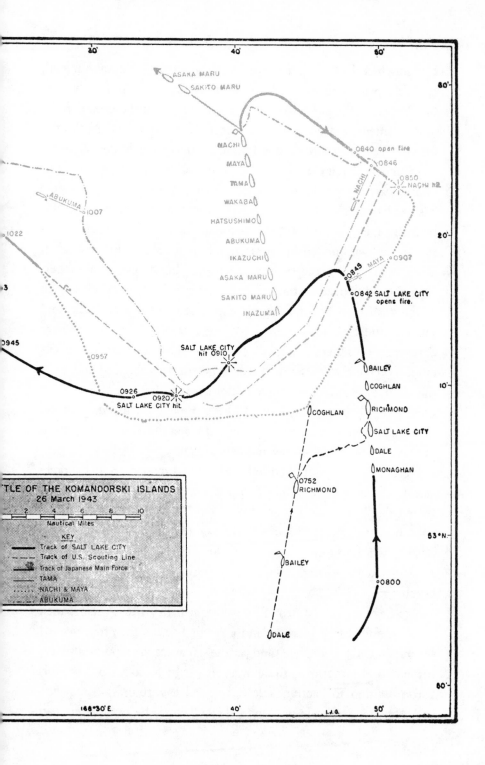

ASAKA MARU
SAKITO MARU

NACHI
MAYA
TAMA
WAKABA
HATSUSHIMO
ABUKUMA
IKAZUCHI
ASAKA MARU
SAKITO MARU
INAZUMA

0840 open fire
0846
0850
NACHI h2.
NACHI

MAYA 0907
0845
0842 SALT LAKE CITY
opens fire.

ABUKUMA 1007
1022

0945
0957

SALT LAKE CITY
hit 0910

0926 0920
SALT LAKE CITY hit

BAILEY
COGHLAN
RICHMOND
SALT LAKE CITY
DALE
MONAGHAN

COGHLAN

0752
RICHMOND

53°N

TLE OF THE KOMANDORSKI ISLANDS
26 March 1943

2   4   6   8   10
Nautical Miles

KEY
——— Track of SALT LAKE CITY
––– Track of U.S. Scouting Line
▨ Track of Japanese Main Force
—— TAMA
..... NACHI & MAYA
-·-·- ABUKUMA

BAILEY

0800

DALE

168°30' E.   40'   L.J.G.   50'

30'   40'   50'   80'
20'
10'
80'

bridge when the O.T.C. received a message from Admiral Kinkaid, at Adak, promising to get Army bombers out to help him "within five hours," and "suggesting that a retiring action be considered."

Retirement, indeed, was now the only thing to do. McMorris first steered west under good smoke cover which the Japanese rangefinders, having no radar, were unable to penetrate. But this course carried the Americans nearer and nearer to the Japanese base at Paramushiro. So at 1100 McMorris turned his force south to disengage. No sooner done than *Salt Lake* suffered a serious 8-inch hit which flooded the after engine room. She continued firing, at declining speed, for twenty miles and almost one hour longer; then she went dead in the water. McMorris reacted by closing in *Richmond* to make smoke and help defend Old Swayback, and (in a magnificent but desperate gesture), ordering three of his four destroyers to deliver a torpedo attack on the fast-approaching enemy. Everyone who could help damage control on board *Salt Lake* did, and everyone else prayed. Before the destroyers had been gone five minutes, what looked like a miracle occurred. Admiral Hosogaya broke off action and turned his entire force west, hotly pursued by *Bailey, Coghlan* and *Monaghan.*

Hosogaya really funked out. He was anxious to get home; smoke concealed from him *Salt Lake*'s desperate plight, and he feared that American air bombers from Dutch Harbor would arrive shortly. Destroyer *Bailey* gave *Nachi*'s superstructure a good dusting with close-in 5-inch fire to firm up his decision to depart. It is no wonder that this Japanese admiral was shortly put on the beach.

Salt Lake recovered propulsion as eight bells struck, then shaped a course for Dutch Harbor, and a repair base. *Nachi,* too, needed several jobs done on her; and as the Japanese transports also returned to Paramushiro, there was no doubt as to who won this battle. During the action *Salt Lake* fired 832 rounds, *Nachi* 707 and *Maya* 904 rounds of 8-inch shell. *Bailey,* the only American destroyer to get close enough to the retiring enemy to use torpedoes, fired five, which missed; the Japanese ships fired 43, and all missed. So this battle deserves a place in the history of naval warfare as the last heavy gunfire daylight action, with no interference by air power, submarines or torpedoes. The demonstration of superior gunnery was tremendously heartening to the United States Navy.

Before leaving Alaska's dreary shores for warmer climes, we must briefly mention the recovery of Attu. Amphibious Force North Pacific was set up to accomplish this, under Rear Admiral Francis W. Rockwell; the 7th Infantry Division United States Army had the unhappy ground assignment. Battleships *Pennsylvania* and *Nevada* emerged from naval shipyards in time to act as support group with *Idaho,* and "Soc" McMorris was back again, in light cruiser *Raleigh,* commanding a covering group. The landings, on 11 May 1943, were successful, but the Japanese garrison fought desperately, culminating in a thousand-man screaming suicide charge on 29 May. A big operation to take Kiska was laid on for late July, but the Japanese fooled us by evacuating their 5000-man garrison under fog cover, leaving only three yellow dogs to contest the American landing.

It was bad strategy to throw such heavy forces into capturing a few square miles of muskeg, at a time when troops and ships were desperately needed in the South and Southwest Pacific. Ironically, one of the main reasons for these efforts in the Aleutians was the desire of the Joint Chiefs of Staff to expedite aid to Russia, in the expected event of her going to war with Japan.

During the rest of the war the Aleutians offer little of interest. Harassing air raids on Paramushiro were varied by occasional shore bombardments and feeble Japanese retaliatory raids on Attu, Kiska and Adak. But there was a constant improvement both of bases and of flying efficiency in these difficult northern areas; and that was all to the good. For it may well be that in the future the

Bering, not the Caribbean, will be America's "Sea of Destiny." In any case, it was wonderful practice ground for armed forces; after a tour of duty in the Aleutians, every other field of action seemed good.

3. *Minor Operations in the South and Southwest Pacific, February–May 1943*

About 9000 infantrymen and Marines, lifted from New Caledonia, landed unopposed on the Russell Islands, 30 miles west of Cape Esperance, on 21 February 1943. This overstuffed affair might well have been omitted.

After the Japanese were thrown out of Buna and Gona, they began to strengthen their garrisons at Lae and Salamaua on Huon Gulf, General MacArthur's next objective. On 1 March 1943 a strong reinforcement convoy for Lae, about 7000 troops in eight transports and as many destroyers, departed Rabaul. By this time Major General George C. Kenney, air commander under Mac-Arthur, had beefed-up his own and the Royal Australian Air Force in Papua to 207 bombers and 129 fighters. He had equipped one squadron of B–25s with 500-pound bombs having a five-second delay fuse that permitted a plane to come in on a ship almost at sea level, like a torpedo-bomber, drop its bomb and escape. The Lae-bound convoy was kept under observation and at 1000 March 3 the land-based Allied planes flew in to bomb it from over Papua. The ensuing battle was the most devastating air attack on ships of the entire war, excepting only that on Pearl Harbor. Out of 37 bombs dropped by the first wave of planes, 28 scored; and by noon, over 200 bombs had fallen upon and around the writhing ships. High above sea level, Army Air Force fighters tangled with the Japanese C.A.P.; others flew to Lae to prevent air reinforcement reaching the enemy. All afternoon the slaughter continued. Seven out of eight transports and two of the eight destroyers were sunk; four undamaged destroyers picked up survivors and fled; the sea was spotted with life rafts, rubber boats and swimmers. At daybreak 4 March the Army Air Force returned and sank two damaged destroyers.

Now the motor torpedo boats took a hand. *PT–143* and *PT–150*, after sinking the one transport still afloat, encountered a Japanese submarine taking on survivors from three big landing craft. The I-boat dived, the PTs sank the craft and machine-gunned the survivors. This may sound horrible, but it had to be done, as Japanese soldiers and sailors were trained to resist capture, or, if captured willy-nilly, to seek revenge on their saviors. There were innumerable incidents such as a wounded Japanese soldier at Guadalcanal seizing a scalpel and burying it in the back of a surgeon who was about to save his life by an operation; and a survivor of the Battle of Vella Lavella, rescued by *PT–163*, pulling a gun and killing a bluejacket in the act of giving the Japanese sailor a cup of coffee.

The total score of this Battle of the Bismarck Sea was eight Japanese transports and four destroyers sunk, and three to four thousand men killed — at a cost of two bombers and three fighters out of over 300 aircraft engaged. Unfortunately this smashing victory could never be repeated, because the Japanese never again risked a transport bigger than a barge in waters shadowed by American planes.

During this long lull in major operations, Japan was improving her defensive positions at Huon Gulf and westward in New Guinea, and in the central and upper Solomons. Munda airfield, on New Georgia, was greatly extended; a supporting field was established at Vila on Kolombangara; seaplane bases were set up at Shortlands and Santa Isabel; new airfields were built on Ballale near Shortlands and Kahiki on southern Bougainville. South Pacific cruiser task groups under Rear Admirals A. Stanton Merrill and

Walden L. Ainsworth raided these places frequently ("Tip" Merrill sank two enemy destroyers incidental to bombarding Vila on the night of 5-6 March); Airsols bombed them even more often, but the Japanese kept right on working. And Fleet Admiral Yamamoto was preparing a big campaign, which proved to be his last.

This "I" Operation, as he called it, was meant to be a crushing, annihilating air offensive, from Rabaul, against American ships and bases in Papua and the Solomons. To double the already strong air fleet at Rabaul, Admiral Ozawa contributed some 170 naval planes from four carriers. No fewer than 187 planes pulled off the first strike of "I" Operation, against Tulagi, on 7 April. There was a wild scene in Tulagi Harbor when the bombers roared in. They sank a tanker, a New Zealand corvette and destroyer *Aaron Ward*, losing only 21 of their own planes. On 11-12 April Yamamoto threw the "I" switch to Papua, burned two merchant vessels at Oro Bay, and sent 174 aircraft over the Owen Stanley Range to attack Port Moresby. MacArthur's antiaircraft guns prevented them from doing much damage. Small result for all this effort; but Yamamoto never learned the truth.

By decrypting Japanese communications, Halsey obtained the complete timetable of a forthcoming inspection tour by the Japanese C. in C., and both Nimitz and King encouraged him to profit thereby. Sixteen United States Army Lightnings flew up from Henderson Field to intercept Yamamoto's air cortege, and neatly shot down the two bombers carrying the Fleet Admiral and staff, killing him and five or six others. All Japanese writers admit that this was equivalent to a major defeat, since there was "only one Yamamoto."

4. *The Central Solomons Campaign, June–July 1943*

Everyone in the now crowded American bases at Nouméa, Espiritu Santo, Guadalcanal, Tulagi and Purvis Bay was asking, "When do we go?" Halsey was ready to start the South Pacific ball rolling in mid-April, but General MacArthur was not. He knew very well that military power is like a three-legged stool; if it lacks one of the three legs, land power, air power and sea power, it will be toppled. In 1942, MacArthur was sitting on one leg — land power. A second leg, air power, proved its strength in the Battle of the Bismarck Sea, and on 15 March a third leg, Seventh Fleet under Vice Admiral Arthur S. Carpender, was set up. But, being "at the end of the line," this was the last fleet to get beaching and landing craft and other instruments to enable Rear Admiral Daniel E. Barbey and his new VII Amphibious Force to go places. Everything in the South Pacific was held up until General MacArthur's third "leg," the amphibious force, was ready.

A Joint Chief of Staff directive of 29 March set Southwest Pacific two tasks: (1) to establish airfields on the Trobriand Islands; (2) to seize Japanese positions on Huon Gulf and along Vitiaz Strait, and Cape Gloucester on New Britain, in order to breach the Bismarck barrier at vital points. MacArthur chose the last day of June to start. It was a walkover, since Kiriwina and Woodlark (the two Trobriands) were occupied only by natives. But this was the first time in the Southwest Pacific that air, land and sea power had operated as a balanced team, and Barbey's plan for the Trobriands became the template for all later shore-to-shore leaps along the New Guinea coast. Before the war ended, VII 'Phib would have over fifty amphibious landings to its credit, and its commander would be known as "Uncle Dan the Amphibious Man."

Nassau Bay was occupied the same day, 30 June, by a shore-to-shore operation. General Eichelberger's troops were lifted 40 miles from Morobe in motor torpedo boats and in landing craft manned by the 2nd Engineer Special Brigade, all riding the crest of a southeast gale.

There was jubilation in the South Pacific when the word "Go!" was finally pronounced in the picturesque Melanesian pidgin: "Musket-he-fire-up." Munda on New Georgia, the annoying air base whence the Japanese raided Guadalcanal and Tulagi for months after they had been secured, was the objective. The amphibious forces, under Rear Admiral R. Kelly Turner in *McCawley*, comprised 10 large transports, 12 destroyer transports, 9 LST and 11 LCI, screened by 8 destroyers and supported by battleships, cruisers and escort carriers under Rear Admirals Ainsworth, Merrill and Glenn B. Davis. The major landing took place on Rendova Island across Blanche Channel from Munda. Troops had to be ferried thence to the New Georgia shore, and then fight Japanese step by step through the jungle to get at the coveted airdrome.

The naval part of this campaign for Munda was sparked off by hot clashes up the Slot between Japanese "Tokyo Expresses" to Vila (whence troops were transferred to Munda), and Rear Admiral Walden L. Ainsworth's light cruiser task force. On the night of 4-5 July it bombarded Vila and Bairoko, but lost destroyer *Strong* (Commander J. H. Wellings) to a mine. The following night, ordered back up the Slot by Halsey, Ainsworth fought the Battle of Kula Gulf, against a ten-destroyer force under Rear Admiral Akiyama. American gunfire sank one destroyer and drove another ashore, but cruiser *Helena* was sunk by three explosions of the Japanese "long lance" torpedoes.

On the night of 12-13 July Ainsworth performed his fifteenth combat mission up the Slot, and enjoyed another fight, the Battle of Kolombangara, in almost the same water as that of Kula Gulf. He had light cruisers *Honolulu* (Captain Robert W. Hayler) and *St. Louis* (Captain Colin Campbell), with H.M.N.Z.S. *Leander*

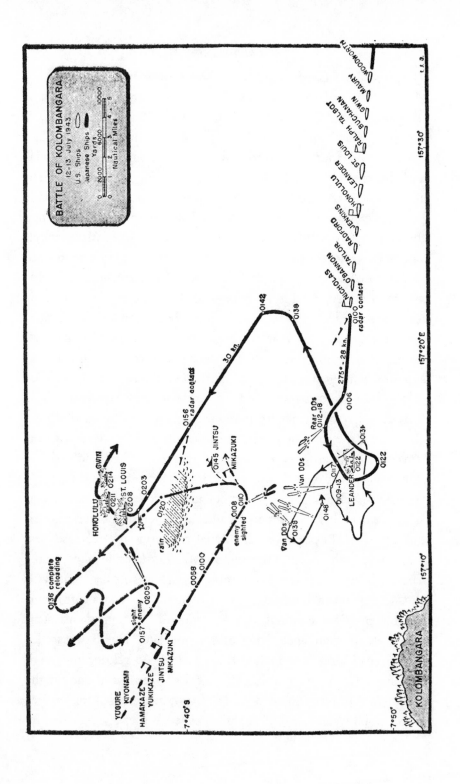

BATTLE OF KOLOMBANGARA
12-13 July 1943

U.S. Ships
Japanese Ships
Yards

Nautical Miles

(Captain C. A. L. Mansergh RN) sister ship to the famous H.M.S. *Achilles* (to replace lost *Helena*), and two destroyer squadrons of five ships each. This time he tangled with Rear Admiral Izaki's support group, comprising Tanaka's old flagship *Jintsu*, five destroyers and four destroyer-transports. Although we had radar and the enemy none, he had a radar-detecting device which enabled him to track Ainsworth's progress up the Slot for an hour before American radar bounced off a Japanese ship. Izaki launched torpedoes at 0108 July 13, one minute before Captain McInerney's van destroyer squadron got off theirs. Ainsworth then waited until range closed to 10,000 yards before ordering his cruisers to commence firing. As usual in early days of radar fire control, the cruisers concentrated on the biggest blip, *Jintsu*, and so smothered her with 6-inch shell that she exploded and went down with all hands. A few minutes earlier a Japanese torpedo crashed into *Leander*, putting her out of the battle and almost out of the war.

While two destroyers stood by *Leander*, Ainsworth sent McInerney's destroyer squadron scampering up the Slot in the hope of catching the retiring Japanese destroyers, and followed with his remaining two cruisers and three destroyers. This bold bid for complete victory was thrown back in his face. The five Japanese destroyers, reloading torpedo tubes under cover of a rain squall in the remarkably fast time of eighteen minutes, countermarched and at 0156 appeared on the American cruisers' radar scopes. Ainsworth hesitated to open gunfire, fearing lest the blips represented McInerney's destroyers returning (I was in flag plot with him, seeing and feeling the agony of decision in such a case); and when at 0205 the Admiral ordered right turn to unmask his main batteries and commence firing, it was too late. The Japanese destroyers had already launched their 31-torpedo reload, and were speeding away. One "long lance" sank destroyer *Gwin*, one caught *Honolulu* and one exploded on *St. Louis*, each so far forward as to kill nobody and do but slight damage. A third, which hit the flagship square in her fantail without exploding, hung there a moment and then dropped out.

Although we who participated in these battles up the Slot felt pretty cocky at the time, thinking we had sunk at least twelve ships in the two actions, sober reassessment indicates that we were not so hot. The Japanese were still tops in torpedo work and night fighting. Incredible as it now seems, the speed, size and range of the Japanese "long lance" torpedo, invented ten years earlier and lavishly employed in every naval action of the war, was still unknown to the Pacific Fleet. One had been salvaged early in 1943 and analyzed by the Bureau of Ordnance, but these findings had not even reached Admiral Halsey. Had Ainsworth been apprised of its capacity, he would never have closed to 10,000 yards before opening gunfire, or maneuvered his cruisers in enemy torpedo water. As it was, he enjoyed good luck in bringing all three cruisers back to Tulagi on their own bottoms.

The Japanese continued to lose planes and ships which they could not replace, to save Munda and Vila; then they continued to lose more planes, ships and men, to get men out of Munda and Vila. Reinforcement and evacuation were very well done; but a string of such victories adds up to defeat.

The land campaign for Munda went very slowly. It was the worst kind of jungle fighting, too many of our troops were raw, and their top commander, until relieved by Major General Oscar W. Griswold, was unequal to the task. It took nearly 34,000 American troops six weeks to wrest this corner of New Georgia from about 8000 Japanese.

Subsequent to the two cruiser actions, the principal naval aid to the New Georgia campaign was contributed by PT boats. They successfully broke up reinforcements by Japanese *daihatsu* armed barges on the nights of 23-24 and 26-27 July. Another action, unsuccessful in a military sense, but important to a future President of the United States, took place on the night of 1-2 August 1943. Fifteen PTs, divided four ways, tried to block Blackett Strait south of Kolombangara to a Japanese destroyer express. They used torpedoes lavishly, but made not one hit on enemy ships going or coming. On the contrary, Commander Hanami of destroyer *Amagiri* had the distinction of running down and knifing in two *PT-109*, commanded by Lieutenant John F. Kennedy USNR. Eleven of the crew of 13 survived, and, with Kennedy swimming and towing a wounded sailor, and the rest on an improvised raft, they managed to reach a small island in five hours. Kennedy refused to give up; he spent most of the next night swimming in the Strait, hoping in vain to intercept a PT. In the morning he sent a message on a coconut shell via a friendly native to an Australian coastwatcher, who dispatched other natives to the rescue. Kennedy and his surviving shipmates were paddled to safety in a well-camouflaged canoe.

The capture of Munda on 5 August did not end the naval campaign up the Slot. For a full year, destroyer officers had been banging fists on wardroom tables and bellowing, "When are they going to cut us loose from the cruisers' apron strings?" In one battle after another the O.T.C. had kept destroyers in van and rear, instead of sending them to make independent torpedo attacks. And the performance of American torpedoes so far had been miserable. But "Just give us a chance!" was the destroyer sailors' reply to every criticism. Now, Rear Admiral Theodore S. Wilkinson, who had relieved Kelly Turner as Com III 'Phib, accepted this challenge from Commander Frederick Moosbrugger, who met it admirably.

The chance occurred because Wilkinson suspected on 5 August that the Japanese would run a Tokyo Express to Kolombangara the following night; and Wilkinson told Moosbrugger to fight the battle his own way. With six destroyers (*Dunlap, Craven, Maury, Lang, Sterett, Stack,* the last two under Commander Rodger Simp-

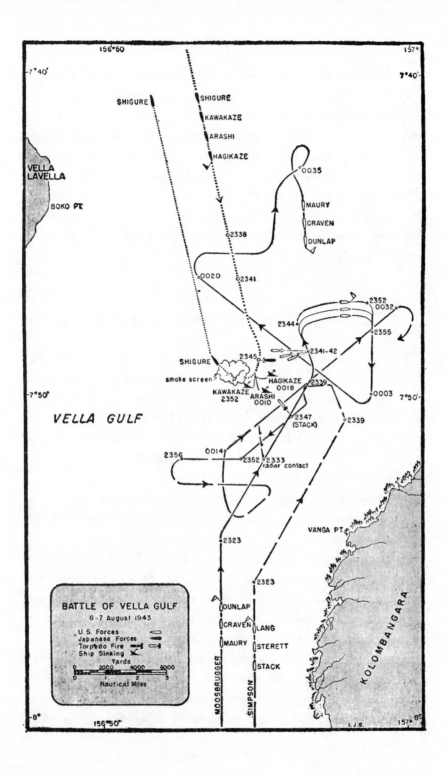

BATTLE OF VELLA GULF
6-7 August 1943

U. S. Forces
Japanese Forces
Torpedo Fire
Ship Sinking
Yards
2000   4000   6000
0   1   2   3
Nautical Miles

son) Moosbrugger gave battle in Vella Gulf, on the night of 6-7 August, to four Japanese destroyers under Captain Sugiura. He surprised them with a flock of torpedoes at a range of 4000 yards, and three of the enemy destroyers exploded with such a flash and roar that sailors on PT boats almost thirty miles away thought that the volcano on Kolombangara had blown its top. There was a brief exchange of gunfire after this initial hit, and lucky *Shigure*, the one that escaped, fired torpedoes; but no Japanese ship laid a finger on Moosbrugger. His Battle of Vella Gulf was one of the neatest victories of the war.

5. Leapfrogging Begins, August–October 1943

July of 1943 was a month of Allied victory in Sicily, on the Russian front, and in the Atlantic sea lanes. Japanese resistance at Munda, threatening to slow up the Pacific war, led to a notable acceleration in tactics. So far, MacArthur's strategy in New Guinea, like Halsey's in the Solomons, could not unfairly be described as "island hopping." If we had continued at that pace, it would have taken at least ten years to reach Japan, and the enemy's strategy of tiring us out by sheer stubbornness might have worked. But about this time, "leapfrogging" was substituted for "island hopping."

General Tojo, shortly before his death, told General MacArthur that leapfrogging was one of the three principal factors that defeated Japan; the other two being the depredations of United States submarines and the ability of fast carrier forces to operate for long periods away from their bases. There was nothing new about leapfrogging or bypassing enemy strong points or, as General MacArthur and Admiral Wilkinson called it in baseball phraseology, "Hitting 'em where they ain't." Wilkinson, a student of naval strategy, had long been eager to take advantage of Pacific topography, bypass the strongest Japanese garrisons, seal them off by air and sea, and leave them to "wither on the vine." So were General MacArthur's staff. Captain Harry R. Thurber of Halsey's staff advocated the bypassing of Munda early in 1943, but we had to take it instead, because there was then no place to leapfrog into.

The first demonstration of leapfrogging came about inadvertently, in the Aleutians. Admiral Nimitz skipped over Kiska to take the more important Attu, and the enemy then secretly evacuated Kiska. Nimitz on 11 July 1943 suggested to Halsey that Kolombangara be given the Kiska treatment — land troops on Vella Lavella to the northwest and skip the island with the long name. A plan was promptly drafted to place Vila airfield under the fire of American artillery, to sever the enemy's supply lines to Kolombangara, and seize lightly held Vella Lavella for a fighter-plane base.

The Vella Lavella landings, on 15 August at Barakoma Bay on the eastern foot of the island, were uncontested except from the air. During two weeks after the landings, Wilkinson's III 'Phib delivered 6305 men and 8626 tons cargo on the island, fought off Japanese planes in scores of air attacks, and turned back one enemy reinforcement echelon. Land operations continued slowly but systematically. On 18 September the American troops were relieved by the 3rd Division New Zealand Army, Major General Barrowclough. The New Zealanders pushed a pincer movement up both coasts, and by 1 October had cornered about 600 of the enemy on the northwest shore. There they stayed for another week, when the effort to evacuate them brought about the Naval Battle of Vella Lavella.

This battle occurred because the Japanese endeavored to evacuate the 600 waifs and strays left on that island. Rear Admiral Ijuin marshaled nine destroyers and a dozen small craft to rescue them, on the night of 6-7 October. Admiral Wilkinson sent Captain Frank R. Walker in command of six destroyers to intercept. Each side had a destroyer with a charmed life — *Shigure*, which had escaped Moosbrugger's slaughter at Vella Gulf and which would be the sole survivor of the Battle of Surigao Strait; and *O'Bannon*, which probably acquired more "hash marks" than any destroyer of the U. S. Navy.

In the ensuing Battle of Vella Lavella on the night of 6-7 October Walker won both the tactical maneuvering and the draw, launching torpedoes at 2255, range 7000 yards, one of which disembowled *Yugumo;* but a torpedo from that very destroyer had already exploded in *Chevalier's* forward magazine, tearing off her bow as far aft as the bridge, and dooming her, besides causing a collision with *O'Bannon* which put that destroyer out of the battle. In the meantime the other two Japanese destroyers had registered on Captain Walker's radar screen. After them he galloped full cry in his now lone *Selfridge*. The range, over 10,000 yards, was too great for the sluggish products of the Newport Torpedo Station, but not for the Japanese long lances, sixteen of which at 2306 were boiling viciously around *Selfridge*. One caught her forward, exploded, and she shuddered to a stop. Eventually she had to be scuttled.

A Japanese plane sighted in the moonlight three destroyers dashing up to help Walker, and passed the word to Admiral Ijuin. That cautious commander then ordered retirement, and the three destroyers arrived a quarter-hour too late to engage. In the meantime the subchasers which Ijuin sent to rescue the Vella Lavella garrison quietly embarked them and got out.

Thus Ijuin performed his mission and inflicted the greater damage; but Captain Walker showed skill and guts in accepting the short end of three-to-one odds, and depriving the Japanese Navy of one more destroyer. It had now lost more than 40 by enemy action since the beginning of the war.

This battle concluded the Central Solomons campaign, second phase of Operation WATCHTOWER. It had cost the United States Navy six warships, and the Imperial Japanese Navy seventeen. It had brought us 250 miles nearer Rabaul — but three months was too much time to spend on getting less than one tenth of the way to Tokyo. Nevertheless, the Allies now had the strategic initiative: they would call the tunes, selecting where and when to fight.

6. *The Bougainville Battles, October–November 1943*

The next hop toward Rabaul from the South Pacific was to Bougainville. This operation was planned by the staffs of Rear Admiral Theodore S. Wilkinson and Lieutenant General Vandegrift, the last two at Guadalcanal. "Ping" Wilkinson, a scholarly officer with an excellent combat record, went into Bougainville as if he had been preparing for it all his life. He had, in fact, won a school prize some forty years earlier with an account of an amphibious operation by Alexander the Great.

Empress Augusta Bay, near the center of the long southwest coast of Bougainville, was chosen as target for this big leap. It was near enough Rabaul to be a good base for fighters to join bomber strikes from Munda, and separated from the Japanese garrisons on Bougainville by many miles of dense tropical rain forest. Thus our troops would have time to dig in and build airstrips before sustaining any serious counterattack by land.

Admiral Koga, Yamamoto's successor, guessing that something was coming up, sliced off 173 aircraft from his three biggest carriers to help defend Rabaul. Between 12 October and 2 November the Southwest Pacific air forces under General Kenney attempted to knock out Rabaul with eight massive raids of 54 to 349 planes each. Rabaul survived this treatment, but Kenney's raids were useful in diverting Japanese attention from Bougainville.

Although the Gilbert Islands operation was being mounted simultaneously in the Central Pacific, Admiral Wilkinson had enough transports and supporting warships for the task at hand. For ground forces he had a superb outfit, the I Marine Amphibious Corps commanded by General Roy S. Geiger usmc, comprising the 3rd Marine Division, the 37th Infantry Division U. S. Army, and a brigade group of New Zealand troops. Equally diverse was Airsols, comprising aircraft of the United States Army, Navy, Marine Corps and the Royal New Zealanders, the command rotating monthly between officers of the first three.

The landing at Cape Torokina, Empress Augusta Bay, of 14,000 Marines and 6200 tons of supplies from 12 transports, was pulled off successfully 1 November 1943. Wilkinson was not bothered by the local defense force, which consisted of 270 Japanese troops and one ancient *soixante-quinze*. But, remembering what happened when enemy planes from Rabaul attacked transports at Guadalcanal on 7-8 August 1942, he insisted on combat-loading his transports so that first things came out first, making for a quick landing and an even quicker getaway. How right he was! The first boat wave hit the beach at 0726; the first counterattack from Rabaul came in at 0735. Air cover from Vella Lavella and Munda took care of that, but about 100 more Japanese aircraft attacked at 1300. They were frustrated by 34 savagely aggressive Airsols fighters which were beautifully handled by a fighter-director team in destroyer *Conway*. In spite of these two interruptions, which forced the big transports to get under way, all but four were completely unloaded by 1730 and departed — a record performance.

Successful as the landings were, everyone expected the Japanese Navy to attempt another Savo Island, and they had not long to wait. Rear Admiral Omori, who hoped to repeat Mikawa's ex-

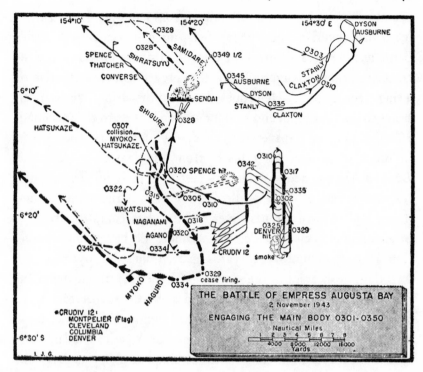

THE BATTLE OF EMPRESS AUGUSTA BAY
2 November 1943
ENGAGING THE MAIN BODY 0301-0350

ploit, was given like him a pick-up task group to break up the
landings. He had his own heavy cruiser division (*Myoko* and
Haguro), two destroyer divisions (one commanded by Rear Admiral Ijuin, the victor at Vella Lavella), two light cruisers and six
destroyers, including indestructible *Shigure*. Omori was steaming
hell-bent to get the American transports in Empress Augusta Bay
when he was intercepted by Rear Admiral Merrill's Task Force
39 — four light cruisers (*Montpelier, Cleveland, Columbia, Denver*) and two destroyer divisions of four ships each, one under
Commander B. L. Austin and the other commanded by Captain
Arleigh A. Burke, who had just won the nickname "31-knot
Burke" for fast stepping on a recent bombardment mission. "Tip"
Merrill certainly had plenty of talent under him.

The situation was now similar to that before the Battle of Savo

Island, with one important difference: from scout planes the Americans had accurate knowledge of Japanese movements. Merrill's battle plan was "to maintain the cruisers in a position across the entrance to Empress Augusta Bay and to prevent the entry therein of a single enemy ship." He proposed to push the enemy westward in order to gain sea room and to fight at ranges close to the maximum effective range of Japanese torpedoes, say 16,000 to 20,000 yards, in order to protect his cruisers from the fate of *Helena* and *Leander*. He planned to detach his destroyer divisions for an initial torpedo attack, to hold cruisers' gunfire until the "fish" struck home, and to give his destroyer commanders complete freedom of action once they were detached. Omori was in cruising disposition, in three columns 5000 yards apart; Ijuin's destroyers on the left, the two heavies in the center, other destroyers on the right. Some of the Japanese ships had radar, but the operators were green and Omori relied wholly on visual sighting. This time, Japanese eyes and binoculars were not equal to American radar.

The maneuvering in this Battle of Empress Augusta Bay was complicated. Actually there were three battles — one waged by Merrill's cruisers against the enemy cruisers, one by Burke's destroyers, and one by Austin's.

Initial torpedo salvos from both sides failed to score. The American cruisers' radar-controlled gunfire converged on the nearest ship, light cruiser *Sendai*, at 0250 November 2, and made five or more hits which jammed her rudder. At 0301 Merrill led his cruisers on a colossal figure eight, to hold an advantageous range, and spoil the enemy's aim. His cruisers dished out 6-inch gunfire as they zigzagged violently at 30 knots, but did little damage; and by 0315 Omori's 8-inch fire began to improve, straddling repeatedly. *Denver* alone was hit, but only by duds.

Japanese planes now approached Merrill's force and dropped both white and colored flares. At that point in the battle a cloud ceiling hung high over the cruisers, acting as a silver reflector to the flares and star shell. These brilliantly lighted up the four graceful vessels as their prows hissed through the black waters, in which their salvos were reflected as broken splashes of orange light. Geysers from the enemy's 8-inch misses rose deliberately from the sea like fountains in a princely garden. They flashed red, green and gold as they reflected the flares and the cruisers' gunfire, poised immobile for a split second, then tumbled in a shower of phosphorescent spume. It was one of those rare moments of awful beauty sometimes vouchsafed to those who do business in great waters.

Optimistic Omori, thinking that he had sunk two cruisers and completed a good night's work, ordered retirement at 0337.

The two destroyer divisions, although given the freedom of action that destroyer men craved, did not do well; they were like lusty children stumbling when just released from leading strings. Desdiv 45 became separated and it took Burke a full hour to get his ships back in formation. By that time there was not much left for them to do except pump a couple of torpedoes into disabled *Sendai*. Desdiv 46 finished off destroyer *Hatsukaze*, which had been damaged in a collision with Omori's flagship; but *Foote*, on the other hand, took a torpedo intended for the cruisers and lost her fantail. Both division commanders wanted to "chase the Japs back to Rabaul." But Merrill, expecting an air attack from that hornets' nest at dawn, called all units to him and started to retire at 0500. Three hours later his disposition was attacked by over 100 of the Japanese carrier planes now based at Rabaul. Merrill maneuvered his ships so nimbly that they received only two hits, neither lethal.

He thoroughly deserved victory over a force greatly his superior in torpedo power and gunfire. In a constantly changing tactical situation, he kept his poise and power of quick decision. His cruisers functioned as a well-drilled team. The Battle of Empress Augusta Bay is a refreshing contrast to earlier cruiser night actions.

Admiral Halsey now seized the initiative by ordering carrier strikes on Rabaul to eliminate the great number of aircraft still based there, and to bomb seven heavy cruisers which Koga had sent south from Truk, in the fatuous expectation of "cleaning up" on Merrill's "remnants." Rear Admiral Frederick Sherman's task force, built around *Saratoga* and the new light carrier *Princeton,* so damaged these ships on 5 November that the Japanese never again committed heavy cruisers to those waters. This performance was more than bettered on 11 November by Rear Admiral Alfred E. Montgomery's task group, built around *Essex, Bunker Hill* and *Independence,* which here made their debut. The Japanese counterattacked with Rabaul-based planes, but lost heavily, and Koga withdrew his crippled ships and the few remaining carrier planes, from Rabaul to Truk. He had expended another naval air group for nothing, and the Pacific Fleet had proved that carriers could profitably be pitted against a powerful land air base.

In the meantime, fresh echelons were pouring into the Bougainville beachhead. By 14 November 33,861 men and 23,137 tons of supplies had been landed at Empress Augusta Bay. But could the defensive perimeter set up around the beachhead be defended while the Seabees built airstrips and a full-fledged airdrome? The Marines were equal to it. A Japanese infantry regiment, first to press through the jungle and try Guadalcanal tactics on them, got "the treatment" on Thanksgiving Day.

On that same day, the 25th, there was even greater cause for thanksgiving, when Arleigh Burke's Desron 23, now reduced to five destroyers (two of them "Count" Austin's)[3] intercepted a Japanese five-destroyer team running reinforcements into Buka. Off Cape St. George, New Ireland, they clashed at 0156. The surprised Japanese lost two new 2000-ton destroyers from torpedo explosions, and a third by gunfire, without making a single hit. It was as good a cleanup as Moosbrugger's at Vella Gulf.

[3] *Charles F. Ausburne, Claxton, Dyson, Converse, Spence.*

The Allies were not long permitted to enjoy their Bougainville toehold in peace. General Hyakutake, the island commander, had some 40,000 soldiers and 20,000 sailors under him. All through January and February 1944 he was moving them along jungle trails, and in barges that hid out by day and crawled along shore by night, in the hope of rubbing out the Allied perimeter. General Griswold, to defend it, had about 27,000 combatant troops, the "Bougainville Navy" of small craft and PTs, commanded by the redoubtable Captain O. O. ("Scrappy") Kessing, and about one hundred Airsols planes. Halsey sent him six destroyers for naval gunfire support, and these were credited with defeating one of several enemy attacks on what was intended to be the fatal day — 9 March 1944. Two more attempts, both failures, were made by the Japanese within a week. Their losses were in the proportion of twenty to our one.

7. *Ringing Around Rabaul,*
September 1943–April 1944

During July and August 1943, while Halsey and Wilkinson slowly masticated the Central Solomons, MacArthur and Barbey had to be content with digesting their easily won gains in the Trobriand Islands and Nassau Bay. To that minor landing the Japanese reacted by setting up a barge line to carry troops from New Britain to the threatened New Guinea bases. General MacArthur wisely decided to take both places and Finsch-hafen too. His prerequisite for success was local air superiority. MacArthur, at 64 somewhat elderly for active duty, was air-minded as the youngest pilot in the A.A.F. He had learned a great lesson of the air age — never needlessly to expose troops or ships to an enemy supreme in the air. A contingent of the Southwest Pacific air forces raided Wewak, the principal Japanese base in New Guinea, 17-18 August, and destroyed over 100 planes; General Kenney seized the Japanese airstrip at Nadzab on 5 September by a surprise paratroop drop of 1700 men. Next day, Australian troops, lifted by Dan Barbey's VII 'Phib from Milne Bay, landed on beaches near Lae, and seized that place on the 16th; Salamaua had already fallen to another group of Aussies; Finschhafen succumbed to a repeat performance by 2 October, 1943.

Seventh Fleet was now in reasonably full control of Vitiaz Strait, but General MacArthur wanted Dampier Strait too, in order to dominate all passages between New Britain and New Guinea. That was his reason for landing the 1st Marine Division (Major General Rupertus) on Cape Gloucester. It was a big shore-to-shore operation, mounted in beaching craft by VII 'Phib in Papua and covered by a mixed United States Navy and Royal Australian Navy cruiser group commanded by Admiral Crutchley RN. After passing a hot and stuffy Christmas at sea, the Marines were landed at Cape Gloucester on the 26th. They found that place to be even worse than Guadalcanal, because the rain never stopped. After suffering heavy losses they secured a beachhead and a perimeter, by 16 January 1944.

Since Rabaul had always been the main objective of Operation WATCHTOWER, it was a shock to General MacArthur when General Marshall on 21 July 1943 suggested that he leap-frog Rabaul instead of assaulting it. The Combined Chiefs of Staff at their Quebec meeting in August directed Halsey and MacArthur to do just that, and as Rabaul's substitute occupy Kavieng in New Ireland and Manus in the Admiralties. This major leap, coupled with a later decision to bypass Kavieng as well, proved to be fortunate. Rabaul still had close to 100,000 defenders under a tough and resourceful general. Since it had been a stockpiling base for various invasions which never came off, the Japanese garrison had plenty of provisions, munitions, weapons and

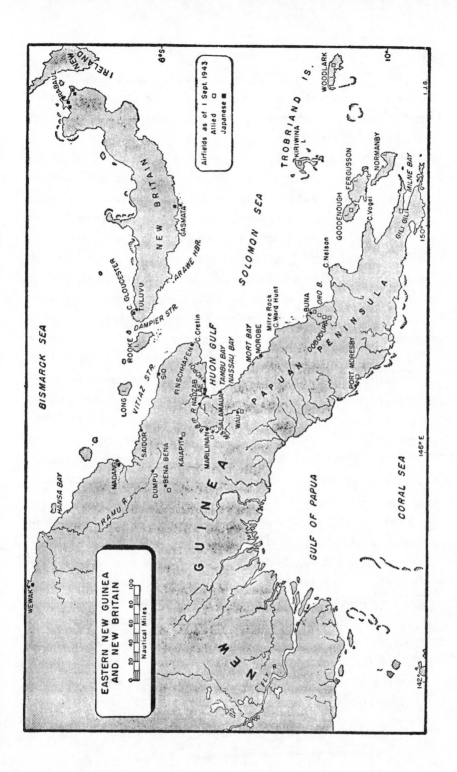

EASTERN NEW GUINEA
AND NEW BRITAIN

0 20 40 60 80 100
Nautical Miles

Airfields as of 1 Sept. 1943
Allied □
Japanese ■

NEW IRELAND

RABAUL

NEW BRITAIN

BISMARCK SEA

C. GLOUCESTER
ROOKE
TULUVU
DAMPIER STR.
ARAWE HBR.
GASMATA

LONG

VITIAZ STR.

SIO
C. Cretin
FINSCHHAFEN
R. NADZAB
MARILINAN
SALAMAUA
WAU
NASSAU BAY
TAMBU BAY
MORT BAY
MOROBE

HUON GULF

SAIDOR
MADANG
DUMPU
BENA BENA
KAIAPIT
RAMU R.

HANSA BAY
WEWAK

NEW GUINEA

PAPUAN PENINSULA

Mitre Rock
C. Ward Hunt
ORO B.
BUNA
C. Nelson
DOBODURA
PORT MORESBY

GULF OF PAPUA

FLY R.

CORAL SEA

SOLOMON SEA

TROBRIAND IS.
WOODLARK
KIRIWINA I.
GOODENOUGH
FERGUSSON
C. Vogel
NORMANBY
GILI GILI
MILNE BAY

6° S.

10°

150°

146° E.

142°

I.J.G.

supplies. They kept busy, digging caves and concealed gun positions and constructing fields of fire and booby traps that should have enabled them to repulse any amphibious operation that the Allies could have laid on.

The last important leap that isolated Rabaul was made by MacArthur into the Admiralty Islands. This was not supposed to come off until 1 April 1944, but on the basis of a B–25 pilot's report that the islands were empty of Japanese, General Mac-Arthur decided to pull off a reconnaissance in force, and to accompany it himself. This kind of reconnaissance means that you send enough men to stay if the target is weakly defended, but not too many to make a brisk retreat if the enemy is there in strength. The 1st Cavalry Division United States Army supplied over a thousand troopers (minus boots, saddles and sabers); Barbey's VII 'Phib lifted them as usual. The troopers were landed on Los Negros Island without opposition, on 29 February. It turned out that the B–25 pilot was wrong. About 4000 of the Japanese were present, and started making trouble that very night. But Mac-Arthur decided to let the troopers stay and to reinforce them quickly, because from his knowledge of Japanese ground tactics he rightly predicted that the enemy would commit his army piecemeal, and that each small package could be defeated.

With the aid of almost the entire Seventh Fleet, abundant air power, and sundry ground troops, the Americans moved from Los Negroes into Manus, the biggest island of the group. By 3 April they were in control of the magnificent, deep, landlocked Seeadler Harbor, fifteen miles long and four wide. Far better as a base than Rabaul, and nearer Japan, the Admiralties became one of the most important staging points in the last fifteen months of the Pacific War.

In the meantime, there had been big doings along the other road to Tokyo — through the Central Pacific.

CHAPTER X

Gilberts and Marshalls

November 1943–July 1944

1. *The Gilberts — Operation* GALVANIC

IN ALLIED CIRCLES, very little was known of enemy activities in the Gilbert Islands, which the Japanese Navy captured in September 1942, and even less of the Marshalls, for which Japan obtained the mandate after World War I. Photographic reconnaissance could not stretch up to the Marshalls, even from Funafuti, which the United States occupied on 2 October 1942. Submarines *Pompano, Stingray* and *Plunger* reconnoitered Rongerik, Bikini, Eniwetok and several minor atolls in February–March; but a fish-eye view does not reveal what is going on ashore. Combined Fleet might have rendezvoused in Kwajalein Lagoon and half a dozen new airfields might have been constructed without the news reaching Pearl Harbor.

Admiral King, always alert to seize opportunities, on 9 February 1943 invited Admiral Nimitz's comment on an operation to secure the Gilbert Islands. Cincpac thought the suggestion premature. No ground troops were yet available, and no naval forces could be spared from the Central Solomons operation, coming up in June.

Modern warfare has to be planned far ahead; improvisation may lead to disaster. Why then did the Marshalls become a priority target in the Joint Chiefs' 20 May plan for the defeat of Japan? Their object was to attain positions in the Western Pacific from which Japan's unconditional surrender could be forced, possibly by air action alone, probably by invasion after repeated air strikes on her industrial cities. The key target to this plan, short of Japan itself, was a base at or near Hong Kong; and although that key fell — owing to Japan's sealing off the entire coast of China — a good part of the plan endured. In brief, it amounted to this: —

Parallel, simultaneous carrier and amphibious operations through (*a*) Gilberts and Marshalls, (*b*) the Bismarck Archipelago, and (*c*) from the Indian Ocean into Burma. The first (*a*) we are about to relate. Operation WATCHTOWER, which (as we have already told) was concluded with the neutralization of Rabaul, is (*b*); Burma (*c*) was postponed again and again. The basic idea was this: an offensive through Micronesia (Gilberts, Marshalls, Carolines) must be pushed at the same time as MacArthur's New Guinea–Mindanao approach to Japan. The one would support the other, and the fast carrier forces, now being augmented by the *Essex* class, could free-wheel between the two. It was a very bold plan. Nothing in past warfare told how amphibious forces could advance in great leaps across an ocean where the enemy had dozens of island bases. The series of operations we are about to relate were one of the finest achievements in World War II.

Cincpac, after a good photo reconnaissance of the Gilberts, convinced the J.C.S. that we had better take Tarawa and Makin for air bases before trying the Marshalls, and the J.C.S. issued the directive on 20 July 1943. Operation GALVANIC was now definitely on the timetable for November.

Fifth Fleet, organized 15 March 1943 from what had been the Central Pacific component of the Pacific Fleet, was at last formidable. It had the new *Lexington*, the new *Yorktown*, three light carriers, twenty new 2100-ton destroyers, and the new fast battleship *Alabama*. The J.C.S. informed Admiral Nimitz that by October he might count on double or triple these numbers, besides 27 transport types and a flock of new Kaiser-built escort carriers.

(Yamamoto was right: the Pacific Fleet had to be "annihilated" in 1942, or not at all.) Vice Admiral Raymond A. Spruance left Nimitz's staff to become Commander Fifth Fleet, and Rear Admiral R. Kelly Turner commanded the V Amphibious Force set up in August — leaving Rear Admiral Wilkinson to carry on, as we have seen, in the Solomons. The ground troops, the V Amphibious Corps, although not all Marines, were commanded by Major General Holland M. Smith USMC.

Planning and training for a big amphibious operation is probably the most difficult branch of military preparation. It never even approaches perfection because the units employed cannot be trained as a team; no one base is big enough to hold them all. In an operation requiring the most detailed planning and the nicest timing, Admiral Turner commanded men of the Army, Navy and Marine Corps attached to ships, planes and ground forces in points as far apart as New Zealand, Hawaii, San Diego and Alaska, organized in units very few of which he could even see before D-day.

There were preliminary carrier-plane strikes on Tarawa and Makin, submarine and photographic reconnaissance, and diversionary strikes on other islands such as Wake and Marcus, to confuse the Japanese. Every day for the week 13–20 November, Army and Navy Liberators bombed Tarawa and Makin. The sortie of surface forces from Pearl Harbor began as early as 21 October. Never before had there been such intensive activity in Pearl Harbor, in the Fijis and in the New Hebrides as during the last days of October and the first of November 1943. Then, suddenly, every harbor and roadstead was deserted. Over two hundred sail — the Fifth Fleet carrying 108,000 American soldiers, sailors, Marines and aviators under the command of taut Raymond Spruance, gallant Harry Hill, and bristling Kelly Turner — were on the high seas. By various and devious routes, they converged on two coral atolls whose names will be remembered as long as men prize valor: Makin and Tarawa.

We may dispose of the easier task first. This was Butaritari Island, Makin Atoll, defended by only 300 Japanese combat troops, with no higher officer than a lieutenant, and 500 labor troops. The landing was easy, but the ground troops made "infuriatingly slow" progress, as General "Howling Mad" Smith put it, despite a 23 to 1 superiority. These were two regiments from the 27th Infantry Division, a New York National Guard outfit that had gone stale from too long training. Thus, it was not until the fourth day of the assault, 24 November, that their commander could signal "Makin taken." The taking cost the Army 64 killed and 150 wounded; it was the Navy that paid dear. Admiral Koga, C. in C. Combined Fleet, committed nine submarines to break up the massive forces supporting the Gilbert Islands landings, and, owing to the slow work of our ground troops, which required naval forces to stay near the island, submarine *I–175* scored heavily. She torpedoed and sank escort carrier *Liscome Bay* on 24 November, taking the lives of Captain I. D. Wiltsie, Rear Admiral Henry M. Mullinnix, and 642 others.

All Japanese air counterattacks were thwarted by planes from aircraft carriers that Admiral Spruance brought up for that very purpose; their presence was a major factor in persuading Admiral Koga to keep Combined Fleet snug in Truk. But he fleeted up a few dozen land-based planes from Truk to Kwajalein; and these, after sunset Thanksgiving Day, 25 November, put on a beautiful show, a night attack on Admiral Turner's force of battleships, cruisers and escort carriers, operating about 60 miles east of Makin. The technique of Japanese night air attacks at this period of the war was spectacular. First, snoopers dropped strings of colored float lights to guide bombers to the enemy ships. When the bombers approached, the snoopers flew high over the ships and

dropped parachute flares, of a brilliance that none of our pyro-
technicians could match. Then the dive- and torpedo-bombers
bore in. Turner, an old hand at evading air attack, won this
contest of wits. His ships had been intensively drilled in radical
simultaneous turns on the voyage from Pearl Harbor, and they
performed so many that night as to afford the enemy no opportunity to score.

On the same Thanksgiving Day night, when Arleigh Burke was
sinking Japanese destroyers off Cape St. George, a group of Japanese planes attacked Rear Admiral Radford's Northern Carrier
Group (*Enterprise, Belleau Wood, Monterey*), which had been
furnishing air support for the Gilbert Islands operation. "Raddy"
had trained a radar-equipped night combat air patrol, and a group
of night fighters as well; they saw to it that not one hit was made
on the carriers. But Commander E. H. ("Butch") O'Hare, one of
the best pilots in the Navy, was shot down.

Thus, Makin was taken at slight cost by the Army, but at considerable cost to the Navy. It provided vivid proof of the necessity of speed in conquering an island, so as to release the covering
naval forces promptly. But, in marked contrast to Guadalcanal,
the main Japanese fleet was never committed, because it had been
temporarily paralyzed by the air attacks on Rabaul.

2. *Tarawa, 19–23 November 1943*

Betio Island, at the southwest corner of Tarawa Atoll, in shape
resembles an old-fashioned muzzle-loading musket, complete with
stock, lock and barrel, pointing a little south of east. The total
length is only 3800 yards; the width, 500 yards at the stock, 600
at the lock, tapering off to a point on the barrel; the area is less
than 300 acres. An airfield occupied the wide center part; and the
rest of the island was covered with a stand of coconut palms under

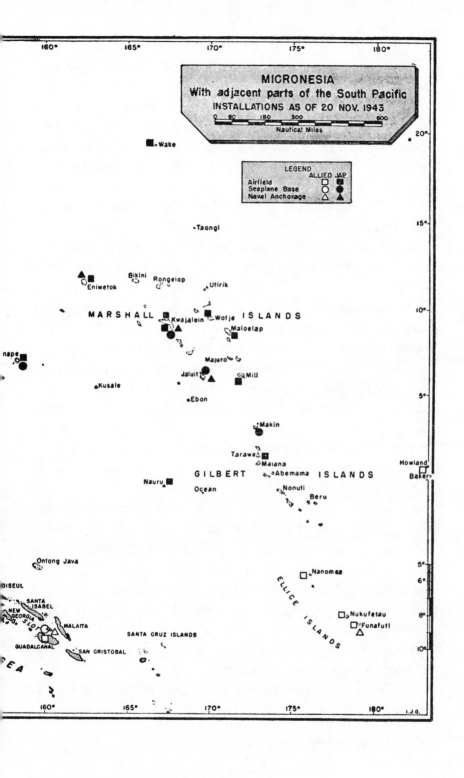

which a complete defensive system had been installed. The atoll commander, Rear Admiral Shibasaki, had 4500 picked troops under him, tough as mountain goats, and indoctrinated to fight to the last man, as they did — only 17 were taken prisoner. These troops had been there over a year with nothing to do but pepper the island with strongpoints. They had plenty of weapons, even 8-inch British naval guns captured at Singapore, and enough bomb-proof shelters to hold the entire garrison. No small island was ever so well protected or stubbornly defended as Betio.

Rear Admiral Hill commanded the Southern Attack Force that took Tarawa. In contrast to the dour and saturnine Turner, Harry Hill was a sanguine, genial officer who thought and talked like a young man and preferred to lead rather than drive. The landing force, the 2nd Marine Division, reinforced to about 18,600 men, was commanded by Major General Julian C. Smith, a student of the art of war and of human nature, who had the complete confidence of his officers and men. Admiral Hill and General Smith came up in battleship *Maryland*, a rehabilitated victim of Pearl Harbor. Pacific Fleet as yet had no specially equipped amphibious command ship, such as Hewitt enjoyed in Sicily, and *Maryland's* communications system, inadequate at best, had an annoying habit of conking out with each main battery salvo.

Beaches on the lagoon side of Betio were chosen as the least difficult of three tough places. The planners hoped that by landing on a three-battalion front the Marines could sweep across the island and capture the airfield in short order. The trouble with this lagoon-side landing was that transports had to unload outside, so that a ten-mile trip with a turn was required for landing craft. And, if the boats could not float over a wide shelving coral reef, the troops would have to wade. Tarawa tides at this season were unpredictable, and we drew the worst.

The Navy badly miscalculated the amount of softening-up that could be done in two and a half daylight hours' bombardment on the morning of D-day, 20 November, preceded and followed by air bombing from the attendant carriers. All coast defense guns were silenced and some destruction was done — but not nearly enough; nobody yet realized how much punishment the Japanese could take when protected by heavy concrete or several layers of coconut logs and coral sand.

This was the first operation to use a large number of amphtracs, LVTs. These, developed from "alligators" used in the Florida Everglades before the war, were 25-foot amphibious tractors that could carry 25 men and two machine guns, make 4 knots in the water, climb over coral reefs if necessary, and operate as tanks on land. Ninety-three LVTs — of which 90 were expended — made up the first three assault waves commanded by Colonel David M. Shoup. Delayed by a heavy chop and westerly set of current, they began hitting the beach at 0913. That was already 28 minutes after an already once-postponed H-hour.

This delay wrecked the landing timetable, to which an amphibious operation has to stick rigidly for success. Admiral Hill did not dare deliver gunfire support after 0855, because both island and lagoon were under a pall of smoke, and he feared hitting the landing craft. The cease-fire afforded the Japanese twenty minutes' grace, which they employed to transfer troops from the south shore to rifle pits and machine-gun nests on the lagoon side. Many Japanese guns had the LVTs under crossfire before landing. After the amphtracs came a wave of tank-loaded LCMs from LSD *Ashland*. These, stranded on the coral apron by an unexpectedly low tide, had to discharge Sherman tanks in three to four feet of water, which drowned out some of the engines. And as no landing craft could float over the reef, troops had to wade for 400 to 500 yards under heavy fire, in water waist-deep, which meant death by drowning for a wound or a stumble.

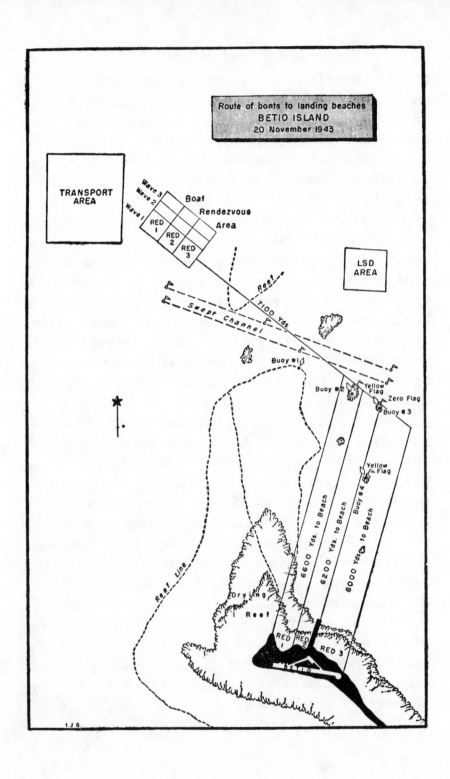

Route of boats to landing beaches
BETIO ISLAND
20 November 1943

Between noon and 1400, the situation ashore was very critical. Some 1500 Marines were pinned down on a narrow beach under a wall of coconut logs and coral blocks, behind which the enemy was shooting everything he had at men wading ashore. General Julian Smith at 1330 radioed General H. M. Smith, who was in battleship *Pennsylvania* off Makin, requesting release of the reserve, and ending with the ominous words: ISSUE IN DOUBT.

By the end of D-day, about 5000 Marines had landed, but at least 1500 had been killed or wounded. Intrepid officers led small squads inland, rooting out defenders as they advanced, and established a 300-yard-wide beachhead by evening.

Next day, 21 November, Major L. C. Hays's battalion of the divisional reserve fought its way ashore, losing 13 officers and 331 men in so doing. Around noon that day, when the laggard tide finally rose and landing craft could steam right up to the beach, the tide of battle turned. Next day the Japanese were thrust into two or three pockets, and by the end of the 23rd these had been eliminated. The first American plane landed on the airstrip at noon. It only remained to send a squad of Marines up the atoll to rescue the Catholic mission station in the northern part, and to exterminate the last of the Japanese garrison.

Tarawa was ours, at heavy cost — the lives of over 1000 Marines and sailors, with more than double that number of wounded. They were not wasted. As a result of intensive study of reports by everyone, from admirals and generals down to boat wave ensigns, many valuable lessons were learned, and these rendered most later amphibious operations in the Pacific, in comparison, pushovers. The relatively easy conquest of Kwajalein in January 1944 is owed to lessons learned at Tarawa; to a perfect take-off position, the triangle Tarawa–Makin–Abemama,[1] captured in November; and to

[1] Abemama, 75 miles southeast of Tarawa, was occupied 21 November by 78 Marines, lifted in submarine *Nautilus*. In three weeks Seabees built O'Hare Field, which became very useful in the Marshalls operation.

using this position, as well as carrier planes, for photographic reconnaissance and for neutralizing enemy air power in the Marshalls before D-day.

All honor, then, to the fighting heart of the United States Marine. Let the battle for that small stretch of coral sand called Betio of Tarawa be remembered as terrible indeed, but glorious, and the seedbed for victory in 1945.

3. *Kwajalein* (*Operation* FLINTLOCK), *January–February 1944*

Although it had long since been decided that the Marshalls would come next after the Gilberts, it was not determined until December what would happen after that. Should the now vastly stronger Pacific Fleet combine with Kinkaid's Seventh Fleet to help General MacArthur roll up the back of the New Guinea bird into the Celebes Sea, and on to Mindanao? Or should the General be left to do that with his own Navy, and Admiral Nimitz continue to hew out a second road to Tokyo across the Central Pacific? Admiral King won the approval of the C.C.S. in its "Sextant" Conference at Cairo, on 3 December 1943, for the Nimitz plan of dual approach. Their principal directive was as follows: —

"The advance along the New Guinea–N.E.I.–Philippine axis will proceed concurrently with operations for the capture of the Mandated Islands. A strategic bombing force will be established in Guam, Tinian and Saipan for strategic bombing of Japan proper."

This bombing force meant the Superfortresses, the B–29s. The need of a base for them in the Marianas was a principal reason why the King-Nimitz idea prevailed over the all-under-MacArthur plan. Other reasons were (1) the planned all-British amphibious operation to retake Burma as a "second front" against Japan had been scrapped; (2) fast carrier forces of the Pacific Fleet were not suitable for employment in the narrow seas south of the Philippines, with Japanese air bases on all sides; (3) Saipan would make an ideal advanced base for United States submarines, which with new and more effective torpedoes had finally got into their stride and were rapidly reducing Japanese merchant tonnage.

Momentum, a word that continually recurs in strategic discussions, was a great consideration. For, the closer that one offensive steps on the heels of the other, the greater will be one's gain and the enemy's loss and confusion. Japan had proved that in early 1942; we now intended to turn the same principle against her. Momentum settled the question of which Marshall atolls should be taken, and which leapfrogged. Nimitz's bold plan provided that undefended Majuro be taken first, for the sake of its anchorage; that both ends of Kwajalein, the hub of the enemy's defense system, be assaulted simultaneously the second day; and that Eniwetok be taken as soon as possible thereafter. All the rest of the atolls, even those with airfields, would be skipped. Admirals Spruance and Turner and General H. M. Smith argued against the plan as too bold, but Nimitz correctly estimated that his fast carrier forces, together with aircraft based on the Makin-Tarawa-Abemama triangle, could neutralize Japanese air power in the Marshalls before operation began. And he now had enough battleships and heavy cruisers to take on the Combined Fleet in case it sortied from Truk.

Fast Carrier Force Pacific Fleet had become really formidable by the first of the new year. Besides old "Big E" and "Sara," Rear Admiral Mitscher had *Essex* and three more of her class, six light carriers of the *Independence* class, with new *Iowa* class battleships and plenty of cruisers and destroyers to screen them. Divided into four task groups, they raided one or more atolls in the Marshalls every day from 29 January to 6 February, virtually destroying enemy air and sea power in the archipelago before the amphibious operation began. And they covered it thereafter. Escort carriers were also present, to furnish close air support.

Rear Admiral Turner (at last in an amphibious command ship, *Rocky Mount*) commanded the entire expeditionary force. Rear Admiral Conolly, fresh from participation in the Salerno operation, took charge of the northern half, lifting the new 4th Marine Division to occupy Roi and Namur Islands on Kwajalein Atoll. Turner himself commanded the southern half, lifting the 7th Infantry Division to take Kwajalein Island.

Japan made almost no attempt to counter this massive onslaught. The Halsey-MacArthur campaign against the Bismarcks Barrier had thrown her forces off balance. Admiral Koga dared not commit Combined Fleet, because his carrier air groups had been expended to defend Rabaul. The Marshalls were only a "holding" front for the Japanese; Imperial Headquarters decided to expend the garrisons and strengthen the next defensive perimeter, Timor–Western New Guinea–Truk–Marianas. A force of submarines was sent up from Truk to do what it could; but not one got a lethal hit, and four, including *I–175* which had torpedoed *Liscome Bay* off Makin, were sunk by our destroyers or destroyer escorts.

Majuro, the undefended atoll, was occupied 31 January 1944, by the attack group under Rear Admiral Hill which later went on to take Eniwetok. Compared with other atolls where the garrison had to camp among the debris of battle, Majuro proved a paradise for American soldiers and sailors. Its spacious lagoon, well served the new mobile supply force of auxiliaries, under Captain Worrall R. Carter, who became SOPA Majuro.

Kwajalein is the world's largest coral atoll, composed of a string of one hundred islands and islets, enclosing an irregularly shaped lagoon 66 miles long and at places 20 miles wide. At the southeast corner is Kwajalein Island, where the Japanese were constructing a bomber strip; at the northern tip were two small connected is-

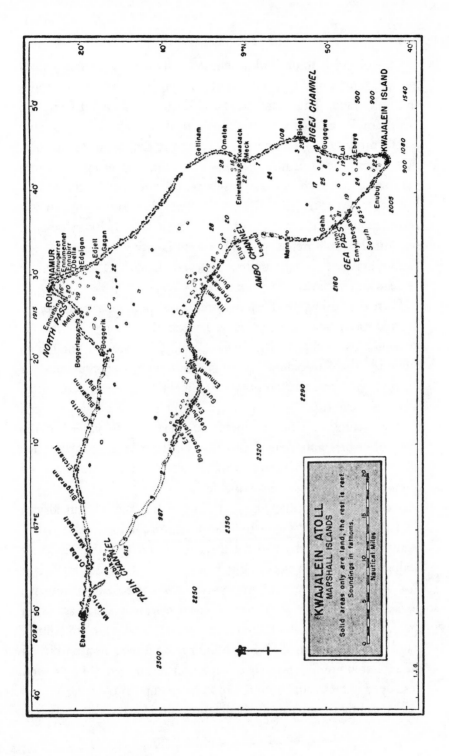

KWAJALEIN ATOLL
MARSHALL ISLANDS

Solid areas only are land, the rest is reef

Soundings in fathoms.

Nautical Miles

lands, Roi and Namur, within whose small area, a mile and a quarter long and three quarters wide, the Japanese had 3500 troops and an airfield. This pair was the objective of Admiral Conolly's Northern Force. Since it was impractical to make a surf landing on the outer coast, it was necessary to boat the assault troops outside, where the atoll made some sort of lee, and bring them into the lagoon through narrow passes which fortunately the enemy had neglected to fortify. But the landing plan had to be so fussy and complicated that plenty of things went wrong. Every foul-up was finally straightened out and every D-day (31 January) objective attained shortly before nightfall. Casualties amounted to 24 dead and missing and 40 wounded.

Then the real agony began. Three days' preliminary air bombing and naval bombardment (this at such close range that the admiral got the nickname "Close-in Conolly") were not enough to pulverize the Roi-Namur rectangle, although a vast amount of damage was done and possibly half the Japanese defenders killed. The rest had to be rooted out, man by man. Roi was secured by the evening of 1 February; Namur next day. It was a stinking mess of debris and dead Japanese. Hardly a tree was left alive in what had been a pretty wooded island, and of the hundred or more buildings not one was usable.

A dismal prospect met the garrison group when it steamed into the lagoon a few days later to relieve the 4th Division. All air protection was removed when the carriers retired, and the particular Seabee outfit sent in with the garrison was so lazy and inefficient that by 12 February the runways were not yet ready to receive planes. That day, these islands received a stinging backlash from the Japanese. A flight of several 4-engined bombers from Saipan, staged through Ponape, hit Roi-Namur and with its bombs touched off an ammunition dump whose explosion killed many Marines and destroyed immense quantities of food and equipment.

The southern attack, on boomerang-shaped Kwajalein Island,

was characterized by a large contingent of LVTs and dukws, and by perfect coöperation between Army and Navy. Here, too, D-day (31 January) was devoted to securing islets adjacent to the objective and basing artillery thereon for the main assault. Admiral Turner, first to admit that Tarawa had not been bombarded long enough or well enough, was determined that this island should be properly pulverized. To execute this worthy object, he started it with four battleships, three heavy cruisers, eleven destroyers and three escort carriers, on 30 January. He continued it all next day and on D-day, 1 February, from 0618 to 0840 and from 0905 to H-hour 0930. And a drop of 2000-pound bombs, flown up from Tarawa, was thrown in.

A well-executed amphibious assault is as beautiful a military spectacle as one can find in warfare, and this one was superbly done in a setting of deep blue white-capped sea, fluffy tradewind clouds, flashing gunfire and billowing smoke over the target, gaily colored flag hoists at the yardarms of the ships and on the signal halyards of the control craft. At 0928 all four LVT waves were approaching the beach in line, not one of the 84 amphtracs falling behind more than a couple of lengths, their cupped tracks churning the blue water into curling sheepskins of white foam, their square bows throwing spray until everyone on board was drenched, but nobody cared. This was what the 7th Division had come for, to kill more of those you-know-what who had cost them so many buddies on Attu. LCI gunboats were flashing and crackling; battleships off shore were booming and belching huge gobs of orange-tinted smoke, and on the island palm trees and parts of buildings were rising in the air.

First wave hit the beaches right at H-hour — 0930. Within twelve minutes, 1200 officers and men had landed without a single casualty. But the Japanese were not wiped out; Rear Admiral Akiyama, the island commander, had prepared his defenses well, and at least half of his more than 5000 troops were still alive.

In the center was a complex of trenches, antitank traps, pillboxes, blockhouses and air-raid shelters, and here the invading infantrymen ran into trouble. The island had to be taken inch by inch, and was not secured until the morning of 5 February. Except for about 35 men, who surrendered, the garrison was annihilated. It only remained, in this southern sector of the bit atoll, to take Ebeye, where there was a garrison of 400, and a few lesser islets.

By 7 February Kwajalein Atoll was entirely American. One of the most complicated amphibious campaigns in history, involving landings on 30 different islets, fights on at least ten, and bloody battles on three, had come to a successful conclusion within a week. The price was far less than had been paid for the Gilberts. The Navy suffered negligible casualties. Out of 41,000 troops committed, 372 soldiers and Marines died on this atoll; on the Japanese side, 7870 men out of 8675 were wiped out.

4. *Truk Bombed, Eniwetok Taken, February 1944*

With Kwajalein in the bag, flag officers and generals turned their attention to Eniwetok Atoll. Admiral Spruance asked Nimitz to let him push right on to this western outpost to the Marshalls, 326 miles WNW of Roi, and only 1000 miles from the Marianas. The very name Eniwetok, meaning "Land between West and East," suggests strategic importance. For the primitive Micronesians it had been a place of call and refreshment in their long canoe voyages from west to east; now it would become an important staging point for the United States Army, Navy and Marine Corps in their spectacular progress from east to west.

Spruance had his wish, and detailed planning began on board Turner's command ship *Rocky Mount* on 14 February. Captain D. W. Loomis's Reserve Force, waiting at Majuro Lagoon, was al-

ready tagged for CATCHPOLE — code name for the Eniwetok operation — and Admiral Hill eagerly assumed the top command. But
the destructive attack of 12 February on Roi-Namur by Japanese
long-range bombers from Saipan, staged through Ponape, proved
that this island, and Truk, needed attention before Eniwetok could
be captured. Liberators of General Willis Hale's VII Army Air
Force, based at Tarawa, pounded Ponape between 15 and 26 February, to such good purpose that there could be no interference
thence. And on Eniwetok D-day (17 February) the fast carrier
forces began a two-day visit to Truk which rendered this "Gibraltar of the Pacific" little more use to Japan, and unnecessary for us
to capture.

An Airsols reconnaissance plane on 4 February found a good
part of Combined Fleet in Truk Lagoon, but Admiral Koga got
most of his ships out in time. Light cruiser *Agano*, however, was
sunk by U.S. submarine *Skate* (Lieutenant Commander W. F.
Gruner) as she sortied. Mitscher's fliers found some 50 merchant
ships in the lagoon and 365 aircraft on the airfields when they
jumped the atoll at dawn 17 February. Their first strike of 72
fighters, followed by 18 Avengers dropping incendiaries, left fewer
than 100 Japanese planes operational. In the meantime Mitscher's
dive-bombers were merrily knocking off ships in the lagoon. That
evening the enemy got off his one and only counterattack, and
managed to make a hit on carrier *Intrepid*, whose propensity to
collect Japanese bombs and torpedoes earned her a nickname,
"The Evil I."

In the meantime, Admiral Spruance in battleship *New Jersey*
was conducting a round-the-atoll cruise with *Iowa*, two heavy
cruisers and four destroyers, to catch escaping ships. They sank
light cruiser *Katori* and destroyer *Maikaze;* but destroyer *Nowaki*,
straddled by the battlewagons' 16-inch salvos at ranges between
17 and 20 miles, managed to escape unhurt, and even launched a
spread of torpedoes. That night Mitscher started bombing with

specially equipped Avengers. Flight operations were resumed by *Enterprise, Yorktown, Essex* and *Bunker Hill* at dawn 18 February; and by noon, when Mitscher decided to pick up and retire, his aviators had destroyed 200,000 tons of merchant shipping, two destroyers and some 275 planes.

This two-days-and-one-night raid on Truk was one of the most successful of the war. For the first time a major enemy base was beaten down without the aid of land-based air power or an amphibious invasion. Truk was still usable for planes, and the buildings were not too badly damaged, but it had become as vulnerable to the Japanese as Pearl Harbor had been to the Pacific Fleet on 7 December 1941. Never again would the eight-rayed flag of C. in C. Combined Fleet meet the rising sun in Truk Lagoon.

The capture of Eniwetok could now proceed without interference from a single enemy plane. The landings at Engebi Island in the north on 17 February by the 22nd Marine Regiment (Brigadier General T. E. Watson USMC) were similar in character to those at Roi-Namur, and even more complicated. The thousand or more Japanese defenders were rendered punch-drunk by the preliminary bombardment and offered comparatively light resistance. Engebi was ours by 1640 February 18, at the cost of 85 Marines killed. But the southern operations against Parry and Eniwetok Islands turned up a number of surprises. The Japanese neatly fooled the invaders into believing that these islands were unoccupied. They had concealed themselves and their weapons from photo interpreters of the Pacific Fleet, and from the eyes of Admiral Hill's lookouts when his ships passed only a biscuit-toss from Parry to enter the lagoon. An Intelligence team, combing through the debris on Engebi, found papers indicating that Eniwetok and Parry Islands were actually defended by 2155 men of Major General Nishida's 1st Amphibious Brigade, a veteran unit of the toughest fighters bred in Japan. Faced with this situation, General Wat-

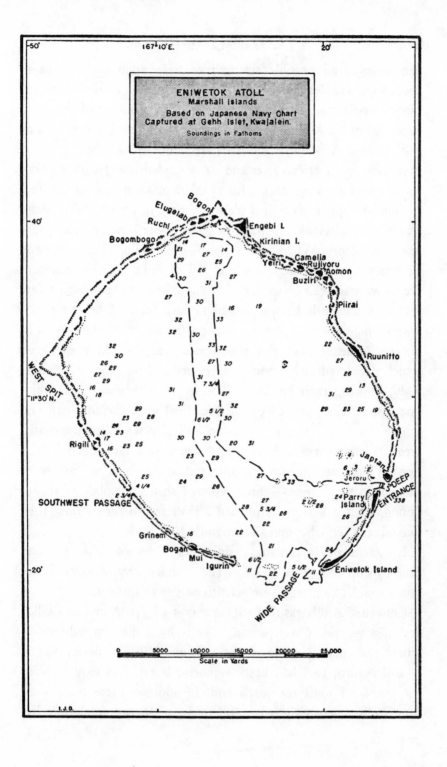

ENIWETOK ATOLL
Marshall Islands
Based on Japanese Navy Chart
Captured at Gehh Islet, Kwajalein.
Soundings in Fathoms

son brought all possible strength to bear upon each island in succession. He decided to throw both battalions of the 106th Infantry Regiment into Eniwetok Island, southernmost of the atoll, together with a Marine reserve battalion brought down from Engebi. Eniwetok Island was not secured until 1630 February 21. It cost only 37 American lives and 94 wounded; the Japanese garrison of about 800 men, except for 23 taken prisoner, was annihilated.

Gunfire support ships had plenty of time to pound Parry Island north of Eniwetok, fortunately, since 1350 hidey-hole Japanese were there. When the Marine Corps landings began at 0900 February 22 the enemy was still full of fight, and his emplacements were so well concealed as to be difficult to spot even a few feet away. Assault troops pushed rapidly forward behind tanks, with demolition and flame-thrower parties directly behind to burn out each enemy nest. But the terrain was studded with mines which detonated on 35 pounds' pressure and tore men apart horribly, blowing their bodies to bits. In the afternoon, in skirmish line, the Marines pushed on to their final goal, the southern end where the enemy was in the open. "Finally we killed them all," wrote Lieutenant Cord Meyer. "There was not much jubilation. We just sat and stared at the sand, and most of us thought of those who were gone — those whom I shall remember as always young, smiling and graceful, and I shall try to forget how they looked at the end, beyond all recognition."

It was one of those many, many times in the war when you had time to stop and think about it, and wonder why mankind is not wise enough to end this senseless suffering and slaughter.

Eniwetok Atoll was secured, at a cost of 339 Americans killed and missing, and 2677 Japanese. Four atolls of the Marshalls group where the enemy had air bases — Jaluit, Mili, Maloelap, Wotje — and Nauru, too, had been bypassed; but it was easy to keep them isolated until the war's end. In addition there were some fifty atolls where only a handful of Japanese, or none, were living; the now famous Bikini, for instance, was occupied by a detachment of Marines in one landing craft after the garrison of five Japanese had committed suicide.

Looking back, Admiral Dick Conolly said: "The Marshalls really cracked the Japanese shell. It broke the crust of their defenses on a scale that could be exploited at once. It gave them no time adequately to fortify their inner defense line that ran through the Marianas." Operations CATCHPOLE and FLINTLOCK and the strikes on Truk enhanced the reputation of the United States Navy. Courage and determination it had shown from the first; but in the Marshalls it demonstrated mastery of the art of amphibious warfare; of combining air, surface, submarine and ground forces to project fighting power irresistibly across the ocean.

CHAPTER XI

New Guinea and the Marianas

April–August 1944

1. *The Conquest of New Guinea*

WHILE SPRUANCE'S FIFTH FLEET and Turner's V 'Phib Force were crashing through the Central Pacific to Eniwetok, Kinkaid's Seventh Fleet and Barbey's VII 'Phib were making equally spectacular leaps along New Guinea. These were shore-to-shore operations, performed largely in the three leading types of beaching craft — LST, LCT and LCI, of which Mac-Arthur never had enough. The last two types, the 114-foot Landing Craft Tank and the 173-foot Landing Craft Infantry, had to perform long hauls and house crews for months on end in compartments designed for a night run across the English Channel. Fast converted destroyer-transports were also used. The covering forces were meager compared with the array of powerful gunfire ships disposed of by Spruance. Rear Admiral Crutchley RN had two heavy cruisers (H.M.A.S. *Australia*, flag) and a few destroyers; Rear Admiral Berkey had three light cruisers (*Phoenix*, flag) and a few more destroyers. Seventh Fleet had four squadrons of amphibious Catalinas, each with its tender; but for air support it depended mainly on General Kenney's Southwest Pacific Air Force, with its many bases and ample strength on New Guinea. Under MacArthur, Generals Eichelberger and Krueger were in command of the ground operations.

We left the Southwest Pacific forces at Manus in the Admiralties in March 1944, after finally breaching the Bismarck Barrier and sealing off Rabaul. General MacArthur's next plan was to leap-frog the strong Japanese garrison at Wewak into Hollandia, and set up new advance headquarters there. Some 215 vessels, mostly beaching craft, were divided into three attack groups, commanded by Rear Admiral Barbey, Rear Admiral Fechteler, and Captain A. G. Noble, each in a destroyer — no luxurious amphibious command ships here. But each attack group had an LSD to bring pre-boated tanks to the targets.

By this time, it had become clear that the success of an amphibious operation depended in great measure on preliminary pounding of enemy air power at the target. By the end of March the Japanese had assembled 351 aircraft on the airfields about Hollandia. On the 30th and on 3, 5, and 12 April, General Kenney made massive air attacks, which almost completely knocked out Hollandia as an enemy air base; carrier aircraft added frosting to the cake on 21 April. For General MacArthur had obtained an order that Mitscher's flattops must support him at Hollandia. It turned out the help was not needed. Not one enemy plane rose from the five target fields to intercept the carrier-borne bombers.

The Hollandia operation was perfectly planned and smoothly executed. D-day was 22 April, and by 3 May the Japanese airfields at Lake Sentani in the hills above the town were in our possession.

Supreme Allied Commander Southwest Pacific needed no urging to push his westward advance rapidly along the New Guinea coast. General MacArthur had already outlined to his planning staff a series of assaults, all pointing toward Mindanao, target date 15 November. Four operations — Wakde, Biak, Noemfoor and Sansapor — carried him and his forces to the northwest point of New Guinea's Vogelkop, 550 miles west of Hollandia, in a little more than three months. Seventh Fleet handled the highly important seaborne aspects of this advance, since the ocean was the only possible road. Motor torpedo boat squadrons, as eager as the Army Air Force to secure forward bases, also took part in this breathless race.

Before the next operation came off — an invasion of the Wakde-Sarmi area on 17 May — the disquieting discovery had been made that heavy bombers could not use the Lake Sentani airfields, and that no site suitable for them existed in Dutch New Guinea, short of Biak Island. Hence, until Biak could be taken, the heavies would have to continue operating from Nadzab, 440 miles east of Hollandia, or from the Admiralties. The need for full speed ahead being evident, General MacArthur decided to simplify the Wakde-Sarmi operation and move on into Biak as soon as possible. Rear Admiral Fechteler, who commanded VII 'Phib in Admiral Barbey's absence, promised to assault Biak ten days after Wakde, which was taken by Captain Noble's group of VII 'Phib and the 163rd RCT, Brigadier General Jens Doe, after two days' fighting, on 19 May. Army engineers had made the airstrip operational even for Liberators. But it was a long, tough job for the Army to capture the adjacent mainland.

Biak is one of the Schouten Islands that close in Geelvink Bay, at the neck of the New Guinea bird. The occupation of this big, reef-fringed island started on 27 May. The landing force under Major General Horace F. Fuller USA and VII 'Phib under Admiral Fechteler were fortunate to get away with it, since the 10,-000 Japanese defenders were amost as numerous as the attacking force and were not surprised. Colonel Kuzume, their commander, denied to us for a month the two Biak airfields within ten miles of the landing beaches by a skillful defense in depth — tactics later developed at Peleliu and Iwo Jima.

The Japanese Navy here tried to interfere with an amphibious operation for the first time since Bougainville. Admiral Toyoda[1]

---

[1] Admiral Koga, Yamamoto's successor as Commander in Chief Combined Fleet, was killed in an airplane accident around 1 April, and was succeeded by Admiral Soemu Toyoda, a much more aggressive character.

realized that heavy bombers based at Biak would be a handicap to his plan for a big naval battle in mid-1944 — a plan of which we shall hear more shortly. He therefore decided to transport 2500 amphibious troops from Mindanao to Biak. Three attempts were made by a reinforcement echelon of destroyers under Rear Admiral Sakonju, who was no Tanaka. Once he was turned back by a false report of an aircraft carrier, and on 8 June he was chased off by Crutchley's cruiser-destroyer force. Toyoda now assembled a really powerful striking force, built around superbattleships *Yamato* and *Musashi*, which should have been able to sink anything in Seventh Fleet. Three days before it was to head for Biak, C. in C. Combined Fleet decided, correctly, that Spruance's Fifth Fleet was about to land in the Marianas, and pulled all naval forces north into the Philippine Sea.

Colonel Kuzume's stubborn but hopeless defense of Biak continued until 22 June. The capture of this island cost Allied ground forces 438 killed, 2300 battle wounded, and 3500 cases of typhus. It became an important air base in subsequent operations for the liberation of the Philippines.

When Biak was proving difficult, General MacArthur's planners began looking for airfield sites on the Vogelkop, the head of the New Guinea bird. They first pitched upon the almost circular island of Noemfoor, about eleven miles in diameter, midway between Biak and Manokwari. A task force was hurriedly assembled, a naval bombardment delivered on the morning of 2 July, and the landing made that afternoon. An important component of the assault force was boated in LCMs, the 50-foot open Landing Craft Mechanized, manned by amphibious Army engineers; it took them 12 days to make the 700-mile passage from Finschhafen.

To complete his control of New Guinea and prepare for the invasion of Mindanao, MacArthur wanted one more air base on the Vogelkop. This was obtained at Sansapor on 30 July by Admiral Fechteler, commanding 16 destroyer types and numerous beaching craft, mounted at Wakde. There was no opposition. Sansapor was MacArthur's last stop in New Guinea on his long return journey to the Philippines.

This advance of 550 miles from Hollandia to Cape Sansapor required little more than three months, with three big Japanese air bases—Hollandia, Wakde, Biak—picked up en route, and a fourth, Wewak, leapfrogged. Expert planning and a high order of teamwork between Army, Navy and Air Forces of the United States and Australia produced these results; but it is questionable whether they could have been attained under any other commander but Douglas MacArthur. Everyone who served under him, in whatever arm of the service or from whatever country, acquired a great respect for his military judgment and leadership. We have seen how smartly his operations were executed, on or very close to the target dates set, with few of the snarls usual in military affairs. We shall now leave him consolidating his positions and preparing for his heart's desire — his return to the Phillippines — while we shift our attention to great doings around the Marianas and in the broad reaches of the Philippine Sea.

2. *The Marianas* (*Operation* FORAGER), *February–June 1944*

The fifteen Mariana or Ladrone Islands stretch for some 425 miles in an arc, of which the 145th meridian east longitude is the chord. Starting with Farallon de Pájaros, 335 miles southeast of Iwo Jima, and ending with Guam, 250 miles north of the Carolines, this chain forms with the Bonins the upright bar of the big Micronesian "L," the foot of which is the Carolines and Marshalls. The four biggest Marianas — Saipan, Tinian, Rota and Guam, all at the southernmost end — are those with which we are concerned; only they had any military or economic value.

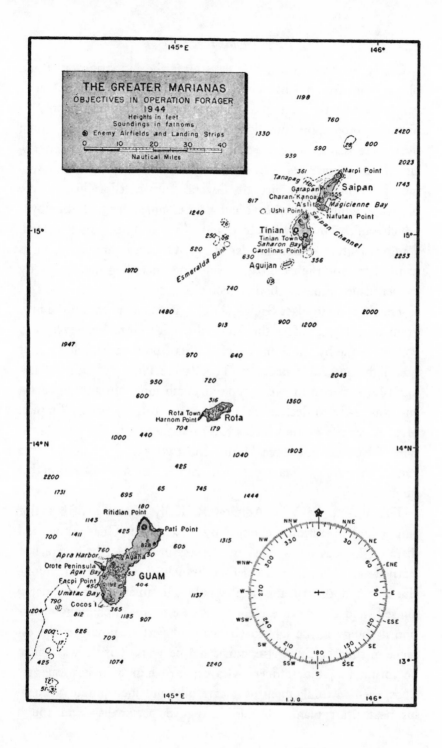

THE GREATER MARIANAS
OBJECTIVES IN OPERATION FORAGER
1944
Heights in feet
Soundings in fathoms
⊕ Enemy Airfields and Landing Strips

0   10   20   30   40
Nautical Miles

On 23 February 1944, five days after the big strike on Truk, planes from Admiral Mitscher's carriers dropped the first American bombs on the Marianas. Cincpac ordered this raid mainly to obtain photographic intelligence, no Allied plane having flown over these islands since the fall of Guam in December 1941. Pacific Fleet submarines were stationed around them to shoot surface game flushed by aircraft. Several ships sailed right into the periscope sights of *Sunfish* (Lieutenant Commander E. E. Shelby), which sank two *Marus* before and after daybreak on the 23rd. *Tang* (Lieutenant Commander R. H. O'Kane) sank four, in as many days; and the total bag of shipping, including those sunk by carrier planes, came to about 45,000 tons.

The decision to place Saipan, Tinian, and Guam next on the program of conquest after the Marshalls, with target date 15 June, was not made by the Joint Chiefs of Staff until 12 March 1944. It was high time for a decision. The Pacific Fleet had become immensely powerful in every type of combatant ship and auxiliary, and was ready to deal another hard blow to the Japanese Empire. Most American ground forces had been allotted to the great invasion of Europe, but three Marine and two Army divisions in the Pacific were ready to take part in a major amphibious operation that summer.

This was to be Vice Admiral R. Kelly Turner's fifth major amphibious operation. Schooled by adversity at Guadalcanal and Tarawa, he was not spoiled by success in the Marshalls. He had learned more about this specialized branch of warfare than anyone else ever had, or probably ever would. He supervised every detail himself; and there were plenty, because in an amphibious operation nothing can be left to chance, and perfect timing is the essence of success. Energetic, quick and nervous, Turner was apt to be abrupt to junior officers who came to him with new suggestions, then to think them over carefully and incorporate them in his next draft plan. For all his rugged personality and rough tongue, "Kelly" had a keen intellect and complete intellectual honesty. He drafted the concept, dated 4 April, on which Operation FORAGER was based: "The objective is the capture of Saipan, Tinian and Guam, in order to secure control of sea communications through the Central Pacific for the support of further attacks on the Japanese."

No amphibious operation on so vast a scale, with a final thousand-mile "hop," had before been planned, although Operation TORCH was a close approximation. Inherent difficulties peculiar to amphibious warfare were enhanced by the distance of the Marianas from any Allied continental base, and by the operation's size. Some 535 combatant ships and auxiliaries carried 127,571 troops, of which over two thirds were Marines. The destination lay 1000 miles' steaming from Eniwetok, the nearest advanced base, which was little more than an anchorage, and 3500 miles from Pearl Harbor. Logistics problems alone would have condemned this operation as impossible in 1941, for the distance meant that the entire expeditionary force had to be afloat at the same time, and that the ships allotted could do nothing else for at least three months.

It is difficult to change logistic plans for a series of naval offensives after the procession of shipborne supplies has started. The flow may be slowed down or diverted to alternate harbors and warehouses if available, but it cannot be reversed without immense confusion and waste. Operations of the magnitude and complexity of FORAGER and its successors were so new to American (or to any) logistics planners that few were capable of planning beyond the assault phase.[2] Fortunately, Admiral Spruance, Commander Fifth Fleet, was one of these few. He understood that

[2] The planning for OVERLORD (Normandy) may be cited to the contrary. But a cross-Channel operation, under various names, had been in the planning stage since early 1942, whilst Nimitz received his directive for FORAGER only three months before its D-day.

FORAGER was but a means to a further end; and he saw to it that his and Turner's plans for the assault were coördinated with those for base development in the Marianas. In this he had the intelligent coöperation of Vice Admiral William L. Calhoun, Commander Service Force Pacific Fleet, and his subordinates, Commodores W. R. Carter of the floating service force and Augustine Gray, "the oil king of the Pacific."

While the Joint Expeditionary Force was at sea, the Pacific Fleet was being reorganized, to accelerate the tempo of the Pacific war. The old South Pacific command was maintained at Nouméa, now a rear base, but Admiral Halsey was placed under Nimitz, with the title Commander Third Fleet, in the same echelon as Admiral Spruance. Thus, the Pacific Fleet command was divided into two teams, the first Spruance's and the second Halsey's. One would plan and train while the other fought, reducing time between operations. Vice Admiral Mitscher's Fast Carrier Force, designated TF 58 when under Spruance's command, and TF 38 when under Halsey's, operated almost continuously, together with most of the gunfire support ships. As Admiral Nimitz put it, "The team remains about the same, but the drivers change."

To invade Saipan was the greatest challenge that the Allies had yet thrown at Japan. She regarded that island as part of her home land, as well as a link in her inner defense perimeter. Yet, owing to the newly won command of the sea by the Pacific Fleet, Japan was unable to reinforce Saipan after April 1944. General Saito, the Army commander, had only 22,700 troops under him when the Americans landed. Admiral Nagumo, who had lost his carriers at Midway, was also on Saipan in command of a small-craft fleet and about 6700 sailors. We have Pacific Fleet submarines to thank for Saito's lack of reinforcement; one Japanese regiment lost all its weapons and ammunition and most of its men when several ships of the convoy lifting it to Saipan were sunk by *Shark*, *Pintado* and *Pilotfish*.

From 11 June Admiral Mitscher's four fast carrier groups carried the ball with heavy bombing attacks on the Marianas airfields. Seven new battleships under Admiral Lee's command were detached from Mitscher's TF 58 on 13 June to bombard Saipan. But this shore bombardment was a failure; the new battlewagons simply did not know how to do it. Next day, the old "Pearl Harbor survivors" did much better, and under their cover the Underwater Demolition Teams of "frogmen" charted channels through the lagoon that bordered the beaches on the leeward coast of Saipan. There were no boat mines or other obstacles such as those that did so much damage on the Omaha beaches in Normandy — the reason being that the Japanese never expected to defend anything, only to conquer, so they were not prepared with defensive matériel other than coast defense guns.

3. *Saipan Invaded, June 1944*

We have now reached Saipan D-day, 15 June. At 0542 Admiral Turner made the signal: "Land the Landing Force." Chaplains offered a last prayer and a blessing — over loud-speakers. Amphtracs laden with troops, taken on board at Eniwetok, poured from the maws of the LSTs. From the big transports other Marines crawled down landing nets into boats. Those who gazed at the shoreline through binoculars could see a narrow beach backed by sandy soil and low scrubby trees, with an occasional palm grove or flame tree blooming with vermillion flowers. The land rose in a series of low escarpments like steps, and Mount Tapotchau dominated the scene. It was not in the least like anything the Marines had assaulted before.

The landings took place on a two-division front on eight beaches, almost four miles long. The line of departure was established 4000 yards off shore, and fifteen hundred yards to seaward were stationed 64 LSTs with the assault troops. Twenty-four gunboats preceded the initial wave to deliver close 40-mm fire support. As the long waves of amphtracs, each trailing a plume of white spray, raced with their supporters toward the beaches, the fire support battleships, cruisers and destroyers, anchored only 1250 yards off shore, delivered frontal and enfilading fire on beach defenses. And as the amphtracs began crawling over the barrier reef, 72 planes from escort carriers, including 12 Avengers armed with rockets, came down in vicious, hawklike swoops to strafe the beaches and the area just behind, the rockets making a sound like the crack of a gigantic whiplash.

At 0844 the initial wave touched down and at once came under intense fire, but pressed resolutely on. Within eight minutes there were troops on every beach, and some were fighting their way across the Charan Kanoa airstrip. As the second wave came in, around 0857, amphtracs of the first were beginning to retract, passing through the second, third and fourth waves with expert helmsmanship. Among these 600 and more LVTs and landing craft, tearing to and fro for the space of two hours, there was not a single serious collision, so well had the training center done its work, and so expertly did Commodore Theiss and his 50 control craft direct the movement. Despite all hazards, 8000 Marines got ashore in the first 20 minutes; and all day long, and after dark, landing craft were plying furiously between the transports and the beaches.

Little, however, went according to plan after the troops were ashore. The reason for landing on so broad a front was to seize a big enough beachhead to allow deployment. Subsequent waves were to mop up behind the first, dig in for the night, next day capture the airfield and strike cross-island to Magicienne Bay. Saipan would be "in the bag," and the assault on Guam could start. But it did not work out that way. The No. 1 objective line was not reached for three days, nor Saipan secured for three weeks, and the assault on Guam had to be delayed until 21 July.

The main reason for this miscarriage was the skill of Japanese artillery and mortar fire, which prevented amphtracs from fulfilling their assignment to carry troops well inland, and forced most of them to disgorge their passengers near the water's edge. By nightfall, although 20,000 assault troops had been landed, one tenth of them were casualties, and only half of the planned beachhead had been occupied.

Unhappy hours lay ahead for the Marines. There is something particularly terrifying about the first night on a hostile beach, when you are the underdog. The Japanese saw to it that nobody slept for more than a few minutes. After a series of probes, their big effort was announced at 0300 June 16 by a bugler; and with much screaming, brandishing of swords and flapping of flags the enemy launched an attack that was supposed to drive the Marines into the sea. As the Japanese fell others replaced them, and the fighting on this flank did not reach its climax until sunrise, at 0545. Five Marine Corps tanks then stopped the last attack, and the Japanese withdrew under a blanket of gunfire from cruiser *Louisville* and destroyers *Phelps* and *Monssen*, leaving about 700 dead on the battlefield. Dawn came none too soon for the Marines — but it found them still there.

This was General Saito's last chance to "destroy the enemy at the beachhead." But he was far from downhearted, since he had been assured that an irresistible fleet was about to bring him succor. Unfortunately for him, Fifth Fleet had the same warning.

On D-day Admiral Spruance received word from submarine *Flying Fish* that a Japanese carrier force was heading in his direction from San Bernardino Strait; and at 0400 June 16 he received submarine *Seahorse*'s contact report on a second Japanese force, steaming north off Surigao Strait. Rightly assuming that these ships meant business, Spruance promptly canceled the 18 June date

330 The Two-Ocean War

for landing on Guam and went on board Turner's flagship to confer with him and General Holland Smith. There, the decision was made to commit at once the reserve (the 27th Infantry Division) to Saipan, to detach certain cruisers and destroyers from the fire support ships to augment the fast carriers' screen, to continue unloading until dark 17 June, and then to send the transports safely eastward until the anticipated naval battle was over.

4. Preparations for a Decisive Naval Battle

While the forces under Nimitz, Halsey and MacArthur were advancing in the Central, South and Southwest Pacific, the Japanese Combined Fleet was swinging around the hook — either in Truk Lagoon, or at Lingga Roads off Singapore, or in the Inland Sea of Japan.

The explanation of this inactivity lay in America's vastly increased air power, while Japan was in the sad position of having a carrier fleet with no planes, having sacrificed them in the fruitless defense of Rabaul. But by the spring of 1944 new air groups were at least partially trained, and Admiral Toyoda felt strong enough to resume Yamamoto's strategy of annihilating the United States Pacific Fleet in one decisive battle. The right person was chosen to do that, if it could be done — Vice Admiral Jisaburo Ozawa. After relieving Admiral Nagumo in command of the carrier striking force in November 1943, Ozawa also became C. in C. First Mobile Fleet, which comprised at least 90 per cent of the surface part of the Japanese Navy. He was an officer with a scientific brain as well as a seaman's innate sense of what can be accomplished with ships; a worthy antagonist to Mitscher and Spruance.

On 3 May his immediate superior, Admiral Toyoda, issued preliminary orders for Operation A-GO, to annihilate Spruance. The intended victim was to be "lured" into waters between the Palaus,

Yap and Woleai, where both land-based and carrier-based planes could slaughter him. But in any event Fifth Fleet must be attacked.

Ozawa's six carriers, five battleships, seven heavy cruisers, 34 destroyers and six oilers rendezvoused at Tawi Tawi, westernmost island of the Sulu Archipelago, on 16 May. In that open roadstead they were snooped by submarines *Bonefish* and *Puffer*, and the latter sank two of Japan's dwindling tanker fleet. Submarine *Harder* (Commander S. D. Dealey) did even better, sinking three destroyers between 3 and 8 June. This was the first installment of the contribution by United States submarines to the forthcoming battle. The second was their two above-mentioned contact reports on Ozawa, which caused Admiral Spruance to postpone the invasion of Guam and prepare to give battle. These sightings were indeed vital, because even our Liberators' 1100-mile air searches from Manus failed to pick up Ozawa's approach; he was too cagey to pass within their range.

In preparation for the "decisive battle," Japan deployed several hundred land-based naval aircraft in the Marianas and Carolines with orders to sink at least one third of the American carriers before they clashed wth Ozawa's. The achievements of this First Air Fleet were miserably disappointing, and equally so were some 25 Japanese submarines deployed during the Marianas campaign. They gathered no valuable information; they hit not one ship. According to Japanese submarine doctrine, these boats were positioned in May in the "NA" line to bar waters into which the high command expected — and wanted — the American fleet to be "lured." Spruance, as at Midway, did not accommodate his movements to the enemy's wishes. On the contrary, Pacific Fleet found out where the enemy RO-boats were deployed, sent a flock of destroyer escorts to get them, and sank no fewer than 17. Of these, six were sunk in the last twelve days of May by destroyer escort *England* (Lieutenant Commander W. B. Pendleton), one of a hunter-killer group under Commander Hamilton Hains. This ex-

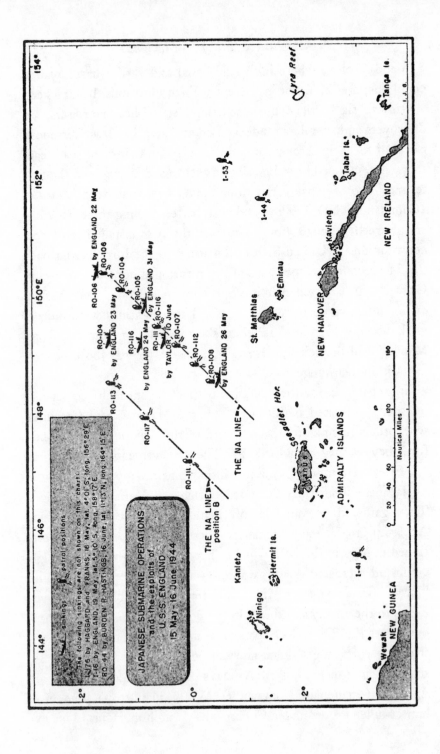

JAPANESE SUBMARINE OPERATIONS
and the exploits of
U.S.S. ENGLAND
15 May - 16 June 1944

The following sinkings are not shown on this chart:
I-176 by HAGGARD and FRANKS, 16 May, lat. 4°01' S., long. 156°29'E.
I-16 by ENGLAND, 19 May, lat. 5°10' S., long. 158°17'E.
RO-44 by BURDEN R. HASTINGS, 16 June, lat. 11°13' N., long. 164°15' E.

ploit exceeded any of those in the Atlantic that we are about to record in the next chapter.

On 15 June, when Admiral Toyoda got news of the landings on Saipan, he activated Operation A-GO for the decisive battle. No more talk of "luring" the enemy south.

Between 15 and 18 June the two carrier forces were warily feeling for each other. Here is a tabular comparison of them: —

SHIPS

	Fleet Carriers	Light Carriers	Battle-ships	Heavy Cruisers	Light Cruisers	Destroyers
Japanese	5	4	5	11	2	28
United States	7	8	7	8	13	69

AIRCRAFT STRENGTH

	Fighters	Dive-bombers	Torpedo-bombers	Total CVs	Float Planes	Grand Total
Japanese	222	113	95	430	43	473
United States	475	232	184	891	65	956

Thus, Ozawa was inferior to Spruance in every naval category except heavy cruisers. But he possessed three tactical advantages that made him confident of victory. First, he intended to give battle within range of his 90 to 100 land-based planes at Guam, Rota and Yap, whilst Spruance could look to no such assistance. Second, Japanese carrier planes, owing to lack of armor and self-sealing fuel tanks, had greater range than the Americans. Ozawa's aircraft could search out to 560 miles, Mitscher's only to 325 or 350; Japanese planes could profitably attack at 300 miles, ours not much beyond 200, although they had to fly 300 on 20 June. And, third, the easterly tradewind gave Ozawa the lee gauge, enabling him to approach his enemy while launching and recovering planes. A further tactical advantage for Japan, of which Ozawa was ignorant, lay in the fact that he had but one objective, to destroy the enemy fleet; whilst Spruance's primary duty was to cover and protect the American invasion of Saipan. That tied him fairly closely to the vicinity of the Marianas.

These tactical advantages for the Japanese were more than offset by the poor training of their aviators. In the United States Navy at that time every naval aviator had two years' training and over 300 hours' flying time before he was considered fit to fly from a carrier, and most of Mitscher's air groups were already veterans. But the air groups of Ozawa's best carrier division had had only six months' training when they left Tawi Tawi; those of Cardiv 3, only three months; and those of Cardiv 2, only two months. Moreover, the month spent at Tawi Tawi before the sortie was wasted, because the fleet lay at anchor to save fuel, and, without an airfield or a moving flattop to practise from, aviators went stale.

Admiral Spruance, victor at Midway, Commander Fifth Fleet since mid-1943, was tried by experience and unspoiled by victory. Modest by nature, he had a prejudice against publicity in any form, and closed up like a clam in the presence of news correspondents. Spruance's leading characteristics were attention to detail, poise, and power of intelligent decision. He envied no man, regarded no one as rival, won the respect of all with whom he came in contact, and went ahead in his quiet way winning victories for his country. Typically, he chose for flagship no big new battleship but twelve-year-old heavy cruiser *Indianapolis*, because she was expendable.

Vice Admiral Mitscher, too, was a simple, unassuming gentleman with a soft voice and quiet manners. He, too, would have avoided publicity if he could; but his slight, wiry figure and leathery, wizened face, usually seen under a long-visored lobsterman's cap, "made copy" in spite of him. A pioneer of naval aviation, Mitscher had, as it were, grown up with the flattop. Since March 1944 he had commanded Fast Carrier Forces Pacific Fleet. He gained devotion and admiration, partly by exceptionally good performance, partly by unusual consideration for his officers and men. Rescue operations for him were as important as battle operations; preservation of aviators' lives as important as risking their lives to attain victory. Admiral Mitscher, in carrier *Lexington*, was in tactical command throughout the Battle of the Philippine Sea; but the major decisions were made, or concurred in, by Admiral Spruance.

Of the four task group commanders under Mitscher, Rear Admiral John W. Reeves, CTG 58.3 (*Enterprise*, flag) was senior. A stern, steady, dependable officer, he could always be counted on to get the most out of his men. Slightly junior to him but of longer aviation experience was Rear Admiral Alfred E. Montgomery, CTG 58.2 (*Bunker Hill*, flag), who had already commanded *Ranger* and an escort carrier division. Next, in *Hornet*, was Rear Admiral Joseph J. ("Jocko") Clark, part Cherokee Indian and part Southern Methodist, but all fighter. A picturesque character who looked more like a western desperado than a naval officer, he knew his business thoroughly and had more than his share of energy and dogged determination. A specialist in naval air, promoted to flag rank at the age of 50, he had just relieved Rear Admiral Frederick C. Sherman as CTG 58.1. Rear Admiral W. K. Harrill, an aviator since 1921, had recently relieved Rear Admiral Ginder as CTG 58.4, in *Essex* (Captain R. A. Ofstie).

As a good instance of Spruance's coolness, when he knew from submarine reports that the enemy was in the Philippine Sea, he calculated how long it would take him to cross, and let "Jocko" Clark perform a scheduled strike on Iwo Jima and Chichi Jima away up north. It was fortunate that he did, for Clark's planes destroyed dozens of Japanese aircraft waiting to attack the landing forces at Saipan.

Kelly Turner, agreeing with Spruance on the 16th that all signs pointed to a big sea battle for the supremacy of the Philippine Sea, lent him five of his heavy cruisers, three light cruisers and 21 destroyers, to augment his screen. Since "Jocko" was then engaged in pounding Iwo, Spruance set a rendezvous for the entire fleet at a point about 160 miles west of Tinian for 1800 June 18. At 1415 on the 17th, he issued this simple battle plan to Mitscher:

Our air will first knock out enemy carriers, then will attack enemy battleships and cruisers to slow or disable them. Battle Line will destroy enemy fleet either by fleet action if the enemy elects to fight or by sinking slowed or crippled ships if enemy retreats. Action against the enemy must be pushed vigorously by all hands to ensure complete destruction of his fleet. Destroyers running short of fuel may be returned to Saipan if necessary for refueling.

Desire you proceed at your discretion selecting dispositions and movements best calculated to meet the enemy under most advantageous conditions. I shall issue general directives when necessary and leave details to you and Admiral Lee.[3]

Spruance also cautioned Mitscher and Lee that "TF 58 must cover Saipan." Its movements were tied to that major objective.

All day 18 June the two forces continued to feel for each other, and the Japanese, owing to their greater search range, obtained much more information about Spruance than he did of them. Ozawa changed to a southerly course at 1540, intending to keep Vice Admiral Kurita's van (light carriers *Chitose*, *Chiyoda* and *Zuiho*) at a distance of about 300 miles, and his Main Body (including the five big carriers), about 400 miles, from Fifth Fleet. This would enable the Japanese to benefit by the longer range of their planes and choose their own time to fight. By 0415 June 19 Ozawa's battle disposition was complete, and all was set to hurl

---

[3] In every carrier campaign, starting with the Gilberts, a Battle Line of battleships, heavy cruisers and destroyers was set up under Vice Admiral Willis A. Lee, to be pulled out from the carrier groups' screens to engage Combined Fleet in a gunfire action, if need be. In this action, Mitscher formed Lee's Battle Line on 18 June and stationed it about 15 miles west or south of the carriers, to help them by its antiaircraft fire.

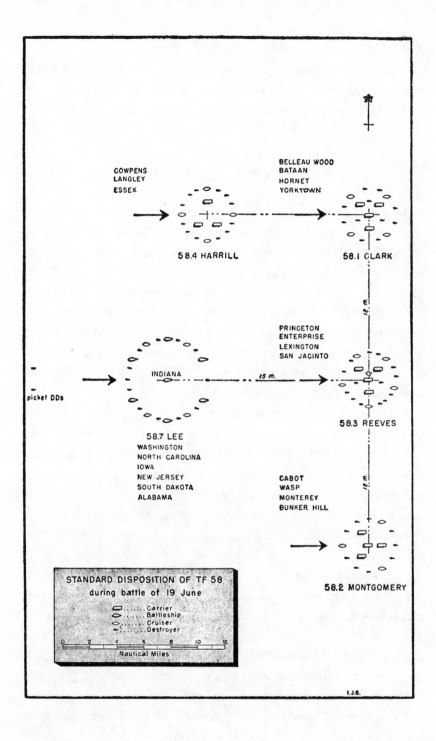

COWPENS
LANGLEY
ESSEX

BELLEAU WOOD
BATAAN
HORNET
YORKTOWN

58.4 HARRILL

58.1 CLARK

12 m.

PRINCETON
ENTERPRISE
LEXINGTON
SAN JACINTO

picket DDs

INDIANA

15 m.

58.3 REEVES

58.7 LEE
WASHINGTON
NORTH CAROLINA
IOWA
NEW JERSEY
SOUTH DAKOTA
ALABAMA

CABOT
WASP
MONTEREY
BUNKER HILL

12 m.

58.2 MONTGOMERY

STANDARD DISPOSITION OF TF 58
during battle of 19 June

☐ ......Carrier
◇ ......Battleship
○ ......Cruiser
▬ ......Destroyer

0   2   4   6   8   10   12
Nautical Miles

t.J.8.

300 planes at Spruance. He, still ignorant of Ozawa's position, was steering east, apprehensive that the Japanese might try an "end run" around him to get at the amphibious forces off Saipan.

5. *The Battle of the Philippine Sea, 19–21 June*

June the 19th, to be as memorable as the 4th in naval annals, broke warm and fair around 0430, with a last-quarter moon in the sky. At a little before six the sun rose over a blue ocean, kindling the carriers' topsides to pure gold for a brief moment. Night clouds soon dissolved, and by the forenoon watch the sea had become all azure with argent high lights, and clouds so few as to afford no cover for pouncing aviators. Wind remained in the eastern quadrant, varying from ENE to ESE, with a strength of 9 to 12 knots. Ceiling and visibility were unlimited; from *Lexington's* high superstructure one could see forty miles all around.

Fifth Fleet was on a north-south line of bearing, each task group in a circle four miles in diameter, their centers 12 miles apart, Lee's Battle Line lay 15 miles to the westward, so that the entire disposition covered an ocean area about 25 by 35 miles.

Flagship *Lexington* at sunrise was about 90 miles NW of Guam, and 110 miles SW of Saipan. As no enemy had yet been spotted, Spruance suggested to Mitscher a morning neutralization strike on Guam. Ozawa (as he rightly guessed) was counting on help from the land-based air forces there, and on using Guam fields to refuel his planes; it was an excellent idea to deprive him in advance of this backlog. First phase of the Battle of the Philippine Sea was a series of dogfights, starting about 0830, over and near Guam. Some 33 Hellcats accounted for more than their number of Japanese planes, but many more were taking off from Orote Field when the Hellcats found something better to do.

"The Great Marianas Turkey Shoot," as an aviator named the

principal phase of this battle, opened at 0959 June 19, when American radar picked up an attack group 150 miles to the westward. This was the first of four massive raids from Ozawa's carriers. At 1023 Mitscher's carrier groups sounded General Quarters, swung east into the wind, launched full teams of fighters to intercept and, to keep flight decks clear, sliced off bombers to orbit on call. This first Japanese raid was 69 planes strong. Hellcats from *Essex, Cowpens, Bunker Hill* and *Princeton* intercepted it well west of the Fleet, and shot down at least 25. As about 40 of them continued toward their targets, more Hellcats came out and destroyed 16 more. One that got through to Lee's Battle Line scored a direct hit on *South Dakota*. None reached the carriers, and of the 69 only 24 survived.

Ozawa's second raid, of 130 planes, was launched by his own carrier division around 0900. Immediately after it took off, submarine *Albacore* (Commander J. W. Blanchard) torpedoed fleet flagship *Taiho*, the newest and biggest flattop (33,000 tons) in the Japanese Navy, exceeded only by our *Saratoga*. *Taiho* was sunk by this single torpedo, plunging so suddenly as to take down three-quarters of her crew. And *Shokaku*, one of the two survivors of the Pearl Harbor strike, had preceded her to the bottom. She was victim of submarine *Cavalla* (Lieutenant Commander H. J. Kossler).

Ozawa's second raid did even worse than the first — 98 of the 130 planes never returned. About 20 closed Admiral Lee's Battle Line, gave his picket destroyer *Stockham* a terrific tussle, and near-missed three battleships. About six planes got through to the carriers, to be knocked down by C.A.P. and antiaircraft fire.

Of Ozawa's third raid of 47 planes, launched from *Junyo* and *Ryuho* at 1000, the greater part, luckily for themselves, made for a false contact point,[4] failed to find their enemy and returned safely.

---

[4] The point called "3 Ri" on the chart.

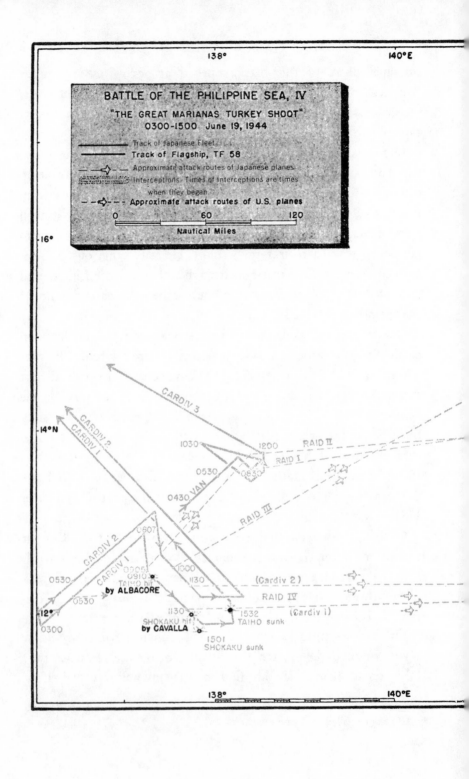

BATTLE OF THE PHILIPPINE SEA, IV
"THE GREAT MARIANAS TURKEY SHOOT"
0300-1500 June 19, 1944

Track of Japanese Fleet
Track of Flagship, TF 58
Approximate attack routes of Japanese planes
Interceptions. Times of interceptions are times when they began.
Approximate attack routes of U.S. planes

0   60   120
Nautical Miles

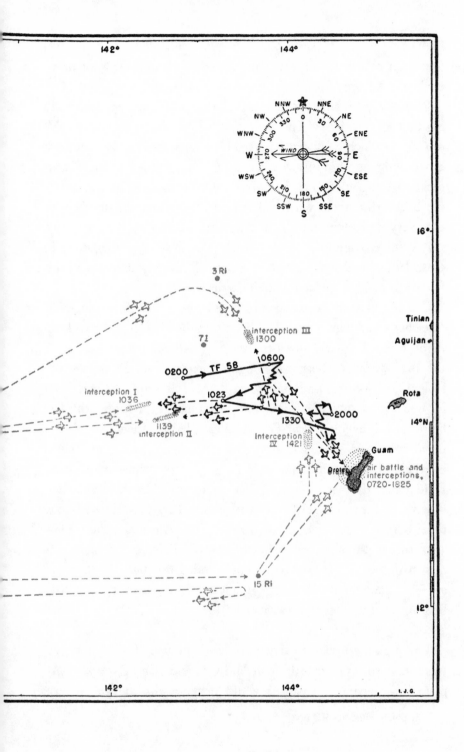

Only ten or twelve engaged, and seven of them were shot down by Hellcats from *Hornet, Yorktown* and other carriers.

Zuikaku, Junyo and *Ryuho* at 1100 began launching the fourth big raid, of 82 planes. These were sent to a phantom contact SW of Guam, which had been reported by a Japanese search plane with a bad compass.[5] Finding nothing there, they turned north. Six attacked Montgomery's carrier group, did no damage, and only one got back; 18 tangled with Hellcats and lost half their number; 49 when trying to land on Guam were attacked by 27 Hellcats from *Cowpens, Essex* and *Hornet,* which shot down 30; the other 19 crash-landed and were knocked useless. Thus only nine out of this raid of 82 planes returned to their carriers.

Guam and Rota were not neglected during the four big raids. Mitscher's bombers, which had been sloughed off in order to keep flight decks clear, were used to destroy grounded planes and to put the airfields out of business. A fighter sweep from *Yorktown* patrolled Guam until sundown, when it was relieved by planes from *Hornet* and *Essex.* On these fell the honor of fighting the last battle of this eventful day. Four Hellcats, led by Lieutenant Commander Brewer, who had distinguished himself in the morning's interception of the first Japanese raid, were patrolling over Orote Field when they saw a "Jill" coming in low. As the F6Fs flew down to pounce on her, they were jumped by an estimated four times their number of land-based Zekes. The American pilots managed to cut down the odds, but not before Brewer and his wingman had been killed. When darkness ended this fight at 1845 the air was completely clear of Japanese planes, except for those limping back to their own carriers.

This was the greatest carrier battle of the war. Forces engaged were three to four times those in Midway, and victory was so complete that Japanese naval air could never again engage on any

[5] The point called "15 Ri" on the chart.

other terms than suicidal. In the "Great Marianas Turkey Shoot" of 19 June Ozawa lost 346 planes and two carriers; the United States Navy lost 30 planes and sustained one bomb hit on a battleship, which did not even stop her. For over eight hours there was fierce, continuous action in the air, directed and supported by action on board ship. The brainwork of the carriers' combat information centers in tracking Japanese raids, and of the fighter-director units (in destroyers) arranging interceptions; the skilled energy of deck crews in rapid launching, recovering and servicing planes; the accuracy of antiaircraft gunners in Lee's Battle Line — all contributed. But, above all, the skill, initiative and intrepid courage of the young Hellcat pilots made this day one of the high points in the history of the American spirit.

Now the hunter became the hunted. At 2000 June 19, having recovered all planes, three out of four American carrier groups started west in search of the enemy, at the low speed of 23 knots to economize fuel. Harrill's TG 58.4, which was due to refuel next day, stayed behind to interdict remnants of the land-based aircraft on Rota and Guam.

Again, American air search failed. Not until 1540 June 20 did an Avenger pilot from *Enterprise* report Ozawa's position, 275 miles away. Mitscher then made the quick decision to launch an all-out strike, even though he knew that recovery must take place after dark. At 1620 TG 58 turned into the wind and completed launching full deckloads — 216 planes from ten carriers in the amazingly short time of ten minutes. At 1840 these aircraft sighted the enemy. Nature had provided a perfect setting from an artistic point of view, but from no other. The lower limb of the setting sun was just touching the horizon, and about half the sky was covered with brilliantly colored clouds. The thinnest golden sliver of a new moon was setting, promising a dark night for aviators' homing. American planes — after flying 300 miles — were so near the end of their tether that there was no time to organize coördinated attacks. Fortunately for them, Ozawa had not yet re-formed his battle disposition to receive air attack.

Six oilers, protected by as many destroyers, were the first group of enemy ships encountered; these had been left astern when Ozawa turned up speed. Some American dive-bombers concentrated on the oilers and disabled two, which had to be scuttled. Four Avengers from *Belleau Wood*, led by Lieutenant (jg) George B. Brown USNR, got two torpedoes into carrier *Hiyo* and sank her; but Brown lost his life. Hits were made on *Zuikaku* and other ships — none lethal. This action cost Ozawa 65 of the 100 carrier planes which had survived the "Turkey Shoot"; only 20 of the 216 American attackers were lost in action.

Many more were lost landing in a pitch-black night, between 2045 and 2300 — although Admiral Mitscher, disregarding carrier doctrine and defying submarines, ordered every ship to light up to make recovery easier. Almost half the aircraft landed on the wrong carriers, fourscore planes crashed, or ditched because they ran out of gas. Fortunately rescue work by destroyers was very efficient.

At midnight Spruance again turned his force westerly, not so much in hope of catching Ozawa as of recovering more splashed aviators and encountering crippled enemy ships. Ozawa, with the engineering plants of his ships still intact, opened distance during the night. Spruance called off the chase at 1920 June 21 and ordered course shaped for Saipan. On the return passage his ships, aided by tender-based planes from Saipan, rescued 59 floating aviators who otherwise would have perished in the Philippine Sea. Thus, all but 16 pilots and 33 crewmen who had taken part on 20 June were eventually recovered. Total losses of American aircraft on the two days of battle, from all causes, were 130; of airmen, 76.

A dispirited and defeated Japanese Mobile Fleet anchored at

Okinawa 22 June, with only 35 serviceable carrier planes out of the 430 which it had possessed on the morning of the 19th. In addition, 31 out of the 43 cruiser and battleship float planes were destroyed in action or crashed on landing, besides about 50 of those based on Guam. The three largest carriers had been sunk, some 480 planes destroyed, and almost that number of aviators. This was the third time that the Japanese carriers' air groups had been virtually wiped out, and there was no time to replace them by October, when the Battle for Leyte Gulf came up.

Although Admiral Spruance was criticized — bitterly so, by self-styled air strategists — for not taking the offensive on 18 June or pursuing more vigorously on the 20th, there can no longer be any doubt that his strategy was correct. If he had thrust aggressively westward instead of awaiting attack off Guam, as his pervading sense of a mission to cover Saipan compelled him to do, he could have accomplished no greater destruction of the enemy air groups, and might have lost some of his own ships. The one thing in this great battle on the American side which can be criticized is Mitscher's failure to send out searches for Ozawa after sundown 19 June. If he had, the air battle of the 20th could have been delivered in the morning, with better results. But Mitscher's refusal to fly night searches is a tribute to his humanity; he felt that his aviators, after fighting all day, were entitled to a little rest. All honor, then, to him for his tactical brilliance and his consideration for human lives; and to Spruance for his strategical savvy. He made the best dispositions to inflict maximum damage on the enemy, and lost not one of his own ships. Nor may we forget the submarines, who coöperated so vigorously and intelligently to make this Battle of the Philippine Sea one of the most decisive of the entire war.

6. *The Marianas Secured, June–August 1944*

After this battle, the fate of the Marianas was sealed, but the Japanese refused to admit it. Two weeks of tough fighting lay ahead on Saipan; Tinian and Guam remained to be taken. The main work at Saipan was done by the foot soldiers of one U. S. Army division and two Marine divisions; but the Navy was in there helping every day with gunfire support. As General Saito, the island commander, recorded, "If there just were no naval gunfire, we feel that we could fight it out with the enemy in a decisive battle."

Equally impressive was the quantity and quality of naval air support. At the beginning of the campaign the escort carriers of the expeditionary force, under the command of Rear Admirals Bogan, Sallada and Stump, maintained from dawn to dusk about 16 fighters and 20 bombers orbiting two air stations some eight miles off shore, to deliver call strikes promptly; a new wrinkle in amphibious warfare. From the 22nd, escort carrier planes of both groups of carriers and Army P-47s based on Isely (ex-Aslito) Field, Saipan, supplied this highly important component. Captain R. F. Whitehead, Commander Support Aircraft, directed the show from Admiral Turner's flagship *Rocky Mount*, receiving calls from shore fire-control parties with the advanced troops and relaying them to orbiting aircraft.

A battalion of Marines led by Colonel R. M. Tompkins captured the top of Mount Tapotchau on 27 June, but the Japanese continued to contest every yard of the island. By the time the last desperate banzai charge flickered out, both Saito and Nagumo, the admiral who in 1941 and 1942 had ranged victoriously with his carriers from Pearl Harbor to Trincomalee, had committed suicide.

The capture of Saipan cost the United States Army and Marine Corps 3426 killed and missing in action. About 24,000 Japanese were killed, by burial count, and 1780 (more than half Koreans) taken prisoner. Hundreds of Japanese civilians committed suicide by jumping off the cliffs of northern Saipan, and for days our patrolling warships sighted their floating bodies — grim reminders of Japanese no-surrender mentality.

The landing on Tinian, 24 July, was perfectly planned and almost faultlessly executed by the same Marine and naval units that had won Saipan. The Marines, unhampered here by slower-moving Army units, drove ahead with their customary *élan*, and in seven days secured the island, incurring casualties of 389 killed and 1816 wounded.

Guam, most important of the Marianas, an American possession for over forty years before the war, was the last to be secured. The unexpected toughness of the Saipan fight showed that the recovery of Guam would require three divisions instead of the two on hand. That meant lifting from Oahu the 77th Infantry Division, but it also meant no respite for the Japanese on Guam, as it gave Admiral Conolly time to plan and carry out the most meticulous prelanding bombardment of the war.

Amphibious operations are difficult and dangerous for people unfamiliar with the technique, but easy and formidable when both naval officers and troops are at home with the work, by constant and well-ordered practice. Rear Admiral Richard L. Conolly, robust, genial, thorough and methodical, loved planning as well as fighting, and he did a great deal of the planning for Guam himself at the Guadalcanal headquarters of Major General Roy Geiger, who was to command the landing force. Daily naval bombardment and air bombing began on 8 July and continued until D-day, the 21st. The UDTs cleared the way for almost faultless landings over difficult reefs. Marines and GIs alike fought with skill and courage against a tenacious enemy, where terrain was all on his side. Casualties, though heavy (1435 killed or missing in action, 5646 wounded) were less than half those on Saipan. Guam was a fitting climax to Operation FORAGER, completed in exactly two months from the first shot. On 12 August 1944, the Eastern Philippine Sea and the air over it, and the major Marianas, were under American control. These islands were as formidable and well defended as Guadalcanal and New Georgia had been — but what a difference in the time it took to take them!

General Tojo and cabinet resigned on 18 July, the day that the loss of Saipan was announced. This was the first move on the Japanese side toward peace; but so reluctant were the Japanese to face defeat that there was no peace for thirteen months.

We can now take a breather from the Pacific war and return to operations on the other side of the world. Throughout the Atlantic Ocean, in Italy and France, the Atlantic Fleet of the United States Navy had been doing its utmost to implement the great strategic decision of 1941: to beat the European Axis first.

CHAPTER XII

Mediterranean and Atlantic

August 1943–June 1944

1. *The Navy at Salerno (Operation* AVALANCHE), *September 1943*

O N 26 JULY 1943, when Sicily was almost overrun and Mussolini had fallen, the Combined Chiefs of Staff ordered General Eisenhower to plan an invasion of Italy — "landings in the Bay of Salerno, to be mounted at the earliest possible date, using the resources already available to you." This last clause registered American reluctance to become more deeply involved in Mediterranean operations. But the futility of resisting that involvement, once we had consented to TORCH, was soon evident. At the C.C.S. conference at Quebec in August, the 26 July directive was confirmed with the significant exception that the General need not be restricted to "resources already available" if he needed more — as of course he did.

Marshal Badoglio began negotiating for the surrender of Italy immediately after relieving Mussolini. If this dicker could have been quickly concluded, Italy might have been ours before August; but it was so protracted by the Italian propensity for bargaining that when a secret armistice was finally signed, on 3 September, it was no secret to the Germans. Even so, the greater part of Italy might have fallen into the Allied lap if an airdrop on Rome by the 82nd Airborne Division, simultaneous with the Salerno landings, had come off. It was canceled because the Italian general in command at Rome, a pro-German Fascist, convinced General Maxwell Taylor that there were too many German troops near Rome to make it a probable success. Rome underwent enemy occupation for eight months, and the Allies had to "crawl up the boot" of Italy, fighting Germans all the way.

The effects of the Italian surrender, upon which Churchill had set his heart, were not too favorable to the Allies. It enabled the Germans to take over most of Italy together with Rhodes and Leros in the Aegean. The Italian Navy did indeed surrender, but added little to Allied naval strength because the ships lacked radar and other modern improvements.

The Gulf of Salerno was chosen for the first important landing on the Italian mainland because it lies about 30 miles south of Naples, and at the then extreme limit of Allied fighter-plane support. Owing to the poor tactical air support provided by the A.A.F. and R.A.F. in Sicily, the Royal Navy added four escort carriers and their planes, as a support carrier force. The over-all commanders — Eisenhower, Cunningham, Alexander and Tedder — were the same as in Sicily. Vice Admiral H. Kent Hewitt commanded the entire amphibious force, which was divided into a Northern Attack Force, mainly British, under Commodore G. N. Oliver RN and Rear Admiral Richard L. Conolly; and a Southern Attack Force, mainly American, commanded by Rear Admiral John L. Hall. These landed, on two sets of beaches about eight miles apart, X Corps British Army and VI Corps U. S. Army. The two together made Fifth Army, General Mark W. Clark USA. The Royal Navy provided the covering force of four battleships and two fleet carriers. Assault convoys were mounted at four ports in North Africa, and Palermo and Términi in Sicily.

Of all decisions about Operation AVALANCHE, the most unfortunate — except giving up the airdrop — was the Army's insistence on no preliminary bombardment, in order to obtain tactical surprise. Admiral Hewitt argued against this in vain, as he had before HUSKY. He pointed out that the Germans were "on"; that it was fantastic to assume that we could surprise them. Implicit in the Army's denial was a fear that preliminary bombardment would attract German forces to Salerno. But on 6 September Marshal Kesselring had already sent there the 16th Panzer Division, which had several days to site artillery, cut down trees, build strongpoints, sight machine guns and fieldpieces on the beaches and their exits, bring up tanks, and cram nearby airfields with German planes. A good selective shoot on strongpoints on the edge of the Salerno plain, for a day or two before D-day, would have rendered the landings much less arduous.

At 1830 September 8, as both attack forces were approaching the Gulf of Salerno, they heard a broadcast in the familiar voice of General Eisenhower, announcing the armistice with Italy. This was singularly ill-timed with reference to the Allied troops. They proceeded to relax, mentally and otherwise; and instead of the tenseness that one usually feels before an amphibious assault, the approach continued under a sort of spell. It was a beautiful, calm, bright night. Capri was visible, swimming in a silver sea; the jagged outline of the Sorrento peninsula made a dark cutout against the star-studded heavens. Lookouts could even see the twinkling lights of Positano, and the flares of the Amalfi fishermen. The illusion of a pleasure cruise, to be followed by a peaceful landing and joyous reception by the Italians, lasted until the transports began easing into their release points at one minute past midnight. Then orders rang out, boatswains' whistles shrilled, and the clang and clatter of lowering landing craft broke the spell.

Admiral Hall's landings of the Southern Attack Force were directed to beaches overlooked by the famous temples of Paestum, all that was left of the Greek colony of Poseidonia destroyed by Saracens over a thousand years ago. As first light broke at 0330 on D-day, 9 September, the initial waves of landing craft were

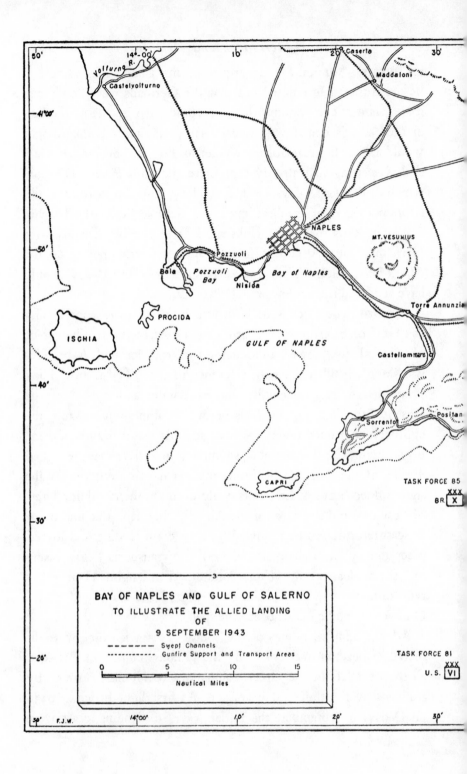

BAY OF NAPLES AND GULF OF SALERNO
TO ILLUSTRATE THE ALLIED LANDING
OF
9 SEPTEMBER 1943

------ Swept Channels
······ Gunfire Support and Transport Areas

0   5   10   15
Nautical Miles

TASK FORCE 85
BR. X

TASK FORCE 81
U.S. VI

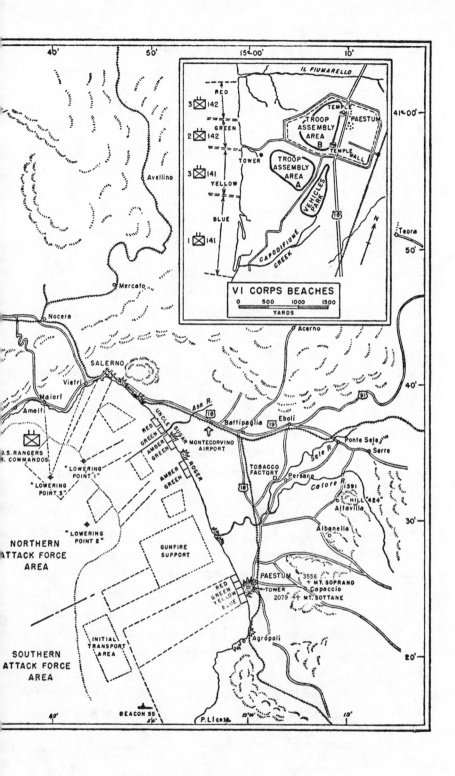

VI CORPS BEACHES

Il Fiumarello

RED 3 ☒ 142

GREEN 2 ☒ 142

TOWER

3 ☒ 141 YELLOW

BLUE

1 ☒ 141

TROOP ASSEMBLY AREA B

TEMPLE PAESTUM

TEMPLE

WALL

TROOP ASSEMBLY AREA A

VEHICLES PARK

18

Capodifiume Creek

N

Teora

50'

0 500 1000 1500

YARDS

41°00'

Avellino

Mercato

Nocera

Acerno

Salerno

Vietri

Maiori

Amalfi

Asa R.

16

Battipaglia

19 Eboli

91

40'

U.S. RANGERS
M. COMMANDOS

"Lowering Point 1"

"Lowering Point 3"

"Lowering Point 2"

UNCLE SUGAR ROGER

RED
GREEN
AMBER
GREEN
AMBER
GREEN

MONTECORVINO AIRPORT

Ponte Sele

Serre

Sele R.

TOBACCO FACTORY

Persano

Calore R.

1391

HILL "424"

Altavilla

30'

NORTHERN ATTACK FORCE AREA

GUNFIRE SUPPORT

18

Albanella

SOUTHERN ATTACK FORCE AREA

INITIAL TRANSPORT AREA

RED
GREEN
YELLOW
BLUE

PAESTUM

TOWER

3556 MT. SOPRANO

Capaccio

2079 MT. SOTTANE

Agropoli

20'

BEACON SS

P. Licosa

40' 30' 10'

nearing the end of their eight- to ten-mile run over a calm sea. All hit their respective beaches on time; second and third waves followed at the proper intervals. These craft had no close fire support or rocket craft or gunboats, as all landings had in the Pacific, because the United States Army would have none of it; imagining that they could obtain tactical surprise if they landed in the dark silently, and ignoring the fact that landing craft engines are the noisiest things afloat. Thus, for want of close fire support, many soldiers in the boats were killed by German gunners ready and waiting.

Fortunately, the assault troops, an RCT of the 36th Infantry Division, were not easily discouraged. Working under fire to their prearranged assembly area, they made it by sunrise, 0436. Dukws carrying 105-mm howitzers arrived from three British LSTs at 0530. No fewer than 123 dukw landings were made on the American beaches in the first two hours — a remarkable achievement. LSTs carrying tanks were no more fortunate than they had been in Sicily; heavy gunfire kept them off, and the 36th Division got very little armor ashore on D-day. German tanks, on the contrary, were active from 0700. The GIs, with the aid of bazookas, howitzers, and naval gunfire, prevented them from reaching the beaches.

Rear Admiral Lyal A. Davidson in *Philadelphia* commanded naval gunfire support in the American sector. He had cruiser *Savannah* and four destroyers at his disposal, while H.M.S. *Abercrombie*, screened by Royal Netherlands gunboat *Flores*, stood by to serve when 15-inch shell was wanted. (It is curious that the Royal Navy went right on building monitors, a type invented by the United States Navy in 1862, long after we gave them up; the type proved to be valuable in World War II for shore bombardment.) Unfortunately, *Abercrombie* struck a mine that afternoon, and had to retire to Palermo. *Savannah* and *Philadelphia*, shortly after 0900, established communication with their shore fire-control parties, and spent D-day pleasantly and profitably silencing or destroying enemy batteries, tanks, and even bridges. For spotting, the cruisers used their own SOC float planes, as well as Army Mustangs, which flew over from Sicily. These P–51s, flying in pairs, turned in an excellent performance; one would spot while the other covered against enemy air attack. When two SOCs discovered a covey of German tanks hiding in a thicket, *Philadelphia*'s 6-inch guns flushed 35 of them, followed them with salvos as they rumbled to the rear, and destroyed about seven. Outstanding support was also given by destroyers *Bristol*, *Edison*, *Ludlow* and *Woolsey*, driving in through minefields to deliver accurate shoots. Their performance inspired a message from the 36th Division artillery commander, "Thank God for the fire of the blue-belly Navy ships. . . . Brave fellows these; tell them so."

Landing craft crews functioned even better here than in Sicily, although enemy fire on the boats was far more severe. Training counted — the men stuck by their craft, and worked around the clock to unload transports. When the operation was over, the incredibly small number of eleven boats had to be abandoned, and all but one of these had been knocked out by enemy action.

In the British Northern sector, the pattern of assault was similar and amphibious technique almost identical; the troops were aggressive and gunfire support ships assiduous. By the evening of D-day the British right flank joined the coast four miles northwest of the Sele River's mouth, leaving a gap of seven miles between their X Corps and the United States VI Corps. That gap proved to be serious; for if anyone imagined that the Germans had shot their bolt, he was destined for a great disappointment. They had at least partial control of the air, and full control over the roads and railways of southern Italy. Reinforcements were rolling in from the mountains, and an armored division was coming south from Naples; leading elements of another panzer division reached the Salerno beachhead at 1900, less than twenty-four hours after they had been ordered to break off contact with Montgomery's Eighth Army, which was marching along the coastal road from Calabria not much faster than Belisarius had done in A.D. 536.

Salerno beachhead ranks with those of Anzio, Tarawa and Normandy as the most fiercely contested in World War II. Few soldiers came under such severe fire on landing as did those of the American VI and the British X Corps, or came through it so well. Yet even these "valiant men of might" could not have carried on without naval gunfire. For three days, 10-12 September, as the tide of battle swept to and fro over the Salerno plain, both navies delivered gunfire support to the troops ashore. During this period the Luftwaffe attacked ships in the roadstead with a new glide bomb, radio-directed to its target from a high-flying plane. One put *Savannah* out of action and almost sank her, but she managed to make Malta under her own power. *Philadelphia* sidestepped two; H.M.S. *Uganda* was struck by one that penetrated seven decks and exploded below her hull, but she too was saved.

By 12 September General Vietinghoff, the local German commander, had built up his forces on the Salerno plain to three divisions with 600 tanks and mobile guns, with which he proposed to throw Mark Clark's Fifth Army into the sea before slow-motion "Monty" arrived to relieve him.[1] The Germans recaptured much of their lost ground that day, and on 13-14 September delivered repeated tank attacks on several parts of the beachhead. These were defeated by the combined efforts of infantry, field artillery and naval gunfire. Vietinghoff reported to Marshal Kesselring on the 14th: "The attack this morning . . . had to endure naval gunfire from at least 16 to 18 battleships, cruisers and large destroy-

1 General Alexander on the 10th ordered Montgomery to hurry, and on the 12th sent his chief of staff to explain the urgent situation; but Monty's advance patrols did not make contact with VI Corps until 1400 September 16, after the crisis had passed. General Clark went so far as to request Admiral Hewitt to make plans for reëmbarking VI Corps and landing it in the British sector; but it is not true, as stated in Bernard Fergusson *The Watery Maze* (1961), that the General's headquarters actually did reëmbark.

ers. . . . With astonishing precision and freedom of maneuver, these ships shot at every recognized target with overwhelming effect." *Philadelphia* was to the fore. *Boise* relieved her, at 0844 September 14, firing almost continuously at tanks and troops. She and *Philadelphia* and the destroyers continued to spell one another until 0530 next morning. In the British sector gunfire support by four light cruisers and four destroyers was equally brisk and enterprising.

On 15 September German armored units made their last attempt to dislodge the Allies from the Salerno beachhead. Next day Marshal Kesselring ordered a general retirement, "in order to evade the effective shelling from warships," as he says in his memoirs.

2. *Naples and Anzio* (*Operation* SHINGLE), *October 1943–June 1944*

Fifth Army on 1 October entered Naples, which the Germans had done their best to destroy. Commodore William A. Sullivan, with a mixed Anglo-American salvage team, did a remarkable job clearing the bay and the waterfront, so that by the end of the year more tonnage was being discharged in Naples than in time of peace.

At the Volturno line north of Naples, with the great harbor secured, and the Foggia airdrome on the other side of Italy in Allied hands, the Italian campaign should have been halted. But Winston Churchill and Field Marshal Sir Alan Brooke, whose idea it was to fight all the way up the "boot," justified continuing on the ground that the battle of Italy pinned down and used up German divisions which might resist the Normandy landing in 1944. Actually the Italian campaign failed to draw German reserves from France, and by June 1944 the Allies were employing in Italy double the number of Germans in that area. It developed, as General Sir Henry Wilson ("Ike's" relief) said, into a "slow, painful advance through difficult terrain against a determined and resourceful enemy, skilled in the exploitation of natural obstacles by mines and demolition." Marshal Kesselring, fighting a series of rear guard actions along prepared mountain entrenchments, used every natural advantage to the full; and no Allied general except Guillaume, who commanded a French army corps, showed much ability to cope with him. From Naples to Rome is but a hundred miles; yet the Allies, with numerical superiority on land and in the air, and with control of adjacent waters, took eight months to cover that ground.

Churchill persuaded the C.C.S. to order an attempt to break the stalemate by an amphibious landing in the rear of the Germans at Anzio, 37 miles from Rome. This Operation SHINGLE was planned as an end run around the German Winter or Gustav Line, which ran through Monte Cassino, where the Allied advance had stalled. The original concept of SHINGLE was to land a division or two in the enemy's rear to coöperate with the Allied armies when they reached Frosinone on the road from Naples to Rome, by seizing the Alban Hills. Eisenhower accepted it reluctantly and with this assumption.

Fifth Army started its drive toward Frosinone on 1 December 1943, but bogged down at the base of Monte Cassino. The Anzio operation, accordingly, was canceled; but Churchill promptly revived it, on Christmas Day, as one of his favorite peripheral jobs. Eisenhower would have done well at that point to have uttered an emphatic "No!" — as Marshall did when Churchill demanded an attack on Rhodes; for the Anzio operation made no sense except to support Fifth Army, which was still too far away to profit by it.

The landings between Anzio and Nettuno on 22 January 1944 of one British and one American division, under Rear Admiral Frank J. Lowry USN and Major General John P. Lucas USA, were completely successful. The troops were lifted from the Bay of Naples, largely in beaching craft, and had ample gunfire support.

Since the concept of this operation was British, but the execution largely American, and most of the troops in the end were Americans too, it has been very tempting to British writers to pin the failure of Operation SHINGLE on their allies. General Lucas should, it is argued, on D-day itself, have ordered one column into the Alban Hills and another into Rome itself, which would have fallen like a ripe plum; Patton would have done just that.[2] Over-extension, however, is one of the worst military blunders and the initial assault forces allotted to Anzio were much too weak to be stretched that far; reinforcements came too late to do anything but save the beachhead. Kesselring, though tactically surprised, had a plan ready both to contain Lucas's VI Corps on a narrow beachhead, and hold Clark's Fifth and Montgomery's Eighth Army as well. That is just what he did. Failure to appreciate the Germans' capability in rapid troop movement was a major lapse in Allied Intelligence. The air forces reported that their preliminary bombings had disrupted all rail and road communications in central Italy, but they had not done so. R.A.F. and A.A.F. firmly believed in the concept of "isolating the battlefield" by bombing bridges and the like; but it was not until the Normandy operation that such tactics, implemented by airdrops, seriously deterred enemy movements.

Even more quickly than Kesselring, the German Air Force reacted to the landings. On 23 January H.M.S. *Janus* was exploded and sunk by one of their new glide-bombs. Two days later over 100 bombers attacked the transport area repeatedly, making several hits and sinking a brightly illuminated British hospital ship.

There is no need here to dwell on the distressing details of the

---

[2] Actually Patton regarded the operation as suicidal. He flew to Naples to say good-by to Lucas, blurting out: "John, there is no one in the Army I hate to see killed as much as you, but you can't get out of this alive. Of course, you might be badly wounded. No one ever blames a *wounded* general!"

Anzio operation. The Germans turned an amphibious assault into a siege; even the Okinawa campaign in the Pacific was shorter. Four more American divisions and one more British division were sent in to beef up VI Corps. All through February, March, April and most of May there was trench warfare of World War I type on the beachhead. Off shore the two Navies stood by, bringing up supplies and reinforcements, rendering gunfire support, and beating off attacks by the Luftwaffe. Deadlock on the beachhead was a severe trial to the soldiers, and to sailors in ships standing by. Cold, drenching rains and gusty winds made any movement ashore difficult. Beaching craft in the roadstead rolled and tossed in the steep Mediterranean winter seas. Evening brought no rest to the weary sailor, who, like as not, had been at General Quarters since dawn, for twilight air attacks were the rule rather than the exception. The Germans had an air observation post high in the Alban Hills, from which they could identify and follow any ship and dispatch a guided missile attack from the Roman airfields at a few minutes' notice.

Special praise is due to the 450 American dukws employed. These "proved an invaluable asset in unloading Liberty ships moored at a distance off shore," recorded General Wilson; and British naval officers praised the Negroes who drove these dukws "for their cheerfulness, cleanliness and courage. Shelling or no shelling . . . those American Negroes and their white comrades kept the unending chain of 'ducks' running to and from the anchorage."

It was Mark Clark's Fifth Army which finally broke the deadlock on 11 May by an all-out attack on the Gustav Line.

Cisterna, which the Germans had turned into a miniature Monte Cassino, was captured by the Anzio forces on 25 May after two days' bitter fighting. *Brooklyn* fired her last shot in this campaign on the 26th, evoking complimentary comments from her spotters. French cruiser *Émile Bertin*, relieving *Philadelphia*, acquitted her-

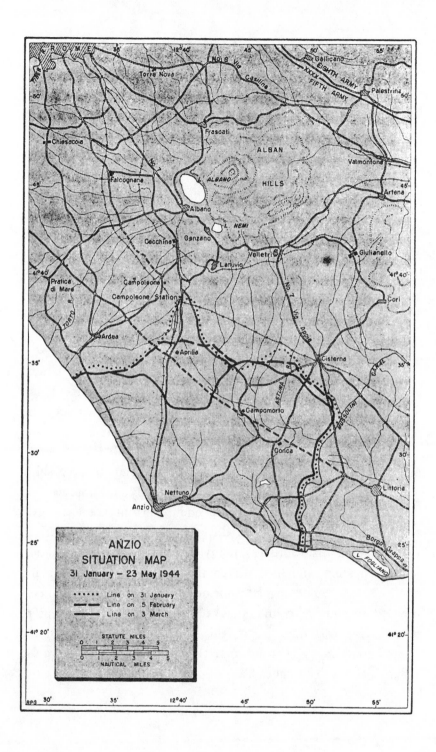

ANZIO
SITUATION MAP
31 January — 23 May 1944

• • • • • • Line on 31 January
— — — Line on 5 February
———— Line on 3 March

STATUTE MILES
0 1 2 3 4 5

NAUTICAL MILES
0 1 2 3 4 5

self with equal skill. With two United States destroyers screening, she silenced three enemy gun emplacements on the 27th. For the next two days these ships supported the Allied left flank at extreme ranges.

No more cruiser fire was wanted, but destroyers took over fire support as the Germans withdrew. From 31 May to 3 June, *Kendrick, Parker, Mackenzie, Champlin* and *Kearny* took turns pouring hundreds of rounds upon guns, vehicles and troops of the retreating enemy around Ardea and Practica di Mare. H.M.S. *Dido* and French *Émile Bertin* came up on 4 June, just in time to hear that it was all over. That night, 19 weeks after Admiral Lowry had landed VI Corps at Anzio, the Germans marched out of Rome and the Americans and British rolled in.

Operation SHINGLE was expensive to both Allies. The United States lost 526 sailors and about 3400 soldiers, the United Kingdom lost 366 sailors and about 1600 soldiers. German mines and bombs sank two cruisers, three destroyers, three LST, one LCI and a hospital ship of the Royal Navy, and two minecraft and six beaching craft of the United States Navy, besides two Liberty ships. Thus Churchill's baby turned out to be a costly and unrewarding brat. But Anzio beachhead should endure in our memories as a symbol of heroic tenacity on the part of British and American soldiers and sailors. Moreover, the two Navies performed an almost faultless landing, and then played the parts of ferry, feeder and gunfire support. The dogged valor of the foot soldiers and gunners repelled formidable counterattacks and eventually broke out to Rome. This was their battle, this their victory; of which the United States Navy is proud to say, "We helped you; and we too suffered, at Anzio beachhead."

3. *Sardinia, Corsica and Elba, September 1943–June 1944*

When the surrender of Italy was announced in September 1943, it became a matter of immediate concern to the Germans to withdraw their garrisons from Sardinia and Corsica, and to the Allies to get theirs in. Marshal Kesselring managed the former with his usual dexterity. By moving to Sardinia the ferries and other small craft used in the evacuation of Sicily, he transferred 25,800 men, hundreds of cannon, and 62 tanks to Corsica by 18 September. And on the same day the evacuation of Corsica to Leghorn began.

The responsibility for occupying Corsica was gladly accepted by the Fighting French. Using their own warships, cruisers *Jeanne d'Arc* and *Montcalm*, destroyers *Le Fantasque* and *Le Terrible*, they poured 6600 French and North African troops into one end of that island, while the Germans streamed out at the other. Over 30,000 enemy troops with their weapons and armor were transferred to the mainland, in one of the notable evacuations of the war. The oversight of the United States and Royal Navies in not attempting to attack this Bastia-Leghorn ferry route, covering 60 miles of deep water, is even more astonishing than their failure to halt the Sicilian evacuation; for here were no deterrents such as narrow seas and powerful coastal batteries.

American Army engineers were soon working on bomber bases in Sardinia and Corsica, which became useful to cover the invasion of Southern France the following year. And both islands were put to good use by Allied small craft. The Royal Navy established an advanced base for coastal forces at Maddalena before the end of September, and Lieutenant Commander Stanley M. Barnes reported there with his veteran MTBron 15 in early October. A second base was established at Bastia, Corsica. United States PTs operated thence with their British partners, under Royal Navy command, to the end of the war in the Mediterranean.

They conducted almost continuous hostilities with the heavily armed German F-lighters — 163-foot beaching craft similar to the LST — and R-boats — 85- to 115-foot escort vessels. These the enemy used to supply his forces in central Italy from Genoa and ports on the French Riviera. The Navies also contended with 30-knot Italian torpedo boats which the Germans had taken over.

The PTs here showed exemplary energy, courage and cunning. Operating with the British boats in mixed patrols, alternately under Commander Barnes and Commander R. A. Allan RNVR (known as "the Corsican Brothers"), they left a gallant record. Penetrating where larger vessels could not venture because of mines, they proved that properly designed and armed small naval craft have an important and useful function in modern warfare.

The most consistently unsung naval heroes of World War II, however, were the minecraft. U. S. Mine Squadron 11 (*Improve*, flag),[3] based since 27 August at Saint-Tropez and from 25 November at Cagliari and Bastia, was very active. In conjunction with British and French minesweepers and destroyers, they quietly pursued their dull, dangerous, but necessary work of clearing the coasts and sea lanes of the Mediterranean from anchored and floater mines which were constantly being planted or released by the retreating Germans.

Elba, least important of the three larger islands of the Tyrrhenian Sea, was not voluntarily evacuated by the Germans. Hitler insisted, probably because of its association with his hero Napoleon, on holding it "to the last man and the last cartridge." And the French Army of Liberation in Corsica insisted on taking Elba, because they wanted something to do before helping to liberate

---

[3] Successive C.O.'s were Capt. H. G. Williams and Cdr. Allan M. Robinson USNR.

their own country. So Operation BRASSARD, to capture Elba, was set up for a D-day of 17 June 1944.

The troops under General Henry-Martin, 12,000 in number, were French, North African and Senegalese. Since this was a shore-to-shore operation mounted in Corsica, the men were lifted in beaching craft and LCPRs towed by motor launches. The naval commander, the portly, genial and vigorous Rear Admiral Thomas Troubridge RN, had for flagship a converted LCI. His invasion flotilla included the ubiquitous Barnes with three PT squadrons, 40 or more Navy-manned LCI, and a few LST of the United States Navy. Gunfire support, in small supply, was rendered by three antique British river gunboats and three other small craft.

This rugged little island, about 30 miles long, was garrisoned by about 3000 Germans — many times the Intelligence estimate — and they were so well provided with coastal and mobile batteries that the convoy, steering into Golfo di Campo on the south shore, was met by murderous fire. Several LCI were sunk and for a time it looked as if nobody would get out alive; but the British SNOL (Senior Naval Officer Landing), Captain Errol Turner, gamely ordered troop-loaded craft to land on other beaches, the six small gunfire support craft did wonders, and by noon all beachheads were joined and only one battery was still giving trouble. The Germans, as soon as they saw the black faces of the *Sénégalais* and heard the wild whoops of the *goumiers* and *tabors*, surrendered in droves; and by 19 June the entire island was in French hands.

4. *The Escort Carriers and the U-Boats, May–December 1943*

Some people regarded the war against the U-boats as won because of the Bay Offensive and the spirited defense of northern transatlantic convoys. That was far from the truth. On 24 May 1943 Doenitz signaled to all U-boat captains, "The situation in the North Atlantic now forces a temporary shift of operations to areas less endangered by aircraft." He chose two areas of American responsibility, the central transatlantic convoy route and the South Atlantic; and one British theater, the Indian Ocean. If the Navies had now failed the merchantmen, there would have been a tonnage slaughter comparable to that of 1942. As it was, the Central Atlantic became the scene of a major tactical triumph over the U-boats, wrought by the American escort carriers.

On 26 May the Grossadmiral, having selected the horse latitudes as the best waters for filling his empty bag with merchant tonnage, ordered Group "Trutz" of 17 U-boats to form north-south line along the 43rd meridian between latitudes 32° and 39° N. Here the United States Navy was convoying hundreds of troop transports, fast tankers and slow freighters crammed with military supplies, in preparation for the invasion of Sicily. But we were well prepared to protect these convoys; and as soon as Group "Trutz" was on station it became the victim of an antisubmarine offensive unique for the rapidity with which tactical innovations were introduced.

The principal innovation was a roving U-boat killer outfit — a group composed of an escort carrier (CVE) equipped with Wildcat fighters and Avengers which could use bombs, depth charges or torpedoes, screened by old destroyers or destroyer escorts. In May 1943, Admiral Ingersoll, C. in C. Atlantic Fleet, gave the commanders of CVE groups discretion to hunt down submarines wherever HF/DF fixes indicated their presence. These orders were a joy to the young escort carrier commanders, making them feel as free off soundings as John Paul Jones or Lord Nelson.

First to profit was Captain Giles E. Short of *Bogue*, which, with four destroyers, departed Argentia 30 May under orders to conduct offensive operations in wide support of North African convoys. On 5 June a Wildcat and an Avenger executed a well-coordinated attack on *U-217* of Group "Trutz," then some 63 miles from *Bogue*. At 1507 June 8, a clear, calm day with glassy sea, a *Bogue* Avenger sighted *U-758* moving "at extremely high speed." She happened to be the first of the German submarine fleet to be equipped with a quadruple mount of 20-mm antiaircraft guns, and to have orders from Doenitz to fight planes on the surface instead of diving. This U-boat drove off two Avengers, then circled slowly on the surface, tempting one Wildcat pilot after another to try his luck. All were forced out of range except Lieutenant (jg) Phil Perabo USNR. He piled in, jammed the German 20-mm Oerlikons with strafing bullets, and mowed down most of the gunners. The C.O. then decided it was time to dive; and as he did so, at 1528, an Avenger dropped a load of bombs which should have been fatal, but were not. Heavy antiaircraft fire and smart tactics saved *U-758*; and incidentally encouraged all her teammates in the fatal belief that "fight back" doctrine was the answer to a German submariner's prayer.

Not until 1147 June 12 did one of *Bogue*'s patrol teams make a fresh contact: *U-118*, a 1600-ton fueling "milch cow" cruising 20 miles astern of the carrier. She did not fight back with anything like the vigor of *U-758*, but it took seven planes to sink her. Grossadmiral Doenitz, exasperated by the failure of Group "Trutz" to intercept convoys, ordered his boats to set up a new barrier south of Flores. After this had been successfully evaded by two convoys, he dissolved the group. No organized patrol line replaced frustrated "Trutz," but by 12 July there were 16 U-boats, including several milch cows, in waters east and south of the Azores.

Escort carrier *Core*, commanded by Captain Marshall R. Greer, stood out from the Capes of the Chesapeake 27 June on her first war cruise. Screened by destroyers *Bulmer*, *George E. Badger* and *Barker*, she remained within hailing distance of Convoy UGS-11 until 11 July when it was about 700 miles south of São Miguel.

Captain Greer than received a signal from Cinclant to join west-bound Convoy GUS–9. On the afternoon of 13 July one of *Core*'s Wildcat-Avenger patrol teams, about 720 miles SSW of Fayal, sighted the 1600-ton tanker *U–487*, and sank it, losing one plane and pilot in the fight. Three days later, the *Core* group made a second kill, of *U–67*.

Santee (Captain Harold F. Fick), with destroyers *Bainbridge*, *Overton* and *MacLeish*, was equally successful. An Avenger-Wildcat team, patrolling about 150 miles north of the carrier at 0803 July 14, sighted *U–160*. *Santee*'s air squadron was now equipped with the homing torpedo "Fido," for which a new form of attack had been worked out. The Wildcat forced the sub to dive; the Avenger dropped a Fido which quickly smelt its target and sent *U–160* to the bottom with all hands. Next day, the same tactics disposed of another 740-tonner, *U–509*, about 180 miles south of Santa Maria. Fick joined a Gibraltar-Norfolk convoy, recognized as still the best bait for U-boats. Upon reaching mid-ocean on 30 July, a Wildcat pilot sighted two submarines: *U–43* playing milch cow to *U–403*. The fighter plane's strafing runs forced both boats to submerge; and while the larger still had decks awash an Avenger dropped two depth bombs and a Fido near enough to do the trick.

All these kills had been made by the escort carriers' aircraft; but on 23 July a member of *Bogue*'s screen, the 1920-vintage destroyer *George E. Badger* (Lieutenant Thomas H. Byrd USNR), scored. *U–613*, Florida-bound with a load of mines to close off the mouth of St. John's river, was the victim. After three depth-charge attacks there were heard on board *Badger* sounds that are music to a submarine hunter's ears — the horrible roarings, rumblings, cracklings, belchings and bubblings that mark the breaking up of a U-boat. Debris appeared on the surface: shattered woodwork, mattresses and clothing, dismembered and mutilated human bodies. Finally and appropriately the sea spewed up a German translation

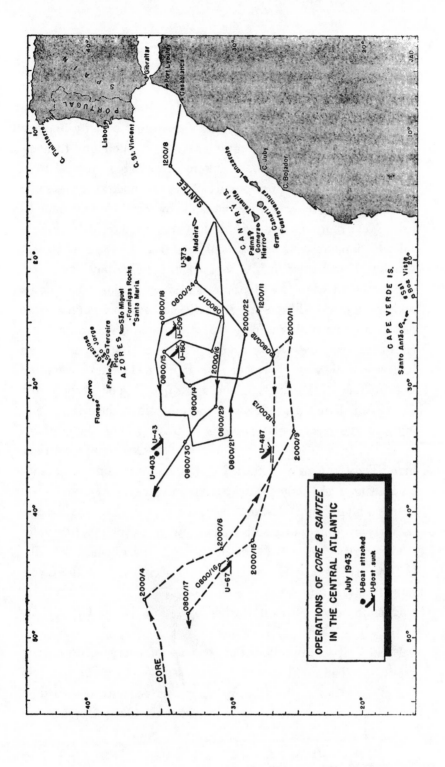

OPERATIONS OF *CORE & SANTEE*
IN THE CENTRAL ATLANTIC

July 1943

● U-Boat attacked
⚓ U-Boat sunk

of Poe's *Murders in the Rue Morgue*. On the same day, one of *Bogue*'s Avengers sank *U–527*.

Escort carrier *Card* (Captain Arnold J. Isbell) and her screen of old four-pipers, *Barry*, *Goff* and *Borie*, now began a five-day battle with U-boats. On 7 August an Avenger, piloted by Lieutenant (jg) A. H. Sallenger USNR, spotted *U–66* about to fuel from *U–117*. With the help of two other planes the milch cow was sunk, but the other got away — to be sunk by *Buckley* nine months later. Next morning, Sallenger and a Wildcat piloted by Ensign John F. Sprague USNR spotted another brace, *U–664* and *U–262*, which had just battled their way past Jack Slessor's boys in the Bay of Biscay and were full of prunes and vinegar. They shot down both planes and killed Sprague; Sallenger and his gunner were picked up on a rubber raft by *Barry*. At noon 9 August, another patrol team spotted *U–664* charging batteries. Captain Isbell had been up all night working out new attack techniques to smother U-boats that tried to fight it out, and to such good purpose that *U–664* was bombed helpless and the crew abandoned ship, leaving 44 floating survivors for *Borie* to pick up. On the 11th, another Wildcat-Avenger team put down *U–525* for keeps with a Fido. The *Card* group returned to the Azorean hunting grounds on 27 August. At noon a three-team patrol sank *U–847*, which had been supplying other U-boats for over a week. She was the sixteenth submarine and eighth milch cow that Admiral Ingersoll's escort carrier groups had sunk in 98 days. In the same period the U-boats had sunk only one ship out of a convoy that the CVEs supported.

Doenitz now called off further operations in the Central Atlantic.

Lacking space to follow the fortunes of every escort carrier group, we shall continue wih Captain Isbell's *Card*. She had two weeks' overhaul at Norfolk in September 1943, then sortied in wide support of a Gibraltar-bound convoy. On 4 October this group hit the jackpot, four U-boats fueling within a radius of 500 yards, sank two of them then and a third on the 13th. After putting in at Casablanca, *Card* sortied and on 31 October sank one of a pair some 660 miles north of Flores. The other, *U–91*, escaped, and Captain Isbell sent destroyer *Borie* (Lieutenant Charles H. Hutchins USNR) to get it.

At 0200 November 1, *Borie* blew a different submarine, *U–405*, to the surface by a shower of depth charges. Hutchins opened fire with main 4-inch battery and machine guns at 1400 yards, closed range, tried to ram, and actually rode his destroyer right up over the U-boat's forecastle. The two ships remained locked in deadly embrace, one under the other, for ten minutes. Two of *Borie*'s 4-inch and three machine guns kept up continuous fire on the sub's conning tower and that part of her deck still above water. Negro mess attendants who manned a 20-mm battery fired right through the metal weather screen; bluejackets not otherwise occupied fired tommy guns, pistols, shotguns, rifles, or whatever they could lay hands on, at the Germans. A sheath knife hurled by a fireman buried itself in the belly of a submariner running to man a gun. In a heavy sea the two vessels pounded and rolled against each other, adding the noise of grinding steel to the roar of gunfire, the clatter of machine guns, and human shouts and screams. All this time *Borie*'s "black gang" was making a gallant fight to keep up steam. The destroyer's plates, light enough at her birth in 1920, had by now been chipped and rusted almost paper-thin, and the whole port side became crushed and holed as it ground against the U-boat's hard pressure hull. All hands, working in water chest-high, stuck to their stations and engineer officer M. R. Brown USNR managed to keep up full power even when salt water was lapping the boilers.

After ten minutes of this mêlée, the submarine managed to back out from under and opened the range to 400 yards; then went into a tight turn. *Borie* circled the submarine, trying to get into position to ram, firing furiously and launching a torpedo which missed. *U–405* straightened out and tried to escape. Now, ordering depth charges set shallow, Hutchins bent on 27 knots, turned on the searchlight and closed to ram. The U-boat skipper, Korvettenkapitän Hopman, had the same thought. Hutchins, with great presence of mind, ordered hard left rudder and, with port engine backing full and starboard engine stopped, slewed *Borie*'s fantail with its depth-charge projectors right across the path of the approaching submarine. Three charges made a perfect straddle around the conning tower, lifting *U–405* bodily and stopping it dead when its stem was only six feet from *Borie*'s stern. The submarine backed full and attempted to pull out. *Borie* swung rapidly to port and pursued, firing. One 4-inch shell blew the German bridge crew overboard; another shell hit the U-boat's exhaust tube, and the boat glided to a halt. Submariners were now coming on deck with hands raised, crying, "*Kamerad!*"

At 0257 November 1, one hour and twelve minutes after the first contact, *U–405* plunged stem-first and exploded under water. A yell of triumph went up from the deck of battered *Borie*.

The victor was in a bad way. When fuel for the radio's auxiliary generator was on the point of exhaustion, it was spliced with lighter fluid, kerosene, and rubbing alcohol so that a message could be put through to the escort carrier at 1100: "Commenced sinking." Captain Isbell got a bearing on this far-from-cheery message and immediately launched two Avengers. One sighted the destroyer at 1129, dead in the water, wallowing heavily and down by the stern. Next he sent *Goff* with hose and handy-billies to pump fresh water for *Borie*'s boilers, but it was now so rough, with swells up to 40 feet, that she could not close. Shortly before sunset 1 November, Lieutenant Hutchins reluctantly gave the word to abandon ship. Captain Isbell sent *Barry*, his one remaining escort, to assist this difficult process, leaving his carrier stripped of her screen. All night *Goff* and *Barry* searched for survivors in heavy seas, until 7 officers and 120 men were rescued. Throughout those hours of heroism and misery, *Card* circled nearby at 10 knots, a fair target for a roving submarine. Finally, an Avenger's depth bombs sent the gallant old destroyer to the bottom, at 0954 November 2.

This memorable battle took place in one of the loneliest stretches of the Atlantic, about halfway between Cape Race, Newfoundland, and Cape Clear, Ireland.

Captain Joseph B. Dunn's task group, composed of escort carrier *Bogue* and destroyers *George E. Badger*, *Osmond Ingram*, *Clemson* and *DuPont*, had the honor of delivering the final blows to German supply submarine activity in mid-Atlantic. On her eastward passage, *Bogue*'s aircraft ended the career of *U-86*. On 9 December she sortied from Casablanca with orders from Admiral Ingersoll to support a convoy until it had cleared a concentration of U-boats near the Azores. The object of Cinclant's present interest and of *Bogue*'s hunting was a 1600-ton milch cow, *U-219*, about to fuel *U-172*, outward bound to the Indian Ocean.

U-172 did not get any nearer the Indian Ocean than that, but she made a good try, sinking only after a fight which lasted intermittently from 0723 December 12 to 1021 next day. She received 14 depth-charge attacks by one destroyer, and gunfire attacks by all three. *U-219*, the milch cow, did escape, and ended the war under Japanese colors. *U-850* was sunk by *Bogue*'s planes 170 miles distant from her, on the 20th.

Captain Dunn now turned west to keep Christmas in Bermuda, while *Card*, with a new screen, destroyers *Schenck*, *Decatur* and *Leary*, again picked up the ball. This time, briefly, the hunters became the hunted, as Doenitz had directed one of his wolf-packs especially to get the escort carrier that had caused him so much grief. At 2200 December 23 *Card* ran afoul of this pack. In the early hours of the day before Christmas, *Schenck* sank *U-645* with depth charges, but *U–245* exploded two torpedoes on *Leary*, and sank her. The skipper, Commander James E. Kyes, gave his life-jacket to a mess attendant who had none, and was drowned — as were 41 others of the 100 who lived to abandon ship. The rest of the wolf-pack let *Card* alone to go after another convoy. But it was a sad Christmas at sea for the group, although they had sunk 11 U-boats as against 8 for *Bogue*, 5 for *Core*, 3 for *Santee*, and 2 each for H.M.S. *Tracker* and *Biter*.

In accordance with Admiral Doenitz's doctrine that it was the duty of his submarine fleet to score off merchant tonnage, no matter where, he began in February 1943 to send U-boats to operate off the Cape of Good Hope and in the Indian Ocean. They did very well, since the Royal Navy had not yet enough escorts to establish convoys in the Indian Ocean. Five U-boats sank 21 vessels of 125,000 tons, including two Liberty ships, in that ocean during the last four months of 1943. Doenitz set up a Far-Eastern submarine base on Penang, off the Malay Peninsula, for future operations. At the same time a number of Japanese I-boats conducted a blitz against Allied shipping in the Indian Ocean, and the Germans took over three Italian submarines. These, the I-boats, and U-boats returning to Germany, sank over 184,000 tons of neutral and Allied shipping in the first three months of 1944.

In order to service and fuel these high-scoring submarines out and home, Doenitz established two filling stations. He sent two supply ships to hang around Mauritius, and milch cows to operate among the Cape Verde Islands. Both supply ships were discovered and sunk by the Royal Navy in February–March 1944; and Admiral Ingersoll sent an escort carrier group built around *Block Island* (Captain Francis M. Hughes) to take care of the others. Her screen was composed of four new destroyer escorts, two of which, *Bronstein* (Lieutenant Sheldon H. Kinney) and *Thomas* (Lieutenant Commander D. M. Kellogg USNR), between them sank three U-boats en route, on 1 and 17 March 1944. On the 19th, having arrived in the Cape Verdes, two of the escort carrier's planes caught an 1100-ton milch cow, *U–1059*, surfaced with the crew in swimming. Lieutenant (jg) N. T. Dowty dropped a bomb right into the boat's ammunition locker and the explosion sank it, but Dowty's plane splashed and he was lost.

Block Island's next cruise, in May 1944, was to be her last. One of her night-flying pilots stalked *U–66*, and homed in DE *Buckley* (Lieutenant Commander Brent M. Abel USNR) of the screen. She opened gunfire on the U-boat in moonlight, at 0320 May 6, closed and rammed. There then ensued a hand-to-hand battle like *Borie*'s. Several of the German submariners attempted, 1812 fashion, to board the destroyer. Abel's merry men repelled them with small arms, shell cases, coffee cups and bare fists in a brawl lasting several minutes. The two vessels parted; *U–66* rammed *Buckley*, scraped clear and made off at high speed, burning furiously with open hatches. Shortly she went down sizzling, and *Buckley* recovered 36 survivors.

U–66 was amply revenged before the month was out. *Block Island* at 2013 May 29 was blasted by three torpedoes from *U–549*, which had slipped inside her screen, and went down quickly. Destroyer escorts recovered 951 survivors, and *Eugene E. Elmore* sank the U-boat. This action took place about 320 miles WSW of Funchal.

Four weeks later, at a point about halfway between the Canaries and the Cape Verdes, Captain Dan Gallery, commanding the *Guadalcanal* escort carrier group, performed the unusual feat of boarding and salvaging a U-boat. At 1110 June 4 a DE of his screen, *Chatelain* (Lieutenant Commander Dudley W. Knox Jr.) made a sound contact on *U–505*. Brisk action followed. Two other DEs bore in to assist, Wildcats circled overhead like hawks, and *Guadalcanal* swung clear at top speed since, as Captain Gallery wrote, "A carrier right smack at the scene of a sound contact is like an old lady in a barroom brawl. She has no business there, and can do nothing but get out of the way." *Chatelain* delivered a full depth-charge pattern which caught the Germans just as lunch was being served, holed the outer hull and rolled the boat on its beam ends, dumping crockery, food and sailors into the bilges. Some of the men, panic-stricken, rushed up to the conning tower shouting that the boat was sinking; the skipper, taking their word for it, blew his tanks and surfaced. A boarding party from DE *Pillsbury*, specially trained to profit by such circumstances, swarmed on board, closed sea cocks, disconnected demolition charges, and took over. *Guadalcanal* passed a towline and, until relieved in mid-ocean by a fleet tug, towed the captured boat toward Bermuda. *U–505*, after serving as a "tame submarine" during the remainder of the war, found a final resting place in the Chicago Museum of Science and Industry.

5. *Fighting U-Boats in Other Waters, May 1943–August 1944*

Between 18 May and 18 September 1943, 62 convoys comprising 3546 merchant ships crossed between America and Britain by the northern transatlantic route, and not one ship was lost. Winston Churchill reported this to the House of Commons with unusual gusto, even for him. He also declared that the excess of new merchant tonnage construction over all losses, since 1 January, was 6 million tons, and that the crisis in food and other imports for the United Kingdom was past. But he rightly predicted that the struggle was not yet over, and that Doenitz was about to spring another surprise.

This was the *Zaunkönig* (wren) homing torpedo, attracted to an escort vessel's propellers as our Fido was to a submerged hull. Doenitz first tried this new device on two northern transatlantic convoys which combined on their westward passage in September. He sank three Canadian and British destroyers and six merchant ships; but the other escorts, assisted by land-based Liberators, sank three of the 21 U-boats deployed against them.

After this convoy attack, Doenitz decided to call off surface warfare for his U-boats and kill time until he could get new and deadlier submarine types into production. One of his time-killing operations was an unsuccessful attempt of 13 U-boats, between June and October 1943, to mine harbor channels from St. John's, Newfoundland to the St. Johns River, Florida. Two of the boats were lost, and their total bag (including that of the mines) was four merchant ships and gunboat *Plymouth*. But they certainly gave a much-needed scare to Eastern Sea Frontier, which was getting careless after nine months' enemy inactivity in its teeming waters.

Doenitz also tried a summer blitz in the Caribbean and off Brazil. *U-615* spent the second half of July prowling about Curaçao in search of tankers. In a space of nine days she beat off attacks by a dozen aircraft and a PC, and sustained such serious damage that when destroyer *Walker*, dispatched from Port of Spain, sighted her on August 7, the skipper, knowing that his time was up, ordered all hands into life rafts, and grimly took his boat down for the last time. *Walker* rescued 43 of the crew. For the Germans, this Caribbean blitz was a disaster. Ten U-boats in six weeks sank only 16,231 tons of shipping, a bag that would have been considered small for one boat in 1942. Five U-boats were sunk in the Caribbean and two more never got home.

After withdrawing the battered remnants of this group in August, Doenitz left the Caribbean undisturbed until late October, when he tried a series of mine-planting missions that accomplished nothing; and, in November, tried a three-boat attack on Caribbean shipping. *U-516* (Kapitänleutnant Hans Tillessen) made the most sensational raid on the Isthmus of Panama since the days of Drake;

and, although he carried off no pieces of eight, he made a bigger bag of merchantmen than had all ten boats of the summer blitz. In the Pacific the Bougainville campaign was now on, Tarawa was coming up, and every day warships, tankers, LSTs and all manner of ships were passing through the Canal to reinforce Pacific Fleet, while troop transports were returning empty from San Diego. Plenty of targets for an enterprising U-boat, which *U-516* was. And, at the very moment when she paid her unexpected call on the Caribbean side, all Panama Sea Frontier forces were engaged in a tactical exercise on the Pacific side.

On 5 November 1943 the boat was sighted north of Curaçao and bombed unsuccessfully by a Ventura. Sea frontier officers sent out three submarine chasers to look for her, but Tillessen eluded them by hugging the coast. On 12 November he sank a small Panamanian freighter, and on the 17th a Colombian schooner; on the 23rd he torpedoed and sank a loaded tanker shortly after it had departed Cristobal, and the following night downed a Liberty ship seventy-five miles off the Canal entrance. Every available plane, including Avengers from an escort carrier transiting the Canal, was ordered out to look for *U-516*; but Tillessen eluded them all and sank another freighter off the Gulf of San Blas, on 8 December. The Aruba and Trinidad sectors now got into the act with minecraft, minesweepers, coast guard cutters and aircraft; Tillessen replied by sinking another tanker off Aruba on 16 December. Sonobuoys, which register propeller noises like a ship's sonar, were dropped around spots where *U-516* was sighted, but she escaped every attack and celebrated Christmas submerged off Saint Eustatius. She then steamed into the open sea by a narrow passage which sea frontier commanders had not troubled to patrol. Tillessen even brought *U-516* back next year and sank two more tankers.

Off Brazil and in the South Atlantic, Vice Admiral Ingram's Fourth Fleet waged relentless war against raiders, blockade run-

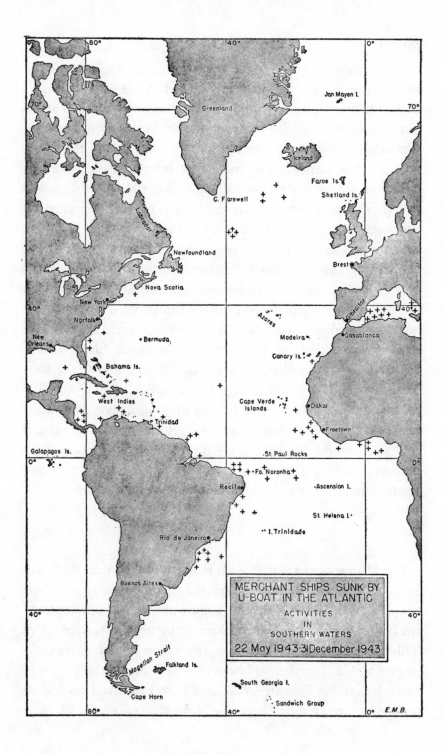

MERGHANT SHIPS SUNK BY
U-BOAT IN THE ATLANTIC

ACTIVITIES
IN
SOUTHERN WATERS
22 May 1943-31 December 1943

ners and submarines, with the coöperation of the Brazilian government and armed forces. Jonas Ingram and President Vargas were thick as thieves, and everything that he wanted the Brazilian armed forces to do was done. The small, closely knit Fourth Fleet, less diluted by replacements than almost any other part of the Navy, ranked high in morale and aggressiveness. It included only five light cruisers of the twenty-year-old *Omaha* class, eight destroyers, and several small craft, but its air arm by the end of 1943 comprised ten squadrons of amphibious Catalinas, Venturas, Liberators and Mariners, located at five different bases on the Brazilian coast. There was also a squadron of Army bombers and some Navy Liberators on the lonely island of Ascension. Air forces were so much stronger and more mobile than surface forces, which were largely employed in escort duty, that all the antisubmarine fights in this theater were aircraft vs. U-boat. From Ascension Island, *U–848* was sunk on 5 November, her sister *U–849* on the 25th, the same Thanksgiving Day which Arleigh Burke was celebrating off Cape St. George in the Bismarcks. Fourth Fleet paid special attention to blockade runners which were trying to bring rubber, tin and wolfram from the Far East to Germany. *Weserland* was sunk by destroyer *Somers; Rio Grande* and *Burgenland* by *Omaha* and *Jouett*. This virtually ended blockade-running for the war.

The Mediterranean was an even more critical sea than the South Atlantic. Between December 1942 and March 1945, twenty-four troop convoys, escorted by the United States Navy, transported 536,134 troops from the United States to the Mediterranean; thirty "Oil-Torch" fast-tanker convoys, with an average of seven tankers each, sailed from the Caribbean to the Mediterranean at 32-day intervals between February 1943 and June 1944. And no loss or damage to any of them. Between November 1942 and VE day,

11,119 merchant ships were convoyed in 189 U.S.-Gibraltar and Gibraltar-U.S. slow convoys, with the loss of only nine ships sunk while under United States naval escort.

Although the largest number of U-boats present in the Mediterranean at any one time was eighteen, in February 1944, this was eighteen too many for the Allies. Staff officers of Cincmed (now Admiral Sir John Cunningham RN), Commander Eighth Fleet (Vice Admiral Hewitt) and Northwest Africa Coastal Command R.A.F. (Air Vice Marshal Hugh Lloyd) devised what they called "the SWAMP Operation," to keep submarines down to the point of exhaustion and attack them when forced up to breathe. On 13 December 1943 SWAMP scored an initial success on *U–593*, after a stubborn, persistent search lasting 72 hours by British and American destroyers and Wellington bombers. *U–73* succumbed a few days later to the efforts of four United States destroyers and SOC planes from *Brooklyn*, which happened to be lying at Oran. In May 1944 *U–371*, which had sunk H.M.S. *Penelope* in the Anzio operation, was downed after a 24-hour hunt. Next day the hunted became the hunter when *U–967* attacked a 107-ship convoy east of Gibraltar and sank destroyer escort *Fechteler*. But, during the same month, *U–616* succumbed to a 90-hour chase in which several British and American destroyers and numerous planes participated.

In April 1944, the German air offensive grew more intense. It was aimed at the big U.S.-Gibraltar-Suez convoys, principal means of supplying Allied armies in the Italian campaign, of building up for the invasion of Southern France, and of carrying matériel to India and Russia. Marshal Goering used all resources that he could spare from the Italian and Russian fronts and all the tactical ingenuity he could muster. His aircraft attacked only at night or in twilight. Elaborate tactics were worked out, with lines of acetylene float lights as long as sixty miles, and intensely bright flares, and coördinated bombing attacks similar to those that we have described the Japanese using off Makin. They were frustrated by a sufficient number of escorts well trained in antiaircraft fire, proximity-fused shells, smoke; and, perhaps even more by Coastal Command Beaufighters vectored out from Algerian fields to intercept the bombers. The only convoy roughly handled was an eastbound one on 20 April, in which destroyer *Lansdale* was sunk and S.S. *Paul Hamilton*, carrying 500 men of the Army Air Force and a crew of eighty, blew up with the loss of all hands. The escort commanders of the other convoys, Commander Jesse C. Sowell in U.S.C.G.C. *Campbell*, Commander W. R. Headden in DE *Stanton*, Captain H. S. Berdine uscg in *Decatur*, Captain Adelbert F. Converse in *Ellyson*, and Captain Charles C. Hartman in *Mervine*, rank high among our antisubmarine fighters. By 1 August, with operation DRAGOON coming up, German airfields in Southern France were interdicted, and the Mediterranean became so peaceful that, beginning with a convoy which passed Gibraltar 27 November 1944, all dispersed at Point Europa and the ships proceeded independently to their terminal ports.

The few U-boats that managed to slip past the Cape Verdes in 1944 did so by grace of the snorkel, which enabled them to cruise continuously submerged and escape the attentions of escort carrier groups and land-based planes. But the chief theater of activity for snorkel-equipped submarines was the North Atlantic. This device, which the Germans stole from the Royal Netherlands Navy, was a combined air-intake and gas-outlet that allowed submarines to run their diesels submerged, charging batteries if needed. It took the shape of a streamlined steel cylinder which was provided with an automatic float-valve to keep out sea water, and a small radar grid. When the snorkel was in use, it made a "feather" on the water scarcely bigger than that of a periscope head — almost impossible to pick up by the radar sets in use in 1944.

Doenitz regarded the snorkel as a mere stopgap until he had Type XXI, with diesel-electric propulsion and new, much more powerful batteries, in operation. In the spring of 1944 he began to send snorkel-equipped boats on nuisance raids to the East Coast of America in hope of sinking strategic cargoes destined for the invasion of Normandy. They accomplished nothing and, in spite of the snorkel spurt, total losses of merchant ships to U-boats fell, in May 1944, to an all-time low of four ships. The most dramatic evidence of Allied mastery of the U-boat came in the Normandy operation of June 1944. Doenitz alerted 58 U-boats to break it up, but not one got near the invasion area. Liberators of R.A.F. Coastal Command, including United States Fairwing Seven, in which Joseph P. Kennedy Jr., brother of the future President, was a pilot, operated a 24-hour patrol across the chops of the Channel, in conjunction with small warships, so close that every part of the surface was inspected by a plane every 35 minutes. All had microwave radar, and sonobuoys to drop if they spotted a U-boat after dark — and there isn't much dark in those northern waters in June. Thirteen U-boats were sunk by planes or surface craft in the Channel approaches in June; and their only successes were two British frigates, one corvette and one empty transport. In early August, after General Patton's breakthrough isolated the Brittany peninsula, the U-boats had to evacuate their Breton ports to operate from Norway.

But whenever the Allies thought they had the U-boats licked, Doenitz uncorked something new; and he was to give us many anxious hours in 1945.

CHAPTER XIII

The Navy in the Invasion of France
1944

1. *Preliminaries, January–June 1944*

IT WAS NO EASY MATTER to get the cross-Channel operation firmed-up for 1944. At the Casablanca Conference in January 1943, the Americans succeeded only in getting a vote to set up
a Combined Planning Staff. That was done in March, when the able
and enthusiastic Lieutenant General Sir Frederick E. Morgan became "Cossac" — Chief of Staff to Supreme Allied Commander
(Designate). In May, at the "Trident" Conference in Washington,
a tentative date was set for a twelvemonth thence, and in August
at the Quebec "Quadrant" Conference, the J. C. S. persuaded the
C. C. S. to accept Cossac's plan for OVERLORD, as the cross-Channel
operation had been named, and to declare that it should be first
charge on Allied resources in 1944.

The British chiefs of staff, especially General Marshall's opposite
number, Field Marshal Sir Alan Brooke, never seemed to understand why Americans had to have commitments well in advance.
Their own logistics problems being relatively simple, they thought
we were unnecessarily inflexible. They did not appreciate the
enormous difficulties of procurement, shipbuilding, troop training and supply necessary to place a million and a half troops in
England, with armor, tanks and troop-lift ready to invade the Continent. The general idea in Britain seems to have been that America
had an inexhaustible pool of man power, weapons, landing craft,

aircraft and other lethal weapons which could be deployed at short notice. American production schedules had been upset in April 1942, to give top priority to landing and beaching craft for the cross-Channel operation that was canceled, and again in January 1943 schedules were upset to give top priority to ships for anti-submarine warfare. That is why there was a landing and beaching craft shortage in 1944. Admiral King was always loyal to the major strategic decision to "Beat Germany first," but he saw no sense in piling up men, landing craft and matériel in England while Mr. Churchill and the British chiefs of staff were making up their minds what, if anything, should be done with them. Too many high strategists in England regarded American and Canadian troops in Britain as a mere army of opportunity, to be thrown across the Channel if and when Germany showed signs of weakening.

Even after December 1943, when OVERLORD was refirmed at the Teheran conference between Roosevelt, Churchill and Stalin, the P.M. tried to have it postponed in order to get in a few more thrusts "around the ring," such as a landing on the island of Rhodes. Churchill told an American general in April 1944 that, had *he* been planning OVERLORD, he would first have recovered Norway, taken some Aegean islands and ensured Turkey's support. General Morgan had difficulty in inducing his planning staff to take OVERLORD seriously, because so many of his countrymen believed it would never be necessary, hoping that something would turn up, such as a crack in German morale, or bombing them into subjection, or the death of Hitler, to make it unnecessary. Planning for OVERLORD was also hampered by Roosevelt's procrastination. From August through December 1943 he was balancing the respective merits of Generals Marshall and Eisenhower as Supreme Commander. He selected "Ike" only at Christmastide, having been persuaded that Marshall was a key member of the Joint Chiefs of Staff who could not be spared from Washington.

After this appointment, which gave the hitherto headless Cossac an energetic director, the planners were absorbed into Shaef (Supreme Headquarters Allied Expeditionary Force). By New Year's 1944 Shaef's staff, at Norfolk House, St. James's Square, London, comprised 489 officers, about half American and half British, and 614 men, two thirds of them British.

The chain of command of naval and ground forces decided on to execute the final plan for NEPTUNE-OVERLORD, as the great cross-Channel operation came to be called,[1] may best be represented by a diagram, in which I have shown the assault elements only of the troops that landed on D-day.

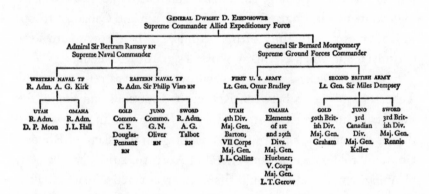

Before describing the vital air plan for the invasion, we must touch on Operation POINTBLANK, the R.A.F. and A.A.F. strategic air offensive against Germany. Its original purpose, in accordance with the Douhet-Mitchell theory of air warfare, was to render an invasion of Germany unnecessary by bombing her into submission. Judged by the results, this was a failure. Even the attacks on Hamburg, in July-August 1943, which wiped out over half the city, killed 42,000 and injured 37,000 people, did not seriously diminish Germany's well-dispersed war production, and failed to break civilian morale.

[1] The code NEPTUNE was generally used for the amphibious phase of the operation.

During 1944, with General Carl Spaatz commanding the U. S. Strategic Air Force in Europe, POINTBLANK was better directed. In the "Big Week" of 19-25 February 1944, 3300 heavy bombers of the England-based VIII, and over 500 of the Italy-based XV Army Air Forces, escorted by about the same number of fighter planes, pounded factories of the German aircraft industry, as far south as Ratisbon and Augsburg. Our losses were 226 bombers, 28 fighters and about 2600 men; but some 600 German planes were shot down, denying their use to the enemy when he needed them most. By 14 April, when Operation POINTBLANK ended and air operations with immediate reference to OVERLORD began, the Allied air forces had established a thirty-to-one superiority over the Luftwaffe. On D-day "Ike" told his troops, "If you see fighting aircraft over you, they will be ours," and they were.

Besides taking a terrific toll of the Luftwaffe, the air forces gave vital prior support to the invasion by their "transportation plan" to cripple the enemy's communications system. This was a sustained bombing of roads, railroads and marshaling yards in France, Belgium and western Germany. Results were spectacular. Some 600 trains carrying German army supplies were back-tracked, and by the end of May all rail traffic between Paris and the Channel was stalled. The Air Forces contributed heavily to blockading the Channel to U-boats. And they destroyed stockpiles of the newly invented German V–1 guided missiles (the so-called "buzz-bombs"), and some of their launching sites. These were too small — many of them mobile — and too well protected by antiaircraft guns to be eliminated by air bombing alone. But the result of this air operation CROSSBOW which cost the A.A.F. and R.A.F. hundreds of lives, was to destroy so many missiles that the Germans were unable to start them off until 12 June, when most of the invasion forces were already in France.

Finally, an essential part of the assault plan was two night airdrops of unprecedented size, two divisions in each sector. In the

American, behind Utah Beach, the 82nd and 101st Airborne, commanded by Major Generals Matthew B. Ridgway and Maxwell D. Taylor made the drop. The object was to confuse the Germans and seal off the land approaches to the Utah beachhead, which they did admirably. Thus, the air power leg to the Allied military tripod was more than sufficiently stout; it was unbreakable.

So, too, was the naval leg. Admiral Ramsay, the top Allied naval commander, after notable service in World War I, had been recalled to active duty at the age of fifty-six, to be Flag Officer, Dover. As such he had been the main instrument in the evacuation of the British Army from Dunkirk in 1940. After serving as Cunningham's chief naval planner for Operation TORCH, he took an important part in later Mediterranean amphibious operations. Rear Admiral Hall, who served under Ramsay, described him as "quiet, brilliant, intelligent, determined and easy to get on with."

Rear Admiral Alan G. Kirk as Commander Western Naval Task Force was the key American naval figure in NEPTUNE-OVERLORD, from the time of his reporting in mid-November 1943. At the age of fifty-six he was rounding out his thirty-ninth year of service in the United States Navy. While chief of staff to Admiral Stark in 1942, he had become thoroughly conversant with English ways, problems and personalities. As Commander Amphibious Forces Atlantic Fleet he had made himself master of that branch of naval warfare, and in the Sicilian operation he led the difficult assault on the eastern flank.

The essence of the over-all plan was to land two American and three British divisions simultaneously on a sixty-mile stretch of the coast of Normandy, on 5 June; with quick, strong reinforcements to keep up momentum and expand the beachhead. Although this was a shore-to-shore operation which required only one night spent in the English Channel, big transports with landing craft on davits were employed in addition to beaching craft. The shortage of what Churchill referred to as "some goddam things called LSTs" provoked the only sharp unpleasantness between Allies over this operation. The British accused the Americans of starving Europe of beaching craft in order to feed the Pacific; Admiral King denied this and accused the British of dragging their feet in producing or repairing their own beaching and landing craft.

A memorandum of the C.C.S. Planning Staff gives the only reliable figures on the deployment of beaching and landing craft. It tells how many of each nation was both operational and serviceable on 1 June 1944, eliminating those building, having shakedown, crossing the ocean, under repair, and so on. Here it is, for the six principal types used in the two operations for the invasion of France: —

1 June 1944	LST	LCI(L)	LCT	LCM	LCVP	LCA[2]
U.S.N. in United Kingdom	168	124	247	216	1089	0
R.N. in United Kingdom	61	121	664	265	0	646
U.S.N. in Mediterranean	23	59	44	185	395	0
R.N. in Mediterranean	2	32	64	95	0	138
U.S.N. on East Coast, U.S.	95[3]	89	58	57	341	0
U.S.N. on West Coast, U.S.	0	41	1	60	181	0
U.S.N. in all Pacific Areas	102	128	140	1198	2298	0
R.N. on E. Indies Station	0	4	2	67	0	46

The first two lines represent what went into Operation NEPTUNE-OVERLORD. Comparing these with the last three lines, it will be seen that the J.C.S. were far from niggardly in allotting beaching craft to the European theater, and that the only types of which the Pacific may be said to have had a superfluity were the LCM and LCVP, together with the LSM (Landing Ship, Medium, not in this table), which was not wanted for OVERLORD. It is also relevant to point out that 115 LST, 220 LCI(L), 171 LCT, 671 LCM, and 1333 of the smaller landing craft, were built in the United States for the Royal Navy during the war.

[2] A British landing craft similar to our LCVP.
[3] Of these, 93 were just completed and not yet allocated.

A legitimate complaint of both British and American officers in Shaef was Admiral King's tardiness in allocating battleships, cruisers and destroyers for gunfire support. This was crucial, since nothing was more certain than that very heavy naval gunfire would be necessary to break down Germany's Atlantic Wall; air bombs couldn't get at it. After Admiral Hall had sounded off on the subject to King's planning officer, C.N.O. allocated three old battleships, three cruisers and 31 destroyers. Yet even with these in hand, the Royal Navy supplied the lion's share of gunfire support, a majority of the minecraft, many specialized types of small craft, and all the Fairmile motor launches and dan-buoy layers.[4]

Rear Admiral John L. Hall had the most varied duties of any attack force commander. He not only commanded XI 'Phib Force, but supervised the training of ships in Force "U" as well as his own assault force. All United States fire support ships reported to him and conducted shore bombardment exercises under his command. "Jimmie" Hall was not only able; his calm, assured temperament spread confidence. Two nights before D-day, when the foul weather and the postponement were giving almost everyone the jitters, the Admiral said to a friend of mine, "I do not expect to be repulsed on *any* beach."

Training centers, supply depots and repair bases for the American troops and landing craft crews were established at Rosneath on the Clyde, at Plymouth, Dartmouth, Salcombe, Exeter and Tiverton in Devonshire, at Falmouth, Fowey, St. Mawes, Launceston, Calstock and Saltash in Cornwall, at Deptford on the Thames below London, and in a base hospital at Netley near Southhampton. Rear Admiral John Wilkes, with headquarters at Devonport, was responsible for the training and readiness of all landing and beaching craft and for amphibious training exercises. These started as early as December 1943 at Slapton Sands and Torquay, Devon-

---

[4] The French and Netherlands Navies between them contributed three cruisers, five destroyers and two gunboats.

shire. Admiral Kirk reported on 1 June that, owing to Wilkes's "splendid efforts," 99.3 per cent of all types of United States beaching and landing craft were ready to go. The corresponding British figure was 97.6 per cent. Both indicated an unusually high order of readiness.

On 26 April 1944 Admiral Ramsay and staff took up headquarters at Southwick House, an old country mansion seven miles from Portsmouth. Here Ramsay was frequently visited by Admiral Kirk, and by Generals Eisenhower and Montgomery. Southwick House now became the nerve center for NEPTUNE-OVERLORD, where the great decisions were made.

The culmination of the joint training program was a couple of full-scale rehearsals in late April and early May. Troops and equipment were embarked in the same ships, and for the most part in the same ports, whence they would leave for the Far Shore, as everyone now called the coast of Normandy. One rehearsal was ruined by German E-boats bursting into it in Lyme Bay and sinking two LSTs, with a loss of almost 200 sailors and over 400 soldiers.

Rehearsals completed, the troops returned to their embarkation ports and marshaling camps, where they were held until it was time for the assault. English harbors have never been so full of ships and sailors, or the English land so heavy with troops, as on the eve of NEPTUNE. Some 1,627,000 "Yanks" were bedded down on British soil before the invasion began, and the Admiralty estimate for sailors then afloat in the harbors or at sea was 52,889 Americans, 112,824 British. The latter assembled at Portsmouth, Southampton, Poole, the Solent and Spithead. American forces were assigned to harbors on the south coast between Portland and Falmouth, with the center of gravity at Plymouth. But these West Country ports were too small to hold all American forces afloat. The naval gunfire support ships and many destroyers were based on Belfast Lough in Northern Ireland, where they had plenty of room for maneuvering and training.

On 28 May Admiral Ramsay from Southwick House sent out the signal that started this vast operation in motion: "Carry out Operation NEPTUNE!" All crews were now "sealed" in their ships and craft. The troops had already been placed behind barbed wire in their long marshaling camps, with Counterintelligence Corps keeping a tight watch to prevent leaks and to stifle loose talk.

2. The Start and the Crossing, 1–6 June

"For now sits Expectation in the air." By 1 June 1944 southern England began to swarm with British, Canadian and American soldiers in battle uniform, with their weapons and field equipment, marching along country roads by day, rolling in trucks and tanks by night through blacked-out villages and towns, whose citizens had been cautioned to reveal nothing.

All night long, no sound was heard but the clatter of army boots on paved streets, the "*Hup*, two, three, four; *hup*, two, three, four" of sergeants, the rattle of vehicles and the roar and putter of engines, as men marched and machines rolled to the water's edge, there to board beaching craft on the "hards," and transports at the docks. Gunfire support ships converged from northern ports in England and Ireland, and at a score of airfields paratroops climbed on board transport planes and gliders. No music, no flags, no crowds; only women and old men offering a last cup of tea and a hearty "God bless you!" Thus, efficiently and in silence, supported by the prayers of the free world, began the great invasion to crush Germany and liberate France.

Vast, unprecedented, was the press of shipping. From Felixstowe on the North Sea, around the South Coast to Milford Haven in Wales, English harbors were crowded with ships. By 3 June almost every vessel assigned to cross on her own bottom — and there were 931 of them for the American beaches and 1796 for the British — was in her assembly port awaiting the word to go.

Would the capricious June weather of northern Europe allow it to go? Forecasts on Saturday June 3 were unfavorable, even alarming. By 0400 Sunday, when Eisenhower met the generals and admirals at Southwick House, it seemed hopeless. The Supreme Commander then postponed D-day from the 5th to the 6th of June, and vessels which had already started were recalled. At 9 o'clock Sunday evening all top commanders met in Southwick House. The weather chart still looked foul, but the staff meteorologist predicted moderating wind and sea for the 6th. If D-day were postponed further, it would have to be postponed for two weeks, when the tide would be right again for landing; that would never do. So, one hour before midnight 4 June, orders were issued to all ships of both Navies to sail to meet a 6 June D-day, and, at 0415 June 5, General Eisenhower made it definite with the laconic order: "O.K. We'll go."

Almost every one of the thousands of ships and craft was under way by noon June 5. At 1800, off Portland Bill, as far as the eye could reach, the Channel was covered with vessels "fraught with the ministers and instruments of cruel war," the small ones tossing and heaving, the great ones steadily advancing. In Portland itself, as midnight approached, the only assault forces left were the motor torpedo boats, to dash across after daybreak. Portland Bill lighthouse was the point of departure for 925 transport planes carrying 13,000 American paratroops, who preceded the seaborne assault. Groups of 18 aircraft each, flying at about 500 feet, came in with running lights on; as they converged on the darkened lighthouse tower, they blacked out and altered course for the Far Shore, streaming away from the towered headland like the wings on the Victory of Samothrace. Cross-Channel they flew, and at

0136 June 6 began dropping troops in the swampy region behind Utah Beach.

The surface crossing was so well planned, with so many different lanes for the 2727 ships and small craft, that in spite of rough water there were no collisions and few arrived late.

Even more astonishing, the Germans were unaware of the impending invasion. The Allies' secrets never leaked. In the tall, conspicuous lighthouse at Cape Barfleur, the powerful lamp was burning brightly. No Luftwaffe reconnaissance plane had seen anything unusual in the Channel. No German E-boats patrolled — because the local naval commander, Admiral Krancke, considered the weather too foul both for them and for us; and he was easy in his mind because, in his book, the tides were not right for a landing between 4 and 6 June.[5] Not until 0309 June 6 did German search radar pick up anything, although many ships had reached their transport areas an hour earlier. The shore batteries waited until first light, shortly after 0500, when they opened up on destroyers *Corry* and *Fitch*.

To repel any possible invasion, General Dollman's Seventh Army at or near the landing beaches had one armored, two "attack" (fully equipped) infantry divisions, and three "static" or vehicle-less divisions. Six armored and 19 other divisions (the Fifteenth Army) were deployed from the mouth of the Seine to the Pas de Calais. Assuming that these could help, the Germans would outnumber the Allies for at least two weeks; and as standard amphibious doctrine required a three-to-one superiority of attack over defense, the success of Operation NEPTUNE was no foregone conclusion.

Over all German forces was Field Marshal Rommel, "Monty's" old desert antagonist; and over him, Field Marshal von Rundstedt.

---

[5] The Germans wanted us, and apparently expected us, to land at high water, when the boats would be hung up or blown up by the obstacles; we, naturally, did the contrary.

Rommel believed in those favorite shibboleths of his oriental ally, to "annihilate the enemy at the beachhead," "hurl him into the sea," and so on, and he had more dirty means of doing that than the Japanese ever thought of. First, a line of underwater mines, then all manner of mined obstacles on the beaches designed to trip up landing craft and disembowel men; then the "Atlantic Wall" of casemated and mobile guns, so placed as to enfilade the dry parts of the beaches, with plenty of land mines planted behind them. Hitler supported this water's-edge defense concept of his favorite general — whom he was to liquidate shortly. The Fuehrer, in an impassioned speech to his principal commanders on 20-21 March, declared that the enemy assault must be repelled within a few hours in order to "prevent the reëlection of Roosevelt," who "with luck, would finish up somewhere in jail!" Churchill, too, would be "finished," and the Allies would never be able to launch another invasion.

Thus, D-day caught the Germans in France unready to meet an invasion, and with only one stout leg to their strategic tripod — the army. More than half of that was pinned down in the Pas de Calais because of a successful deception by the British; the creation of a phantom army around Dover. But the Atlantic Wall — that crust of steel and concrete girdled with mined obstacles — inadequate as it proved to be for stopping the American, Canadian and British troops, was the most formidable barrier encountered by any amphibious assault in history. It might even have been a fatal barrier but for the Allies' priceless asset of surprise, which they maintained right up to H-hour of D-day.

3. The Landings, D-day, 6 June

The nine-mile stretch of beach on the east coast of the Cotentin (Cherbourg) Peninsula, which we named (and the French still call)

Utah, is featureless: a shelving beach backed by dunes, such as one finds in a thousand places from Canada to Key West. The Germans had not paid as much attention to this — fortunately for General Collins's VII Corps — as to Omaha, or to the British sector; but they had built a concrete wall along the edge of the dunes, planted thousands of underwater mines, and had some sections of beach swept by fields of gunfire.

At 0200 June 6, 34 British and United States minesweepers under a veteran minecraft officer, Commander M. H. Brown RN, began sweeping the transport area ten miles off shore, the fire support areas, and the approach channels for boats and bombardment ships. These mines, of the type that required several sweeps to deactivate, proved to be the most dangerous enemy weapon of the Utah assault; two minecraft, two destroyers, a DE, two LCIs, a PC and three LCTs carrying tanks were sunk by them.

First wave of troops touched down exactly at H-hour, 0630. A curious feature of this landing was that the whole thing "slipped" a mile south of the designated points. A ten-mile boat trip against head wind and sea, and a strong southerly set of current, were responsible. This mistake — which Brigadier General Theodore Roosevelt discovered — was a lucky break, as the "right" beaches were enfiladed by casemated German batteries and the "wrong" ones were lightly defended. Twenty-six assault waves were landed before noon, dumps were quickly established inland; by 1800, over 21,000 troops and 1700 vehicles were ashore, and the big transports were not only unloaded by midnight, but, most of them, back in Portland. The 4th Division, with the essential help of the paratroops who dropped well behind Utah, had reached their first objective line, and suffered only 197 casualties.

A principal factor in breaking down German resistance at Utah was abundant and accurate naval gunfire support, especially on the remote and large-caliber batteries that the assault troops could not get at. This was directed by Rear Admiral Morton L. Deyo

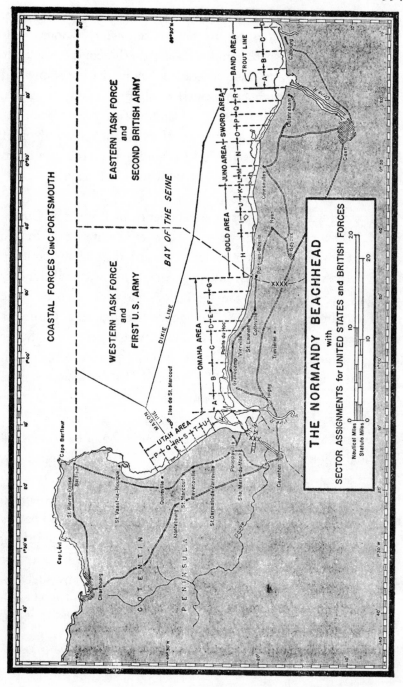

THE NORMANDY BEACHHEAD
with
SECTOR ASSIGNMENTS for UNITED STATES and BRITISH FORCES

in heavy cruiser *Tuscaloosa*. The flagship, *Nevada*, and H.M.S. *Black Prince* and *Erebus*, for 50 minutes following H-hour, bombarded heavy German batteries north of the beachhead, using air spot. After completing these scheduled shoots, the big ships fired on targets of opportunity on request of shore fire-control parties. The new method of air spotting by land-based fighter planes, devised at Salerno, was used. *Nevada*, that gallant old survivor of Pearl Harbor, even answered a call for gunfire from the paratroops well inland, and received the thanks of General Ridgway.

Very different indeed was the experience of landing at Omaha Beach.[6] This six-mile-long stretch between Pointe de la Percée and Port-en-Bessin was far better defended than Utah, both by fixed defenses and troops; and no American airdrop behind it engaged the attention of the Germans, who were two or three times as numerous as Allied Intelligence had reported. Casualties were staggering, but General Gerow's V Corps United States Army (1st and 29th Divisions) got through, thanks to their own valor, the landing well planned by Admiral Hall, and naval gunfire support rendered by Admiral Bryant's ships.

The coast here trends easterly and takes on a more rugged character than the Utah area of the Cotentin Peninsula. The land is a bold, high plateau which the sea has abruptly chopped off, leaving steep, sandy bluffs, at the foot of which are wide sandy beaches of gentle gradient. According to plan, the troops landed along this coast at or near low water, so that UDTs would have a chance to blow beach obstacles while the flats were dry, and rising tide (which rose to 22 feet on D-day) would make it easier for reinforcements to get in. Thus, the assault echelons, after debarking at low water, had to tramp across a wet beach planted with booby-trapped obstacles. Above the beach was a ruff of "con-

---

[6] For a fine detailed narrative, see S. L. A. Marshall "First Wave at Omaha Beach" in *Atlantic Monthly* for November 1960.

certina" barbed wire, against an artificial seawall. Having sur-
mounted that, the GI found himself on a level, grassy area 150 to
300 yards wide, heavily mined and devoid of cover. On the inland
side of this level shelf was a line of bluffs, through which there
were only four exits, deep ravines eroded through the plateau.
Each exit was thoroughly covered by gunfire from concealed concrete emplacements which could not be reached by naval guns.

Altogether, the Germans had provided the best imitation of hell
for an invading force that American troops had encountered anywhere. Even the Japanese defenses of Tarawa, Peleliu and Iwo
Jima are not to be compared with these. Moreover, the protective
works for Omaha had hardly been touched before D-day, owing to
the imperative need for tactical surprise. Allied air power had concentrated on isolating, not pounding, the beachhead; and the Navy
was not given the time to do much damage on D-day morning.

Minesweeping by British and Canadian minecraft began before
midnight and was effectively concluded by 0355. The fire support
ships, led by 32-year-old *Arkansas* and including two French
cruisers, arrived at 0220. The assault elements of the 1st and 29th
Divisions — 16 big transports, 205 beaching craft and numerous
small craft — arrived half an hour later. By 0430 the initial boat
waves were on their way to the beach from the big transports, anchored eleven miles off shore.[7] There was no enemy reaction until 0530, half an hour before sunrise, when a light battery began
firing ineffectively at *Arkansas* and several destroyers. For 35 minutes, beginning at 0550, *Texas* and other gunfire support ships
worked over the beach exit that led to Vierville; *Arkansas* and
H.M.S. *Glasgow* plastered the Les Moulins area; French cruiser
Georges Leygues and other ships smacked the Saint-Laurent

[7] Admiral Kirk was criticized for placing his transports so far out; the reason
he did so was to protect them from coast defense guns on the lofty Pointe du Hoc
near the western end of the Omaha area. This point was captured by Lt.
Col. Rudder's 2nd Ranger Battalion United States Army on D-day morning, only
to find that the dreaded cannon were "Quaker guns" made of telephone poles.

plateau where the military cemetery is now located. All this did some good, but not nearly enough; and the 484 B–24s of VIII Army Air Force, which were supposed to bomb the major enemy strongpoints after the ships lifted their fire, missed the beach altogether and dropped their stuff on crops and cattle three miles inland.

At H-hour, 0630, when the naval bombardment ceased, a new and ominous noise was heard. From Pointe de la Percée to Port-en-Bessin, German automatic weapons and artillery began belching fire on landing craft at the water's edge.

A bloody morning lay ahead. First casualties were the DD (dual drive) amphibious tanks, scheduled to land five minutes ahead of the infantry. These were fitted with "bloomers," canvas water-wings which were supposed to afford enough flotation to enable them to churn ashore if launched from LCTs a mile or more off the beach. On this occasion the bloomers failed to bloom in the rough water, and 27 out of 32 tanks destined for the eastern half of Omaha Beach went straight to the bottom, carrying most of their crews with them. Those for the western part, owing to the good judgment of Captain Lorenzo S. Sabin, were landed on the beach directly from LCTs, but most of them were shot up by German artillery before they could support the American infantry.

As landing craft of the first assault waves grounded and dropped ramps, the GIs came under intense enemy gunfire. They had to wade through 50 to 100 yards of water, then cross 200 to 300 yards of beach, dodging the fixed obstacles, to the protection of the seawall. Some drowned after one wound or a stumble, others were blown to bits by the mines or, if only wounded, lay on the beach until the flood tide drowned them; so many company officers were killed or wounded that survivors, crouching under the seawall, knew not what to do next. Only two companies out of the eight in the first assault wave were on the beaches where they were supposed to be. By 0800 not a man or a vehicle had moved in-

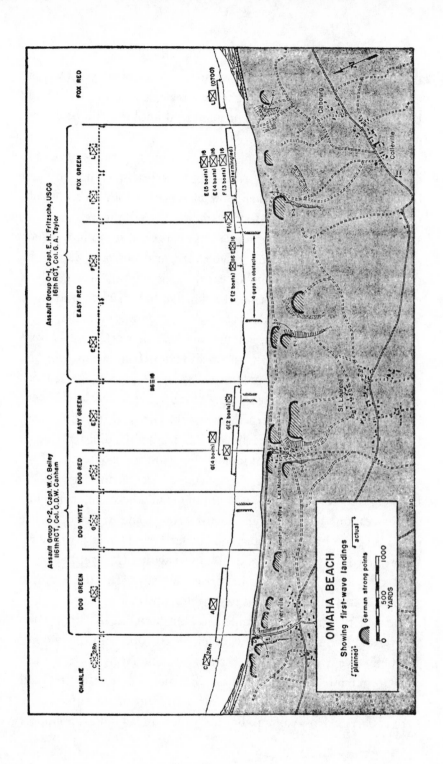

OMAHA BEACH

Showing first-wave landings

planned

actual

German strong points

0   500   1000
YARDS

land in the western sector, and very few had done so in the eastern; and the congestion became so great that at 0830 the head beachmaster ordered no more boats to land until it could be cleared up.

The busiest people in this phase of the assault were the 16 UDTs of seven sailors and five Army Engineers each, trying to blast boat channels through beach obstacles before they became submerged by the rising tide. One team was wiped out by an enemy salvo just as it landed. Another had its charges all set to blow when a direct hit set them off and killed every man but one. Before the flood tide, rising twelve inches every eight minutes, forced them to vacate, these brave men had blown five big channels and three partial ones through the hideous array of murderous obstacles.

Once the assault started, landing and beaching craft crews were completely on their own, with no direction from senior officers; they had to use their own judgment. Neither admirals nor generals could learn what was going on. Three troop-laden LCIs were hit by artillery fire and burned; their survivors had to swim for it. For two hours after the beachmaster suspended landings, about 50 LCTs and LCIs milled about looking for gaps in the obstacles. Two young skippers then broke the stalemate. Lieutenant (jg) S. W. Brinker USNR crashed *LCT–30* through and beached, her automatic weapons blazing at an enemy strongpoint, which shot her up so that she had to be abandoned; but her vehicles got ashore. Lieutenant E. B. Koehler USNR followed with *LCI–554*, but managed to retract after landing his passengers; and after this example the shoreward movement was never interrupted.

Most of the artillery scheduled to land between 0800 and 0900 was boated in dukws, which were unable to cope with the choppy sea. Only five made the beach; hence only one Army battery managed to get into action on D-day. But the place of the drowned artillery was proudly taken by the 5-inch guns of the support destroyers. At 0950 Admiral Bryant called to all gunfire support

ships over TBS: "Get on them, men! Get on them! They are raising hell with the men on the beach, and we can't have any more
of that. We must stop it!" Magnificently they complied, although
hampered by the want of shore fire-control parties with the troops
— these had been shot up or their radios drowned out. In their
eagerness to help, the destroyers incurred the risk of running
aground time and again; several actually did scrape the bottom, but
got off. *Frankford, Doyle, Harding, Thompson, Baldwin, McCook*
and *Emmons* all got into the act; the first-named fired from shoal
water up to 800 yards off the beach, often with but a few inches
between her keel and the sand. Captain Sanders led his "cans"
this close to shore in order to see profitable targets with the naked
eye. The battleships and cruisers, using air spot by pairs of Spit-
fires as off Utah, took on inland strongpoints and batteries; and
Texas in the afternoon helped materially to clear one of the beach
exits with shellfire. She and "Arky" between them shot off 771
rounds of 14-inch on D-day. "Without that gunfire," wrote the
chief of staff of the 1st Division to Admiral Hall, "we positively
could not have crossed the beaches."

Around 1100 the situation at Omaha improved. Surviving company officers began leading their men inland and smoking Germans
out of their casemates. Enemy artillery fire on the beaches diminished during the afternoon. Engineers bulldozed two new roads inland, and tanks started rumbling along them. Army artillery began
to come ashore in strength. By dark the better part of five regimental combat teams were ashore, and the beachhead extended a
mile or more from highwater mark.

Admiral Kirk, thinking over D-day ten years later, said, "Our
greatest asset was the resourcefulness of the American sailor."
Throughout the confusion created by heavy enemy fire on the
boats and explosions of mined obstacles, the bluejackets kept their
heads, found means to beach (not always on the right beach), re-

tracted, brought in another load under fire, never flinched, never failed. Destroyer sailors risked grounding and being pounded to pieces by shore batteries. Battleship sailors did their best to knock out strongpoints. Minecraft sailors were in there first, sweeping. UDTs, the "naked warriors," sacrificed themselves to help the others. Courage there was in plenty; but the resourcefulness of these young sailors made courage and training count. That evening, when General Gerow set up headquarters on the beach, his first message to General Bradley, still on board *Augusta*, was: "Thank God for the United States Navy!"

Although we cannot tell the story of the Eastern Naval Task Force commanded by Rear Admiral Sir Philip Vian RN in anything like the detail it deserves, we remind the reader that it was an essential part of Operation NEPTUNE-OVERLORD, and a bigger part than that assigned to Admiral Kirk's Western Naval Task Force — a three-division as compared with a two-division landing. All troops concerned were British or Canadian, but many beaching craft of the United States Navy participated, just as British landing craft, minecraft and support ships were used in the American sector.

The British assault area extended from Port-en-Bessin, where Omaha ended, about twenty-five statute miles eastward to Ouistreham at the mouth of the River Orne. The three assault landing beaches (Gold, Juno, and Sword) were separated from one another by reefs which prevented access to the shore.

Landings in this sector, as at Utah, were preceded by a paratroop drop. The 6th Airborne Division British Army dropped during the night of 5-6 June, and seized bridges over the Orne and the Caen Canal.

Because the reefs and the foul ground off the British beaches were bare at low water, it was necessary to postpone H-hour until the flood tide had been running between 60 and 90 minutes. This gift of time was well improved by the Royal Navy to bombard selected strongpoints with high-caliber shell for almost two hours by daylight — four times as long a bombardment as the United States Navy had opportunity to deliver at Utah and Omaha. H.M.S. *Warspite*, veteran of the Battle of Jutland, was particularly effective. Owing to this two-hour pounding of beach defenses and strongpoints, and the fact that only one "static" German division was defending the British area, these landings were a pushover. But elements of a German panzer division were about to be committed, and Caen, which optimists thought might fall on 7 June, would be captured only after more than a month of heavy fighting. The Germans here made their bitterest stand against the invasion, to block the road to Paris. All this was expected, and in accordance with Montgomery's plan to draw upon the British Army the weight of German countereffort, giving the United States Army time to capture Cherbourg.

The Royal Navy kept busy delivering gunfire support in its area, as the United States Navy did off Omaha and Utah. There was not a day and hardly an hour after 6 June when one or more British battleships, cruisers or destroyers were not supporting Sir Miles Dempsey's Second Army. Since the British sector lay close to Le Havre, a German advanced naval base, the British gunfire ships were subjected to frequent night raids by enemy torpedo boats, and lost several ships. At Admiral Ramsay's request, Bomber Command R.A.F. hit Le Havre harbor with 2000 tons of bombs shortly before midnight 14 June. The effects were catastrophic. Three torpedo boats, 10 E-boats, 15 R-boats, several patrol vessels and harbor defense vessels, and 11 other small craft were sunk; others were badly damaged. And at dusk 15 June, the R.A.F. hit Boulogne with a similar raid, sank 25 R-boats and small craft, and damaged 10 others. Thus, within two days, the German surface fleet threatening the Allies in the Bay of the Seine was wiped out. But there were more to come. E-boats were shipped into

Le Havre by rail, 47 one-man "human torpedoes" came out in July and sank three British minecraft; remote-controlled explosive motor boats were employed with some effect. All these "secret weapons" were mere fleabites to the British, annoying them without even delaying the invasion. British coastal craft, aided by American motor torpedo boats, set up a close blockade of Le Havre which squelched that source of nuisance.

These events on the east flank are an interesting commentary on Admiral Mahan's doctrine of the ineffectiveness of special devices and a mosquito fleet against a seagoing navy. The British were shuttling thousands of men and hundreds of ships between the English coast and the Far Shore every day and night, under the noses of the Germans at Le Havre, a city that had land, sea and air communications with Germany. The enemy had plenty of torpedo boats, small craft and secret weapons; but they availed him naught. And his U-boats, which might have raised havoc among the invasion fleet, were kept out of the Channel by a tight air and surface patrol.

4. *Consolidating and Supporting the Beachhead,* *7–18 June*

Consolidation of the American beachhead and the beginning of a massive buildup began on 7 June. Although the troops had scanty artillery and tank support from their own elements that day, they enjoyed ready and accurate naval gunfire support, which frustrated the enemy's attempts to counterattack. Behind Utah, Generals Barton and Collins devoted their efforts to cleaning out pockets of resistance and the 4th Division extended its line about two miles to the north. Admiral Deyo's gunfire support group had another busy day: *Nevada* broke up a troop concentration; *Quincy* obliged the Army by smashing a few bridges over the Douvres River; *Tuscaloosa* took on a 155-mm coastal battery near

Saint-Vaast which was straddling destroyer *Jeffers,* and which *Nevada* finally demolished. The same sort of thing went on at Omaha, as the beachhead enlarged.

So well had the airdrops and deception done their work that no German reinforcements reached the American battle area before June 8. By that time, the original defenders had been all but obliterated. These reinforcements afforded the gunfire support ships plenty more shoots during the next six days. Army aviation engineers had a 3500-foot runway good enough for transport planes ready by 2100 June 8. Four full divisions were ashore at Omaha on the 9th, and two at Utah — not counting the paratroops, who were fighting harder than anybody. Six more divisions were landed on the American beaches by 22 June, and the millionth Allied soldier to arrive in France got there on the Fourth of July.

Unloading at Omaha was greatly facilitated by "Mulberry A," an artificial harbor composed of concrete caissons that were towed across the Channel and sunk, enclosing a sheltered harbor as big as Gibraltar's, with three pontoon-section runways where LSTs could unload at any stage of tide. In addition, both Omaha and Utah had a "Gooseberry," a sheltered harbor for small craft created by sinking a line of old ships parallel to the shore. Both were British projects and British built. Those at the American beaches were functioning by 16 June. The aspect of these lonely stretches of beach, where nothing bigger than a small fishing boat had ever landed, was astounding; Omaha's Mulberry A had become the most active port in Europe, with the British Mulberry B a close second.

Leaving it to others to describe the movements of troops ashore, we must record German counterattacks on the naval forces, which stood by for call fire for two weeks. The German Air Force flew up about a thousand aircraft from Germany and Italy, and expended them freely in a vain endeavor to hamper the Allied buildup. Their attacks began on the night of 7-8 June, when they sank destroyer *Meredith* with a glide-bomb, and next day they got a Liberty ship. Within a few days, fighter interception became so well organized that Luftwaffe raids became less frequent.

The German weapon that gave sailors the greatest concern was the mine. One of the most fortunate things that happened to the Allies was the enemy's delay in planting the "oyster" mines that he had recently developed; these lay on the bottom and were exploded by the pressure applied by a ship going over them. Most of the mines that did the damage off the beaches were delayed-action magnetic or sonic mines, laid before D-day. At 0820 June 7, *Susan B. Anthony* exploded one of these while approaching Omaha, and went down quickly. Her troops were rescued by small craft. Next day saw the loss by mines of destroyer escort *Rich* and of destroyer *Glennon*. Up to 3 July, 261 mines were swept in the American sector and 291 in the British.

5. *The Great Storm and the Capture of Cherbourg, 18 June–16 July*

On D-day plus 12, June 18, everything in both sectors was "all tickety-boo," to use a favorite phrase of Field Marshal Montgomery for describing military perfection. By the end of that day 314,514 troops, 41,000 vehicles and 116,000 tons of supplies had been landed over the American beaches; 314,547 troops, 54,000 vehicles and 102,000 tons of supplies over the British beaches. Then Nature intervened with the worst June storm in forty years.

At midnight 18-19 June, a strong wind with heavy rain began to blow on the assault beaches. During the day the wind increased and the sea built up so rapidly that by midafternoon unloading had to stop on Omaha beach. This state of affairs continued for two more days. Heavy surf pounded the beaches, small craft took shelter behind the block-ships, all work stopped, ships anchored off shore dragged anchors and fouled one another, beaching craft were driven ashore, Mulberry A began to break up, and the crash of small craft, dukws, vehicles and derelict units grinding together was heard above the din of war. When the wind abated, on 22 June, the Omaha beaches were a shambles of stranded and wrecked craft, coasting vessels, barges and Mulberry fragments. General Bradley was "appalled by the desolation." Yet, even before the wreckage was surveyed, unloading had to be resumed, since almost nothing had been landed during those three days; it had been necessary to ration ammunition among the troops ashore. Unloading soon recovered momentum, and on 24 June 15,525 troops, 3321 vehicles and 11,562 tons of supplies were landed over the Omaha beaches alone.

Mulberry A was so thoroughly broken up that Admiral Kirk decided to make no attempt to repair it. Mulberry B at Arromanche was far less damaged, owing to its partial protection by the off-lying reefs and capes. Most of the "gooseberry" breakwaters of sunken ships at Omaha and Utah held fast.

This storm warned all hands that their hold on Normandy was precarious. Until the Allies could capture Cherbourg, the nearest major port, they would be at the mercy of tricky English Channel weather. "We've *got* to get to Cherbourg in a hurry," was the theme of every staff conference at First Army headquarters. "Fortress Cherbourg" contained a garrison of over 40,000 men. The German commander had been charged by Hitler to make it impregnable. The Fuehrer knew that the Allies must have a port to supply their armies, and thought he could stop the invasion by denying it to them.

By 22 June General Collins's VII Corps, now beefed-up to six divisions, two squadrons of motorized cavalry and two tank battalions, was ready to advance. The three divisions which did most of the fighting lost over 2800 killed and 13,500 wounded in liberating Cherbourg. But it will not detract from the Army's glory to point out that the United States Navy delivered an important Sunday punch on 25 June.

Admiral Deyo commanded the bombardment force, which comprised most of his Utah fire-support ships, together with others from Omaha. They silenced a coast defense battery of 150-mm guns at Querqueville, and delivered carefully air-spotted fire on German strongpoints in the town, into which the American troops were now breaking. The four 280-mm (11-inch) pieces of Battery "Hamburg" east of the city, which had a range of 40,000 yards, were taken under fire by *Texas*, *Arkansas*, and a number of destroyers, two of which were hit, as was *Texas*, none of them lethally. Only one gun of the Hamburg's 4-gun battery was knocked out; but that helped, in conjunction with shoots on other batteries. Both German commanders at Cherbourg, and Admiral Krancke, regarded this "naval bombardment of a hitherto unequaled fierceness" as one of the main factors which led to the surrender of the city next day. A number of isolated forts and units still held out, and the Navy helped mop them up.

Operation NEPTUNE, the amphibious part of OVERLORD, was now concluded. On 25 June Montgomery opened his drive to take Caen, which fell on 9 July. The American First Army, after eleven days' heavy fighting in the *bocage* country, entered Saint-Lô on 18 July. Patton "busted loose" on the 30th, and the rest of the great story of the drive across France and into Germany is the Army's.

The Allied Navies' first task in France was now the clearance of Cherbourg, which the Germans had left a demolished, ruined and booby-trapped port. The inner harbor was a mass of scuttled ships, thickly sown with mines. All cranes and other harbor works which could have been useful were destroyed. Commodore William A. Sullivan and part of his salvage outfit arrived around 1 July, followed by Rear Admiral John Wilkes as Commander United States Naval Bases, France, with a capable staff and a few hundred Seabees. Six British and three American salvage vessels, 20 United States Navy coastal minesweepers, two flotillas of similar British craft and four flotillas of British motor minesweepers were allocated for the clearance. Commodore Sullivan, who had already cleared North African and Italian ports, found German sabotage and demolition to be more spectacular than effective, but their mining of both outer and inner harbors was thorough beyond belief.

The first Allied cargo landed at Cherbourg from lighters on 16 July. By the end of that month, 12 to 14 Liberty ships could be discharged at once, together with six LSTs. By autumn, Cherbourg had become second only to Marseilles as a port of logistic supply to the United States Army in Europe. Proudly the Cherbourgeois refer to their city as the first French port to be recovered, and the starting point of the *chemin de la libération* which led to Paris and the Rhine.

6. *The Invasion of Southern France,* *15 April–15 September 1944*

The Southern France amphibious operation — ANVIL, as it was originally called, DRAGOON as Churchill renamed it, because he said he was "dragooned" into it by Roosevelt and Eisenhower — is one of the most controversial of the entire war. The dispute, unlike those over Tarawa and Anzio, is not about how it was carried out — everyone admits that DRAGOON was done perfectly — but whether a different operation, which might have beaten the Russians to the Danube, should not have been substituted, as Churchill ardently desired.

Since the Allies had not sufficient troop-lift or gun power for a simultaneous invasion of both Northern and Southern France, the latter had to be postponed to 15 August. General Eisenhower insisted on this southern invasion for two good reasons. He knew that the armies would need another major port — Marseilles — to handle their logistic supply; and he was right, for Cherbourg could not do it all, and Antwerp was not secured until 1945. In addition, "Ike" wanted General Patch's Seventh United States Army and General de Lattre de Tassigny's First French Army deployed on his southern flank to take part in the invasion of Germany. Churchill and the British Chiefs of Staff opposed the Southern France invasion because many of the troops would have to be taken out of the Italian campaign, Alan Brooke's pet baby; and also because they wanted any amphibious operation in the Mediterranean to be directed to Trieste. From that port at the head of the Adriatic, troops would march through the Ljubljana Gap in the Balkans and reach Budapest and Vienna before the Russians.

All American strategists, planners, generals and admirals, and (naturally) the French, were appalled at the idea of shifting this amphibious assault to Trieste, a thousand miles farther than Marseilles from Gibraltar. Eisenhower rejected it, not once and again but again and again. Hanson Baldwin supports Churchill in denouncing the American refusal to make this switch as a major blunder, assuming that we could have liberated Hungary and Austria ahead of the Russians, and perhaps even have kept Rumania and Bulgaria from going Red. But — could we have? The Ljubljana Gap, narrow, tortuous, dominated by mountain peaks, would have been a tactical cul-de-sac. The railway runs through innumerable tunnels which the Germans, who were there in force, could easily have blown; and the road was a two-lane affair, over which the logistic support of more than two divisions would have been impossible. Moreover, Tito's partisans, had we attempted to march through Yugoslavia, would have joined the Germans against us.[8] At best, the operation could not have started before the

---

[8] Wilhelm Hoettl, in *The Secret Front* (1954) p. 165 and ff. tells of intercepting a courier from Stalin to Tito *ordering* him to join forces with the Germans if the Allies tried a landing on the Yugoslav coast; and Anthony Pirie in *Operation Bern-*

end of August, when the Russians were already in Bucharest. Thus, an operation which secured Marseilles, brought in a French Army to help liberate their own country, and provided two more armies for the invasion of Germany, if Churchill and Alan Brooke had had their way, would have been sacrificed in favor of a Balkan safari with very slight chance of success.

Throughout this period of indecision, which lasted right down to D-day minus six when Churchill made his final plea for reconsideration, planning for DRAGOON continued at Admiral Hewitt's headquarters on the Naples waterfront, assuming that it would take place. Training and rehearsals were so thorough that, as Admiral Lowry remarked, all hands "could have made the landing without an operation order." That is as it should be in an amphibious operation, and generally was, too, when Admirals Turner, Wilkinson, Kirk or Hewitt were in charge.

Marseilles, the No. 1 objective, and Toulon, were too well protected by 240-mm coast defense batteries to be the targets of a direct assault. Five yellow sand beaches between pineclad rocky headlands were chosen on the coast of Provence for the initial landings, starting at the Îles d'Hyères and extending to Calanque d'Anthéor, bracketing the gulfs of Saint-Tropez and Fréjus. Knowledge of these spots was easy to obtain from French officers at headquarters and from aërial photographs; and the F.F.I., the patriotic French resistance forces which were very active in Provence, provided abundant data on enemy movements and emplacements. These last were formidable, but not in a class with those of Normandy. The Germans made good use of heavy coast artillery and big guns from French warships, emplaced in heavy concrete casemates. Thousands of land mines were planted on the beaches and behind them, with a density found nowhere else but in Normandy. Underwater obstacles were far less formidable

---

hard (1961) p. 91 tells of Gen. Velebit, one of Tito's closest collaborators, going to the German Ambassador at Agram with that very proposal.

than on the northern coast, and the Navy, after its experience there, was better prepared to cope with them. Germany had about 30,000 troops in the assault zone and over 200,000 near enough to be committed, if the coastal defense could manage to hold up the invaders for a few days. A vain hope, indeed.

The Western Naval Task Force was predominantly American in composition as well as in command, but the Royal Navy made a substantial contribution of gunfire support ships, transports, minecraft, tugboats and LCTs. The French Navy used most of its ships that had been in OVERLORD, and several more. The Royal Canadian Navy provided two fast converted transports and several hundred commandos.

As Eighth Fleet included nothing bigger than light cruisers, five battleships (U.S.S. *Nevada, Texas, Arkansas,* H.M.S. *Ramillies,* French *Lorraine*); three heavy cruisers (*Augusta, Quincy, Tuscaloosa*), and many destroyers and beaching craft were sent down from the English Channel. Also, a number of destroyers manned by Polish and Greek sailors, and flying the flags of these countries, were assigned.

The command organization[9] may be represented as follows: —

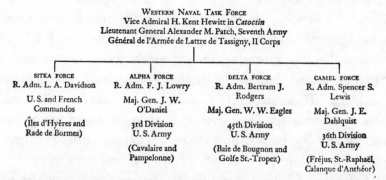

WESTERN NAVAL TASK FORCE
Vice Admiral H. Kent Hewitt in *Catoctin*
Lieutenant General Alexander M. Patch, Seventh Army
Général de l'Armée de Lattre de Tassigny, II Corps

SITKA FORCE R. Adm. L. A. Davidson	ALPHA FORCE R. Adm. F. J. Lowry	DELTA FORCE R. Adm. Bertram J. Rodgers	CAMEL FORCE R. Adm. Spencer S. Lewis
U. S. and French Commandos	Maj. Gen. J. W. O'Daniel	Maj. Gen. W. W. Eagles	Maj. Gen. J. E. Dahlquist
(Îles d'Hyères and Rade de Bormes)	3rd Division U. S. Army	45th Division U. S. Army	36th Division U. S. Army
	(Cavalaire and Pampelonne)	(Baie de Bougnon and Golfe St.-Tropez)	(Fréjus, St.-Raphaël, Calanque d'Anthéor)

[9] The statement in Fergusson *The Watery Maze,* that the top Allied Mediterranean commanders, General Maitland Wilson, Admiral Sir John Cunningham and General Ira Eaker, controlled DRAGOON from Ajaccio, is incorrect. These gentlemen simply approved the plan drafted by Admiral Hewitt's and General Patch's staffs, and exercised no control whatsoever over the operation.

The main landings were preceded by a successful parachute drop from almost 400 planes of a provisional air division U.S. Army, between 0315 and 0515 August 15. There were also Commando raids in the light of a last-quarter moon; one to deceive the Germans (which it didn't do) into believing that the big landings were to be near Toulon, and the other, led in person by Lieutenant Commander Douglas E. Fairbanks, to cut the Corniche road from Cannes (which they failed to do). "Sitka" Force, a double-Commando affair, was more successful. One part seized most of the Îles d'Hyères, and the other, composed of picked men from four nations, blocked the road from Toulon and scared the daylights out of all German troops in the vicinity. Between 0600 and 0730 there was the usual minesweeping, air bombing, and naval bombardment, which proved to be adequate to discourage the defenders.

In this operation, to do away with having to supplicate Army Air Force for air support, Admiral Hewitt had strengthened Western Naval Task Force by two groups of escort carriers: five of the Royal Navy under Rear Admiral Troubridge in H.M.S. *Royalist*, and four of the United States Navy under Rear Admiral Durgin in *Tulagi*. These operated off shore for two weeks without being subjected to a single enemy air or submarine attack. The primary mission of their air groups was to spot for naval gunfire; a secondary one, in which they were highly successful, was to bomb the retiring enemy.

D-day for DRAGOON, 15 August, broke fair, calm and misty. The summits of the Alpes Maritimes could be seen above the haze. Aërial bombing ceased at 0730, to let the Navy deliver the final licks. At that moment the first troop-laden LCVP were speeding down the boat lanes. Fire support destroyers opened a heavy drenching fire on the land behind the beaches. Rocket-equipped LCT spouted missiles onto the beaches themselves. Then compara-

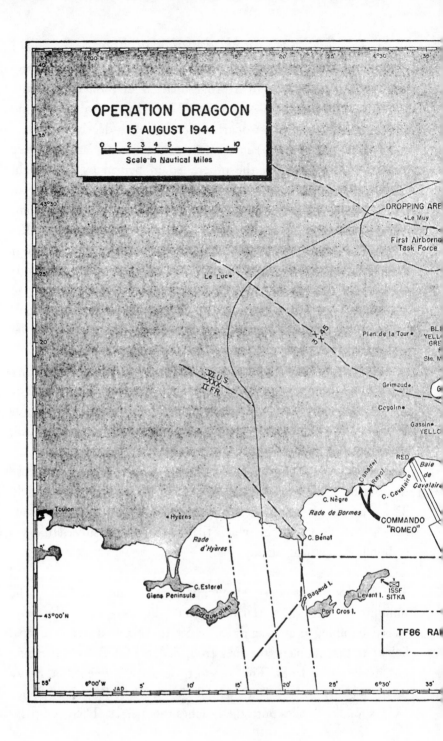

OPERATION DRAGOON

15 AUGUST 1944

0 1 2 3 4 5 — 10
Scale in Nautical Miles

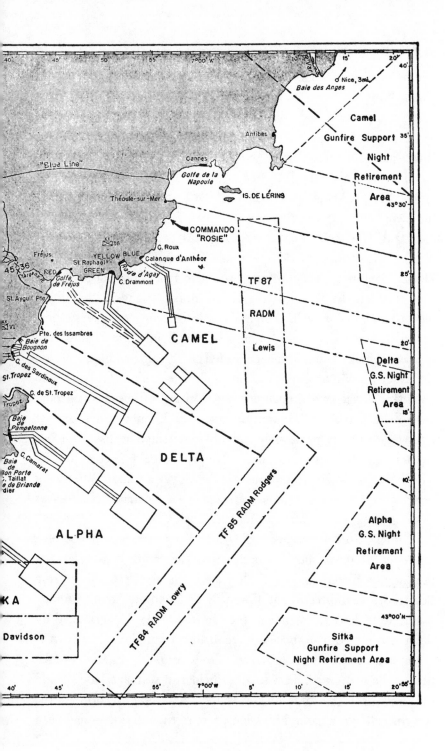

tive silence, when one heard only the hum of landing-craft engines. Now the first wave of landing craft began hitting the beaches on the thirty-mile front. One minute after H-hour, at 0801, signals reached Admiral Hewitt that assault troops had landed on one beach after another, all the way from Baie de Cavalaire to Calanque d'Anthéor.

The "Alpha" landings on each side of Cap Camarat were almost too easy; nothing went wrong. By nightfall D-day, some 16,000 men and 2150 vehicles were ashore, and the Germans had been cleared out of this wooded peninsula. Admiral Rodgers found the "Delta" landings a very different problem from conning *Salt Lake City* through the Battle of the Komandorski Islands, but he handled them equally well. Admiral Bryant's strong gunfire support group battered down the principal strongpoints and enabled the troops to make what someone called a "dream landing," before the resort town of Sainte-Maxime. Contre-Amiral Jaujard, who commanded the two French cruisers in the gunfire support group, gave high praise to Admiral Bryant. "By his pluck, his perfect knowledge of his profession and his leadership, he has won our admiration and our gratitude." "Delta" Force unloaded on D-day the contents of all its transports and over a hundred beaching craft, carrying some 33,000 men and 3300 vehicles. No loss of landing or support craft, and no casualties.

"Camel" Force, however, did not find Operation DRAGOON a pushover. It drew the only section of the target coast that was thoroughly mined and well defended, an area extending from Pointe des Issambres to the Golfe de la Napoule, facing Cannes. On its west flank the shores of the Golfe de Fréjus, overlooked by the town of Saint-Raphaël, were badly wanted by the Army. Here, where the sluggish Argens flows into the sea, the French before the war had built a small airfield and seaplane base behind the beach; the only one on the water's edge in Provence. As the Argens valley is a natural invasion route to the interior — had been so used for at least 1500 years — the Germans guessed that we would land there and had prepared a hot reception. Since Intelligence predicted this, Admiral Hewitt's staff selected beaches east of Saint-Raphaël for the initial assault, but postponed landings at the head of the gulf until the afternoon in order to allow time for coast defenses near Saint-Raphaël to be taken out and mines to be swept.

Admiral Deyo's gunfire support group banged away at pre-arranged targets until 0800, and succeeded in neutralizing many strongpoints. The landings of the 36th Division on Beach Green met with no opposition whatever; Beach Blue, at the head of Calanque d'Anthéor, was a little tougher. After these two points had been taken, the gunfire support ships helped the troops' successful fight to occupy Saint-Raphaël and the rest of the Golfe de Fréjus. On D-day 17,390 troops and 2790 vehicles were landed in the "Camel" area.

The Navy's task in Operation DRAGOON was only half accomplished by the successful landings on 15 and 16 August. Follow-up convoys from Italy, North Africa, Corsica, and even from the United States were scheduled for the next two and a half months; and many of these had to be speeded up, or their composition changed, owing to Seventh Army's requirements in its rapid advance. Admiral Hewitt vested primary control of follow-up convoys in Captain James P. Clay, Comdesron 7. Initially he had 62 escort vessels at his disposal, and by 21 August almost as many more. Captain Clay accelerated the arrival of two French divisions by several days, which enabled General de Lattre de Tassigny to maintain momentum. By the end of 2 September, 190,565 men, 41,534 vehicles, and 219,205 tons of supplies had been landed over the DRAGOON assault beaches. By the 25th, when the last assault beach closed, these figures had been almost doubled.

The Navy also coöperated with the French II Corps, whose

primary mission was to liberate Toulon and Marseilles. Most of the gunfire support ships steamed over to that flank; and a nice job they had to knock out a casemated battery of two 340-mm (13.5-inch) naval guns on Cap Cépet which protected both cities. It took several days' battering by *Nevada, Augusta, Quincy,* H.M.S. *Ramillies* and French battleship *Lorraine* to do it.

On 28 August Toulon and Marseilles surrendered.

Thus, the great objectives of Operation DRAGOON were secured within two weeks of D-day, and in less than half the time that the planners expected. Although intensive minesweeping and salvage operations were necessary before Marseilles and Toulon could be used, unloading of supplies in the larger port began as early as 3 September; and by the 15th a greater volume of troops and matériel was being discharged in these two harbors than was sent over the assault beaches. On that day, when the Allied troops had reached Lyons, all ground forces in Southern France were incorporated in Lieutenant General J. L. Devers's Sixth Army Group and placed under the operational control of General Eisenhower. By V-E Day (8 May 1945), 4,123,794 long tons of cargo and 905,512 troops had been landed at Marseilles, Toulon and Port de Bouc; the lion's share of them at Marseilles. We must also add the men and matériel landed on the DRAGOON beaches: 380,000 troops, 306,000 tons cargo, 69,312 vehicles and 17,848 tons gasoline to 25 September, when they were closed.

In such wise did Operation DRAGOON justify itself. It may stand as an example of an almost perfect amphibious operation from the point of view of training, timing, Army–Navy–Air Force coöperation, performance and results. But it met no opposition comparable to that which Operation NEPTUNE encountered in Normandy. Moreover, DRAGOON was launched two weeks after the big breakthrough, on a flood tide of victory. Its greatest accomplishment was to swell that tide by an entire Army group, which made the Allied advance into Germany irresistible.

U-1229, with snorkel raised, under attack by aircraft of VC-42

U.S.S. *Bogue*

U.S.S. Bogue *and One of Her Victims*

"Ike," "Alan," and "Mort"
General Dwight D. Eisenhower, Rear Admiral Alan G. Kirk,
and Rear Admiral Morton L. Deyo
On board U.S.S. *Tuscaloosa* at Belfast Lough, May 1944

From water color by Lieutenant Dwight Shepler USNR

U.S.S. Emmons *Delivers Gunfire Support,*
off Omaha Beach, D-day

Admiral Thomas C. Kinkaid USN

U.S.S. *McDermut*

Night Action, taken from U.S.S. *Pennsylvania*
The nearest line of flashes are gunfire from the U.S. cruisers; the
farthest, hits on *Yamashiro* and *Mogami*

The Battle of Surigao Strait

Hit and straddled but still under way

Dead in the water

Note Japanese heavy cruiser on horizon, shooting

Left behind by rest of Taffy 3

Taken from *Kitkun Bay*. These are the only daylight photographs of the Pacific War that show Japanese and U. S. ships on same plate

The Last Fight of Gambier Bay

Rear Admiral Theodore S. Wilkinson USN
Commander Amphibious Force, South Pacific

Admiral Richard L. Conolly USN

The First Flag-raising on Mount Suribachi, Iwo Jima

The Marine Corps men grasping the pole are Sgt. H. O. Hansen,
Pl. Sgt. E. I. Thomas and 1st Lt. H. B. Shrier. Pfc. J. R. Michaels holds
the carbine, Cpl. C. W. Lindberg stands behind

Avengers over the beaches

Kadena Airfield under No. **57**

LVTs passing U.S.S. *Tennessee*

L-day at Okinawa

U.S.S. *Laffey*, after hits on 16 April

U.S.S. *Aaron Ward*, after hits on 3 May

Kamikaze Victims at Okinawa

Third Fleet off Coast of Japan, 17 August 1945

CHAPTER XIV

Leyte

September–December 1944

1. Pacific Strategy Again

WE LEFT THE PACIFIC WAR at the end of July 1944, with the Battle of the Philippine Sea won, Saipan, Tinian and Guam secured, and General MacArthur in control of Biak and the New Guinea Vogelkopf, poised to cross the Celebes Sea into Mindanao. But the question whether the liberation of the Philippines should precede or follow the defeat of Japan had not yet been resolved. Whilst both armed services planned to strike Japan repeatedly by sending B–29s "up the ladder of the Bonins," Admiral King and the Navy generally wished to bypass the Philippines, invade Formosa, and then set up a base either on the Chinese mainland or in the Ryukyus for the final assault on Japan. General MacArthur was firmly insistent on liberating the Philippines and using Luzon for the final or semi-final springboard to Japan. He made the strong plea that the United States was honor bound at the earliest possible date to liberate the Philippines, where he had been nourishing resistance forces against the Japanese puppet government; and that if we failed the Filipinos, no Asiatic would ever trust us. He also made the sound strategic argument that loyal Luzon, sealed off by Allied sea power, would be a more suitable base to gather forces for the final assault on Japan than hostile Formosa, which the Japanese could readily reinforce from China.

General MacArthur's strategic plan was sound, even if stripped of its political overtones. From what we learned of the defenses of Formosa after the war, it would have been a very difficult island upon which to obtain a lodgment. And its contemplated use as a steppingstone to the mainland could never have come off, since by the end of 1944 Japan controlled almost the entire coast of China.

The first approach to a decision on this knotty question was made at Pearl Harbor in the last week of July, 1944, at a conference between President Roosevelt, General MacArthur and Admiral Nimitz. In this conference the General not only converted the willing President, but the dubious Admiral Nimitz, to his concept — "Leyte, then Luzon." An understanding was reached, not a decision; but, as in the case of the Mediterranean, when once you put your foot on a strategic ladder it is difficult to get off, unless the enemy throws you off. Admiral King and Rear Admiral Forrest Sherman (Admiral Nimitz's top planner), might still argue in the J.C.S. for bypassing Luzon, and throw ridicule on General MacArthur's contention that Manila could be captured in two weeks after a landing at Lingayen; they lost their case.

At the Quebec Conference, in September 1944, the following timetable was drawn up by the Combined Chiefs of Staff. *September:* MacArthur to take Morotai, Nimitz to take Peleliu. *October:* Nimitz to take Yap in the Carolines, Ulithi a few days later, then to move into Talaud. *November:* MacArthur to occupy Sarangani Bay, Mindanao. *December:* MacArthur and Nimitz in concert to invade Leyte. But it was still left open whether the securing of Leyte would be followed by a landing on Luzon, or on Formosa.

Within a week this timetable was torn up, the plan changed, and the tempo of advance accelerated, owing to Admiral Halsey's carrier raids on the Philippines in September 1944. His *Essex* class carriers steamed up to within sight of shore, pounded Japanese airfields and destroyed the few Japanese planes that they encountered. These carrier strikes dissipated the myth created by

Billy Mitchell-minded airmen to the effect that aircraft carriers could not safely venture within flight distance of enemy airfields, and exposed the enemy's then air weakness in the Philippines. So Halsey sent a message via Nimitz to the Joint Chiefs of Staff, then sitting at Quebec with the British Chiefs of Staff, the President, the Prime Minister, and Mr. Mackenzie King. Halsey recommended that the Peleliu, Morotai, Yap and Mindanao operations be canceled, and that Pacific Fleet and Seventh Fleet make a joint assault on Leyte on 20 October, two months ahead of schedule. The J.C.S. received MacArthur's consent to this acceleration on the night of 15 September; and in an hour and a half they made this decision; MacArthur and Nimitz to invade Leyte on 20 October, and Wilkinson's amphibious force, already embarking to take Peleliu and Yap, to join them after taking Peleliu only.

This sudden change of objectives and of timing was a notable instance of strategic flexibility. The logistic plan, of course, required radical changes, but they were made; and the amphibious assault on Leyte became one of the most successful of the war.

Another important decision at Quebec in September 1944 had to do with participation of the Royal Navy in the Pacific War after the defeat of Germany, which most strategists at that particular moment thought would take place before the end of the year. The British Chiefs of Staff for a year or more had been discussing plans for this participation. Admiral King wished the Royal Navy to operate eastward from the Indian Ocean, recapture Singapore and help puncture the bloated Japanese Empire from the south. This concept was pleasing neither to Churchill nor to the First Sea Lord. They wished the Royal Navy to get into the thick of the fighting alongside the United States Navy as it approached the Japanese home islands. General MacArthur did not want the Royal Navy under his command unless it were in the form of a task force attached to the United States Seventh Fleet, under Admiral Kinkaid. Admiral King did not want the Royal Navy in the Central Pacific at any price; and said so, frankly, creating unnecessary offense. It was not that King was anti-British, or that he disliked sharing the anticipated spoils of a Pacific victory. The root of his objections, purely and simply, was logistics. Ships of the Royal Navy were short-legged — accustomed to putting into a base for replenishment and upkeep about every two or three weeks. American war ships were long-legged — staffed with technicians capable of making extensive repairs at sea, and able to fuel at sea while making twelve to fifteen knots' speed. For the Fast Carrier Forces Pacific Fleet there had been developed a Mobile Service Base of auxiliary craft which provided the fighting ships with everything they needed at sea, from replacement aircraft and spare engines to cigarettes, so that these vessels could, and did, keep the sea literally for months. Since the Royal Navy did not enjoy these facilities, Admiral King feared it would become a drain on us for logistic supply.

President Roosevelt, for the sake of preserving good Anglo-American relations, overruled the Admiral's objections and required American planners to find a place for a British fleet in the final operations against Japan in 1945. That they did; and the United States Pacific Fleet was grateful for Royal Navy support at Okinawa and later.

2. *Preliminaries — Morotai, Peleliu, Formosa Air Battle–15 September–19 October 1944*

Before invading the Philippines, a few islands were considered necessary as advanced bases: Morotai, Peleliu and Ulithi.

Morotai was wanted as a stepping-stone to Mindanao (before the Mindanao invasion had been canceled) and as a base whence the nearby big island of Halmahera, where the Japanese had a large garrison and some eight airfields, could be neutralized. Landings there were carried out on 15 September by units of Admiral Barbey's VII 'Phib, lifting the 31st Infantry Division, with Rear Admiral Russell S. Berkey commanding the support force. They were virtually unopposed. Army Engineers and two airfield construction squadrons of the Royal Australian Air Force moved in, and the first airfield was ready 4 October.

Morotai played an important role in the great operation coming up, because it was the only Allied air base from which short-range fighters and light or medium bombers could be staged up to Leyte. The V A.A.F. used it as a springboard, and had 162 aircraft ready to go in as soon as the airstrip was ready.

On 15 September Vice Admiral Wilkinson's III 'Phib landed on Peleliu, southernmost island but one of the Palau group. This was a very different proposition from Morotai. Admiral Halsey proposed to bypass Peleliu as well as Mindanao, but Admiral Nimitz declined to authorize this because the invasion forces were already at sea, and he felt that the Palaus would be necessary as staging-points for aircraft and ships to Leyte. They did prove useful, though hardly necessary; and, considering that the capture of Peleliu and the adjacent small island of Angaur cost almost as many American lives as the assault on Omaha Beach, it would seem that Cincpac here made one of his rare mistakes.

Wilkinson's III 'Phib, comprising big transports and beaching craft lifting the veteran 1st Marine Division (Major General W. H. Rupertus) was selected for the assault on Peleliu. Naval bombardment of the island began on 12 September and the UDT "frogmen" had plenty of time to work over the reefs off beaches selected for landing, clearing out coral heads, blowing the primitive (compared with the German) antiboat wooden obstacles, and chipping away at the coral to make over the reef for the LVT and berths for the LST.

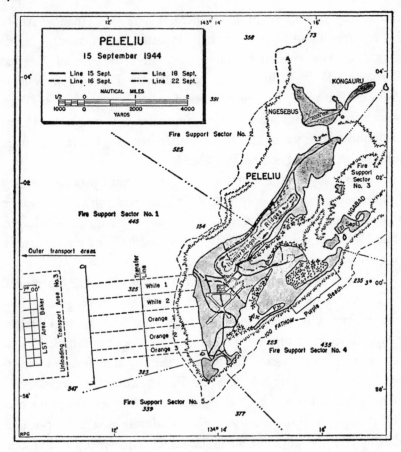

The Japanese defenders under Colonel Nakagawa, numbering 5300 fighting men and as many more construction troops, had no intention of selling Peleliu cheap. Imperial General Headquarters had been giving special attention to defense against amphibious assault. The old tactics of meeting the enemy on the beach had failed everywhere. The new tactics were to prepare a main line of resistance and defensive positions well in the rear of the beaches, place substantial forces in reserve to mount counterattacks at opportune moments, and offer token defense only at the beach. The defenders of Peleliu were the guinea pigs for these new tactics (the reverse of Rommel's on Omaha Beach), which proved hideously successful in prolonging the Iwo Jima and Okinawa operations. Natural caves in the jagged limestone ridges north of the airfield were developed into an interconnected series of underground strongpoints, so strongly protected by sand and concrete as to be almost impervious to aërial bombing or naval bombardment.

Colonel Nakagawa, however, tried both the old and the new. His men so stoutly contested the landings that the Marines lost 210 killed and 900 wounded on D-day, 15 September. By the 18th they had occupied the airfield, but not secured it. Stretching northeasterly from the airfield for two miles was the high Umurbrogol Ridge. Here the Japanese, with the aid of professional miners, had excavated a system of interlocking caves in the soft coral rock, too deep for naval bombardment or air bombing to reach. The Ridge could not be ignored, for several cave entrances overlooked the airfield only a few hundred yards away, and the Japanese were well provided with food, weapons and ammunition. They had to be rooted out or sealed off. The Marines — and a regiment of the 81st Division which was sent to help — would reach a cave mouth after a bloody battle, only to find that it was deserted, or capture a peak and smell cooking being done by cave-dwelling Japanese resting comfortably beneath. The biggest cave, encountered on 27 September, contained more than a thousand Japanese. The only weapon to cope with them was a new long-range flame-thrower, first mounted on LVTs and later on Sherman tanks, which threw a wicked tongue of fire that could penetrate 40 or 50 feet and even lick around a corner. Attrition by this means gradually reduced the enemy.

On the night of 24-25 November occurred the last organized resistance, and Colonel Nakagawa, having done just what the Emperor commanded, committed suicide. His garrison was exterminated, but he had cost the Marines and Army 1950 lives.

Angaur, the two-mile-long island south of Peleliu, wanted for a bomber strip, was captured by the "Wildcat" 81st Division from 1600 die-hard Japanese by 23 October. Kossol Passage, some 60 miles north of Angaur, became a patrol and search base for three squadrons of long-range Mariners, which, with five PBM units equipped for air-sea rescue, arrived on 16-17 September with four tenders. Their searches, extending to 775 miles on October 8, were very useful in the Leyte operation, during which Kossol Passage was extensively used for ships seeking replenishment from service force vessels.

Ulithi Atoll, where Admiral Wilkinson landed an RCT of the 81st Division on 23 September, was wanted for its big, deep lagoon, a perfect fleet base. It was promptly developed as such, and from it sortied on 4-6 October Fast Carrier Forces Pacific Fleet (TF 38) under Halsey and Mitscher: *Enterprise* and eight *Essex* class carriers, eight *Independence* class light carriers, with an ample screen of new battleships, heavy and light cruisers, and destroyers. Shortly before dark 7 October, about 375 miles west of the Marianas, this great carrier task force made rendezvous. The modern age has afforded no marine spectacle comparable to a meeting of these big warships, which have become as beautiful to the modern seaman's eye as a ship of the line to his bell-bottomed forbears. The great flattops, constantly launching and recovering aircraft; the new battleships with their graceful sheer, tossing spray and leaving a boiling wake; the cruisers bristling with antiaircraft guns; the destroyers darting, thrusting and questing for lurking submarines, all riding crested seas of deepest ultramarine; the massy trade-wind clouds casting purple shadows — all together composed a picture of mighty naval power. It corresponded to a fleet of ships of the line with their attendant frigates and sloops majestically sailing across the Caribbean in the eighteenth century.

On 12 October began the really big business for Task Force 38: a three-day effort to knock out Japanese air strength on Formosa, and to deny it to the enemy as a staging base toward Leyte. The carriers arrived before dawn at their launching position, 50 to 90 miles east of Formosa. At 0544, an hour before sunrise, the first strike, a fighter sweep to gain command of the air over Formosa and the Pescadores, was launched. Flying weather throughout these three days was perfect. On 12 October no fewer than 1378 sorties were flown on Formosa from all four American carrier groups, followed by 974 on the morning of the 13th. In the afternoon, Japanese planes struck back, making one hit on carrier *Franklin* and a second on cruiser *Canberra*, neither lethal. On the third day, 14 October, when TF 38 made only 146 sorties against Formosa, XX Bomber Command (109 B–29s) carried the ball from China fields. Japanese counterattack crippled but did not sink cruiser *Houston*, and she was towed clear.

The results of this three-day Formosa air battle were over 500 enemy planes destroyed, some twoscore freighters and small craft sunk, and many others damaged; and an enormous destruction of ammunition dumps, hangars, barracks, shops and industrial plants. In the counterattacks, TF 38 engaged nearly a thousand land-based enemy aircraft, and beat off all except those that made the three hits. The cost to the Navy was 79 planes, 64 pilots and crewmen, and a number of seamen killed in the three ships that were hit.

Japanese aircraft losses in the week of 10-17 October were tremendous, but the government consoled itself by the myth — broadcast and stated in official communiqués — that their "eagles" had sunk 11 carriers, 2 battleships and 3 cruisers. Japan was swept by a sudden wave of exhilaration which dispelled the dismay over the loss of the Marianas. The Army even assumed that the American invasion would be given up. Imperial General Headquarters, believing its own propaganda, had actually started planning on that assumption, when the vanguard of American invasion forces for Leyte was sighted off Suluan on 17 October.

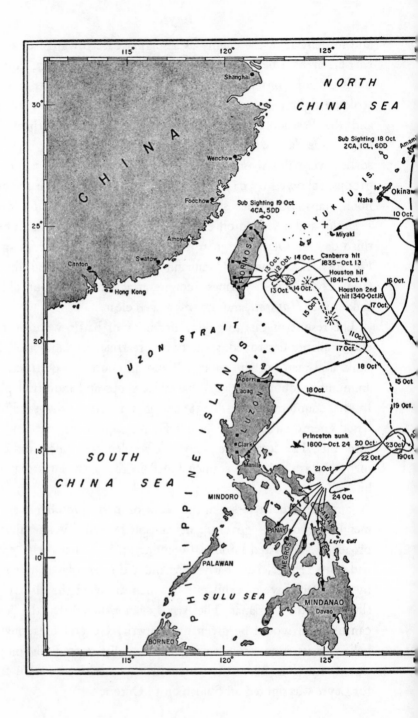

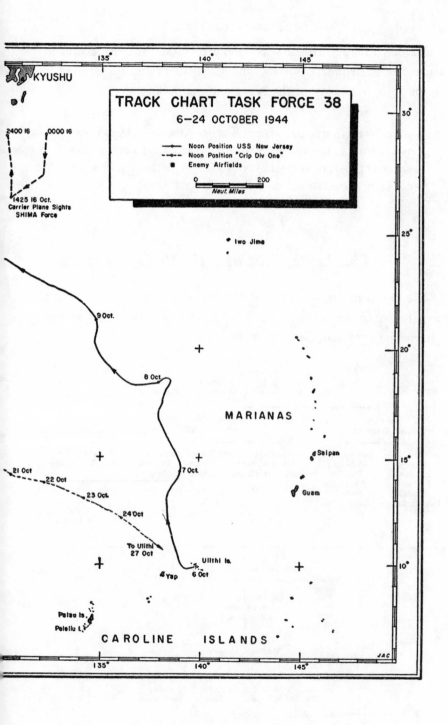

KYUSHU

TRACK CHART TASK FORCE 38
6–24 OCTOBER 1944

—○— Noon Position USS New Jersey
—•— Noon Position "Crip Div One"
■ Enemy Airfields

0   200
Naut. Miles

2400 16   0000 16

1425 16 Oct.
Carrier Plane Sights
SHIMA Force

Iwo Jima

9 Oct.

8 Oct.

MARIANAS

Saipan

21 Oct

22 Oct

23 Oct.

7 Oct.

24 Oct

Guam

To Ulithi
27 Oct

Ulithi Is.

Yap   6 Oct

Palau Is.
Peleliu I.

CAROLINE   ISLANDS

JAC

Admiral Halsey made a witty reply to these Japanese claims in a message to Admiral Nimitz, and Cincpac promptly released it on the 19th, to the joy of the Navy and the public: —

ADMIRAL NIMITZ HAS RECEIVED FROM ADMIRAL HALSEY THE COMFORTING ASSURANCE THAT HE IS NOW RETIRING TOWARD THE ENEMY FOLLOWING THE SALVAGE OF ALL THE THIRD FLEET SHIPS RECENTLY REPORTED SUNK BY RADIO TOKYO.

3. *The Leyte Landings, 17–20 October*

The command setup for the invasion of Leyte — which lasted with few changes through the Battle for Leyte Gulf — was not (unfortunately) a unified but a dual one: —

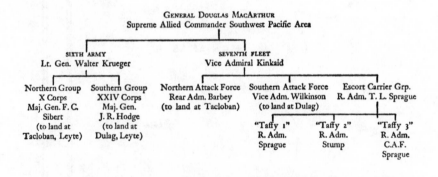

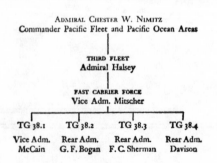

MacArthur and Nimitz had come together at the summit, as it were, and the President did not dare put one over the other.

A large part of Seventh Fleet was "borrowed" for this operation from Third Fleet; Wilkinson's III 'Phib, for instance, was placed under Admiral Kinkaid.

Early in October, General MacArthur's military forces and Admiral Kinkaid's Seventh Fleet began to concentrate at Manus, Hollandia and other places along the coast of New Guinea. Seven hundred and thirty-eight ships were in the attack force; fewer than those that took part in the invasion of Normandy in June, but mounting a heavier striking power.[1] Adding the 17 fleet carriers, six battleships, 17 cruisers and 64 destroyers of TF 38, this made the most powerful naval force ever assembled. But this record would be equaled at Lingayen Gulf in January 1945, and surpassed off Okinawa in April.

On 10 October the northward movement began; slow minecraft which were to sweep safe channels for the transports, in the van. Commander Wayne R. Loud's minesweeping and hydrographic group arrived off Leyte Gulf 17 October and at 0630 began sweeping the approaches to Dinagat and three smaller islands, Calicoan, Suluan and Homonhon, which divided the entrances to Leyte Gulf from the Philippine Sea. Air reconnaissance showed that the enemy had installations on them, probably search radar whose electric feelers would signal the approach of the forces of liberation. They did. At 0750 this Dinagat group was sighted by the Japanese garrison on Suluan, whose commander promptly notified Admiral Toyoda, C. in C. Combined Fleet. He issued the alert for SHO-1, his planned naval battle, at 0809, and ordered important elements of Combined Fleet to get under way at once.

By noon 18 October, all islands commanding the entrances to Leyte Gulf had been secured by the Rangers. Rear Admiral

[1] These comprised 157 combatant ships, 420 amphibious types, 84 patrol, minesweeping and hydrographic types, and 73 service types.

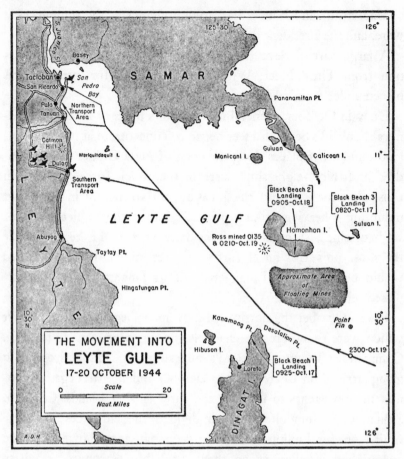

THE MOVEMENT INTO
LEYTE GULF
17-20 OCTOBER 1944

Jesse B. Oldendorf, who commanded the gunfire support ships, then steamed boldly into the Gulf and commenced bombarding the landing beaches to cover operations of the UDTs.

As Assault day (A-day), 20 October, broke, Admiral Wilkinson led the "parade," as he called it, from a rendezvous point 17 miles outside Desolation Point. Admiral Wilkinson's Southern Force was now steaming toward its transport area off Dulag, and Admiral Barbey's Northern Force for its anchorage in San Pedro Bay, as the northern, inside bight of Leyte Gulf is called. A Japanese patrol plane approached to take a look and was shot down. The sun rose out of a yellow haze over Samar, and light spread over the calm green waters of Leyte Gulf. Mist dissolved from the mountains, and the palm-fringed beach, behind which lay the enemy, became clearly visible. In villages and hideouts ashore, Filipinos — and the few Americans who had managed to survive the tragic events of 1941-1942 — peered out through coconut palms at this mighty fleet. Joy filled their hearts, and prayers went up to Heaven; for they knew that the hour of deliverance was at hand.

President Roosevelt, in a message broadcast to the Philippine people that morning, declared: —

On this occasion of the return of General MacArthur to Philippine soil with our airmen, our soldiers and our sailors, we renew our pledge. We and our Philippine brothers in arms — with the help of Almighty God — will drive out the invader; we will destroy his power to wage war again, and we will restore a world of dignity and freedom — a world of confidence and honesty and peace.

The Leyte Gulf landings were easy, compared with most amphibious operations in World War II — perfect weather, no surf, no mines or underwater obstacles, slight enemy reaction, mostly mortar fire. Admiral Wilkinson's Southern Attack Force landed XXIV Corps on a 5000-yard stretch of beach which began about eleven miles south of the Northern Force left flank. A welcome addition to the amphibious fleet now was the Landing Ship, Medium (LSM), 203 feet long, 900 tons, which had the vehicle capacity of an LCT but was faster, more seaworthy and more comfortable. This Southern landing, too, was relatively uneventful. Dulag was captured by the 7th Division around noon, and the 96th Division drove the Japanese out of their principal strongpoint on "Hill 120" and raised the flag there at 1042, less than an hour and three quarters after the first troops landed.

Liberation of the Philippines was off to a good start.

Dulag and Tacloban airfields fell into American hands on 21 October, and Army Engineers promptly went to work improving them. The 24th Division took Mt. Guinhandang by 0900; and Tacloban itself, with the only docking facilities on Leyte, was captured that day. By midnight, 132,400 men and almost 200,000 tons of supplies and equipment had been landed by the assault echelons of the Northern and Southern Attack Forces, and most of the ships had departed. Now only the three admirals' amphibious force flagships, one AKA, 25 LST and LSM, and 28 Liberty ships, remained in Leyte Gulf. All fire support battleships, cruisers and destroyers were advancing up Surigao Strait to meet the enemy. Lieutenant General Krueger had set up Sixth Army command post ashore, and the amphibious phase of the Leyte operation was over. And the first phase of the great naval Battle for Leyte Gulf had already been fought.

4. *The Battle For Leyte Gulf — Opening Actions, 23–24 October*

As the amphibious vessels completed unloading on the Leyte shore and Sixth Army extended its beachhead, Japanese naval forces were sallying forth to give battle. The four-part Battle for Leyte Gulf [2] that followed comprised every type of naval warfare invented up to that time — heavy and light gunfire; bombing, strafing, rocketing and torpedoing by land-based and carrier-based planes; torpedo attacks by submarines, destroyers and motor torpedo boats. Every naval weapon but the mine was employed by

[2] This official name comprises four naval actions: in the Sibuyan Sea on 24 Oct., Surigao Strait 24-25 Oct., Battle off Samar 25 Oct., and Battle off Cape Engaño 25-26 Oct. 1944. Regarding these as parts of a whole, this was the greatest naval battle of all time. In the Battle of Jutland (1 June 1916), 250 ships (151 British, 99 German) engaged. In the Leyte Battle, 282 ships (216 U.S.N., 2 R.A.N., 64 Japanese) engaged. The air component at Jutland was only 5 seaplanes; at Leyte it was hundreds of planes of all types. Estimates of numbers of officers and men engaged are, U.S.N. and R.A.N., 143,668; Japanese, 42,800. There were more American sailors in this battle than there had been in the entire Navy and Marine Corps in 1938.

both sides, and the Japanese introduced new and deadly air tactics. In every part the action was memorable and decisive, resulting in the destruction of the Japanese Fleet as an effective fighting force. But before victory was won the situation was puzzling, mistakes were made on both sides, and anything might have happened.

Japanese naval ambition to fight a "general decisive battle" with the United States Pacific Fleet was not quenched by the signal defeats sustained at Midway and in the Philippine Sea. Imperial General Headquarters expected its enemy to invade the Philippines, but was uncertain which island would be the initial target. Consequently, it prepared four SHO plans (SHO meaning Victory), and, as we have seen, Admiral Toyoda activated SHO-1, the plan for a decisive naval action off Leyte, on 18 October after Commander Loud's minesweepers were sighted from Suluan. But owing to lack of tankers to carry fuel north, the Combined Fleet was so widely dispersed — from the Inland Sea of Japan to Lingga Roads off Singapore — that a good week elapsed before it could reach the waters off Leyte. Thus the Japanese Navy missed a great chance to attack the Leyte landings in their "naked" phase when troops were being boated ashore and the Gulf was full of vulnerable shipping.

The Japanese Navy's task organization for SHO-1 is on the next page — the words in italics being the somewhat simplified names given by us to the three principal forces, and place names being the locations of these several forces when Operation SHO-1 was activated.

The general outline of the SHO-1 plan was this: —

Ozawa's Northern Force, built around carriers *Zuikaku, Zuiho, Chitose* and *Chiyoda*, would decoy Halsey's Third Fleet up north and out of the way. Then Kurita's Force "A" or Center Force, which included super-battleships *Musashi* and *Yamato*, and nine heavy cruisers, would debouch from San Bernardino Strait, at the same time as the Nishimura-Shima Force "C" or Southern

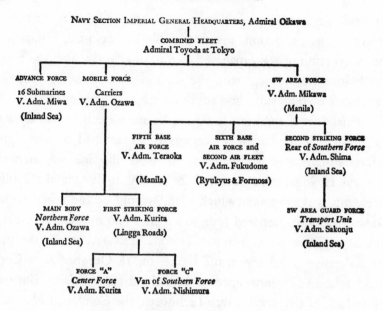

NAVY SECTION IMPERIAL GENERAL HEADQUARTERS, Admiral Oikawa

COMBINED FLEET
Admiral Toyoda at Tokyo

ADVANCE FORCE
16 Submarines
V. Adm. Miwa
(Inland Sea)

MOBILE FORCE
Carriers
V. Adm. Ozawa

SW AREA FORCE
V. Adm. Mikawa
(Manila)

FIFTH BASE
AIR FORCE
V. Adm. Teraoka
(Manila)

SIXTH BASE
AIR FORCE and
SECOND AIR FLEET
V. Adm. Fukudome
(Ryukyus & Formosa)

SECOND STRIKING FORCE
Rear of *Southern Force*
V. Adm. Shima
(Inland Sea)

MAIN BODY
Northern Force
V. Adm. Ozawa
(Inland Sea)

FIRST STRIKING FORCE
V. Adm. Kurita
(Lingga Roads)

SW AREA GUARD FORCE
Transport Unit
V. Adm. Sakonju
(Inland Sea)

FORCE "A"
Center Force
V. Adm. Kurita

FORCE "C"
Van of *Southern Force*
V. Adm. Nishimura

Force debouched from Surigao Strait, to put a pincer on the amphibious ships in Leyte Gulf, destroy them, and then (presumedly) annihilate Halsey. Thus, General MacArthur would be left out on a limb as at Bataan in 1941-1942. This was a typical Japanese strategic plan, employing division, deception, and forces popping out at unexpected places. It required better timing and communications than the Japanese fleet was capable of, but with good luck it might have worked except for starting too late, and *complete lack of air power*. The two Japanese base air forces noted in the above task organization, had not even 200 aircraft available on 22 October, Ozawa's carriers had only 116 planes on board when they sortied from the Inland Sea, and most of these were flown off to land bases before the battle. The Japanese simply did not have time to train new air groups after the destruction wrought by the Spruance-Mitscher forces in the Battle of the Philippine Sea.

Kurita's First Striking Force sortied from Lingga Roads on 18 October and called at Brunei Bay, Borneo, to fuel. On the 20th, it split: the Center Force with the big battleships and most of the heavy cruisers departed at 0800 October 22 for the Sibuyan Sea and San Bernardino Strait, while Nishimura's van of the Southern Force, including two battleships, made for Surigao. At the same time, as an afterthought, Shima's Second Striking Force was ordered south from the Inland Sea to "support and coöperate" with Nishimura. Ozawa's Northern Force, the carriers, sortied from the Inland Sea 20 October, undetected by the United States submarines which had been sent to intercept it.

Kurita's was the first to suffer, in the Palawan Passage between the long island of that name and the reefs that border the South China Sea. In the small hours of 23 October, as Center Force entered Palawan Passage, it encountered U. S. submarines *Darter* (Commander David McClintock) and *Dace* (Commander B. D. M. Claggert). The submarines sent off a contact report to Admiral Halsey — first word any American had of what the enemy was up to — and at 0630 *Darter* got two torpedoes into Kurita's flagship *Atago*, which sank her, and two into *Takao*, which disabled her. *Dace*, shortly after, sank *Maya* in a torpedo attack. *Darter* ran aground on Bonbay Shoal and had to be abandoned, but *Dace* took off all her crew. Kurita proceeded, minus three heavy cruisers. And the submarines' contact reports prepared a heavy reception for him in the Sibuyan Sea.

By noon 24 October three of the Halsey-Mitscher fast carrier groups were deployed on a broad front: Sherman's Group 3 to the northward, Bogan's Group 2 off San Bernardino Strait, Davison's Group 4 about sixty miles off southern Samar.[3] The stage was set for an air-surface engagement, the Battle of the Sibuyan Sea, first

[3] McCain's Group 1 had been sent to Ulithu to refuel, but was promptly recalled, and its planes got into the battle on 25 October.

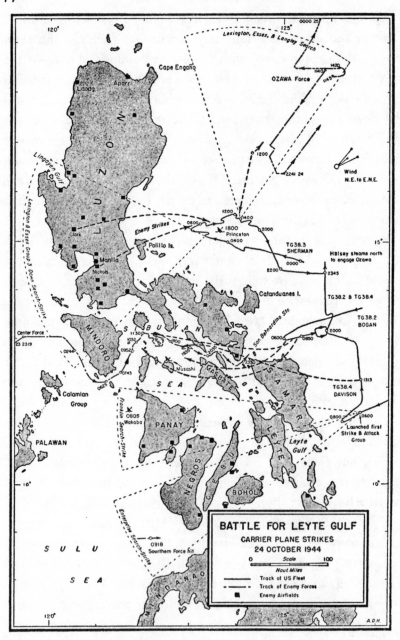

Battle for Leyte Gulf, Carrier Plane Strikes, 24 October 1944

120°   125°   0000 25
                    Lexington, Essex, & Langley Search

Cape Engaño   1420
Aparri   1400
Laoag   1425   OZAWA Force

                                                  Wind
                                                  N.E. to E.N.E.
Lingayen Gulf   1200   2241 24

Clark   1200
                         1400
         Enemy Strikes 0800 1800 2000
Manila   0400 Princeton   TG 38.3
Nichols   Polillo Is.   SHERMAN
                                        Halsey steams north
                                        to engage Ozawa
                                   0000
                              2200   2345
                                              Catanduanes I.
                                                  TG 38.2 & TG 38.4
         MINDORO   S I B U Y A N   TG 38.2
                          1130   BOGAN
Center Force   1052   San Bernardino Str. 2000
23 2319   0244   0952D   0600 0850
                0743 Musashi 2330
                    0605   *MASBATE*   S A M A R   1313
Calamian   Wakaba   S E A   TG 38.4
Group   0805   DAVISON
PALAWAN   Franklin Search-Strike   0800 0600
              PANAY   Launched first
                                                   Strike & Attack
                              LEYTE   Group
              NEGROS   C E B U   Leyte
                              Gulf
                    BOHOL
S U L U
                         BATTLE FOR LEYTE GULF
  S E A   CARRIER PLANE STRIKES
         0918   24 OCTOBER 1944
         Sourthern Force hit
                         0   Scale   100
                             Naut Miles
                         ———— Track of US Fleet
M I N D A N A O   – – – Track of Enemy Forces
120°   125°   ■ Enemy Airfields

                                                      A.D.H.

of the four major engagements that constitute the Battle for Leyte Gulf. But before Mitscher's planes could strike Kurita's ships, Japanese land-based planes attacked Admiral Frederick Sherman's TG 38.3. Most of them were intercepted and shot down, but one "Judy" made a lucky hit which went through several decks of light carrier *Princeton*, exploded the torpedoes stowed below, and did her in. Cruiser *Birmingham*, which had closed the carrier to help fight fires, was badly damaged by a tremendous explosion of *Princeton*'s torpedo stowage, but eventually was saved.

While *Princeton* was vainly struggling for survival, some 259 sorties of Mitscher's planes were wreaking vengeance on Kurita's ships in the Sibuyan Sea. Kurita had no combat air patrol — Base Force being too heavily engaged in counterattacking TF 38 — and super-battleship *Musashi*, after taking 19 torpedo and 17 bomb hits from *Intrepid, Cabot, Essex, Lexington, Franklin* and *Enterprise* aircraft, rolled over and went down at 1935, with great loss of men. Other ships received hits, but all except heavy cruiser *Myoko* were able to proceed. Moreover, the milling around, and evasive courses of Kurita's Center Force in this attack, which lasted intermittently most of the day, delayed the SHO-I timetable by seven hours. It was no longer possible for Kurita to rendezvous with Nishimura and Shima inside Leyte Gulf at break of day, even if the last two got through; and neither did.

5. *The Battle of Surigao Strait, 24–25 October*

Both parts of the Southern Force (Admiral Nishimura's Force "C" or Van) comprising battleships *Fuso* and *Yamashiro*, heavy cruiser *Mogami* and four destroyers, and Admiral Shima's Second Striking Force or Rear, comprising two heavy cruisers, a light cruiser and four destroyers, were sighted by carrier planes before noon 24 October. Vice Admiral Kinkaid, Commander Seventh Fleet, correctly estimated that Southern Force would try to penetrate Leyte Gulf via Surigao Strait that night, and took measures accordingly. At 1443 he ordered Rear Admiral Jesse B. Oldendorf, who commanded all Seventh Fleet fire support ships at the Leyte landings, to prepare to meet the enemy.

Oldendorf disposed of his force of overwhelming strength with deadly effectiveness, remembering the old California gambler's adage, "Never give a sucker a chance." A Battle Line of six battleships, five of them survivors of Pearl Harbor, together with four heavy cruisers (one, *Shropshire*, of the Royal Australian Navy) and four light cruisers, under Rear Admirals Hayler and Berkey, were so disposed as to cross the fifteen-mile-wide waters between Leyte and Hibuson Island, where Surigao Strait debouches into Leyte Gulf. Two destroyer divisions, under Captains McManes and Coward, were to thrust down the Strait to deliver torpedo attacks, while a third under Captain Smoot was to follow up, and a fourth to stand by Battle Line. Thirty-nine motor torpedo boats, under Lieutenant Commander R. A. Leeson, were sent south to patrol the entire strait, and its approach via the Mindanao Sea.

For want of night-flying, radar-equipped patrol planes, these PTs were the "eyes of the fleet." Their orders were to report all contacts, surface or air, visual or radar, and attack independently. The boats lay-to on station, so as to leave no wake. The sea in the Strait was smooth and glassy, just what they wanted. The atmosphere was clear until a quartering moon set shortly after midnight; then the sky became partly overcast and the night went pitch-black. There were not many rain squalls; it was a fairly dry night for the eastern Philippines. On such a night as this the Pacific Fleet had swapped punches with the enemy in Ironbottom Sound, up the Slot, and off Empress Augusta Bay. But it had never before been so well prepared, with a flock of PTs to intercept, three destroyer squadrons to deliver torpedo attacks and a Battle Line to cap the enemy's column.

Since the Japanese Southern Force was really two independent groups which had no tactical connection, we may follow the ill fortune of the first before turning to the better luck of the second. Vice Admiral Nishimura's van, which included the two battleships, was supposed to arrive in Leyte Gulf before dawn at the same time as Kurita's Center Force. This timing was essential to the success of SHO-I battle plan. Whether Nishimura imagined he could get through Surigao Strait without a fight, we do not know; but any hope he may have had of joining Kurita in a merry massacre of amphibious craft and transports, which he believed to be present in great numbers, must have vanished around 1830 October 24 when he received a signal from Kurita that he had been delayed by the air battle of the Sibuyan Sea. Nishimura, nevertheless, maintained course and speed, and felt confirmed in this decision around 1900 by an order from Admiral Toyoda: "All forces will dash to the attack." He made no attempt to wait for Shima's rear to catch up with him, probably reflecting that his best chance of penetrating the Gulf lay under cover of darkness, since he had no aircraft to protect him after dawn.

First contact of the Battle of Surigao Strait came at 2236 October 24, when *PT-131*, operating off Bohol, picked up Nishimura's battleships on her radar, and, with the other two boats in her patrol, closed to attack. At four minutes before midnight they were taken under gunfire by destroyer *Shigure* and driven off with some loss; but not before they got off a contact report to Admiral Oldendorf. It was the same story for fifty miles across Mindanao Sea and up the Strait. Nishimura encountered successive PT patrols, each three-boat section observed gun flashes of the previous fight, made contact itself, attempted to get off a report (and sometimes did), attacked with torpedoes (all of which missed), became brightly illuminated by enemy searchlights, came under brisk gunfire, and retired under a smoke screen. They neither stopped nor confused the enemy, but they performed an indispensable service in alerting Admiral Oldendorf.

At six minutes past midnight the moon set — the last moon that Nishimura and most of his sailors were destined to see. After chasing off the last PT attack at 0213, Nishimura steamed quietly along for three quarters of an hour; then he ran into something more serious than motor torpedo boats — Captain Jesse G. Coward's Desron 54.

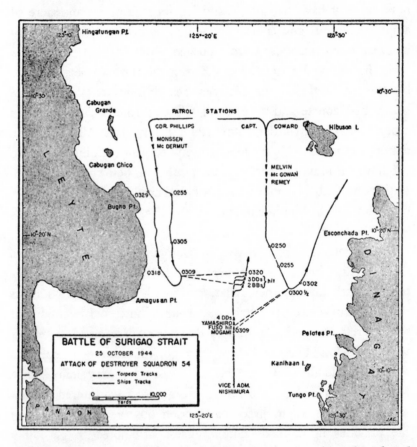

Coward set up a "left-and-right" torpedo attack and ordered his five destroyers to withhold gunfire, which would disclose their position. The two divisions, one under Commander Richard H.

Phillips and the other under Coward himself, started south at 0230 and picked up Nishimura on the radar 15 minutes later. Southern Force van was in single column. Four destroyers led, next came Nishimura's flagship, battleship *Yamashiro*, then, at one-kilometer intervals, *Fuso* and *Mogami*. At 0300 Coward's division (*Remey*, *McGowan*, *Melvin*) commenced launching torpedoes, at ranges of 8200 to 9300 yards. They got one into battleship *Fuso*, which sheered out of column and began to burn and explode. Phillips's flagship *McDermut* had the distinction of torpedoing three destroyers, of which *Yamagumo* blew up and sank, *Michishio* started on her way to the bottom, and *Asagumo*'s bow was knocked off. *Monssen* made a torpedo hit on *Yamashiro* which forced the flooding of two magazines, but failed to stop her. All five American destroyers retired unhurt.

Ten minutes after the Japanese ships had taken these blows, they were subjected to a similar attack from the west side of the Strait by Captain McManes's Desron 24 (*Hutchins*, flag). His ships sank disabled *Michishio* and *Killen* scored a second torpedo hit on *Yamashiro*.

During both destroyer attacks, Nishimura continued to steam stolidly along, neither taking evasive action nor paying attention to the knocked-out ships. His one object, it seems, was to break into Leyte Gulf, being ignorant of the massive forces Admiral Oldendorf had deployed across the entrance to stop him. These amounted to a left flank of three heavy and two light cruisers, a right flank of one heavy and two light cruisers, a line of six battleships, and another destroyer squadron. It was a War College game board setup. The enemy column, now reduced to battleship *Yamashiro*, cruiser *Mogami* and destroyer *Shigure*, made a very short vertical to a very broad T, but Oldendorf was about to cap it, as Togo had done to Rozhdestvenski in 1905 at the Battle of Tsushima Strait, an action which thousands of naval officers had since hoped to emulate.

At 0323, American radar screens began to register the enemy disposition. Oldendorf, whose cruisers were two or three miles nearer the enemy than the battleships, ordered all to open fire at 0351. Two minutes later, *Yamashiro* slowed to 12 knots, but continued on her northerly course, firing at visible targets, since she had no fire control radar. Nishimura was steaming boldly into a terrific concentration of gunfire, supported feebly by *Mogami* astern and *Shigure* on his starboard quarter. His last message, to *Fuso* at 0352, asked that sinking battleship to come along at top speed.

West Virginia, Tennessee and *California*, equipped with the newest Mark-8 fire control radar, were responsible for most of Battle Line's action. *West Virginia* opened fire at 0353, range 22,800 yards. These three battlewagons got off 225 rounds of 14-inch armor-piercing shells, fired in six-gun salvos so as to conserve their limited supply. The other three, equipped with Mark-3 fire control radar, had difficulty finding a target. *Maryland* picked up the enemy by ranging on *West Virginia*'s splashes and got off 48 rounds. *Mississippi* fired a single salvo and *Pennsylvania*, with a primitive type of radar, never fired.

While the elusive and lucky *Shigure* dodged salvos, receiving but one hit during the action, *Yamashiro* and *Mogami* were being battered by every size projectile from the light cruisers' 6-inch up to *Maryland*'s and *West Virginia*'s 16-inch AP. They gamely returned fire; *Mogami* until 0355, when her skipper decided to retire; *Yamashiro* until after 0400. The doomed battlewagon directed her 14-inch fire at the nearest group, "Count" Berkey's right flank cruisers, and fired her secondary battery fire at retiring destroyers; she made hits only on destroyer *Albert W. Grant*.

At 0400, when eight bells marked the end of this eventful midwatch, the battle began to reach a climax. *Yamashiro*, which had been zigzagging in a northerly direction during the last ten minutes, firing doggedly, straightened out on a W by S course. She was burning so brightly that even her 5-inch mounts stood out against flames which seemed to arise from her entire length. *Shigure* turned south to retire; *Mogami*, which had already done so, launched torpedoes at 0401, which missed. A minute later a salvo from cruiser *Portland* exploded on the cruiser's bridge, killing the C.O. and all officers present; other hits were scored in engine and firerooms and *Mogami* slowed almost to a stop. Captain Roland Smoot's Desron 56, having advanced into the fray, launched 13 torpedoes at *Yamashiro* at 0404, and it was two from *Newcomb* which achieved the battleship's ruin.

The American Battle Line changed course from ESE to W by simultaneous turns, and as this maneuver closed the battleships' range, their volume of fire became even greater and more accurate.

"Most beautiful sight I ever witnessed," reported Captain Smoot; "The arched line of tracers in the darkness looked like a continual stream of lighted railroad cars going over a hill." But this show did not long continue. At 0409 Admiral Oldendorf, receiving word that *Albert W. Grant* was being hit by "friendlies," ordered Cease Fire, in order to give Smoot's destroyers a chance to retire. Nishimura and the officers and men of *Yamashiro* must have regarded this cease-fire as God's gift to them and the Emperor. In spite of the punishment their battleship had been taking, she increased speed to 15 knots, turned 90 degrees left, and began to retire southward. But she had less than ten minutes to live. At 0411½ *Newcomb*'s two torpedoes exploded in her, and eight minutes later, as her list increased to 45 degrees, the C.O. ordered Abandon Ship and she sank, taking down the Admiral and all but a few members of the crew.[4]

Mississippi's one salvo, fired at *Yamashiro* just after Admiral Oldendorf ordered Cease Fire, concluded this major phase of the

---

[4] Lieut. S. Ezaki, the senior survivor, interviewed in 1961, insists that it was the four torpedo hits that sank his ship; the shell hits merely hastened her end.

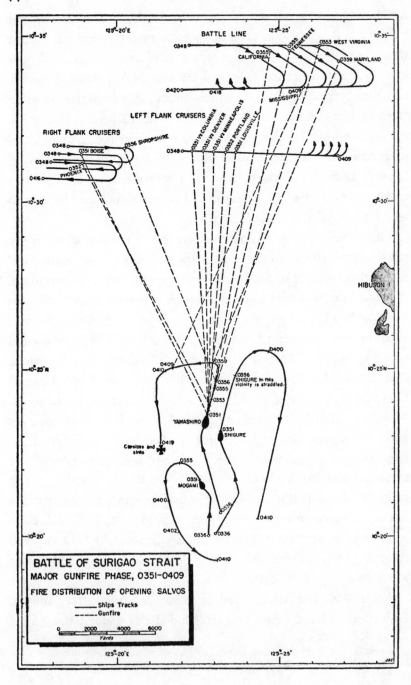

BATTLE OF SURIGAO STRAIT
MAJOR GUNFIRE PHASE, 0351–0409
FIRE DISTRIBUTION OF OPENING SALVOS

Ships Tracks
Gunfire

0   2000   4000   6000
Yards

battle. Silence followed, as if to honor the passing of the tactics which had so long been foremost in naval warfare. The Battles of Lowestoft, Beachy Head, the Capes of the Chesapeake, Trafalgar, Santiago, Tsushima, Jutland, every major naval action of the past three centuries, had been fought by classic line-of-battle tactics. In the unearthly silence that followed the roar of Oldendorf's 14-inch and 16-inch guns in Surigao Strait, one could imagine the ghosts of all great admirals, from Raleigh and De Ruyter to Togo and Jellicoe, standing at attention to salute the passing of the kind of naval warfare that they all understood. For in those opening minutes of the morning watch of 25 October 1944, Battle Line became as obsolete as the row-galley tactics of Salamis and Syracuse.

Admiral Nishimura's van was done for, all but limping *Mogami* and lively *Shigure;* but Admiral Shima's rear group had not yet put in an appearance. As his column was rounding the southern point of Panaon Island to enter Surigao Strait, light cruiser *Abukuma* was hit by a torpedo from *PT–137* and fell out of formation. Although he passed the burning hulks of some of Nishimura's ships, Shima still thought, at 0420, that he was hastening to the support of what was left of the van. Observing two ships on his radar screen — probably *Louisville* and a left flank cruiser — he ordered *Nachi* and *Ashigara* to attack with torpedoes. They turned east and fired eight torpedoes each. No hits were made, and two of the torpedoes were later recovered on Hibuson Island.

This futile action was Shima's only contribution to the battle. Possessed of unusual discretion for a Japanese admiral, he now decided to retire "temporarily" and await developments. In so doing, *Nachi* collided with *Mogami,* which, miraculously, had managed to turn up enough speed to fall in with Shima's column. *Shigure* followed suit.

The pursuit phase of the battle commenced at 0432 when Admiral Oldendorf started south through the Strait, with his left flank cruisers, screened by Captain Smoot's destroyers. Day was now breaking. In the gray half-light, one could just see the high, verdure-clad shores of Dinagat and Leyte Islands. Filipinos had been gazing seaward all night, wondering what the flashes meant, trusting they were ships of the hated *Hapon* Navy going down. Small groups of Japanese survivors began swimming ashore, to find a reception committee ready with sharp knives and bolos. On board the United States ships, everyone who could be spared topside came up for a breath of cool morning air, a look-around, and a discussion as to whether any of "them bastards" were still afloat. It was good that morning to be alive and with a deck under your feet, in Surigao Strait.

Louisville, Portland and *Denver* caught up with *Mogami* around 0530 and added several hits to her collection. But, although the Japanese cruiser appeared to be "burning like a city block," the last of her nine lives was not yet expended. She even drove off two PT attacks after sunrise, and turned up high speed. And "Oley" — who, as his chief of staff "Rafe" Bates frequently reminded him, might have to fight another battle with Kurita's Center Force that very morning — decided to retire at 0537 to keep out of Japanese torpedo water. He turned south again at 0617, and half an hour later sent Bob Hayler with *Denver* and *Columbia* "to polish off enemy cripples." They sank destroyer *Asagumo*, whose bow had been knocked off by Coward's torpedo attack, and then retired.

Admiral T. L. Sprague's escort carriers, which were to bear the brunt of the Battle off Samar, joined in the pursuit as early as 0545. Three hours later, 17 of their Avengers found Shima's retreating rear in the Mindanao Sea, and finally disposed of *Mogami*. Light cruiser *Abukuma*, slowed by a PT torpedo, put in temporarily at Dapitan but was sunk at noon the following day by bombers of the V and XIII Army Air Forces based on Noemfoor and Biak. Shima's two heavies and four destroyers made good their escape. *Shigure,* sole survivor of Nishimura's van, made Brunei Bay safely.

In no battle of the entire war did the United States Navy make so nearly a complete sweep as in that of Surigao Strait, or at so little cost — 39 men killed and 114 wounded, most of them in *Albert W. Grant.* But in no other battle except Halsey's off Cape Engaño, that same day, did the United States Navy enjoy such overwhelming power. The tactical dispositions and battle plan of Admiral Oldendorf were perfect, using his mighty force to best advantage. On the Japanese side, the only alleviating circumstances were the stubborn bravery of *Yamashiro* and *Mogami,* and the intelligent discretion of Vice Admiral Shima in retiring.

6. *The Battle off Samar, 25 October*

One of the strangest incidents in this or any modern war occurred on 25 October, 40 miles off Paninihian Point, Island of Samar, about fifteen minutes after sunrise. An escort carrier group known by its code name "Taffy 3," under Rear Admiral Clifton A. F. Sprague in *Fanshaw Bay,* having launched routine patrols to cover the ships in Leyte Gulf, had secured from General Quarters, and the deck crews were eating breakfast. At 0645 lookouts observed antiaircraft fire to the northward. What could that possibly be? At 0646 the flagship's radar screen showed something odd. One minute later the pilot of a plane on antisubmarine patrol reported that he was being fired upon by a force of battleships, cruisers and destroyers at a position some twenty miles' distant. "Check identification!" yelled Admiral Sprague to air plot. But before verification of this astonishing contact could be obtained, sailors on lookout sighted the unmistakable tall masts of Japanese battleships and

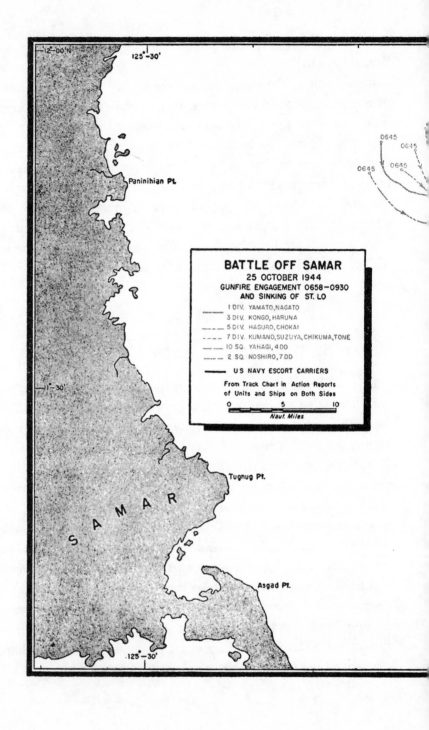

BATTLE OFF SAMAR
25 OCTOBER 1944
GUNFIRE ENGAGEMENT 0658—0930
AND SINKING OF ST. LO

1 DIV.	YAMATO, NAGATO
3 DIV.	KONGO, HARUNA
5 DIV.	HAGURO, CHOKAI
7 DIV.	KUMANO, SUZUYA, CHIKUMA, TONE
10 SQ.	YAHAGI, 4 DD
2 SQ.	NOSHIRO, 7 DD

—— US NAVY ESCORT CARRIERS

From Track Chart in Action Reports
of Units and Ships on Both Sides

0   5   10
Naut. Miles

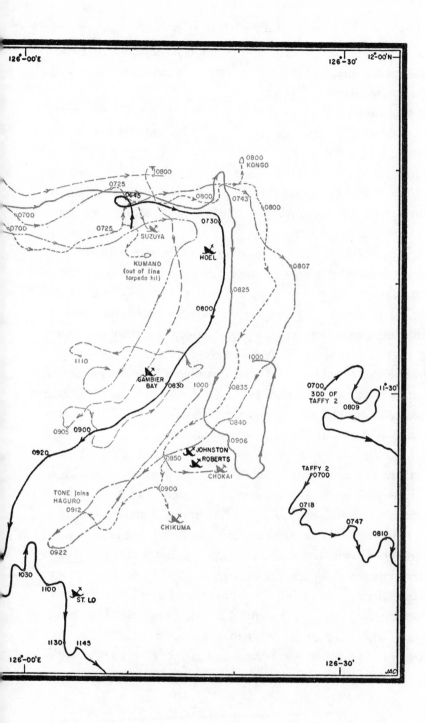

126°-00'E 126°-30' 12°-00'N

0800 KONGO

0800

0725

0645

0700 0725 0730 0743 0800

SUZUYA 0800 0807

KUMANO
(out of line
torpedo hit)

HOEL

0825

0806

1110

1000

0700
3DD OF
TAFFY 2 0809 11°-30'

GAMBIER
BAY 0830 1000 0835

0840

0905 0900 0906

0920 JOHNSTON
ROBERTS
0850 CHOKAI TAFFY 2
0700

0900 0718

TONE Joins
HAGURO
0912 0747 0810

CHIKUMA

0922

1030

1100 ST. LO

1130 1145

126°-00'E 126°-30' JAC

cruisers pricking up over the northwestern horizon. At 0648 these ships opened fire, and a minute later splashes from their shells began rising all around Taffy 3.

It was Admiral Kurita's powerful Center Force. He was every bit as surprised as Sprague. He thought he had run smack into Mitscher's Task Force 38.

How could this formidable fleet have covered 125 to 150 miles from *inside* San Bernardino Strait, down along the ocean shore of Samar, in the last seven hours — undetected by ship, search plane or coastwatcher?

Admiral Halsey was informed by a night-search plane from *Independence* that Kurita's Center Force would sortie from San Bernardino Strait. Sightings on it heading that way reached the Admiral as late as 2120 October 24. But he simply did not care. Estimating that his carrier pilots' exaggerated reports of their sinkings in the Battle of the Sibuyan Sea were correct, he assumed that Center Force "could no longer be considered a serious menace to Seventh Fleet," in or outside Leyte Gulf, and did not even warn Kinkaid to watch out. By the time Halsey received the night-sighting reports, his Third Fleet — less McCain's TG 38.1 sent south to fuel — was high-tailing north, hellbent after Ozawa's Northern Force. That was exactly what the Japanese wanted it to do. Halsey might have spared one carrier group and Admiral Lee's Battle Line (*New Jersey, Iowa, Washington, Massachusetts, Alabama*) to guard San Bernardino Strait; but he left not even a picket destroyer. That is why Kurita's Center Force was able to debouch unseen into the Philippine Sea at 0030 October 25, and steam south unseen off the Samar shore, until intercepted by Clifton Sprague's escort carriers. And that is why Taffy 3, composed of six escort carriers with no guns bigger than 5-inch, screened by three destroyers and four destroyer escorts, had to fight Kurita's four battleships, six heavy cruisers and numerous destroyers.

Taffy 3 was supported by the aircraft of two other groups of nearly the same strength: Rear Admiral Thomas L. Sprague's Taffy 1, which was operating well to the southward off Mindanao, and Rear Admiral Felix B. Stump's Taffy 2, off the entrance to Leyte Gulf. The total plane complement of these 16 carriers was 235 fighter planes (Hellcats and Wildcats) and 143 Avenger torpedo planes; and it was they, in addition to Clifton Sprague's skillful tactics, and the intrepid attacks by his screen, which enabled him to win this battle against an overwhelming surface and gunfire superiority. But few of these planes were available at the moment of surprise. Taffy 1 had already launched a strike group to pursue Japanese ships fleeing from Surigao Strait; all carriers had launched planes for routine patrol, or for odd jobs such as delivering cans of fresh water to the troops on Leyte.

The Battle off Samar, thus unexpectedly joined at 0648, was the most remarkable of the Pacific war, since the tactics had to be improvised. Prewar training prepared the United States Navy to fight battles such as Surigao Strait; but there was no preparation, no doctrine, for a force of "baby flattops" fighting a battle fleet such as Kurita's. Their training was all for supporting amphibious operations by strikes, C.A.P., and antisubmarine patrol, not for bearing the brunt of a major battle. Rear Admiral Clifton A. F. Sprague, known as "Ziggy" in the Navy, an able and conscientious officer forty-eight years old, had commanded fleet carrier *Wasp* in the Battle of the Philippine Sea, but now he faced a unique challenge.

Weather gave the escort carriers their first break. Wind blew from the eastern quadrant, permitting them to steer away from the enemy while launching planes, and rain squalls afforded occasional cover. Clifton Sprague, knowing very well what a pickle he was in, acted with cool and correct decision. He turned Taffy 3 due east, upped speed to the flattop maximum of 17½ knots, ordered every plane to be launched and to attack, and broadcast an urgent plea for assistance. Admirals Tom Sprague and Felix Stump responded quickly; but Taffy 1 lay 130 miles distant; could the planes get there in time?

Kurita fumbled from the moment the battle joined. His staff told him that the escort carriers were fleet carriers, the destroyers cruisers, and the DEs destroyers. At the moment of impact, he was changing the disposition of Center Force from cruising to antiaircraft formation; he should promptly have formed Battle Line with his fast, powerful ships and committed light forces to torpedo attack. Instead, he ordered General Attack — every ship for itself — which threw his force into confusion and made the battle a helter-skelter affair, ships committed piecemeal and defeated piecemeal, just as the Japanese Army was wont to do ashore.

Clifton Sprague formed his six carriers into a rough circle 2500 yards in diameter, his screen patrolling outside the engaged sector, as Japanese salvos edged closer and closer. At 0706, to quote his Action Report, "The enemy was closing with disconcerting rapidity and the volume and accuracy of fire was increasing. At this point it did not appear that any of our ships could survive another five minutes of the heavy-caliber fire being received." His task unit being faced by "the ultimate in desperate circumstances," he saw that counteraction was urgently required. He ordered all escorts to a torpedo attack. And, also at 0706, compassionate providence sent a rain squall, under which the carriers, in conjunction with the smoke that they and the escorts were making, were protected for about fifteen minutes. During this respite the Admiral decided to bear around to the south and southwest, in order to bring his disposition nearer to the hoped-for help from Leyte Gulf. But no help appeared. Admiral Oldendorf, his ammunition depleted by the night battle, had to replenish from supply ships in Leyte Gulf; and by the time he was ready to sortie it was too late to reach the flattops. Sprague's tactics were risky, since they invited the enemy to take the inside track, but they proved to be correct. Kurita was so obsessed with keeping the weather gauge that, instead of cutting corners, he maintained course until he was due north of the carriers, and then bore down. And most of his ships, repeatedly dodging air and torpedo attacks, could not catch up. The Japanese admiral was sadly bewildered by the way everything we had afloat or airborne went baldheaded for him.

Clifton Sprague ordered Taffy 3 screen to counterattack the Japanese heavy ships at 0716, after the escort carriers had entered the rain squall. The three destroyers were *Hoel*, flying the pennant of Commander W. D. Thomas, and *Heermann* and *Johnston* — all 2100-tonners of the *Fletcher* class. *Johnston* was already counterattacking. Her skipper, Commander Ernest E. Evans, was a fighting Cherokee of the same breed as "Jocko" Clark — short, barrelchested, loud of voice, a born leader. As soon as the Japanese ships were sighted he had ordered all boilers to be lighted, called all hands to General Quarters,[4] and passed the word, "Prepare to attack major portion of Japanese Fleet." As *Johnston* sheered out to lay a smoke screen, she commenced firing at a range of 18,000 yards. Closing to within 10,000 yards of a heavy cruiser column, she launched torpedoes and got one hit on *Kumano*. The Japanese flag officer on board shifted to *Suzuya*, which had already been slowed down by air bombing, and both cruisers dropped astern and out of the battle.

About 0730, *Johnston* took three 14-inch and three 6-inch shell hits. "It was like a puppy being smacked by a truck," recalled her senior surviving officer. The after fireroom and engine room were knocked out; all power to the after 5-inch guns was lost. A rain squall gave her ten minutes to repair damage. At this stage of the battle confusion reigned supreme. *Johnston*, having

[4] The sailors called *Johnston* "G. Q. Johnny," owing to her frequent General Quarters signals.

expended all torpedoes, used manually-controlled 5-inch gun-fire against battleship *Kongo;* and, as if this were not enough, she played the major part in frustrating Kurita's destroyer attack on the carriers. After that, said the survivor, "We were in a position where all the gallantry and guts in the world could not save us." Three cruisers and several destroyers, overtaking her in her slowed-down situation, poured in an avalanche of shells and she went dead in the water. Commander Evans ordered Abandon Ship at 0950. The same Japanese destroyer squadron whose attack on the carriers she had thwarted, now made a running circle around her, shooting rapidly. At 1010 she rolled over and began to sink. A destroyer closed to give her the *coup de grâce.* A swimming survivor saw the Japanese skipper on her bridge salute as *Johnston* took the final plunge.

Hoel and *Heermann* were fighting just as vigorously, their skippers' one object being to inflict maximum damage on the enemy in the hope of diverting major-caliber fire from the carriers. *Heermann* (Commander A. T. Hathaway) at one point was engaging four battleships. She was too nimble for them to hit but her spread of six torpedoes caused the mighty *Yamato* to reverse course for ten minutes, which took those 18.1-inch guns out of the fight. *Hoel* (Commander L. S. Kintberger), with one engine and three 5-inch guns knocked out, was not so lucky. She took over 40 hits, even 16-inch, which went right through her hull without exploding, but knocked her so full of holes that at 0855 she rolled over and sank. Her crew, wrote her C.O., "performed their duties cooly and efficiently until their ship was shot from under them."

In the second torpedo attack Clifton Sprague ordered, at 0742, the three destroyer escorts of his screen also took part. *Samuel B. Roberts* was sunk, after exchanging gunfire with several heavy cruisers. Here is the tribute of her C.O., Lieutenant Commander R. W. Copeland USNR, to his men, one which may apply equally well to the entire screen:

To witness the conduct of the average enlisted man on board this vessel . . . with an average of less than one year's service, would make any man proud to be an average American. The crew were informed over the loudspeaker system at the beginning of the action of the C.O.'s estimate of the situation: i.e., a fight against overwhelming odds from which survival could not be expected, during which time we would do what damage we could. In the face of this knowledge the men zealously manned their stations . . . and fought and worked with such calmness, courage, and efficiency that no higher honor could be conceived than to command such a group.

For two hours after 0743, when they emerged from the rain squall, the six escort carriers of Taffy 3 were making best speed of 17½ knots around an irregular arc, subtended by a chord almost parallel to the coast of Samar. Their own planes, helped by many from Taffy 2 and Taffy 1, were continually attacking the Japanese with bombs, torpedoes, machine-gun bullets and making dry runs when they ran out of ammunition. Kurita's ships were capable of twice the speed of Sprague's, but their frequent evasive maneuvers to escape destroyers' torpedoes and carrier-plane attacks canceled the advantage; while the flattops, except for some quick salvo-chasing, plodded steadily along. Hence the enemy's main body never appreciably closed range. The three Japanese battleships still advancing at 0820 were astern of the carriers, slowly firing salvos with armor-piercing projectiles which, if they hit, failed to detonate on the thin-skinned flattops. The heavy cruisers were much more deadly: they made thirteen 8-inch hits on *Kalinin Bay,* and she was the only carrier hit by a battleship; heroic efforts of damage control kept her in formation. Boatswains' crews worked in five feet of water to plug holes below the waterline. Black gang worked knee-deep in oil, choked by the stench of burning rubber and threatened by scalding steam, to repair ruptures in the power plant. Main steering control conked out and quartermasters steered the ship by hand from far down in her bowels, like helmsmen in the ancient Spanish galleons.

Aircraft for the most part made individual attacks, as they were too hastily armed and launched to be coördinated. Avengers used torpedoes as long as torpedoes lasted; when these gave out they armed with bombs — even little 100-pounders — and made dry runs to divert the Japanese gunners. Lieutenant Commander Edward J. Huxtable, Air Group Commander in *Gambier Bay*, guided his Avenger for two hours through the flak to make dry runs, once flying down a line of heavy cruisers to divert them from their course and throw off their gunfire for a few precious minutes. The Wildcat pilots strafed topsides or ran interference for an Avenger; and they too made dry runs. Lieutenant Paul G. Garrison USNR made ten such out of a total of twenty. Since the carriers were now scudding and could not afford to luff up to recover, when aircraft ran out of fuel they had to land on a carrier of Stump's Taffy 2 about 25 miles away, or the more distant Tacloban field, Leyte, which Army Engineers had providentially made usable. There they refueled, picked up 500-pound bombs and flew out to sea to attack again.

The battle reached a crisis when Kurita's four remaining heavy cruisers *Chikuma, Tone, Haguro* and *Chokai*, more enterprising than his battlewagons, pulled ahead on the port quarter of the carriers and closed range. *Chikuma* began a steady pounding of *Gambier Bay*, from which even attacks by the intrepid *Johnston* and *Heermann* did not divert her. The escort carrier, after a salvo-chasing snake dance lasting 25 minutes, began to take 8-inch hits, and dropped astern. The other three heavies, light cruiser *Noshiro*, and a Japanese destroyer now concentrated on *Gambier Bay*. As she began to sink Captain Vieweg gave the order Abandon Ship. *Chikuma* continued to pound her at short range, and at 0907 she capsized and went down.

On to the southwestward plunged the other five American flat-tops. *White Plains* fired her single 5-inch guns at each cruiser which closed within 18,000 yards, and made at least six hits on

Chokai. "Hold on a little longer, boys," sang out Chief Gunner's Mate Jenkins. "We're sucking 'em into 40-mm range!" And they almost did, or would have, but for an attack on that heavy cruiser by four Avengers led by Commander R. L. Fowler of *Kitkun Bay*'s air group. These planes scored ten hits and had the satisfaction of seeing *Chokai* go down. Next, *Chikuma* was sunk by a well coördinated Wildcat-Avenger attack from Felix Stump's Taffy 2; and down she went. Clifton Sprague's harried and beset carriers, now threatened by high-caliber battleship fire as well as by *Haguro* and *Tone*, saw to their amazement both heavy cruisers break off their pursuit. A moment later a signalman on the bridge of *Fanshaw Bay* yelled "Goddammit, boys, they're getting away!" The entire Center Force was retiring.

Kurita had ordered the break-off at 0911. The air and destroyer attacks had cost his force three heavy cruisers.[5] His communications were so bad that he never knew how near *Tone* and *Haguro* had closed the flattops. At that time, he intended merely to reassemble his dispersed and disorganized force, ascertain damage, and resume the march to Leyte Gulf. But the more he thought it over, the less he liked the prospect, and the better he relished the idea of going home the way he came. Center Force had been battered for three days — by submarines on the 23rd, fast carrier aircraft on the 24th, and in the battle just over. Kurita and his staff were so muddled as to estimate that the escort carriers were making 30 knots (instead of their maximum of 17.5) so that it would be impossible to catch them. "I knew you were scared," said another admiral to Clifton Sprague after reading this postwar statement by Kurita, "but I didn't know you were *that* scared!"

Kurita had already received a radio signal from Admiral Shima indicating that Southern Force, with which he was expected to coöperate, was all washed up. So he figured that his prospects in Leyte Gulf were both thin and grim. American transports and

[5] Including *Suzuya,* which was going down.

amphibious craft would have departed by the time he could get there; he feared massive land-based air attacks from Tacloban Field on Leyte Gulf, and heavy carrier-based air attacks from TF 38, and he did not care to fight Oldendorf's victorious gunfire force (which lay outside the entrance to Leyte Gulf waiting for him until 1300), in order to sink maybe a few LSTs and sprinkle shellfire on American troops ashore. A fresh air attack by 70 Wildcats and Avengers from Taffys 2 and 3, which came in on Center Force at 1230, and made hits on battleship *Nagato* and heavy cruiser *Tone*, helped Kurita to make up his mind to retire. At 1236 he signaled C. in C. Combined Fleet at Tokyo that he was heading for San Bernardino Strait.

Kurita's retirement did not end this day's battle for the escort carriers. While Clifton Sprague's Taffy 3 was fighting to the northward, Tom Sprague's Taffy 1 was receiving the dubious honor of first target of the Kamikaze Corps. Postponing to next chapter a description of this formidable suicide club, we may note here that *Santee* was crashed by a member at 0740, and hit by a torpedo from submarine *I-56* at 0756; but these converted-tanker flattops were tough, and by eight bells *Santee* was making over 16 knots. Sister *Suwannee* received a second kamikaze shortly after, but was able to resume flight operations at 1009. Taffy 3's turn came at 1050 when she hoped that the battle was over. One crashed Rear Admiral Ofstie's flagship *Kitkun Bay* but bounced into the sea; two that made for *Fanshaw Bay* were shot down; two were exploded by antiaircraft fire when diving at *White Plains* and *Kitkun Bay*; two crashed *Kalinin Bay* but inflicted comparatively little damage. But one broke through the flight deck of *St. Lo*, burst into flames, exploded the bombs and torpedoes on the hangar deck, and sank her.

An hour later, Kurita's Center Force was attacked by aircraft from Admiral McCain's TG 38.1. Admiral Halsey, at Kinkaid's urgent request, had ordered this. McCain, fueling when he got the word, turned up flank speed and commenced launching at 1030 when distant 335 miles from Kurita. This was one of the longest-range carrier plane attacks of the war; too long, for Avengers could not carry heavy bombs or torpedoes that far, and they suffered considerable loss without inflicting additional damage.

By noon the Battle off Samar was over. It had been a glorious but expensive victory: two escort carriers, two destroyers and a destroyer escort sunk; several other ships badly damaged, and heavy casualties: —

	Killed & Missing	Wounded
Taffy 1 Ships' Crews	283	136
Taffy 3 Ships' Crews	792	768
Aviators, all escort carriers	43	9
Aviators, TG 38.1	12	0
TOTAL	1130	913

Kurita's successful retirement was small consolation for the complete failure of his mission. His defeat was due, in last analysis, to the indomitable spirit of the escort carriers, their screen, and their aviators. It was they who stopped the most powerful gunfire force which Japan had sent to sea since the Battle of Midway.

7. *The Battle off Cape Engaño, 25 October*

All day 24 October Admiral Halsey's Third Fleet search planes were eagerly looking for Admiral Ozawa's Northern Force, and Ozawa was equally anxious to be seen, in order to carry out his mission to bait Halsey up north out of Kurita's way. Yet the Japanese were unable to get themselves sighted until 1540.

Ozawa's Northern Force comprised four carriers with 116 planes on board; the two "hermaphrodites" *Hyuga* and *Ise*, battleships whose superstructures had been shorn abaft the stack to make a short flight deck, but carried no planes; three light cruisers, nine destroyers and a tanker unit. They sortied from Bungo Suido, Inland Sea, on 20 October. During the forenoon watch on the 24th they located a group of Mitscher's TF 38, and at 1145 Ozawa launched a 76-plane strike on Frederick Sherman's TG 38.3. It accomplished nothing. Some planes were splashed, 15 to 20 landed on Luzon fields, and the 29 which returned on board were all that Ozawa had during the battle.[6] Halsey received his search planes' contact reports on Ozawa around 1700; and at 2022, as we have seen, ordered his entire Third Fleet — less McCain's TG 38.1, which had been sent away to fuel — up north. Admiral Mitscher in *Lexington*, next in command under Admiral Halsey in *New Jersey*, had 64 ships and 787 planes (401 fighters, 214 dive-bombers, 171 torpedo-bombers)[7] opposed to Ozawa's 17 ships and 29 aircraft. Surely, enough for him to have spared Lee's Battle Line, or part of it, to guard San Bernardino Strait; but Japanese carriers gave Halsey blood in the eye, and he was taking no chances of letting one guilty flattop escape.

Rendezvous of the three American carrier groups was made around midnight at lat. 14°28′ N, long. 125°30′ E, off central Luzon. All three proceeded north in company, *Independence* sending five night fliers ahead to search. Around 0220 October 25 they sighted the two groups into which Ozawa had divided Northern Force: one under Rear Admiral Matsuda with the two hermaphrodites, a light cruiser and four destroyers; the rest of the force under Ozawa himself. They were then about 200 miles E by N of Cape Engaño, Luzon.

At 0430 October 25 Mitscher (O.T.C. from now on) ordered all carriers to arm a deckload immediately and be prepared to launch at earliest light. Throughout morning watch, deck crews

---

[6] Apparently the 40 other planes on board had also been flown ashore.

[7] Exclusive of the complement of *Princeton*, sunk that day; but many of her surviving planes had been received on board the other carriers.

were arming and spotting planes and aviators were either taking a last nap or eating an early breakfast. Not since the Battle of the Philippine Sea in June had these air groups had a crack at enemy carriers. This was what they had been looking and praying for. And the new battleships were longing for some good floating targets to test the power and accuracy of their main batteries.

First strike reached the enemy around 0800. Helldivers first, strafing fighter planes next as the dive-bombers overshot, and Avengers last, releasing torpedoes from 700 to 1000 feet, at ranges from 1400 to 1600 yards. Commander David McCampbell of the *Essex* Air Group acted as target coördinator. Admiral Ozawa was not taken aback, but there was nothing he could do except use antiaircraft fire, which was brisk and intense. Despite this, carrier *Chitose* and one destroyer were sunk by a cluster of bomb hits, and big *Zuikaku*, veteran of Pearl Harbor, the Coral Sea and the Philippine Sea, took a torpedo which knocked out her communications and caused Ozawa to shift his flag to light cruiser *Oyodo*. A good beginning indeed.

Strike No. 2 was already in the air. Upon its arrival at the target, around 0945, the enemy force presented a picture of wild confusion. *Lexington*'s and *Franklin*'s planes made bomb hits on *Chiyoda*, setting her heavily afire; a third hit disabled her engines. *Hyuga* attempted to take her in tow, but was frustrated by Strike No. 3. *Chiyoda* was abandoned with her crew still on board, and sunk by gunfire of Admiral DuBose's cruisers at 1630.

Strike No. 3, launched around noon from Sherman's TG 38.3 (*Essex*, flag) and Davison's 38.4 (*Franklin*, flag), comprising over 200 aircraft (about 150 of which had been in Strike No. 1), stayed over and around Ozawa's ships for an hour. *Zuikaku*, as a result of three torpedoes which hit her simultaneously, rolled over and went down. *Zuiho*, her flight deck quaintly camouflaged to make her look like a big-gunned battleship from aloft, took a lot of punishment from this strike, and 27 more planes of Strike No. 4

were required to sink her. Strike No. 5, consisting of full deckloads from five carriers, concentrated on *Ise* but got nothing but
near-misses and only slightly damaged that tough old hermaphro-
dite. She threw up remarkably heavy antiaircraft fire, and her
C.O., Rear Admiral Nakase, was an expert at evasive manuever-
ing. Strike No. 6, by 36 planes from Davison's group, took off at
1710 and claimed a few hits, but sank nothing more.

After the war, Admiral Ozawa said that the first three strikes
did the most damage, and his chief of staff remarked, "I saw all
this bombing and thought the American pilot is not so good." He
was not too bad — having sunk four carriers and a destroyer with
a total of 527 plane sorties, 201 of them fighters. Yet it must be
admitted that, blow for blow, the escort carrier planes in the Battle
off Samar inflicted more damage than did the aircraft of any two
fast carrier groups. A comparison of this battle with that of the
Philippine Sea in June suggests that the American fast carrier
planes were much better at intercepting enemy aircraft than at
hitting ships. The old SBDs did better at Midway than the SB2Cs
off Cape Engaño; but Japanese antiaircraft fire had vastly improved since 1942.

Now came the surface part of the battle, and the controversial
"Where is TF 34?" incident. Admiral Halsey at 1512 October 24
had organized Task Force 34, including most of his gunfire ships,
under Admiral Lee. The dispatch, headed "Battle Plan," named
the battleships, cruisers and destroyer divisions which "will be
formed as Task Force 34" and "will engage decisively at long
ranges." Admirals Kinkaid in Leyte Gulf, Nimitz at Pearl Harbor, and Cooke, deputy C.N.O. in Washington, all misread Halsey's future indicative for present imperative. They assumed that
TF 34 was not only set up on paper but detached to guard San
Bernardino Strait; and Kinkaid was not informed of the contrary
by Halsey until 0705 October 25. From 0822, following the surprise off Samar, Halsey received a series of plain-language pleas

from Kinkaid for any kind of assistance, air or surface, that he could spare; and Halsey complied, as we have seen, to the extent of ordering Admiral McCain to belay fueling his TG 38.1 and hasten to strike Kurita's Center Force. But he did not detach Lee's TF 34 to block Kurita's escape, because he wanted to keep all heavy ships for a gunfire battle up north after his aircraft had done their worst.

Admiral Nimitz, also amazed at the surprise off Samar, wanted information and sent a dispatch asking for it. The encoding yeoman at Pearl Harbor, who apparently had been reading "The Charge of the Light Brigade," put in as padding (to throw off possible enemy decrypters), "the world wonders." The decoding yeoman on board *New Jersey*, taking this to be a part of the message, handed it to Admiral Halsey at 1000 in this form:

From Cincpac Action Com Third Fleet info Cominch CTF 77 X where is RPT where is Task Force Thirty-four RR the world wonders.[8]

Halsey was furious. He thought that Nimitz was criticizing him, and that, too, before Admirals King and Kinkaid (CTF 77) by making them addressees. He brooded over the supposed insult for almost an hour, then at 1055 ordered the major part of Lee's TF 34 south to help Seventh Fleet, went along himself in *New Jersey*, and picked up Bogan's carrier group en route. It was too late by several hours for them to reach San Bernardino Strait ahead of Kurita. When they arrived at 0100 on the 26th, there was only one crippled destroyer of Center Force outside the Strait. Kurita had got through three hours earlier.

This was a bitter disappointment to Admiral Lee, as to all battleship sailors. Adept at handling battlewagons, as he had proved in the Battle of Guadalcanal, Lee had planned to form Battle Line between Kurita and the Strait, so that the Japanese would be

---

[8] Potter and Nimitz *The Great Sea War* p. 390n.

forced to fight. What a brawl that would have been — with *Ya-mato, Nagato, Kongo* and *Haruna* on one side, and *Iowa, New Jersey, Massachusetts, South Dakota, Washington* and *Alabama* on the other! And it proved to be the last opportunity to find out what *Yamato*'s 18.1-inch main battery could do against the 16-inch guns of the *Iowa* class.

When Halsey sent the major part of TF 34 south at 1045, he detached cruisers *Santa Fe, Mobile, Wichita, New Orleans* and nine destroyers to continue northward with the carriers. Mitscher at 1415 ordered this cruiser group, under command of Rear Admiral Laurance T. DuBose, to pursue Ozawa's limping units. They sank abandoned *Chiyoda,* then encountered *Hatsuzuki* and two smaller destroyers in the twilight. *Mobile* opened fire from very long range at 1853. *Hatsuzuki* returned fire and worked up speed to escape. The cruisers pursued at 28 knots, gradually over-hauling the group, and at 1915 DuBose sent three destroyers ahead to make a torpedo attack, which slowed up *Hatsuzuki.* The cruis-ers closed to 6000 yards, illuminated with star shell, brought the destroyer under gunfire, and saw her explode and sink at 2059. She had absorbed a tremendous amount of punishment.

Half an hour later, two *Independence* night flyers sighted Ozawa's ships steaming north at 22 knots abreast of Bashi Chan-nel, the northern entrance to Luzon Strait. A simple calculation showed that even if DuBose pursued at 30 knots he could not overhaul them before daylight, when they would be under the pro-tection of land-based aircraft on Formosa. So he retired. The black gangs in *Oyodo, Hyuga, Ise* and five destroyers were "pouring it on" to escape. They ran the gantlet of two wolf-packs of Pacific Fleet submarines, whose torpedoes missed (though *Jallao* sank lag-ging light cruiser *Tama*, earlier bombed), and made harbor in the Ryukyus on 27 October.

Admiral Ozawa had performed his mission of baiting Halsey and saving Kurita, as well as his own force, from annihilation. The

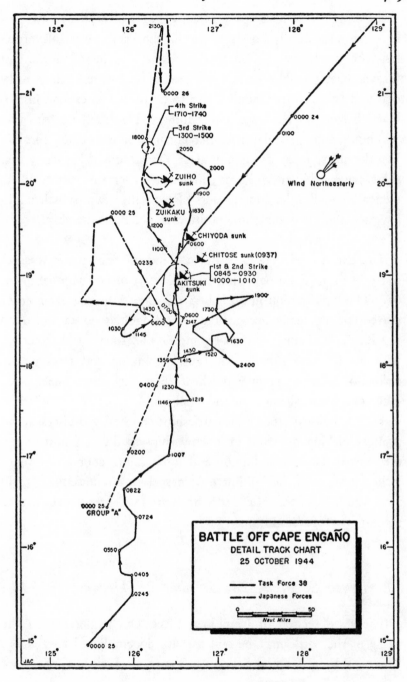

BATTLE OFF CAPE ENGAÑO
DETAIL TRACK CHART
25 OCTOBER 1944

——— Task Force 38
—·—·— Japanese Forces

0 ⊢⊢⊢⊢⊢⊢ 50

Naut. Miles

antiaircraft fire of his ships, especially *Ise*'s and *Hyuga*'s, was perhaps the most deadly on either side in the Pacific war. Nevertheless, the battle was a "bitter experience," as he admitted. For Ozawa, protagonist of carrier warfare in the Japanese Navy, to be defeated twice in five months, and to be forced to expend his beloved flattops as bait, was bitter indeed. He faced the situation without flinching; and his former enemies, now friends, consider him the ablest Japanese admiral after Yamamoto. What irony that this sacrificial Northern Force should have been superbly handled, tactically; whilst the commanders of the other two, which might have accomplished something positive, fumbled so miserably!

The Battle for Leyte Gulf did not end the war, but it was decisive. And it should be an imperishable part of our national memory. The night action in Surigao Strait is an inspiring example of perfect timing, coördination and almost faultless execution. And the Battle off Samar had no compeer. The story of that action, with its dramatic surprise, the quick thinking and resolute decisions of Clifton Sprague; the little screening vessels feeling for each other through the rain and smoke and, courting annihilation, making individual attacks on battleships and heavy cruisers; naval aviators making dry runs on enemy ships to divert gunfire from their own; the defiant humor and indomitable courage of bluejackets caught in the "ultimate of desperate circumstances," will make the fight of the "Taffys" with Kurita's Center Force forever memorable, forever glorious.

8. *Leyte Secured, 26 October–25 December 1944*

One small section of Combined Fleet which operated on the verge of the battle may be said to have accomplished its mission. This was Vice Admiral Sakonju's Transport Unit. It lost heavy cruiser *Aoba*, torpedoed but not sunk by United States submarine *Bream* outside Manila Bay on 23 October, lost a destroyer next day to plane attack from TF 38, and another destroyer and light cruiser *Kinu* to Tom Sprague's planes on the 26th. But on the day of the big battle, it embarked 2000 troops in destroyer-transports at Cagayan, Mindanao, and landed them next morning at Ormoc on the back of Leyte. That was the beginning of a series of reinforcements by quick, fast thrusts, similar to the Tokyo Expresses at Guadalcanal. They ran 'em in daily, without opposition, until 30 October, when B-24s from Morotai sank an unloaded *Maru* in Ormoc Bay. Two large convoys from Manila were badly bombed on 11 November by planes from three of the fast carrier groups, sinking six destroyers and drowning about 10,000 troops.

Two weeks elapsed before the Japanese could send in more reinforcements. But, before these back-side Leyte convoys were stopped, about 45,000 troops and 10,000 tons of supplies had been landed on the west coast of Leyte, more than 100 per cent increase over what was there on 20 October. The 101,635 American troops ashore by 1 November still outnumbered them, but Japan had some 365,000 troops elsewhere in the Philippines to draw on. The situation bore a distressing resemblance to that on Guadalcanal two years earlier. We had won a great naval battle and secured our sea communications; but without round-the-clock air supremacy it was impossible to prevent the running in of reinforcements by Tokyo Express.

As soon as the Japanese high command caught its breath, it began staging aircraft south into Luzon fields, to harass General Krueger's Sixth Army ashore, and the supply ships constantly coming and going in Leyte Gulf. Admiral Halsey made up for any earlier mistakes through nobly standing by for many days after the big battle, since Army Engineers were unable to get the boggy airstrips on the Leyte beachhead fit to receive Army Air Force until November — and not many planes even then. Admiral Bogan's

TG 38.2 and Admiral Davison's TG 38.4 struck the airfield complex around Manila on 29-30 October; in return, kamikazes crashed carriers *Intrepid, Franklin* and *Belleau Wood,* injuring them so badly that they had to retire to Ulithi. Task Force 38 held rendezvous there on 1 November — first rest for the sailors and aviators who had been fighting three days out of four since their last sortie on 6 October.

Upon the departure of the Halsey-Mitscher forces, the air situation over Leyte deteriorated, since troops and ships had for protection only the few Army planes which Tacloban airstrip could accommodate. One destroyer was sunk by a kamikaze and three were damaged by conventional bombers on 1 November. TF 38 was back in the area by 5 November — Bogan's group even earlier — and in two days' strikes on the airfields around Manila they destroyed over 200 enemy planes at the cost of 25 of our own, and a kamikaze crash on *Lexington* which killed 50 and wounded 132 men but did not seriously injure the ship. These efforts brought about a marked improvement in the air situation at Leyte.

On 13-14 November Halsey, at MacArthur's urgent request, resumed air strikes on Luzon. This time he concentrated on reinforcement shipping, sinking a light cruiser, four destroyers and seven *Marus.* Again, on the 25th, *Ticonderoga*'s planes sank heavy cruiser *Kumano* in Dasol Bay and broke up two coastal convoys. The kamikazes then made a really vicious counterattack. Carriers *Intrepid, Cabot* and *Essex* were crashed — "Evil I" twice — with a loss of over a hundred men.

This action of 25 November concluded fast carrier support of the Leyte operation, which had begun on 8 October. This support had been prolonged for four weeks after the originally planned date of its termination, owing to the disappointingly slow work on Tacloban airfield. Not counting its two short calls in Ulithi lagoon, TF 38 had been at sea almost continuously for 84 days. The resulting strain on all hands was severe. No ship except *Princeton* had been lost, but five carriers needed extensive repairs. Under these conditions, wrote Admiral Halsey, "further casual strikes did not appear profitable."

In the meantime, General Krueger's Sixth Army had been slashing ahead on Leyte, through foul weather and continual rain. Not since the Guadalcanal and Buna-Gona campaigns had fighting been as arduous as on Leyte. In spite of the victories of 25 October, soldiers, sailors and aviators were dying daily for the liberation of that island.

By December 1, Sixth Army controlled most of Leyte except the San Isidro Peninsula and a semicircular sector with a 12-mile radius from Ormoc. The Japanese still had about 35,000 men on the island, but they could no longer reinforce it, and General Krueger's effective strength had risen to 183,242. His losses up to 2 December were 2260 killed and missing and several thousand laid up from wounds, dysentery, "immersion foot," skin diseases and other ills incident to campaigning in tropical mud. Over 24,000 enemy dead had been counted. It was time to finish.

A preliminary to the finish was a series of destroyer sweeps, commanded by Captains Robert H. Smith and W. M. Cole, into Ormoc Bay and the Camotes Sea, and minesweeping the Canigao Channels between Bohol and Leyte. The PTs got into this, too. There were numerous night and day encounters during the first week of December, in which destroyer *Cooper* was lost after sinking Japanese destroyer *Kuwa;* their rafted survivors drifted together next morning and even conversed in English. There was a shore-to-shore amphibious landing on Ormoc Bay, commanded by Admiral Struble, on 7 December, in which destroyers *Mahan* and *Ward* were sunk by kamikazes. But the 77th Division was landed near Ormoc; and that, as General Krueger commented, "Serving to split the enemy forces and to separate them from their supply base, proved to be the decisive action of the Leyte Operation."

Re-supply echelons now had to be sent from Leyte Gulf through Surigao Strait into Leyte; and the one on 11-12 December under Captain J. D. Murphy took a bad beating from kamikazes, losing destroyer *Reid;* and *Caldwell* was twice crashed but not sunk.

The shore fighting, of which we have no space to tell, culminated in the capture of Palompon on Christmas Day. General MacArthur, congratulating General Krueger on the event, said: "This closes a campaign that has had few counterparts in the utter destruction of the enemy's forces with a maximum conservation of our own. It has been a magnificent performance on the part of all concerned." Next day, the General declared, "The Leyte-Samar campaign can now be regarded as closed, except for minor mopping-up operations." These "minor" operations went on until 5 May 1945; but General MacArthur was unconsciously corroborated by General Yamashita, who, on Christmas Day from his headquarters at Manila, notified General Suzuki on Leyte that he had written off that island as a loss and had decided to concentrate on the defense of Luzon, shedding "tears of remorse" for the tens of thousands of his countrymen who must fight to the death on Leyte.

On the American side, mopping-up operations were conducted under Commanding General Eighth Army, Lieutenant General Robert L. Eichelberger, veteran of the Papuan campaign. General Hodge's XXIV Corps remained to finish the job. All naval supporting forces were withdrawn for the Mindoro and Lingayen operations; the Engineer Special Brigade craft did whatever convoy work was required.

The outstanding tactical lesson of the Battle for Leyte Gulf is the utter helplessness of a modern fleet without air support. Tha' is why "jeep carriers" and their thin screen were able, off Samar, to defeat a powerful fleet of battleships and heavy cruisers. Spruance's victory in June and Halsey's October strikes on Formosa were responsible for the accelerated assault on Leyte, catching Japanese air forces at their lowest ebb. If the original timetable for that assault (20 December) had been strictly maintained, Ozawa would have had new air groups trained, and the Japanese Navy could have put up a far better fight. Halsey was responsible for the accelerated timetable; so let us, in retrospect, remember that strategic inspiration of the grand old admiral, and forget his mistake on the fateful night of 24–25 October, which was fully compensated by the gallantry of Kinkaid's escort carrier groups next morning.

CHAPTER XV

The Philippines and Submarine Operations

13 December 1944 to 15 August 1945

1. *Mindoro*

THREE WEEKS BEFORE the Battle of Leyte Gulf, on 3 October 1944, the Joint Chiefs of Staff decided to liberate Manila and Luzon. That was as General MacArthur had always wished. Admiral King long held out for taking Formosa, which would "put the cork in the bottle" of the South China Sea, isolate Japan, and provide an advanced air and naval base for the final assault. But the Army estimated that at least nine divisions would be required to capture even a part of Formosa; and, owing to involvement in Europe, it could not get nine divisions. However, the five divisions in Leyte should be ready for another amphibious operation before the end of 1944; and these, it was thought, would be enough to invade Luzon. The J.C.S. put the landings at Lingayen Bay, Luzon, on the program for 20 December, ordered Admiral Nimitz to invade Iwo Jima on 20 January 1945, and the Ryukyus on 1 March.

It was impossible to keep to this timetable, largely because of the prolonged Japanese resistance on Leyte, and their revived air power with kamikaze tactics. Admiral Kinkaid finally persuaded General MacArthur to postpone Lingayen to 9 January 1945.

Mindoro was considered an essential stepping-stone to Luzon, where Army Engineers could build airfields to help cover Lingayen convoys and landings. Rear Admiral Arthur D. Struble was appointed commander of the Visayan Attack Force, to bring up 12,000 combat troops, 10,000 A.A.F. and 6000 service troops from Leyte Gulf. Everyone knew that this was going to be a bold and dangerous thrust, since a score of Japanese airfields were within easy range of the route to Mindoro. Accordingly an escort carrier group was attached in wide support, as the one means of protecting the convoy during hours when the A.A.F. at Leyte could not be overhead.

The approach from Leyte Gulf was very eventful. Shortly before 1500 December 13, as the convoy was about to round the southern cape of Negros into the Sulu Sea, a kamikaze sneaked in low from astern and crashed cruiser *Nashville* on her port side abaft Admiral Struble's cabin. Fires immediately broke out; flag bridge, combat information center and communications office were wrecked. No fewer than 133 officers and men — including the Admiral's and the commanding General's chiefs of staff — were killed, and 190 were wounded. Two hours later, a kamikaze crashed destroyer *Haraden* and she too had to return to Leyte. For next day the Japanese prepared an attack by 186 planes on the Visayan Attack Force, but missed owing to an assumption that it was aiming to land on Negros or Panay instead of Mindoro.

The mission of Admiral Struble and General Dunckel was to establish a perimeter embracing the village of San José in southwestern Mindoro, there to begin airstrip construction. The landings on 15 December were uneventful, since there were only a few hundred Japanese troops on Mindoro, and none in that part of the island. But an amphibious landing is only the first step in an overseas operation. Supplying the men with food, clothing and matériel is a great effort, especially where, as in Mindoro, an airfield has to be built promptly. The resupply echelons for Mindoro provided the Kamikaze Corps with rich targets for three weeks. The Corps sank three LST en route to Mindoro, two at the beachhead, and five Liberty ships. Not since the Anzio operation had the Navy experienced so much difficulty supporting an amphibious operation after the initial landing.

By Christmas Eve Army P–38s were operating from the new San José airfield. But a Japanese bombardment force commanded by Rear Admiral Kimura, including heavy cruiser *Ashigara,* light cruiser *Oyodo,* and six destroyers, was on its way to break up the landings. This was all that the Japanese Navy could assemble after the destruction it had sustained in the Battle for Leyte Gulf. Admiral Toyoda may have intended to use his new 27,000-ton carrier *Unryu* in this raid, but she did not survive long enough. On 19 December, as she was steaming southerly toward Formosa Strait, submarine *Redfish* intercepted her in the East China Sea in broad daylight, scored two torpedo hits and had the satisfaction of seeing her go down.

Kimura's force was reported on 26 December by a Leyte-based Liberator, and the entire strength of the V A.A.F. at Mindoro — 92 fighters, 13 B–25s and a few P–61s — took the air to meet the enemy. The situation looked much like that in Empress Augusta Bay on the night of 1-2 November 1943, but with no "Tip" Merrill in sight. The only Allied naval vessels near the beachhead were a score of motor torpedo boats under Lieutenant Commander N. Burt Davis, who also had to protect the merchant ships present. Planes and PTs in concert did a beautiful job, diverting the attention of Japanese gunners so that their shore bombardment went wild. *PT–223,* commanded by Lieutenant (jg) Harry E. Griffin USNR, sank the new destroyer *Kiyoshimo,* and both PTs and planes damaged so many other ships that Kimura put about for home in the early hours of 27 December.

Mindoro was a tough little operation from start to finish, because we lacked complete control of the air, but it was well worth the effort. Army air forces based on Mindoro could not waft the Navy into Lingayen Gulf unmolested, but they may well have saved that bloody passage from becoming a mass slaughter.

2. *The Kamikazes and Lingayen Landings,* 1–12 January 1945

What was this Kamikaze Corps, whose sacrificial crashes had already caused so much agony? It was a special air corps organized by Rear Admiral Arima in 1944 to meet a desperate situation for Japanese air power. The air groups of the Imperial Navy had been largely wiped out in the Battle of the Philippine Sea and land-based aircraft too were in short supply. A new tactical situation had been created by the growing competence of American fighter planes at interception, and by the American invention of a proximity-armed fuse for antiaircraft shells. After the United States Navy had been liberally furnished with these fuses, which exploded a shell automatically when near enough to an attacking plane, it became nearly impossible for a conventional bomber to get near enough to a ship to hit her. Hence the Kamikaze Corps. The name (meaning "Heavenly Wind") came from a famous historical event. In 1570 an Emperor of China organized a huge amphibious force for the invasion of Japan, and there was little preparation to resist him. But the gods sent a Heavenly Wind in the shape of a typhoon which scattered and destroyed the Chinese Fleet.

The new tactics for aircraft were to crash an enemy ship, set it on fire by the spread of gasoline, and explode it with the bombs. The pilot had to be expended, but this sort of sacrifice appealed to the Japanese temperament and thousands of young men volunteered for a duty certain to be fatal to themselves, but expectantly fatal to the United States Navy. These tactics had the additional advantage that obsolete types of aircraft, like biplanes and the Val with nonretractable landing gear, could be used; that the pilots needed very little training, and that even if a pilot were killed by a proximity-fused shell before he crashed, the momentum of the plane would usually take it to the target. The first organized kamikaze attack was the one on escort carriers *Santee* and *Suwannee* on 25 October during the Battle off Samar, which we have already related. And, as we have seen, the kamikazes enjoyed considerable success on convoys plying between Leyte Gulf and Mindoro in December 1944. But their full fury was first unleashed against the expedition proceeding to Lingayen, and at the beachhead itself, in early January 1945.

The Luzon Attack Force included most of the ships which had taken part in the Leyte invasion. Vice Admiral Kinkaid commanded it in AGC *Wasatch*, with Lieutenant General Walter Krueger, Commanding General Sixth Army, on board. There were two main amphibious groups, comprising big transport types and beaching craft, commanded respectively by Vice Admiral Barbey and Vice Admiral Wilkinson. Vice Admiral Oldendorf commanded the bombardment and fire support group of battleships, heavy cruisers and destroyers; Rear Admiral Berkey had a close covering group of light cruisers and destroyers; Rear Admiral Durgin (veteran of Operation DRAGOON) the escort carriers; Commander W. R. Loud a minesweeping group of 22 large and 42 small minecraft.

Admiral Oldendorf in battleship *California* took charge of all operations en route to Lingayen Gulf, and until Admiral Kinkaid arrived with the amphibious forces. "Oley" had 6 battleships, 6 cruisers, 19 destroyers, 12 escort carriers screened by 20 destroyers and destroyer escorts, a big minesweeping group, 10 destroyer transports carrying the underwater demolition teams, and 11 LCI gunboats. These made rendezvous at Leyte Gulf on New Year's

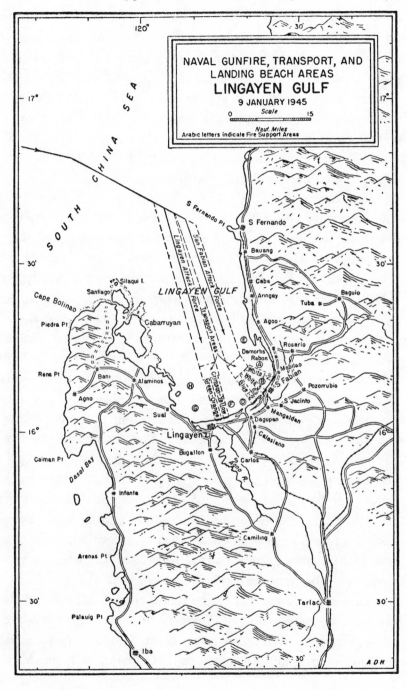

NAVAL GUNFIRE, TRANSPORT, AND
LANDING BEACH AREAS
LINGAYEN GULF
9 JANUARY 1945
Scale
0   15
Naut. Miles
Arabic letters indicate Fire Support Areas

Day, formed cruising disposition, and passed through Surigao Strait, scene of Admiral Oldendorf's recent victory, into the Sulu Sea. Heavy fighter cover from the CVEs and Tacloban knocked down most of the 120 Japanese planes from Luzon committed against this convoy; but, on 4 January, a kamikaze crashed escort carrier *Ommaney Bay* and sank her, with a loss of 100 men. A severe attack of 16-plus kamikazes developed next day. Cruisers *Louisville* and H.M.A.S. *Australia*, escort carrier *Manila Bay* and destroyer escort *Stafford* were crashed, but survived.

The operation plan for the Lingayen landings called for a three-day interval between Oldendorf's arrival and that of the amphibious forces, to allow plenty of time for minesweeping and shore bombardment. These were three hellish days for ships present. At noon 6 January, when battleship *New Mexico* was bombarding the shore, she was crashed on the port wing of her navigating bridge by a Japanese plane already in flames. The C.O., Captain R. W. Fleming, Lieutenant General Herbert Lumsden (Winston Churchill's liaison officer at General MacArthur's headquarters) and his aide, and *Time* magazine correspondent William Chickering, were instantly killed. There were 26 other fatalities and 87 men wounded; but *New Mexico* continued shooting. Destroyer *Walke*, attacked by four planes in rapid succession, knocked down two, but a third crashed the bridge. The C.O., Commander George F. Davis, drenched with the plane's gasoline, burned like a torch. Sailors smothered the flames and he conned his ship, exhorting all to save her; and, still on his feet, saw his guns in local control destroy a fourth kamikaze. Then, when the safety of his ship was assured, he consented to be carried below. But his burns were too terrible to be borne, and a few hours later he died.

Minesweeper *Long* was crashed and sunk; *Southard* and destroyers *Barton* and *Allen M. Sumner* were crashed but survived. *California* took one at the base of her foremast. A kamikaze crashed the main deck of light cruiser *Columbia* (Captain M. E.

Curts) at top speed. Plane, pilot and engine penetrated the deck and the bomb went through two more decks before exploding. Several fires blazed up, but prompt flooding of magazines saved the ship from a major explosion. Within an hour all fires were out, and at 1828 her forward 20-mm gunners shot the tail off a plane trying to crash H.M.A.S. *Australia*. Despite flooded compartments and loss of two main battery turrets, *Columbia* completed her fire support assignments. *Australia* received a crash at 1734, adding another 14 killed and 26 wounded to her already high casualties of the previous day. But, like her neighbor "The Gem of the Ocean," she kept on shooting. Heavy cruiser *Louisville* was too heavily damaged by a crash abreast the bridge structure to do that, and the flag officer on the bridge, Rear Admiral Theodore E. Chandler, was frightfully burned by the flaming gasoline. He helped handle a fire hose and took his turn with the enlisted men for first aid; but as the flames had scorched his lungs every effort to save him failed, and next day he died. Thirty-one shipmates went with him, and 56 more were wounded; but for an ample supply of blood plasma most of those, too, would have perished.

Not only Admiral Oldendorf but all responsible officers off Lingayen were seriously concerned when they contemplated the results of this 6th day of January, three days before the landings. It was the worst blow to the United States Navy since the Battle of Tassafaronga in November 1942, and the more difficult to bear because the recent naval victory at Leyte Gulf had made men believe that Japan was licked. With the kamikazes she had sprung a tactical surprise which would cost the Allied armed forces dear.

Next day, while bombardment and minesweeping continued, was not so bad; but minecrafts *Hovey* and *Palmer* were crashed and sunk. On the 8th, H.M.A.S. *Australia*, favorite target of the kamikazes, took a third and a fourth crash, but still carried on.

The approach of the two amphibious forces, Barbey's for San

Fabian and Wilkinson's for Lingayen, was comparatively uneventful. Seven ships, including cruiser *Boise* with General MacArthur on board, were attacked, Admiral Ofstie's flagship *Kitkun Bay*, was disabled, but none were sunk.

As S-day, 9 January, dawned over Lingayen Bay, ships could be seen in every direction. At 0700 the combatant ships began hurling high explosives at supposed enemy installations. A few minutes after 0700 a kamikaze crashed *Columbia* and added 92 more casualties to her list; but her valiant crew quenched the fires and resumed bombardment half an hour after the hit. The landings were virtually unopposed.

A hot night followed in the Gulf, as the Japanese pulled what we called the suicide boat out of their bag of tricks. Port Sual, protected by a point of land stretching down from the north, was the concealed anchorage for 70 of these 18½-foot plywood motor boats. Each carried two 260-pound depth charges, one light machine gun and a few hand grenades, with a crew of two or three men, to destroy Allied shipping. They managed to sink two LCIs and to damage four LSTs, but were so severely shot up themselves by destroyers *Philip* and *Leutze* and other intended victims as to be incapable of further operations.

The Lingayen landings were a terrible ordeal for all hands, not excepting troops in the transports and other auxiliaries. Here is an extract from the diary of Lieutenant G. R. Cassels-Smith in transport *Harris* for 11 January:

"Two more burials at sea this evening — that makes four who have died so far and there are several more who may die. They are so badly burned or mangled that they are really better off dead. The doctors . . . are always amazed at the remarkable bravery and fortitude of those wounded men. They never complain and are pathetically grateful for everything that is done for them. The enlisted men of the crew are wonderful too. They labor under a terrific strain unloading hundreds of tons of cargo, then stand their watches at the guns all night without sleep, and then donate their blood to the wounded and volunteer their services to help feed the helpless by hand."

On 10 January, convoys began to depart, the Lingayen airstrip was ready for emergency landings, and Rear Admiral Conolly's Reinforcement Group brought up another infantry division. The kamikazes returned on the 12th to damage DE *Belknap* in Lingayen Gulf, and four Liberty ships in a returning convoy. A crash next morning on escort carrier *Salamaua*, which failed to sink her, was the last successful kamikaze attack in Philippine waters. For the Japanese had expended almost every aircraft they had in the Philippines, excepting 47 units which Admiral Fukudome evacuated to Formosa. Ground crews were forced to join the infantry defending Luzon, and surviving pilots flew north as best they could. After 15 January only ten Japanese planes were left on the entire island of Luzon. For the Allies the kamikazes now seemed but a horrible dream. Unfortunately, like other bad dreams, this one was to recur.

3. *Luzon Secured, 13 January–30 June*

Generals MacArthur and Krueger and their staffs went ashore 13 January; and from then on the story of the campaign that captured Manila and all Luzon, except the mountains to which General Yamashita retreated, is largely the Army's story.

Seventh Fleet still had plenty to do. With the help of Halsey, Admiral Kinkaid set out to secure a difficult sea lane, the Mindoro-Lingayen line, upon which the success of the Luzon campaign and the lives of thousands of American soldiers depended. They were unnecessarily anxious about a possible Japanese naval attack on this line, similar to the one on Mindoro in December. The

Japanese Navy was now incapable of anything like that. Nevertheless, Admiral Halsey made a memorable incursion into the South China Sea, with almost his entire Third Fleet, on 10-20 January. It was a bold and beautifully handled operation, underlining the ability of our fast carriers to take fire power anywhere and supply themselves from the floating service force at sea. The sought-for Japanese warships were not there; but TF 38 planes sank 44 vessels, mostly of the merchant marine, totaling 132,700 tons. Very few of our own planes were lost. The carrier planes took another crack at Formosa on their way out; and here the kamikazes again showed their hands, crashing but not sinking *Langley*, *Ticonderoga* and a destroyer.

Third Fleet support of the Luzon campaign is impressive. During January some 300,000 tons of enemy shipping was sunk or destroyed, and the number of aircraft destroyed exceeded 500. The cost to the United States was 201 carrier aircraft, 167 pilots and aircrewmen, and 205 sailors who were killed in the kamikaze crashes of 21 January. As Halsey wrote, "The outer defenses of the Japanese Empire no longer include Burma and the Netherlands East Indies; those countries are now isolated outposts, and their products are no longer available to the Japanese war machine except with staggering and prohibitive losses en route." In *New Jersey* he arrived at Ulithi on the afternoon of 25 January and two days later Admiral Spruance assumed command of the Fleet, which under him was numbered the Fifth. He had a wonderful reputation to live up to, and that he did.

On 12 January 1945 MacArthur, now a five-star General of the Army, called Admirals Kinkaid and Wilkinson and General Krueger to a conference on board *Boise*, off the beachhead. He stressed the urgency of occupying Manila as early as possible in order to free the Allied prisoners and internees, who were slowly starving to death. He emphasized that our losses so far had been small and predicted that the enemy would evacuate Manila rather

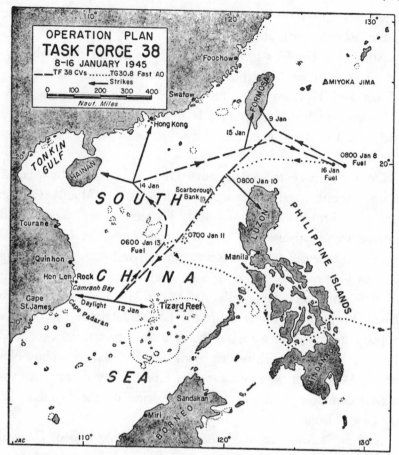

OPERATION PLAN
TASK FORCE 38
8-16 JANUARY 1945
—— TF 38 CVs ········TG30.8 Fast AO
◄── Strikes

0   100   200   300   400
Naut. Miles

than defend it. Such indeed was General Yamashita's intention, but his orders were not carried out.

The advance on Manila was slow; by 29 January, after two weeks' progress, XIV Corps had only reached San Fernando. The Navy then lent a hand by landing XI Corps on beaches forty-five miles across the mountains from that town; a landing formidable in size, but uncontested. Admiral Struble was pleased to find the area already in friendly hands, with American and Philippine flags displayed by the natives. Indeed, everywhere in the Philippines the Americans were received as liberators and with touchingly enthusiastic demonstrations.

Admiral Fechteler's group of VII 'Phib landed the 11th Airborne Division at Nasugbu, Batangas Province, on the last day of January. This operation was ordered by the General to establish a line of advance on Manila from the southwest. Except for a little trouble from Japanese midget torpedo boats, it was uncontested.

On 1 February the 1st Cavalry Division, covered by Marine Corps aircraft, spearheaded a XIV Corps dash to Manila. On the 3rd they broke into the suburbs, liberating over 5000 Allied internees and prisoners of war. General Yamashita had ordered Manila to be evacuated, but Rear Admiral Iwabachi, commanding a naval base there of 20,000 troops, declined to obey and fought to the bitter end, fanatically defending Manila from house to house. In this month-long battle the Japanese defense forces were wiped out almost to a man; but the beautiful city was wrecked, and Intramuros, the Spanish walled town, was reduced to rubble. Not until 4 March was the city cleared of Japanese. By that time it was a more complete picture of destruction than Cologne, Hamburg or the City of London.

At least it was free. Even before the fighting ended, General MacArthur caused a provisional assembly of Filipino notables to be summoned to Malacañan Place — where his father, General Arthur MacArthur, had lived when military governor — and in their presence declared the Commonwealth of the Philippines to be permanently reëstablished. "My country has kept the faith," he said; "your capital city, cruelly punished though it be, has regained its rightful place — citadel of democracy in the East."

There were still about 1400 Japanese troops on Bataan and 5000 on "The Rock," Corregidor. It took a shore-to-shore amphibious operation from Subic Bay, under Admiral Struble, to take Mariveles (15 February) against considerable opposition, and a parachute drop next day to get a foothold on Corregidor. The Japanese there used a maze of tunnels and caves and had to be dug out or sealed in. For ten days, Desdiv 46 (Captain R. W. Cavenagh in *Converse*) kept two ships on station to support the troops ashore. The destroyers moved in to half a mile from the beach, and, spotted from ashore, shot up pillboxes and fired directly into the mouths of caves full of Japanese. "We were so close," wrote the division commander, "that we could see the Japs get up and run between salvos." By 26 February The Rock was again in American hands, and General MacArthur on 2 March presided over an impressive flag-raising on the island, which he had left under such different circumstances almost three years earlier. Caballo Island held out until 15 April.

Since 9 March Commodore William A. Sullivan had been working on the problem of clearing Manila Harbor of hundreds of sunken ships. He had done this for at least five harbors in Europe, but Manila was the worst, the Japanese being more efficient demolitioners than the Germans. With the aid of the Army Engineers' Special Brigade, two battalions of Seabees, and several salvage ships and minecraft, Sullivan raised some wrecks, destroyed others, and, for future action, buoyed many more. Minesweepers *Scuffle* and *Cable*, with 15 YMS under Lieutenant Eric A. Johnson USNR, worked the harbor and bay; they swept 615 square miles of water and destroyed 584 mines. By 1 May, 350 of the sunken vessels had been removed and the waterfront was progressively cleared until, in mid-August, 24 Liberty ships could berth simultaneously.

For Sixth Army the campaign for the liberation of Luzon had lasted 173 days, during which it lost 8297 killed or missing and had 29,557 wounded. Losses to the U.S. and Australian Navies in the Luzon campaign, mostly due to kamikaze attack, were more than 2000. On 30 June General Eichelberger's Eighth Army took over from Krueger's Sixth the mission of destroying the rest of the

Japanese troops, holed up in the mountains. General Yamashita and about 50,500 men finally surrendered after the close of hostilities on 15 August.

4. *Liberation of the Central and Southern Philippines, 28 February–22 July*

General of the Army Douglas MacArthur was not satisfied with the liberation of Leyte, Samar and Luzon. He felt obligated to expel the enemy from the entire Archipelago. His plan of February 1945 envisaged two series of operations: the Visayas and Mindanao, to be liberated by Seventh Fleet and Eighth Army; Borneo and Java to be liberated by Seventh Fleet and the Australian Army.

The Joint Chiefs of Staff did not see eye to eye with the General in these plans. At the Yalta Conference in February 1945, General Marshall told the British that he did not contemplate employing major United States forces to mop up in the Philippines or the Dutch islands; he assumed that the Filipino guerillas and the newly activated Army of the Philippine Commonwealth could take care of the rest of their country, and that Anglo-Australian forces would cover the N.E.I. But, as Seventh Fleet and Eighth Army were not required for the invasion of Iwo Jima and Okinawa, the J.C.S. simply permitted MacArthur to do as he chose, up to a point.

Herein strategic mistakes were made both by MacArthur and the J.C.S. The General could, as it turned out, have used his leapfrog strategy to bypass the Visayas and Mindanao. The Filipinos in these islands were not suffering greatly at the hands of the Japanese garrisons, which were now cut off from reinforcement and would have surrendered anyway at the end of the war. The forces used to liberate the Visayas and Mindanao could have been thrown immediately into Java and Sumatra, where the Dutch colonists were suffering acutely and the Japanese were cannily nourishing Sukarno's independence movement. Even if General MacArthur did not choose to put the Netherlands East Indies first, the J.C.S. should have found him the necessary shipping when he did propose to do it. But nobody then expected the Pacific war to end with a big bang in August.

At the Quebec Conference of September 1944, the Combined Chiefs of Staff predicted that it would take eighteen months after the defeat of Germany to procure the unconditional surrender of Japan. Actually it took only a little more than three months. It was assumed that we would have to invade Kyushu in October, Honshu in January 1946, and then fight the Japanese on their own soil; so there would be plenty of time to liberate Indonesia. MacArthur presented to the C.C.S. in February 1945 a plan to do it in June. But the C.C.S. fiddled around with this plan until August, when it was too late; MacArthur then had all he could attend to with the occupation of Japan. Not until a full month after the surrender did Allied warships even put in at Batavia (renamed Jakarta), and in the meantime the country was given over to rabid nationalists who, unlike the Filipinos, had no training in self-government.

It may also be observed that Admiral Lord Mountbatten, the Allied commander in Southeast Asia, was ready and eager to liberate Indonesia early in 1945, but could not get at it while the Japanese controlled Singapore and the Strait of Malacca. Admiral King was eager to have Admiral Sir Bruce Fraser's Pacific Fleet help MacArthur and the Australians do the job, but this was vetoed by Churchill. For prestige reasons he wanted the Royal Navy to be "in at the death" of Japan, alongside the United States Navy. That it was, and very helpfully too; but King had the right idea. It was far more important for the future to liberate Indonesia and set up a stable government there before the war's end than to help American forces to capture Okinawa and bombard Japan.

Amphibious operations in the Southern Philippines and Borneo were conducted by General Eichelberger's Eighth Army, and by Rear Admiral Barbey's VII 'Phib. They followed the pattern established in 1944 — preliminary air bombing and naval bombardment, assault troops landing from APDs and beaching craft, Japanese retiring to the jungle and having to be rooted out. VII 'Phib by this time had been divided into groups, of which the 8th, commanded in succession by Rear Admirals W. M. Fechteler and Albert G. Noble; the 6th, commanded by Rear Admiral Forrest B. Royal; and the 9th, commanded by Rear Admiral Struble, did most of the work. Rear Admirals Berkey and Ralph S. Riggs commanded the covering and support groups, comprising two or three light cruisers such as *Denver*, *Phoenix*, H.M.A.S. *Ho-*

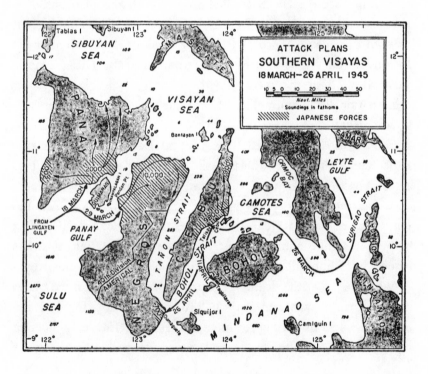

ATTACK PLANS
SOUTHERN VISAYAS
18 MARCH–26 APRIL 1945

Naut. Miles
Soundings in fathoms
JAPANESE FORCES

bart, and a number of destroyers. Motor torpedo boats also were very active and useful. The Japanese were able to commit but few and ineffective air forces, from the Netherlands East Indies and Malaya, and no kamikazes; hence these assaults were relatively easy. Rooting out the Japanese defenders from the mountains and jungles was another matter — that cost Eighth Army thousands of casualties.

These ten Southern Philippines and Borneo operations may be represented briefly in tabular form: —

SUMMARY OF OPERATIONS IN SOUTHERN PHILIPPINES AND BORNEO,
1945

Target	D-day 1945	Major Units Engaged		Commanders			Objective Secured 1945
		Naval	Military	Naval Attack Group	Covering Group	Military	
Palawan	28 Feb.	8th 'Phib Group	41st Div.	Fechteler	Riggs	Haney	22 April
Zamboanga	10 Mar.	6th 'Phib Group	41st Div.	Royal	Riggs	Doe	15 August
Panay, W. Negros	18 Mar.	9th 'Phib Group	40th Div.	Struble	Riggs	Brush	4 June
Cebu	26 Mar.	TG 78.2	Americal	Sprague	Berkey	Arnold	18 April
Bohol	11 Apr.	TU 78.3.3	164th Inf.	Deutermann	none	Arnold	20 April
S.E. Negros	26 Apr.	TU 78.3.3	164th Inf.	Deutermann	none	Arnold	12 June
Mindanao	17 Apr.	8th 'Phib Group	X Corps	Noble	Riggs	Sibert	15 Aug.
Tarakan	1 May	TG 78.1	Aus. I Corps	Royal	Berkey	Morshead	30 May
Brunei Bay	10 June	TG 78.1	9th Aus. Div.	Royal	Berkey	Wootten	1 July
Balikpapan	1 July	8th 'Phib Group	7th Aus. Div.	Noble	Riggs	Milford	22 July

5. *Submarine Operations, 1942–1943*

The United States submarine was destined to be one of the most devastating weapons in the Pacific. General Tojo, after the war, said that the destruction of her merchant marine was one of three factors that defeated Japan, the other two being leapfrog strategy and fast carrier operations. We have already noted the principal instances in which submarines supported the Fleet — especially in the Battles of Midway and of the Philippine Sea — but have said little about their steady, unremitting attrition of the enemy merchant marine. Nearly one third of all Japanese combatant ships destroyed and nearly two thirds of merchant tonnage sunk was the work of United States submarines.

These operated under Commander Submarines Pacific Fleet at Pearl Harbor, and Commander Submarines Southwest Pacific at Fremantle and Brisbane, Australia. Comsubpac, during the greater part of the war, was Vice Admiral Charles A. Lockwood; his opposite numbers were Captain John Wilkes, and Rear Admiral Ralph W. Christie from March 1943. Each exercised full administrative control, but only a limited operational control over his boats[1] once they were committed to an operation. The admirals did not attempt to carry on daily conversations with their boats over radio as Grossadmiral Doenitz did with his U-boats; partly because they wished to give the skippers maximum initiative, and partly because radio transmissions are apt to help the enemy locate a submarine. The submarine service was almost a navy in itself, manned exclusively by volunteers and commanded by ambitious and intelligent young officers.

The American concept of submarine operation, dictated by our few and far-between bases, required that they be capable of self-sustained cruising for long periods over great distances. We had nothing resembling the German milch cows. Thus the Navy entered the war with a preponderance of large fleet-type submarines, of greater endurance, reliability and comfort than the smaller types favored by European powers. These rugged vessels displaced in the neighborhood of 1500 tons. Variations from this mean tonnage were the older and smaller S-boats of 800 to 1100 tons, which were mostly retired by late 1943, and *Argonaut, Narwhal* and *Nautilus*, which ran up to 2700 tons' displacement. The average fleet-type submarine was manned by a crew of 7 officers and 70 men. It had a cruising range of 10,000 miles and carried supplies for 60 days. Surface speed was 20 knots; submerged speed 9 knots. Underwater

---

[1] United States submarines are traditionally referred to as "boats," not "ships," supposedly because the original ones were only boat size.

endurance at 2½ knots was 48 hours. Power on the surface was derived from a diesel-electric engine and motor combination; storage batteries furnished juice to the electric motors when submerged. During 1942 the installation of both air-search and surface-search radars greatly increased the effectiveness of American submarines. Their initial armament consisted of six to ten 21-inch torpedo tubes, one 3-inch 50-caliber deck gun and two .50-caliber machine guns — more deck guns were added later. About 18 spare torpedoes were carried. Initially all torpedoes were propelled by turbines, operated by hot gases resulting from the combustion of a jet of alcohol and compressed air mixed with steam. Later in the war, electric torpedoes, valuable for the absence of the tell-tale wake, were introduced. The warheads were loaded with TNT, later with the more powerful torpex, and were supposed to detonate whether the torpedo struck a target or passed close to the magnetic field of a metallic hull.

Unfortunately, for reasons explained in Chapter I, American torpedoes at the beginning of the war had grave defects in the depth-control mechanism and the exploder. These did not come to light until the war was well along. The first defect caused the torpedo to run ten feet deeper than set, usually so far under a ship's hull that the magnetic feature was not activated. The contact exploder was a detonating mechanism fitted into the warhead before launching. Its firing pin, supposed to function under physical impact, proved too fragile to stand up under a good, square, 90-degree hit; normally it would set off the charge only if the warhead hit a ship at an acute angle. Thus, the best shooting was rewarded by duds, and submarines returned from war patrols with sad tales of hearing as many as nine torpedoes go bang against the hull of a Japanese ship, without a single one exploding. Admiral Nimitz in June 1943 ordered the magnetic mechanism to be used no longer; and Admiral Lockwood, by conducting a series of tests with torpedoes against the cliffs of Kohoolawe Island, found out what the trouble was with the exploder and fitted stouter firing pins. But it was not until September 1943 that United States submarines had dependable torpedoes.

Before the war, United States and Japanese doctrine of submarine employment was identical — to use the boats primarily to destroy enemy warships. In practice the United States Navy, apart from special missions and supporting a fleet offensive, employed its boats as the Germans did, to reduce the enemy merchant marine. But the Japanese I-boats, which were as big as ours and almost as numerous initially, and which mounted far more powerful torpedoes, rigidly concentrated on sinking enemy warships. They were fairly successful at this in 1942, as we have seen; but as American antisubmarine doctrine improved they seldom got in a shot. For instance, the 16 Japanese submarines which were deployed before and during the Battle of Leyte Gulf managed to sink but one vessel, a destroyer escort. And much of Japan's submarine potential was wastefully diverted to special missions. They made long cruises to conduct nuisance bombardments, as on Midway, Johnston and Canton Islands and (in 1942) the coasts of Vancouver Island and Oregon. They carried scouting aircraft great distances to make reconnaissance flights of no value. But the mortal blow to a successful undersea war was the Japanese Army's discovery that submarines were useful to carry supplies to bypassed garrisons. Thenceforth more and more were pulled off patrols to serve isolated Army garrisons with rice and bullets. By 1943 the United States Navy was able to stop convoying merchant ships in the Pacific and employ escort vessels to better purpose.[2]

Equally strange, and verging on the idiotic, was Japan's failure as an island nation to protect her own merchant marine lifeline. This can be explained only by the assumption that the Japanese

[2] According to Masanori Ito *The End of the Imperial Japanese Navy* (1962) p. 182, Japan had 64 submarines in Dec. 1941 and built 126 during the war, but by the time of the Battle for Leyte Gulf she had only 32 operational. These figures do not include midgets.

war lords refused to face the fact that they might have to wage a defensive war. By the same token, the Japanese Navy in 1942-43 decided to construct twenty aircraft carriers, which are of no use in defensive strategy, and to convert a *Yamato* class battleship hull to the super-carrier *Shinano*. From the same materials they could have built hundreds of destroyers and smaller escort vessels. Not until the end of 1943 was an escort fleet organized, and it never amounted to much. The Japanese ended the war with the same antisubmarine equipment that they had at the beginning — not very accurate depth charges and aircraft bombs; and they never solved the largely mathematical problem of where to drop a depth charge to do damage. They had no method of assessing anti-submarine attacks, and smugly assumed that they were sinking a United States submarine whenever they attacked one. They did manage to sink a good many, as our chart indicates, but never enough to win.

The changing pattern of submarine tactics was illustrated by *Tarpon*'s cruise. Near Tokyo Bay on the night of 1 February 1943, she picked up a radar contact, ran it down on the surface and sank an 11,000-ton *Maru* without using her periscope. In darkness on the 8th she picked up a radar contact, chased it on the surface, and using radar ranges and periscope sighting put four hits into 17,000-ton *Tatsuta Maru*, and that pride of the Japanese merchant marine went to the bottom.

For the entire year 1943 the score by United States submarines in the Pacific was 22 warships and 296 *Marus*, the merchant loss amounting to 1,335,240 gross tons. Since Japanese shipyards had produced a little over half a million tons of new shipping in 1943 and captured or salvaged about 100,000 tons more, the net loss was 718,000 tons. The United States Submarine Force that year lost 15 boats and 1129 officers and men, a heavy toll indeed; yet the three submarine commands in the Pacific, based at Pearl Harbor, Brisbane and Fremantle, had 75 boats on their rolls on New

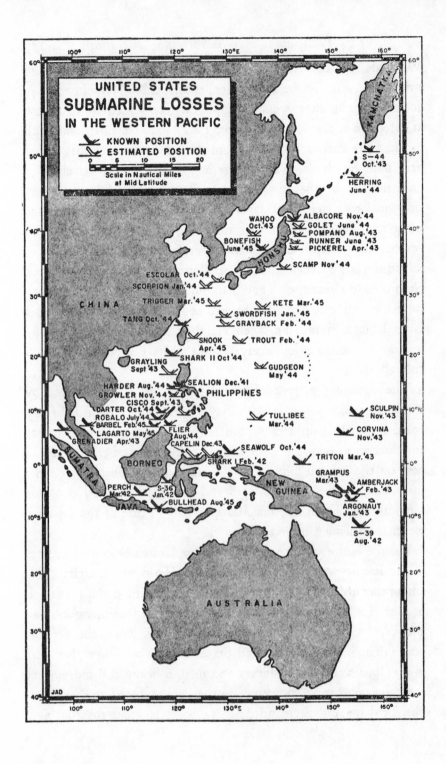

Year's Day 1944, as against 53 on 1 January 1943. And these 75 were almost all fleet submarines, as most of the aged S-boats had been retired to training centers. In the same twelvemonth, Japan lost 23 submarines.

General MacArthur kept contact with Filipino guerillas and unsurrendered members of his army, by Fremantle-based submarines. During the period 8 February 1943 to 5 March 1944, 19 such missions were performed, seven by the big 2700-ton *Narwhal*, which was especially assigned to this work, and others by fleet submarines. These carried important contact men, such as Lieutenant Commander C. Parsons, to the guerillas, together with arms, money, munitions, radio sets and miscellaneous supplies. *Narwhal* on one voyage took 90 tons to Mindanao and Samar and, on another, evacuated 32 civilians from Panay. These missions were of inestimable value in obtaining intelligence of enemy ship and troop movements, supplying guerilla forces with munitions and medicaments, and counteracting Japanese propaganda to the effect that America had forgotten the Philippines.

In May 1943 *Tautog* received a special assignment to land two pro-Allied Javanese agents on the Celebes. Both were pious Mohammedans, which created difficulties not anticipated by the *Submarine Officer's Manual*. Spam, ice cream, fried eggs and other staple submariners' food were tabu; canned tuna fish and salmon had to be provided; and the navigator acquired a new duty of giving his passengers four times daily the course for Mecca. Thus history came full circle; for the science of celestial navigation evolved from this necessity that all Sons of the Prophet were under, to project their prayers in the right direction.

The vicissitudes of a submariner's life are illustrated by the loss of *Sculpin* (Commander Fred Connaway), which was stationed between Truk and Ponape during the Gilberts operation to report Japanese fleet movements. On the night of 18-19 November 1943

Sculpin sighted a fast enemy convoy and at dawn attempted to attack it, submerged, but was detected and forced deep. When she surfaced an hour later, she was immediately forced down and depth-charged by destroyer *Yamagumo*. When the diving officer tried to bring her to periscope depth the depth gauge stuck at 125 feet and *Sculpin* broached. As *Yamagumo* roared in to attack, the submarine dove deep but 18 depth charges followed her down. The explosions threw the boat out of control, distorted her pressure hull, started leaks, jammed her rudders and diving planes. As a desperate expedient Commander Connaway ordered, "Blow all ballast!" and then, as *Sculpin* rose from the depths, gave the signal for gunfire action: "Battle Surface!" *Sculpin*'s one 4-inch and two 20-mm guns had no chance to fight off a Japanese destroyer with six 5.1-inch guns, torpedo tubes and numerous automatic weapons. She took one lethal hit in the main induction valves. A second, penetrating the conning tower, killed the C.O., his exec., and the gunnery officer. The senior surviving officer ordered Abandon Ship. All vents were opened and *Sculpin* dove for the last time. Captain John P. Cromwell, a passenger on board, and a dozen others rode her down, Cromwell deliberately sacrificing his life because he was familiar with operation plans and feared lest information be extorted from him by torture. Forty-two of *Sculpin*'s crew were picked up by *Yamagumo* and with the exception of one wounded man, who was thrown overboard, were taken to Truk, where they were transferred to escort carriers *Chuyo* and *Unyo*. En route to Japan *Chuyo* fell victim to a torpedo attack by United States submarine *Sailfish,* and only one of the prisoners survived. He and 20 prisoners in *Unyo* were forced to work in the copper mines at Ashio until released at the end of the war.

6. *Submarine Operations, 1944–1945*

On 1 January 1944 the Japanese still had 300,000 more tanker tonnage than on 7 December 1941; United States submarines made a special effort to correct this. That month eight more enemy tankers were downed, one to a Navy carrier plane and the other seven to submarines. Greater misfortunes overtook the Japanese oiler fleet next month. The 17 February carrier strike on Truk put five tankers totaling 52,183 tons under the surface; and then along came submarine *Jack* (Commander Thomas M. Dykers), "Jack the Tanker Killer," as she was known in the submarine fleet. In the South China Sea at 0338 February 19, Dykers made a radar contact on an enemy convoy of five tankers and three escorts. In a series of attacks that lasted all day and almost until midnight *Jack* sank four of them, totaling over 20,000 tons.

Grayback (Commander John A. Moore), patrolling between Luzon and Formosa, was lost with all hands on 27 February 1944 after sinking 11,500 more tons of shipping. Probably an enemy plane was responsible. *Trout*, the veteran boat which had carried gold out of Corregidor early in the war, was on her eleventh patrol with Lieutenant Commander Albert H. Clark as skipper when, on 29 February, SSE of Okinawa, she picked up a Japanese convoy carrying troops from Korea to reinforce the Marianas. She damaged a new 11,500-ton transport and sank a 9245-tonner which contained 4124 troops and a crew of 105, half of whom went down with the ship. In the flurry of depth-charge attacks that followed, *Trout* was lost with all hands.

Sandlance (Commander Malcolm E. Garrison) on her maiden voyage patrolled in rough waters. En route Pearl Harbor to the Aleutians in February 1944, she encountered two tempests within four days and, when surfaced, quickly became sheathed in ice, which she could slough off only by submerging. Arriving on station off Paramushiro 24 February, *Sandlance* found herself completely surrounded by drift ice. The temperature dropped so that the sea water froze over the periscope in a film of ice. Despite these difficulties, Commander Garrison conned his boat along the Kuriles and Hokkaido, knocking off a freighter on 28 February and another on 3 March, evading all attacks by patrol craft and planes. Eventually he entered the Japan current, and water temperature promptly rose from barely freezing to 70° F. *Sandlance* passed Honshu and down along the Bonins. During the midwatch 13 March, when his sound operator reported echoes, Garrison brought his boat to periscope depth to view a "sight beautiful to behold — worth the past four weeks of battling typhoons, blizzards and ice-fields. We were completely surrounded by ships." He had run into a second Marianas-bound Japanese reinforcement convoy. A full moon enabled him to select the best targets, light cruiser *Tatsuta* and a large freighter. At 0310 *Sandlance* shot two torpedoes at each, then swung 180 degrees and fired her last two "fish" at a second *Maru*. In a jiffy she was surrounded by wildly depth-charging escorts which could not locate her. Garrison coolly kept his boat at periscope depth for 15 minutes to watch developments. In that time he observed that *Tatsuta* was sinking and that the first *Maru* was burning, decks awash; and he saw the victim of his Parthian shot go down rapidly, bow first. The destroyers then forced him down and kept him down for 18½ hours; after which, with all torpedoes expended, *Sandlance* shaped a course to Pearl Harbor, where Pacific Fleet submariners enjoyed a little recreation between patrols.

By April 1944 the scorekeepers in Washington concluded that the Japanese Navy must be getting short of destroyers, since it had lost 64, and few new ones had been built. Admiral King decided that it was time to decrease the small number left. On 13 April he issued an order to Pacific Fleet submarines to give enemy destroyers No. 2 priority as targets, after capital ships but ahead of transports, tankers and freighters.

United States submariners hardly needed this to persuade them to turn on their traditional enemies. *Albacore* had already sunk *Sazanami; Skipjack* had sunk *Suzukaze* in January; *Guardfish* put *Umikaze* down for keeps and *Pogy* sank *Minekaze* in the East China Sea in February; *Tautog* sank *Shirakumo* off Hokkaido 16 March and *Redfin* disposed of *Akigumo* in April, all before Admiral King issued his order. And the very day that he did, *Harder* (Commander Samuel D. Dealey), after a long duel with *Ikazuchi* off the Marianas, was able to add another good phrase to the book of traditional United States Navy sayings: "Range 900 yards. Commenced firing. Expended four torpedoes and one Jap Destroyer."

In the meantime Rear Admiral Christie's Southwest Pacific submarines, based at Fremantle, were finding good hunting in the Sulu and Celebes Seas. A convoy carrying an infantry division to reinforce the Japanese positions on the Vogelkop lost three transports to *Gurnard* (Commander Charles H. Andrews), and thousands of soldiers were drowned; this discouraged the relief of Biak. *Lapon* and *Raton* made a good bag in the South China Sea in May, 1944. *Rasher* (Commander Henry G. Munson) hit the jackpot on 18 August, sinking escort carrier *Taiyo*, which had been used to furnish C.A.P. for the big battleships.

Southwest Pacific submarines continued to keep Filipino guerillas informed and supplied, evacuating marooned Americans and endangered Filipinos on the return passage. *Angler* (Lieutenant Commander R. I. Olsen) was ordered to rescue "about 20" Filipinos, on whom the Japanese were closing, from a point on the coast of Panay. When Olsen surfaced off the rendezvous on 20 March 1944, he was informed that 58 men, women and children had been assigned to him as passengers. After hiding from the Japanese in the jungle for over two years, many of these unfortunate people were sick and all were undernourished, dirty and lousy; many had tropical ulcers and one woman was expecting a baby. But a submariner is never nonplussed. The entire crew of *Angler*, during the 12-day run to Darwin, was berthed in the after-battery compartment, male passengers in the forward torpedo room, and women and children in the after torpedo room. It was on this passage that the bluejackets felt that they had "seen everything" when a nursing mother, after smoking a large cigar while nursing her infant, let the suckling take a few drags at it, after he had finished feeding. Food had to be strictly rationed, but all passengers were landed without a casualty.

In June 1944, when the Battle of the Philippine Sea was over, more submarines were released for the pursuit of Japanese merchant shipping, and the area which Comsubpac named "Convoy College" — extending across the East China Sea from Luzon Strait to Formosa and the coast of China — became the scene of great destruction. The "Mickey Finns" (*Guardfish, Piranha, Thresher,* and *Apogon*), a wolf-pack under command of Captain W. V. O'Regan, were the first "freshmen" to cross this watery campus, and their five-day semester cost the Japanese some 41,000 more tons of merchant shipping.

A night battle fought in Luzon Strait during the early hours of 31 July 1944, between *Steelhead, Parche* and *Hammerhead* and a big convoy, accounted for a tanker, two transports and two passenger-cargo ships, totaling over 39,000 tons. By this time, Saipan being secured, tender *Holland* moved up there to afford the submarines a forward fueling and repair base 3600 miles west of Pearl Harbor. With hunting grounds restricted by the westward advance of American sea power, and Japanese shipping accordingly canalized to the narrow seas, convoys became larger and hunting more profitable.

The first day of September found Subpac boats vigorously and successfully combing waters around Formosa. Captain E. R. Swinburne's wolf-pack, *Barb, Tunny* and *Queenfish*, was enjoying a profitable term in Convoy College, whose campus extended from Pratas Reef south to Swatow through Luzon Strait to long. 130° East. A transport, a 10,000-ton tanker and a destroyer escort fell to their bag. Commander G. R. Donaho's pack, consisting of *Picuda*, *Redfish* and *Spadefish*, on 8 September, east of Formosa, sank three or four merchant ships out of a single convoy. By the time Donaho had concluded his patrol, on 21 September, he had eliminated 64,456 tons of enemy shipping, the highest wolf-pack score so far. A third wolf-pack in this scholarly area during September was Commander T. B. Oakley's: *Growler*, *Pampanito* and *Sealion II*. During the night of 11-12 September they picked up a Singapore-Japan convoy of nine ships with seven escorts, about halfway between Hainan and Cape Bojeador, Luzon. After *Growler* had blown up frigate *Hirado*, *Sealion* at 0524 torpedoed three ships, one of which, unfortunately, had on board 1350 English and Australian prisoners of war. In the meantime *Growler* at 0653 sank destroyer *Shikinami*, after which the convoy turned and fled toward Hong Kong. But *Pampanito* hung on all day 12 September and at 2240 sank a tanker and 10,509-ton *Kachidoki Maru*, in which were 750 prisoners. The Japanese escorts picked up their own survivors next day but left the prisoners struggling in the water. Many managed to survive by clinging to wreckage, and some were rescued by the submarines.

In October 1944, 68 United States submarines sank 320,906 tons of Japanese merchant shipping, the highest monthly score of the war; and almost one third of it consisted of tankers. In November 214,506 more tons were sunk.

In early October, a bold raid into the Formosa Channel was performed by Commander Richard H. O'Kane in U.S.S. *Tang*. This was her fifth war patrol. After safely weathering a typhoon on 6 October, *Tang* threaded an enemy mine field between Formosa and the Sakashima Gunto and passed close aboard the northern extremity of Formosa. At 0400 October 11, she finished off her first victim, a small, heavily loaded diesel freighter. That night, close to the shore, another small freighter was sunk. *Tang* now steered for Turnabout Island off Haitan, the landmark where, for thousands of years, shipping northbound through Formosa Strait had changed course for Foochow. Shortly after midnight 23-24 October a convoy for the Philippines — four deeply laden freighters carrying planes, a transport with crated planes piled high on deck, a destroyer, and several small escort vessels — headed right for *Tang*. O'Kane maneuvered his boat inside the screen to a firing position where the ships seemed to overlap, bow and stern, on both sides of her. In a few minutes three freighters were floating torches. The unhit freighter and the transport promptly converged on *Tang* with intent to ram.

Tang, under a shower of small-arms fire, slipped between the converging stems of these two ships and had the humorous satisfaction of seeing them collide after she had escaped. O'Kane headed north to relax for a few hours, surfaced before dawn 24 October, then turned in again toward Turnabout.

After dark, the biggest convoy anyone on board had ever seen was tracked close to the jagged coast of Fukien; and, as *Tang* closed, the Japanese escort commander obligingly illuminated his charges with a large searchlight, revealing two big transports and several tankers. These O'Kane selected as preferred targets, and sank one. *Tang* then turned to fire three stern torpedoes at a tanker astern of the first victim, at ranges of 600-700 yards. The tanker was nicely hit and blew up, scattering burning gasoline over the Formosa Channel.

After putting five miles between himself and the milling escorts, O'Kane slowed down to check his two remaining torpedoes. Both appeared to be in order, so *Tang* returned to the scene of her recent exploits to fire her 23rd and 24th torpedoes. The last, launched at about 0200 October 25, broached, porpoised, reversed course, and within half a minute struck the submarine abreast her after torpedo room, and exploded. *Tang* immediately sank by the stern and hit the bottom 30 fathoms down. Sailors in the control room succeeded in closing the conning tower hatch, leveled off the boat by flooding tanks, and destroyed secret publications by burning. Thirty officers and men reached an escape position in the forward torpedo room, where smoke from the burning documents as well as lack of oxygen knocked half of them out. Enemy escorts were depth-charging all about but failed to discover the motionless sunken boat. At 0600 October 25 thirteen men, the only ones still strong enough to make the attempt, started leaving the escape trunk. Eight reached the surface through 160 feet of water. Five of them, together with O'Kane, an officer and two sailors who floated off topside when she sank, were the sole survivors. These men were picked up by an escort vessel and given fairly good treatment, according to Japanese standards. They were liberated at the close of the war.

Bold fight-back tactics saved *Salmon* of Commander Harlfinger's pack from becoming a victim of enemy escorts off the southern cape of Kyushu on the night of 30 October. After she had sent two torpedoes into a tanker, four screening Japanese frigates forced her down, depth charges damaged her hull, and sent clocks, gauges and other detachable objects hurtling about her compartments. Commander H. K. Nauman decided that his only chance was to fight it out with gunfire. Surfacing at 2030, *Salmon* enjoyed a precious respite which gave the skipper and crew time to correct her list, plug holes, pump bilges and get the engines turning up 16 knots. Around 2200 one Japanese frigate began jabbing at *Salmon* like a dog attacking a bear, closing repeatedly to bark and retire. After this had happened several times, and the other frigates began to show signs of closing, Commander Nauman felt ready to take the offensive. *Salmon* attacked the frigate that had been dogging her, passing parallel on opposite course only 50 yards distant, raking topsides clear, knocking all the fight out of the Japanese and scaring away the other escorts. She then ducked into a rain squall, repaired battle damage, and made Saipan safely.

American submarines hotly pursued enemy shipping in November, but found fewer targets. The enemy had become more wary. Singapore-Japan convoys no longer followed the west coast of Luzon but hugged the western shore of the South China Sea, even as close as a mile or two. This month, however, brought rich increase in the bag of combatant ships. Four submarines dogged a big convoy carrying an infantry regiment from Manchuria to Luzon, sinking two troop-filled transports; then (by *Picuda*, Commander O. O. Underwood) escort carrier *Jinyo*. *Sealion II* (Commander G. T. Reich) sank destroyer *Urakaze* and tough old battleship *Kongo* north of Formosa.

Archerfish (Commander J. F. Enright) made the biggest single kill of the submarine war on 29 November: the new 59,000-ton carrier *Shinano*. This leviathan, converted from a *Yamato*-class battleship hull, had taken over four years to build. Provided with a 30-cm thick steel flight deck over a layer of concrete, she should have survived any amount of bombing, and her compartmentation was so complete that she was supposed to be unsinkable. Screened by three destroyers, *Shinano* sailed from Tokyo Bay on her maiden cruise at 1800 November 28. Only two hours later, Enright made radar contact and dogged her, making 20 knots, until 0300 when she presented a perfect target at 1400 yards' range. *Archerfish* launched six torpedoes, four of which exploded on the carrier, whose skipper, believing her unsinkable, maintained speed and course for some eight hours. She then rolled over and sank, taking down most of her crew. *Shinano* was surely the shortest-lived big warship in history.

On 9 December at 0134 *Redfish* (Commander L. D. McGregor), west of Kyushu, got two hits on 24,000-ton carrier *Junyo*. She was the carrier whose planes had bombed Dutch Harbor in

1942, and damaged battleship *South Dakota* in the Battle of the Santa Cruz Islands, and which had survived the Battle of the Philippine Sea. She was now so badly damaged as to be out of the war. *Redfish* was really in the money; on 19 December she had a crack at another carrier, new 17,500-ton *Unryu*, escorted by three destroyers. The group conveniently zigged toward *Redfish*, which at 1635 fired a spread of four torpedoes. One hit the carrier aft, stopping her dead and causing her to burst into flame. While destroyers milled about, dropping depth charges indiscriminately, Commander McGregor reloaded his tubes and at 1650 fired a torpedo which hit just abaft the carrier's island. *Unryu* went down within twenty minutes. Her escorts gave *Redfish* some heavy jolts from a cluster of depth charges, but she escaped by lying on the bottom until dark.

Admiral Halsey's foray into the South China Sea in mid-January 1945 almost completely halted Japanese ship movements in those waters. But Rear Admiral James Fife, who had just relieved Admiral Christie as Commander Submarines Southwest Pacific, was taking no chance of missing anything. He maintained about 20 boats in that sea, and around Borneo. On 24 January 1945 one of them scored well. *Blackfin*, Commander W. L. Kitch, picked up a convoy, made a surface approach and one hit, which sank destroyer *Shigure*, miraculous survivor of many battles, including Surigao Strait.

Blackfin's exploit was emulated by *Pargo* (Commander D. B. Bell) off the coast of Indochina on 19 February. A night torpedo attack on a zigzagging destroyer was followed by a tremendous explosion which tore the destroyer apart. That was the end of *Nokaze*, the 39th and last Japanese destroyer to be destroyed by an American submarine. *Flasher* (Commanders R. I. Whitaker and G. W. Grider), the same month, completed her sixth war patrol, establishing a record for tonnage sunk by any United States submarine — 21 ships totaling over 100,000 tons.

So much for the last operations of Southwest Pacific Submarines, whose main base had now been moved up to Subic Bay, Luzon. It was much the same story — growing scarcity of targets — for Pacific Fleet Submarines, now mostly operating from Guam. Small escort vessels, coastal Marus and the like were the usual victims, but *Balao* (Commander R. K. R. Worthington), operating in the Yellow Sea on 19 March, bagged a 10,413-ton transport.

One of the most successful and carefully planned submarine offensives of the war was Operation BARNEY, the invasion of the Sea of Japan — the only remaining body of water where enemy shipping still moved freely. This project of Admiral Lockwood's completed the ring around Japan by shutting her off from the Asian mainland. A wolf-pack under Commander E. T. Hydeman in *Sea Dog*, known as "Hydeman's Hellcats," was selected for the first penetration of the Sea of Japan. Sailing from Guam on 27 May, these nine submarines headed for the Strait of Tsushima. En route Hellcat *Tinosa* picked up ten survivors from a B–29 which had splashed south of Kyushu; but when the rescued aviators learned of this boat's mission they expressed a unanimous desire to return to their rubber raft and wait for a different rescue! *Tinosa* and her eight sister boats passed through Tsushima Strait on 5-6 June. After reaching their assigned patrol stations on the 9th, they began knocking 'em off — in eleven days, 27 merchantmen for a total of 57,000 tons. The Hellcats made their exit by La Pérouse Strait, between Hokkaido and Sakhalin; but without *Bonefish*, which had mysteriously perished. Admiral Lockwood followed up this foray, and six more submarines operated in the Sea of Japan until V-J Day.

During the waning months of the war, the aircraft lifeguard service by submarines was an even greater contribution to victory than the destruction of enemy shipping. This system, originally set up during the Gilbert Islands operation in November 1943 in order to rescue downed aviators from carrier strikes, had picked up no fewer than 224 airmen by the end of 1944. By the close of that year, when the air effort had became one of the principal offensive elements against Japan, and B-29s were striking the Japanese home islands, it was necessary to step up lifeguard service. For each B-29 mission against Japan at least three submarines, and usually more, were stationed along the flight route and near the targets to pick up aviators who were forced to ditch. During the eight months that the Pacific war lasted in 1945, 86 different submarines rescued a total of 380 aviators. They were not the only means of air-sea rescue. Toward the end of the war there was no point on the B-29 route that could not be reached by a "Dumbo" rescue plane in half an hour, or by a destroyer or submarine in three hours. When the last B-29 strike on Japan was made on 14 August, the air-sea rescue team on station consisted of 14 submarines, 21 Navy seaplanes, nine Dumbos and five ships.

Merchant tonnage owned by Japan declined from about 6 million tons at the beginning of the war to about 2.5 million on 1 December 1944, despite the addition of some 800,000 tons by conquest early in the war, and 3.3 million tons of new construction. At the end of the war she had only 1.8 million tons left in her merchant marine, mostly small wooden vessels in the Inland Sea. United States forces were responsible for the sinking of 2117 Japanese merchant vessels of 8 million tons during the entire war. Of this destruction, submarines accounted for 60 per cent, aircraft 30 per cent, mines and surface ships 10 per cent. Other Allied forces, mainly British and Dutch submarines, sent another 73 merchant ships of 211,664 tons to the bottom. And United States submarines accounted for 201 of the 686 Japanese warships sunk during the war.

JAPANESE TONNAGE SUNK BY UNITED STATES SUBMARINES
Last 4 Months of 1943, 1944, and First 8 Months of 1945

1943	Number of Warships	Displacement	Number of Marus	Gross Tons
Sept.	3	3,085	31	135,540
Oct.	–	——	26	128,088
Nov.	4	3,992	47	228,313
Dec.	3	22,120	33	130,097
1944				
Jan.	3	9,230	53	285,672
Feb.	4	12,092	52	252,016
Mar.	5	8,322	29	121,213
Apr.	9	12,203	24	98,199
May	6	6,960	54	236,700
June	11	76,570	44	189,611
July	8	15,689	40	220,089
Aug.	11	41,089	45	232,028
Sept.	7	26,905	48	152,505
Oct.	9	27,662	66	320,906
Nov.	18	125,877	56	214,506
Dec.	13	43,047	18	81,206
1945				
Jan.	8	5,703	27	96,165
Feb.	9	7,085	19	47,878
Mar.	4	3,086	37	89,859
Apr.	12	13,336	32	67,725
May	5	4,550	24	31,222
June	7	12,582	48	83,418
July	11	7,896	18	28,488
Aug.	4	3,900	6	18,297

CHAPTER XVI

Iwo Jima and Okinawa

February–August 1945

1. *The Assault on Iwo Jima, 19 February 1945*

THE JOINT CHIEFS OF STAFF on 3 October 1944 issued a directive to General MacArthur and Admiral Nimitz, in pursuance of which the operations described in this chapter were carried out: —

1. Admiral Nimitz, after providing covering and support forces for the liberation of Luzon, will occupy one or more positions in the Bonins-Volcano Group, target date 20 January 1945, and one or more positions in the Ryukyus, target date 1 March 1945.

2. General MacArthur will provide support for subsequent occupation of the Ryukyus by Admiral Nimitz's forces.

The strategic concept herein was to secure island bases for a final assault on Japan. Tokyo, Saipan, and Formosa make an isosceles triangle with legs 1500 miles long. The eastern leg, Saipan-Tokyo, was about to be used by B–29 Superforts to bomb the Japanese homeland; but a halfway house was wanted, and Iwo Jima alone fitted the bill. Formosa having been rejected as too difficult to capture, the western angle of the strategic triangle was shifted to Okinawa in the Ryukyus, several hundred miles nearer to Japan and less stoutly defended. Owing to the unexpectedly prolonged and bitter defense of Leyte and Luzon, target dates in the 3 October directive could not be kept, and this gave the Japanese another month to make Iwo Jima almost impregnable.

The Iwo Jima operation was placed first because it was expected to be easier than Okinawa. The same Pacific Fleet would have to cover and support both, while Seventh Fleet and Amphibious Force were engaged in covering and liberating the Southern Philippines, as described in our previous chapter.

Iwo Jima, central island of the Volcano group of the Nanpo Shoto or Bonin Islands, was uninhabited except by the Japanese garrison. Shaped like a bloated pear, Iwo is only 4½ miles long and 2½ miles wide. The inactive volcanic crater of Mount Suribachi rises 550 feet above sea level. The northern part of the island is a plateau with rocky, inaccessible shores, but beaches extend from the base of Mount Suribachi for more than two miles north and east. These beaches, the land between them, and a good part of the terrain are deeply covered with brown volcanic ash and black cinders which look like sand, but are so much lighter than sand that walking is difficult and running almost impossible. This grim island, which cost us so dear to wrest from the enemy, was wanted for one thing only: to provide for emergency landings of the B–29s on their bombing missions from the Marianas to Tokyo (which began 24 November 1944), and to base fighter planes for their escort, since no fighter plane could fly the entire distance.

Iwo Jima underwent the most prolonged and also the most disappointing air bombing and naval bombardment of any Pacific island. The VII Army Air Force (Major General Willis H. Hale) raided it ten times in August, 22 times in September, 16 times in October. On 8 December it began daily strikes. Three heavy cruisers (*Chester*, flag) under Rear Admiral Allan E. Smith, bombarded Iwo on 8, 24 and 27 December and 5 and 25 January. Chichi and Haha Jima were also pounded in order to prevent reinforcements from reaching Iwo — but they did. For two weeks from 31 January VII A.A.F. bombed the island night and day, and the B–29s bombed it twice. Some 6800 tons of bombs and 22,000 rounds of shell from 5-inch up to 16-inch were aimed at Iwo Jima before the invasion.

Unfortunately, Iwo's defenses were of such a nature that neither air bombing nor naval bombardment, no matter how prolonged, could neutralize them. The slopes of Mount Suribachi contained a labyrinth of dug-in gun positions for artillery, mortars and machine guns. These were accompanied by elaborate cave and tunnel systems to provide living quarters and storage space for weapons. From the volcano's rim, everything that went on all over the island could be observed. The main feature of the bulbous part of the island was an intricate network of excavated caves, connected by deep tunnels. In some places there were five levels of these caves, each with several entrances, and most served the double purpose of protecting men and positioning weapons. A mortar could be set up at a cave or tunnel mouth, fired and then withdrawn out of sight. Many of the surface positions were so cleverly prepared that they were impossible to spot until they opened up, or until the protective camouflage was blown away by gunfire.

This system, an elaboration of the new Japanese defense tactics first revealed at Peleliu, followed a battle plan drawn up by Lieutenant General Tadamichi Kuribayashi in September 1944. He was to "transform the central island into a fortress." When the landings took place, the garrison must aim at "gradual depletion of enemy attack forces, and even if the situation gets out of hand, defend a corner of the island to the death." What happened is a lesson in the value of speed in securing strategic objectives. We could have walked into Iwo in September, right after securing the Marianas; but at that time the J.C.S. was still arguing over "What next?" The original target date of 20 January would have been far better than the actual one of 19 February, but Sixth Army's pace in taking Leyte dictated the month's postponement.

The Japanese Navy's only contribution to the defense of Iwo Jima was in the form of submarines bearing the "human torpedoes"

— directed by one swimmer — which they called *kaiten*. An initial success of this gimmick, sinking a fleet oiler in Ulithi Lagoon on 20 November, was not repeated. A *kaiten* unit composed of three I-boats sailed for Iwo Jima 22 February. One ran afoul of destroyer escort *Finnegan* (Lieutenant Commander H. Huffman USNR), when escorting a convoy from Iwo Jima to Saipan, and was sunk.

In preparation for protecting the Iwo operation from submarine attack, escort carriers *Anzio* (Captain G. C. Montgomery) and *Tulagi* (Captain J. C. Cronin) were made nuclei of hunter-killer antisubmarine units, similar to those which had done such good work against U-boats in the Atlantic. *Anzio*'s planes sank one *kaiten*-bearing submarine a few miles west of Iwo Jima. The third reached Iwo waters, but was kept down by destroyers for over 48 hours, almost suffocating the crew, and then returned to base. Another, after a frustrating cruise around Iwo, constantly harassed by antisubmarine craft, was recalled. It seems odd that the Japanese Navy had not learned, from our S-boats' lack of success in stopping their original invasion of the Philippines, that submarines are no good against an amphibious operation which has plenty of alert escorts.

During the last three days before Iwo D-day there took place a series of carrier-borne air strikes over and around Tokyo. These were laid on not only as a shield for Iwo Jima, but to destroy enemy planes and reduce Japanese capability for launching air attacks. They were successful in both objects, delivering a powerful two days' attack on Tokyo airfields and aircraft plants on 16-17 February — but this did nothing to reduce the defenses of Iwo Jima.

This was a Fifth Fleet show, with the same Spruance-Turner-Mitscher team that won Saipan and the Philippine Sea. Major General Harry Schmidt commanded the Marines. Pre-landing activities at the objective were under Rear Admiral William H. P. Blandy. "Spike" Blandy was the sanguine Celtic type, with a humorous Irish mouth overhung by a large red nose. As Chief of the Bureau of Ordnance his quick mind, grasp of essentials and driving energy had served the Navy well, especially in developing and manufacturing the Swedish Bofors and the Swiss Oerlikon as the 40-mm and 20-mm antiaircraft weapons. And he had commanded an amphibious group at Saipan. Blandy now had a fair-sized fleet: eight battleships, including four which had helped cover the invasion of France; five heavy cruisers, and a flock of destroyers. They bombarded Iwo vigorously on 16 and 17 February, evoking no reply from the defenders until seven LCI gunboats, advancing in line abreast to cover the underwater demolition teams, drew a torrent of gunfire. All were hit and one was sunk, with an aggregate loss of 76 men; but they stuck to it and recovered the "frogmen," who, after all this fuss, had discovered no underwater obstacles or mines. Another day's bombardment followed on the 18th.

D-day, 19 February, opened with the heaviest pre-H-hour bombardment of World War II, by "Spike" Blandy's ships. "Kelly" Turner ordered "Land the Landing Force" at 0645. H-hour was easily met. Iwo was shrouded in the dust and smoke created by the bombardment, but weather conditions were almost perfect. The operation looked like a pushover. Optimists predicted that the island would be secured in four days, but the Marines were skeptical. A chaplain on one of the transports had printed on cards, and distributed to each Marine, the words of Sir Jacob Astley's famous prayer before the Battle of Edgehill in 1642, which well fitted the mood of United States Marines three centuries later: —

> O Lord! Thou knowest how busy I must be this day:
> If I forget Thee, do not Thou forget me.

At one minute short of H-hour naval gunfire shifted to targets about 200 yards inland, at 0902 it moved another 200 yards inland and thereafter formed a modified rolling barrage ahead of the troops, constantly adjusted to conform to their actual rate of advance. This barrage was fired by the secondary batteries of the heavy ships, to each of which was assigned a shore fire-control party with the troops.

At 0830 the first assault wave, consisting of 68 LVT(A), the amphtrac tanks, left the line of departure. It hit the beach almost precisely at H-hour, 0900. Within the next twenty-three minutes the remaining assault waves landed on schedule, and at 0944 twelve LSMs, carrying medium tanks, beached.

Up to the point of actually touching down, everything went off like a parade. Then trouble started. The LVT(A)s found their way blocked by the first terrace, which rose as high as fifteen feet. The volcanic ash and cinders afforded poor traction, and men of the first wave were slowed down to a walk. A few amph-tracs advanced through breaches blasted by naval gunfire, some backed into the water and fired their turrets at inland targets; but many bogged down on the beach. The volume and accuracy of enemy mortar fire increased heavily. A situation developed some-what similar to the one at Omaha Beach, but here there was not even a sea wall for protection to the troops, who found it virtu-ally impossible to advance in the face of withering fire.

General Kuribayashi's static defense now began to show itself. His troops cozily sat out the naval bombardment. As soon as gunfire lifted they returned to their well-protected positions and opened up on the advancing troops. As the volume of enemy fire on the Marines increased, the gunfire of supporting ships off shore stepped up. *Santa Fe* was the star of the fire support cruisers. She laid almost continuous 5-inch and 6-inch shellfire within 200 yards of the battalion on the left flank of the 5th Division, with the re-sult that hardly a shot was fired by the enemy from the base of Mount Suribachi, commanding their line of advance. *Nevada* be-came the sweetheart of the Marine Corps. Her skipper, Captain H. L. ("Pop") Grosskopf, an old gunnery officer, had set out to make his battleship the best fire support ship in the Fleet, and did.

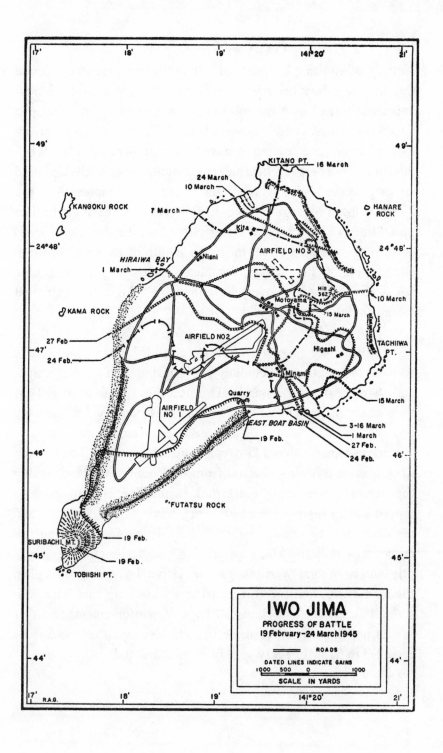

KITANO PT. 16 March
24 March
10 March
7 March

KANGOKU ROCK

HANARE ROCK

24°48'

Kita

Nishi

AIRFIELD NO 3

HIRAIWA BAY
1 March

Motoyama
Hill 362
10 March

15 March

KAMA ROCK

TACHIIWA PT.

27 Feb
47'
24 Feb.

AIRFIELD NO 2

Higashi

Minami
15 March

Quarry
AIRFIELD NO 1

EAST BOAT BASIN

19 Feb.

3-16 March
1 March
27 Feb.
24 Feb.

46'

FUTATSU ROCK

SURIBACHI MT.
19 Feb.
45'
19 Feb.
TOBIISHI PT.

IWO JIMA
PROGRESS OF BATTLE
19 February–24 March 1945

——— ROADS

DATED LINES INDICATE GAINS
1000   500   0   1000

SCALE IN YARDS

R.A.G.

Nevada, when firing her assigned rolling barrage about 0925, found that her secondary battery could not penetrate a concrete block-house and turned over the job to her main battery. This damaged a hitherto undisclosed blockhouse behind the beach, blasting away its sand cover and leaving it naked and exposed. At 1100 when this blockhouse again became troublesome the battleship used armor-piercing shells, which took it completely apart. At 1512 *Nevada* observed a gun firing from a cave in the high broken ground east of the beaches. Using direct fire, she shot two rounds of 14-inch, scoring a direct hit in the mouth of the cave, blowing out the side of the cliff and completely destroying the gun. One could see it drooping over the cliff edge "like a half-extracted tooth hanging on a man's jaw."

Approximately 30,000 troops were landed on D-day. There were 2420 casualties, including 519 killed or missing in action; and 47 more died of wounds. The beachhead established fell far short of the planned phase line, but it already contained six infantry regiments, as many artillery battalions and two tank battalions.

Darkness finally closed D-day, a day such as Iwo had never seen since it arose a hissing volcano from the ocean. The Marines dug themselves in where night overtook them. Gunfire support ships moved out to night withdrawal areas, leaving only *Santa Fe* and ten destroyers to supply star shell illumination and harassing fire on enemy positions. The expected big counterattack never came off; banzai charges were no part of General Kuribayashi's plan. He intended to conserve his man power, knowing that American sea and air power had closed all hope of reinforcement, and that it was hopeless to try to drive the Marines into the sea. But he intended to fight for every yard of ground, and did.

2. *Iwo Jima Secured, 20 February–16 March*

The reduction and capture of Iwo Jima is a story of yard-by-yard advance against a tough, resourceful enemy who allowed no let-up, and who used his terrain to extract the maximum price in blood. The Marines, advancing in the open with little natural shelter, had to fight their way against an enemy burrowed underground and protected from everything but a direct hit. It was a costly and exhausting grind, calling for higher qualities of courage, initiative and persistence than a campaign full of charges, countercharges and spectacular incidents that maintain morale. It was like being under the lash of a relentless desert storm, from which there was no shelter, day or night; but this storm lasted six weeks and rained steel, not sand. General Holland Smith said that "Iwo Jima was the most savage and the most costly battle in the history of the Marine Corps." And Admiral Nimitz observed that on Iwo "uncommon valor was a common virtue."

A pattern for the island campaign was promptly cut out. For daytime direct support, each Marine battalion had attached to it one or more destroyers with a liaison officer on board, and a Navy shore fire-control party stayed with it ashore. At daybreak the heavy support ships closed the island to fire a preliminary bombardment on targets selected by divisional and regimental commanders the evening before. After the Marines jumped off, the ships stood by for deep support on targets designated by the troops' shore fire-control parties or by spotting planes. A special feature of gunfire support during the first week was the LCI mortar unit. With their shallow draft these LCI(M)s could work close inshore, often in a position to shoot up gullies at enemy targets invisible to the Marines.

Escort carrier planes acted as winged workhorses of this campaign. While Task Force 58 raided Tokyo and Okinawa, the "jeeps," almost within sight of Mount Suribachi, fed out call-bombing and rocketing missions, and provided C.A.P. and anti-submarine patrol, from before D-day to 9 March. "The daily task of providing air support," observed their commander, Admiral Durgin, "is not broken even for replenishing and refueling. It is a continual grind from dawn to dark each day."

Owing to Iwo's distance from Japanese air bases, the Navy there was not much bothered by kamikazes. One, however, crashed *Saratoga* about 35 miles NW of Iwo on 21 February, and five more attacked, adding a bomb to her collection. She lost 42 planes burned, jettisoned or splashed, 123 men killed and 192 wounded, but she was able to steam under her own power to a West Coast yard. It took a "friendly" atomic bomb at Bikini to put much-bopped old "Sara" down for keeps. Also on the evening of 21 February, escort carrier *Bismarck Sea* was crashed by a kamikaze starting gasoline fires and explosions that did her in and killed 218 of her crew. Simultaneously, several Japanese torpedo-bombers attacked escort carrier *Lunga Point*. All torpedoes missed but one plane skidded across the flight deck with propeller chewing up the planking, and plunged into the sea. The damage was slight and nobody but the pilot was killed. These, together with hits on net cargo ship *Keokuk* and *LST–477*, make up the total enemy aircraft damage in the Iwo Jima operation. It seemed a good omen for Okinawa, but it was not.

On 23 February came the successful scaling of Mount Suribachi. Colonel Harry ("the Horse") Liversedge sent a 40-man detachment from the 28th Marine Regiment, commanded by 1st Lieutenant H. G. Schreier, to scale the volcano. As they scrambled over the rim of the crater they were challenged by the last Japanese survivors on the opposite edge, and a hot little fight developed. Before it ended, at 1020, a Marine picked up a length of iron pipe, lashed to it a small American flag that he had brought in his pocket, and raised it. This flag was too small to be seen through the fog of battle, but already a bigger one was coming up, a battle ensign from *LST–779*, which had beached near the base. A Marine carried it up the mountain, and an Associated Press photographer arrived in time to take the famous picture of the second flag-raising.

Beginning 25 February the Marines made slow but steady progress, gradually pushing the Japanese into the northern part of the island. The final drive was made three divisions abreast. On 4 March the former Japanese airfield, improved and extended by Seabees, received its first call from a B–29, returning from Japan low on gasoline. General Schmidt announced Iowa Jima secured on 16 March, and operation completed on the 26th. But there was plenty of ground fighting between these two dates, and even later. General Kuribayashi's radio informed Chichi Jima on the 21st: "We have not eaten or drunk for five days. But our fighting spirit is still high." It was indeed. His men continued to do all the mischief they could. On 26 March, before dawn, about 350 Japanese tried to brawl their way through an A.A.F. and Seabee camp, killing 53 and wounding 119 American officers and men before being annihilated themselves.

General Schmidt closed his command post 27 March and the 3rd Marine Division departed. The 147th Infantry Regiment U. S. Army, which had been arriving since 21 March, now took over responsibility for mopping-up and garrison duty.

Down to 1800 March 27, the Marine Corps and Navy casualties incurred in capturing Iwo Jima were as follows: —

	MARINE CORPS		NAVY
	Officers	*Men*	*Officers and Men*
Killed in action	215	4,339	363
Died of wounds	60	1,271	70
Missing, presumed dead	3	43	448
Wounded in action	826	16,446	1,917
Combat fatigue casualties	46	2,602	?

Up to and including 26 March the count of Japanese killed and sealed up in caves was 20,703, and only 216 had been taken prisoner. It was then estimated that only 100 to 300 of the enemy were left alive on the island. This proved to be far too optimistic. The Army netted 867 more prisoners in April and May, during which time 1602 more Japanese were killed. Isolated pockets held out even longer in various parts of the island.

The United States Marines conducted this, one of the toughest battles in their entire history, with exemplary endurance, skill and valor. And it was not a spectacular battle, but one of steady slugging against a relentless enemy. Battle casualties amounted to 30 per cent of the entire landing force, and 75 per cent in the infantry regiments of the 4th and 5th Divisions. The Seabees, who began to land on D-day and to restore the No. 1 airstrip five days later, and 7600 of whom were on the island 20 April, did the major work in making Iwo Jima useful to the Army Air Force. By the end of the war about 2400 B–29 landings had been made on the island, carrying crews of many thousand men.

There is no doubt that the capture of Iwo Jima became a major contribution to victory over Japan. One B–29 pilot said, "Whenever I land on this island, I thank God and the men who fought for it."

3. *The Approach to Okinawa, 9–31 March*

Okinawa in the Ryukyus, a name unknown to the vast majority of Americans before 1945, signifies an island where American forces seem destined to remain until the cold war waxes hot or the Communist menace fades. Under an earlier name, "The Great Loochoo," Okinawa became well known to Americans when, in that happy era before "imperialism" and "colonialism" became pejorative words, Commodore Matthew C. Perry was sailing about the Orient. In 1853 the Commodore raised the American flag near Shuri on one of the hills that cost us so dear to capture in 1945. He forced the King of the Ryukyus to sign a treaty guaranteeing friendly treatment to American ships, and even established a temporary coaling station at Naha harbor. Japan only took over the group in 1879 and the Okinawans have never been completely assimilated to the Japanese.

In 1945 the island, with a small rural economy, was overpopulated with almost half a million people. The countryside, with steep limestone hills, umbrella-topped pines, small cultivated fields and patches of woodland, recalls those Italian landscapes seen through the windows of Tuscan and Sienese paintings; but neither tower nor dome breaks the skyline. The soft limestone structure of the island lent itself to a deep, prolonged defense such as General Kuribayashi's on Iwo Jima.

Planning for this massive Operation ICEBERG, described by British observers as "the most audacious and complex enterprise yet undertaken by the American amphibious forces," began with a Cincpac-Cincpoa staff study dated 25 October 1944. The detailed operation plan of Vice Admiral Turner was issued on 9 February 1945.

Admirals Spruance, Mitscher and Turner, and Lieutenant General Simon Bolivar Buckner USA, commanding Tenth Army, were the

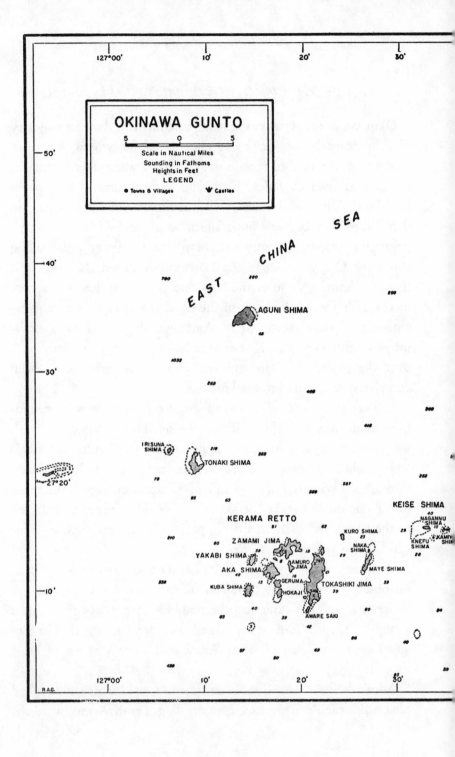

four principal commanders. Tenth Army was a powerful invasion force, comprising III 'Phib Corps (Major General Roy S. Geiger) of three Marine divisions, and XXIV Army Corps (Major General John R. Hodge USA) of four infantry divisions with a fifth in reserve — a total of about 172,000 combatant and 115,000 service troops.

D-day for Okinawa was set for 1 April 1945. Planners and commanders were highly apprehensive of what enemy air might do to us before we could secure our own airfields on Okinawa. For the Japanese had several airfields there and in the nearby islands, airdromes 150 miles away in the Amami Gunto, about 230 miles away on the Sakishima Gunto, and 65 airfields on Formosa, as well as 55 on Kyushu. Since no other operation would be going on at the time except in the southern Philippines, the enemy could concentrate an estimated 2000 to 3000 planes on the expeditionary force, and employ kamikaze tactics, which is exactly what Imperial General Headquarters planned to do. The island commander, Lieutenant General Mitsuru Ushijima, who had 77,000 to 100,000 troops in his garrison, was ordered to employ the same defense-in-depth tactics as at Iwo Jima.

Air power was not one-sided. Even before the bloody scroll of the Iwo Jima campaign was completely unrolled, the B–29s had begun a series of air raids, with incendiary bombs, on large urban areas of Japan. These, in the words of the Japanese collaborators to General MacArthur's *Historical Report*, "rocked the nation to its very foundations." The attack on the night of 9-10 March, in particular, was "indescribably horrifying." Well over 250,000 houses were destroyed, rendering more than a million persons homeless, and 83,793 people were burned to death. Compared with these, the results of fast carrier raids on Japan on 18-21 March were unimportant; and the kamikazes got in some good licks on *Wasp*, *Yorktown* and *Franklin*. The first-named lost 101 dead and 269 wounded, but continued her flight operations; *Franklin* (Captain Leslie H. Gehres) was very badly damaged, had to be towed clear by heavy cruiser *Pittsburgh* (Captain John E. Gingrich) and lost 724 killed and 265 wounded. *Franklin* was in much worse shape than old *Lexington* in the Coral Sea or old *Yorktown* at Midway; but the outstanding skill, heroism and stamina of damage control parties enabled her to make the 12,000-mile voyage to New York with only one stop.

Neither *Franklin* nor many other ships crashed by kamikazes off Okinawa could have been saved but for the firefighting schools and improved technique instituted by the Navy 1942-1943. The initial impulse came from the New York City fire department, which interested Rear Admiral Edward L. Cochrane, Chief of the Bureau of Ships, in a new "fog nozzle," which atomized water to a fine spray and quenched a blaze much more quickly than a solid stream could do. New York and Boston fire-fighters trained over 260 officer instructors and established schools with mock-up ships at every continental naval base. The damage control party of every new warship was trained at one of these before going to sea. The major object of this instruction was to "get the fear of fire out of the sailor"; to teach him that, if properly equipped with fire mask and helmet, handling an all-purpose nozzle and applicator, he could boldly advance to the source of a blaze and not get hurt. All ships were equipped with 160-pound handy-billies, and the destroyers and larger types with 500-pound mobile pumps, each operated by its own gas engine. Portable oxyacetylene steel-cutting outfits and rescue breathing-apparatus were provided. A foamite system was placed at every hundred feet of a carrier's deck. Foam generators in destroyers were moved topside. Salvage vessels (ARS) were especially fitted out to help fight fires in other ships.

Japanese authorities admit that losses from these carrier raids were "staggering": 161 out of 193 aircraft committed shot down, in addition to an indeterminate number destroyed on the ground. These losses, luckily for us, prevented heavy participation by Japanese air forces in the defense of Okinawa until 6 April.

Two naval bombardment forces were brought up to the Ryukyus eight days before the landings, in order to give Okinawa and the vicinity a complete working-over. Admiral Blandy's amphibious support force of escort carriers, minecraft, light gunboats and the like, and Admiral Deyo's bombardment group of battleships and cruisers, were given this job. Also under Blandy's command was a complete attack group, lifting an infantry division, to take the Kerama Retto, a cluster of small islands 15 miles west of Okinawa. This preliminary operation was the idea of Admiral Turner, in order to secure the Kerama roadstead before the main show, as an advanced naval base for fueling, repairs and ammunition replenishment. The Kerama Retto landings, which would have been considered a major amphibious operation in 1942, went off like clockwork, and the group was secured on the 27th.

Between 28 March and 8 April, seven fleet tankers and three station tankers issued 940,000 barrels of fuel oil and 203,000 barrels of diesel, together with large quantities of lube oil and avgas, to 277 ships. Inside the roadstead, despite frequent air alerts, one had a feeling of security, like having a roof over your head in an air raid. As Rear Admiral Allan Smith wrote, Kerama "gave a firmness to the Okinawa tactical situation . . . We were there to stay, with a place to tow damaged ships, look after survivors, replenish and refuel, drop an anchor."

Aye, drop an anchor! For that boon alone, sailors blessed Kelly Turner, whose bright thought made it possible.

4. *The Okinawa Landings, 1 April 1945*

L-day, as D-day for Okinawa was called, came on Easter Sunday, 1 April. It was preceded by five days of naval bombardment and air bombing. The five-to-six-mile-long strip of Hagushi beaches had been chosen for the landings because they gave ready access to two landing fields, Yontan and Kadena, and it seemed inconceivable that the enemy would abandon these without a fight. For aught we knew, the Japanese were holed up immediately behind the beaches, ready to give the boys hell when they stepped ashore. These beaches were bisected by Bisha River, which flows into the sea between two outthrusting limestone bluffs. The cliff faces were honeycombed with caves and tunnels from which the landing beaches could have been enfiladed by gunfire. Behind every beach was a thick six- to ten-foot-high sea wall of masonry and concrete. Both airfields were dominated by tunneled and fortified hills. It looked as if landing on the Hagushi beaches would be as bloody an affair as Omaha, and that the three days allowed in the operation plan would be too little time for capturing the airfields.

Everyone was wrong. What they thought to be difficult proved to be easy, and after the easy part was over the tough fighting began.

The Paschal sun rose over heavy, low-lying clouds around 0640 April 1. It was a beautiful morning, perfect for an amphibious operation: calm sea, just enough offshore wind to blow the smoke away and to float the varicolored banners of the control craft. As the sun rose over the clouds it cast a peachlike glow over the water and on the multitude of ships, some painted solid gray, some with striped Atlantic Ocean camouflage. These last had not had time to change clothes, as it were, having been hustled more than halfway around the world to meet Okinawa L-day.

At 0600 Vice Admiral Turner in *Eldorado* took over from Rear Admiral Blandy the command of all forces afloat except the fast carriers. After wresting one position after another from the enemy, Turner was in fine fettle. He had just been attacked in the American press for wasting lives at Iwo Jima and compared unfavorably with General MacArthur, but little he cared for that. He was still the same driving, swearing, sweating "Kelly" whose head could conceive more new ideas and retain more detail than any other flag officer in the Navy. His complicated landing plan could hardly go wrong, based as it was on two years' combat experience.

In order not to overwhelm the reader with detail, yet do justice to the magnitude and complexity of this last amphibious operation of the war, I shall describe one quarter part of it, the landing of one infantry division by boats and craft of Transport Group "Dog," Commodore M. O. Carlson. "Dog" formed half of the Southern Attack Force, which was commanded by Rear Admiral "Jimmie" Hall of Normandy fame. His job was to land Major General Hodge's XXIV Corps. The "Dog" transports, which had the 7th Infantry Division on board, were to land it on a front of 3000 yards, the so-called Orange and Purple beaches.

Very early the big attack transports (*Harris*, flag) heave-to about seven and a half miles off shore. Beaching craft proceed to an area four miles nearer, control craft mark the line of departure 4000 yards off shore, and 17 "specialist" beaching craft (supply, water, hospital, and so on) together with LSD *Epping Forest* carrying boated tanks in her womb, heave-to seaward of the LSTs. Each control craft displays a banner of the same color as the beach, with vertical stripes to distinguish between Nos. 1 and 2 of the same color. This is carried out consistently. Every boat wave's guide flies a pennant of similar color and design, and each landing craft

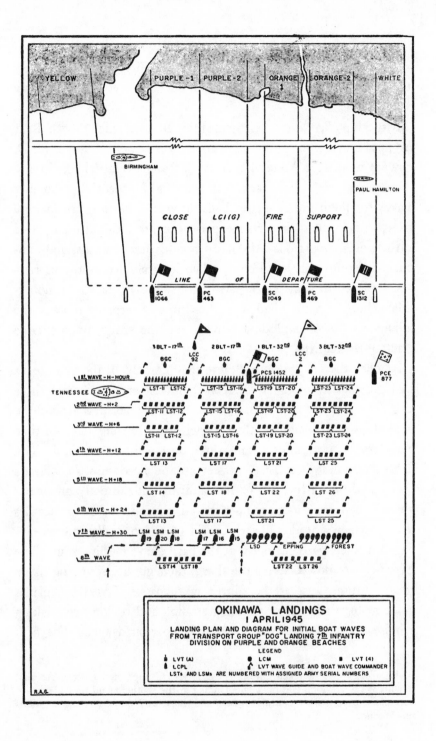

OKINAWA LANDINGS
1 APRIL 1945

LANDING PLAN AND DIAGRAM FOR INITIAL BOAT WAVES
FROM TRANSPORT GROUP "DOG" LANDING 7th INFANTRY
DIVISION ON PURPLE AND ORANGE BEACHES

LEGEND

LVT (A)   LCM   LVT (4)
LCPL   LVT WAVE GUIDE AND BOAT WAVE COMMANDER

LSTs AND LSMs ARE NUMBERED WITH ASSIGNED ARMY SERIAL NUMBERS of the initial waves has it painted topside. First wave ashore sets up corresponding beach markers about ten feet high, brightly painted on canvas.

Battleship *Tennessee* (Captain John B. Heffernan) with Rear Admiral Deyo embarked, and cruiser *Birmingham* (Captain H. D. Power) with Rear Admiral Bertram J. Rodgers embarked, close to 1900 yards from the beach. En route, a Japanese dive-bomber makes for them but is splashed just astern of *Birmingham,* whose crew, in view of their earlier experiences, are pleasantly surprised at their escape.[1] At 0640 the naval bombardment opens, and continues intermittently until 0735, when it is raised to allow carrier-based planes to play their part. The sound of naval cannon is stilled, but the air is filled with the drone of airplane motors, the rolling rumble of exploding bombs, and the sharp, unmistakable crack of rocket fire.

At 0800 the cry goes up, "Here they come!" In the van are 12 LCI gunboats, moving in perfect alignment at a deliberate three knots in order not to outdistance the LVTs. They pass around the battleships and open fire, their 3-inch guns rattling like old-time musketry. In ten minutes' time three boat waves, each flanked by flag-flying guide boats, have swept around Battleship *Tennessee's* bow and stern, re-forming on her landward side directly under her guns, which are shooting 14-inch, 5-inch and 40-mm projectiles over the men's heads. The troops in green coveralls and camouflaged helmets gaze curiously at the battleship's flashing guns. The LCI(G)s are now close to the shore; their gunfire sounding like a roll of drums. Just as the fourth wave passes *Tennessee,* planes come in for their last pre-landing strafing and rocket fire, making a noise like a gigantic cotton sheet being ripped apart. The fifth

[1] Kamikazes also attacked the "Demonstration Group" under Rear Admiral Jerauld Wright, which laid on a fake landing at the southern end of Okinawa to distract the enemy. Two crashed an LST and transport *Hinsdale,* killing 40 sailors and Marines.

boat wave passes, troops standing on the after deck to see "what goes on." And a marvelous sight it is, these waves of landing craft extending parallel to the coast as far as the eye can see, all moving with a precise deliberation that well represents the stout though anxious hearts that they are carrying.

At 0828 word arrives that the first wave is 75 yards from the beach. Admiral Deyo orders Cease Fire. The LCI gunboats have halted outside the reef over which amphtracs of Wave 2 are already crawling to begin their last dash through the lagoon. At 0832 comes word, "First wave has hit the beach!" Waves 2 and 3 are on the reef, 4 and 5 take off from Line of Departure; others are forming up as far as you can view seaward.

As *Tennessee* winds ship, in order to give her starboard secondary battery a chance to shoot, the first signs of enemy opposition appear. Plumes of white water rise up between her and the beach. A mortar battery on the bluffs of the Bisha River is trying to get the range, but never does. Sixth wave is composed of LCVPs whose troops will have to be transferred to retracting LVTs to cross the reef. Seventh wave includes six landing ships, medium (LSM) for the Purple beaches. These little sisters to the LST are camouflaged by great blobs of green, yellow and brown paint, which light up to a modernist fantasy when seen in echelon; yet there is also something curiously medieval about them. Nearly amidships rises a tall, cylindrical pilothouse like the turret of a castle, with round ports; and the numerous gadgets which crown the turret have the effect of battlements protecting the helmeted sailors. Can it be a coincidence that the control craft for Purple 1 is numbered 1066? As the LSMs pass, their bow gates are already open, ready to disgorge the newest amphibious vehicle, a medium Sherman tank supported by pontoons. Nine centuries of warfare and military architecture seem to come to a focus off the beaches of Okinawa.

Nine o'clock. The sun has burned away the mist, disclosing an almost solid mass of transports to seaward, beaches swarming with amphtracs and men, troops moving through cornfields toward the tableland, landing craft forming waves, earlier waves retracting. Tanks can be seen swarming up the slope, orange and purple beach markers are clearly visible, landing craft bearing bulldozers and cranes pass; one is labeled PRESS in large white letters. Wind and sea have made up; no whitecaps yet but enough chop so that landing craft pitch and throw spray.

At 1100 word reached *Tennessee* that the Marines in the northern sector had taken Yontan airfield, and that the troops in the Army sector were on Kadena. All hands were stunned by the lack of opposition. Where are the Japanese? What is wrong with their elaborate installations? . . . No one knew the answer. Officers looked at one another and shook their heads. The big joke that morning was the word passed by some Corps humorist: "The Marines are going so fast that they have already contacted the Russians coming up the other side of Okinawa!"

Throughout the afternoon unloading on the beaches continued unopposed, and at 1600 Admiral Turner reported that about 50,000 troops had been landed. The big transports were then withdrawn seaward for the night, and while they were retiring, *Alpine* and *Achernar* were crashed by kamikazes, losing 21 men killed. But they were able to discharge the undamaged part of their cargoes next day before retiring for repairs.

Altogether, this Easter Sunday saw the most successful amphibious landing of the war — not so much owing to our own foolproof plan and tactics as to the enemy's decision to retire from the beach area. What could be his idea?

5. Yamato *and the Fast Carriers, 6–12 April*

The answer is that General Ushijima was rigorously applying the defense-in-depth tactics laid down by his superiors, and practiced at Iwo Jima, for opposing a landing force of superior strength. The idea was to "lure" the enemy into a position where he could not be supported by naval gunfire, and then wipe him out. The General concentrated most of his troops on the southern quarter of the island; hence the Marines, who were given the northern three quarters to conquer, overran that part easily. For several days General Hodge's XXIV Corps felt its way south, and not for a week did the real land battle begin.

In the meantime the Navy had effectively sealed off the big island from any possible reinforcement — there would be no Tokyo Express to Okinawa. The enemy did try one desperate surface lunge at the amphibious forces, but Task Force 58 dealt effectively with that sacrificial sortie.

United States submarines *Threadfin* and *Hackleback*, on the evening of 6 April, reported a sizeable force debouching from Bungo Suido, the southern entrance to the Inland Sea. It consisted of *Yamato*, light cruiser *Yahagi* and eight destroyers. Their objective, in concert with the opening day of Operation TEN-GO — the massed kamikaze attack — was to knock off whatever ships the kamikazes left afloat. They were not expected to return, and only four destroyers did so; *Yamato* had only fuel enough for a one-way trip, and *Yahagi* had food for only five days. But their magazines were fairly bursting with ammunition; *Yamato* had over 1000 rounds for her main battery. This mammoth battlewagon, which had been through the Battles of Midway, the Philippine Sea and Leyte Gulf with little damage and still less effect, was 863 feet long and displaced 72,908 tons when fully laden. Her main battery consisted of nine 460-mm (18.1-inch) guns which threw a projectile weighing 3200 pounds and had a maximum range of 42,000 meters (22½ miles). Her complement was 2767 officers and men. She had radar and 150 antiaircraft and machine guns. Four turbine engines, developing 150,000 horse power, gave her a maximum speed of 27.5 knots. This surprising ratio of speed to weight was attained by a unique hull design. *Yamato* was a very beautiful ship, with a graceful sheer to her flush deck, unbroken from stem to stern, and a stream-lined mast and stack. She and her sister *Musashi* (sunk in the Battle of the Philippine Sea) would have inaugurated a new standard for battleship construction — as H.M.S. *Dreadnought* had done forty years earlier — if air and missile power had not doomed the big-gunned capital ship. So this last sortie of *Yamato* has a sentimental interest for all sailors. When she went down, five centuries of naval warfare ended.

This "Special Surface Attack Force," as it was called, under the command of Vice Admiral Seiichi Ito, sailed through the Inland Sea. It sortied from Bungo Suido at 2000, naked of air cover. That rendered this forlorn hope of the Japanese Navy completely hope-less. With exceedingly bad judgment, the now unified Japanese air command hurled all available fighter planes against the amphibi-ous forces around Okinawa, and at Task Force 58, instead of covering *Yamato*.

Mitscher's fast carriers were in fine shape and vast strength, despite the recent crashes which had sent *Franklin, Wasp* and *Sara-toga* home for repairs. He was in *Lexington*, while Spruance flew his flag in *New Mexico* of the bombardment and fire-support group. Both admirals expected *Yamato* to sortie, and assumed that she would approach through the East China Sea, which we dared not enter owing to the mines, and make a night run to Okinawa. Consequently she might escape notice of the TF 58 search planes, operating from east of Okinawa. But Spruance prepared to get her one way or another. The submarines' report of her coming out of the Inland Sea on the evening of 6 April enabled Mitscher to get three of his task groups up north within striking position, and to fly searches at dawn. An *Essex* plane at 0823 April 7 flushed *Yamato* and her consorts after she passed through Van Diemen Strait, making 22 knots, and working west in the hope of keeping out of carrier planes' range. As soon as he heard this, Spruance signaled to Mitscher "You take them," and he did. At the same time he ordered Admiral Deyo's bombardment force to prepare for a surface action northwest of Okinawa, in case the Japanese broke through the air barrier. So, at 1530 April 7, out lumbered the old battlewagons, none too cheerfully; Deyo's chief of staff "Rafe" Bates taking care to point out that *Yamato*'s guns had a range of 45,000 yards as compared with 37,000 for *Tennessee*'s main battery.

But by that time *Yamato* was no more.

It was a mizzling day with low overcast, ideal for air attack. Two tender-based PBMs from Okinawa shadowed the Japanese force for five hours, sending valuable information to Mitscher and coaching-in the carrier plane strikes. The first of these struck at 1232 April 7. Within ten minutes, *Yamato* had received two bombs and one torpedo hit, one destroyer was sunk and the light cruiser knocked out. Between 1300 and 1417 the force was under almost continuous air attack. Antiaircraft gunners, for want of practice, were unable to shoot down more than half a dozen of the American planes which piled in one after the other, in deuces and treys, bombing and torpedoing, reducing *Yamato*'s topsides to a shambles, knocking out every gun. Ensign Yoshida, a survivor, has vividly described the scene in the final attack, when her list had increased to 35 degrees: —

I could hear the Captain vainly shouting, "Hold on, men! Hold on, men!" . . . I heard the exec. report . . . "Correction of list hopeless!" . . . Men were jumbled together in disorder on the deck, but a group of staff officers squirmed out of the pile and crawled over to the Com-

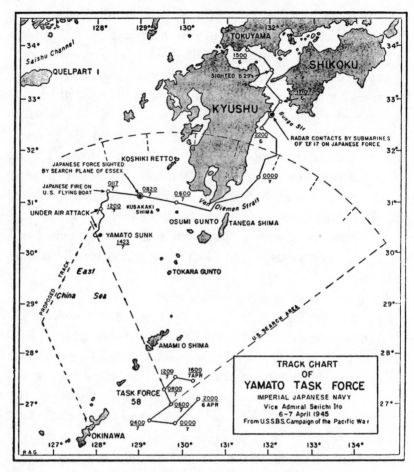

TRACK CHART
OF
YAMATO TASK FORCE
IMPERIAL JAPANESE NAVY
Vice Admiral Seiichi Ito
6–7 April 1945
From U.S.S.B.S. Campaign of the Pacific War

mander in Chief for a final conference. [Admiral Ito] struggled to his feet. His chief of staff then arose and saluted. A prolonged silence followed during which they regarded each other solemnly. The deck was nearly vertical and *Yamato's* battle flag was almost touching the billowing waves. . . . Shells of the big guns skidded and bumped across the deck of the ammunition room, crashing against the bulkhead and kindling the first of a series of explosions. [At 1423] the ship slid under completely, [followed by] the blast, rumble, and shock of compartments bursting from air pressure and exploding magazines already submerged.

Light cruiser *Yahagi* proved almost as tough as the battleship, taking 12 bomb and seven torpedo hits before going down. Four destroyers were sunk or scuttled; four others, damaged, managed to get back to Sasebo. *Yamato* alone lost 2488 officers and men, and the other ships, 1167. Our losses, including those from a kamikaze crash on carrier *Hancock* at noon, were about 15 airplanes and 84 sailors and aviators.

So, farewell to the battlewagons! Japan had only one left, *Haruna*, shortly to be taken apart by air bombing. Most of those of the United States and Royal Navies were still prancing about with the carriers, unconscious that they too would soon be headed for the boneyard; although one would be honored as the scene of Japanese surrender. But not another battleship was ever built. Their long day was now closing, the roar of the big guns would never again be heard, because weapons a thousand times as destructive were to take their place.

A Japanese aviator rescued from the sea boasted to his captors in *Hancock* that they would all be killed by a second massed kamikaze attack on 11 April. So TF 58 got ready for them. True enough, *Missouri* was crashed once, *Enterprise* twice, and destroyer *Kidd* once; but they suffered comparatively slight damage.

Since 26 March the Royal Navy's Pacific Fleet contingent, including carriers *Indomitable*, *Victorious*, *Illustrious* and *Indefatigable*, under Vice Admiral Sir Bernard Rawlings in H.M.S. *King George V*, was performing a useful mission of covering the Sakashima Gunto, pounding down airfields, and intercepting Japanese planes from Formosa. In so doing the British carriers were proving the value of steel decks, which American naval architects had rejected on account of their weight. A kamikaze crashing a steel flattop crumpled up like a scrambled egg, and did no damage beyond its immediate vicinity; but a kamikaze crashing an American wooden deck started serious fires and its bombs penetrated the ship's interior. On the other hand, the Royal Navy carriers were short on fuel capacity and had to retire to refuel every week or so. During that time Admiral Durgin had to send four of his escort carriers from off Okinawa to take the places of the British off Sakashima Gunto. This pattern of wide support by the British carrier forces continued throughout the Okinawa campaign.

6. *The Ordeal of the Radar Pickets, 6–12 April*

The peculiar prolonged hazard to the Navy during this Okinawa campaign was the kamikaze. A series of massed kamikaze attacks, for the first of which *Yamato* was supposed to mop up, were laid on between 6 April and 22 June, constituting Operation TEN-GO. Prior to and in between these *kikusui* (floating chrysanthemum) massed attacks, as the Japanese called them, there were individual kamikaze exploits. Besides those already noted on the landing day, the following were successful during 2–5 April: destroyer transport *Dickerson* was crashed on her bridge, killing her skipper, Lieutenant Commander Ralph E. Lounsbury USNR, the exec., and 52 more officers and men, and she had to be scuttled. Transports *Telfair*, *Goodhue* and *Henrico* were crashed; and the last-named lost the division commander, the skipper, two Army colonels and 45 other sailors and soldiers. The ship survived, but she was out of the war.

Admiral Turner's screening plan for protecting the expeditionary force in and around Okinawa was unusually comprehensive. He set up two antisubmarine destroyer screens, an inner and an outer, a destroyer screen to cover possible approaches of surface raids, a "flycatcher screen" to catch suicide motor boats, and, most important, the radar picket screen, composed primarily of destroyer types[2] but supported by LCI(G)s and other small craft. These

[2] Destroyer types include DDs, DEs, DMs (DDs converted to minecraft) and APDs, destroyer transports.

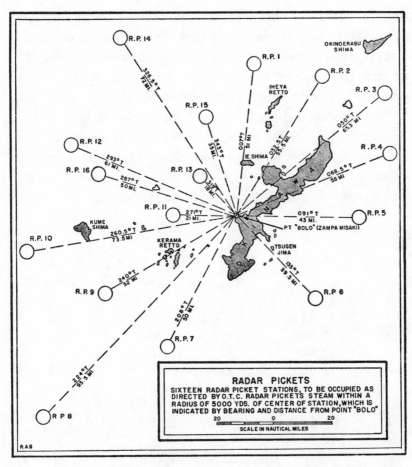

radar picket stations were the posts of greatest danger. They were disposed around Okinawa at distances of between fifteen and one hundred miles from land, so as to pick up flights of approaching enemy planes and, with the aid of C.A.P., to intercept them. From 26 March on, each station was kept by a destroyer type with a fighter-director team on board. This controlled the C.A.P., maintained all day by Admiral Durgin's escort carrier planes. The picket vessel patrolled night and day within 5000 yards of her station, and when bogeys appeared on her radar screen, the fighter-director officer vectored out C.A.P. to intercept. By this means a large proportion of enemy planes approaching Okinawa was shot down before they reached the island, and our forces engaged in landing, unloading or fire support were given timely warning of an air raid. Hundreds of sailors lost their lives and about a score of ships and craft were sunk rendering this service.

The fast carrier forces, too, had their radar pickets; and the casualties to these, while less serious than to those around Okinawa (because more difficult for enemy planes to locate), were formidable. They are included in this table of ten *kikusui* attacks which constituted the better part of Operation TEN-GO.

Attack No.	Date	No. of Planes Kamikaze	Other[3]	Sunk	U. S. Ships Damaged A	B[4]
1	6-7 April	355	341	6	10	7
2	12-13 April	185	195	2	3	6
3	15-16 April	165	150	1	4	2
4	27-28 April	115	100	1	3	1
5	3-4 May	125	110	6	4	2
6	10-11 May	150	125	0	4	0
7	23-25 May	165	150	3	5	1
8	27-29 May	110	100	1	5	2
9	3-7 June	50	40	0	2	1
10	21-22 June	45	40	1	3	1
TOTAL		1465	1351	21	43	23

Counting all planes in these mass attacks, together with individual kamikaze attacks not included in the table, over 3000 sacrificial sorties were launched against American naval forces in the Okinawan campaign. In addition there were hundreds of attacks by conventional dive-bombers and torpedo planes. The total number

[3] Data in this column (after No. 2) are estimates.

[4] A, scrapped or decommissioned as result of damage, or repairs incomplete at end of war; B, out of action for over 30 days. The complete table, including ships sunk or damaged between *kikusui* attacks and by causes other than air, will be found in my *History of United States Naval Operations in World War II* Vol. XIV: *Victory in the Pacific* pp. 390-392.

of Japanese aircraft involved is not known, but the Japanese Navy counts 3700 sorties by Navy planes, including fighter escorts and conventional bombers. The sorties of Army planes, if in the same proportion to Navy as in the *kikusui* attacks, would add some 2600 more. A book might well be written about each of the six greater *kikusui* attacks, with inspiring details of heroism and suffering on the part of the crashed ships' crews. We shall have to content ourselves here with samples only.

In the first and biggest *kikusui* attack, to which no fewer than 355 kamikazes were committed, destroyers *Leutze* and *Newcomb* bore the brunt. In quick succession one kamikaze crashed *Newcomb*'s after stack, a second was splashed, and a third, carrying a large bomb, crashed her amidships, gouging deep into her bowels with a tremendous explosion that cut off all remaining sources of power and blew both engine rooms and the after fireroom into a mass of rubble. "With intentions of polishing us off," wrote her skipper, Commander I. E. McMillian, "a fourth plane raced toward *Newcomb* from the port beam and although under fire by her forward batteries came through to crash into the forward stack, spraying the entire amidships section of *Newcomb*, which was a raging conflagration, with a fresh supply of gasoline." Flames shot up hundreds of feet, followed by a thick pall of smoke and spray which so completely covered the destroyer that sailors in nearby battleships thought that she had gone down.

Destroyer *Leutze*, closing rapidly to render assistance to *Newcomb*, observed with astonishment that she was still holding together. A solid mass of flame swept from bridge to No. 3 gun, but her valiant skipper and crew showed no intention of abandoning ship. Lieutenant Leon Grabowsky, C.O. of *Leutze*, gallantly risked his ship to help her sister, closed her weather side ten minutes after the first crash and passed hose lines on board to help fight fires. Then a fifth plane approached, heading for *Newcomb*'s bridge. One of her 5-inch guns, fired in local control, made a hit which tilted the plane just enough so that it slid athwartship and on to *Leutze*'s fantail, where it exploded, jamming the rudder.

Now *Leutze* too was in trouble. While one of her repair parties continued fighting fires on board *Newcomb*, two others checked flooding on their own ship and jettisoned topside weights. Seventeen compartments laid open to the sea by the Japanese bomb let in so much water that *Leutze* began to settle. Destroyer *Beale*, fire hoses streaming, now closed the disengaged side of *Newcomb*, and *Leutze* signaled, "Am pulling away, in serious danger of sinking." But minesweeper *Defense* (Lieutenant Commander Gordon Abbott USNR), already damaged by two kamikaze hits shortly after 1800, towed *Leutze* to Kerama Retto. Both destroyers had to be scrapped; they were lucky to lose only 47 men killed or missing.

These ships belonged to the gunfire support screen. Radar picket destroyers fared even worse. *Bush* (Commander R. E. Westholm), on radar picket station No. 1, and *Colhoun* (Commander G. R. Wilson), on station No. 2, were the first to be encountered by "floating chrysanthemums" flying southwest along the Nansei Shoto. Advance elements of the massed air attack heckled them all through the midwatch and *Colhoun* was subjected to eleven bombing attacks, all of which missed, between 0230 and 0600 April 6. The forenoon watch was fairly quiet. Around 1500, 40 to 50 planes flew down from the north, stacked at various altitudes between 500 and 20,000 feet, and began orbiting and attacking *Bush*, while about 12 others went after *Cassin Young* at station No. 3, next to the eastward.

Bush shot down two Vals and drove off two more. Thirteen minutes later a Jill was sighted heading low for her. Fire was opened at a range of 7000 yards. The plane jinked and wove at an altitude of 10 to 35 feet above the water; and although every gun on the destroyer was firing, it kept coming and crashed between the two stacks. The bomb exploded in the forward engine room, killing every man there and in the two firerooms. Flooding started immediately and *Bush* took a 10-degree list, but escaping steam smothered the fires and power was regained as the auxiliary diesel generator cut in. Handy-billies were used to control the flooding, the wounded were treated on the fantail or in the wardroom, and, although the ship had gone dead, everyone expected to save her. All hands cheered when a C.A.P. of four planes appeared overhead.

Colhoun, learning by radio that *Bush* needed help, began to close at 35 knots, bringing along her C.A.P. for the short time it could remain. At 1635 she closed *Bush*, apparently foundering. She signaled a support craft, LCS–64, to rescue the crew and tried to interpose herself between the sinking ship and a flight of about 15 Japanese planes. They approached, and one went for *Bush* at 1700. Commander Westholm ordered about 150 of his men fighting fires topside to jump overboard for self-protection, and trailed knotted lines for them to climb on board again. All his 5-inch guns that would bear were jammed in train, but his 40-mm guns opened fire. *Colhoun* shot every gun she had at an approaching Zeke, which splashed midway between the two ships. Another was hit by a 5-inch shell at 4000 yards, and caught fire. *Colhoun*'s guns Nos. 1, 2 and 3 were quickly trained on a third diving at her starboard bow, and the first salvo hit him square on the nose; he splashed 50 yards abeam. Just then Commander Wilson received a report that a fourth Zeke was about to crash his port bow. Too late he ordered full left rudder. The plane, already aflame, hit *Colhoun*'s main deck, killing the gun crews of two 40-mm mounts. Its bomb exploded in the after fireroom, killing everyone there and rupturing the main steamline in the forward engine room. A quick decision by the engineer officer to open the cross-connection valve enabled *Colhoun* to maintain a speed of 15 knots. She was already getting fires under control when the fifth attack within 11 minutes came in. Two kamikazes were splashed but a third crashed, blowing a great hole below the waterline and breaking the ship's keel. While the damage control parties were working, and three 5-inch guns were being fired manually, a sixth attack came in. Two planes were splashed but a third and a fourth crashed *Bush*, killing all the wounded in the wardroom and starting a fierce fire. Still, neither C.O. would give up his ship. At 1800 a kamikaze crashed *Colhoun*, already so badly damaged that this additional misfortune did not make things much worse.

It was now dark. At 1830 a big swell rocked *Bush*, whose structure was now so weak that she jackknifed and slid to the bottom. Commander Wilson of *Colhoun* now decided to abandon his ship. At 1900 *Cassin Young* closed to take off survivors and recover swimmers, and then sank *Colhoun* by gunfire. *LCS–64*, a fleet tug, and a PC, did their best to rescue *Bush*'s swimmers, and those in floater nets and rubber life rafts; but complete darkness had set in, a high, crested sea had made up, and very many were drowned. *Bush* lost 94 officers and men out of 307 on board. *Colhoun*, owing to *Cassin Young*'s prompt rescue work, lost only 35 killed or missing.

There was air-surface action all around Okinawa that afternoon and evening of 6 April. Destroyer *Emmons*, an LST and two Victory ships carrying ammunition were sunk. Six other destroyer types were crashed. Every one of these put up a good fight; most of them splashed four to six kamikazes before one got in. The massed attacks petered out on 7 April, but total casualties to the ships sunk and badly damaged in this No. 1 *kikusui* assault were 466 killed and 568 wounded. And it must be remembered that most of the wounded in these attacks were horribly burned. They suffered excruciating agony until given first aid; for a man blown overboard, hours might elapse until a pharmacist's mate could relieve him. The medical officers did wonders if the wounded survived long enough to receive attention. And many men in rear hospitals, who looked like mummies under their bandages, breathing through a tube and being fed intravenously while their bodies healed, were cured by virtue of new methods of treating burns.

Japanese losses were equally heavy — 355 kamikazes, none of which returned, and 341 conventional bombers, an uncounted number of which were shot down; but if the enemy could keep up attrition at this rate, the objects of Operation TEN-GO would be attained. Some destroyer officers insisted that a pilot bent on crashing could not be stopped by anything smaller than 5-inch shell, and that under the existing system of gunfire control, it was impossible to knock down planes in one-two-three order. Radar picket duty could be as suicidal for the picketing sailors as for the attacking Japanese, unless two or more destroyers were placed at each station and C.A.P. were provided at dawn and dusk, which the escort carrier planes were unable to do. But an encouraging factor was the prompt buildup of a land-based air force. Yontan and Kadena fields were no beds of roses for tired airmen. Japanese artillery shelled them daily; strafers and bombers paid frequent visits. Yet, by the evening of 8 April, 82 Marine Corsairs and seven night fighters were based on Yontan field, and more were brought up within a day or two by escort carriers. Of this number, 41 were already available for C.A.P.; in another week if all went well these would be increased to 144. The land-based night fighters could not be used for C.A.P. before 14 April, as their radar and calibration gear had not yet been unloaded. So the holes in the Fleet's air cover, at dawn and dusk, were not yet filled. Close support duties for Operation ICEBERG tied down TF 58 until well into June; it got away only to sink *Yamato* and strike Kyushu airfields.

The reserve infantry division, the 27th, was landed on 9-10 April, bringing the total number of American troops ashore up to 160,000. Really tough ground fighting now began. The troops were now up against lines that the enemy intended to defend, the edge of a complicated and heavily fortified region across the three-mile-wide waist of the island, from a point south of the beaches to the Nakagusuku Wan. This area included pillboxes with steel doors impervious to flame-throwers. And Japanese artillery fire was increasing in volume and accuracy.

On 12 April opened the second *kikusui* attack, of 185 kamikazes and 195 other planes. It was bad but far less destructive than the first. Radar picket station No. 1, where Captain C. A. Buchanan was O.T.C. in destroyer *Purdy*, first took the rap. On station No. 4 destroyer *Mannert L. Abele* (Commander A. E. Parker) had the dubious honor of being sunk by the first *baka* bomb seen by our forces in action. This little horror was a one-way glider with three rockets as boosters, only 20 feet long with a wing span of 16½ feet and a warhead carrying 2645 pounds of tri-nitro-anisol. *Baka* arrived in the combat area slung under the belly of a two-engined bomber. Its pilot had an umbilical communication with the bomber's pilot, who released him near the target. The suicide pilot had to pull out of a vertical dive into a glide toward the victim, if necessary increasing speed by the rockets to over 500 knots. The small size and tremendous speed of *baka* made it the worst threat to our ships that had yet appeared, almost equivalent to the guided missiles that the Germans were shooting at London.

This initial *baka* attack was well timed. At about 1445 April 12, *Abele* was crashed by a Zeke which penetrated the after engine room. Its bomb exploded, breaking the keel and the shafts, and *Abele* went dead in the water and lost power. About one minute later, in came a *baka* at 500 knots. It hit the ship on her starboard side beneath the forward stack, penetrated No. 1 fireroom, and exploded. The ship's midship section disintegrated, bow and stern parted, and *Abele* went down so quickly that five minutes later there was nothing on the surface where she had been except wreckage and survivors, who were being bombed and strafed by other Japanese planes. Fortunately, their picket station was also manned by two LSM(R)s which closed to pick up survivors and rescued all the destroyer's crew but 79.

On that same day destroyer *Zellars* and battleship *Tennessee* were crashed, but carried on.

Friday, 13 April, broke bright and clear, but in every other respect it was a Black Friday. Just as first light dawned over Okinawa, devastating news came over ships' loudspeakers: —

"Attention! Attention! All hands! President Roosevelt is dead. Repeat, our Supreme Commander, President Roosevelt, is dead."

Half an hour after the morning watch came on duty, Franklin D. Roosevelt had breathed his last. "We were stunned," recorded one bluejacket in attack transport *Montrose*. "Few of us spoke, or even looked at each other. We drifted apart, seeming instinctively to seek solitude. Many prayed, and many shed tears." In no section of the American people was the President so beloved as in the Navy. Bluejackets went about their duties sadly, officers looked anxious, mess attendants appeared as if they had lost their only friend. The question frequently asked of officers, "What will become of us now?" indicated that sailors had looked to Franklin Delano Roosevelt as their champion in peace, their leader in battle, and their guarantee of a better world after victory.

Radio Tokyo reported the President's death simply and decently; but Hitler, in his Berlin bunker, received the news with maniac glee, thinking it would end the war.

Under Harry Truman, now President of the United States, the war effort did not slacken for a moment.

7. *Ordeal by* Kikusui, *16 April–28 May*

On 16 April hell broke loose again in the third *kikusui* attack, 165 planes strong. Destroyer *Laffey* (Commander Frederick J. Becton), in radar picket station No. 1, was the first to catch it, at 0827. Probably no ship has ever survived an attack of the intensity that she experienced. The kamikazes came in from every quarter of the compass. C.A.P. accounted for a number outside the ship's gun range, and boldly flew into the orbit of her gunfire to intercept. During a period of 80 minutes, in 22 separate attacks, *Laffey* was hit by six kamikazes and four bombs, as well as being near-missed by a bomb and by a seventh kamikaze which splashed close aboard. Her guns, fired in local control after the director was knocked out, splashed eight would-be crashers. *Laffey* lost 31 men killed and 72 wounded in this memorable action, well described by Admiral Joy as standing out "above the outstanding." But the ship lived. Towed into Hagushi roadstead, she was patched up and proceeded to the new repair base at Guam under her own power.

Radar picket destroyer *Pringle* was sunk in this attack with a loss of 65 killed and 110 wounded; four others were badly damaged, and out in Task Force 58 *Intrepid* took her usual beating, losing ten killed and 87 wounded.

The little island of Ie Shima, west of northern Okinawa, wanted for land-based search radar, was invaded 16 April by a landing force of the 77th Division, and secured on the 21st. It was here that the beloved war correspondent Ernie Pyle was killed by machine-gun fire when closely following the troops.

After the 16 April attack, radar pickets had a respite of twelve days while the Japanese were readying more "floating chrysanthemums." The fourth *kikusui* attack of 115 kamikazes was spread over 27 and 28 April. One ammunition ship was sunk, one transport and two destroyer types were badly damaged, and the fully lighted hospital ship *Comfort* was crashed, with a loss of six Army nurses, seven wounded patients and 23 others killed and 52, including four nurses, wounded.

Ashore there was bitter fighting during the last week of April, forcing the Japanese back to another series of caves and entrenchments. Each line of defense was stubbornly held by the Japanese until the sheer weight of attack penetrated and forced abandonment. Then the process was repeated. The battle for Okinawa was the toughest and most prolonged of any in the Pacific war since Guadalcanal.

"Naval gunfire," state the Army historians, "was employed longer and in greater quantities in the battle of Okinawa than in any other in history. It supported the ground troops and complemented the artillery from the day of the landing until action moved to the extreme southern tip of the island, where the combat area was so restricted that there was a danger of shelling American troops." [5] Night illumination with star shell, delivered by destroyers, was also a great help to the troops, thwarting Japanese tactics of infiltration and night attack. *Mississippi*, whose special assignment was the demolition of Shuri Castle (where Commodore Perry had been entertained in 1853) fired 2289 rounds of 14-inch and 6650 rounds of 5-inch in six weeks' duty off Okinawa.

The fifth *kikusui* attack, on 3-4 May, proved to be one of the worst. Destroyer *Luce* was crashed and sunk at radar picket station No. 12. Station No. 1, manned by two destroyers, three LCI(L) and *LSM(R)-194*, really had it. *Morrison*, crashed by two Zekes simultaneously, and immediately after by two antique wood-and-canvas biplanes, had to be abandoned in a hurry and lost 159 officers and men, over half her complement, besides some 100 wounded. The other destroyer, *Ingraham*, was crashed but survived; the rocket LSM was crashed and sunk. Total losses to

[5] R. E. Appleman and others *Okinawa: The Last Battle* p. 253.

the fifth attack were two destroyers, two LSM and 370 officers and men. The sixth big attack, of 150 kamikazes on 10-11 May, more powerful than the fifth, did even greater damage. *Bunker Hill* caught it in TF 58, losing almost 400 officers and men killed; destroyer *Hugh W. Hadley* at radar picket station No. 15 beat off almost as many attacks as had *Laffey*. She lost 28 killed and 67 wounded, including her C.O., Commander Byron J. Mullaney, who survived long enough to write an eloquent report on the performance of his ship's company: —

No captain of a man of war had a crew who fought more valiantly against such overwhelming odds. Who can measure the degree of courage of men who stand up to their guns in the face of diving planes that destroy them? . . . I know of no record of a destroyer's crew fighting for one hour and thirty-five minutes against overwhelming aircraft attacks and destroying twenty-three planes. My crew accomplished their mission and displayed outstanding fighting abilities.

The seventh *kikusui* attack on 23-25 May, of 165 kamikazes, was mostly beaten off by the radar pickets but some planes penetrated the fire support area, where they sank destroyer transports *Bates* and *Barry* and *LSM-135*, and knocked out five more vessels. The eighth, on 27-29 May, the last to which more than a hundred planes were committed, knocked out *Braine* and *Anthony* and sank *Drexler* at picket stations 5 and 15, with heavy casualties — 290 killed and 207 wounded.

Few missiles or weapons have ever spread such flaming terror, such torturing burns, such searing death, as did the kamikaze in his self-destroying onslaughts on the radar picket and other ships. And naval history has few parallels to the sustained courage, resourcefulness and fighting spirit that the crews of these vessels displayed day after day after day in the battle for Okinawa.

8. *Okinawa Secured, 29 May–3 July*

The eighth *kikusui* attack coincided with the relief of Admiral Spruance by Admiral Halsey on 27 May, when Fifth Fleet again became Third Fleet, and TF 58, TF 38. Since 17 March the fast carrier forces had been at sea dishing it out and taking the rap, exposed to the threat of air attack day and night. With a count so far of 90 ships sunk or damaged badly enough to be out of action for more than a month, this operation had proved to be the most costly naval campaign of the war. Throughout the ordeal Admiral Spruance clung tenaciously to the principle that Okinawa must be secured. He never flinched, and no more did the officers and men of his command. A less serene and courageous man might, before reaching this point, have asked "Is this island worth the cost? Is there no better way to defeat Japan?" But no such doubts or questions ever even occurred to Raymond A. Spruance.

After two months of bitter fighting on the big island, a company of Marines on 29 May captured the shell of Shuri Castle. Naha, the capital, had already been occupied. At the outset of the final push, General Buckner was killed by Japanese artillery. The two last *kikusui* attacks, on 3-7 and 21-22 June, were small and relatively undestructive.

On 21 June, when Tenth Army drove through to the southernmost point of Okinawa, it could be announced that organized resistance had ceased. General Ushijima committed suicide next day.

Base development began by Seabee battalions soon after L-day. Buckner Bay (formerly Nakagasuku Wan) and Kimmu Wan were transformed into seaports, with docks and other cargo handling facilities. New airfields and a seaplane base were built on the eastern side of Okinawa, and airfields on Ie Shima. The face of the island was changed more than it had been for thousands of years, by multi-lane roads, traffic circles, water points, quonset villages, tank farms, storage dumps and hospitals. And by the end of the war in mid-August, base development had progressed to the point where Okinawa could well have performed its original purpose of serving as an advance base for the invasion of Japan proper.

Although your historian himself has been under kamikaze attack, and witnessed the hideous forms of death and torture inflicted by that weapon, words fail him to do justice to the sailors who met it so courageously. Men on radar picket station, to survive, not only had to strike down the flaming terror of the kamikazes roaring out of the blue like thunderbolts of Zeus; they were under constant strain and intense discomfort. In order to supply high steam pressure to build up full speed rapidly in a destroyer, its superheaters, built only for intermittent use, had to be lighted for three and four days' running. For days and even nights on end, the crew had to stand general quarters while the ship was kept "buttoned up." Men had to keep in readiness for the instant reaction and split-second timing necessary to riddle a plane bent on sacrificial death. Sleep became the rarest commodity and choicest luxury, like water to a shipwrecked mariner.

The capture of Okinawa cost the United States Navy 34 naval vessels and craft sunk, 368 damaged, over 4900 sailors killed or missing in action, and over 4800 wounded. Tenth Army lost 7613 killed or missing in action and 31,800 wounded. Sobering as it is to record such losses, the sacrifice of these men is brightened by our knowledge that the capture of Okinawa helped to bring Japanese leaders to face the inevitable surrender.

As Winston Churchill put it, in a message of 22 June to President Truman, "This battle [is] among the most intense and famous of military history. . . . We make our salute to all your troops and their commanders engaged."

CHAPTER XVII

The End of the War

November 1944–September 1945

1. *The U-Boats' Comeback and Defeat, November 1944–May 1945*

THE FEELING OF SECURITY from U-boats which had long existed on the Eastern Sea Frontier of the United States was dissipated by several incidents in the fall of the year 1944.

U–1230 landed on the Maine coast a German and a renegade American who had been given a thorough course of training in Nazi sabotage schools. This big snorkel-equipped submarine shaped a course for Mount Desert Rock, where it escaped the notice of fishermen, coastal pickets and air patrol, steamed into Frenchmans Bay on the calm night of 29 November and debarked the spies in a rubber boat. Landing at Hancock Point, they were observed by a smart lad who notified the police; trailed by F.B.I. agents to New York, they were there picked up. *U–1230* sank a Canadian steamer, 44 members of whose crew died in the icy waters of the Bay of Fundy, and then took up weather-reporting duties.

During December large numbers of U-boats began leaving their Baltic and Norwegian bases, to discover that with snorkel they could operate successfully in coastal waters. They appeared off the East Coast of Britain and in the Western Approaches. Taking advantage of currents and unfavorable sound conditions in shallow waters, they often eluded the antisubmarine vessels and did a good deal of damage. Their active range also extended into the English Channel. Around 10 January 1945 the snorkelers moved into the Irish Sea, where they sank several merchantmen and a British escort carrier. This activity became of great concern to the Allied high command. In spite of the repeated bombing of German plants where U-boats were built, the Germans had so cleverly dispersed production as to raise their average monthly output, December-March, to 27 U-boats, greater than it had been since 1942. By 1 February at least 25 snorkelers were moving into British coastal waters; and this was the first time since 1941 that shipping in the narrow seas had been so troubled. The Admiralty had to deploy over 400 escort vessels and 800 Coastal Command planes to deal with these boats. They sank 51 ships of 253,000 tons in the Atlantic from January through April 1945. The German Army was collapsing under Russian, American and British advances into Germany, but Doenitz was trying to do as much damage as possible before he and the gods of Nazidom passed into the twilight. The snorkel blitz was his counterpart to the kamikaze — a weapon that could only postpone, but could not possibly prevent, Allied victory.

The Royal Navy, assisted by Coastal Command — which now included several United States Navy Liberator squadrons — had to cope with this offensive in the narrow seas, and finally brought to book most of the snorkelers abroad. The R. A. F. and A. A. F. Bomber Commands helped by destroying 24 more in German harbors in March and April.

Four snorkelers moved across the Atlantic early in the New Year. All were sunk by the persistence of hunter-killer groups composed of destroyers and DEs. But this was not Doenitz's final effort in the Western Atlantic.

Early in 1945, tales of the captured spies from *U-1230* and other intelligence items, created a serious apprehension that U-boats were preparing to launch attacks on East Coast cities with robot rocket bombs such as those then falling on London. Admiral Jonas Ingram, who had relieved Admiral Ingersoll as Cinclant, feeling that the American public was becoming too complacent, created a sensation by announcing this unpleasant possibility. Doenitz was indeed planning a final blitz on the Eastern Sea Frontier, but the six 740-ton snorkel U-boats which made up this Group "Seewolf" carried no secret or unconventional weapons. In fact he had none; and in late March 1945, when he dispatched these boats from their Norwegian bases, armies under Eisenhower and Zhukov were battering their way into the heart of the Reich.

Doenitz however, had the satisfaction of giving Cinclant and Tenth Fleet a big scare. Admiral Ingram, who as commander in Brazilian waters had successfully barred the Atlantic Narrows to German raiders and U-boats, tried similar tactics here. He organized a Barrier Force of twenty destroyer escorts to maintain a 120-mile picket line along the meridian which passes between Fayal and Flores, supported by an escort carrier with a screen of DEs, cruising forty to fifty miles to the westward. The first barrier, with Commander Morgan H. Harris USNR commanding the picket line, and Captain Kenneth Craig as C.O. of the *Croatan* carrier group, was set up in exceedingly rough weather on 11 April. *Frost* and *Stanton,* skillful hunters from the carrier screen, sank *U–1235* and *U–880* in a fog-mull on the night of 15-16 April. A second night attack in heavy fog on 21 April by DEs *Carter* and *Neal A. Scott* sank *U–518.* The "creeping" tactics which enabled these destroyer escorts to make kills on foggy nights were worked out by Commander F. D. Giambattista, who had commanded the screen of *Croatan* when that carrier's C.O. was a great U-boat hunter — Captain John P. W. Vest.

The *Croatan* group was now relieved by one built around *Bogue,* commanded by Captain George J. Dufek. A third, of which *Core* (Captain R. S. Purvis) was the nucleus, operated near by. It was still so foggy that aircraft could give no help; five out of six boats of Group "Seewolf" were destroyed by DEs. But one of these gallant little ships was sacrificed in the effort. On 24 April *Frederick C. Davis* detected *U–546* trying to slip through the screen to get *Bogue,* and when hunting it was herself torpedoed and sunk, with great loss of life. The U-boat, after being intensively hunted, hedgehogged and depth-charged for 12 hours, came up fighting, and was then sunk by *Flaherty's* gunfire, helped by that of three other DEs. And on 6 May *U–881* was sunk by DE *Farquhar.*

These destroyer escorts did their designers and their crews proud in the last months of the war. The final battle in the Western Atlantic was the sinking of snorkeler *U–853* by DE *Atherton* and frigate *Moberly*, off Block Island on 6 May, a few hours before Germany surrendered.

Doenitz's most formidable aces in the hole, the new Type XXI, XXIII and XXVI U-boats, never got into this war. Type XXI was a 1500-tonner with diesel-electric engines, new and powerful batteries, and a beautifully streamlined hull so that she could make 17½ knots submerged. No. XXIII was the same. The first boat of Type XXI was launched in April 1944 on Hitler's birthday, and 119 units were completed before the end of the war; but they were so badly built that they had to be recalled after their training cruises, even during initial war patrols, for extensive repairs and alterations. Only three of these actually departed on combat missions, too late to accomplish anything. An even greater menace was Type XXVI, the "Walter boat," powered by a hydrogen-peroxide turbine which required no air, and capable of steaming 158 miles submerged at 25 knots. Three of these were completed before the end of the war but never got to sea. Fortunate indeed that the war in Europe ended when it did; for a couple of hundred U-boats of these new types might have ruptured Allied sea communications and prolonged the struggle into 1946.

On 30 April 1945, before Group "Seawolf" had been liquidated,

Hitler died a coward's death in his Berlin bunker. Deserted at the last by all top Nazis trying to save their skins, the Fuehrer designated his loyal C. in C. Navy, Grossadmiral Doenitz, as his successor. On 4 May Doenitz had his first surrender offer in the hands of Field Marshal Montgomery, and ordered every German warship at sea to stop fighting and give up, or return to port. The surrender papers were signed at Rheims at 0241 May 7 Central Europe time, Russia signing next day, which is the official V-E day.

The total number of U-boats sunk by Allied forces or lost by marine casualty during the war was 781, together with some 32,000 officers and men. The German submarine fleet sank 2575 Allied and neutral merchant ships, totaling 14.5 million tons.[1] The sailors killed or drowned in these ships numbered just under 30,000 for the British merchant marine alone; and to this we must add at least 15,000 American merchant mariners, passengers, and sailors of the warships sunk.

Of the 398 U-boats still in commission, 217 were destroyed by their own crews. Most of the others began popping up all over the Narrow Seas, off Iceland and Gibraltar, and off the East Coast of the United States, flying the black flag of surrender as Admiral Burrough RN, acting for General Eisenhower, ordered them to do. "They surfaced above their handiwork, in hatred or in fear: sometimes snarling their continued rage, sometimes accepting thankfully a truce they had never offered to other ships, other sailors."[2] They broadcast their positions and were escorted into port with a prize crew on board to prevent scuttling. Of four submarines thus brought into Portsmouth, New Hampshire, *U-234* was a 1600-tonner en route to Tokyo with a German technical mission. The skipper of *U-234* gave permission to two Japanese officer passengers

[1] Italian submarines (of which 85 were lost) sank 94 ships of 532,393.
[2] Nicholas Monsarrat *The Cruel Sea* (1951) p. 501.

to commit suicide before he surrendered; but to his disgust they dosed themselves with luminal instead of performing the traditional *seppuku,* and died slowly and ignobly. Two diehard skippers sailed their boats all the way to Buenos Aires, where they expected to obtain asylum; instead they were surrendered by the Argentine government to the United States Navy.

On 28 May 1945 the Admiralty and C.N.O. issued a joint announcement that convoys were abolished, and that all merchant ships "at night will burn navigation lights at full brilliancy and need not darken ship." This did not, of course, apply to the Pacific; but to sailors in the North and South Atlantic, the Arctic and the Indian Oceans, it meant that the war was really over, and completely won.

There is no denying that the submarine was the greatest threat to Allied victory over the Axis. Doenitz was a competent tactician, and he fought clean; for all his adulation of Hitler, he was a good, solid German and a great leader. The morale of the U-boat crews, which had broken down badly in World War I, kept high to the very end in 1945. But his "integral tonnage concept," which he defends as sound strategy, was a failure. The graph of Allied and neutral merchant ship losses was overtaken by that of new construction in July 1943, and the two never again converged. Doenitz's idea that a ton of shipping lost to the Allies, no matter where or how employed, gained that much to Germany, was unsound; in order to make a score he (fortunately for us) sent to the South Atlantic and Indian Oceans U-boats which, to have decisive effect, should have been hurled at the transatlantic troop and merchant convoys, bridges of ships between the Old World and the New. Admiral Lord Cunningham declared that "Doenitz was probably the most dangerous enemy Britain has had to face since

De Ruyter," a compliment indeed from this great Sea Lord. Admiral King, I think, would have considered Admiral Yamamoto our most competent enemy, with Doenitz a good second.

One boon Doenitz lacked which his enemies enjoyed was a close coöperation with air forces and scientists. It was the unbeatable combination of surface and air power and scientific research that enabled the British and American antisubmarine forces to win. Quantity also entered into it; "more and better of everything" — more and better escorts, more and better planes, better training, improved and vastly more numerous weapons, finally smothered the U-boats. But let us never forget that the initial successes and surprises effected by the U-boats fell not far short of rendering Germany invincible on the seas, while her armies were carrying everything before them on the continent of Europe.

2. *Last Actions in the Pacific, 10 July–15 August*

In Admiral Nimitz's plan of 15 May 1945, Admiral Halsey's Third Fleet was given the mission to "attack Japanese naval and air forces, shipping, shipyards and coastal objectives," as well as to "cover and support Ryukyus forces." On 1 July, after organized resistance on Okinawa had ceased, Task Force 38 sortied from Leyte Gulf to operate close to Japan; and there it stayed until Japan surrendered. The first strikes against Tokyo took place on 10 July. These took the Japanese by surprise, and surprised our pilots too, since they encountered no opposition from the air, very little anti-aircraft fire, and grounded planes were well hidden and cunningly camouflaged. For the Japanese were husbanding aircraft to be used in mass kamikaze attacks on the amphibious assault on Kyushu which never came off, thanks to the atomic bomb.

On 14 and 15 July TF 38 planes struck hitherto untouched targets in Honshu and Hokkaido. They completely disrupted the Aomori-Hakodate car ferry system, which carried the coal trade across Tsugaru Strait.

Simultaneously with the air strikes, and for the first time, a naval gunfire force bombarded a major installation within the home islands of Japan. This was the iron works at Kamaishi, one of the seven plants of the Japan Iron Company. Rear Admiral John F. Shafroth commanded the bombardment unit, which comprised battleships *South Dakota, Indiana* and *Massachusetts,* two heavy cruisers and nine destroyers. This bombardment caused a loss of the equivalent of two and one half months of coke production and one month of pig iron production.

On 16 July another task unit under Rear Admiral Oscar Badger, comprising battleships *Iowa, Missouri* and *Wisconsin,* two light cruisers and eight destroyers, bombarded the Nihon Steel Company and the Wanishi Ironworks at Muroran, Hokkaido. This was conducted at exceedingly long range, around midnight, in a heavy overcast and rain which precluded plane spot or illumination. A record number of 16-inch shell was expended. Astern of Admiral Badger's unit steamed H.M.S. *King George V* and two British destroyers, to bombard a plant about eight miles north of the city. The damage resulting from this bombardment cannot be isolated from what was inflicted by B–29s in June and again on 19 July; but the cumulative effect was to cut production almost to zero, and to interrupt rail service, electricity and water supply.

By the end of July the Japanese surface and air navies were knocked out or impotent; but, just as German U-boats swarmed into the Western Atlantic up to the very end of the war, so Japanese submarines continued active in the Western Pacific, and they were much more successful than the U-boats.

The final Japanese naval offensive comprised six I-boats, each carrying six *kaiten* one-man midget submarines, better known as the "human torpedoes." A *kaiten* from *I-53* on 24 July sank destroyer escort *Underhill* when escorting a convoy, with a loss of 112 officers and men. Most disastrous was the loss of heavy cruiser *Indianapolis* (Captain Charles B. McVay), when steaming unescorted across the Philippine Sea to join a training unit off Leyte Gulf. Shortly before midnight 29 July she was torpedoed and sunk by *I-58*. Out of 1199 men on board, some 800 got into the water or into life rafts alive; but, owing to carelessness on the part of authorities ashore, the nonarrival of the cruiser was not noted; the report of an Army aircraft pilot who saw Very lights fired from Captain McVay's life rafts was neglected; and an intercepted contact report from the I-boat's skipper to Tokyo was dismissed as Japanese boasting. The floating survivors were sighted by a Navy plane 84 hours after their ship had gone down, and only 316 were rescued alive.

From this tale of routine stupidity and unnecessary suffering it is pleasant to return to the big carriers. Probably the largest logistics operation ever performed on the high seas was the refueling and replenishment of TF 38 on 21-22 July, along lat. 30° N and between longs. 147° and 142° E. Rear Admiral Beary's floating service force provided the flattops and their screen with 6369 tons of ammunition, 379,157 barrels of fuel oil, 1635 tons of stores and provisions, 99 replacement aircraft and 412 replacements of officers and men.

Replenishment completed 23 July, TF 38 proceeded to launching points for entering the Inland Sea. These strikes, delivered on 24 and 28 July, were among the heaviest of the war and the most destructive of shipping. At Kure and Kobe most of the heavy ships still left to the Imperial Navy were moored in coves and difficult of access to bombers, which nevertheless scored heavily on warships that had been slugging it out with the United States Navy since 1942. Battleships *Haruna*, *Ise* and *Hyuga*, veterans of numerous fights, and battle-scarred heavy cruisers *Tone* and *Aoba*,

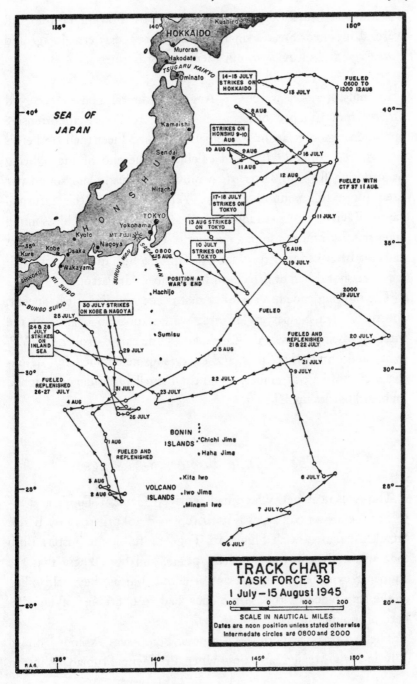

TRACK CHART
TASK FORCE 38
1 July – 15 August 1945

100   0   100   200

SCALE IN NAUTICAL MILES
Dates are noon position unless stated otherwise
Intermediate circles are 0800 and 2000

were now so heavily damaged that they settled on the bottom and were abandoned. Strikes on the new aircraft carriers *Amagi* and *Katsuragi,* and on *Ryuho,* put them out of business.

In mid-forenoon watch 15 August, Admiral Halsey received orders from Cincpac ordering the Navy to "cease all offensive operations against Japan." Commander Third Fleet then broke his four-starred admiral's flag and celebrated the end of the fighting by ordering flagship *Missouri* to blow her whistle and sound her siren for a full minute, at 1100. Yet, even while this informal paean of victory was sounding and starry flags were blossoming on every flag officer's ship, a number of enemy planes, whose pilots had not been ordered to cease fire, approached to attack TF 38. All were shot down or driven off by Combat Air Patrol.

The fighting ended so abruptly that peace was difficult to accept, and the Allied Navies in Japanese waters took no chance of the surrender being a ruse. Air search, antisubmarine patrol and C.A.P. continued on wartime basis, and every ship maintained full defensive alert until 2 September, when the formal surrender was signed on board battleship *Missouri.*

3. *The Atomic Bombs, 6–9 August*

The Koiso cabinet, which had replaced General Tojo's as a result of the loss of Saipan, was itself replaced 7 April 1945 by Baron Suzuki's cabinet, with Shigenori Togo as foreign minister. Both men were advocates of a speedy peace, and both knew that the Emperor expected them to bring it about; but as they held office at the sufferance of the Army, they had to continue making die-hard pronouncements.

The American experimental atomic bomb was exploded on 16 July in New Mexico, at a time when President Truman, Winston

Churchill and the Combined Chiefs of Staff were meeting in Potsdam. The use of the bomb against Japan as soon as possible, without warning, had already been recommended to the President by a committee of high officials and top atomic scientists. And on 25 July the President issued the directive.

In the meantime, Suzuki and other Japanese statesmen were playing with the idiotic notion of getting out of the war through the friendly mediation of Stalin, who had already decided to go in on the other side. Anything to save face! Everyone in the government knew that the war was lost, and that the B–29s were capable of wiping out one Japanese city after another. But nothing was done to prepare the people for the inevitable. On the contrary, Suzuki issued a statement that the loss of Okinawa "improved Japan's strategic position," and dealt America a "severe spiritual blow." "Peace agitators" were threatened in official broadcasts, efforts were made to increase war production, a program of building underground shelters was announced to protect the people from air bombing, and of stockpiling food to render them self-sufficient.

All these foolish calculations were upset by the Potsdam Declaration of 26 July by Truman, Churchill and Chiang Kai-shek, stating conditions under which Japan could end the war. The essential ones were: surrender of all conquests made since 1895; Japan not to be "destroyed as a nation, but stern justice shall be meted out to all war criminals"; "Freedom of speech, of religion, and of thought, as well as respect for the fundamental human rights, shall be established"; Allied occupation of Japan, to be withdrawn "as soon as these objectives have been accomplished, and there has been established a peacefully inclined and responsible government." The Japanese government was called upon "to proclaim now the unconditional surrender of all Japanese armed forces," the alternative being "prompt and utter destruction."

Still, the Suzuki government could not bring itself to face facts and accept the inevitable. One little word at that point could have averted the horror of Hiroshima, since the President's directive to use the bomb could not be executed for at least a week, and at any time could be countermanded. Truman and Secretary Byrnes listened eagerly for that word; but all that came from Suzuki was a silly statement that the Potsdam Declaration was unworthy of notice.

B–29 "Enola Gay" was commanded by Colonel Paul W. Tibbets; Captain William S. Parsons, a naval ordnance expert, went along to make the final adjustments to the bomb. She took off from Tinian at 0245 August 6 and toggled out the bomb over Hiroshima, headquarters of the Japanese Second Army, at 0915.

A new chapter then opened in the history of warfare, and a new challenge to mankind to avert his own destruction.

4. *The Surrender of Japan, 10 August–2 September*

Even after the second atomic bomb was exploded over Nagasaki on 9 August, the same day that Russia declared war on Japan, members of the Imperial Conference, the highest authority in Japan, tried to evade surrender. Admiral Toyoda, the Navy chief of staff; General Umezu, the Army chief of staff; and General Anami, the war minister, all insisted not only that guarantees be given of the Emperor's inviolability, but that there be no military occupation of Japan, no disarming of Japanese troops overseas, no trial of war criminals except by Japanese courts. Foreign Minister Togo pointed out that they could never get Allied consent to such conditions. At a second meeting of the Conference, which lasted until 0230 August 10, the Emperor intervened. He it was who decided, provisionally, to surrender according to the Potsdam terms. That decision was sent to the Allied governments via Switzerland at 0700, and was accepted by them.

Even then there was shuffling of feet among the war lords

in Tokyo; understandably it was a terrible shock to military men with their long tradition of victory to accept defeat short of annihilation. At a third Imperial Conference, opened at 1100 August 14, Anami, Umezu and Toyoda urged the Emperor to fight "one last battle" for the defense of Japan itself, to save national honor. The Emperor then spoke the thoughts that he had long held. Continuing the war would merely result in additional destruction; the nation would be reduced to ashes. The Allied reply to his note of 0700 August 10 indicating positively that he was to continue to reign, showed evidence "of the peaceful and friendly intentions of the enemy." It was the Imperial desire that his ministers of state accept it. They must at once prepare an Imperial rescript broadcasting this decision directly to the people.

The deed was done. At 1449 August 14 (East Longitude date) Radio Tokyo flashed the Emperor's decision around the world. The official notification reached President Truman at 1550 August 14, West Longitude date. He announced it from the White House at 1900 the same day, and declared a two-day holiday of jubilation.

It was a very near thing. That night a military plot to seize the Emperor and impound his recording of the Imperial rescript (which was to be broadcast on the 15th) was narrowly averted. Attempts were made to assassinate Suzuki and others. But the Emperor's message to his people went out in the morning. It ended on the dignified note, "We charge you, Our loyal subjects, to carry out faithfully Our will." Even after the Emperor's will had been made public, it was touch and go whether the Japanese actually would surrender. Hirohito had to send members of the Imperial family to the principal Army commands to ensure compliance. Prince Takamatsu was just in time to make the Atsugi airfield available for the first occupation forces on 26 August, and to keep the kamikazes grounded — they were boasting that they would crash *Missouri* when she entered Tokyo Bay. If these elements had had their way, the war would have been resumed with the Allies feeling that the Japanese were hoplessly treacherous, and with a savagery on both sides that is painful to contemplate.

When these facts and events of the Japanese surrender are known and weighed, it will become evident that the atomic bomb was the keystone of a very fragile arch. Certainly the war would have gone on, and God knows for how long, if the bomb had not been dropped. It has been argued that the maritime blockade would have strangled Japanese economy, and that the B–29s and naval bombardment would have destroyed her principal cities and forced a surrender without benefit of atomic fission. I do not think that anyone acquainted with the admirable discipline and tenacity of the Japanese people can believe this. If their Emperor had told them to fight to the last man, they would have fought to the last man, suffering far, far greater losses and injuries than those inflicted by the atomic bombs.

The probable effects of the projected invasions of Kyushu and Honshu (Operations OLYMPIC and CORONET) in the fall and winter of 1945-1946, and of a desperate hand-to-hand, place-to-place defense of Japan, stagger the imagination. It is simply not true that Japan had no military capability left in mid-August. She had plenty of ammunition; the United States Army after the war found thousands of tons holed up in Hokkaido alone. She had over a million men under arms in the home islands. Although 2550 kamikaze planes had been expended, 5350 were still left, together with as many more ready for orthodox use, and 5000 young men were training for the Kamikaze Corps. All aircraft were to be dispersed on small grass strips in Kyushu, Shikoku and western Honshu, and in underground hangars and caves, to be readied for kamikaze crashes on the Allied amphibious forces invading Kyushu. It requires no prophetic sense to foresee the horrible losses that would have been inflicted on our invading forces, even before they got ashore. After accepting these losses there would have been protracted battles on Japanese soil, which would have cost each side very many more lives, and created a bitterness which even time could hardly have healed. Moreover, Russia would have been a full partner in this final campaign, Japan would have been divided like Germany, and so completely prostrate that the Communists would have had little difficulty in taking over the country.

President Truman announced that General of the Army Douglas MacArthur would be Supreme Commander of the Allied Powers (SCAP) for the surrender and occupation of Japan. This set in motion the wheels of an occupation which rolled smoothly but not quite so fast as that of Germany. For the Imperial government was intact and the Japanese Army, still undefeated, was in a position to resist any premature attempt of the Allies to take over. General MacArthur, who understood the situation perfectly, was responsible for the sequence of events which gave time for the Emperor's commands to reach all his armed forces, as well as time for his own command to prepare the first landings of occupation troops. On 15 August the General directed the Japanese government by radio to order "immediate cessation of hostilities" and to send "a competent representative" by air to Manila to receive instructions for the formal surrender and the reception of occupation forces. An Imperial order went out at 1600 16 August "to the entire Armed Forces to cease fire immediately." This, it will be observed, was thirty hours after Admiral Nimitz had ordered all United States forces to cease fire.

Admiral Halsey decided to anchor major units of Third Fleet in Sagami Wan, under the shadow of Mount Fuji. His own flagship *Missouri*, H.M.S. *Duke of York* wearing the flag of Admiral Sir Bruce Fraser RN, and other ships of Third Fleet and of the British Pacific Fleet, entered Sagami Wan 27 August and proceeded to selected berths. From the anchorage, the sun appeared that evening to set directly into the crater of Mount Fuji. It seemed symbolic — a dismal setting of that sun which had risen triumphant over Oahu on 7 December 1941.

On 29 August, Admiral Nimitz arrived by air, and next morning landings began at the Japanese forts guarding the entrance to Tokyo Bay and at Yokosuka naval base. General MacArthur arrived by air at Atsugi airfield the same day, and set off for Yokohama, where final arrangements were made for the formal signing of the instrument of surrender, at 0900 September 2. General MacArthur, having obtained his wish, the prior occupation of Japan, yielded to Admiral Nimitz the choice of place. Battleship *Missouri* (Captain S. S. Murray), became the scene of the ceremony. She anchored in Tokyo Bay about four and a half miles from Commodore Perry's old anchorage, and on a bulkhead overlooking the ceremony was displayed the 31-star flag that Perry carried into Tokyo Bay in 1853. There were now anchored in that Bay 258 warships of all types from battleship to beaching craft, representing the Allied nations which had been at war with Japan. Most of the aircraft carriers remained outside in order to launch planes at the appropriate moment of this "V-J Day."

Sunday, 2 September, dawned with scattered clouds that dissipated during the morning. The "Mighty Mo," as the bluejackets called her, was especially rigged for the occasion. At Morning Colors the flag that had flown over the Capitol in Washington on 7 December 1941 was raised on the battleship's flagstaff. Destroyer *Buchanan* closed her starboard side at 0803 to deliver high-ranking officers and Allied representatives. When Fleet Admiral Nimitz came on board at 0805, his five-starred flag was broken at the main, Admiral Halsey having shifted his four-starred flag to *Iowa*. General MacArthur's flag was promptly broken alongside that of Admiral Nimitz.

At 0856 the Japanese delegation, lifted from Yokohama in destroyer *Lansdowne*, mounted the starboard gangway. They were headed by the Foreign Minister, Mamoru Shigemitsu, followed by

General Umezu, the diehard chief of the Army general staff, to sign on behalf of Imperial General Headquarters; Rear Admiral S. Tomioka, chief Navy planner for Imperial General Headquarters, and other representatives of the Foreign Office, the Army and the Navy. The civilians were in formal morning dress with top hats, in contrast to the ill-fitting uniforms of the military members and to the khaki uniforms with open-neck shirts worn by the United States Navy and Army officers. Sideboys were stationed and the Japanese delegation were piped on board. As they arrived on deck, their faces expressing no emotion, complete silence fell over the assembled multitude.

Immediately abaft the table on which the documents lay stood representatives of the Allied Nations to sign for their respective governments. On their right and under *Missouri's* No. 2 turret stood a score of flag and general officers of the United States who had taken a leading part in the war against Japan. The atmosphere was frigid. The Japanese, performing an act unprecedented in their country's history, preserved their dignity. After three or four minutes had elapsed, General MacArthur appeared with Admirals Nimitz and Halsey. The General took his place before the microphones to open the ceremony. At his side were Lieutenant General Jonathan M. Wainwright USA, who had surrendered the Philippines in 1942, and Lieutenant General Sir Arthur E. Percival, who had surrendered Singapore the same year. Both had been flown from prison camps in Manchuria. General MacArthur made a short speech stating the purpose of the occasion, concluding with a ringing expression of hope for the future: —

It is my earnest hope — indeed the hope of all mankind — that from this solemn occasion a better world shall emerge out of the blood and carnage of the past, a world founded upon faith and understanding, a world dedicated to the dignity of man and the fulfillment of his most cherished wish for freedom, tolerance and justice.

Mr. Kase of the Foreign office was profoundly moved by the General's words. It transformed the battleship's quarterdeck, he recorded, "into an altar of peace."

Appropriately, it was Foreign Minister Shigemitsu who, after a year's quiet working for peace, first signed the instrument of surrender at 0904 September 2, officially ending the war. It had lasted exactly 1364 days, 5 hours and 44 minutes from the attack on Pearl Harbor. General Umezu, who in contrast to Shigemitsu had held out for fighting to the last, signed next for Japan. General Mac-Arthur signed the acceptance for all Allied powers; then came the individual signers for each of the nations that had been at war with Japan: the United States (for which Admiral Nimitz signed), Great Britain, Russia, Australia, Canada, France, The Netherlands, and New Zealand.

After all had signed, General MacArthur spoke a final word:

"Let us pray that peace be now restored to the world and that God will preserve it always."

As the formalities came to an end, at 0925, the sun broke through, and a flight of 450 carrier aircraft, together with several hundred of the Army Air Force, swept over *Missouri* and her sister ships.

That Sunday evening Admirals Halsey and Wilkinson attended an impressive sunset ceremony held by Admiral Sir Bruce Fraser on board flagship H.M.S. *Duke of York*, anchored not far from *Missouri*. The flags of all Allies, flying from the signal yards, were handsomely lowered in unison as massed bands from all British ships present played the music of Ellerton's sunset hymn: —

> The day thou gavest, Lord, is ended,
> The darkness falls at thy behest;
> To thee our morning hymns ascended,
> Thy praise shall sanctify our rest.

So be it, Lord; thy throne shall never,
  Like earth's proud empires, pass away:
Thy kingdom stands, and grows for ever,
  Till all thy creatures own thy sway.

Nothing could have been more appropriate to the occasion than this Sunday evening hymn to the "Author of Peace and Lover of Concord." The familiar words and music, floating over the now calm waters of the Bay to American and British bluejackets, touched the mystic chords of memory, reminding all hands of the faith that had sustained them through travail and sacrifice. It made sailors feel that their Navies had achieved something more than a military victory.

They were right. If victory over Japan meant anything beyond a change in the balance of power, it meant that eternal values and immutable principles, which had come down to us from ancient Hellas, had been reaffirmed and reëstablished. Often these principles are broken, often these values are lost to sight when people are struggling for power or survival; but to them man must return, and does return, in order to enjoy his Creator's greatest gifts — life, liberty and the pursuit of happiness.

CHAPTER XVIII

Conclusion

IN CONCLUSION, your historian may be allowed a few estimates and remarks on how the United States Navy conducted
itself in this, the greatest of all wars in which it has ever been
engaged.

On the whole, gloriously. But certain faults and lapses must be
remembered, if we are to maintain high standards and meet the
challenge of the atomic age. The Navy was caught unprepared
mentally for the attack on Pearl Harbor, largely owing to routine
and lack of imagination in the higher echelons. It was caught unprepared, both materially and technically, to cope with the U-boat
menace — despite benefit of British experience in over two years of
antisubmarine war. The Navy's fighter planes and torpedo-bombers were inferior to those of the Japanese, whose night-fighting
tactics were superior to ours until mid-1943. Although certain strategists in the United States Navy anticipated the use of aircraft
carriers to project striking power deep into enemy-held waters,
too many envisaged this war as a succession of Jutlands, to be decided by big guns on battleships. Consequently our gunfire became
highly effective, but warships greater than destroyers had no torpedo tubes. Torpedoes themselves underwent no development between wars, and the testing of those we had was so inefficient and
misleading that United States submarines long had the mor-
tification of making hit after hit with no explosion to follow. The destroyers, fortunately, retained their torpedoes, but
the tactical employment of destroyers for surface action was infer-

ior to that of the Japanese prior to the Battle of Vella Gulf in 1943.

Although the *Iowa* class battleships never had a chance at a long-range gunfire battle (and what a beauty there would have been off San Bernardino Strait had Halsey released Lee in time!) the accuracy and efficiency of our naval gunfire was a great asset in the war. Gunfire support almost opened a new dimension to amphibious operations. Antiaircraft fire, helped by the proximity-fused shell, became so deadly that the Japanese were forced to adopt suicide tactics. Although aircraft bombing tolled the bell for long-range battleship action, naval gunfire will always be wanted to cover amphibious landings, which are likely to be necessary as long as there is war.

The United States Navy quickly adopted and developed the English invention of radar; but it was not until well into 1943 that officers generally appreciated its capabilities and limitations, and made best use of it. Nevertheless, the prior possession of radar turned out to be a great asset.

In antisubmarine warfare it was long before the United States Navy caught up with its teacher, the Royal Navy of Great Britain. But we made full use both of British experience and the contributions of American scientists and mathematicians. This was only the second war that the Navy fought as part of a coalition, and its relations with the British and Royal Canadian Navies were far closer and more effective than in World War I. In the Pacific the United States Navy, owing to its overwhelming strength, called the tune, but was loyally followed by the smaller Navies of three British Commonwealths.

Admiral Ernest J. King was the Navy's principal architect of victory. A stern sailor of commanding presence, vast sea-knowledge, and keen strategic sense, he was so insistent on maintaining the independence of the Navy, not only from our great Ally but from the Army, that he seemed at times to be anti-British and anti-Army. Neither was true; but King's one mistaken idea was his steady opposition to "mixed groups" from different Navies in the same task force; an idea strengthened by the unfortunate experience of the

ABDA command. Mixed groups were of necessity adopted on the convoy routes, with American, Canadian and even an occasional Free French or Polish destroyer in the same escort unit, and they worked well; whilst in the Pacific, ships of the Royal Australian and New Zealand Navies operated perfectly with those of the United States. All three services of the same country worked well on one team in forward areas where the real fighting went on. The in-fighting between services and the disputes between British and American representatives were largely confined to Washington, London or wherever the Combined Chiefs of Staff met.

We may, however, concede to Admiral King a few prejudices, for he was undoubtedly the best naval strategist and organizer in our history. His insistence on limited offensives in the Pacific to keep the Japanese off balance, his successful efforts to provide more and more escorts for convoys, his promotion of the escort carrier antisubmarine groups, his constant backing of General Marshall to produce a firm date for Operation OVERLORD from the reluctant British; his insistence on the dual approach to Japan, are but a few of the many decisions that prove his genius. King's strategy for the final defeat of Japan — the Formosa and China Coast approach, rather than the Luzon-Okinawa route — was over-ruled; but may well, in the long run, have been better than Mac-Arthur's, which was adopted. King was also defeated in his many attempts to interest the Royal Navy in a Southeast Asia comeback; and in this he was right. The liberation of Malaya before the war's end would have spared the British Empire a long battle with local Communists and would have provided at least a more orderly trans-fer of sovereignty in the Netherlands East Indies.

After King, Nimitz was our greatest naval strategist and leader, and, as Cincpac-Cincpoa, he had, after King, the biggest responsi-bility. Nimitz engineered, as it were, the Battles of the Coral Sea and Midway; patiently but stubbornly he held out for the dual approach to Japan. He proposed the bold plan to go right into Kwajalein after securing the Gilberts, and he put it across, con-trary to the advice of others. He made only two possible mistakes in the war — detaching Admiral Kinkaid prematurely from his South Pacific task force, and rejecting Halsey's proposal that Peleliu be bypassed. Nimitz probably inspired a greater personal loyalty than did any other admiral in the war. Every commanding officer, when his ship, no matter how small, put in at Pearl Harbor, was encouraged to call on Nimitz at the Cincpac-Cincpoa headquarters in Makalapa and express his views. Knowing that the finest test of a commanding officer is (in Churchill's words) "the quality of his effort," and that mistakes in battle are inevitable, Nimitz was slow to relieve any commanding officer who failed; he believed in the adage that every dog should be allowed two bites. It may be conceded that he allowed one bite too many to certain task force commanders before he relieved them; but it was fortunate for the cause that he allowed two bites to Kelly Turner, who turned out to be a practitioner of amphibious warfare second to none.

In the same web-footed class with Turner were Wilkinson and Barbey in the Pacific, and Hewitt and Kirk in the Atlantic and the Mediterranean. The last two, having to deal with high officers of the Royal Navy who were more used to ordering subordinates than conferring with equals, had to double as diplomats. Ingersoll and Ingram became very competent commanders of the Atlantic Fleet. There was an immense amount of talent in the lower echelons of flag rank. Rear Admirals Hall, Deyo, Conolly, Joy, Fechteler, Blandy, Low, McMorris, Merrill, Denebrink, DuBose, to mention only a few, were fully equal to exercising even higher commands which seniority denied to them. Of these who were killed in action or as a result of it, we remember Kidd, Scott, Callaghan, Mullinnix, Chandler, and Royal.

When we come to the admirals who commanded at sea, and who directed a great battle, there was no one to equal Spruance. Always calm, always at peace with himself, Spruance had that ability which marks the great captain to make correct estimates and the right decisions in a fluid battle situation. He was bold and aggressive when the occasion demanded offensive tactics; cautious when pushing his luck too far might have lost the fruits of victory. Spruance in the Battle of Midway, with his instinct for the enemy's jugular vein — his carriers — deciding to launch planes at the right moment, retiring at night when further persistence would have risked an encounter with Yamamoto's massed gunfire, was superb; there is no other word for it. Spruance in the Battle of the Philippine Sea, overriding Mitscher the carrier expert in letting the enemy planes come at him instead of going in search of them, won the second most decisive battle of the Pacific war. And, off Okinawa, Spruance never faltered in face of the destruction wrought by the kamikazes. It is regrettable that, owing to Spruance's innate modesty and his refusal to create an image of himself in the public eye, he was never properly appreciated.

Halsey, the public's favorite in the Navy, will always remain a controversial figure, but none can deny that he was a great leader; one with the true "Nelson touch." His appointment as Commander South Pacific Force at the darkest moment of the Guadalcanal campaign lifted the hearts of every officer and bluejacket. He hated the enemy with an unholy wrath, and turned that feeling into a grim determination by all hands to hit hard, again and again, and win. His proposal to step up the Leyte operation by two months was a stroke of strategic genius which undoubtedly shortened the Pacific war. Unfortunately, in his efforts to build public morale in America and Australia, Halsey did what Spruance refused to do — built up an image of himself as an exponent of Danton's famous principle, "Audacity, more audacity, always audacity." That was the real reason for his fumble in the Battle for Leyte Gulf. For his inspiring leadership in 1942-1943, his generosity to others, his capacity for choosing the right men for his staff, Halsey well earned his five stars, and his place among the Navy's immortals.

Admiral Kinkaid, after being allowed one "bite" — the loss of *Hornet* in the Battle of the Santa Cruz Islands — rose to be one of our greatest seamen as Commander Seventh Fleet. He had a difficult role to play as head of "MacArthur's Navy," since that great general, for all his genius, at first imperfectly understood the limitation and capabilities of sea power. But he learned from Kinkaid. In the Battle for Leyte Gulf Kinkaid had an unfortunate position in the chain of command, under MacArthur but unable to control Halsey; within these limitations he acquitted himself very well, and is entitled to no small part of the glory reaped by Oldendorf in Surigao Strait and Clifton Sprague off Samar.

In a special category of excellence are the flag officers of fleet carriers, with Mitscher *facile princeps*. Under him, McCain, Reeves, Bogan, Clark, Frederick Sherman and Radford showed qualities of greatness; and the Battle off Samar proved that the escort carrier admirals, the two Spragues and Felix Stump, were in no way inferior. And we must not forget two great chiefs of staff, Burke and Carney.

Above all these sailors was the Commander in Chief, Franklin D. Roosevelt — a remarkable leader indeed. Unlike Winston Churchill, Roosevelt never imagined himself to be a strategist. In general he followed the advice of the Joint Chiefs of Staff, which included King, Marshall, and his own chief of staff, wise old Admiral Leahy. Thrice at least he went over their heads — refusing to redeploy American forces into the Pacific in 1942, insisting that Guadalcanal must be reinforced and held at all costs, and inviting a British fleet to participate in the Okinawa campaign. He also threw his influence in favor of MacArthur's desire to liberate Leyte and Luzon against the Navy's wish to bypass them. He was a tower of strength to Marshall, King and Eisenhower against insistent British pressure to postpone OVERLORD and shift DRAGOON from Marseilles to Trieste. The Navy was his favorite service — I heard him once, in true regal style, refer to it as "my Navy" — and he did his utmost to build it up and improve its efficiency both before and during the war.

In operations, there were several things that the Navy did superlatively well. Instigated by the Marines, it studied and developed the technique of amphibious warfare well before 1939. In this important branch the United States Navy was behind the Japanese but ahead of the Royal Navy when war broke; but the Japanese, thrown on the defensive, had no chance to practise amphibious warfare after the Java campaign, and the Royal Navy, thanks largely to Mountbatten's combined operations unit, caught up with us in Sicily and Normandy. In carrier warfare the United States Navy was supreme, because it successfully resisted (as the Royal Navy had not) the efforts of the Army to obtain control over all combatant planes, and because admirals like Mitscher and McCain made constant efforts to improve carrier tactics and profited by early mistakes. In order to service the fast carrier forces and enable them to keep the sea, fighting, for many weeks on end, the Navy devised the at-sea logistics system, one of the principal instruments of victory. For this, credit is primarily due to Admirals Calhoun and Beary, and Commodores Gray and Carter.

The planning of operations, too, was very well done, even though it often had to be done in a hurry. The supreme planning job of the war was that for Operation NEPTUNE-OVERLORD, in which British and Americans both took part; but for purely United States Navy operations, the top planners — "Savvy" Cooke on King's staff and Forrest Sherman on Nimitz's — deserve a special accolade. Kelly Turner was an amazingly meticulous, thorough and accurate planner for his own amphibious operations, and oversaw every detail himself. Once Turner gave the word "Land the Landing Force!" everything went like clockwork; one felt that anybody could have done it, not knowing the immense amount of skill and thought which had gone into the plan. Wilkinson was Turner's peer in the Central, as Barbey in the Southwest Pacific. Foul-ups (which the Navy called by a harsher word) had always been expected in amphibious operations, even when uncontested, and it was a tribute to our new tactics that the Japanese finally decided not to contest these operations, but to hole up and sell their lives dear.

One feels particular admiration for the officers of the destroyers, the "tin cans" which operated in every theater of the war. They not only had to be first-rate seamen and ship handlers, but men of science to assimilate the new techniques of antisubmarine warfare and air defense. Although overwhelmed with paper work, these young officers maintained something of the port and swagger of the oldtime frigate skipper; they were good for a lark ashore as for a fight at sea. In every theater and every kind of operation, as we have abundantly seen, destroyers were the indispensable component. Whether in convoy duty or in a hunter-killer group in the Atlantic, or supporting amphibious operations, delivering torpedo attacks in a night battle, or taking the rap from kamikazes off Okinawa, the men who manned these ships proved themselves to be the most versatile and courageous of sea warriors. It is no wonder that so many have risen to high command in the new Navy.

Equally admirable were the submariners, an even more scientific and specialized branch of the Navy, and their great leaders, Admirals Lockwood, Christie and Fife. Owing to wartime secrecy, they seldom received public credit; this was the true "silent service." The submarines not only dogged the Japanese merchant navy to its death and sank more than their share of warships; in both oceans they scouted in advance of amphibious landings, and in the Pacific they maintained contact with Philippine patriots. The submarines lost an even greater proportion of their numbers than did the brave naval aviators. And the "boats" named after fishes, whose exploits we have told all too briefly, were immediate ancestors of the nuclear-powered, polaris-armed underwater warships which have become the prime protectors of the free world.

Let us also remember the "small boys" — the gunboats, minecraft, destroyer escorts, PTs, beaching and other lettered craft, even the lowly "yard-birds" and small cutters. These, largely officered by reservists, were forced to perform functions and make long voyages for which they had not been designed. The production of thousands of these in wartime, the training of them at special schools set up for that purpose, the operation of them under the most hazardous conditions, are beyond praise; but we may not forget that when the war involved us the Navy was woefully deficient in escorts and small craft, and should resolve never to be caught short again.

On 1 July 1940 the Navy had only 13,162 officers and 744,824 enlisted men; on 31 August 1945 it had 316,675 officers and 2,935,695 enlisted men. Similar figures for the Marine Corps are 1819 officers and 26,545 enlisted men in 1940; 36,851 officers and 427,017 enlisted men at the end of the war.[2] In spite of this immense dilution of all ranks and ratings, the Navy did a superlative job in making fighting sailors out of young Americans fresh out of school, farm, or minor shore jobs, teaching them the manifold skills necessary to operate and fight a modern warship, pride in their ships, courage to face the most hideous form of death, by burning.

The vastly expanded American merchant marine, too, deserves high praise for its world-wide operations, which were indispensable to support of the Navy, the Army, and our Allies. Merchant mariners and the Naval Armed Guards on the ships showed exemplary courage in convoy duty, in actions with German raiders and U-boats, and in replenishing the Fleet off Okinawa under constant threat of kamikaze attack. We must never forget that, since one of the main functions of a navy is to protect trade and communications both in peace and in war, it can never function properly without a strong and efficient merchant marine, or without the know-how of master mariners and seamen.

So, thanks to all; and, no matter what the atomic age brings, America will always need sailors and ships and shipborne aircraft to preserve her liberty, her communications with the free world, even her existence. If the deadly missiles with their apocalyptic warheads are ever launched at America, the Navy will still be out on blue water fighting for her, and the nation or alliance that survives will be the one that retains command of the oceans.

[2] To these should be added 8399 women officers and 73,685 enlisted women (the "Waves"); 813 officers and 17,350 enlisted women Marines, and 10,968 nurses, all at the end of the war.

Index

Names of Combatant Ships in SMALL CAPITALS
Names of Lettered Combatant Ships such as LSTs, and of
Merchant Ships, in *Italics*